2

"A NEW KIND OF WAR"

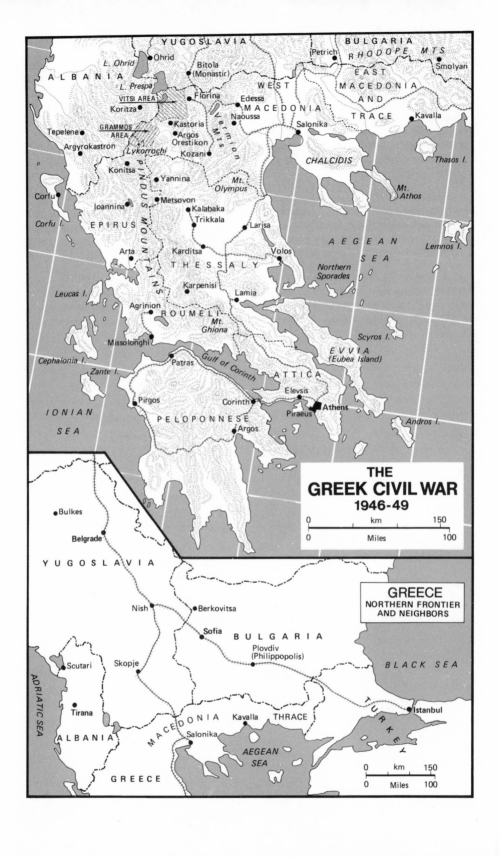

**THE
GREEK CIVIL WAR
1946-49**

| 0 | km | 150 |
| 0 | Miles | 100 |

GREECE
NORTHERN FRONTIER
AND NEIGHBORS

| 0 | km | 150 |
| 0 | Miles | 100 |

"A NEW KIND OF WAR"

America's Global Strategy
and
The Truman Doctrine in Greece

HOWARD JONES

New York　　　Oxford
Oxford University Press
1989

Oxford University Press

Oxford   New York   Toronto
Delhi   Bombay   Calcutta   Madras   Karachi
Petaling Jaya   Singapore   Hong Kong   Tokyo
Nairobi   Dar es Salaam   Cape Town
Melbourne   Auckland

and associated companies in
Berlin   Ibadan

Copyright © 1989 by Howard Jones

Published by Oxford University Press, Inc.,
200 Madison Avenue, New York, New York 10016

Oxford is a registered trademark of Oxford University Press

Library of Congress Cataloging-in-Publication Data
Jones, Howard, 1940–
"A new kind of war": America's global strategy and the Truman
Doctrine in Greece / Howard Jones.
p. cm. Bibliography: p. Includes index. ISBN 0-19-504581-5
1. United States—Foreign relations—1945–1953. 2. United States—
Foreign relations—Greece. 3. Greece—Foreign relations—United
States. 4. World politics—1945–1955. 5. Truman, Harry S.,
1884–1972—Views on Greece. 6. Greece—History—Civil War,
1944–1949. 1. Title. II. Title: Truman doctrine in Greece.
E813.J63 1988 973.918—dc 19   88-4220 CIP

Portions of Howard Jones, "The Diplomacy of Restraint: The United States' Efforts
to Repatriate Greek Children Evacuated During the Civil War of 1946–49."
Journal of Modern Greek Studies 3 (May 1985):65–85.
are reprinted with the permission of the Johns Hopkins University Press.

2 4 6 8 9 7 5 3 1

Printed in the United States of America
on acid-free paper

For Howie

Preface

At precisely 1:00 p.m. on March 12, 1947, President Harry S. Truman briskly walked down the aisle of the chamber of the House of Representatives, prepared to deliver a major address before a joint session of Congress. Carrying only a black folder, he made his way to the speaker's rostrum and, after the applause came to a close, began a speech that would help to shape the nation's present and future security policy. As he read from his notes, members of Congress recognized the gravity of the moment. The British government had announced an end to its aid program in Greece and Turkey, and the congressmen knew that the President was calling upon them to do something never done before in peacetime: approve a massive military and economic foreign assistance program that would involve the United States in European political and military affairs.

The situations in Greece and Turkey, the President declared, demanded America's immediate attention. The Greek government was in danger of collapsing to communist guerrillas pursuing terrorist activities in the north, and it had appealed to the United States for aid. If the call went unheeded, the only democratic country in the Balkans would fall to totalitarian rule. Conditions in Turkey were not as immediately serious, but that country's independence and integrity were likewise crucial to the maintenance of order in the Middle East. Unless the United States defended these "free peoples," no nation would be safe from the forces of totalitarianism. The collapse of Greece and Turkey would "undermine the foundations of international peace and hence the security of the United States."

Over halfway into the address, the President highlighted the principle underlying what became known as the Truman Doctrine: "I believe that it must be the policy of the United States to support free peoples who are resisting attempted subjugation by armed minorities or by outside pressures."

As leader of the Free World, the United States had a duty to protect the right of free peoples to decide their destiny. Such assistance "should be primarily through economic and financial aid, which is essential to economic stability and orderly political processes." If Greece and Turkey should fall, shock waves would reverberate throughout the Middle East and Europe, sending a message to the beleaguered people of those parts of the world that the United States's assurances of self-determination were mere rhetoric. The President asked Congress to appropriate $400 million in economic and military aid for Greece and Turkey and to approve the assignment to each country of American civilian and military advisers to implement the program. "If we falter in our leadership, we may endanger the peace of the world—and we shall surely endanger the welfare of our own nation."

At the conclusion of his short address, the President acknowledged the applause, shook hands with several of those present, and left the chamber.

In less than twenty minutes, President Truman had urged the nation to break its longstanding tradition against political and military intervention in Europe during peacetime and to accept the responsibilities of world leadership thrust upon the United States by the Second World War. Though the President had specifically mentioned only Greece and Turkey, he had left room for a general application of his principles by emphasizing that those two countries were only part of a broader problem resulting from the decline of British power. Even though he had not referred to the communists as the "armed minorities" and to the Soviets as the "outside pressures," his remarks left no doubt about their direction. The President sought congressional approval to help any free people who were resisting totalitarian rule.

The Truman Doctrine marked the beginning of a global foreign policy that was flexible, restrained, and not recklessly military in tone. More than a decade before President John F. Kennedy introduced his program of "flexible response," Truman and his advisers (some of whom would also advise Kennedy) developed a foreign policy that was adaptable in strategy to the shifting challenges to democracy. Though Turkey was included in the aid program, most of the problems there had eased in late 1946 as the Soviets withdrew their diplomatic pressure. But an emergency prevailed in Greece. The Truman administration's policy in that country was realistic in application and idealistic in purpose. Its composite thrust was military, economic, and political, allowing for adjustments as the nature of the threat changed. The policy rested on the fundamental premise that freedom was indivisible and that wherever it was endangered, so also was America's future in jeopardy.

By 1947 Greece was the only Balkan nation professing democracy, making its welfare a test of America's will and a symbol of the Free World's struggle against totalitarianism. The crucial issues in Greece were constitutional and economic. However, the White House perceived a larger threat: the Soviet Union and its Balkan allies were exploiting the country's troubles for their own purposes. Policymakers in Washington ultimately recognized the need to extend immediate military aid because the situation had deteriorated to the point that economic assistance could come only after the government in Athens had established political stability in the face of growing bands of guerrillas. The resurgence of civil war in Greece thus assumed Cold War significance as the country provided a microcosm of East-West differences and left the impression that both the United States and the Soviet Union were at least indirectly involved. America's sole possession of the atomic bomb, advisers believed, had forced the Soviet Union to adopt short-of-war tactics in pursuing expansionist goals. The central concerns for the United States became whether the communist guerrillas would undermine the government in Athens, force the country's collapse, set an example that would break the will of other governments, and encourage further Soviet expansion. The Truman Doctrine served notice to the world that America intended to accept the new challenges to self-determination during the atomic age.

The following is a study in American policy toward Greece as the focal point in the development of a global strategy designed to combat totalitarianism. It is not a study in Anglo-American relations, for I have relied on other historians who have provided fine works on the subject. Nor is this a study of Greece, Russia, Yugoslavia, Albania, or Bulgaria; the Greek government's archives are restricted until 1995, and none of the other countries' papers are open. Consequently, this work covers America's understanding of events, which in turn was shaped by its policymakers' perceptions of Soviet behavior, by prior Soviet actions in Iran, Poland, and Eastern Europe, by known Soviet interests in the Near East, eastern Mediterranean, and Middle East, and by the best available U.S., British, and Greek governmental and public analyses and observations. Additionally, since the Turkish problem had somewhat calmed by October 1946, that subject will be treated here as the Truman administration treated it then—as peripheral to Greece.

Thus, this work is necessarily limited in scope, more often guided by contemporary perceptions than by whatever the reality might have been at the time. In regard to Greece and Turkey, the United States, of course, developed a strategy based on the White House view of the problem. The fundamental assumption was that the Kremlin sought expansion, whether for security or self-aggrandizement, whether for reasons stemming from ideology or *Realpolitik*. The United States's atomic monopoly during the immediate postwar years had seemingly forced an alteration in Soviet tactics from confrontation to infiltration and subversion. The Truman administration concluded that the Soviets were using every means short of war to promote the fall of Greece. Only when that country's army began winning and American involvement became increasingly military in nature did Soviet Premier Joseph Stalin order an end to the guerrilla war. He also knew that a communist defeat in Greece, coming at the same time as the defection of Yugoslavia's leader, Marshal Josip Broz Tito, might lead to a further corrosion of the Soviet alliance system in Eastern Europe. Without Soviet and East European documents, who can today determine the extent of Soviet involvement in Greece? In truth, the question is academic: the Truman administration *believed* that the Soviets were at least indirectly involved in that nation's affairs. American documents reveal considerable insight into Soviet behavior during the period, some of which was substantiated years after the Greek civil war, but most of which may remain forever hidden in foreign archives.

Without the assistance of numerous friends, colleagues, and archivists, this work would not have been possible. John O. Iatrides graciously read the manuscript two times, answered numerous inquiries by mail, by phone, and by personal conversations—in every instance warmly sharing his extensive understanding of Greece and the nature of the American involvement. Forrest and Ellen McDonald again took time from their own research and writing to read the entire work and share their expertise and friendly advice. Peter Maslowski likewise furnished the close and critical reading that can come only from a friend. Others who read all or parts of the manuscript and made countless helpful suggestions include Robert H. Ferrell, Donald Rakestraw, Richard V. Burks, David Brinkley, J. Garry Clifford, William H. McNeill, Arnold Offner, and Hugh Ragsdale. At the National Archives, John Taylor and Wilbert Mahoney located much useful material, while David Wigdor did the same at the Library of Congress. Also of great assistance were the staffs of the Carlisle Military Barracks, the Center of Military History, the Federal Records Center in Suitland, Maryland, the Simpson Library at Maxwell Air Force Base, and the Washington Navy Yard. Dennis Bilger, Erwin Mueller, and Pauline Testerman provided invaluable guidance into the extensive holdings of the Truman Library, as did the archivists at the Franklin D. Roosevelt Library, the Dwight D. Eisenhower Library, the Clemson University Library, the Public Record Office in England, and, in particular, those working in the Interlibrary Loan Service of the University of Alabama Library.

Several contemporaries of the 1940s graciously consented to interviews. These included Loy W. Henderson, George McGhee (who also provided some of the photographs from his collection), Dean Rusk, Lieutenant General Russell L. Vittrup, and General Albert C. Wedemeyer. Repeated efforts to interview General James Van Fleet or to see his private papers proved unsuccessful. But his authorized biographer, Joseph C. Goulden, has assured me that the Van Fleet papers contain nothing additional to that already found in the U.S. Army's official papers in the National Archives.

Parts of this work have appeared in different forms. A segment was read before the annual meeting of the Society for Historians of American Foreign Relations in Annapolis, Maryland. Another part was read before an international colloquium at Queens College in New York that focused on "Greece and the United States: Forty Years Since the Truman Doctrine." An early hypothesis was presented as a paper at the Missouri Valley History Conference in Omaha, Nebraska. Finally, I am grateful to the Johns Hopkins University Press for permission to use materials from my article published in the *Journal of Modern Greek Studies*.

Financial assistance came from several sources. These included the Earhart Foundation in Ann Arbor, Michigan, the Truman Library, the Eleanor Roosevelt Institute, and the Research Grants Committee and the Research Stimulation Grant Fund of the University of Alabama.

The people at Oxford University Press continue to be a source of friendly inspiration and encouragement. Sheldon Meyer supported my work on the Truman Doctrine in Greece from the moment it came to his attention. Rachel Toor displayed her remarkable ability for instilling confidence in a writer struggling to meet a deadline. Stephanie Sakson-Ford furnished superb editorial guidance in the final stages of the manuscript's completion.

On a personal level, I owe the deepest gratitude to those who are closest to me. To Mary Ann, I can only express my warmest appreciation for allowing me to share her life. My daughters were helpful in many ways. Shari provided warm companionship on the long drives to Abilene, Hyde Park, Independence, Montgomery, and Washington, whereas Debbie (who preferred to talk about the research trips afterward rather than take them) repeatedly demonstrated her interest in my work and continually gave moral support. My parents again provided the care and concern that are immeasurable in importance.

If this work has any value, much of the credit goes to all of those mentioned above; the shortcomings belong to the person mentioned below.

Tuscaloosa, Alabama   Howard Jones
Spring 1988

Contents

"A NEW KIND OF WAR"

Let nobody write about Greece lightly. Here is one of the most tragic and painful situations in the world. What is going on in Greece today is real war, though the fighting is desultory and the casualties comparatively light—what is worse, civil war, the most ravaging of all kinds of war. Moreover this is not merely a Greek war but an American war; it is the Americans who make it possible to fight it. Athens is almost like an Anglo-American (mostly American) armed citadel, and neither the Greek army nor government could survive ten days without aid—concrete military aid—from the United States. Not one American citizen in a thousand has any conception of the extent of the American commitment in Greece, the immensity of the American contribution, and the stubborn and perhaps insoluble dilemma into which we—the United States—have plunged ourselves.

John Gunther, *Behind the Curtain* (N.Y.: Harper, 1949), 129.

Introduction

I

In early 1949 the *New York Times*'s veteran correspondent in Athens, Anne O'Hare McCormick, observed that the Truman Doctrine had involved the United States in "a new kind of war" against communist-led guerrillas in Greece.[1] The conflict was dark and murky, a war in the shadows characterized by enemies difficult to define or even to see, and by a search for victory not measurable in territorial terms or human and material loss. The enemy rarely wore uniforms, often fought with confiscated weapons, usually relied upon non-conventional warfare, and nearly always received supplies and shelter from neighboring communist countries. Battlefronts seldom existed, for the guerrillas preferred the terrorist tactics of raiding, pillaging, sniping, and abducting villagers and townspeople into their small but effective force. Communist propagandists kept the atmosphere tense by attacking America for pursuing imperial interests and opposing the popular will. In the United Nations and other public forums, the United States sought to defend its actions while attributing a large measure of the turmoil in Greece to outside communist forces.

The designation of this type of conflict posed problems. In a real sense, of course, guerrilla warfare was the oldest form of fighting; but the Truman administration attached global importance to the conflict in Greece because of its belief in Soviet involvement. The outcome would therefore have a major impact on other nations that had not yet decided to resist communism. Every event took on symbolic meaning as an indication of America's commitment to Free World principles. Even the terms used to describe the unrest in Greece had deep implications. Should White House spokesmen proclaim the trouble in Greece a civil war, international law would permit outside recognition of

3

the belligerents and allow foreign aid. If American policymakers declared the problems external in origin, ensuing events could cause international turmoil and lead to World War III. To contain the conflict within national borders, the Truman administration publicly insisted that the problems were primarily domestic and that the Greek government had to resolve them (albeit with American aid).

The type of war being waged in Greece made it possible for an inferior but motivated army to win by simply avoiding defeat. In a war of wills, these shadowy forces—whether called guerrillas, rebels, insurgents, *andartes*, partisans, or, as the Greek loyalists and some Americans termed them, bandits—recognized that patience was their best weapon.[2] A long and frustrating conflict would wear down the morale and determination of disciplined army regulars or it could break the will of civilians and force an end to the war. As the guerrillas fought and retreated into northern mountainous refuges, leaders of the Greek government realized that to emerge triumphant, their army's pursuit units had to keep on the trail of each guerrilla band until they destroyed it. Victory depended on maintaining the support of the countryside by securing villages through pacification programs while the army encircled and eliminated the guerrillas. Americans found themselves in the uncomfortable position of having to defend the Greek government's brutal actions in destroying a movement allegedly of the people.

The new threat to the Free World was partly attributable to what one writer has called a "revolution in warfare" brought about by the atomic bomb.[3] While both the United States and the Soviet Union searched for more sophisticated weaponry after 1945, paradoxically they found themselves resorting to conventional and often pre-modern warfare. Even had the United States possessed an abundance of atomic weapons, it could not justify their use against countries having no equivalent power and posing no direct and unmistakable threat to American security.

Postwar circumstances forced the Truman administration to develop a broader definition of strategic interests. Traditional geopolitical considerations were still vital—transportation and communication lines, military concerns, fueling installations, natural resources—but the development of the UN and numerous Third World countries caused the power of example to receive greater emphasis than before. To be victorious in this type of warfare, the United States had to protect any part of the world that should and could be preserved for democracy. In Greece anti-communist groups were in the majority and the country's leaders were receptive to aid and advice. Most important, the Greek populace was favorably disposed toward the United States. Greece became a viable testing ground for America's broadened strategic concerns.

Failure to defend Greece, the White House believed, would demoralize other nations and force them either to accept communism or to buy peace by making concessions to totalitarianism. American strategy entailed not only displaying its military strength in Greece but also proving to other nations that it possessed the will to help. The United States had to demonstrate an endurance capable of convincing democracy's enemies that they could not win. In an article in the *New York Times* entitled "Greece Is a Test of Staying Power," McCormick declared that Greece provided a "preview of the front-less, almost faceless, war of tomorrow—a war of Trojan horses pointing the way for machine guns. The battle-line is everywhere and nowhere," for the Kremlin's central directive was "rule or ruin."[4]

America's decision to intervene rested on the best analyses available at the time. Without Soviet, Greek, and other Eastern European documentation, Americans had to act on the bases of circumstantial evidence, first- and second-hand observations, an intelligence network that was not always accurate in its assessments, and a deep suspicion of Soviet communist involvement. Though legitimate doubts have been raised about the Kremlin's post-war capacity for aggression, America's leaders at that time could not have been sure that the Soviets were more concerned about security than expansion. Indeed, one drive can become indistinguishable from the other. Within two years of war's end, Soviet behavior in Iran and in Poland and other Eastern European countries had added to America's concern regarding Greece. More than a few of Washington's spokesmen questioned whether Moscow had a blueprint for conquest in the 1940s; hardly anyone was willing to take a chance that it did not.

The Truman administration suspected the Soviets of extending aid to the Greek guerrillas through the neighboring communist states of Yugoslavia, Albania, and Bulgaria. Direct Soviet involvement was unlikely. During World War II, a Soviet mission had arrived in Greece, undoubtedly to inspect the potential of the communist resistance. Disappointed with the guerrillas, the mission returned to Moscow without hope for establishing a strong Communist party in Greece. In October 1944, Stalin and British Prime Minister Winston Churchill divided Eastern Europe into spheres of interest. By the "percentages agreement" in Moscow, Stalin recognized Britain's control in Greece, even to the point of not intervening in behalf of Greek communists who tried to overthrow the Athens government in the "December Revolution" of 1944.[5] For practical reasons—lack of confidence in the guerrillas and a desire to solidify control over areas already held—Stalin displayed little interest in Greek events.

The Truman administration did not possess proof of Soviet complicity in Greece, but considerable circumstantial evidence suggested that the Kremlin would exploit any advances won by the guerrillas on their own. Thus if matters took a turn for the worse, Stalin could disavow all connection with Greece and let events take their course. When trouble threatened to erupt in Greece at the beginning of 1946, Soviet press and radio attacked Greece and Great Britain. During the first UN session, the Soviet delegation lashed out at Greece for allegedly causing unrest in the Balkans by seeking unwarranted territorial claims in the north. At least in part to counter Western complaints about the continued Soviet presence in Iran, the Soviets criticized the British for maintaining troops in Greece, and expressed interest in Turkey, Iran, and a base in the Dodecanese islands. Greece was the chief obstacle to Soviet penetration of the eastern Mediterranean, making it evident that the antagonistic policies of Yugoslavia, Albania, and Bulgaria toward Greece paralleled Soviet interests in the region and that it was therefore almost unimportant whether a formal, cooperative arrangement existed among the communist states.[6]

Whatever the truth regarding Soviet involvement in Greece during the 1940s, the guerrillas received enough outside encouragement and assistance to leave the impression that a Soviet-American confrontation was developing and that Greece had become a battleground of the Cold War. If the Western-supported government collapsed, the world would perceive the outcome as a communist victory guided by the Kremlin. The actuality of Soviet direction of events was secondary to what observers *thought* that direction to be.

American policymakers repeatedly discussed the possibility of sending combat troops to Greece, particularly after the British indicated that they would soon withdraw their soldiers. The British troop presence, though not important in substance, was emblematic of the West's intention to protect the government in Athens. When the British notified the Truman administration of their military retrenchment and ultimate withdrawal, Americans became concerned about the symbolic importance of such an act. Would not a decision against replacing the British with American forces signal an end to the Free World's commitment in Greece? And yet, to send troops would require a diversion of the already small number of American men in uniform from pressing needs in Germany and Japan. Furthermore, if someone should fire on American soldiers and force an engagement, the communists would have gained excellent material for propaganda accusing the Americans of imperialism. Indeed, such an incident could develop into a full-scale war. The United States had to establish its military presence in Greece short of combat.

The situation in Greece was exceedingly complex. Immediate causes of the unrest were economic and political, the first relating to the destruction during World War II, the second to the constitutional question of whether to restore the monarchical form of government. But, was the struggle internecine in nature and fueled by outside help? Or, was it an internal matter that threatened to become regional in scope because of the fierce, longtime hostilities felt by the Balkan states for one another? Or, was it a localized conflict that threatened to grow into something larger because of the major powers' geopolitical and strategic interests? The Truman administration had to maintain the appearance of an internal conflict—a civil war—by keeping the fighting confined within the country's borders. If the guerrillas established their own regime, neighboring countries and perhaps even the Soviet Union would probably extend recognition and openly authorize military and economic assistance. The problems in Greece would become international and greatly intensify the Cold War.

II

When, in May 1946, Secretary of State James F. Byrnes asked French Foreign Minister Georges Bidault what the foundation of Soviet foreign policy was, he replied, "security through expansion." Two months later the State Department conceded this point but added that the Soviets were so suspicious of others that the results were "the same as if the motive were aggression, indefinite expansion." President Truman asked special counselor Clark Clifford to prepare a study of Soviet violations of the wartime and postwar agreements with the United States that would, according to Clifford, help Americans "find a way to get along with the Soviets." Truman knew this would be difficult, if not impossible, because the Soviets appeared to be pursuing world domination. "What's more," Clifford later insisted, "they were, and we stopped them." America's sole possession of the bomb was "an *enormous* factor."[7]

Maxim Litvinov had publicly admitted that harmony between the nations was a useless quest. The preceding June, the former Soviet ambassador to the United States told a CBS news correspondent that East-West differences were irreconcilable because of an "ideological conception" among Americans of the "inevitability of conflict between [the] Communist and Capitalist worlds." Once the nations might have been able to live together, but recent events had forced the Soviet Union to resort to the "outmoded concept of geographical security." Asked if the West's granting of Russian demands would relieve suspicion, Litvinov replied that this merely "would lead to [the] west being faced after [a] period of time with [the] next series of demands."[8]

Litvinov's prophecy seemed fulfilled, for as far as the Truman administration was concerned, the Soviets had broken their promises in regard to Poland, violated self-determination in Eastern Europe, and provoked trouble in both Iran and Turkey. The preceding February, the American chargé in Moscow, George F. Kennan, dispatched the "Long Telegram" to the State Department, describing the bases of Soviet behavior and calling for a long-range policy aimed at halting the spread of communism. That same month the *New York Times* quoted Stalin's assertion that irremedial differences existed between communism and capitalism. And, in March, former British Prime Minister Winston Churchill delivered a ringing speech before President Truman and a college audience in Fulton, Missouri, warning that the Soviet Union had lowered an iron curtain across Eastern Europe.

By the summer of 1946 the Soviets appeared determined to establish control over Turkey as part of a drive toward the eastern Mediterranean and the Middle East. As early as July 1944 Russian policy toward Turkey was aimed at securing postwar interests in the region. Soviet demands soon concentrated on the Black Sea straits and on Turkey's eastern provinces of Kars and Ardahan, large and populous regions that bordered the Soviet republics of Georgia and Armenia. The Soviets called for a revision of the Montreux Treaty of 1936 that authorized exclusive Turkish control over the straits, and urged the establishment of a new system of joint Soviet-Turkish control. In March 1945, Soviet Foreign Minister Vyacheslav M. Molotov informed the Turks that his government was preparing to terminate the 1925 treaty of friendship between the countries. The following June Moscow launched a press and radio propaganda campaign that lasted a year and called for a base on the straits and favorable border changes in eastern Turkey as a condition for renewing the treaty. In the meantime, the American and British governments expressed interest in a revision in the treaty that would establish international control of the waterways. At the Potsdam Conference of July 1945, the British, Americans, and Russians agreed to conduct individual discussions with Turkey regarding the straits. President Truman repeatedly expressed his interest in the proposed revision over the next few months. The government in Ankara continued to refuse the Soviet demands but notified the United States in December that it would participate in and agree to the decisions of an international conference on the Dardanelles—as long as Turkey's "independence, sovereignty and territorial integrity are not infringed."[9]

In early August 1946 the crisis in the Mediterranean intensified as, in the midst of difficulties elsewhere, the Soviet Union rejected the internationalization approach and repeated its demands for a "new regime" of the straits by "Black Sea powers" and the creation of a defense system under the joint control of Turkey and the Soviet Union. Byrnes was in Paris at another peace conference, repeatedly having to defend the United States against communist accusations of selfish capitalist and imperialist interests. Tensions were growing in the Balkans, as the Yugoslavs stepped up their pressure for Trieste and Bulgaria demanded that Greece turn over Western Thrace. The Soviets had assigned twenty-five troop divisions to the southern Caucasus, where they could exert pressure on both Turkey and Iran. Palestine was degenerating into daily explosions of violence, China was threatening to break out in civil war, and the Yugoslav air force had shot down two American transport planes engaged in regular missions from Austria to Italy. As trouble seemed to be brewing all over the world, the White House feared that the Soviets sought to incorporate Turkey into their alliance system, establish air and naval bases in that country, and go on to seek control over Greece and the entire Near and Middle East. If successful, the Soviets would outflank the West in the Mediterranean and secure the oil of the Middle East. Although American embassy officers in Moscow believed it unlikely that the Soviet Union would go to war, they were convinced that it would seek these objectives through political, economic, and psychological pressures, as well as through military threats. The U.S. ambassador in Ankara, Edwin C. Wilson, warned that the fall of Turkey would open the door for Soviet expansion into the Persian Gulf and Suez area.[10]

On August 15, at a strategy meeting in the White House, President Truman approved recommendations for action that were derived from discussions with the secretaries of war and navy and the chiefs of staff. The administration would encourage the Turks to resist the Soviet demands; to show America's support, the President ordered a naval task force (led by the new aircraft carrier *Franklin D. Roosevelt*) to Istanbul to join the battleship USS *Missouri* that was already there on an unrelated mission. In the White House, Army Chief of Staff Dwight D. Eisenhower asked Truman if he understood that war could result from U.S. resistance to Soviet efforts regarding the Dardanelles. The President opened a desk drawer and took out a big map of the eastern Mediterranean. After asking everyone to gather around, he demonstrated his grasp of the problems by delivering a brief lecture on the strategic importance of the region.[11]

Four days later, on August 19, the White House implemented a policy that ultimately defused the Turkish crisis. The Department of State advised the Turkish government to turn down the Soviet demands, and sent a note to the Soviets emphasizing that Turkey had primary responsibility for defending the straits. Revision of the Montreux Treaty was not the sole concern of Black Sea powers. In the event of a threat to the area, the UN Security Council would handle the problem. The British followed with a similar note two days later. The next day the Turkish government likewise sent a note to the Soviets, rejecting their recommended revisions of the treaty. In September, Secretary of the Navy James V. Forrestal announced that the U.S. Navy would maintain a permanent presence in the eastern Mediterranean. The Soviets eased their pressure by the end of October.[12]

In late September, Clifford presented the White House a long, top-secret report entitled "American Relations with the Soviet Union" that helped to ease Forrestal's repeatedly expressed fears that his nation's defense establishment was unable to uphold the administration's policy of firmness. After receiving the President's directive, Clifford had instructed his assistant, George M. Elsey, to gather the information and write the report. Elsey was already at work on a study of Soviet-American relations and expanded the project to include an analysis of the bases and results of Soviet behavior. He incorporated the thoughts of Byrnes and others in the administration, including the ideas set out in Kennan's Long Telegram. Thus the Clifford-Elsey report called upon the United States to adopt a firm line because the Soviet Union was preparing for war "by many means," both direct and indirect, and had already begun expansionist moves in Europe.[13]

The report substantiated the administration's belief that the Soviets were engaged in a new kind of war against the West. They would seize every opportunity to "foment antagonisms among foreign powers" and to undermine other nations by "discrediting their leadership, stirring up domestic discord, and inciting colonial unrest." They would also use obstructionist

tactics in the UN. The Soviets wanted to establish influence in Greece and
Turkey as steps toward gaining control over the eastern Mediterranean and
the oil of the Middle East. In the meantime they were making every effort to
destroy American prestige by propaganda, subversion, and infiltration of
governments. The United States's opposition to these moves threatened to
lead to war because the Russians sought global supremacy and considered
conflict between communism and capitalism to be inevitable. The September
report set out what Elsey called the "totality" of America's relations with the
Soviet Union. It recommended that the United States "be prepared to wage
atomic and biological warfare" as "the only deterrent to Soviet aggressive
action." The administration had to inform the public of these problems with
the Soviet Union and make it clear that America's policies "must . . . be
global in scope." The President considered the recommendations so explosive
that he told Clifford not to distribute copies to cabinet members.[14]

Clifford disagreed with those who would later argue that the report had
accepted the inevitability of war by calling for a change in American policy
from an economic to a military emphasis. One of the recommendations
contained in the report bore out the principle of flexibility underlying the
study:

> In addition to maintaining our own strength, the United States should support and
> assist all democratic countries which are in any way menaced or endangered by the
> U.S.S.R. Providing military support in case of attack is a last resort; a more
> effective barrier to communism is strong economic support. Trade agreements,
> loans and technical missions strengthen our ties with friendly nations and are
> effective demonstrations that capitalism is at least the equal of communism.

Clifford insisted that the administration's concern was to use any workable
method to halt Soviet expansion. No one considered restricting American
policy to any specific means. "When you are faced with that kind of crisis,
you come up with whatever weapons you have—political, military, economic,
psychological, whatever they might be."[15]

Although Kennan's ideas on Soviet behavior permeated the report, he
probably would have regarded it as too military in tone. That same month he
made his first public reference to the "containment" doctrine when he urged
State Department colleagues to seek "wise and nonprovocative" policies that
would "contain [the Soviets] both militarily and politically." He did not
believe that the Soviets aimed at world revolution or that they intended to
invade Western Europe. He considered it a mistake to argue that the Soviet
Union wanted to establish communist governments all along its borders.
"What [the Soviet leaders] wish to do is to establish in those states governments *amenable to their own influence and authority*. The main thing is that
these governments should follow Moscow's leadership. . . . It should always
be borne in mind that for the Communist leaders, power is the main thing.
Form is a secondary consideration."[16]

Although many members of the Truman administration believed that devastating wartime losses made direct Soviet military aggression unlikely before 1948, others were not so sure. The Central Intelligence Group, forerunner of the Central Intelligence Agency, concluded in September 1946 that the Soviets would probably refrain from outright military actions in the near future. But not everyone agreed. The director of intelligence for the U.S. Air Force admitted to a lack of reliable information that the Soviets would begin a war within the immediate future, but he noted that situations could change—particularly in China, Germany, Italy, and Greece. The Office of Naval Intelligence likewise did not share the Central Intelligence Group's guarded optimism. War could develop if the Kremlin interpreted some American action as a prelude to an attack on the Soviet Union or its allies.[17]

The White House had another indication of coming problems when it learned of a series of secret remarks made in Shanghai in May 1946 by Soviet Vice-Consul Araniev to leaders of the "Soviet colony." An agent from the Central Intelligence Group managed to attend this meeting, and in late September reported that the Soviets sought worldwide communist revolution by means other than war. The report, forwarded to Admiral William D. Leahy, the President's chief of staff, noted that Soviet moves to establish communist cells in China were consistent with activities throughout the world. During Araniev's presentation of the "Three Year Political Plan," he remarked that World War II had been only a truce between Russia and its ideological enemies—the capitalist countries, now led by the United States. "Because of the absolutely different ideology of our 'so-called' allies, only a temporary truce exists, which may collapse at any time, like a house of cards." War was "in the wind." The "new fires" in Greece and China were "rehearsals" and "trials of strength" that were political and psychological in nature.[18]

Araniev insisted that his government had secretly begun a "new war" against the United States and England. In such a contest, the Soviets' weapon was an "organization of millions of working masses in one bulk, under the banner of communism" and seeking the "propagation of communist ideas on a world-wide scale." This plan entailed the establishment of communist cells of three to five members inside trade unions, the army, transport factories, and any other organization of workers. With these cells, the Soviets could "embrace all countries and peoples." Araniev called for an "invincible army among all nations and peoples" that would use "strikes, sabotage and other means" to "discredit capitalist governments." The Soviet Union sought to fulfill the historical mission of Nikolai Lenin and Joseph Stalin by replacing "all the capitalist governments with our communist government." W. Averell Harriman, former ambassador to the Soviet Union and now secretary of commerce, was perhaps aware of Araniev's speech when a few days after the report arrived he asserted that the Russians had declared "psychological warfare" on the United States and that it was a "war of ideology and a fight unto the death."[19]

Other intelligence information affirmed that the Soviets had decided upon a new kind of warfare. A report of early January 1947, entitled "Revised Soviet Tactics in International Affairs," concluded that Moscow had developed a subtle approach in response to the firm policy of the United States. The Kremlin's leaders realized that continued expansion in Europe could cause all-out war and consequently sought to ease tensions with the United States. Such an approach would buy time for Soviet domestic rehabilitation, permit advocates of conciliation toward Moscow to gain a following, provide opportunity for the negotiation of trade agreements with the West, and allow the reduction of Soviet occupation forces.[20]

A cutback in Soviet troops offered numerous attractions. Since the Soviets had already established control over key parts of Eastern Europe, they could reduce the number of soldiers without sacrificing effectiveness—largely because improved mechanization facilitated the mobilization of armies. Such a reduction would alleviate worldwide tension and eliminate local tensions in occupied areas where the people had been embittered by the Soviets' harsh reparations program and by the undisciplined behavior of their troops. Furthermore, Soviet action could furnish grounds for exerting pressure on the West to reciprocate. American and British cutbacks would be difficult to undo, whereas the Soviets could shuffle troops around the European continent with ease and in secrecy. Their men could infiltrate allied armies and police forces, moving in as civilians but ready to mobilize when needed. Soviet troop reductions could also win support at international conferences from smaller nations outside the Kremlin's sphere of control—especially from those who usually took the American and British side of issues. Finally, the Soviets would be in a better position to call for general disarmament. The strength of Western nations lay in navies, modern weaponry, and air forces; a curtailment in Western power would take years to reverse. The Soviet Union, however, depended on land armies and could quickly restore its position by sheer manpower.[21]

Domestic factors were also involved in the Soviets' change of tactics in foreign affairs. The economy was in critical shape: agriculture faced serious shortages and industries had failed to meet quotas set by the Fourth Five-Year Plan. The Kremlin might have to reduce that portion of the country's economic output allotted to the military. Troop reduction would lessen expenses and would have the added bonus of freeing men to work in the internal economic system. Moreover, occupation by Soviet troops had the effect of continuing to expose soldiers to other cultures, which could lead to disturbing repercussions.[22]

Thus, even though the Soviets' tactics had changed, their ultimate goal remained the same. The Kremlin sought a temporary relaxation of hostilities to allow "economic and ideological rehabilitation at home and the consolidation of positions abroad." In the meantime it would use largely non-military means to gain political and economic control over various countries. These "characteristically Soviet techniques" included a political strategy based on the popular front or coalition form of government; infiltration of government positions; liquidation of opposition groups by local communist parties; encouragement of unrest in capitalist states; stripping or expropriating industries and replacing them with cartels under Soviet control. This new phase of Soviet foreign policy included increased communist militance in European countries outside Soviet-controlled areas. The goal was to establish communist regimes by legal or revolutionary means in France, Italy, Spain, and Greece. At the same time, the Soviets sought economic and political penetration of the Middle East, Far East, and Latin America. To obscure these activities, they would engage in propaganda designed to convince the world of their peaceful intentions.[23]

All the while, American intelligence asserted, the Soviets would be developing a long-range military program that included industrial expansion, secret weapons research and military buildups, collection of information on other nations' activities, and efforts to safeguard industry against attack. Though the Soviets would not seek direct military action, they would follow two seemingly contradictory courses: "international collaboration" and "unilateral aggression." To cause confusion and to hamper the opposition's attempts to develop counter-strategies, the Kremlin would shift from one position to another, depending on circumstances.[24]

By early 1947 the Truman administration was convinced that even though the Soviet Union had adopted a set of tactics short of outright military aggression, its ultimate objective was world control. Whether Stalin sought security or expansion, the two motives had meshed to present a formidable challenge for the United States. In this new style of confrontation, the Soviets posed threats on every front—the social, political, and economic, as well as the military. Based on these assumptions, the administration would interpret many troubles in the world as Soviet-inspired and believe that the United States, as leader of the Free World, had the responsibility of coping with them. Putting a stop to Soviet expansion would be expensive, for such a strategy entailed a potential long-range commitment to any peoples threatened by communism and seeking American help. The "Northern Tier" of the Mediterranean, comprised of Greece, Turkey, and Iran, became the testing ground for holding the line against communism. Of these three countries, Greece was the most pressing concern.

III

According to information held by American officials during the early postwar period, Greece was the first objective in Moscow's plan to take over Britain's position of preeminence in the eastern Mediterranean. Policymakers believed that the Soviets hoped to strip Greece of its northern territory by encouraging the establishment of an independent Macedonia, which might become part of the Yugoslav Federation, and by facilitating Bulgaria's acquisition of Thrace.

Thus weakened, Greece might collapse, thereby promoting Soviet control of the Aegean and the entrances to the Dardanelles and forcing neighboring Turkey to grant concessions long sought by the Kremlin. These developments would open the way to Iran and the Persian Gulf, endanger the Suez Canal, and put the Soviets into the strategic position of being able to extract oil concessions from the Middle East. The Central Intelligence Group warned that Greece's fall would have the "most unfavorable repercussions" in countries where "political sympathies [were] balanced precariously in favor of the West, and against Soviet Communism."[25] In addition to these concerns, both France and Italy were in desperate economic and political straits and leaning toward communism. Should they fall, the remainder of Western Europe would follow.

The United States found it imperative to take a stand against what many onlookers in Washington perceived as Soviet-engineered communist aggression. Unless someone devised a solution to Greece's economic and financial problems, a British representative there warned, this "independent democratic state" would be incorporated into "the Soviet system of buffer police states controlled by Communist minorities and dependent on Moscow for economic aid." The Kremlin could then use political means, especially in the UN Security Council, to obstruct Western support to Greece.[26]

Lines of communication into Greece had to remain open: it was the only Balkan country that had not fallen to Soviet pressure and the only one susceptible to Western influence. The State Department believed that the Soviets had been trying to control Greek internal affairs since 1943. Their purpose was to establish a "concealed form of Soviet power" by engaging in a violent propaganda campaign against Britain and the United States. The Kremlin wanted the world to believe that the National Liberation Front (EAM), the Greeks' major resistance organization during World War II, was the only democratic group in Greece and that its opponents were fascists. EAM, the State Department concluded, was not a friend or ally of the Russians; EAM was a communist-led "instrument of Soviet policy."[27]

The domestic issues underlying the unrest in Greece were also tied to the postwar rivalry between Britain and the Soviet Union. Greeks who had supported the monarchy now occupied positions in the government, leaving those who had worked with EAM during the war subject to systematic persecution by government and right-wing parastate organizations. Former EAM members called their monarchical opponents fascists, while government supporters referred to leftists as communists. For support, the Greek right turned to the British, the left to the Russians. In Washington, a State-War-Navy Coordinating Subcommittee for the Middle East confirmed this pattern. The Greek problem was attributable to "an apparently well organized and armed Communist minority, supported by the USSR and Soviet satellites." The Soviets were unquestionably extending military assistance to groups seeking to overthrow the Greek government. America's ambassador to Greece, Lincoln MacVeagh, observed that communist-caused chaos would not necessarily lead to direct Soviet intervention as long as Russian-controlled forces in the states bordering Greece could achieve the same goal. Soviet-inspired interference in Greece's economic and political problems could encourage neighboring nations to position troops along the northern frontier as a psychological threat designed to undermine the government in Athens.[28]

The Department of State warned that a communist takeover of Greece would facilitate the Soviets' "master plan" for the encirclement of Turkey and their penetration into the eastern Mediterranean. In early March 1947, Undersecretary of State Dean Acheson darkly warned cabinet members that the situation in Greece was critical. The United States must see the entire picture. "If Greece fell within the Russian orbit, not only Turkey would be affected but also Italy, France, and the whole of western Europe." Even so, the Department of State emphasized, the struggle must not become one between the United States and the Soviet Union, but between the USSR and the non-Soviet world. In this new type of limited warfare, military force would not be the only measure of strength. America's prestige was tied to "maintaining faith in the U.S. on the part of all key nations not now in the Soviet sphere." Greece had become "an important arena in the contest for favorable world opinion."[29]

The State Department's assessment of Soviet aims in Greece was identical to that presented by the U.S. Army. In December 1946 General Stephen J. Chamberlin, director of Army Intelligence, warned that the Soviets sought control of Greece as a step toward dominating the Near and Middle East. They had refrained from direct interference in Greece only to promote their "current role as champion of peace and cooperation." Yugoslavia, Albania, and Bulgaria were subservient to Soviet policy and were helping the communist subversives and other dissidents in northern Greece. As long as British troops remained in the country, the chances for direct Soviet involvement were remote. The Soviets would resort to anti-imperialist propaganda while continuing "camouflaged intervention." Soviet pressure would remain until either a "subservient Greek regime" took over or the government in Athens developed enough strength to stand on its own. Though Soviet leaders did not want war, they might not be able to control "hotheaded, irresponsible local agents of Soviet policy." The War Department joined the Department of State in insisting that the United States hold the line in Greece.[30]

By 1947 the Truman administration was certain that the course of events in Greece would become the standard by which the world judged the United States's performance in the Cold War. At first glance, Greece—staggered by economic problems, torn by political dissension, besieged by communist guerrillas receiving support from neighboring countries and perhaps even the Soviet Union—seemed an unpromising place to make a stand. But the Greek people were resilient and, for the most part, not attracted by communist ideology. Most important, they *wanted* American help. The United States had to develop a policy that would at once be flexible enough to handle all contingencies and yet be sufficiently restrained to prevent local conflict from erupting into full-scale war. The civil war in Greece provided the first battle-field for this new kind of war.

CHAPTER
1

Holding the Line in Greece

I

The background of the Greek civil war of 1946–49 was extremely complex. Much of the unrest stemmed from the dictatorship of General John Metaxas from 1936 to early 1941, followed by the German occupation of World War II. After Nazi liberation, British military forces put down a communist uprising in the December Revolution of 1944, which culminated in an uneasy truce at Varkiza the following February. At the Potsdam Conference of July 1945, the Soviets complained about the British troop presence in Greece and about the Greek government's harsh policies toward dissenters. In the post-war period, the government in Athens seemed unresponsive to the people's needs, thereby exacerbating longstanding economic and political problems and contributing to an atmosphere conducive to violence. The central question was whether King George II, who had gone into exile first to London and then to Cairo, should reoccupy the throne. This matter became the subject of bitter debate between forces on the left and right; many people believed that the principal issue was whether the small group of communists in the country could take over the government and tie it to Moscow. Indeed, former leaders of EAM were now exercising influence through the Greek Communist party (KKE).[1]

The right easily won the general elections of March 1946, its margin widened by the communists' decision to abstain from voting. The Populists (royalists) took 231 of 354 members of Parliament, whereas the Liberals won 48 seats. The new prime minister was Constantine Tsaldaris, a Populist who favored a rightist regime which would prevent a communist takeover. Doubtless most Greeks did not support the Populists, but had voted for them out of fear of continued internal disorder. An Allied Mission for Observing the

17

Greek Elections, comprised of more than 1,200 British, French, and American observers (invited by the Greek government), witnessed scattered instances of violence and intimidation along with a few irregularities, but judged the elections fair. America's chief observer, Henry F. Grady, insisted that the outcome reflected a "true and valid verdict of the Greek people." The remaining political question was whether a plebiscite, scheduled for early September, would restore the monarchy.[2]

Another problem was a longstanding territorial claims issue. Greece wanted adjustments along the northern frontier that would afford better security, but such aspirations caused friction with Yugoslavia, Albania, and Bulgaria. Before a meeting of the KKE in Athens in May 1946, the party's secretary, Nikos Zahariadis, declared that the Greeks must resolve the national claims question before they could achieve a "Greater Greece." Among other areas, Greece must have Cyprus and the eastern sector of Turkish Thrace. British occupation first had to end, Zahariadis insisted; the government in London was responsible for the wartime arrangements permitting Bulgarian occupation of Western Thrace.[3] But the KKE was caught in a dilemma: northern expansion would involve taking territory from neighboring countries, all of which were under Soviet influence; failure to make these demands would cost the party its influence at home.

Confusion characterized the KKE's leadership. On February 12, 1946, the first anniversary of the Varkiza Agreement and just three days after Stalin delivered a speech in Moscow calling upon his people to make the Soviet Union into a world power, the Central Committee of the KKE decided "to organize an armed struggle against the monarcho-fascist orgy." Early in that same year a KKE delegation had gone to Moscow to seek aid. According to the leader of the group, Mitsos Partsalidis, the KKE was told to focus on political means, participate in the March elections, and "wait and see." Depending on events, the KKE "might sometimes turn to lawful struggle and other times to armed struggle." This meeting in Moscow was a strong indication that Stalin would have been pleased with expanded communist influence in Greece as long as the KKE became a legitimate political party and refrained from armed conflict; but party leaders in Greece read Moscow's recommendations as suggestions and not directives and proceeded to boycott the elections.[4]

The outcome of the March elections virtually assured a resurgence of civil war. Violence broke out on the evening of the elections, March 30–31, when a small group of self-proclaimed defenders of the people attacked the lightly guarded gendarmerie post in the village of Litokhoron, located on the eastern slopes of Mount Olympus. The incident was perhaps isolated and spontaneous, the result of a local group of former ELAS members (the military arm of EAM's resistance during World War II) feeling persecuted by the government and striking out in frustration against its forces in the area. But within a year the attack had evolved into mythology as the birth of the civil war, an image upheld by the KKE by late October 1947.[5]

The guerrillas' activities escalated into raiding and pillaging expeditions in June after they established positions throughout the mainland and the Peloponnese, on the islands in the Aegean and Ionian seas, and along Greece's northern frontier. Geoffrey Chandler, press officer of the British embassy in Salonika, described the scene: "Infiltration from the north, in the form of small armed bands slipping over the Yugoslav border and back again, was now a familiar part of the Macedonian scene and fights between gendarmerie and Communist bands had grown in frequency. . . . Salonika remained insulated from the facts of the situation, although here there was already a thin trickle of refugees bringing the pinpricks of a reality of which Athens was still completely unaware." The Ministry of Public Order in Athens soon complained that the guerrillas had created a desperate situation in the north. Parliament moved to restore order by approving local courts martial, suspending the right of habeas corpus, and authorizing government forces to establish curfews, search houses, and make arrests without warrants. Radio Moscow denounced the measures as attempts to promote the "legitimization" of a "fascist dictatorship," and charged that the Parliament was "illegal and based on fraud and violence." In this atmosphere, unsubstantiated rumors followed of a possible Russian attack on Greece.[6]

Soviet involvement remains problematical, but little doubt exists that the guerrillas received considerable help from the communist states of Yugoslavia, Albania, and Bulgaria. Many of the guerrillas received training and equipment in camps located inside these neighboring countries. Not everything possessed by the guerrillas came from these sources. Their arms, which included machine guns, rifles, grenades, mines, and mortars, came primarily from materials stolen in Greece—weapons the British had furnished to the resistance during World War II and wartime supplies left behind by Italy and Germany. From the United Nations Relief and Rehabilitation Administration (UNRRA) came food, clothing, and motor vehicles. These materials were vital, but there can be little doubt that the assistance of Yugoslavia, Albania, and Bulgaria was essential to the warmaking capacity of the guerrillas.[7]

The first infiltration of guerrillas into Greece probably began as early as March 1946—following a speech by Zahariadis at a training camp in Bulkes, located northwest of Belgrade in Yugoslavia. Just days before, he had attended a Communist party meeting in Prague and received assurances of help from Yugoslavia. Zahariadis had been trained in Moscow and was already considered the KKE's leading exponent of Stalinism. Born in Asia Minor, where he became a schoolmaster, Zahariadis was a stodgy, humorless, and ruthless figure, possessing a huge head, crew-cut brown hair, and square profile. After living nearly three years in Russia, he returned to Salonika in the mid-1920s and became a chief spokesman for the claims of the Macedonian Slavs in the Balkans. Arrested and briefly jailed in 1926 for his communist activities, he again visited Russia upon his release before returning to Greece two years later. In 1934 he became the KKE's general secretary, and was elected to Parliament two years later. Zahariadis spent most of World

War II in prison, the bulk of it in the German concentration camp at Dachau. Returning to Greece in March 1945, he received an enthusiastic welcome by trade union members meeting in Athens Stadium who regarded him as a proponent of the coming social revolution. Indeed, he dominated the Central Committee of the KKE at the Second Plenum of February 1946. Although during the war he had not supported guerrilla activity and had not urged the communists to join the insurgents, he now, in 1946, preferred militant political actions based in Leninist-Stalinist ideology and aimed at achieving revolution in the towns and winning influence in the government.[8]

The guerrillas' first objective was to establish a headquarters somewhere in the secluded mountainous regions of northern Greece. After stepping up their activities in Thessaly and Macedonia, they sought to isolate Macedonia and incorporate it into a Yugoslav federation. To accomplish these goals, the guerrillas had to push government forces south of an area stretching from Mount Grammos on the Albanian border to Mount Olympus close to the Aegean. Though the guerrillas were successful in some places, they could not amass enough power to break the government's hold on that line. The area not taken included Salonika, where British troops were stationed.[9]

To achieve the organization, leadership, and strength needed, the KKE in July 1946 appointed "General" Markos Vafiades as commander-in-chief of what would be called the "Democratic Army." Markos was a forty-year-old former EAM representative in Macedonia and political commissar of ELAS, who, like Zahariadis, was born in Asia Minor; but he became a tobacco worker in Thrace and a staunch member of the KKE before his communist affiliation led to his imprisonment at the outset of World War II. Escaping in 1941, Markos earned a reputation in the mountains as a "military genius," a notoriety marred only by an explosive temperament that he constantly struggled to keep under control. He was 5'7" in height, which was unusually tall for a Greek, and had a mustache, blue eyes, thin and bony features, leathered skin, deeply lined cheeks, and straight brown hair. Dressed in boots, the tunic of an officer, and a roll-neck sweater, Markos conveyed the image of a rugged mountain hero and attracted a fervent following.[10]

According to one source, planning for the Democratic Army had begun as early as mid-December 1945. In the Bulgarian town of Petrich, close to the Greek border, the Central Committee of the KKE met with Yugoslav and Bulgarian army officers to reorganize the Greek partisans and prepare "to fight against the Greek government in power." With the Yugoslavs promising aid, reorganization began around former ELAS officers in the towns of Naoussa in Macedonia and Volos in Thessaly. In early 1946, ELAS gathered arms and ammunition hidden at the time of surrender in February 1945 and relocated them in supply centers just outside Greece. Thus Bulkes was already the Democratic Army's training camp for thousands of ELAS refugees by the time of Zahariadis's visit in March.[11]

Markos later claimed that he had wanted to launch a major offensive during the summer and fall of 1946, but was restrained by party leaders torn by whether to follow military or political tactics. In July the KKE had about 30,000 modern weapons hidden in Greece and 20,000 men in Yugoslavia waiting to be armed. But the KKE was indecisive because the attitude of the Soviet Union and its allies was unclear. Christopher M. Woodhouse, a close British observer of events at the time and author of several works dealing with the subject, now believes that the KKE might have stayed with political methods had the West given the party a chance to take part in the electoral process. The KKE, he speculates, might have taken the paths of the Communist parties in France and Italy by working within the political system.[12]

Thus, even though the reorganization process of the guerrilla army was under way by early 1946, the KKE had not yet made a decision for civil war. Before the summer of that year the guerrillas made no efforts to enhance their numbers. Indeed, many bands had taken to the mountains *without* Communist party instigation. The guiding principle seemed to be armed self-defense against what many considered to be a repressive government in Athens. In July, however, a few guerrillas began scattered operations that gradually raised the level of activity.[13]

The Department of State in Washington was carefully monitoring the growing unrest in northern Greece. The leftists seemed well-organized, highly spirited, and experienced in guerrilla resistance. Furthermore, State Department analysts thought that the guerrillas were receiving the "moral support of Moscow and the latter's Balkan protégés," who had criticized the recent elections and called the new Athens government "monarcho-fascist." Should EAM's friends outside Greece extend military support, the Greek government would face a serious problem in maintaining authority. Two factors seemed to necessitate American aid: the threat from Greece's northern neighbors and a steady decline in the Greek economy.[14]

In July the Greek government made public its complaints about foreign assistance to the guerrillas. A large part of the reasoning behind bringing this matter into the open was attributable to the observations of J. M. Mackintosh, a British soldier who had been a liaison officer with the Soviet army from 1944 to 1946 while a member of the Allied Control Commission in Sofia, Yugoslavia. Mackintosh noted persistent reports of supplies from Bulgaria arriving in the southern part of Yugoslav Macedonia. In July of 1946, he asserted, "immediately after a prolonged visit to Moscow of the Soviet Commander-in-Chief in Bulgaria, the Soviet military authorities in Bulgaria created a 25 kilometre forbidden zone along the whole Greek-Bulgarian frontier." In addition to this potential staging area for guerrilla warfare, huge supplies of arms had been found after the expiration date set by the Varkiza Agreement for the surrender of weapons. Though many arms had been kept in violation of the agreement, others had been confiscated from enemy nations during World War II. The Greek army engaged in a clearing operation in Mount Vermion and Mount Olympus, but the effort was ineffective. By August, minor disturbances had developed into organized guerrilla attacks on Naoussa and other towns, which virtually closed travel between

Thessaly and Macedonia, obstructed economic rehabilitation, and threatened to undermine popular support for the government.[15]

The plebiscite in September probably reflected general sentiment in supporting the return of the king by a two-to-one margin, but the result did not ease the growing pressure on the United States to help Greece. More violence had erupted during the voting process, and the Liberal opposition and others accused the right of stuffing the ballot boxes. Indeed, an Anglo-American mission supervising a revision of the electoral lists cited the dubious figures compiled by Greek officials that nearly 100 percent of the registrants had voted. A monarchy was less threatening than the communists, insisted "The Justice for Greece Committee" in the United States. The Truman administration must take action against the "*intensive aggression of Pan-Slavism and Communism.*" Greece was a bulwark of peace in the Balkans and in the world. Should that country fall to communism, the Soviet Union would close the eastern Mediterranean. Ambassador MacVeagh in Athens agreed that the plebiscite constituted a vote against communism rather than an indication of popular feeling in favor of royalism. A British representative in Greece wrote that economic recovery depended on the Greek government's ability to stamp out the guerrillas. Political concessions had only temporarily eased the situation, for the communists had foreign support and were preparing to intensify their activities. Military force alone could end the threat to Greece.[16]

If military assistance were to come, it would not be from the British; the government in London was moving toward a total withdrawal of its troops from Greece. Despite staggering wartime losses, the British had maintained troops in Greece since 1944. Prestige was involved in the decision to stay after the war, but British spokesmen also considered Greece (and Turkey) a barrier against the Soviet spread into the Middle East. The British military presence, however, had come under attack from the Soviet Union, from left-wing groups in Britain and elsewhere, and from several Labor members of Parliament. A withdrawal would ease the manpower shortage at home, as well as undercut criticisms of the government in London for sponsoring the repressive Populist regime in Athens. In addition, arguments over Iran in early 1946 underlined the importance of withdrawing the troops from Greece before the Russians used the British presence as a pretext for staying in Rumania, Bulgaria, and Iran. Consequently, in autumn 1946, the British government notified Greek officials of the decision to withdraw its military forces (about 14,000 combat troops plus the 1,380 officers and enlisted men of the British Military Mission who were engaged in training the Greek army). The process would begin on September 15 (two weeks after the plebiscite) and would be completed by the end of the following month.[17]

The impending withdrawal had immediate repercussions on the war. Fighting escalated in mid-September as the British began pulling out a division of troops from the Peloponnese and Attica; only a single division was left in Macedonia and a brigade in the Athens area. Increasing hostilities along Greece's northern borders caused the cabinet in Athens to seek British approval for an enlargement of Greek armed forces. But the British refused because the move would necessitate another huge expenditure from a rapidly depleting treasury. They also believed that strategic considerations in the Middle East would ultimately force the United States to cooperate with Britain in safeguarding the entire region from the Soviet Union.[18]

It was clear in London that a withdrawal could assure the loss of Greece unless the United States—which had exasperated British leaders by its indecisiveness—stepped in now and assumed the burden. In November the British chiefs of staff advised Foreign Secretary Ernest Bevin to delay the withdrawal until 1947 to allow time for their military officers to prepare the Greek army for battle. But even this expedient could not guarantee success. Prime Minister Clement Attlee was upset by a recent request by Byrnes to postpone the troop withdrawal; the Americans were all too hesitant about providing the aid required to save Greece. By late December the British cabinet seemed to be leaning toward dropping Greece regardless of whether the United States helped. Hugh Dalton, the chancellor of the exchequer, opposed further aid because of problems at home. A "high military opinion" questioned the importance of Greece to British interests. If the guerrillas were defeated, he noted, the British troops would not be necessary; if the guerrillas won, the troops would have to get out to avoid involvement in the hostilities. The chiefs of staff were willing to allow a brigade to remain as a token presence only until April 1, 1947. In the meantime the Greek army must be reorganized and trained in counterinsurgency warfare. The British government emphasized that economic reconstruction, not military assistance alone, would save Greece, and that the necessary funds must come from the United States.[19]

British leaders were not united on the question of pulling out of Greece; Bevin learned of the growing feeling for an early withdrawal while at the UN in New York and was shocked. Both he and the Foreign Office were opposed to a total withdrawal. The Greek government would come under enormous pressure as the Soviets sought to expand into Turkey, Iran, Italy, the Persian Gulf, and the Middle East. The abandonment of Greece would be another Munich. But such an outcome seemed almost inevitable. Bevin and his supporters could not deny the harsh realities confronting their country, and, they noted with angry frustration, the United States had not demonstrated a willingness to do anything specific to save the situation.[20]

In retrospect, British retrenchment policies in the Near East and the eastern Mediterranean made it incumbent upon the United States to become involved. But that reality was not clear at the time. Congress was in no mood to take on extensive foreign policy obligations, and the American people seemed content to wash their hands of external political and military affairs. Such a myopic view, however, could not change a fundamental truth: a refusal to assume global responsibilities would encourage the spread of totalitarianism—which even isolationist-minded Americans could not accept. In addition, the withdrawal of British forces from Greece would suggest an imminent Western reversal of policy that could only be halted by an injection of American troops. The British decision was monumental in importance, caused by practical realities during the postwar period and by the desire to awaken the United States to duties no longer avoidable.

On October 28, 1946, the situation in Greece became more alarming when Markos announced the creation of the Democratic Army and it soon adopted the battle cry "By Fire and Axe!" The guerrilla forces did not appear formidable. They probably numbered no more than 13,000, and not all of them were in the field. Yet their tactics and experienced leadership from the wartime resistance more than balanced the advantages that government forces had in numbers and matériel. The guerrillas carried on fifth-column activities in the Greek army and among civilians to gather intelligence, spread propaganda, and terrorize the population. The rugged terrain bordering Yugoslavia, Albania, and Bulgaria was laced with mountain trails suitable for moving men and supplies. The surrounding populace included a substantial minority of communists, who had gained control over many local administrative positions. Only three main roads or railways, all of which were easy to sabotage, connected the north with Athens and Salonika. An American intelligence report cautioned that by the following spring or winter the guerrillas might install an "independent pro-Soviet regime" that the "satellite states" would recognize as a prelude to granting open aid. Either Greece would collapse or the great powers would go to war. In the worst possible scenario, both could happen.[21]

By December most observers realized that the Greek army needed vast improvements before it could defeat the guerrillas. The manpower ceiling seemed sufficiently high at 115,000 (along with 35,000 gendarmerie). But the men were poorly led, ill-trained, undisciplined, inadequately provisioned, low in morale, and reluctant to take the offensive. Many regulars were tied to static defense duties, unable and in many instances unwilling to leave their posts. The previous October the Greeks had established an organization called MAY, which was comprised of "units of rural self-defense" in the villages, armed and subordinate to officers or non-commissioned officers of reserves living in the area. But the men had few weapons and little ammunition. The British commander in the Middle East underlined the need for small, mobile commando units and recommended that the army put field divisions on a "semi-pack basis." Unless the situation changed, the guerrillas would establish control over the countryside and move into the towns. When the army launched a daylight offensive, the guerrillas dispersed, only to regroup at night after the regulars had returned to their posts. The immobile Greek forces had to stay in large groups for safety, making it impossible to carry out the scattered pursuit tactics necessary for victory. To alleviate this problem, the General Staff established mobile Units of Pursuit Detachments (MAD) along with army commando groups.[22]

Other branches of the Greek military service were no better prepared. British observers argued that the Greeks needed naval patrols for minesweeping, stopping guerrilla movements by sea, and maintaining supplies for small army forces. But World War II had left the navy in poor shape. The outlook of the Royal Hellenic Air Force was also dismal. It consisted of fifty-four aircraft, all British-manufactured, and fewer than 300 battle-trained pilots. Greek finances precluded the purchase of more planes, and the Germans had confiscated the only state aircraft factory. Greece had no petroleum refineries, no munitions manufacturers, and no facilities for overhauling aircraft or for making replacements and spare parts.[23]

The situation became critical in early 1947 as guerrillas in Thrace sought to join those in the west and broaden their influence along the entire northern frontier. According to the guerrillas, they controlled over a hundred villages and were engaged in conscriptions, collecting taxes, and making laws. Their headquarters were near Lake Prespa, where the Greek, Yugoslav, and Albanian borders met, and their territorial possessions included the Grammos and Vitsi mountains. Americans in Greece urged their leaders in Washington to cooperate with the British in extending economic and financial aid. But the problem was not simply economic. The communists were making political gains by taking advantage of the economic crisis and the ensuing domestic strife. And it is doubtful that the problem was primarily ideological. When asked about Marxism and Leninism, a captured seventeen-year-old guerrilla replied: "I am illiterate. I cannot read or write, and I don't know anything about Marxism and Leninism. But I can tell you what our leader said. Our leader said we're going to get that big white house right on the waterfront in Salonika." Greeks on both sides of the fighting had lost confidence in their government's ability to provide security. The only way to re-establish order, MacVeagh insisted, was for the United States to make clear, especially to the Soviet Union, its determination to prevent aggression. Immediate military measures were necessary to buy time for long-range economic correctives.[24]

By 1946 the Greek government had taken its case to both the Truman administration and to the United Nations. Greek representatives exerted pressure on the State Department to help them achieve territorial and reparations claims. A group in New York urged Byrnes to arrange for wartime reparations, the return of southern Albania (which the Greeks called Northern Epirus), and the rectification of the Bulgarian border so as to assure a natural defense line for Greece. Tsaldaris sent a communication to the secretary-general of the UN, urging the Security Council to investigate charges that Yugoslavia, Albania, and Bulgaria were helping the guerrillas. Heated debates followed, during which those three nations accused the Greeks of violating their borders. In the Security Council, the Soviet Union vetoed an American proposal in September calling for a UN investigation of the Greek border situation. And then, in the following December, the Soviets shocked observers by reversing their posture and supporting a similar American resolution that would permit an investigation on both sides of the border. The reasons became clear: such an inquiry (with Russian participation) would highlight the presence of British troops as well as provide a showcase for the Greek government's repressive policies.[25]

The Security Council appointed a commission to investigate the border violations and submit recommendations. Headed by Mark Ethridge, editor and publisher of the Louisville *Courier-Journal* and the Louisville *Times*, the commission departed for Greece in January 1947 and immediately encountered difficulties. Two months later, after repeated failure to uncover border transgressions, the commission set out on a cold, windy morning from Salonika to meet the guerrillas' leader, General Markos. After several postponements, the commission decided to leave, feeling "exploited as an advertisement of the rebel cause." The dawn departure caused considerable trepidation, especially after the village's guerrilla chieftain read a statement accusing the commission of not giving Markos the opportunity to explain his side.[26]

Ethridge believed that Greece was a "ripe plum ready to fall into [the Soviets'] hands." Confirmation came from British and American political, economic, and military sources. Communist forces were increasing in numbers, while in the Greek army desertions were up and morale was at its lowest. Other commission members—British, French, Chinese, Colombian— agreed with him that Greece's demise would bring not only the collapse of the Near East but of France and Italy as well. After the Soviets had encountered stiff opposition in Azerbaijan and Turkey, they found Greece "surprisingly soft" and adopted measures that went beyond the "probing state." Greece's fall, Ethridge concluded, would destroy "the hope of many other nations, including the small ones who gratefully look on [the] US at the moment as a colossus."[27]

The greatest needs in Greece were economic, for without emergency aid and long-range economic planning the country would collapse and endanger America's strategic and economic interests in the Near East. The White House was aware of the growing importance of the region, both in restraining Soviet expansion and in securing access to oil. It was also cognizant of Britain's sharp decline in economic and military strength. In early April 1946, the U.S. battleship *Missouri* had visited Athens, signifying America's long-standing friendship with Greece. An American embassy official in Athens reported that Greeks viewed the event as a "token of US friendship," a "symbol of US might and US interest in Near and Middle East affairs," and a "friendly reassurance" against the Soviet Union. By the following autumn, the United States was moving toward replacing the British in the Near East. Should the United States fail to assume this responsibility, American policymakers believed, the Greek people could choose communism. A United Press correspondent traveled by jeep behind the guerrillas' lines in December 1946 and warned that they were "strategic pawns in a Russian campaign to outflank the Dardanelles." If Greece were to remain what a *New York Times* editorial called the "Western 'island' in the Balkans," the "Anchor on the lifeline," the "Key to the Straits," the United States would have to grant economic aid.[28]

II

The Greek government had aleady begun a campaign for American economic assistance. In early January 1946 spokesmen in Athens asked the Food and Agriculture (FAO) Mission for Greece to determine whether UNRRA assistance had helped. Mission representatives found the Greek economy dangerously weak, and warned that outside assistance would be necessary after UNRRA's scheduled termination on March 31, 1947. The Greek government should seek aid from the UN Economic and Social Council as well as the American and British governments. For 1947 and 1948, Greece would need $100 million. To spread responsibility and to avert charges of American imperialism, a UN mission should extend technical assistance and advice on the implementation of funds. An international program could replace the British economic mission and eliminate the need for one run by Americans.[29]

While the FAO was conducting its study, Tsaldaris, who was en route to London, stopped in Paris, where at the Council of Foreign Ministers meeting he met with Byrnes and said he received assurances that Greece would not be left to fend for itself. Byrnes recommended that the State Department discuss the matter with Greek representatives in Washington. Tsaldaris left Paris optimistic about the prospects of American aid.[30]

Tsaldaris could not have known that the State Department had already initiated a study of the feasibility of approving economic aid to Greece. In mid-July 1946 analysts reported their findings. The end of UNRRA's involvement in Greece, they warned, would hurt America's commercial relations with that country. During the last half of that year food and rehabilitation matériel would taper off and the Greeks would have to find a way to finance imports. Termination of UNRRA aid would create an explosive situation. A budget drawn by the Greek government also contained problems: its major expenditure was for the army, but income depended on indirect taxes and the sale of UNRRA supplies.[31] A massive overhaul of the country's economic and financial system was essential.

Pressure for American assistance increased as a Greek economic mission arrived in Washington in August. The mission was expected. After Tsaldaris had arrived in London, he informed the American ambassador of his government's interest in an additional loan from the Export-Import Bank. State Department officials consulted the bank, and even though they informed Greece that the time was not good to ask for another loan, they agreed to discuss the country's situation. Members of the Greek economic mission, headed by the prominent political figure Sophocles Venizelos, met with Export-Import Bank officials and submitted a program calling for a credit of $175 million. In meetings with Acheson and Truman, Venizelos warned of worldwide repercussions if the United States deserted Greece.[32]

The Truman administration was not ready to support Greece's appeal. The President was unwilling to put in money until the Greek government brought some semblance of economic stability to the country. Whereas some members of the Treasury Department considered Greece part of the British sphere of interest and were reluctant to take an active role, spokesmen for the Department of State wanted the Greek government to make a greater effort to resolve its economic problems. Acheson wanted Greece first to ease its harsh government practices and give up its northern territorial claims. He considered Tsaldaris a "weak, pleasant, but silly man," who believed that his government could resolve its problems by winning a territorial cession in the north and securing the unrealistic sum of $6 billion in economic aid from the United States. As of July 31, 1946, Acheson wrote the President, UNRRA had furnished $293 million to Greece, and by the end of the year the total would have climbed to nearly $358 million. Greece could meet import requirements in 1947 by resources already in its possession—an evaluation that included a still unused $25 million allotted by the Export-Import Bank. The State Department could not ask Congress for more money through any organization. Eight months had passed since the last Export-Import Bank credit and the Greek government had not yet used all of that fund.[33]

White House opposition to additional credits did not rule out economic assistance; the obstacle was the irresponsible manner in which reconstruction had been administered. Instead of taxing the rich, Greek officials had legislated a system of indirect taxation and made no attempts at long-range planning. Few relief measures had touched the people in the villages—those who needed the most help. Draft animals had been reduced by half from 1945; national production of field crops (corn, wheat, beans) was about half; production of export cash crops (tobacco and dried fruit) had diminished to a third; sheep and goat herds were down to two-thirds. Wartime inflation had driven up the exchange rate of the drachma to 50 billion of the old for one of the new. By January 1946 the drachma was stabilized only for a time with British help. Fields lay untilled, the refugee lines in towns stretched longer, economic unrest threatened to cause political chaos, communist-led groups stood ready to seize the government. Perhaps one writer is correct in asserting that late in the summer of 1946, Byrnes and Bevin made an informal arrangement to assist Greece (as well as Turkey). According to Bevin, the British would handle military assistance in Greece while the United States assumed responsibility for economic aid and perhaps military help. Whether such an arrangement existed, the Greek government was convinced that American aid was forthcoming. A day or so after the September plebiscite, the Greek undersecretary of foreign affairs wrote that he had received assurances from American officials (not identified) that the prerequisite for aid was a broadening of the Greek government to make it more democratic and thus more responsive to economic and political needs.[34]

For reasons that transcended the problems in Greece, the Truman administration was moving closer to an economic aid program. Soviet pressure on Iran and Turkey convinced Acheson of the strategic value of the region. In late September 1946 the United States granted a credit of $10 million to Greece for maritime equipment. Less than a week later, Greece received an additional credit of $25 million for buying other economic goods. A dispatch had arrived from Byrnes, still in Europe, which recommended that the United States help Greece and Turkey. Secretary of War Robert Patterson and Secretary of the Navy James V. Forrestal were supportive, as was the acting director of the State Department's Office of European Affairs, John Hickerson, who declared that the United States should extend economic aid because of Greece's symbolic importance. "The world is watching the support or lack thereof which we furnish our friends at this critical time, and the future policies of many countries will be determined by their estimate of the seriousness or lack thereof with which the US upholds its principles and supports those of like mind."[35]

In mid-December 1946, Acheson informed newspapermen that an eight-member team of economic experts headed by Paul A. Porter would make a firsthand inspection to determine Greece's economic needs. Porter was well-qualified for the task. Former legal counsel for the Department of Agriculture, later for the CBS radio network, he had worked with the Office of Price Administration during the war, and then with the Office of Economic Stabilization, before becoming OPA administrator in 1946. He also was a close friend of Mark Ethridge, who as U.S. representative on the UN border commission would provide his candid assessment of the situation. In mid-January 1947, the Porter economic mission landed in Athens and would soon talk with hundreds of Greek businessmen, engineers, economists, factory workers, farmers, and spokesmen for a large number of organizations. The timing of the mission's arrival was not propitious. The run on gold had regained momentum, and another political crisis had erupted following the resignation of two members of Tsaldaris's cabinet. A few days afterward, Porter grimly informed the press that the Greek government would have to achieve economic stability primarily with its own resources and that his visit did not assure American aid.[36]

Porter admitted that the economic situation was worse than expected. A month of investigations revealed that Greece was verging on bankruptcy and allotting almost half of the national income on non-productive outlets. The government had fed inflation by failing to resist demands for wage raises. The country was stricken with black marketing, speculation, and profiteering. Lack of confidence in the government had impeded investment in long-range reconstruction programs. Politics permeated every part of Greek life, hindering reconstruction of the economy and blocking efforts to guarantee personal security. The Greek people exhibited what Porter termed an "unhealthy psychological condition"—a feeling of helplessness—that leaned toward the belief that the Allies were obligated to extend aid because of the country's suffering in World War II. A dependence mentality had resulted, leading Greeks to believe that America's duty was to save their country. No "state" existed in Greece according to Western definition. Greece was comprised of a "loose hierarchy of individualistic politicians" who were preoccupied with power and had no interest in reforms. Virtually no government services existed, corruption was rampant, and civil service was a "depressing farce." To President Truman, Porter reported that the Greek government was "completely reactionary, . . . incredibly weak, stupid and venal." Unless Greece received considerable outside aid, a certain financial collapse would result that would have serious political implications.[37]

MacVeagh did not agree with Porter's exclusive emphasis on Greece's domestic troubles, and ultimately convinced him that economic rehabilitation could not take place without first clearing up the military situation along the northern border. He complained that Porter was a "new deal" reformer who did not understand that the real threat came from outside the country, not from internal "sins of selfish reactionism and venality." He and Ethridge tried to persuade Porter that Greece was a "soft" spot for Soviet encroachments, and that there was a critical relationship between domestic pacification and the settlement of border disputes. MacVeagh insisted that economic reconstruction could not take place in Greece without first repulsing the "double attack" on the government coming from inside and outside the country. The Greek people felt helpless and demoralized because of the guerrillas' activities and the growing fear of an invasion from the north. Porter finally gave in, but with the stipulation that Washington make its assistance conditional upon the Greek government's institution of major economic reforms. The United States would have to provide financial support, suggestions for reconstruction, and daily leadership in implementing the aid program. It must establish an economic mission in Greece that would be directly administered by Americans and that might have to stay five years. But Porter agreed with MacVeagh that the largest initial expenditure would be military in view of growing domestic violence encouraged from the outside. The next few months would determine whether Greece would survive.[38]

MacVeagh realized that the Greek problem was not solely military, and emphasized that only a more broadly based government could attract enough popular support to implement economic reforms. Tsaldaris, however, still refused to condone participation by opposition forces. Without an immediate move toward a coalition government, a large part of the public, including the moderates, could soon join the opposition. MacVeagh warned that in encouraging the establishment of a broadened government and a liberalized program, there must not be the "least possible publicity" of American pressure.[39]

The new secretary of state, George C. Marshall, supported MacVeagh's recommendation to widen the base of the Greek government. Marshall was a respected and revered military figure, who, during World War II as chief of staff of the American army, had grasped the importance of alleviating economic distress before it became subject to totalitarian exploitation. A more representative government would ease political strife in Greece and stem potential American opposition to aiding a government that lacked popular support. Marshall, however, had just returned from a disheartening experience in China and understood the difficulties in establishing a coalition government. He recognized that the United States could not demand changes in the Greek government's political makeup, but it could—and should— refuse to help any regime leaning toward extremes, right or left. Communists could not become part of the government, for they would infiltrate important posts and be in the position to interfere with government administration. The domestic order vital to economic and political progress would not have a chance. Stability could come only through amnesty and disarmament programs, and by tax reforms, financial controls, and a reorganized civil service.[40]

In late January 1947 the government in Athens seemed to move in the direction desired by the United States: Tsaldaris resigned under pressure, and Greece underwent its thirteenth major change in leadership since Nazi liberation. An elderly banker and former foreign minister, Dimitrios Maximos, became premier, even though Tsaldaris held onto the position of vice premier and maintained control over foreign affairs. The new regime opened the cabinet to leaders of seven political parties in Parliament—all except the Liberals of Themistocles Sophoulis, who refused to serve because of Populist domination—making the government a coalition of rightist groups controlling nearly 90 percent of the votes in Parliament. The government's call for political reforms seemed sincere. Maximos promised to free women and children held as political prisoners, and to grant amnesty and protection to those who surrendered and turned in their weapons within a month. Marshall publicly expressed hope that the recent governmental changes signaled the beginning of political cooperation and a good chance for a resolution of the nation's problems short of deeper American involvement.[41]

But another variable was beginning to sharpen America's focus on the strategic importance of the Near East: the postwar decline of British power, which caused that government to contract its military commitments in both Greece and Turkey, and to ask the United States to assume the burden. To ease the impact of such a drastic retrenchment, Bevin called on the cabinet in late January to approve a grant of two million pounds' ($8 million) worth of equipment to Greece for the reorganization and training of its army. Perhaps the British could also meet part of the costs of maintaining the Greek army after March 31 if the United States picked up the balance. The cabinet soon approved Bevin's recommendation for the special grant, and it agreed to the proposal of the chiefs of staff to reduce British troops in Greece to one brigade by April 1. But Attlee, Dalton, and the Treasury feared for Britain's own financial collapse and opposed going any farther. The cabinet stipulated that military aid to the Greek army would end on March 31, 1947. Though the British would continue helping to organize and train the army, the Greek government would have to turn to the United States for economic assistance. Bevin recommended that nothing be said to the Greeks until he could talk with the United States about that prospect. The Foreign Office would send formal notes to Washington, explaining the situation and urging that the United States assume the responsibility of assistance.[42]

The postwar economic troubles confronting the British were no surprise to Washington. The State Department had received alarming reports in early January 1947. Wartime property damage in Britain caused by air bombardments totaled almost six billion dollars at current replacement costs. Heavy industrial losses had resulted from the government's wartime policy of allowing the depletion of capital goods by deferring all but the most vital maintenance and repairs. Net depletion appeared to have been more than one and a half billion dollars. Reduced exports were especially damaging. The wartime decision to cut the British merchant fleet by 25 percent was an obvious contributor, but another factor was more important. Britain had been experiencing a long-range decline in natural resources and industrial growth that was attributable to its failure to keep pace with changes in mechanization and to a rapidly diminishing supply of coal, which had been the foundation of the country's industrial power.[43]

Other considerations magnified Britain's problems. The war had struck a near mortal blow to manpower. Britain's population in 1947 was slightly lower than it had been in 1939. Overseas assets had fallen, while overseas liabilities had risen. The war had forced the liquidation of more than four billion dollars of foreign investments, a figure that grew to more than five billion in the period afterward. Net income from foreign investments had dropped to half the prewar level. Britain was now a debtor on the international account. Its short-term liabilities to other nations—through accumulated sterling balances—were more than fourteen billion dollars. Finally, little hope existed for rapid recovery. The State Department estimated that for Britain to make up losses in overseas income and pay back debts to the United States and Canada, it would need an economic miracle—an increase in exports to 175 percent of the 1938 volume. This hardly seemed possible, especially since the rationing of gas and electricity forced many industries to shut down and helped push unemployment to over 15 percent. As the British in 1946–47 underwent winter blizzards and record cold followed by summer floods and droughts, they realized that the time had come to reassess their role in foreign affairs.[44]

America's most immediate concern was that British troop removals from Greece would eliminate what Washington's policymakers perceived as a major deterrent to Soviet "satellite action" against the country's northern frontier. The military implications of Britain's economic condition were clear to American military leaders: the British would have to make troop cuts worldwide. A bill before Parliament would allow up to 40 percent of British overseas forces to be of foreign origin. Such a mixture of British regulars with mercenaries would endanger the British life line in the Mediterranean by lowering the level of military performance and damaging national prestige. The decline of the British Empire would have a profound impact on America's foreign policy.[45]

These realities became especially clear on the afternoon of Friday, February 21, 1947, when the series of events began that would culminate in the

Truman Doctrine. The director of the State Department's recently created Near Eastern and African Affairs Division, Loy Henderson, received a call from Hickerson: the first secretary of the British embassy, Herbert M. Sichel, would arrive in an hour. After entering Hickerson's office around 4 p.m., Sichel explained that the British ambassador to the United States, Lord Inverchapel, would visit the State Department the following Monday morning to deliver "a blue piece of paper," which was diplomatic language for a formal message from the British government. In keeping with standard diplomatic practice, Inverchapel was placing copies of two notes—one on Greece, the other on Turkey—in the department's possession beforehand.[46]

The timing of the notes achieved the British purpose: they forced the United States into decisive action. The Truman administration had already decided that the Near East was strategically important. As early as the autumn of 1945, the White House had discussed the possibility of helping Greece and Turkey. But nothing specific had resulted. The British notes brought focus to the crisis in the Mediterranean. Hickerson contacted Henderson, who in turn read them and urged swift action. British aid to Greece and Turkey would cease in six weeks. For strategic reasons, the notes declared, the two countries must not fall to the Soviet Union. The emergency in Greece required an army assault on guerrilla strongholds during the coming spring. Britain would provide two million pounds' worth of military equipment free of charge, but the Americans would have to furnish enough financial aid to enable Greece to meet other civil and military needs by the end of 1947. If State Department analysts were correct in regarding the presence of British troops as "purely symbolic" and a mere "scarecrow against the left," their departure would nonetheless imply the end of Western assistance and invite more trouble. In the meantime Soviet border threats had forced the Turkish government into a state of military preparedness that likewise necessitated aid for military reorganization and economic development. Henderson and Hickerson rushed to Acheson's office. Marshall was already on his way to speak at the bicentennial celebration of Princeton University, but he was well aware of the problems confronting the British. Before leaving his office that afternoon he had responded to an earlier memorandum from Henderson about Greece by instructing Acheson to prepare steps for economic and military aid.[47]

Even though Acheson called the British notes "shockers," they could not have been unwelcome; he and Henderson had repeatedly discussed the importance of taking action in the Near East. Both men had long advocated a firm position against believed Soviet aggression and now, due to this heightened sense of peril, Acheson instructed Henderson to prepare an assistance program for Marshall to examine upon his return to the office on Monday. When the draft was ready, Henderson was to call Acheson at his home in Georgetown, no matter what time of day or night. Concerned that the thrust of the program would be overly economic, Acheson that same evening of February 21 drafted a memorandum for Marshall outlining the crisis and recommending military assistance. Henderson and his staff worked Friday afternoon, late into the evening, and all day Saturday, debating and arguing before finally emerging with a draft of a tentative program. By 10 a.m. on Sunday, they were ready to take their paper to Acheson. As he had expected, the draft emphasized economic aid. Acheson would deliver it to Marshall the following morning, who in turn would show it to the President. Should Marshall approve, Henderson and his staff recommended that Truman call in the army, navy, Congress, and other groups for discussions. Afterward the administration should inform the American people of the Soviet threat in the Near East. They must know "what's going on," Henderson insisted. Although he would have preferred including Iran in the aid program, he could find no justification: no Russian troops were there, and the British notes did not mention Iran (perhaps because the British still had oil concessions). In addition, as Marshall later explained, the United States was able to work through existing channels in helping Iran. The United States planned no "open, blunt attack" on the Soviet Union, Henderson later explained, but his country must save Greece and Turkey. Legislation was needed to authorize American aid beginning on April 1.[48]

When Marshall saw the draft on Monday, he expressed satisfaction and told Henderson and others at the meeting that he would recommend that the President deliver a speech designed "to tell the world the truth." Just before a cabinet luncheon that same day, Marshall told Forrestal that the British notes contained "obvious implications" as to the British successor in the Middle East. President Truman's reaction was unmistakable in meaning: "This is the right line."[49]

Although the Truman administration had decided to assume Britain's peacekeeping role in Greece and Turkey, some advisers remained uncertain about whether London was merely trying to maneuver the Americans into protecting its international interests. The same day the notes were officially delivered, Henderson sought assessments from two Americans in London, Waldemar J. Gallman, the chargé, and H. Freeman Matthews, former head of the State Department's European Affairs Division. Despite his colleagues' apprehension, Henderson did not believe that the British intention was to trick the United States into assuming responsibility for preserving their empire.[50]

Within a week Gallman assured Henderson that the notes were sincere: the British were unable to continue financial aid to the Greek army after March 31. On the question of keeping British troops in Greece, Gallman believed that a few thousand would remain until Russian soldiers withdrew from Bulgaria within the required ninety days after ratification of the Bulgarian Treaty. Indeed, in early March the British embassy notified the State Department that one brigade would remain in Greece but that it would pull out during the summer in accordance with that treaty. The British government, however, would continue financial help on an emergency basis for up to three months after March 31, with a loan of two million pounds per month until American aid began.[51]

To the President's chief of staff, Admiral William D. Leàhy, the issue was clear: aid to Greece and Turkey would lead to America's "open involvement in the political and financial affairs of European Governments."[52] The Truman administration had to convince the American people that intervention in behalf of those two countries was vital to holding the line against communism.

CHAPTER
2

The Truman Doctrine and
the Beginnings of Global Strategy

The Truman Doctrine has been the subject of debate since its announcement in March 1947. Critics have called it the "first shot of the Cold War"; a global license for American imperialism; an exaggerated response to an imagined communist menace that scared Americans with rhetoric and contributed to McCarthyism; a reactionary policy that placed the United States on the side opposite freedom and social, political, and economic reforms; proof of an "arrogance of power" that helped lead the United States into Vietnam.[1] Defenders have hailed the declaration as evidence of America's determination to contain Soviet communism; an assurance of the nation's commitment to Free World principles; a promise by America to safeguard the world against totalitarianism; a generous aid program designed to help first Greece and Turkey and then any nation that could prove need.[2] Yet, in focusing on these issues, writers have not given adequate attention to one of the Truman administration's greatest contributions: the development of a flexible and restrained foreign policy designed to counter the renewed threat to freedom without a resort to all-out conflict.

The Truman Doctrine signaled the administration's willingness to engage in the struggle against communism on all fronts—social, political, and economic as well as military. The result was a foreign policy intended to meet all exigencies. The Truman Doctrine authorized U.S. intervention in European affairs during peacetime; it also constituted a viable response to shadow-like aggressions in which victory lay in convincing democracy's enemies that they could not win. The administration's policy was dramatic but not revolutionary; the ideas contained in the Truman Doctrine appeared in the late nineteenth century and had been growing in intensity since the last days of World

36

War II as the White House reacted to its perceptions of Soviet aggressions. The new policy of firmness toward the Soviet Union was already evident in the administration's policy toward Iran, the Dardanelles, and Eastern Europe, but perhaps most graphically in the incorporation of Kennan's Long Telegram into the Clifford-Elsey report of September 1946. Somewhere the line of defense against communism had to be drawn. Greece became a vital part of that line, the first showcase of the American will.[3]

The greatest danger in this kind of war lay in its endemic trend toward escalation. As the United States explored the limits of the Democratic Army's will, it raised the level of involvement in Greece. Step by step, American intervention grew as the guerrillas countered each move with one of their own. Years afterward, Acheson emphasized that the "limited use of force" was the central principle underlying effective foreign policy. If the struggle at hand was "military in background but really not military in operation," the nation had to have "strong economic and political aspects" in its foreign policy. But if the struggle was on the verge of becoming fully military, the United States had to determine the level of counter-force required without using the "ultimate force."[4] In Greece, victory would come by breaking the will of the enemy while holding the allegiance of the Greek people. Yet each antagonist further confused the complex situation by couching its actions in democratic and patriotic terms. And, as each side intensified claims to being the defender of freedom, it moved in the opposite direction. As Americans became immersed in the struggle, they relied less on democratic methods because of the difficulty in controlling the variables essential to victory. The most baffling complication was that the United States was expected to use democratic methods in a war that, by its very nature, made them ineffective.

I

The same day that the British officially notified Washington of their retrenchment policies in Greece and Turkey, February 24, 1947, Henderson (an admitted "hard-liner" toward the Soviets) chaired the Special Committee to Study Assistance to Greece and Turkey, whose recommendations pointed toward a global strategy designed to curb Soviet expansion. Among those on the committee who shared many of Henderson's views regarding the Soviets were Hickerson, Kennan, and Charles E. Bohlen, a Department of State counselor. When Henderson explained that the British notes constituted an admission to their empire's decline, Hickerson proposed that the United States assume Britain's peacekeeping role in Greece and Turkey. Most others agreed in principle, although General James K. Crain, deputy chairman of the Policy Committee on Arms and Armaments, opposed the economic emphasis of the aid proposal and thought that Washington should warn the Soviets of its willingness to use force in saving Greece and Turkey. Indeed, the United States should prepare for war with Russia. Other committee members,

however, thought such a warning provocative and noted that Greece and
Turkey might be only two of numerous countries requiring American assistance. Gradually a consensus developed that the administration should present the economic approach to Congress as one ingredient of a global program. Hickerson remarked that in doing so the White House must electrify
the American people.[5]

The committee recommended the establishment of a small State-War-
Navy committee to consider the global implications of intervention. There
was no debate concerning whether to act. If the United States failed to do so,
Greece and Turkey could become "Soviet puppets," leaving an example of
democratic failure that would cause the "widespread collapse of resistance to
Soviet pressure throughout the Near and Middle East and large parts of
western Europe not yet under Soviet domination."[6]

In keeping with the committee's recommendation, the secretaries of state,
war, and navy met with their advisers to discuss how to secure congressional
support for the nation's new global responsibilities. The group's central
argument was that the Greek and Turkish problems were "*only part of a
critical world situation confronting us today in many democratic countries*"
and must receive attention "*as a whole.*" From a military perspective, Secretary of War Patterson explained, the independence of Greece and Turkey was
strategically vital because of their location near the crossroads of the world.
Forrestal agreed. Marshall concurred with his two colleagues on the need for
three immediate actions by the administration: extending financial relief to
Greece, even before enabling legislation was enacted; arranging for the Greek
government to make a formal request for American aid; and engaging in
private and frank discussions with both Democratic and Republican
members of Congress. The President must be authorized to extend loans,
credits, or grants. He must be able to approve the transfer of military supplies
not permitted under existing laws. And he must have the power to assign
American personnel to administer the aid program. Finally, the State-War-
Navy Coordinating Committee (SWNCC) on Foreign Policy Information
must establish the program. That same day Marshall explained to the President that similar situations elsewhere in the world would also require American assistance.[7]

The Intelligence Division of the War Department likewise emphasized the
broader nature of the aid program—that American involvement might not be
confined to Greece and Turkey and would not be strictly military. The
assistance effort must be a "psychological and political one in which morale,
and the superficial manifestations of force, such as possession of weapons and
equipment," constituted "the most important element." Economic rehabilitation was needed—under American supervision.[8] Military assistance would be
a means toward that end.

The SWNCC Subcommittee on Foreign Policy Information, also chaired
by Henderson, kept the focus on global strategy. Henderson emphasized the
necessity of halting destructive forces throughout the world, thereby disagree-

ing with Kennan's proposal to restrict the assistance to Greece and Turkey. America's objective, as Marshall believed, was to salvage Greece as a demonstration of America's will. To set this example, Henderson explained, the United States must help the Greek army restore domestic order as the prerequisite to economic reconstruction. Uncertainty remained about British troop intentions, although one report indicated that withdrawal would be gradual and that about 6,000 soldiers would stay for an undetermined time. John Jernegan from the State Department wanted to play down the idea of sending arms. Otherwise, Americans would worry about where the escalation would end. No one contemplated putting American troops in Greece, he insisted; the primary emphasis was economic. To help Americans realize that Greece and Turkey were only part of a worldwide problem, Francis Russell of Public Affairs recommended that the United States speak "in terms of [the] new policy of this government to go to the assistance of free governments everywhere."[9]

The SWNCC Subcommittee wrestled with the question of whether the United States should directly intervene in Greek internal affairs. Rear Admiral Robert L. Dennison, assistant chief of Naval Operations, saw no alternative to Americans exerting influence because of political as well as economic and military considerations. Unless they took charge of the aid program and made sure that the Greek government did its part, critics would accuse the United States of "pouring money down a rat-hole." Jernegan observed that the United States would have more leverage by sinking money into Greece. But the Greek people must not get the impression that the loan was a device to win political control. Llewellyn Thompson from the Office of European Affairs admitted that the United States must exercise political influence but warned that the Soviets would bring charges of imperialism before the UN. To curtail the certain criticism, the State Department issued the following statement: "It is our primary purpose to assist the Greek people, so that they may retain the opportunity to choose the form and composition of their Government in accordance with the wish of the majority."[10]

The ominous point was that Greece's economic needs were intertwined with military problems enhanced by outside interference, which increased the chances of an economic aid program becoming military in orientation. Yet such a change would constitute only a shift in means; the primary objective was to rebuild the nation's economy. In an effort to keep the United States out of Balkan entanglements, the SWNCC Subcommittee stipulated that American aid would be for "the reestablishment of internal order and the necessary political and economic stability to permit Greece to maintain her independence and the form of government desired by the majority of the Greek people." The United States had to establish administrative controls so that the aid program would concentrate on domestic matters and be adaptable to changing circumstances. To ease expected opposition at home, the Greek government should make a formal request for American aid. The United States must meanwhile use existing legislation to arrange the transfer to

Greece of military goods deemed necessary by the state, war, and navy departments.[11]

The SWNCC Subcommittee recommended that the White House alert the American people to the worldwide Soviet challenge facing the United States. General Henry H. Arnold declared that they must recognize the necessity of holding the line against communism in Greece and Turkey. The issue was communism versus democracy. Russell agreed: the United States must "tell [the] story that has to be told." Jernegan emphasized that the administration must present the policy as vital to America's interests. When he recommended including Turkey in the information program, Thompson disagreed, claiming that to place as much emphasis on Turkey would leave the impression that the United States was the aggressor and intended to encircle the Soviet Union. Turkey would be part of the program, but secondary to the central Soviet threat against Greece. Thinking along these lines, when State Department adviser Joseph Jones suggested the inclusion of references to border raids originating out of Yugoslavia, Dennison warned that people might derive the mistaken belief that Greece's neighbors were the principal reason behind American intervention. The United States must keep the focus on the Soviets.[12] To America's policymakers, Britain was not the issue; nor was Turkey or Greece. The issue was whether the Soviet Union would succeed in demonstrating that America's commitment to Free World principles rested solely on rhetoric.

Whether or not the Soviets were directly involved in the problems confronting Greece and Turkey, the Truman administration had concluded that both countries were part of the East-West conflict and in need of immediate assistance.[13] As symbols of Western endurance, as strategic considerations, and perhaps as ideological battlegrounds, Greece and Turkey had become by 1947 the focal points of the Cold War.

The potential for expanding the scope of the Greek struggle quickly became evident as the communists in that country responded to the news of America's impending aid program by appealing for UN help. In early March the communist secretary general of EAM, along with two members of the KKE's Central Committee, announced a formal written protest against American intervention. The document stressed the Greek people's friendship for the United States and objected to economic help seemingly conditioned on Britain's retention of troops in Greece. America's economic aid was welcome but not its influence. To keep Greece outside of international rivalries, EAM demanded "neutralization" of the country under UN auspices.[14]

To MacVeagh in Athens, the communists' appeal to UN intervention had "the ear-marks of Moscow directed strategy." The USSR would rather have a weak UN in Greece than a powerful United States. The Free World was facing the "most ruthless realists" the world had seen. Failure to pursue a tough policy against the Greek communists would encourage the Russians. No one could make peace with communist-directed movements seeking to subvert established governments. Though the present Greek government was "feeble," "foolish," and "even disgraceful," it deserved protection because Western observers had certified that government as having been chosen by the people. The United States must stand firm in Greece, for if the Soviets won control over all of the Balkans, the Near East would fall and the UN would be "killed in its cradle."[15]

Increasing numbers of Americans outside the administration had likewise come to believe that the future of democracy lay in Greece. Columnist Walter Lippmann asserted that "with all the world watching, our ideals and professions will be put severely to the test." The New York *Herald Tribune* insisted that the priority was the West's confidence, which rested on America's willingness to support Greece and to offer a viable alternative to communism. Military analyst Hanson Baldwin warned in the *New York Times* that if Greece fell, the Aegean would become "sovietized" and the Russians would gain a Mediterranean outlet and flank the Dardanelles. Leahy predicted that Soviet control over Europe would lead to the destruction of democratic government on the continent and endanger America's safety.[16]

The Truman administration's global concern over Greece was evident in a paper prepared by SWNCC's Subcommittee on Foreign Policy Information and designated FPI 30. Written by the State Department, the paper contained ideas that Acheson attributed to the White House. FPI 30 declared that the administration must convince the American people that Greece was the starting point of a global conflict between freedom and totalitarianism. America sought a world in which the people determined their own way of life. The policy of the United States was to "give support to free peoples who are attempting to resist subjugation from armed minorities or from outside forces." These universal rights were embodied in the Atlantic Charter, UN Declaration, and Yalta Agreement.[17]

According to FPI 30, the United States could avoid direct military involvement in Greece by concentrating on long-range economic rehabilitation. This program would require American advisers and technicians, which necessitated involvement in Greek internal affairs. Americans sought no special position in Greece: their purpose was to help the Greek people determine their destiny. To counter Soviet propaganda, FPI 30 outlined a public information program. Against the expected Russian accusation that the United States was supporting a reactionary Greek government as part of an anti-Soviet campaign based on "Atom diplomacy" and capitalist encirclement, the study advised the White House to announce the extension of economic aid to a people desiring the right to choose their government.[18]

The President's advisers enthusiastically supported a Greek-Turkish aid program even while noting its interventionist character. Leahy asserted that such involvement in Europe's political concerns was a "direct and positive change in the traditional policy of the United States." Acheson assured his colleagues that the move was necessary because the outcome in Greece was pivotal: it would determine the American public's reactions to similar threats in France, Italy, Hungary, and Turkey. Intervention offered no assurance of success; but, the undersecretary solemnly added, those areas would have no chance against communist subversion should the United States stay home. Patterson, Forrestal, and Harriman agreed.[19]

Three days after the cabinet meeting, the President, Marshall, and Acheson conferred with leaders of both political parties. For some reason that Acheson termed an "accidental omission" (and which Republican Senator Arthur Vandenberg of Michigan, chairman of the Foreign Relations Committee, quickly brought to the President's attention), the administration failed to invite Republican Robert A. Taft of Ohio, who was one of the most influential members of the Senate, the chairman of the Republican Senate Policy Committee, and a leading advocate of isolationism.[20] For considerations that were doubtless encouraged by this slight, Taft would staunchly oppose the aid proposal.

Marshall attempted to explain the problem to the congressional leaders, but he did so in what one White House adviser called "dry and economical terms" that were less than inspiring. When the initial reaction came in the form of sullen questions pertaining to the United States "pulling British chestnuts out of the fire," Acheson leaned over to Marshall and asked in a soft voice, "Is this a private fight or can anyone get into it?" Marshall, Acheson thought, had "most unusually and unhappily, flubbed his opening statement" and left both the secretary of state and the President "equally perturbed" with the congressmen's failure to understand the dimensions of the problem. Marshall secured the President's permission for Acheson to speak.[21]

Acheson's presentation was eloquent and persuasive. Within the past eighteen months, while communist parties were causing problems in France and Italy, the Soviet Union had exerted pressure on the straits and in the Balkans. The Soviets' purpose was to control the eastern Mediterranean and the Middle East. From there they could expand into South Asia, Africa, and Europe. The last obstacle to Soviet expansion was Greece. If that country collapsed, like "apples in a barrel infected by one rotten one, the corruption of Greece would infect Iran and all to the east." Britain's power was gone, leaving only the United States to stand against the Soviet Union. Such a polarization of power in the world had not occurred since the days of Rome and Carthage. Freedom was at stake, not the British Empire, and America's security was integral to the maintenance of that freedom. The United States could accept the challenge, or it could lose by default.[22]

After a long silence, Vandenberg grimly declared, "Mr. President, if you will say that to the Congress and the country, I will support you and I believe that most of its members will do the same." Vandenberg later recorded in his memoirs that the Greek problem was "probably symbolic of the world-wide ideological clash between Eastern Communism and Western Democracy." He realized, as did Acheson and others in the administration, that the February 27 meeting had demonstrated the necessity of making a strong and explicit statement to the American people that emphasized the gravity of the threat to freedom.[23]

To highlight the Greek crisis, the President announced to the press that he had postponed a vacation in the Caribbean. He would address Congress within a week.[24]

Truman told his advisers that aid to Greece marked the beginning of a policy of intervention that would require the "greatest selling job ever facing a President." He had earlier declared that the world had to realize that America's policy was to defend freedom "wherever it was threatened." To Acheson he explained that he saw no reason to restrict the policy to the Middle East and thought it should have a "worldwide application." Truman now took the Greek crisis as an opportunity to announce the willingness of the United States to assume the global responsibilities of power. Cabinet members agreed that the President had to be straightforward with the American people. After considerable discussion, his advisers recommended that he deliver a message to Congress that would explain the world situation in frank terms, while not provoking the Soviet Union. Henderson later claimed that his memorandum had provided the general thrust of the presentation, although Acheson was apparently responsible for the open-ended nature of the aid request. Jones remarked to the undersecretary that the draft of the speech had taken on the air of a general authorization of aid. Acheson responded by leaning back in his chair, thinking a while, gazing at the White House, and then saying slowly: "If F.D.R. were alive I think I know what he'd do. He would make a statement of global policy, but confine his request for money right now to Greece and Turkey."[25]

On March 12 President Truman went before a joint session of Congress to recommend the program of economic and military assistance to Greece and Turkey that became known as the Truman Doctrine. Without mentioning the Soviet Union, he referred to the struggle between two ways of life—one advocating self-determination, the other totalitarian rule, and both having roots in the longtime conflict between "Old World" Europe and "New World" America. Greece and Turkey now stood at the front of the democracies' line of freedom. The fall of those two countries to communism would be potentially devastating to freedom. "I believe," he asserted in a close rendition of FPI 30 that became the central idea of the Truman Doctrine, "it must be the policy of the United States to support free peoples who are resisting attempted subjugation by armed minorities or by outside pressures." He called for $400 million in emergency aid, most of it military and for Greece. He also sought military and civilian advisers to implement the program in each country. Congressional refusal would open the way for totalitarian expansion into the Mediterranean and Middle East.[26]

Within minutes, the President was on his way to the airport to leave for a vacation in Key West and await reaction to his speech.[27]

Reaction came from all sides, but even though the opposition was loud, the preponderance of opinion was favorable. The *New York Times* happily announced that America's "epoch of isolation" was "being replaced by an epoch of American responsibility." Both Anne O'Hare McCormick and

James Reston of the *Times* acknowledged America's strategic interests in the Near and Middle East. A survey of the paper's correspondents across the United States showed the majority in support. *Time* magazine applauded the President's stand for "worldwide freedom" and warned that if the United States did not act, the "Iron Curtain would be moved down to the Mediterranean." Anticipating the administration's policy, *Newsweek* had earlier declared that failure to act would cause the fall of Greece and a disastrous "chain reaction" affecting America's strategic interests all over the world. The Americans for Democratic Action, which included Franklin D. Roosevelt, Jr., Hubert H. Humphrey, Arthur M. Schlesinger, Jr., and Marquis Childs, declared that the United States "*must* assume the responsibilities of greatness" and praised the Truman Doctrine for striking out at "hunger and injustice," for advocating military assistance against only "*external aggression*," and for making America "the world symbol of progressive democracy." Though congressional members were generally supportive, many expressed concern about the unilateral nature of the American action. *Time* magazine noted that the speech brought an "unusually grave" countenance to most congressmen, although Senator Taft yawned "prodigiously" in his front-row seat. Democratic Senator Richard Russell of Georgia saw no reason to change his earlier remark that he was fed up with helping the British. He snidely recommended that Congress admit England, Scotland, Wales, and Ireland into the Union as states. "The King could run for the Senate, as could Winston Churchill."[28]

The opposition in the United States ranged from the extreme left to the extreme right and largely for that reason was unable to mount an attack capable of seriously challenging the administration's policy. The group included *Nation* and *New Republic*, the isolationist New York *Daily News*, the pacifist National Council for Prevention of War, and liberals critical of the administration's "tough" policy such as the former mayor of New York, Fiorello La Guardia, and the onetime secretary of agriculture and later Vice President under President Franklin D. Roosevelt, Henry Wallace. La Guardia had once headed UNRRA and witnessed firsthand the widespread corruption and the repressive practices of the government in Athens. If the United States went into Greece, he warned, it would be there for a long time. Wallace, former secretary of commerce during the early days of the Truman presidency, was now editor of *New Republic* after being dismissed from the administration over a bitter policy dispute. While commerce secretary, Wallace had vigorously opposed the policy of firmness adopted by the White House against the Soviet Union and had delivered what the Truman administration termed an unauthorized speech to that effect in New York's Madison Square Garden in September 1946. His dismissal soon followed. Now, in editorials, over radio, and in speeches in Britain, he called the Truman Doctrine a declaration of war on the Soviet Union and a "global Monroe Doctrine." According to at least one White House adviser, Wallace was the aid program's "most violent and vocal critic."[29]

Walter Lippmann probably expressed the views of many Americans, when he announced support for the aid bill but objected to the methods used. The administration, he argued, should have turned first to the UN to exert moral and global pressure on the aggressors and to avert charges of imperialism. Ideological crusades were nearly always grandly received but nonetheless dangerous because they carried unlimited commitments. There was an old adage: "Today they are ringing the bells; tomorrow they will be wringing their hands." Lippmann insisted that experienced diplomats work by understatement. Otherwise, as Elihu Root once warned, first you shake your fist, and then you shake your finger. Zeal should not replace judgment; the United States could not take over the world's problems. Lippmann's differences with the administration became so acrimonious that at a dinner party in Washington he and Acheson got into an argument that almost led to blows. As observers stood with mouths open, the two men jabbed each other's chests and finally stalked away in anger. Acheson telephoned an apology the next morning.[30]

Outside the country, the reaction was global and primarily favorable, although the assessments varied there almost as much as they did inside the United States. The response generally broke down into those in favor of the policy coming from the center and the right, and those in opposition from the left. The Soviet paper *Izvestia* led the communists' attack in criticizing the United States for adopting a new policy of colonialism and imperialism. The British countered by expressing support for the aid proposal while urging Americans to take the leadership in resolving a problem that belonged to the entire Western world. To American congressmen objecting that the White House was merely assuming responsibility for Britain's possessions, an unnamed British figure in Washington angrily retorted: "You had your men in Greece. They have been sending you reports and figures. By now you should have made up your minds." Had not the time come to drop this senseless babble about "pulling British chestnuts out of the fire? To hell with the British. Forget the British. Can't you finally understand that this is your problem?"[31]

Kennan was concerned that the President had committed the United States to a global crusade that it should not and could not support. His long career as a diplomat had taught him that nations should not make broad and indefensible commitments. Seven years in the embassy in Moscow had convinced him that the United States had to pursue a firm policy against Soviet expansion. But he urged caution in choosing the means for seeking this objective. Already disenchanted with the shift in emphasis from economic to military aid, Kennan denied that the immediate threat in either Greece or Turkey was military. Unrest in Greece was attributable to political and ideological factors and could be handled by economic means. The President's address was "grandiose" and "sweeping," Kennan insisted years afterward. His criticisms found some agreement from Marshall, Bohlen, and Clifford, who supported the program yet believed the speech characterized by anti-communist rhetoric.[32]

Kennan was not convinced, but Truman's advisers were doubtless correct in asserting that the sweeping, global language was necessary to secure congressional approval of the bill. To avoid provocations, the President had not mentioned the Soviet Union, nor did he emphasize Turkey and the strategic importance of the Middle East. White House advisers had warned against alarming the American people about strategic matters in peacetime. Thus he left out references to America's vital interests in the Middle East, emphasizing instead basic principles of hope and freedom. As one presidential adviser later declared, "Military aid to Turkey was not concealed; but it was not emphasized." The President aimed his speech more at the American public than at the world. The Republican-dominated 80th Congress which convened in January 1947 had set out to fulfill campaign promises of raising tariffs and cutting income taxes and spending. Because of domestic issues—in particular the wishes of a few liberals to accommodate the Soviets and the intentions of many Americans to return to the carefully circumscribed economic and military policies of the pre-World War II period—the administration discerned a threat to its foreign policy, which necessitated dramatic warnings of totalitarian threats to the world's freedom. But the administration's faith in the Truman Doctrine rested on controls in which Kennan had little confidence: the ability of policymakers to control the rate and type of escalation and to restrict the nation's involvement to countries both vital to America's security and capable of being saved.[33]

Despite these differences over method, Kennan saw the challenge in the same way as did the White House. His disagreement stemmed from the opposing assessments of the Greek crisis: whereas the White House believed military assistance necessary, Kennan argued that the situation was salvageable by less provocative means. Economic assistance would counter "ideological and political penetration" by encouraging the Greek people to have confidence in their government. In a speech before the National War College in Washington, D.C., Kennan asserted that the Soviets had "taken care to shove forward Balkan communists to do their dirty work for them and to disguise as far as possible their own hand in Greek affairs." Inaction by the United States would "confirm the impression that the Western Powers were on the run and that international communism was on the make."[34]

Ironically, Kennan's position was not much different from that taken by the White House: both would lead the United States to worldwide involvement. If the democratic ideals propounded by the President were indivisible, America's commitment to freedom had no territorial limitations. If the Kremlin, as Kennan claimed, was searching for "soft spots," his call for containment carried the same global implications.[35] Finally, even if the Soviets were not guilty of the motives and actions attributed to them by American policymakers, the perception was more important than whatever the reality might have been. Given Washington's prevailing assumptions that the Soviets were engaged in a new type of war, the global impetus of America's foreign policy was predictable.

II

Both the UN Security Council Commission of Investigation and the Porter economic mission confirmed the administration's belief that the situation in Greece had deteriorated so badly that economic aid without military assistance could not turn things around. As George McGhee, soon to become coordinator of the Greek-Turkish aid program, asked years afterward, "What good was economic reconstruction when the bandits simply blew up bridges and railroads as fast as Americans built them?" A State Department adviser on Greece, Francis Lincoln, noted that many Americans objected to military assistance because it was "essentially negative while economic aid was positive and could build a better life for impoverished people." Few seemed to see that law and order were prerequisites to ending "organized violence" and allowing "civilized life." The problem in Greece was "political-military-economic." Years afterward, Lincoln added, "extremely unsophisticated writers" unfairly criticized the military aspects of the Truman Doctrine while praising the economic nature of the Marshall Plan. "In Greece these were two aspects of the same problem." Only military assistance could achieve the security necessary to economic stability.[36] The White House hoped that the assignment of administrators and technological advisers would be sufficient to prove America's determination to achieve rehabilitation. Greeks first needed security, and that entailed military goods—including weapons—and advice on their incorporation into the war effort.

The process by which the United States deepened its involvement in Greece exemplified the complications inherent in international commitments. The State Department urged the participation of all branches of government and full disclosure of the situation to the American people. Interdepartmental committees were needed to coordinate the decisionmaking process. Acting as a liaison, the State Department established both a Departmental Committee and an Inter-departmental Committee for Aid to Greece and Turkey. The organizations involved in the process comprised a lengthy list: the Departments of Treasury, Agriculture, Commerce, Army, Navy, and Labor; the Social Security Administration; the Public Roads Administration (Federal Works Agency); the Bureau of the Budget; the Federal Security Agency; and the Corps of Engineers. With the State Department delegate chairing the sessions, the Departmental Committee met daily and replied to questions as they arose. The Inter-departmental Committee would draw up policy and present expenditure plans to congressional appropriations committees.[37]

The legislative process for the Greek-Turkish aid bill began with its introduction in the Senate on March 19, followed within a week by a long series of public hearings before both the Foreign Relations Committee and the House Foreign Affairs Committee. Since the necessary monetary allotment probably could not come before the March 31 deadline for Britain's withdrawal from the two countries, the administration had incorporated an emergency provision for Greece into the bill that would authorize the President to grant interim advances from the Reconstruction Finance Corporation. The financial aid program was to continue through June 30, 1948, by which time Greece should have made enough progress to ask the International Bank for a reconstruction and development loan. Once the aid program was in place the President would determine the allocation of funds. An American mission established in Greece would recommend guidelines. To prevent graft and corruption in the Greek purchasing agencies as well as in procurement operations in the United States, the bill provided for centralized control over the program and for careful screening of personnel. According to the plan (which differed from UNRRA procedures), the United States would assign to a single individual—the chief of the mission—the responsibility for overseeing the expenditures and reporting directly to the President. Americans must administer the aid program, MacVeagh insisted. Otherwise, the money would "go down a rat hole."[38]

No part of the aid funds used for non-wealth-producing purposes (consumer or military goods) would be in the form of loans. Greece was not a good credit risk, Acheson remarked. Furthermore, the charter of the International Bank did not allow loans for military purposes. Should any portion of America's funds go for the reconstruction of developmental or wealth-producing assets, that could come in the form of a loan. The Senate expressed concern that granting money to Greece would establish a dangerous precedent, but Undersecretary of State for Economic Affairs William L. Clayton assured the Foreign Relations Committee that the emergency relief would promote only enough economic and political improvement to permit Greece to apply later for a loan that would facilitate long-range stability. About half of the $300 million sought for Greece would furnish its armed forces with munitions, clothing, and rations necessary for counteracting the guerrillas. But another side of the matter was important, warned Democratic Senator Tom Connally of Texas. To forgo a loan in favor of a grant would dramatize the Greek case, making the aid program appear to be a direct thrust at the Soviet Union.[39] The Truman administration was prepared to take that risk. Practical considerations and military necessity prohibited a loan.

The American mission in Greece would constitute a bureaucracy in every sense of the word. Communications facilities alone would require nearly 800 people to staff eight civilian sub-missions. The headquarters of each sub-mission would be in Athens, though separate from the embassy and consular offices, and each headquarters would have a minimum of eight sub-headquarters. In addition to the $300 million for Greece, that country received $50 million as its proportion of the post-UNRRA relief program provided by separate legislation. Of the $350 million for Greek assistance, the Department of the Army, through its military advisory group (assigned to the American mission) of perhaps forty members, would provide the Greek National Army (of about 150,000 men) with advice on the use of $150 million of war matériel. The civilian advisers would use the remainder for relief, reconstruction, and rehabilitation. A high commissioner would head the mission, but he would also be responsible for coordinating the military and civilian advisers. Besides additional staff for existing offices in Washington, a large number of Americans would reside in Greece to supervise the program. One plan called for 250 advisers in the ministries of the Greek government; another required several thousand Americans for planning and advising on programs, as well as giving direction within the Greek government. Detailed directives followed on various aspects of the program: advising, training, procurement, shipping, recruiting personnel, distributing equipment and supplies, and furnishing regular reports.[40]

Before the congressional committees, Acheson repeatedly denied that the Truman administration had made an automatic global commitment for the United States. He assured committee members (with some "sharpness," according to one observer) that the White House would have to consider each applicant for assistance on an individual basis. Do you consider the Truman Doctrine an "extension of the Monroe Doctrine?" asked a House committee member. "No, I do not," Acheson "crisply" replied. Some parts of the world were irretrievable. Wherever self-determination was in danger, the United States would help—if a reasonable chance for success existed. In response to an article by Lippmann questioning whether the United States was stretching itself too thin, Acheson noted that certain areas were inaccessible to American influence. The United States could not be effective in Rumania, Bulgaria, and Poland, for instance, because they fell within the "Russian sphere of physical force." Before the Senate committee, Vandenberg sought clarification: "In other words, I think what you are saying is that wherever we find free peoples having difficulty in the maintenance of free institutions, and difficulty in defending against aggressive movements that seek to impose upon them totalitarian regimes, we do not necessarily react in the same way each time, but we propose to react." Acheson replied: "That, I think, is correct." Joseph Jones declared that these words suggested the "test of practicability" and thereby constituted "the global implications of the Truman Doctrine."[41]

Acheson insisted that America bore the responsibility for supporting the UN's pronouncements of self-determination. To the Senate Foreign Relations Committee, he explained that when the United States signed the UN Charter, it had accepted the global burden of maintaining peace and security. The President's statements before Congress accorded with the UN Charter and the duties of member nations. The proposed aid bill came at the requests of the Greek and Turkish governments. To reject the calls for help would undermine faith in democracy and create fear and uncertainty. A concerned world was watching events in Greece and Turkey. Success would strengthen the bases of peace and the hopes of the UN. America's primary purpose, Acheson told the House Foreign Affairs Committee, was to help people live the way they wanted to live. Failure to guarantee this right would produce a "very strong conviction throughout the world that our professions are mere words."[42]

The administration emphatically denied that the Truman Doctrine was an effort to remake its beneficiaries in the American image. According to McGhee, the United States never sought to recast Greece into an Americanized democracy. Some years earlier, Brigadier General Patrick J. Hurley suggested to President Roosevelt that the United States use "nation building" as a criterion for dealing with states threatened by aggression; but Acheson had opposed the idea then as "innocent indulgence in messianic globaloney." He now reiterated to the congressional committees that the United States sought only to guarantee Greece and Turkey the right to establish the government they wanted.[43] Acheson recognized that serious problems remained in Greece regarding which political group represented the people and what kind of government was wanted. Indeed, the question of legitimacy had not been settled after the March 1946 elections. Nonetheless, critics of Truman's foreign policy too easily dismissed as rhetoric that portion of his March 12 address which read: "I believe that we must assist free peoples to work out their own destinies in their own way."

MacVeagh also appeared before the congressional committees in an attempt to allay their fears that the United States was assuming a worldwide burden of opposing communism. Some areas aroused no interest in the Kremlin, he implied—primarily because the Russians would not pursue unwinnable causes. MacVeagh read the following statement from "The Foundations of Leninism," a series of talks by Stalin published in Moscow in 1934:

> The essential task of the victorious revolution in one country is to develop and support the revolution in others, so the victorious revolution in a victorious country ought not to consider itself as a victory self-contained, but as a means of hastening the victory in another country.

The situation in Greece, MacVeagh maintained, resulted from a communist revolution in neighboring countries that was part of the doctrine of "international communism." If the strategic line of Greece and Turkey snapped, the Near East would stand unprotected and the Soviets would "pick the lock of world dominion." The administration's foreign policy did not rest on the assumption that all trouble spots in the world were attributable to communism. Americans could not become "simple minded" and believe that "a communist [was] under every bed."[44]

The major criticism of the administration's proposal came from those who believed that the Greek and Turkish problems were the UN's responsibility. Indeed, a White House spokesman noted widespread fear that American action in those countries would upstage and weaken the UN. Despite the Truman administration's claim to be acting in the spirit of the UN Charter, skepticism arose among what one observer called "left-wing spokesmen," such as Wallace and Max Lerner, as well as among "more sober commentators," such as Lippmann and Childs. But this feeling also ran deeply among the administration's strongest supporters—the "liberal independents," the idealists, the working classes, and many average Americans for whom the UN had become a symbol of hope.[45]

Defenders of the Truman Doctrine cited many reasons for not acting through the UN. Jones declared that the UN lacked funds and authority to approve military assistance; above all, it could not act quickly. Another presidential adviser, George M. Elsey, explained later that Soviet vetoes in the Security Council would have obstructed UN action. "Time was of the essence," he insisted. "It was not something you could sit around and debate for weeks or months." Acheson and Henderson agreed with Elsey's assessment, as did McGhee. The UN Relief and Rehabilitation Administration, McGhee reminded his colleagues, had not succeeded in Greece primarily because the United States had had no control over the distribution of funds. What hope could there be for the UN? Connally joined in the administration's defense by pointing out that the UN Charter did not authorize loans or grants. He also noted that nothing in the charter prohibited an individual nation from taking the initiative. "To turn this problem over to the UN, which isn't constituted to handle it, would be a buckpassing arrangement, just a dodging and trimming and flim-flamming around." Vandenberg agreed with the administration that the UN could not act for two reasons: it lacked funds for economic aid, and it did not have military reserves authorized by the Charter because of Soviet obstructionist tactics.[46]

Nonetheless, controversy continued to rage over the administration's decision to bypass the UN. Part of the problem lay with the White House: its advisers had not consulted the State Department's Office of Special Political Affairs which dealt with UN matters, nor had they talked with America's ambassador to the UN, Warren R. Austin. Indeed, Austin did not receive his first full statement on the new policy until March 11, 1947—the day before the President's speech. Austin was not happy with the administration's unilateral action. Before the nation made an aid commitment, it should await recommendations from UN field committees. Such a move would strengthen the UN and the cause of collective security. But because of the necessary time involved in UN consultations, Acheson called the failure to contact Austin a "fortunate error." Another of the administration's advisers, Francis Lincoln, was blunt about whether the White House bypassed the UN: "It did." The UN lacked funds and other necessary matériel, and its members could have confused issues and prevented quick and decisive action.[47]

The White House received support from various groups both outside and inside the country, who likewise doubted the UN's capacity to cope with the problems in Greece. Government officials in Athens preferred direct American aid because the UN lacked "the talent, the experience, the experts, the policies, to help in such a difficult program." A spokesman for the British government considered the UN in no position to provide immediate assistance to Greece and warned that such a move would convey a slight to other countries also in trouble. James Reston agreed that the UN lacked funds, troops, and authority. Moreover, because of the veto power in the Security

Council, the UN was not designed to halt the aggressions of big nations. Dean Rusk, at that time a political adviser to the UN, later expressed irritation with the charge that the United States had purposely bypassed the organization in instituting the Truman Doctrine. Most critics, he pointed out, overlooked a major factor in the controversy: Article 33 of the UN Charter provided that parties to an international dispute were to exhaust all other remedies *before* taking the matter to the UN. Only the Security Council could have taken binding action; the General Assembly made recommendations. The UN offered no feasible alternative.[48]

In practical terms, of course, the administration was correct in arguing that the UN lacked the means for resolving the Greek-Turkish problems; but in a symbolic and perhaps idealistic sense, the critics had a just complaint in declaring that the United States had ignored an instrument for peace that the White House itself had fashioned into existence. Had the President authorized his UN representatives to consult that body—either before or immediately following the congressional speech of March 12—opponents of the bill would have lost the basis of their argument. The President would have been in a more defensible position to argue that the emergency in Greece could not await a long debate in the UN over whether to take action. The slightest homage to the UN would have defused much of the controversy.

While the arguments over the UN issue went on, defenders of the administration tried to ward off other critics who admitted to a threat in Greece but expressed skepticism over any danger to Turkey. Acheson told the Senate committee that Turkey was engaged in a "war of nerves" with the Soviet Union that had driven the Turkish government to the verge of bankruptcy because of the necessity of maintaining an army to ward off a feared invasion. The U.S. ambassador to Turkey, Edwin C. Wilson, assured both the Senate and the House committees that the maintenance of Turkish independence was a "vital interest" to the United States. Turkey was the only independent nation along the Soviet border between the Baltic and the Black Sea. Although Moscow had ordered no military buildup during the last three or four months, Soviet troops were still present along the border. Turkey's fall would permit the Soviet Union to expand all over the Mediterranean and Middle East. The result would be another world war. The Joint Chiefs of Staff tied Turkey with Greece as part of the broad challenge to America's security. The Soviets were resorting to political pressures and subversion to achieve objectives in Greece. Similarly, they sought to achieve control of Turkey short of direct military measures. Unless the United States gave sufficient assurance to both countries, the Turks might interpret inaction as Western weakness and yield to Soviet pressure. Turkey held an important strategic position in relation to the Middle East and to the Arab world in general. Turkey was also a "test case."[49]

The chief concern among Americans, however, was that the aid program in Greece would lead to full-scale military involvement—and in support of a repressive government that was only professing to be democratic. In a single morning, nine people testified before the Senate Foreign Relations Committee that the Greek-Turkish aid bill was too military in nature. Similar expressions of alarm came from the press, radio, Congress, and public opinion analyses. Columnist Stewart Alsop warned that the United States, in attempting to stop Soviet expansion, would become a supporter of the status quo. The "easiest course" in foreign policy was to "shore up any regime, however corrupt, merely because it [was] an anti-Communist regime. That course . . . [was] in the long run self-defeating." According to a State Department analyst, Americans understood that their government had responsibilities throughout the world, but were worried that military aid to Greece would increase the chances of war with Russia. The public wanted to help Greece economically but was sharply divided over whether to provide military supplies and advisers. A slim majority favored economic aid to governments resisting armed communist takeovers, but these same Americans were reluctant to approve military assistance.[50]

Acheson assured both congressional committees that the aid bill contained safeguards against the outbreak of war. He reminded the Senate committee that American military figures in Greece would advise only on the use of weapons and supplies and would number no more than forty army officers. The present proposals, he said, "do not include our sending troops to Greece or Turkey. We have not been asked to do so. We have no understandings with either Greece or Turkey, oral or otherwise, in regard to the sending of troops to those countries." Technical personnel would advise the Greeks on the use of trucks, motorized equipment, and other materials furnished by the United States. The British Military Mission would continue training the army and providing small arms, artillery, clothing, and miscellaneous supplies. Acheson's testimony demonstrated that the Truman administration regarded its policy in Greece as restrained and flexible, designed to help the Greeks put down what MacVeagh termed a "subversive political movement against the state."[51]

Still, the fears persisted. The tensest moment came during Acheson's appearance before the House committee. Democratic Representative Mike Mansfield asked whether the administration's policy could lead to war. The crowded room became silent as Acheson rubbed his chin, hesitated, and finally responded: "I was going to say—no possibility it would lead to war." But after a pause, he added: "I don't think it could lead to war. By strengthening the forces of democracy and freedom, you do a great deal to eliminate the friction between big powers."[52]

In this strained atmosphere, the possibility of a total British troop withdrawal from Greece took on such serious ramifications that Brigadier General George Lincoln, from the War Department's Plans and Operations Division, had to assure congressmen that the move would not automatically lead to the use of American soldiers. At the time of the hearings, he explained, about 10,000 British soldiers—along with the supporting force—were still in Greece. Even if they pulled out, the United States expected the

British Military Mission, which was comprised of several hundred officers and men, to remain and to continue training the Greek army. He admitted that neither the Greek navy nor air force offered much hope. The navy was composed of only eight destroyers, a few minesweepers and amphibious craft, three tankers, and a few other items. In addition, the naval vessels needed diesel fuel in order to patrol those coastal areas along which the guerrillas moved. The air force's reconnaissance craft and aged British fighters were fairly helpful in establishing air-to-ground contacts with the army, and in bombing and strafing operations; but even this limited effectiveness rested almost solely on British assistance. Lincoln emphasized that even though a British pullout would hurt the situation, the United States did not anticipate having to send combat forces to Greece.[53]

Despite these disclaimers, the truth was that the White House had thought from the beginning of its direct involvement in Greece that stronger military measures would become necessary. MacVeagh had recognized this possibility as early as December 1946; and now, before the congressional committees, he repeated his fear that America might be "left holding the bag." Widespread feeling had developed in the administration that expanded military help was inescapable because of the pending British troop withdrawal, the dire condition of Greek armed forces, and the strategic and symbolic importance attributed by the United States to the region. Henderson believed that without greater military assistance the Greek government could not sustain its army's spring campaign. Acheson carefully explained that "present plans do not envisage any training program for the Greek armed forces under American auspices, except possibly for limited technical instruction in the use of American equipment." But, as several military experts affirmed, a successful offensive on the battlefield depended upon a thorough reorganization of the Greek army. Such a change, according to a British officer, required the assistance of several hundred American officers.[54]

The Truman administration likewise had difficulty convincing Congress that the military aspects of the aid program were only one part of a broadly conceived response to world problems. Shortly before the President's address to Congress, the War Department assigned Greece a higher priority than Iran for military equipment. But such military aid, Patterson informed Marshall, was only one of the emergency measures forced upon the United States by its need to take preventative action in areas around the world that were vital to security. As Forrestal explained to the Senate Foreign Relations Committee, the administration preferred a general authorization bill that allowed maneuverability. Connally warned, however, that such encompassing terms would give tacit approval to the use of American combat troops. Vandenberg feared that a blank check could lead to war with Russia.[55]

The White House insisted upon a flexible aid bill. Henderson remarked that the President had purposely worded the Truman Doctrine loose enough to be either economic or military in thrust. Indeed, Henderson would have opposed the bill had it ruled out military aid. McGhee declared that the chief quality of the Truman Doctrine was that its administrators could shift the emphasis to either economic or military aid, depending upon circumstances. Bohlen agreed that the Truman Doctrine did not assure the use of armed force. But all argued that the United States should maintain the military option. Rusk insisted that the fighting in Greece necessitated military assistance.[56]

As the hearings continued, McGhee expressed the feelings of many in the administration when he declared that the Truman Doctrine provided the "excitement of a new venture." Clifford argued that the program was an outgrowth of his report of September 1946 setting out patterns of Soviet behavior, and that the President's speech had let the Russians know that "by God, we understood what we were up to." The Truman Doctrine, Henderson insisted, constituted a frank statement of what State Department analysts had long been saying with "subdued voices." Rusk declared that the administration had taken a stand against the "phenomenon of aggression—an insatiable political doctrine backed by force" and resting on a "doctrine of world revolution that also was insatiable because there were no world boundaries." The President was convinced that the Soviet Union rested on a "Frankenstein dictatorship worse than any of the others, Hitler included."[57]

To an administration deeply suspicious of the Kremlin, signs repeatedly confirmed some form of Soviet involvement in Greek affairs. Support for this view came from the British government, whose spokesmen approved all replies given by Acheson to the congressional committees and urged him to recognize that the Soviet threat to Greece was indicative of a worldwide danger to freedom. When America's decision to help Greece became known, the Soviet delegate on the UN Security Council Commission of Investigation, Alexander Lavrishchev, immediately confronted Ethridge with the question: "What does this mean?" "It means," Ethridge crisply replied, "that you can't do it." Lavrishchev smiled and commented, "I quite understand, Mr. Ethridge."[58]

III

The congressional hearings confirmed the Truman administration's need to launch a public information campaign aimed at convincing Americans of the need to help even non-democratic governments in trouble. When Vandenberg asked Acheson if the White House intended to tell the entire story to the American public, the undersecretary replied: "We will have to do it with a certain amount of discreetness, but we will have to do it, yes." Henderson insisted that the administration could not adopt a position of helping only those governments that fitted the American definition of democracy. In a radio discussion of the aid bill, he was asked whether the price of American economic assistance should not be "a government to our liking." "No. We are not going to do that." The administration had attached no strings to the program. Henderson later told the Chicago Council on Foreign Relations that Americans who "expect a political democracy to function perfectly in a country that has been ravaged by two invasions and an enemy occupation and which is now beset by political terrorism and on the verge of economic collapse, are either extremely innocent or extremely calculating."[59]

As part of this information program, Secretary of Labor Lewis Schwellenbach delivered a public address in San Francisco in which he defended the administration's policy as an appropriate response to the situation in Greece. A negotiated settlement always remained an option. But past experiences showed the futility of this approach. The United States had negotiated many times on matters affecting the freedom of peoples in the Middle East and in central and southern Europe. President Truman had referred to the Yalta agreements in protesting Soviet pressures on Poland and other countries. The situation in Greece called for a different level of reaction by the United States. The White House did not categorize all opponents of the Athens government as communists; several opposition groups simply disliked the regime. The United States must convince Europe and Asia that democracy had much to offer. "Our best effort in Greece and Turkey should demonstrate that democracies are able and willing to help each other protect their free institutions and their independence."[60]

Vandenberg meanwhile quieted many objections by securing an amendment that made the Greek-Turkish aid bill compatible with the UN Charter. In his private papers, he had penciled in the claim that the administration had made "a colossal blunder in ignoring the U.N." To rectify the matter, he called for the termination of the aid program if either the Security Council or General Assembly determined that "action taken or assistance furnished by the United Nations makes the continuance of such assistance unnecessary or undesirable." To add strength to this provision, the United States would waive the "exercise," though not the "right," of veto in the Security Council. Although Acheson believed that this proposal was "window dressing and must have seemed either silly or cynical or both in London, Paris, and Moscow," it was a "cheap price" to pay for the support of Vandenberg, Austin, and other skeptics. Under Vandenberg's amendment, the United States also would withdraw aid if either the Greek or the Turkish government, supported by a majority of its people, made the request, or if the President determined that the United States had either accomplished its mission or could not do so. Americans could not "escape war by running away from it," Vandenberg cautioned. To a Michigan resident, he wrote that the democracies had engaged in a fatal policy of appeasement when they chose to "lie down" at Munich in 1938. The Free World could not afford another Munich.[61]

The White House did not try to conceal anything from the public, as the broad nature of the American response came under full discussion in the congressional hearings. When Georgia Democrat Walter George inquired whether American assistance was to be military or economic or both, Acheson replied in a way that only at first glance seemed evasive. "I do not think it is something which it is possible for me to answer," the undersecretary told the committee. "I do not think those words were used." The decision to intervene rested on a consideration of all aspects of the problem. Connally understood Acheson: the United States had to demonstrate will power. "If we do not go to Greece, as the most appealing spot—if we do not go into Greece and Turkey under these circumstances—we will not go in anywhere else except in the Western Hemisphere." Democrat Alben Barkley of Kentucky agreed. Failure to take action would provide the Russians with "evidence of our unwillingness to do much in defense of our principles and the things for which the Allied nations fought this last war at untold cost."[62]

Republican Henry Cabot Lodge, Jr., of Massachusetts perhaps best grasped the importance of having a general authorization bill. In this case "military" assistance did not mean preparation for maneuvers, tactics, field exercises, or combat on any scale; it meant equipping Greek personnel so that they could keep order inside the country. American military personnel would train Greeks in the use of signal equipment, vehicles, and weapons. "We can, therefore, safely conclude that there is nothing whatever in this bill which involves the United States in combat operations in Greece or which by any stretch of the imagination could put Greece in a position to undertake offensive international action." The program did not break down into economic or military compartments because the two forms of assistance were "constantly merging" and interrelated. The best descriptive word for America's efforts, used in the broadest sense, was strategic.[63]

Acheson emphasized strategic considerations in attempting to ease the concerns of those senators who feared that sinister American oil interests were guiding the administration's actions. The assistance program, he assured committee members, did not result entirely from the presence of oil. America's "policy would have been exactly the same in this instance if there had not been a single drop of oil in the Near East." This statement was doubtless the truth, but what few observers realized was that Acheson was not denying the nation's interest in oil; he was arguing that oil was only one aspect of America's strategic concern in the region. The growing American interest in oil was a matter of record, both public and private. Byrnes, Forrestal, and Leahy had all emphasized the importance of Middle East oil in World War II; even though the United States had a surplus at the end of the war, that supply would gradually diminish, making the Middle East (which held 40 percent of the world's reserves) an important part of America's global strategic considerations. A July 1945 survey of the Near East's oil resources revealed that it had reserves of fifteen billion barrels, whereas the United States had twenty billion. Of the fifteen, the British controlled 74 percent and the United States 24 percent. Including its own reserves, the United States controlled 57 percent of the world's oil resources, the British 27 percent, and the Soviets (based primarily on production in the Caucasus) 11 percent. Acheson recognized the importance of the Middle East's oil, but his immediate concern was the impact that the area's collapse would have on morale and security. The Soviets' postwar interests in the region added urgency to the question.[64]

The widespread suspicions of America's private oil interests in the Middle East were not unfounded; but critics failed to realize that the economic interests of the oil companies paralleled, not guided, the strategic concerns of the White House. Primarily for business reasons, these oil firms supported the efforts of the Truman administration to bring order to the region; the result was a unified policy that only appeared to be cynically devised. Nonetheless, even supporters of the proposed aid program raised questions about the administration's motives. *Time* magazine observed that U.S. oil companies were busily investing in Arabia as part of the scheme to control the Middle East's oil, which was the "jackpot" in the "blue-chip game." Although the "loud talk" concerned Greece and Turkey, "the whispers behind the talk were of the ocean of oil to the south." Oil, according to the *New York Times*, was the "big factor" in America's aid to Greece. In an article entitled "U.S. Interest in Mideast Oil is Strategic," Cabell Phillips came close to grasping the real issue when he emphasized the strategic importance of oil in stopping the spread of the Soviet Union. But even Phillips failed to see that the presence of oil alone would not have determined policy. Acheson repeatedly declared that oil was one consideration among many. The administration's policy could not be compartmentalized into different kinds of objectives. Its purpose was to help Greece and Turkey on every front—whether diplomatic, economic, political, or military. The White House was ready to use every means available to protect America's strategic interests along the Northern Tier. There was no distinction between economic and political goals, between ideals and self-interest. They were inseparable parts of a general policy intended to promote national security.[65]

The truth is that the Truman administration found the nation's oil companies to be valuable tools in achieving strategic objectives. If any question exists about whether these companies were more concerned about profits than national security, there can be no doubt that their leaders wanted support—not directives—from Washington in the postwar years. America's oil magnates had established themselves in the Middle East through private and unregulated policies—not as part of a coherent national policy. U.S. government officials now recognized that if they supported the companies in their daily business, the result could be a more effective foreign policy that was in part constructed upon securing the nation's postwar oil requirements. Even though oil had become a "dirty word" by the 1940s, Henderson declared, that product of the Middle East was the "lifeblood" of the West. The administration faced the challenge of developing "a more mature approach" that would put oil in its proper place as a "vitally needed commodity like food" and "not necessarily a symbol of sinister imperialism."[66]

The Iranian crisis of 1945–46 had demonstrated the inseparability of the nation's strategic objectives and its oil policy. President Truman had agreed with Henderson and Clifford that Soviet inroads into Iran would threaten

America's access to the Middle East's oil. Thus the administration could not have been displeased with the spread of American oil acquisitions in the region. By the end of World War II, five of the nation's largest oil companies had huge holdings in the Middle East. Standard Oil of New Jersey and Socony-Vacuum controlled nearly 24 percent of Iraq's reserves along with the oil along the Arabian coast; Gulf Oil controlled half of Kuwait's supply; Standard Oil of California and the Texas Company controlled almost all of the oil of Bahrain and Saudi Arabia. In early 1947, Standard Oil of New Jersey and Socony-Vacuum bought Aramco (Texas and California companies united in Saudi Arabia), thereby consummating a deal that helped make the Persian Gulf the base of the world's price structure for petroleum. Because Aramco needed materials to build a pipeline across the Arabian peninsula, it applied to the Commerce Department in Washington for export licenses. In September, that department authorized a license because of what it called the "strategical, political and economic interests of the United States." The State Department strongly supported the move because the pipeline would aid American policy in the Middle East and Europe by furthering economic and political stability. Oil was one element in the search for peace.[67]

Strategic and economic objectives even meshed on an international level, for the Cold War forced rival Anglo-American oil concerns in the Middle East to shelve their differences in light of the greater Soviet threat. In the postwar period the British government recognized that its interests paralleled those of the United States in the region, and encouraged American oil firms to expand their operations—as long as they did not come into conflict with British holdings. An editorial in *The Economist* in Britain argued that Middle East oil was a "vital interest" to both nations as well as to the entire West. "To represent this interest as sinister or exclusively commercial is silly." Mutual Anglo-American strategic concerns over possible Soviet encroachments in the Middle East had combined with mutual economic interests in the region to constitute the common thread overriding past differences between the nations regarding the oil question.[68]

In retrospect, the White House probably should have confronted the oil issue publicly by proclaiming that the product was essential to the security of America and the Western world. Republican Senator Alexander Wiley thought so. In a long line of questioning of Acheson pertaining to the nation's oil interests in the Middle East, Wiley remarked that he did not believe the American people were as "dumb as we sometimes assume they are." America's self-interest was the vital factor. The U.S. government was trying to stop "the onrush of an ideology that we think is in conflict with us all over the world." In the event of another world war, the United States would require Middle Eastern oil. "That is strategic material. We have depleted our own in the last world war to such an extent that nobody knows what the cost is going to be to us in the future. I think you ought to call a spade a spade. Otherwise I don't think that you can get the American people to understand."[69] Had the administration handled the matter in the way suggested, the American people (who would support the interventionist policy in Greece and Turkey) would doubtless have favored the spread of their nation's oil interests in the Middle East.

While the hearings continued, and even before the Truman administration had won a formal congressional commitment to Greece, the military part of the aid program was virtually in place. By the first of April, the United States had sent the following items to Greece, all of which fell into the category of "surplus property credits": thirty-five AT-6 training planes, nineteen mine-sweepers, one patrol craft, nineteen landing craft, one landing ship dock, and fourteen aircraft engines. General Lincoln explained to the Senate Foreign Relations Committee that additional military goods would include weapons and ammunition; motor vehicles along with oil, lubricants, fuel, and related items; food and clothing; horses and mules; engineering materials; and road building equipment. Patterson added airplane replacement parts and gasoline to the list. The United States would furnish no strategic or tactical training, he declared.[70]

Despite these assurances from the War Department, some congressmen still wanted to incorporate into the aid bill specific limitations on America's military activities in Greece. Republican Karl Mundt of South Dakota sought to set a maximum on the number of military personnel because he feared that the Russians would regard a large American involvement as a virtual declaration of war. Republican Jacob Javits of New York wanted to change the wording, "in advisory capacity only," to "in the instruction and training of military personnel, and in the procurement of military equipment and supplies only." Such changes in the bill, they thought, would prove to the Kremlin that America's only objective in Greece was to promote domestic security without becoming involved in the fighting.[71]

Patterson and Acheson opposed both amendments. The secretary of war explained that when he had earlier announced a probable ceiling of forty in the military mission, he had still held hope that the British Military Mission would remain in Greece after passage of the aid bill. He had merely wanted to attach additional personnel to an economic mission or to enlarge the staff of the military attaché. Patterson did not believe it advisable to set a ceiling because of unforeseen problems, but he later agreed to limit the size of the mission in each country to a hundred. The same principle applied to Javits's call to specify the military's functions. Unanticipated needs might not fit the language of the proposed amendment and yet be vital to the mission's success. When Javits expressed concern that Americans would eventually extend tactical assistance to Greek officers on how to kill guerrillas, Patterson replied that the term "advisory capacity" would be a sufficient restraint. Acheson agreed. The American military missions to both Greece and Turkey would be small and consist only of observers and advisers.[72]

The Greek-Turkish aid bill became law on May 22, 1947, and, in a victory for both the administration and bipartisan foreign policy, it did not contain the restrictive amendments that had risen in both the Senate and House

Committee hearings. The measure passed the Senate by the largest bipartisan support for a major foreign policy bill since war broke out in Europe in 1939. The vote was 67 to 23, the Republicans comprising 35 of those in favor and 16 against. In the House, the bill also passed by a wide margin: 287 to 107, 127 Republicans for the bill and 93 in opposition. As President Truman signed the measure into law, he emphasized that the United States was fulfilling its responsibilities to the UN.[73]

Public Law 75 authorized the establishment of aid missions for both Greece and Turkey, with the American Mission to Aid Greece to be located in Athens and headed by a chief who would supervise all expenditures and administer both civilian and military assistance programs while keeping the ambassador fully informed. The mission in Greece would begin with a staff of forty members (exclusive of military and naval personnel), but that figure would soon grow to about 175. The law empowered the President to provide "loans, credits, grants, or otherwise" in helping Greece (and Turkey) upon that government's request. In accordance with the administration's recommendations, Congress approved $400 million for Greece and Turkey, and authorized the Reconstruction Finance Corporation to make a maximum advance of $100 million to Greece, that amount to be reimbursed when the congressional appropriation went into effect. The appropriated sum came on July 30, 1947, with $300 million of it earmarked for Greece. The monetary allotment for the aid program would extend through June 30, 1948, although Congress could appropriate additional funds at that time. The mission's objective was to maintain the "internal security and the national integrity and survival of Greece as a free self-respecting democracy and thereby to contribute to the security and independence of all freedom-loving peoples."[74]

The military branch of the mission, consisting of the United States Army Group Greece (USAGG) and a small naval section, would serve in an "advisory capacity only." USAGG would have a staff of fifty-four, including officers, enlisted men, and civilians. The naval mission would have no more than thirty men, whose duty would be to train the Greeks in using American minesweepers, tank landing ships, personnel boats, tugs, and other craft no larger than a destroyer. USAGG, organized in Washington over a month before passage of the aid bill, was placed under the temporary command of acting head Colonel Charles Lehner and would be responsible for advising the government in Athens on equipment and supplies needed by the Greek army, air force, and gendarmerie, and for regulating the distribution of American goods in accordance with congressional legislation. Anticipating passage of the aid bill, Lehner left on May 20 with an advance party for Athens, where USAGG was officially activated two days later. The British Military Mission, while in the country, would continue to train the Greek army.[75]

The Department of State supervised the aid program, although numerous government agencies were involved. The missions in each country would operate under a chief, who in turn answered to the coordinator in Washington. Twenty-two offices and divisions took part in planning the effort and delegated eighty-nine personnel to act as liaison with other departments. Operational procedures were subject to the approval of the secretary of state. George McGhee, as coordinator of the program, presided over a staff of seventy people in Washington, all responsible to the undersecretary of state.[76]

The chief of the American mission in Greece was Dwight Griswold, a former governor of Nebraska and a liberal Republican who had served with Truman during World War I and who at the time of his appointment was working with America's military government in Germany. Such a choice was at least partly political; it would facilitate future congressional appropriations, should they become necessary. The cabinet in Washington enthusiastically praised the President's decision. Griswold would spend a month of study in Washington before departing for Athens with a small staff. The immediacy of the problem prevented further delay.[77]

The aid bill had not come without misgivings. Although the administration stressed the need for flexibility, many congressmen remained worried about the open-ended nature of the commitment. The decision to escalate the involvement rested solely in the hands of the President acting through his secretary of state. The aid bill included no limitations on the size and functions of the military mission and did not incorporate specific prohibitions against the deployment of combat forces. Perhaps Republican Representative Francis H. Case of South Dakota voiced the sentiments of many of his colleagues. After chairing the House Committee of the Whole while it considered the bill, he concluded that most of his peers approved the measure only because they saw no choice. About seventy-five members of the House, including himself, voted for the bill because they did not want to hurt the UN cause of collective security. Middle East oil was not a major consideration. The secretary of the interior had assured him that the United States had a surplus and that American companies were seeking import restrictions to keep Middle Eastern oil out of the country. Moreover, the United States could more cheaply resolve future fuel problems by research and expanded production than by policing the Mediterranean and Middle East. But, Case warned, "no country, ours or any other, is wise enough or rich enough, or just plain big enough to run the rest of the world."[78]

The Truman administration recognized the impossibility of guaranteeing self-determination throughout the world. Some regions were crucial for strategic reasons; others would furnish examples of the peoples' capacity to resist aggression; still others were untouchable because they lay within Soviet spheres of influence. But the administration also knew that actual and symbolic considerations had meshed to broaden the definition of America's vital interests. In theory and in ideal, the commitment to Greece and Turkey was part of a global strategy designed to protect freedom wherever challenged. In practice and in reality, that strategy was limited by circumstances—whether the troubled area could and should be saved. As long as ideal and reality remained distinguishable, congressional fears were groundless.

CHAPTER
3

The Need for American Military Assistance

I

By the time the President announced the Truman Doctrine, the military situation in Greece had taken a turn for the worse. The Greek army's first campaign against the guerrillas began in April 1947 with an attack on enemy strongholds near the Gulf of Corinth in central Greece. Bad weather at first brought operations to a halt, but by the middle of the month government soldiers had resumed their move northward through Thessaly and western Macedonia. As the army advanced toward the frontier, it intended to isolate and crush the guerrillas or drive them out of the country and seal the border—over 600 miles in length, desolate, rough, and largely unmarked. To break down resistance, the government authorized the minister of war to grant amnesty to guerrillas who surrendered, leaving those captured to courts-martial. But as the weeks passed, the offensive bogged down due to lack of organization and sheer inability to sustain the operation.[1]

The army's initial successes had only temporarily concealed its endemic weaknesses. From the first encounters with the guerrillas, the army was plagued by poor discipline, training, and leadership. Soldiers preferred safe-guarding villages and towns to a relentless pursuit that could either force a decisive engagement or scatter the guerrillas and keep them cold, hungry, and hunted. The army managed to clear some regions and consolidate control, but it was unable to stop guerrilla raids and sabotage. In the meantime, the communists infiltrated cells of workers into the cities, towns, and large villages. Referred to as "self-defense personnel," the cells built an intelligence and supply network that worked behind the lines of the Greek army in recruiting, raising money, gathering information about troop movements, and terrorizing the population. McGhee, while admitting that the countryside remained dangerous, nonetheless considered the major cities to be generally safe. Most observers agreed that the problem in Greece had become so predominantly military that economic reconstruction could not begin.[2]

The nature of the war afforded numerous advantages to the guerrillas. Based strictly on manpower and matériel, the Greek government should have had little difficulty crushing the opposition. Loyalist forces, including army and gendarmerie, totaled 165,000 men, whereas that of the guerrillas had grown to perhaps 28,000, which included 18,000 operating in Greece and the balance moving in and out of neighboring states. But several other factors offset the guerrillas' numerical disadvantages. No one could determine how many Greek civilians were assisting them. The guerrillas engaged in hit-and-run missions that allowed them to terrorize settlements throughout Epirus, Macedonia, and Thrace. The country's inadequate road system severely limited army pursuit. The Greek army had no armored force, except for a few British Centaur tanks, but these were virtually useless because of the uneven terrain. Few passageways were paved, and once motor vehicles left these main arteries, they had to reduce speeds to less than fifteen miles per hour. In summer the dirt lanes became beds of dust; on rainy days they turned into mud; in winter they were impassable because of snow and ice. A single road connected Athens in the south to Salonika in the northeast; along the west coast the only north-south highway was the Yannina-Arta-Agrinion road. Across the northern part of the country, the single west-east link ran from Yannina to Trikkala to Larisa. Though a railroad followed the east coast, regular troops found it and the roads of no use in pursuing the guerrillas. Moreover, the Yannina road wound through a low-lying coastal stretch between sea and mountains and provided an excellent opportunity for guerrilla sabotage and ambush.[3]

For protection, the guerrillas relied upon the mountains that made up more than 60 percent of the country's surface. Steep slopes made movement perilous, particularly to government forces unfamiliar with the region, and the great number of caves and forested areas provided countless hideouts. In winter these guerrilla bases were especially formidable. Sleet and snow enveloped the area, concealing byways that could easily collapse onto jagged crevices. Cold blasts of central Asian air further sealed the mountainous terrain, making survival tenuous and diminishing accessibility as sharply as visibility. The guerrillas' strongholds became virtually impregnable as trails and passes vanished.[4]

Villages in the mountains were small, numbering from 500 to 2,000 inhabitants, and they were usually located in valleys hidden by trees. Many settlements had no road connecting them with the outside world. Travelers had to use winding, treacherous trails around the mountain sides. The uneven countryside helped to keep the villagers isolated and poor. The enclosed surroundings encouraged them to regard outsiders with suspicion—particularly those representing the government in Athens. Though summer made the guerrillas' villages more vulnerable to attack, the dryness of the weather provided early warning. When soldiers and accompanying motor vehicles approached, their movements raised clouds of dust and enabled guerrillas in the hills to track their path. The brush along mountainsides and valleys furnished camouflage for the guerrillas, while immense patches of reeds hid their movements along the shores. Gorges and other pitfalls in the mountains also deterred pursuers. Not only could one fall into a crevice but the high passes, the rugged and winding cuts into the mountains, and the barren, open expanses facilitated surprise attacks on invading armies.[5]

The sudden death of King George II in early April brought his brother, Paul I, to the throne. The change in the royalty had immediate impact. Whereas George had not been warm and charismatic, his brother was active in politics and attractive to the people. Although Paul had led the National Youth Organization under Metaxas during the 1930s (which was modeled after the Nazi youth and provided no basis for popularity), he was a sportsman who drew a lot of attention by his interest in yachting. The new king was married to Princess Frederika of Brunswick, grand-daughter of Kaiser Wilhelm II and a former leader of the Hitler Youth League. American observers predicted a more visible role for the monarchy—by both heads. An embassy counselor reported that the king and queen had tried to promote better social ties with American representatives by hosting parties and meeting with them more often than did their predecessor. The *New York Times*'s overseas correspondent, Cyrus L. Sulzberger, noted that the queen had "a way with the men."[6]

In the meantime the guerrillas seemed to be building an impressive force. By the time the United States had decided to assist Greece, the Democratic Army was fairly well organized. Markos had most of his guerrilla force operating as bands or "groups," each consisting of seventy to a hundred men and called "Military Formations." These were in turn headed by political commissars or "kapetanios." A general headquarters had been established with Markos in charge. Under him, seven commands were responsible for organizing intelligence and other services in Thrace, eastern Macedonia, Epirus, Thessaly, Roumeli, and the Peloponnese. The guerrillas soon established permanent headquarters in the far north, close to Lake Prespa on the Greek side of the Albanian and Yugoslav borders. From this location, which was near the supply centers outside the country, the Grammos and Vitsi mountain ranges provided a formidable barrier against attack.[7]

Greek leaders in Athens at first underestimated the threat posed by the guerrillas. The army's initial counter-measures were primarily shows of force, for the government maintained that the major remedy was amnesty. But the guerrillas were confident of victory and regarded the offer of amnesty as the government's admission to weakness. Military strategists therefore called on the army to surround guerrilla strongholds, cut off all ways out, and move in for the kill. The strategy rarely worked. In one instance, the army blocked off a two-thousand-square-mile area in the north and closed in, hoping to capture Markos. Government forces imprisoned or killed a large number of the enemy, but many of the captives were elderly men or teenagers. Most of the guerrillas had escaped into the Pindus Mountains. Gradually the Greek government intensified efforts to put down the rebellion. It stepped up amnesty offers, increased mass arrests, called for more men and equipment to encircle and destroy the enemy, and promised a reward to anyone who brought in Markos dead or alive. "Each new effort," BBC reporter Kenneth Matthews wrote, "promises to be the last, as climbers reach a peak only to see a more forbidding one appear above them."[8]

The bitter turn of events escalated the rate of violence, which complicated the efforts of the American aid program. The traditional patriarchal society in Greece had encouraged a vendetta atmosphere, spreading a hatred that seared the country from within. Families closed ranks, seeking to avenge anyone who wronged one of their own. In many cases these feuds developed into small wars—especially when family members divided in loyalties between the guerrillas and the government. Stories abounded of atrocities—by both sides. Supporters of the Greek government pointed to the raiding and pillaging of villages, the forced recruiting practices of the Democratic Army, and the terrorist executions by guns, knives, and axes. Critics of the government denounced its brutal efforts to restore domestic order, and cited instances of Greek army commanders using political prisoners as "mine detectors" by forcing them to precede truck convoys in pursuit of the guerrillas. A London newspaper carried a photo of Greek soldiers on horseback swinging the decapitated heads of female guerrillas by the hair, en route to collect bounties awarded by the government. Although a spokesman for the government noted that this was an "old custom for bandits on whom the State has put a price to be decapitated and have their heads exposed to the public," the custom added weight to those critics in both Britain and the United States who opposed assistance to Greece.[9]

Washington's policymakers realized that longstanding Balkan problems had injected further complexities into the Greek situation, but, like the government in Athens, they did not know how to resolve those problems. The "frontier violations," as the UN Security Council Commission called them, had been going on for centuries. Since the Greek elections of March 1946, government forces had clashed nearly a thousand times with the guerrillas, about 700 of these skirmishes taking place in the Greek provinces near the frontier. The commission was unable to determine whether the illegal crossings were part of a "systematic plan of provocation by one country against another"; but it did note that Greece's northern neighbors had taken advantage of the large numbers of refugees fleeing into Yugoslavia and Bulgaria to train, indoctrinate, and return them to Greece as guerrillas.[10]

The Macedonian question particularly confused the Greek situation. Macedonia was a huge and vaguely marked area that linked Yugoslavia, Bulgaria, and Greece. It comprised the watershed of the Vardar River with the two main towns of Skoplje in Yugoslavia and Salonika in northeastern Greece. Macedonia was strategically and economically important because through it ran the chief transportation and communication route from Central Europe to Salonika and on to the eastern Mediterranean. The Balkan Wars of 1912–13 had brought focus to the issues of nationality and ownership of the area. Afterward, the Slavo-Macedonians were arbitrarily divided into those of Bulgarian (Pirin), Serbian (Vardar), and Greek (Aegean) Madeconia. About 80,000 lived in Greece, mostly in the Florina area in western Macedonia. Inhabitants of Macedonia were primarily Slav except in Greek Macedonia, where the number of Greek "Slavophones" (Slav-speaking Greeks) had been reduced by population changes of the 1920s. Thus the great majority of people in Greek Macedonia were actually Greeks. The Greeks' purpose since winning their independence during the early 1820s was to incorporate all of Macedonia into the national framework. Both the Yugoslavs and the Bulgarians resisted; among many reasons, they sought Salonika as a port on the Aegean Sea.[11]

During World War II, the prevailing thought among the interested peoples was that the Soviets favored an autonomous Macedonia. Thus many Greeks in Macedonia did not support the EAM/ELAS resistance group because its success would mean the eventual wresting of Greek Macedonia from Greece. There was reason for their fear. Yugoslav Partisans (communist guerrillas) had established a resistance organization in Slavo-Macedonia. By late 1943 these Slavo-Macedonian Partisans were urging their people to unite into a separate Macedonian state that would seek admission into a Yugoslav Federation. Yugoslav Partisans also persuaded the communist-led Greek guerrillas to allow the Slavophones to establish resistance groups in Slavo-Macedonia. When the German armies withdrew from Greece, the Macedonian issue reached crisis proportions. Greek royalist forces swarmed into the Slavophone sector of Macedonia, determined to halt any move toward autonomy and eventual incorporation into a Yugoslav Federation. Observers reported tortures, murders, and burnings of villages. As the harsh Greek policies continued, many Slavophones sought refuge farther north.[12]

In the postwar period, the Department of State, while opposing the establishment of a Macedonian state, had to stay clear of an issue that could spread the Greek war into neighboring countries. An independent Macedonia would come at the expense of Greek territorial integrity, which would raise doubts among other nations about the effectiveness of the Truman Doctrine. But if the White House took a firm stand against such a state and it emerged anyway, America's loss in prestige would be even greater. Policymakers in Washington chose to dodge the issue and avoid having the possible establishment of a Macedonian Republic take on the appearance of a diplomatic defeat for the West. The Truman administration insisted that its central goal in Greece was to promote domestic security. The United States could not afford to get involved in a regional controversy that might invite direct Soviet intervention.[13]

Either out of frustration, desperation, or both, the Greek government pursued increasingly repressive policies against dissidents that not only fed the angry national mood but threatened to alienate allies. According to the American member of the UN border commission, Mark Ethridge, these "discriminatory and gangster-like methods" drove many Greeks into the ranks of the guerrillas. MacVeagh warned that the government's actions could have an adverse effect upon the outlook of Americans: the Truman Doctrine would be discredited for supporting a police state. Greek policies were embarrassing to the State Department and others who had praised the government in Athens as the only alternative to the communists. Marshall noted the bad publicity received by the Greek government in the American press and warned that every action was in the "world spotlight." In England, *The Economist* asserted that the activities of the Greek government were causing more people to look upon the communists as their only hope. Confirmation came from the former assistant military attaché of the American embassy, William H. McNeill. After a tour by jeep from Athens into the settlements north, he reported that harsh actions taken by government security organizations and armed rightist groups were costing them popular support.[14]

Furthermore, the government's measures were not working; indeed, they were intensifying the civil war. One observer warned that unless the government changed its ways and provided security and food, more Greeks would push for an autonomous Macedonia. The amnesty program was a failure: only 160 individuals had surrendered under its terms. A Greek intelligence officer admitted that his government could not guarantee the safety of either those who accepted amnesty or their families. In addition, the guerrilla leaders were discouraging desertions by concentrating their forces in larger groups, away from the Greek army and gendarmerie. Some American observers were convinced that the nationalist reaction got out of hand after Napoleon Zervas, the former wartime leader of the Greek resistance group called EDES (National Republican Greek League), became minister of public order in Maximos's Populist government. According to these firsthand reports, Zervas was a "cut throat by common account," who instituted a "white terror" against enemies of the state and swore to kill all communists in the towns. The wave of government actions included mass arrests, executions in the Peloponnese and Salonika, the exile of thousands of Greeks into the islands, and a general disregard for guilt or innocence in meting out punishment. The situation became more alarming as rightist groups pushed for a bill outlawing the KKE. Marshall urged the Athens government to repudiate these policies because the communists would be more dangerous if driven underground. The Greek government, however, was afraid that leniency might undercut the morale of its army.[15]

In late May 1947, the UN commission substantiated Washington's belief that Yugoslavia, Albania, and Bulgaria were supporting the guerrillas. The Truman administration was prepared for these findings; a few days earlier, Ethridge had sent Marshall a draft of the report. Commission members had gathered testimony from nearly 240 witnesses, who claimed that the Yugoslavs were training refugees in guerrilla warfare and providing them with supplies, hospitalization, transportation, and sanctuary. During the spring of 1946, the commission noted, a guerrilla training camp had been established at Bulkes in Yugoslavia. The commission had even procured a copy of a text-book written in the summer of 1945 as a manual for guerrilla tactics. The Greeks likewise received political instruction and military training in an Albanian camp at Rubig, a village located about fifty miles north of Tirana. Bulgaria also provided refuge, hospitalization, arms, and equipment. The Yugoslavs and Bulgarians kept border tensions high by calling for the establishment of an independent Macedonian state and its incorporation into a Yugoslav Federation.[16]

Marshall was alarmed that the UN commission intended to hold the Greek government partly responsible for the border unrest. The commission laid primary blame on Yugoslavia, Albania, and Bulgaria for provoking border incidents and on EAM for breaking the Varkiza Agreement of 1945 by not surrendering arms, by urging members to go underground, by refusing to participate in the March 1946 elections, and by promoting terrorism and outside interference in Greek affairs. Yet the commission refused to exonerate the Greek government. That regime's repressive policies, according to the commission, contributed to border disturbances by encouraging hostility to its rule. After the Varkiza Agreement had brought an uneasy truce to the civil war, over 20,000 Greeks, a substantial number of them Slavo-Macedonians, fled into Yugoslavia while another 5,000 made their way into Bulgaria. The Greek government's persecution of these minorities had caused turmoil in Greek Macedonia, providing a breeding ground for separatist movements. In addition, the Greek government had kept tensions high by its claims to Northern Epirus (southern Albania) and by its refusal to end the state of war with Albania that had begun in October 1940, when Italian forces invaded Greece through Italian-controlled Albania. The commission concluded that both sides shared blame.[17]

The Truman administration exerted influence on the commission to high-light the role of neighboring states in fomenting the unrest in Greece. Marshall urged Ethridge to emphasize the responsibility of Yugoslavia, Albania, and Bulgaria. The commission must not provide the communists with propaganda by criticizing the Greek government. Though Marshall admitted that government persecution and disturbed conditions in Greece helped to explain the problems along the frontier, he persuaded the commission to emphasize the distinction between domestic issues that permitted frontier violations, and outside interference that was responsible for those violations. That point established, Marshall succeeded in convincing the commission to focus attention on the external threat.[18]

The commission report urged Greece to work toward the restoration of good diplomatic relations with Yugoslavia, Albania, and Bulgaria. It called upon the four governments to develop new frontier arrangements; it proposed a commission with investigatory and conciliatory functions; it advocated the voluntary transfer of minority groups; and it recommended steps to solve the refugee problem. In late July the Soviet representative on the Security Council vetoed the recommendations, even though nine colleagues had been supportive.[19] The outcome was predictable: the UN report became part of the permanent record, the border transgressions continued, and the Security Council moved to other business.

II

On May 24, the day after the UN commission submitted its report, the first contingent of American military advisers arrived in Athens as part of the United States Army Group Greece (USAGG). Under the acting command of Colonel Lehner, USAGG immediately began studying the equipment needs of the Greek army, air force, and gendarmerie. By mid-July USAGG had cut Greek General Staff requirements from forty million dollars to sixteen million, established an integrated relationship with the British and Greeks, and made recommendations for supplies and operations. In the meantime, Lehner assumed the position of deputy commander when General William L. Livesay arrived on June 19 to head USAGG. Livesay had had a long military career. After enlisting in the army in 1915, he served in the Mexican border crisis and in both world wars. He graduated from the Army War College in 1933, and at the time of his appointment to Greece was commanding general at Fort Jackson, South Carolina. Livesay's orders placed him under stringent limitations. If the Athens government issued an official invitation, he could attend meetings of the High Greek Military Council—but only as "an observer and in an advisory capacity concerning logistical problems." His responsibility was to advise the Greeks on the use of military equipment.[20]

USAGG's arrival seemed timely. The War Department believed that global attention was on the Truman Doctrine, making America's military commitment "an obligation of the first magnitude." The day following Livesay's arrival, he and Greek officials in Athens formalized the aid agreement by signing the "Aid to Greece" treaty. It affirmed that America's objectives were to "avert economic crisis, promote national recovery, and restore internal tranquility."[21]

Immediately upon arrival, Livesay had to deal with the Greek government's request for an enlarged military force. In early May, Marshall had opposed any expansion of either the army or gendarmerie without further study of the military and economic implications. A diversion of economic allocations to the military, he explained, would appear to have political purposes. Later that same month, the Greek General Staff insisted on a larger military allotment by asserting that its forces were not merely suppressing an armed insurrection but were fighting an undeclared war. The Greek ambassador in Washington explained why amnesty failed. The guerrillas knew that if they won the war they would have Greece; if they lost they would have forgiveness.[22]

Livesay's greatest problem was the Greek government's insistence upon an expanded military force. Its spokesmen considered three items essential: an increase of 10,000 men in the form of "pursuit detachments" comprised of armed villagers; the replacement of 7,000 suspected communists in the army (referred to as category "C" personnel) with men loyal to Greece, and the reassignment of "C" personnel to military labor battalions (thus creating an enlargement); the maintenance in the army of an already approved 20,000-man increase to the end of the year—not for three months as authorized. Maximos also revived an earlier suggestion for providing small arms and ammunition to 20,000 villagers as "military home guard" or "Country Self-Security Units (CSSUs). In the meantime the Ministry for Public Order requested an increase in the gendarmerie. To achieve internal security, Zervas believed that after the army had cleared an area and moved northward, it must leave a large number of men behind to conduct "mopping-up operations." Though these responsibilities were not technically part of the gendarmerie's mission of keeping domestic order, the army needed these units to subdue the guerrillas.[23]

Livesay opposed enlarging the military establishment until he had had time to assess the situation. He knew that the gendarmerie played a vital role in maintaining civil order after the army had cleared an area of guerrillas. But since a gendarme's monetary compensation was four times that of an average soldier, Livesay did not believe that a gendarme should perform a soldier's duty. He recommended no action at that time. On the category "C" question, he agreed that the release of communists screened from the army would further endanger the country. Yet underwriting such personnel in the army did not constitute a proper draw upon American funds. The army should retain communist inductees in service, grant them only those rations that did not disrupt the local Greek market in army goods, and issue essential equipment and clothing from army stocks.[24]

On the other big issue, that of the CSSUs, Livesay had misgivings about spreading small detachments of armed civilians throughout the country to protect villagers. The Greek General Staff had nonetheless formulated a plan designed to organize selected individuals into small units, preferably under a retired officer of the community; they would be armed with German and Italian weapons that had been captured during World War II. The British Military Mission had opposed the establishment of CSSUs because the impression would spread that civilians fighting the communists were part of government-sanctioned "Right Wing bands." Yet in Thessaly during the spring of 1947, the government in effect expanded the CSSUs by authorizing pursuit detachments. After the army cleared an area of guerrillas, it took along local inhabitants who knew the trails and hideouts and who, given arms, could help secure the region. When villagers left their localities, they received pay from small funds allotted by the Greek government. The General Staff claimed that the CSSUs now totaled over 26,000, although that figure was misleading. Many CSSUs were not armed, and a number of those who were armed did not have sufficient ammunition.[25]

Livesay finally approved the use of the CSSUs, primarily because of their success in northern Greece. Many villagers no longer felt unprotected, and they provided the army with information about the guerrillas. Furthermore, the General Staff had eased one of Livesay's greatest reservations about the plan by proposing the return of arms from villagers once an area was safe. He recommended that the chief of the American mission approve the use of military appropriations to expand this civilian support force.[26]

The responsibilities of the mission chief, Dwight Griswold, were no less sensitive than those of Livesay's. From his arrival in Athens in July 1947 until his resignation in mid-September of the following year, Griswold's chief objective was to preserve Greek independence and integrity by promoting domestic security and economic rehabilitation. Marshall's instructions helped to make this task difficult. To avoid criticism in the UN, the mission could not "intervene in Greek political affairs to the extent of imposing a government of our own choice." And yet Griswold was to make every effort to eliminate extremists in the Athens government, whether on the left or right. If government reorganization seemed advisable, Griswold was to work with MacVeagh in making discreet suggestions that would lead Greek leaders to believe that they had made changes on their own. When Griswold found incompetent or non-cooperative Greek officials, he was "to effect [their] removal." But Griswold was to do it quietly and in a way that would cause minimal resentment.[27]

The question of Greek political affairs had potential for causing trouble not only between the American and Greek governments but also between Griswold and MacVeagh. Marshall assured Griswold that the Department of State would welcome his views on amnesty, elections, and changes in the government. But Marshall made it clear that MacVeagh's judgment would continue to be "a principal determinant" in policymaking. In realistic terms, however, Griswold had considerably more power: he had supreme authority over civilian and military aid, and he could offer advice and other help to Greece. If only as implicit leverage, he could suspend aid if the Greek government failed to administer the program in cooperation with the American mission.[28] MacVeagh's authority remained theoretical and elusively defined, whereas Griswold's was specific and more effective.

Given the differing backgrounds and philosophies of the two men, their problems seemed almost inevitable. MacVeagh was once a literary agent and publisher who founded Dial Press. A cultured gentleman, he was cosmopolitan and learned, and had an aristocratic bearing. At Groton and Harvard, he studied Greek and Latin and majored in philosophy. Afterward he continued his studies in philosophy and languages at the Sorbonne in Paris before seeing action in France during World War I. MacVeagh was a mild-mannered and highly sensitive man who had been appointed to the post in Greece by

President Roosevelt. Griswold, however, was gruff and outspoken, a Republican chosen as mission chief in part to satisfy a Republican-controlled Congress and to demonstrate the White House penchant for bipartisan politics. MacVeagh's differences with Griswold concerned methods and not objectives. Both men wanted the United States to demonstrate to the world its support for Greek independence and territorial integrity. But MacVeagh chose a quiet approach through diplomatic channels, whereas Griswold preferred bold, forceful actions that often bordered upon outright interference in Greek domestic affairs. Career officers in the State Department considered MacVeagh a dedicated public servant who held Greek interests uppermost. Many thought Griswold had political aspirations and would use his mission in Greece as an opportunity to prove his organizational and leadership ability. He had been appointed without MacVeagh's knowledge, and over his pleas to Acheson and others in the State Department not to send a "politician" to head the aid mission.[29]

The matter of divided responsibility would soon become an issue between Griswold and MacVeagh.[30] The basis for much of the confusion lay in the directives to the American mission and to the American embassy. MacVeagh was to retain his dominant role in recommending policy, but the truth was that the aid responsibilities assigned to Griswold were inseparable from policymaking. If Griswold could withdraw aid, he automatically had economic and military leverage over the Greek government that MacVeagh did not have. The Department of State would have to deal with these problems lest the aid program collapse from within. For the time being, however, other matters took priority.

The Griswold-MacVeagh difficulties were illustrative of the many unforeseen and baffling problems resulting from the American experience in Greece. Although the Truman administration preferred not to intervene in domestic political matters, it nonetheless expected Griswold and MacVeagh somehow to bring about the establishment of a broadly based government. To avoid charges of U.S. interference in Greek internal affairs, they were only to make suggestions about the structure of that government. Congress, however, had necessitated changes by stipulating that Americans could not support an extremist regime. Many observers assumed that the United States had the leverage to dictate policy in Greece because of the aid program. The Greeks, however, determined a large part of policy because of their awareness that Americans had termed the area vital to their security and did not dare to cancel the assistance. One observer warned: "The Greeks in power will use us for all we are worth. We think we are doing them a favor; they know they are doing us a bigger one."[31] Withdrawal of American aid remained an implied threat, but given the commitment, such action seemed unlikely.

The temptation to forgo the diplomatic approach was strong, for the Truman administration's overriding consideration was that Soviet influence in Greece was real, if only because other nations regarded the events as a test of America's will to combat communism. Despite the probability that Soviet

involvement in Greek affairs was no more than that of interested observer—
and then, only when there was a flicker of hope for success—the prevailing
assumptions among Washington's policymakers about the Kremlin's behavior
prevented them from believing that the guerrillas could have been acting on
their own—and especially without Stalin's blessings.

The White House belief in Soviet complicity in Greece fitted the broad
outlines of Kremlin policy explained by George F. Kennan in an article
entitled "The Sources of Soviet Conduct," which he published in the July
1947 issue of *Foreign Affairs*. Kennan argued that the only way to halt Soviet
expansion was through a policy of "containment." As the Soviets exerted
pressure on the "free institutions of the Western world," the United States had
to respond with the "vigilant application of counter-force at a series of
constantly shifting geographical and political points, corresponding to the
shifts and maneuvers of Soviet policy." Kennan did not specify what counter-
measures he envisioned, but he later insisted that they were primarily economic. This stand was consistent with his argument regarding the type of aid
that should go to Greece and Turkey; his differences with the White House lay
in his belief that the priority should not be military assistance. One member
of the Truman administration, George M. Elsey, claimed that Kennan's ideas
did not mold policy so much as they followed a path already taken; even if so,
Kennan's article substantiated the White House belief that the Soviets were
engaged in a global policy of expansion that the United States had to
counteract.[32]

Conceivably, the critics were correct who charged that the Truman Doctrine had provoked the Soviets into challenging America's credibility in
Greece. Since the President's declaration, according to American intelligence
sources, the Soviets had been increasing indirect support to the Greek communists. "Soviet-Satellite authorities" had assumed control over guerrilla
operations with the purpose of undermining the Truman Doctrine by maintaining chaotic conditions in Greece and supporting an independent Macedonia. The Greek embassy in Washington, probably in a self-serving effort,
warned of a widening war. Reports (never substantiated) indicated that an
"international brigade" had left Yugoslavia and Albania, en route to northern
Greece.[33] Lack of Soviet documentation makes it impossible to determine the
validity of these allegations, but the truth was less important than prevailing
perceptions. Policymakers in Washington were convinced that the communists had stepped up activities in Greece in almost direct proportion to the
American aid effort. For practical purposes, appearances of Soviet involvement in Greece had become reality.

The Truman administration was determined to contain the communists in
Greece and elsewhere. Marshall emphasized to Griswold and to the American
ambassador at the UN, Warren R. Austin, that events in Greece were part of
a "world-wide Communist effort to subvert governments and institutions not
already subservient to the Soviet Union." The War Department asserted that
the Kremlin had "a plan of expansion—ideologically and territorially"—that

sought gains without a resort to war. America's strategy was to safeguard North America, Britain, the Cairo-Suez area, essential Atlantic islands, the Bering Sea-Japan Sea-Yellow Sea connection, and important lines of communication throughout the world.[34]

But America's assurances to Greece came into question as stories spread of an international brigade preparing to launch an invasion from the north. In July, 2,500 guerrillas crossed the border out of Albania, isolated the town of Konitsa and laid siege, and appeared to be heading next toward Yannina. They carried heavy arms, traveled with pack animals and supplies, and were well trained in taking cover at the approach of a plane. Evidence seemed to support the Greek government's assertion that an international brigade had been formed. Both *Time* and *Newsweek* seemed to believe so, with the latter reporting that the Russians were organizing a brigade north of Greece to aid the free government that the Greek guerrillas expected to establish in the mountains. In the UN Security Council, America's deputy representative, Herschel Johnson, warned of an "explosion any day" and demanded emergency meetings dealing with the "invasion." The Greek government claimed that Albanians had participated in the attack on Konitsa, and that an international brigade was poised just across the border in Albania. Speculation was that the guerrillas intended to establish Konitsa as the capital of a new free state. Both British and American observers were skeptical about the charges of a brigade and Albanian participation, but the rapidity of events did not allow time for examination and reflection.[35]

The Greek conflict threatened to take on international proportions as the guerrillas prepared to establish a new government of "Free Greece" in the north. In June, Zahariadis appeared at the annual meeting of the French Communist party in Strasbourg, and received a thundering ovation when he declared that "all of the political, military and international conditions existed for the creation of a Free Government in Greece." With him was Miltiadis Porfirogenis, a high official of the KKE, who asked the congress for international assistance in fighting "Anglo-American intervention and monarcho-fascist intransigence." If no compromise were possible, he declared, a "Free Greek Government" was needed. Soon after the conference, Democratic Army radio broadcasted Markos's proclamation calling for a "provisional democratic government in free regions" of Greece. The establishment of a guerrilla regime would compromise the Athens government's claim to legitimacy, permit open assistance to the guerrillas from the outside, and vastly improve their chances for winning the war.[36]

Domestic matters likewise took a more serious turn. Greek police had searched the port of Piraeus, where they found revolvers, explosives, and revolutionary proclamations in the headquarters of the communist-dominated National Liberation Movement (or EAM). Such terrorist intentions, Marshall told the Joint Chiefs of Staff, were connected to the violations of Greece's northern borders by armed forces. A few days afterward, a fire in Athens took several lives in the building housing the offices of the American and British missions and the Greek air force. Within a week the government authorized a series of arrests that eventually netted nine thousand suspects. All were imprisoned and accused of participating in a communist coup planned in Athens with the help of an international brigade. When MacVeagh warned the Greek government that these indiscriminate arrests were creating a bad impression abroad, its response was that to expect "anything like western standards would be unrealistic."[37]

By the summer of 1947 the KKE's last efforts at a political settlement ended in failure, and all-out guerrilla warfare began in Greece. Until that time, the party's leaders had sought negotiations aimed at winning seats in the Greek cabinet. The preceding spring, the elderly leader of the Liberals, Themistocles Sophoulis (in his eighties), had talked with the KKE about determining some basis for preventing an expanded conflict. Sophoulis was left of center and a former prime minister, a charming and popular anti-royalist who smoked a pipe and always seemed calm and self-possessed. But he was also ambitious and shrewd, and doubtless saw a chance to win high office again if he could get the two sides together. And yet, even he could find no middle ground between the opposing forces. By July Sophoulis had become exasperated and announced his opposition both to the communists and to government policies. The KKE representative had expressed verbally to Sophoulis what MacVeagh called the "final terms for calling off the civil war": resignation of the Greek government; dissolution of Parliament; estab-lishment of a "pure center government" led by Sophoulis; an agreement between the new government and the KKE on the basis of what MacVeagh termed "Sophoulis's policy of appeasement"—general amnesty, assurances of security to those laying down arms, and new elections based on revised electoral lists. Since MacVeagh had learned of these terms from the British (who had been told by the Liberals), he wondered whether Sophoulis was "playing square" with Maximos, or "following at least to some extent, [the] well-known Communist tactics of trying to use [the] UK against [the] US." Less than a week later, Marshall informed MacVeagh that the terms were "insincere and dangerous, and that any serious discussion of them could only strengthen [the] Communists' hand." The Greek center lost interest, the KKE broke off relations with the Liberals, and the civil war began in earnest as the party adopted military tactics.[38]

Prolonged conflict was likely if the communists succeeded in establishing a government along the border. Truman directed Leahy to inquire into the possibility of sending the Mediterranean Squadron to Greece on what would be called a routine visit. Such a show of force, Forrestal agreed, might deter the guerrillas. Marshall asked Griswold about military reports from the Yannina-Konitsa area that the guerrillas held the initiative, and expressed concern that a proposed border commission then under debate in the UN Security Council would not be equipped to prevent large-scale invasions. At present, neither the United States nor the UN was capable of safeguarding Greece. If the situation continued to worsen, the Truman administration did not want to be in the position of hampering Greek attempts to defend the country. The installation of a Free Greek regime would obscure the reality—that the fighting was threatening to escalate into "open hostilities between the Soviet-dominated Balkan States and Greece." If the communists persuaded the world that the fighting in Greece constituted a civil war between two established governments, the Truman Doctrine would assume the appearance of blatant interventionism.[39]

By the end of July, just before the first American goods arrived in Greece, General Livesay was moving toward the position that deteriorating conditions necessitated an enlarged Greek infantry and more pack artillery. The infantry was vital in clearing an area of guerrillas and in setting up an occupation force to prevent their return until the gendarmerie could take charge. The irony was inescapable: without additional men, each military success ensured ultimate failure in the war. As the army cleared and occupied areas, its infantry was drained, becoming progressively smaller and losing the capacity to continue the offensive. Figures for the size of the army were deceiving. Many of the men were not in the field because of static defense assignments. In fact, nearly half of the forces were unavailable for combat. Another problem was that the functions of the army and the gendarmerie had been reversed. The army was performing occupation responsibilities, whereas the gendarmerie had assumed control over the army's mission and was now, along with the infantry, seeking army ordnance, signal, and transportation equipment. The most important objective was to get more men involved in combat, both by increasing the size of the fighting force and by re-orienting those already in uniform to the offensive.[40]

That same month, the government in Athens stepped up its demands for an expanded army when the British appeared on the verge of pulling out the last of their troops from Greece. At the Greek First Army's headquarters in Volos, the commander of the British Military Mission made clear that his government was moving closer to withdrawing its final five thousand soldiers. Still hoping that a larger Greek army would prove unnecessary, Livesay lamented that senior officers thought the problem lay in insufficient man-power—an argument that seemingly gained credibility with the imminence of British withdrawal.[41]

A note of encouragement came in late summer of 1947, when the Truman administration took a major step toward extending massive economic aid to Europe through the proposed Marshall Plan. At Harvard University the previous June, Marshall had outlined the widespread wartime damages on the continent and called on his nation to lead the way in reconstruction. After the Soviets refused to participate, sixteen European nations, including Greece, sought assistance from the United States. In response, President Truman appointed a committee in late June, headed by Secretary of Commerce Harriman, which proposed at least $12 billion of aid over four years. Later that summer a House committee went to Europe to investigate and came back supportive of Marshall's proposal.[42]

Despite the high hopes stemming from American aid, the Truman administration recognized that the key to success against the guerrillas was a major
military offensive, not an enlarged Greek army and the injection of American
military and economic goods. But this reality got lost in the excitement over
the impending arrival of American matériel. BBC reporter Kenneth Matthews capsulized the misguided optimism in Greece. The United States
brought the "prestige of limitless resources and an air of knowing how to put
things straight in no time—in no time at all." Every problem would disappear.
"Corruption in the administration?" The Americans "would plant their men
inside the Greek ministries. Morale in the army? They would stiffen it with
American officers, not sitting on their rumps at a headquarters desk, but
slogging it right up there with the front-line fighters." Victory seemed certain
as the initial shipment of American military and economic supplies arrived in
Piraeus on August 2.[43]

CHAPTER

4

The Call for American Combat Troops

The most controversial aspect of the Truman Doctrine in Greece was its military orientation. According to critics, the administration exaggerated the dangers to convince Congress and the American people to support a policy of interventionism. Yet even if the rhetoric was strong, policymakers in Washington did not give light regard to the military question; their many discussions of the matter provide a model of analysis and decisionmaking. They examined the availability of personnel; they scrutinized the impact that direct military involvement would have, both domestically and internationally; and they considered the repercussions of either success or failure. Even more important, they examined the steps toward terminating involvement if events did not follow the desired course. At a crucial time in the war, during the autumn of 1947, the Truman administration debated the wisdom of sending American soldiers to establish the domestic order vital to the long-range economic reconstruction of Greece.

The insertion of American military and economic supplies into Greece would not ensure victory—a point that took on ominous implications during the summer of 1947, when the British notified Washington that they intended to pull out the last of their troops. Unless the United States could persuade the British to delay their troop withdrawal, the Truman administration had the choice of either continuing the aid program and hoping the Greek army could improve its field performance, or assuming a greater responsibility in the war. As conditions worsened, the debate intensified over expanding the American military role. Should the United States provide operational advice to Greek soldiers in the field? Or should it send Americans to fight the war?

The Truman administration was in a quandary. It regarded the British troops, though few in number, as a symbol of Western opposition to the spread of communism in both Greece and the surrounding Balkan region.

Their withdrawal would be emblematic of a concession by the West to Soviet encroachments that could spread to other parts of the world. The "hot question" of the period, asserted *Time* magazine, was whether the United States would send troops to Greece and thus meet the "test" of fulfilling America's obligations in Europe. The British soldiers were not capable of warding off an invasion by a combined force of neighboring countries, but they were a deterrent to overt Soviet actions because their presence carried the implication that increased support by the British and perhaps other Western powers might be forthcoming. If the British soldiers pulled out of Greece, the United States would have to decide whether to replace them with its own troops. But, to do so would require withdrawing Americans from other areas. The United States had cut its armed forces so drastically after World War II that it could not send enough men to hold off an invasion of Greece. Postwar demobilization had reduced America's armed forces from 12 million in June 1945 to a bare one and a half million by June 1947. In Europe America's troops were down from three and a half million to 200,000.[1] And yet, failure to send some soldiers to Greece would leave the impression that the Free World had capitulated to totalitarianism. For the Truman administration to send the large number of men necessary for effective combat, it would have to take the politically unpopular step of mobilizing manpower and resources.

As the nation's involvement in Greece deepened, the United States more keenly grasped the essence of limited conflict: the necessity of convincing the enemy (as well as other nations) that America possessed the will to resist communist aggression without resorting to all-out war.

I

The imminent British troop withdrawal angered the United States. Of the remaining 5,000 men (excluding those assigned to the British Military Mission), the combat troops only numbered 3,500, which consisted of an infantry brigade of three battalions in Salonika and one infantry battalion in Athens.[2] Though the British military presence was small, the United States regarded it as a necessary component in a global strategy of combatting aggression.

The British chiefs of staff offered the Americans several suggestions to offset the "political effect" of the impending withdrawal. They called for the establishment of an aggregate force of 150,000 in the Greek army that would result from raising its present ceiling to 120,000, making permanent the already sanctioned temporary addition of 20,000 men, and eventually adding another 10,000. They recommended increases in the air force and urged that the gendarmerie assume their "correct role" of maintaining domestic order rather than clearing an area of guerrillas in the wake of the advancing army. The United States must approve an immediate increase in the Greek army.[3]

British officials insisted that their decision to pull out did not signal a change in policy. In Washington, Bohlen complained to the British chargé, Sir John Balfour, that his government had not first discussed the matter with the United States. The White House was concerned that the British were caving in to communist pressure, especially since the decision came so soon after a Soviet veto in the UN Security Council of the proposal to continue the border commission. Balfour offered assurances that this was not the case. His government that very day was telling newsmen and others in London that the troop removal was part of a general retrenchment. Bevin told the American ambassador in London that the withdrawal could not be delayed until after the Security Council had dealt with the Greek border issue—particularly since the United States was proposing that the matter go before the General Assembly.[4]

Marshall was upset that the British had not first consulted the United States. The withdrawal was poorly timed and would remove one of the "stabilizing factors" in Greece. It would cause "acute embarrassment" for the White House by endangering the continuation of public and congressional support for Greek-Turkish aid. Because the British troop presence was "symbolical" of the West's determination to halt the spread of communism, the withdrawal would weaken the entire Anglo-American strategic position in the Mediterranean. As Marshall reminded his cabinet colleagues, the United States was in a precarious position because congressmen had made clear their opposition to military occupation. The British move would necessitate a careful reassessment of America's strategic position and economic commitments. The nation's foreign policy was dependent upon Britain's contributions.[5]

Marshall was "disturbed and puzzled" about the "present trend" of British policy. Though aware of Britain's dire financial position, he expressed doubt that "the full story has been conveyed to us. We fear we are being faced with the first of a series of actions stemming from new policies unknown to us." The United States must inquire whether "these actions presage a basic revision of British foreign policy involving a progressive withdrawal from previous commitments and previously held positions." The psychological consequences of the withdrawal would far outweigh any gains the British might make in either manpower or economics. The problem was greater than merely having to balance British troop withdrawals with increases in the Greek army. The British had to cooperate with the United States in pursuing a global strategy designed to halt Soviet expansion. They were "far too casual or freehanded in passing the buck of the international dilemma" to the United States.[6]

Marshall searched for a way to soften the impact of a British troop withdrawal. He explored the possibility of raising the number of America's naval forces in the Mediterranean and increasing their visits to Greek ports. Though opposed to bluffing, he thought that such moves "might smoke out the depth of the Russian purpose." Marshall wanted the British troops to remain until both the Security Council and General Assembly had given final appraisals of the Greek border issue. In a cabinet meeting, Harriman advocated dealing "roughly" with the British. The United States "should not aid a move further to the left by the British." With "sharp resentment," Marshall remarked that the British could reduce their forces in Japan and Germany without serious repercussions. The British were "overdrawing on our feelings and sympathies" in an effort to have the United States "get them out of the hole."[7]

Marshall's suspicions were unfounded. Britain's retrenchment policy rested on a realistic assessment of the nation's capabilities and was not an attempt to maneuver the United States into protecting British interests. Some British officials regarded the general strategic picture in the same way as did the United States: Anglo-American cooperation was essential to keeping the Russians out of the Middle East, but because of Britain's problems the chief burden in the shared responsibility had shifted to the United States. In late 1946, an American adviser to UNRRA wrote a paper for the State Department that urged cooperation between the Atlantic nations in safeguarding the Middle East from Russia. The British ambassador in Washington sent a copy to the Foreign Office, where it was circulated for a wide reading. An unidentified British official scrawled on the paper: "An admirable paper for an American to have written. It might have been composed in the F.O. [Foreign Office]."[8]

MacVeagh did not suspect the British of deception, but he considered their move "astonishingly ill-timed" and hoped for a delay until the Greek government could take appropriate security measures. The British troop presence provided a "precious deterrent" to trouble in the north from the Slavs. The withdrawal could furnish a "specious pretext" for a Free Greek regime to appeal to the "satellite states" for help. The decision, following so closely the Soviet veto in the UN, would leave the "appearance of fundamental weakness and lack of unity of [W]estern democracies." The communists' morale would soar in the local areas—especially when they already anticipated that Moscow would order its allies to increase aid. A "highly placed US military officer" in Greece warned that unless American forces replaced the British, the United States "might as well pack up and go home."[9]

The Joint Chiefs of Staff thought the British withdrawal might necessitate the use of American soldiers as replacements. To balance the loss with an increase in the Greek army would involve "impracticable modifications" of America's aid plans. Should the United States send a small combat force as a token commitment to Greece? Or a contingent large enough to hold off an armed attack? No in-between course—a display of air or naval power in the eastern Mediterranean—would halt outside aid to the guerrillas or stop them from establishing a regime in northern Greece. The United States might have to send armed forces "as a show of strength in the Eastern Mediterranean and as tangible evidence of U.S. determination to uphold its policy by military action if necessary." Either British or American troops must be in Greece.[10]

America had to maintain its commitment to Greece. The United States had taken a strong stand before the UN and was committed to the Truman Doctrine. These endeavors, the joint chiefs declared, demonstrated America's determination to prevent Greece from falling into the "Soviet orbit." After these public stances, "failure in Greece would lead to a dangerous weakening of resistance to communism in the non-Soviet world." British withdrawal would undermine the Truman Doctrine and jeopardize America's strategic position in the Mediterranean. The absence of a military force might encourage a full-scale insurrection as well as an invasion from the north.[11]

Other American military figures recognized that Britain's decision had major ramifications for the United States. General Livesay warned that observers would regard the move as "Anglo-American weakness" and wanted the British to remain until the Greek army had cleared the country of guerrillas. Brigadier General Walter E. Todd, deputy director of intelligence, noted that Britain's retrenchment effort must ultimately come at the expense of the United States. The British would become more reliant on the proposed Marshall Plan of economic aid for Europe, and would call upon America to assume more of the occupation load in Germany. They probably would ask the United States either to furnish more dollar credits or relax loan requirements. The United States would lose intelligence on Greece produced by the British "for which the British Forces there [were] a cover." In addition, British withdrawal from Greece would leave the United States as the only target of communist propaganda.[12] Every foreign policy decision made in London had potential impact on America's strategy.

Acting Secretary of War W. Stuart Symington recognized the global implications of British retrenchment. Troop reductions in Italy would pose difficulties for the Allies in that area, and the probable request for American replacements would drain an already small reserve and have an adverse effect on the question of sending Americans to Greece. The British should leave their troops in Greece and instead remove a corresponding number from Germany. The main impact of present intentions would be strategic: British withdrawal from Greece would damage the "generally accepted concept of combined British and American collaboration" against "Soviet expansionist and subversive activity."[13]

American intelligence sources added a sense of alarm when, in the midst of this controversy, they confirmed the administration's suspicions of Soviet aims. An operative from the Central Intelligence Group microfilmed a copy of a Russian paper entitled "Soviet Intentions," which he had temporarily removed from the safe of the mission chief of one of the Russian allied states (unnamed). According to the paper, which the agent claimed had an "undeniable ring of truth," the Politburo was engaged in a struggle over whether to follow a hard-line foreign policy until the United States sank into the postwar economic crisis that the Soviets expected by 1949. Those advocating an intransigent policy included Foreign Minister Vyacheslav M. Molotov, the general staff, the generals in command of the Soviet occupation armies in

Europe, and the Communist parties of Central Europe. They believed that a refusal to make concessions during this period would allow time for American influence to decline, resulting in the end of capitalism in Europe. To promote this outcome, the hard-liners wanted to preserve what the writer of the paper called "Soviet conquests and Soviet jumping-off bases in Europe, in the Far East and in the Near East." According to Molotov, the first step in the Balkans would be to "liquidate the opposition." After a series of general strikes and "social agitations," "Greek partisans" would engage in a "general offensive . . . toward Salonika and the proclamation of an autonomous Macedonian Republic." These measures would "check" the Truman Doctrine.[14]

Molotov feared that if the United States expanded its European influence, it would be in a position to attack the Soviet Union. According to the author of the paper, Molotov regarded the Marshall Plan as "only the Truman Plan skillfully disguised and destined to check Soviet and Communist influence in Europe." The Russians believed that if they were able to restrain the United States, they could inherit its influence. "To be sure of this, the USSR now must hold all possessions which it now has and must re-enforce itself by all means possible, politically, militarily, economically, as well as by the increase of Russian industrial potential."[15]

Those Soviets favoring a moderate policy, in particular Foreign Trade Commissar Anastas Mikoyan, warned that a hard-line stance would lead to economic isolation for the Russians at a time when they needed trade. Mikoyan criticized the "casualness" with which Molotov predicted the imminent collapse of capitalism and declared that even though the Soviets' "conquered countries" had strategic importance, "politically and economically they [were] burdens." Success lay in negotiating more economic agreements with various countries. But even here Mikoyan agreed with Molotov that the common goal was to preserve Russia's security until the "inevitable American crisis."[16]

Stalin's problem, the writer argued, was to take a stance somewhere between the groups. Though the premier approved the majority position of Molotov, he admitted to the necessity for signing economic pacts with Europe. Indeed, Stalin had eased his hard-line attitude in part because of the military threat implied by the Truman Doctrine. He was now in the uncomfortable position of having "to prove Molotov wrong without proving Truman right."[17]

If General Cortland T. van R. Schuyler was aware of this document, he received the wrong signals. He was correct in warning Admiral C. D. Glover that the Soviets' indirect attempts to achieve their objectives in Greece might lead to direct American military involvement. The USSR, through its "satellites," wanted to establish an "independent Communist State in Northern Greece" and "increase the uneasiness existent throughout the world." Toward these ends, Schuyler asserted, the guerrillas used "extensive subversive, sabotage and espionage activities," hoping to "involve U.S. and/or British forces in armed action.''[18] The latter claim, however, is highly dubious. The guerrillas could not have wanted Anglo-American military involvement in the conflict. They had already had a disastrous confrontation with British military power during the December Revolution of 1944. In addition, the document cited above supports the argument that Soviet involvement in Greece was at the most indirect and cautious. Stalin would have welcomed a communist state in Greece; but he realized that the chances of that happening were slim and maintained a hands-off policy that would allow the guerrillas to succeed or fail on their own. The Soviets' military potential was limited in comparison with that of the United States, and he could not have favored any action by the guerrillas that would have encouraged the White House to support direct American military involvement in Greece. If Stalin had any control over the situation, it was doubtful that he would permit events to reach that point.

II

The most far-reaching effect of the impending British troop withdrawal was its impetus to heightened guerrilla activity and to deeper American military intervention. Army intelligence warned that the British move would encourage additional guerrilla actions and more infiltration from "Soviet satellite countries." The United States would inherit the full burden of stabilizing Greece. Secretary of War Kenneth C. Royall feared that the withdrawal would disrupt Anglo-American unity in a "test case against communist aggression" that had worldwide ramifications. Lieutenant Colonel Walter T. Kerwin emphasized, however, that the British decision did not necessarily entail the assignment of American troops and recommended that Royall make that point with Livesay. Kerwin warned of "especially grave implications, both foreign and domestic," in deciding whether to send troops to Greece.[19]

The question of sending combat forces to Greece was still a matter of debate, but the War Department had begun preparing contingency plans for such an eventuality. These precautions, Schuyler explained, were necessary to avoid "a possible blitz solution." Studies were under way concerning the training of Greek forces, the protection of American interests and nationals in Greece, and the undertaking of other missions assigned by the Joint Chiefs of Staff that might, in the words of a military spokesman, "include active combat against all enemy forces short of the Russians, initially against guerrilla forces in Greece, possibly against an International Brigade in Greece (if such a command exists), and subsequently against the Soviet satellites." Though Schuyler considered the chances of sending American soldiers "quite remote," the United States might have to use military force to demonstrate political commitments.[20]

Practical problems became apparent in a decision to send combat troops. The commanding general of the U.S. Army Air Forces was asked to determine the maximum air lift available for the movement of soldiers to Greece within ten days of receiving detachment orders. He found that to achieve full capability, air units would have to be diverted from other foreign and domestic responsibilities, leading to security threats elsewhere. Schuyler observed that "Overseas Theaters" were at "rock bottom" strength and that reassignments would have serious implications. The problem was double-edged: on the one side, the size of the ground force determined the number of air force units required, since air operations would be coordinated with those on the ground; on the other side, the low number of frontline aircraft limited the size of the combat force that could be sent.[21]

Another consideration was the predictably negative reaction from European nations. In late August an American delegate to the UN and later secretary of state, John Foster Dulles, told Senator Vandenberg that the United States might ask the General Assembly for approval to "send troops into Greece to patrol the northern boundaries," but this would be "a reckless thing to do and contrary to the spirit . . . of the Greek Assistance Act." European nations "would not want to be invited to back up what might appear to be a more or less private undeclared war between the U.S. and Russia, leading from what originally was a unilateral act of ours."[22]

Yet these military considerations were necessary because of the widespread perceptions concerning Soviet objectives. MacVeagh had recently reported that the situation in Greece was "deteriorating—steadily and dangerously." In a White House conversation relating to the Marshall Plan, President Truman listened to Acheson and Clayton discuss the Soviet danger. The Kremlin intended to spread its influence into Eastern Europe through Red troops and puppet governments and into Western Europe through the Communist party in each nation. Part of America's impulse behind the Marshall Plan was humanitarian, the two advisers admitted, but the nation's security was inseparable from the results.[23] The problem would not go away without increased American involvement.

The UN offered little avenue for hope. If that body's machinery failed to resolve the border crisis, *Time* magazine declared, the United States might have to send troops. Inside the UN, Soviet delegate Andrei Gromyko had vetoed (along with Poland's representative in the Security Council) an American recommendation for a two-year "peace watch" by the United States on Greek borders. He then engaged in a heated attack on both Greece and the United States that, according to *Time*, was intended for the "gulliberals of the Henry Wallace school." Gromyko blamed the Greek government for the border problems and called for the withdrawal of all outside military missions. He urged the creation of a commission with Russian membership which would supervise foreign economic aid to Greece. Intervention by Yugoslavia, Albania, and Bulgaria, he exclaimed, was a "myth. Intervention cannot be concealed in bushes." The U.S. delegate to the Security Council, Herschel Johnson, wryly responded: "So . . . the innocent little Slavic-Albanian brothers . . . are menaced by this wicked fascist Greek wolf. It is curious and almost like a fairy tale come to life." When the Colombian delegate later recommended a compromise by creating a modified Balkan commission, Gromyko dismissed it as the same old U.S. resolution with a "wash, a haircut, powder and lipstick."[24]

Additional pressure for American action came from the government in Athens, which again was headed by Tsaldaris and again appealed to the United States to underwrite a bigger army. If the White House decided against American troops, the best alternative, according to the Greek foreign minister, was to strengthen his country's army enough to withstand an invasion. The White House was not happy with either the new government or the request. Efforts to arrange a coalition regime had failed after popular dissatisfaction with the war effort had combined with Zervas's security crackdown to encourage the fall of the Maximos government in August. Before Tsaldaris took office, Griswold had told one of Tsaldaris's men that a Populist government was "inadmissible" and warned in a memorandum of a possible termination of American aid. The next evening, Tsaldaris went to MacVeagh's residence and bitterly complained that Griswold's assertion implied an obstruction of constitutional procedure. "Does this mean you declare war on us?" MacVeagh tried to calm him and called in Griswold, who explained that the word should have been "inadvisable." In response to Tsaldaris's request, MacVeagh recorded in a letter given to Tsaldaris that "inadmissible" meant "inadvisable." The prime minister nonetheless told the press that he had received "small comfort, indeed, for his plans from Ambassador MacVeagh and Griswold, especially from Griswold." Now, according to the *New York Times*, Greek spokesmen and the press regarded Tsaldaris's new government as "defiance of the Americans." Tsaldaris made clear that he would officially ask for American troops if he could have advance assurances that the United States would approve his request.[25]

Griswold agreed with Washington in opposing an enlargement of the Greek army; but he could not understand his government's hesitancy in replacing British troops with its own soldiers "of slightly greater strength." Failure to do so would increase communist pressure in Athens and inflict a severe blow to American prestige. After the Americans were in place, the British Military Mission should withdraw, leaving the Greek army's training under American guidance. The United States must assume responsibility for upgrading the Greek soldiers' performance in the field. Furthermore, it must coordinate the military program and bolster Greek morale by implementing the changes at the same time the British began their withdrawal.[26]

Griswold also wanted to use American military intervention as leverage to secure political changes. The assistance effort would have a better chance if Greek political leaders first brought unity to the country by agreeing to broaden the makeup of their cabinet. In addition, Griswold was willing to go before the cabinet and "demand" an end to political interference in the country's military forces. Charges of interference did not concern him. The United States was susceptible to these accusations regardless of its actions.[27]

MacVeagh, however, thought the United States should use "every non-interventional influence" to achieve political unity in Greece. No leaders in Athens could succeed if they came under foreign control. The United States should continue its policy of "detailed non-involvement." Contractors should use more Greek personnel to promote "public relations and greater public confidence in Greece." Americans should only *encourage* the Greeks to remove unsatisfactory officials. Greek politicians had an understanding of America's strategic interests in the area and would not put stock in threats to cut off aid. The United States must use its prestige in "direct but discreet action."[28]

MacVeagh's opposition to Griswold's call for intervention in political matters caused a furor that reached the White House. McGhee urged the men to work out their differences. Griswold, however, had gotten the impression that Tsaldaris believed that the United States would help his country regardless of its government. Griswold remained adamant in his desire to use America's aid as pressure to resolve political problems. And MacVeagh, just as firmly, continued his call for a broadened government while expressing disapproval of Griswold's methods.[29]

Despite MacVeagh's displeasure, Griswold forwarded his monthly report with a recommendation for increased American involvement in Greek political affairs. Had it not been for "Greek dependence on the American Aid Program," the report declared, the United States would have had "no club with which to force the Greek political leaders into a program of unity." The threatened withdrawal of American money forced Tsaldaris to drop his partisan intentions. An ambassador had "no such pressure to exert," and the political leaders were "too tough to penetrate with reason only."[30]

Griswold took a strong stand against enlarging the Greek army. Its mission was to put down the guerrillas, not to resist an invasion. Many infantry battalions were smaller than their authorized strength, but the problem lay in performance, not numbers. The army was not effectively using nearly forty companies trained as commandos. Additional soldiers would further dilute the combat units by requiring a shift of veterans from the battlefield to train and organize the new men. Besides, the time needed for preparation would mean that the new units could not have an impact on the military campaign until winter. As long as the problem remained domestic, the army as currently constituted was satisfactory. If a large-scale invasion occurred, foreign soldiers would be required anyway.[31]

British and American observers in Greece shared Griswold's reservations about expanding the army. Though the Greek General Staff urged a ratio of five soldiers to one guerrilla, British military spokesmen thought two to one sufficient as long as the reinforcements were properly trained. Americans noted that the only way to defeat guerrillas was to encircle them and prevent escape. In some geographical areas, the ratio might have to climb to ten to one for success, although such large-scale operations could not take place in several regions simultaneously. For planning purposes, the American mission recommended three to one.[32]

Most American military representatives concurred with Griswold that, barring a surge of outside help to the guerrillas, the solution to the problem was to improve the performance of the present army. But all agreed that the situation would change if the Soviets' allies extended recognition to a government of Free Greece and sent recruits and supplies. Recruiting was reportedly taking place in various countries for sending international brigades to Greece. American observers in Rome had gotten word that the guerrillas were receiving arms and munitions from Italy. Should they also receive air power, artillery, and other heavy matériel, Greek military forces would be no match.

The Truman administration did not know the details at the time, but during that month of August, Yugoslavia's Communist leader, Marshal Josip Broz Tito, met with his Bulgarian counterpart, Georgi Dimitrov, at the summer resort of Bled in northwest Yugoslavia to establish an independent Macedonia and incorporate it into a Balkan Federation. Publicly, their talks led to a Yugoslav-Bulgarian treaty of friendship similar to other treaties of that period within the Soviet sphere. Privately, the other arrangements made at Bled were ominous in regard to the ongoing Greek conflict. The KKE was to agree to the formation of a Slavo-Macedonian state by renouncing claims to Aegean Macedonia and Pirin Macedonia. The new state would become part of a Balkan Federation, which would include Albania, Bulgaria, and Greece. For giving up Pirin Macedonia, Bulgaria would receive Greek Thrace and an outlet into the Aegean. The KKE, in exchange for accepting the new Macedonia, would win assistance from the three neighboring countries in its war against the royalists in Athens. Such a program included refuge and hospital aid for the guerrillas, sanctuary in Vardar Macedonia (Yugoslav section of Macedonia), arms, artillery, trucks, technical assistance, and help from the Slavophones in the war. According to one writer, the conferees established a Joint Balkan Headquarters with Democratic Army officers under it.[34]

Washington's assumption of communist unity makes it unimportant how Stalin regarded the Bled agreements. Whether he knew about them before or afterward, he must have reacted bitterly. Not only did the meeting reflect independent behavior by both Tito and Dimitrov but the promise of assistance to the KKE assured a widened war and a greater chance for direct American involvement. Stalin's feelings, however, are not the point. Whatever his attitude toward a Balkan Federation, an independent Macedonia, and the Greek war, policymakers in Washington *believed* that cohesion within the communist alliance was undeniable. They perceived as another signal of such unity the Soviet and Yugoslav breaks in diplomatic relations with Greece before the end of the month.[35]

Livesay, of course, was unaware of the Bled agreements, but he had for a different reason adopted the Greek position of enlarging the army. He still maintained that the present army could defeat the guerrillas—*if* it were "properly and vigorously utilized." But too many units were still engaged in static defense. Attempts to withdraw soldiers from the towns met vehement opposition from politicians seeking to protect their constituencies. Livesay reluctantly concluded, "I do not now believe the Army will be able to overcome this political pressure and exterminate the bandits until it has greater strength." To achieve the peace and order necessary to economic reconstruction, he first called for a permanent increase of 20,000 men as long as the Greek government provided a steady flow of fresh replacements for the troops in the field and the specialists in training centers. Second, he recommended an additional 10,000 men to constitute an occupation force in cleared areas until the gendarmerie could take over. And third, he urged a limited increase in men and equipment for the Greek air force. His proposals required the diversion of twenty million dollars from the economic aid program.[36]

Livesay emphasized to Greek political and military figures that he had no intention of taking over the war. His mission in Greece, he declared at a meeting of the Supreme National Defense Council, was to advise on logistical matters and the use of American equipment. His recommendations were personal observations only.[37]

III

Despite his advisory limitations, Livesay found it difficult *not* to assume a greater role in the Greek war effort. He tried to work closely with the British Military Mission to maintain the appearance of unity, but he came into repeated disagreement with its members over matters of training, operations, and administration. As one American military officer noted, Livesay found it almost impossible "to refrain from assuming leadership in the direction and employment of our matériel." Livesay recommended that to safeguard American interests in Greece, "we must eventually consider assuming entire responsibility for the reconstitution and employment of the Greek National Army." This in mind, he requested four more American officers to assist in staff and planning matters.[38]

The American military presence in Greece was increasingly evident by late August. After the initial shipload of military supplies arrived in Piraeus, ten more had followed before the month was over. By the end of the year, nearly $40 million of such goods had reached Greece. The main items unloaded and distributed were motorized vehicles, horses, and subsistence supplies. The training section of USAGG was already in place, manned by American civilians attached to the Greek staffs and prepared to instruct in the installation, operation, and maintenance of technical equipment. The men were "not [to] become involved in military combat action of any character."[39]

The presence of USAGG, however, did not improve the military situation. Lieutenant Colonel Allen C. Miller, assistant military attaché at the embassy in Athens, reported that the "house is on fire, but few in Athens or Washington seem to realize how fast [the] flames are spreading." Despite sweeps by the army, the guerrillas continued to dominate the region lying close to the Pindus Mountains and stretching from the Albanian border through central Greece and to the Bay of Corinth. American army intelligence did not believe that the guerrillas sought permanent control over any area because this would enable the Greek army to stabilize its rear and establish effective lines of warfare. Present government communications, especially in Thrace and Macedonia, had no front and no rear and were vulnerable to guerrilla interference. Rumors spread that the guerrillas were under orders to assassinate "Monarchofascists" and to drive people from the fields into the cities, making them wards of the state and further burdening the economy, heightening frustration, and hindering the war effort. Demoralized Greek soldiers had abandoned their posts along the Bulgarian border, leaving an escape route for the guerrillas. Political pressure was growing to maintain additional troops in the towns and villages, leading to what an American observer called a senseless game of "hide-and-seek."[40]

With growing desperation, Livesay noted that foreign aid to the guerrillas was becoming dangerously effective. Civilian morale was low and would decline even more should the army withdraw from the villages. The April offensive had ground to a halt because of troop shortage, physical exhaustion, and poor planning. The army had not engaged in "really bitter fighting" because of a "lack of offensive spirit" and a "disinclination to come to grips with the bandits." Though the army had not been beaten anywhere, morale was low among both officers and soldiers. Command and staff officers were frustrated by the absence of "determined political leadership." Morale in the air force was the "poorest of all." Squadron leaders were under orders to save their aircraft "at all costs" and to fly sorties only on demand from the army. Even though they could take the initiative in emergencies, Livesay sarcastically remarked, "there appears to never be an emergency." Despite these problems, he asserted that, with continued American help, the government would win—but not within at least another year.[41]

In a move supported by both Griswold and General Stuart Rawlins of the British Military Mission, and with which General Omar Bradley of the U.S. Army "seemed satisfied," Livesay made a far-reaching recommendation: American officers should supervise the field operations of the Greek army. Greek military officials recognized the need for "practical direction and guidance" in using their armed forces. They were fearful that British troop withdrawals meant that Greece was "being abandoned" by the allies. Livesay warned that if American assistance stopped on June 30, 1948, as stipulated in the aid bill, this would force a dramatic cut in Greek armed forces and guarantee a victory for communism. To raise morale and ensure effectiveness in the field, the army required "firm guidance in the planning and conduct of operations."[42]

Livesay's involvement in Greek internal affairs was nonetheless increasing by early September, even while the situation was slipping out of control. USAGG's supply and training duties were too closely integrated with the

strategic, tactical, and political aspects of the Greek army to expect a clear
separation of functions. As Livesay explained, a number of "logical sequen-
ces" had enlarged the scope of USAGG. "Upon its arrival in Greece the
USAGG has become at once intimately involved in the political problem of
developing the GNA [Greek National Army] into a more effective fighting
force." The sheer occurrence of daily events dictated growing military and
political involvement.[43]

Continued lack of success in the war heightened the pressure for a greater
American military role. During a meeting in the American embassy in
Athens, British military observers agreed with Colonel Miller that about
twenty-five specially trained American officers should take operational command of the Greek army and prepare for an offensive before winter. Lack of
progress in the war now seemed to override MacVeagh's doubt that Congress
had given the Americans in Greece such authority. The embassy counselor,
James Keeley, wrote Marshall in Washington that the United States had to
act—and soon.[44]

Operational advice seemed the only alternative; army intelligence had
already concluded that a decision to send American soldiers would have little
positive impact on the war. Provisions of the aid bill were "broad enough to
permit flexibility in enlarging and revising the nature and allocation of
military assistance." But such expansion must be in an advisory capacity and
aimed solely at ending the guerrilla threat from within the country. The
northern frontiers of Greece were indefensible against attack. Neighboring
countries could enter Greece through any of six major passes scattered from
the Adriatic Sea to Turkey. Since the natural entrances into northern Greece
ran north to south, the frontier between the Adriatic and Turkey had no land
features suitable for lateral communications. Along Greece's eastern half of
the border—from the Vardar River valley to Turkey—the army had little
chance of establishing defense posts because of the short distance between the
frontiers and the Aegean. In the central part of the country the unfavorable
prevailing winds and rough terrain near the sea would hamper landing
operations and the construction of truck routes into the interior. Government
forces could develop communications along the western areas served from the
Adriatic and Gulf of Patras, and in the east at Piraeus and the Gulf of Volos.
The island of Corfu could serve as an air and naval base for the purposes of
protecting Salonika and launching a counter-offensive against guerrillas
along the Albanian coast. But if the mainland fell to the guerrillas, Greek and
American control of the sea could do little to dislodge them.[45]

The dispatch of American combat forces to Greece offered some advantages, but the potential disadvantages were far greater. On the positive side,
the presence of troops would show the Kremlin that the United States "meant
business," perhaps even easing the "war of nerves" along the Greek frontier.
Deployment of American soldiers would also encourage the Turks and Iran-
ians to resist Soviet aggression. Though a token force would have little
tactical value and would be unable to resist an attack, it could serve as a

"deterrent to direct or indirect Soviet action in Greece because the Soviets [were] not yet prepared to become involved in an all-out war with the Western Powers." But on the negative side, the chief danger was that any kind of troop dispatch could lead to a full-scale war that the United States would find unwinnable in view of Soviet military superiority in the Balkans. According to estimates, the Soviets had 14,000 operational aircraft, 4,800 of which were in Eastern Europe and could change their insignia and easily prevail over the Greek air force. The Soviet Black Sea Fleet was in position to support ground and air forces in Greece. If the Soviets seized the straits, the Greek navy would become ineffective. The Red armies were "almost without limit" and could "overrun Greece in ten days to two weeks."[46]

Even if a major war did not erupt, the presence of American troops would cause greater unrest in both the Balkans and the eastern Mediterranean. The division between East and West would widen, for the Soviets would encourage reprisals against America's supporters. The Balkan communist regimes would accuse the United States of international violations and move closer to each other and to the Soviet Union. Anti-American propaganda and psychological warfare would make the United States "Enemy Number 1" among the Soviets' allies in the Balkans. Furthermore, the assignment of troops might cause apprehension among Arab states over America's broader intentions— especially in light of a probable UN partition of Palestine that was adverse to Arab interests. The dispatch of American troops would leave the impression that the White House was setting a precedent for equivalent military action in Palestine and other troubled spots in the eastern Mediterranean. As in the Balkans, "Soviet-oriented groups" would intensify propaganda against American imperialism and call for Red Army intervention in "Soviet-oriented and peripheral states."[47]

According to army intelligence, the Truman Doctrine had put the Soviet Union on the defensive, causing it to adhere to indirect tactics in an effort to hide involvement in Greece. The Kremlin would not resort to war at this time, but it still sought to frustrate the American aid program, discredit the Athens government and keep the country in turmoil, and use Greece as an "object lesson" for other governments desiring American help. In the UN, the Soviet and Polish delegates had used the veto and other obstructionist tactics to keep the Greek situation unsettled. To maintain tension, the communists relied upon a "triple threat" of a Balkan Confederation, international brigades, and the establishment of a Free Greek regime. The Soviets were working through the Greek guerrillas and neighboring communist states to subvert the Truman Doctrine.[48]

Army intelligence concluded that the sending of American troops was not advisable. Though the ultimate aim of the Soviet Union was to dominate a communist world, its immediate objectives were to control peripheral areas through the establishment of "friendly governments" run by organizations "transparently disguised as Communist-controlled Front coalitions." A White House decision to send troops to Greece would give substance to communist charges of American aggression. The basic ingredient of success—economic equilibrium—could come only after the "communist directed guerrilla warfare [was] liquidated." But this had to take place without the deployment of American soldiers.[49]

Thus America's military establishment strongly opposed direct military intervention in Greece. Indeed, General Lauris Norstad emphasized, "[I]t was usually the military people who had to hold back the sporadic and truculent impulses of political people and diplomats who [did] not realize the consequences of aggressive action."[50] Army intelligence had focused on the practical and realistic possibilities of using American troops to preserve Greek independence and American prestige. The analysts did not pin hopes on ingenuity or luck. They did not argue that the mere threat of direct American military intervention would frighten the guerrillas into submission. They examined all features of the Greek situation and concluded that American combat forces could not guarantee a favorable outcome. Only the Greek army could win (or lose) the war.

With the option of sending American soldiers at least temporarily shelved, the Truman administration chose two other courses. First, it approved an enlargement of the Greek army, and second, it began an assessment of whether American officers should accompany Greek army units in the field and offer advice on operations.[51]

CHAPTER
5

The Decision to Extend Operational Advice

I

In Washington on September 17, 1947, the Department of the Army made the decision to send General Stephen J. Chamberlin as special representative of the chief of staff to study the military situation and make recommendations on a course of action. Those in attendance at the meeting—including Chamberlin, Henderson, Norstad, and Schuyler—agreed that the special mission should focus on several issues: the wisdom of arming villagers in areas secured by the army; the role of the gendarmerie; the use of American officers as observers to accompany Greek units in the field; and the desirability of advising the army on operations. On the most sensitive matter—that of providing operational advice—the group recommended that the White House first ask the British Military Mission to assume this responsibility. Should the British refuse, the United States would consider sending another 125 to 200 officers to carry out this task. If British military forces and the mission pulled out of Greece, the United States would explore the possibility of replacing both.[1]

The Department of State meanwhile approved some of Livesay's suggestions to expand America's military role in Greece. Nine million dollars would be transferred from the economic allocations within the aid program to permit two changes: a three-month extension in duty time of the 20,000 men recently added to the army, and an increase of 10,000 in the army ceiling. Griswold urged the Department of State to broaden Livesay's advisory authority to the "maximum extent permitted by law." Griswold saw no real difference between operational advice and the logistical assistance already furnished by USAGG. The implementation of such advice would improve the efficiency of the Greek armed forces. Furthermore, if American troops be-

95

came necessary, the presence of American army officers would facilitate the replacement of British soldiers.[2]

In the midst of these complexities, the White House had to send Henderson to Athens to resolve another problem: the Tsaldaris government's repressive measures were threatening to undermine the entire aid effort. The British Foreign Office agreed with this assessment; according to American sources, the British considered Tsaldaris a "fool" and his government "deplorable." On September 1, Henderson and MacVeagh talked with the prime minister about pursuing moderate policies. According to MacVeagh, they "emphasized" to Tsaldaris that if the Greek people did not install a "government having wide support," the United States "might well refuse" to continue the assistance program. MacVeagh did not intend to push for "a one-sided centrist solution"; he wanted to leave "to the Greeks themselves the actual setting up of their Government or at least the luxury of thinking that such action is their own." That evening, in a discussion with other Greek political leaders, Henderson called for a National Government comprised of the center and right. Within a week the Greeks complied. The Liberals' leader, Themistocles Sophoulis, became head of a coalition government that did not contain "Communists or Communist sympathizers." The cabinet would be primarily Populist, but among the Liberals was Constantine Rendis, who replaced Zervas as minister of public order. The real power, however, rested with Tsaldaris, who remained as deputy prime minister and foreign minister.[3]

Henderson's action constituted interference in Greek internal affairs; whether the move was unwarranted remains a subject of debate. The aid program appeared to be in danger because of the Greek government's harsh policies; President Truman had considered the problem so urgent that he had given Henderson only a few hours' notice before sending him to Athens. White House instructions had come by phone from Undersecretary of State Robert Lovett: "The President wants you to leave for Greece this evening." If the Greeks did not establish a coalition government, Lovett warned Henderson, Greek-Americans in the United States might persuade Congress to hold back money for the aid program. Henderson was to work with MacVeagh in letting Tsaldaris know that the continued success of the Truman Doctrine was dependent upon the establishment of a broadly based government. Henderson admitted that his mission constituted "indirect intervention." But he insisted that he did not specifically call for Tsaldaris's resignation or for the establishment of a coalition government. Years afterward, however, Henderson made the following concession: "It can be argued, I suppose, that in telling him frankly what our problem was, I was really inviting him to resign."[4] Little question exists that the White House had engineered the demise of the Tsaldaris government. Such action seemed unavoidable, however, given the political realities inside the United States.

The new government in Athens at first offered hope for a change in direction; but the Americans' repeated calls for a greater offensive in the field again encouraged the Greek government to intensify its pleas for an even larger military force. In mid-September Sophoulis announced another amnesty program that, like the earlier attempt, had no measurable impact. His government also attempted to free the army from village defense duties. To do this, Sophoulis called for an increase in the army to 150,000 and the establishment of a 50,000-man Home Guard. Livesay pointed out, however, that the present American pipeline was unable to service an army larger than 120,000 men and that the request would create enormous practical problems. Griswold emphasized the necessity of eliminating political interference. Numbers was not the problem; the soldiers must pull out of the villages and pursue the guerrillas.[5]

Rather than enlarge the Greek army, General Rawlins of the British Military Mission preferred that the United States provide operational advice. The army's basic weakness was direction in command. Though the attitude of the soldiers in the ranks seemed improved, the officers were discouraged, exhausted, and frustrated. They were certain that ceilings on the army were obstacles to the military effort and that their British and American allies were ready to pull out. Since the British lacked authorization to advise on field operations, Rawlins hoped the United States would assign the responsibility to USAGG. The Greek forces, as now commanded and constituted, could not end the communist threat by the time the Truman Doctrine was scheduled to expire. Americans must supervise the anti-guerrilla campaign.[6]

Additional support for such a move came from Washington, where both the National Security Council and the Central Intelligence Agency noted the global importance of escalating America's military involvement in Greece. In the National Security Council, Lovett (now acting secretary of state) warned that if the Russians seized control of the Mediterranean, the American position in the Middle East would be in jeopardy, forcing Iran, Iraq, and Saudi Arabia to re-evaluate their policies regarding the Soviet Union. According to the CIA, Greece was the place of "utmost urgency." The oil of the Persian Gulf was a consideration, but the region was more important as a strategic connection between East and West and an obstacle to Soviet expansion. If Greece fell to communism, the Soviets would secure a base in the eastern Mediterranean. Such a result would have a worldwide psychological impact. The United States might have to use armed intervention to save Greece.[7]

Griswold likewise maintained the pressure on the White House by repeating his argument that the United States must provide operational advice and that, to avoid the appearance of a "war-like gesture," the new duty should be assigned to the American mission. He drew support from Leonard Cromie of the American embassy in Athens, who agreed that military, political, and economic matters should remain integrated. The White House had to free Livesay to do everything he could to bring about a better field performance by the Greek army. If the British stopped providing planning and tactical advice, Griswold warned, the United States must send a planning staff of up to two hundred officers, along with tactical observers to accompany Greek forces in the field. If the British withdrew their troops, American soldiers had to replace them. In the event of full-scale combat, the responsibility for American military aid should be transferred to the War Department. But the outcome depended on the continued coordination of military and economic efforts under the mission's supervision. The establishment of a separate military mission would seem provocative.[8]

Impetus for an expanded American military role also came from a seemingly related development in the Balkans: Soviet representatives met with Eastern European Communist parties in Belgrade to establish the Cominform (Communist Information Bureau) in October. Although the KKE was not present at the meeting and was bitter over its exclusion, outside observers were unaware of these realities and feared an internationalization of the war in Greece. The Greek government believed that the purpose of the new organization was to unify the region's communists against Greece. The Truman administration considered the location of the meeting important in signifying Soviet support of Yugoslav actions regarding the war. Despite these fears, the evidence seems conclusive now that no one there mentioned aid to the Greek guerrillas. One of Tito's officers, Vladimir Dedijer, later noted that many of the communists in attendance expressed wonder that no Greek Communist party representatives were present; but, he added, this absence should have been no surprise in light of the spheres-of-interest agreement of 1944 between Stalin and Churchill. "Stalin did not invite the Greeks." Another of Tito's close cohorts, Svetozar Vukmanović-Tempo, recalled that even though Yugoslavia tried to secure a statement favorable to the Greek guerrillas, "Soviet leaders did not allow the Resolution of the first meeting of the Cominform to include a single sentence which might aid the people's revolutionary fight in Greece." The Cominform said nothing about events in Greece. "Was that not all a consequence of the fact that the leadership of the Bolshevik Party had been against the revolutionary struggle of the Greek people from the outset?"[9]

The White House was doubtless wrong in believing that the Cominform was evidence of growing Soviet involvement in the Greek war. In fact, the Belgrade meeting should have signaled the exact opposite meaning. Stalin had probably wanted the organization created in Yugoslavia as a means of keeping a close watch on Tito, who appeared to be moving toward an independent stance in Eastern Europe. He and Dimitrov had met at Bled the previous August to discuss the prospects of a Yugoslav Federation. A few days before the October meeting in Belgrade, Tito had visited Bulgaria and Rumania, where he delivered a speech urging more militant communist expansion and criticizing other communist nations. The Kremlin was angry with Tito for assuming an international role.[10] But, of course, American policymakers were not privy to these developments, and were understandably

alarmed by the apparent cohesion among the communists that the establishment of the Cominform had demonstrated.

Tension mounted that same month as more stories (again, never substantiated) spread of an international brigade preparing to invade Greece. The
American ambassador in Paris, Jefferson Caffery, reported the first "concrete
evidence" of the recruitment in that city of such a force. A "trustworthy
American source" said that seven young men with American accents and a
"rough appearance" had urged him to join. The men claimed that they had
been recruited in Brussels and were en route to Albania and Yugoslavia for
guerrilla training. Signees were promised a thousand dollars per month.
British intelligence soon informed Caffery that the Cominform was recruiting
Poles in France to comprise an international brigade.[11]

The White House realized that such accounts, whether or not true, could
substantiate the critics' claim that America's involvement in Greece was the first
step in an interventionist policy that would alienate other countries and culminate in all-out war. Henderson assured the Wellesley Club in Washington, D.C.,
that the Greek-Turkish aid program did not imply that the United States was
ready to intervene everywhere; the approval of assistance depended upon the
circumstances in each case. The White House had not entered the "business of
overthrowing or setting up governments." Over CBS radio, McGhee defended
his nation's growing military involvement in Greece. Lasting change could not
occur in that country without domestic stability. An improved military situation was vital to economic rehabilitation: "If order is not restored there can be
no recovery."[12] The central problem remained—how to resolve the issues in
Greece without allowing them to spread beyond its national borders.

Operational advice became a certainty when the Joint Chiefs of Staff
confirmed the findings of their intelligence committees: the United States had
so few men in uniform that they could not have a favorable impact on the
war. American and Greek ground forces were far fewer in number than those
in "adjacent Soviet satellite states." The U.S. air force could establish supremacy over the combined air forces of Yugoslavia, Albania, and Bulgaria—
even if they received Soviet equipment and crews. But fighting in the Balkans
would be primarily on the ground. The day after the joint chiefs drew their
conclusions, another study showed that marines might constitute a "show of
force in the Eastern Mediterranean as evidence of U.S. determination to
uphold its policy in Greece." But even then, such a move would be "primarily
a political decision." The joint chiefs concluded that the United States was
"not now capable of deploying sufficient armed forces in Greece to defeat an
attack into Greece by the combined forces of Albania, Yugoslavia and Bulgaria; most emphatically not if these countries receive either covert or active
Soviet support." This situation could change only through "time-consuming
and drastic action, including reinstituting selective service."[13] The rapid postwar demobilization by the United States left a shortage in manpower that
now had potential impact on events in Greece.

II

Amid growing controversy, General Chamberlin completed his report on the military situation. The columnist Joseph Alsop, although urging the Truman administration to protect Greece, revealed unauthorized knowledge of the purpose of Chamberlin's mission. He warned that the institution of operational advice would constitute "open acknowledgment of an almost unlimited American strategic and political liability in Greece." Lovett was incensed because Alsop's dispatch from Athens contained classified information. While this matter smoldered, Chamberlin and representatives of the air force and army general staff returned to the United States. They had talked with Greek commanders and staffs in the field, including soldiers on the division, brigade, and battalion levels. They had also conferred with MacVeagh, with British representatives in Greece, and with numerous Greek cabinet members.[14]

On October 20 Chamberlin submitted his findings to the army chief of staff, General Dwight D. Eisenhower. Certain political measures were vital to military success: stabilizing the government; creating a sense of national emergency; ending domestic subversion; re-establishing respect for Greek military leaders; ordering a halt to political interference with military officials. The guerrillas received support from the "communist movement, aided, abetted and directed by the Soviet and Soviet satellite nations." Indeed, the guerrilla effort would collapse without the help of "Soviet agencies." The most dangerous development would be the establishment of a Free Greek regime, because neighboring communist states would extend recognition and provide direct assistance. If the new state asked the UN to resolve the problem, that organization would inadvertently promote "Soviet under-cover activities" by prohibiting outside aid (including that under the Truman Doctrine) until its inquiry was completed.[15]

Chamberlin reported that the American assistance program in Greece was in confusion. Though the entire effort was under the supervision of the Department of State, the command was divided between the ambassador and the chief of the aid mission. Both MacVeagh and Griswold were concerned with political issues, and both had requested advisory and observation teams on military operations. But their overlapping responsibilities were leading into a personal feud that was threatening to break down the aid effort. As matters stood, the curtailment of American assistance after June 30, 1948, would promote a victory by the guerrillas. Long-range policies were necessary; but these could come only if the United States resolved its administrative difficulties in Greece and made a continuing commitment.[16]

The reduced role of the British Military Mission also endangered the situation. Until more Americans arrived, Chamberlin wanted the British to stay and continue organizing, training, and advising the Greek army. But British instructors had received orders to leave the training centers, and British observers no longer worked in the forward areas of army operations.

The mission was therefore unable to discern problems and make recommendations to the Greek army. Diminished control over training led to a loss of contact with the Greek General Staff and a resulting loss of guidance over the army.[17]

To win the war, Chamberlin emphasized, the British troops would have to remain in Greece to promote the "united front aspect" of Anglo-American relations. The decline in British prestige seemed to have mixed blessings, for American control over the aid program would have a better chance of receiving support from the American people and Congress if they saw no "British monitoring." However, most equipment used by the Greek army was British, and a sudden change in control would disrupt field operations. American personnel could not handle British equipment without their advice. The British presence in Salonika had maintained stability in the north. The "most disadvantageous course" would be for the British troops to withdraw immediately.[18]

Despite Griswold's insistence upon assigning operational advisory responsibilities to the mission, Chamberlin favored the establishment of a separate "high level advisory and planning group." Such a change required enough field personnel to promote "positive coordination and timely execution of operational plans and directives." Operational guidance could not come from USAGG; that body was under the auspices of the mission chief, and Griswold was not qualified to command a military group. There were other drawbacks to working through USAGG: the aid law placed a limit on the number of American military personnel in Greece, and it restricted their duties to advisory work. A new group was necessary.[19]

Chamberlin explained how the advisory and planning group would function. It should be composed of no more than twenty officers, who would be nominally controlled by the ambassador but directly responsible to the Joint Chiefs of Staff. The group's mission would be to provide operational advice, but only in coordination with the British and upon request of the government in Athens. In addition, Chamberlin recommended sending another group of American army observers who would join the Greek army in the field for the purposes of instilling an offensive spirit and advising on planning and operations. They would be composed of sixty-nine officers and eighty-three enlisted men, including the personnel in the advisory and planning group. To facilitate the offensive, the United States should approve the formation of fifty Home Guard Battalions and allot more mountain artillery and more machine guns to the Greek army. If the British refused to leave their troops in Greece, the United States should send in an Allied or American force—*before* Britain's withdrawal. Greek civilians should not be armed, and the gendarmerie should be returned to civil police duties. USAGG should receive an additional eight officers and twelve enlisted men to expedite supply distribution and to offer technical advice. Finally, Chamberlin recommended the coordination of military efforts through an Anglo-American Armed Forces Committee of senior representatives of the army, navy, and air force in Greece.[20]

Barring a British troop departure, Chamberlin did not recommend that the United States send combat replacements or that the UN authorize an international force. The military and political disadvantages of dispatching American soldiers outnumbered possible benefits. Once the troops arrived, their withdrawal for any reason except total success would have "the most serious consequences as regards the position of the U.S. among the world powers." An international force likewise seemed inadvisable because the Soviet Union would probably veto the proposal in the Security Council. If the General Assembly approved such a measure, the other governments would probably refuse to allot enough money to improve conditions in Greece. A congressional appropriation would doubtless include the stipulation that Americans disburse the funds and use the equipment.[21] As long as the British troops remained, a military escalation short of American soldiers seemed advisable.

The Truman administration was moving toward a stopgap measure—that of operational guidance—which would hopefully resolve the military problem without a resort to combat troops. A decision to extend such advice nonetheless had dangerous ramifications. Besides subjecting Americans to capture and death, the move provided them with a place of leadership in the war that would make the United States at least partly responsible for the outcome. Yet the Greek army could not win without more guidance.[22] The United States was caught in a serious dilemma: on the one hand, its soldiers were not numerous enough to have a positive impact on the fighting; on the other, in the event of British withdrawal, a refusal to send at least a small contingent could suggest that the administration had dropped its commitment to Greece. The only way to emerge victorious was to convince the British to remain and hope that the Truman Doctrine and operational advice would be sufficient to enable the Greeks to win the war.

III

Eisenhower agreed with Chamberlin's recommendations and urged the Truman administration to make a public announcement explaining the reasons behind an increased military involvement. The White House should follow the lead of Secretary of War Patterson, who had assured the House Foreign Affairs Committee in April 1947 that he would notify that group of any changes in the army advisory group. Chamberlin's proposals necessitated heavy draws from economic funds. But Eisenhower knew that the distinction between the types of aid had become blurred. Economic rehabilitation could not take place without first taking sterner military measures.[23]

Like Chamberlin, MacVeagh recognized the need for a separate military group that would *not* fall under the American mission's supervision. The new group must provide operational advice to the Greek army, and it must engage in forward planning because of the increased chance of more involvement by the Soviet allied states and perhaps even that of the Soviet Union. The advisers must formulate policy on the highest level. Assigning the responsibility of military plans and operations to the aid mission would disrupt coordination. Indeed, MacVeagh insisted, a unified effort could come only by placing both the mission and the new military group under the ambassador. The White House must remove the mistaken idea that the mission had an independent status that allowed it to operate on the same level as the embassy.[24]

MacVeagh's feelings guided the thinking of his home office, for the Department of State issued a directive (which he partly drafted) declaring that the embassy would be the only channel for working with either the Greek government or other foreign officials on high policy matters. The ambassador could consult the mission chief and his major military and naval subordinates in Greece, and he was to keep them informed on policy. But the ambassador was to retain authority in matters affecting a "high policy decision," which the State Department defined as "major political factors or repercussions apart from the technical desirability or undesirability of the action proposed." Such matters included changes in either the Greek cabinet or high military command; major alterations in size of the military; differences with Greek or British officials which could impede the aid program; Greek relations with the UN or foreign nations; governmental policies toward political parties, trade unions, subversive groups, guerrilla activities (including issues of punishment and amnesty); questions on holding elections. If a disagreement developed between the ambassador and the chief of mission or his major military and naval officers, the issue would go to the State Department for resolution.[25]

Griswold was not happy with the directive. He thought it a mistake to leave the impression that the mission lacked power and was not involved in Greek internal affairs. Congress intended that the mission control expenditures, which entailed involvement in Greek affairs.[26]

The Truman administration approved the extension of operational advice to the Greek army, but, because of the controversy over supervision of that task, it did not immediately establish a separate agency. The Department of State preferred that both operational advisers and additional planning and observing personnel be responsible to the chief of USAGG. The National Security Council wanted the advisory and planning group to be part of the mission in Greece but to have direct communication with the Joint Chiefs of Staff. Chamberlin continued to insist that advice to the Greek army should come from a separate military agency controlled locally by the ambassador but reporting directly to the joint chiefs.[27]

The military attaché in Athens, Colonel Harvey H. Smith, meanwhile appeared before the House Armed Services and Appropriations Committee to present General Livesay's views regarding the need for greater American supervision in Greece. USAGG's mission was to secure supplies and equipment for the Greek army. Americans offered only technical training to make sure the Greek soldier knew how to use the equipment; they had no operational responsibilities. The army wanted heavy machine guns and additional mountain artillery, but Livesay opposed the latter. Not only was it expensive, but the Greeks had a "tendency to start shooting at a great distance and if they get more mountain artillery they will set up the guns and start shooting them out." Livesay preferred a greater reliance on the infantry. In answer to why a large army could not defeat a small guerrilla force, he had once explained: "If you attack a bandit concentration on a hill you cannot approach them from one side because if you do, when you get there they are not there. They disperse and there is nobody there to fight. When the army goes down the hill again they reassemble and there they are. In order to destroy them you must completely surround them and close in on them. After each operation, when the army clears an area of bandits and moves on to the next area they have to leave some of the army to guard the villages. After a few such operations the army is practically all dispersed guarding villages."[28]

Livesay insisted that the United States could not resolve the problem without extending operational advice. The guerrillas were close to establishing a regime in the north and winning recognition. They were already receiving everything but rations from Yugoslavia and Albania; food was not provided in an effort to force the guerrillas to continue raiding villages. To the present, all guerrillas captured were Greeks. But this could change. "What we have here and what we have planned to come here is not sufficient to cope with such a situation. Just as soon as the northern countries start sending help in we would have to bring men in or we would have to get out. There is no force in Greece that could stop the Yugoslav Army." On whether the Soviets were training the guerrillas, Livesay declared, "I don't think there is any doubt but that the Soviet Union is backing Albania and Yugoslavia in training the bandits. But," he added, "they [the Soviets] are not across the border directing operations." Livesay asserted that he wanted to do more. "I would like to follow every piece of equipment right down to the combat area. I do not have personnel to do it and, of course, I cannot get into combat areas." The best available solution was to extend operational advice to the Greek army.[29]

Griswold was not pleased when the Truman administration approved the establishment of a separate agency in Greece and assigned the coordination of operational advice to the secretary of state. Claiming to be "completely in [the] dark" over the recommendations, he wrote Marshall that all he knew was what he had read in *Time* magazine. Military and economic matters were interrelated and of equal importance, Griswold declared; a larger focus on military concerns would come only at the expense of economic aid. Chamberlin's recommendations ignored the economic aspects of the mission. Indeed, the general, "reportedly dubbing [the] Mission a failure," never talked with anyone associated with it.[30]

Griswold's pique was not justified. The purpose of the Chamberlin mission was military in nature, and Griswold was a civilian who had no reason to feel snubbed. As mission chief, he was responsible for civilian and military aid to the Greek government; his duties did not encompass the Greek army's operations in the field. Griswold was not qualified to offer the type of military advice that Chamberlin sought. It is true that all aspects of the aid program were interrelated, as Griswold repeatedly emphasized, but Chamberlin's task was not to assess the overall thrust of the assistance program. His job was to evaluate the military effort and make recommendations on how to improve its performance. This task did not involve Griswold.

While Griswold nonetheless bristled over the White House decisions, the Greek government worked toward eliminating another obstacle to a military offensive: the establishment of a National Defense Corps. The corps would provide a village defense system by replacing the MAY and MAD commando units, free the army to pursue the guerrillas, and put a stop to political divisions over local protection. But USAGG funds were too small to allow both the previously approved permanent increase of the army by 10,000 and the establishment of a National Defense Corps. Accordingly, the Greek Higher Military Council, with the concurrence of USAGG, canceled the army increase and allotted the money for a National Defense Corps. The Department of State thereupon approved the formation of thirty-two battalions, or 16,000 men. To assure the men's dedication, the Supreme National Defense Council informed USAGG and the British Military Mission that each part of the corps would secure provinces "from which its troops were called up."[31]

As these changes were being implemented, the Greek government had sought to stabilize the military situation in September by launching the second phase of a small-scale offensive northwest of Athens called "Lailaps" (Whirlwind). The drive's early successes had offered encouragement about clearing central Greece. Soldiers surrounded nearly 1,500 guerrillas and seemingly left them no escape. By the first week of October, however, three hundred of the guerrillas eluded their captors by infiltrating government lines, while most of the remainder escaped to the southwest between government troops and the gendarmerie. The guerrillas then split into small bands to avoid another encirclement. The results of Lailaps were similar to those of other army operations. Government forces seized several supply depots but did not capture the guerrillas.[32]

The impact of this operation was more serious in the north. The army's commitment to Lailaps had weakened the area around Trikkala, allowing the guerrillas to intensify activities there and in the northwest. Some of those who had survived the offensive joined others to comprise a force of 2,500 that attacked the army battalions at Metsovon in late October. Additional government forces sent to help the entrapped soldiers were hampered by heavily mined roads, booby traps, and guerrilla attacks along the way. The guerrillas apparently sought to cut the road between Epirus and Thessaly and to establish a stronghold in the Grammos area. Their concentrated artillery assault on Metsovon was the first on an army unit of battalion size and might have been a step toward the establishment of a headquarters for Free Greece. By month's end the guerrillas escaping northward had crossed the Ioannina-Metsovon road through two corridors. Those guerrillas in Metsovon came under attack and withdrew to the heights in the north, where they consolidated along ten miles of what took on the appearance of a battlefront. About 3,000 guerrillas were above the town, intending to withdraw no farther.[33]

As winter closed in, Livesay was optimistic even though the Greek army had still not opened a major offensive. By the end of October, however, a force of 6,000 men was preparing for a three-pronged assault. Five hundred mules had arrived from the United States, the first installment of many that were specially trained for mountain operations. American military assistance funds had been raised from $150 million to $171 million; the Greek army had been increased from 100,000 men to 132,000; and the number in the National Defense Corps had grown to 50,000. In cooperation with the gendarmerie, the corps would perform garrison duties and free the army for field operations. Even the army's leadership problem seemed on the way to a solution. Sophoulis had recently sought the advice of USAGG and the British Military Mission on the choice of Greek officers to head the army chief of staff and command the First Army. This offensive, if combined with American field advice and air force support, had the potential for victory. Livesay observed that "it remained for the new Army Commander, with American supplies, American-trained technicians, and an American-developed defense corps, to reveal what strength there lay in the Greek armed forces as they moved into the difficult phase of winter operations."[34]

CHAPTER
6

The Joint U.S. Military Advisory and Planning Group

I

By early November the Truman administration was moving toward the establishment of an advisory and planning group in Greece. Following the President's approval of the program, the National Security Council worked out the details. The group would be comprised of ninety officers and eighty enlisted men divided among the army, navy, and air force, and would be part of the military section of the aid mission but have direct communications with the Joint Chiefs of Staff. The head of USAGG as senior army officer would be director of planning and operations and responsible to the chief of the American mission. Final authority, however, would rest with the ambassador, who would approve decisions and continue to deal with the Athens government on high policy. Military matters relating to such policy would come to his attention by the director and through the mission chief's office. Forrestal, now secretary of defense, directed the joint chiefs to select the men for the operational advisory task force.[1]

The White House had to offer assurances that the expanded military role did not signal a more dangerous involvement. Marshall assured cabinet colleagues that the move would not enlarge the war. Royall noted that the Greek government's failures had necessitated operational advice; its leaders in Athens had asked for help. Captain J. B. Carter of the U.S. Navy was certain that the decision was correct; more than military supplies and training were needed to re-establish internal security. That very day in the Senate Office Building, Royall admitted to Vandenberg that serious repercussions could develop from America's expanded participation in the war. He nonetheless thought the chances remote that Americans would become casualties in combat.[2]

Congressional leaders had mixed feelings. Vandenberg asserted that had Congress known of this possibility the preceding May, it might not have passed the aid bill. He would take the matter before the Foreign Relations Committee the following morning where, he warned, the press would learn of the buildup because the committee meetings were public. Marshall supported the move. That same day, Royall joined Generals W. H. Arnold and Wilton B. Persons in revealing the administration's intentions to the chairman of the House Committee on Foreign Affairs, Charles A. Eaton. He expressed no objections. To downplay the matter, Arnold wanted it "handled as a routine Department of the Army affair." A brief press release would follow on the morning of November 14.[3]

The escalated military involvement should not have come as a surprise; the Truman administration had left its options open during the congressional hearings on the aid bill. Acheson had emphasized that the kind of assistance depended on the prevailing situation. The White House had hoped to resolve the emergency in Greece by economic and military aid. But it had also insisted upon a policy flexible enough to permit adaptations to changing circumstances. White House spokesmen did not welcome a graduated involvement, but they had been consistently straightforward in asserting that an open-ended aid bill was necessary because more stringent measures were conceivable.

Less than a week after the army's announcement of the change in Greece, Griswold held a press conference in Athens during which he handled questions that suggested both his own irritation with recent events as well as a growing fear among reporters of an expanded war. American military personnel had come to Greece with authorization to advise only on matters relating to materials and equipment. "That authority has now been broadened" to include operational advice. The result was a "joint Greek-American operation." But, he quickly added, the Americans would "not be taking command" of the Greek army. Griswold did not know how many additional Americans the program would require, but he did not foresee "a great increase." The administration was "not going to send in thousands of people here." Asked the purpose of the new military men, he crisply replied: "[W]inning the civil war." The British had possessed only the authority to train the Greek army; they could not give advice in the field. A reporter expressed concern that the American military men would not leave when the aid statute expired: "Practically speaking now, doesn't their presence as almost a joint partner in the defense against a civil war mean almost unlimited commitment to stay until the war is over?" Griswold answered: "Such a commitment can only be made by Congress."[4]

The reporters' major worry was American participation in the war. Would officers accompany the Greek soldiers on combat operations? Griswold explained that Americans would be with them down to and including divisions.

But, he quickly emphasized, even though a division commander could go out with the units, that did not mean he was engaging in the war. "It is difficult to say that a division headquarters is actually engaged in combat operations. Ordinarily—I won't say a division headquarters is out of the range of fire—but you don't ordinarily refer to the division staff as being in combat. It depends on the definition of the word 'combat.'" Pausing a moment, he added: "After all, in a sense, all of Greece is a combat area." The United States was *not* a belligerent; it was "merely helping the Greeks to quell a rebellion within their own borders." A reporter asked: "I don't suppose it would be possible to publish the exact terms of the new directive, since American troops are involved not in combat but on the edge of combat?" Griswold did not have access to the full directive. Another wanted to know the title of the new American officers: "Is the word as you have been using it liaison officers, or observers—that will be attached to division headquarters?" Griswold sharply replied: "Don't get into a dictionary battle now. I don't know what they will be called." When someone remarked that Tsaldaris referred to them as "observers," Griswold noted: "They will be advisers; they will be observers and advisers. They will undoubtedly observe and report to the planning staff here—I mean our people—and they will be permitted to advise the Greek commanders."[5]

Several reporters inquired about the role of the British. Griswold explained that they would continue to train the Greek army. The relationship between the British and the Americans had been good—the British training the army and the Americans furnishing the equipment. On the question of British withdrawal, Griswold noted that the British Military Mission was supposed to have left the previous summer. But, he added, "I have no reason to believe that they will withdraw." Would some British troops remain? "I know of no plan to change the present situation as far as the British are concerned." No one should assume that the arrival of American officers was necessarily related to the possible withdrawal of the British. What did the British troops contribute? Their presence suggested that the venture in Greece rested on joint cooperation. "Off the record," Griswold declared, the United States should not engage in any "unilateral action." After the UN refused to take over the problem, the practical approach was for the British and Americans to share responsibility. They had worked together in the past; their cooperation would continue.[6]

Asked when the civil war would be won, Griswold replied, "I don't know. There is no use asking that question."[7]

At another press conference two days later, the primary subject again was America's expanding role in Greece. Griswold admitted that the aid statute restricted the mission to advisory work, but he insisted that the enhanced responsibilities fell within the law. Another reporter noted that Tsaldaris recently stated that the new officers would advise on arms but only reluctantly admitted that they would give strategic and tactical advice. Was this true? Griswold declared, "They are authorized to give military advice and of course that includes the use of equipment and arms and so forth—but it includes everything." Until now, the White House did not permit Americans to offer either tactical or strategic advice. But the military situation had gotten worse. "Certainly what we want to do is to advise the Greeks so that they can pick up the job and do it themselves." The following day a reporter inquired whether the establishment of a joint planning staff marked the beginning of a general staff that would have full military command. Griswold emphasized that Americans would be giving no orders. The Greeks would make final decisions.[8]

The reporters' anxiety about direct American participation in the war was not unfounded: besides the administration's repeated discussions and studies of that prospect, a proposal was before the White House to establish a "Guerrilla Warfare School." The State Department had investigated the political and military factors involved in guerrilla warfare and recommended that the three services cooperate in creating a "U.S. Guerrilla Corps." An ad hoc committee of the Joint Strategic Plans Committee would meet in early December to discuss the proposal. Some practical matters had already been worked out. If the United States sent its own guerrillas to Greece, the army would arrange a "Cover Plan" to maintain secrecy until their arrival. Since the nation's armed forces were so limited in number, any change in their location might cause speculation injurious to international relations. The initial movement of men must be "completely disguised" to allow a surprise landing in Greece. The "deception plan" would depend upon phony army-navy-air force maneuvers in the Antilles that included a landing on Puerto Rico. Since planning agencies would suspect that Puerto Rico was not the target, the White House must emphasize some emergency other than Greece.[9] Nothing came of the proposal.

Support for sending American troops was weakening; but it would not die. Eisenhower and others in the army had talked with the State Department about deploying soldiers in Greece—for occupation duties and not necessarily for combat. A War Department memorandum again dampened the idea by warning that the move might provoke war: "A decision to send U.S. troops to Greece should be made only after exhaustive evaluation of the best available intelligence estimates as to whether the USSR is willing to risk general warfare by permitting her satellites to make an overt attack against Greece while U.S. troops are present in that country."[10] Faced with that challenge, the White House could withdraw and lose prestige, or expand the troop involvement by general mobilization. Since neither option was attractive, the only feasible approach was operational advice.

The Greek government had meanwhile tried to halt the deteriorating military situation by instituting a village evacuation plan intended to undermine the enemies' sources of recruits and supplies in the north; but, like so many of the government's efforts, it failed because of lack of guidance and follow-through. The army evacuated the villages and moved the people to safety. Once the villagers were relocated, however, the army assumed no responsibility for them. Evacuees soon numbered over 300,000, along with thousands of refugees—all wanting to return home, all feeling abandoned by their government, and all susceptible to communist propaganda. In November the Athens government ended the evacuation program.[11]

Difficulties came not only from the Greek government; the imminent establishment of the planning and advisory group caused another eruption of problems between the mission and the embassy. In a telegram to Marshall but marked "Personal for President Truman," Griswold complained about the directives coming out of the National Security Council. He was especially unhappy that the ambassador would be the sole channel for dealing with the Greek government. Griswold claimed that his original instructions had given him exclusive authority over American aid and therefore awarded the mission a status separate from the embassy. The new instructions set up a two-headed mission: the ambassador would be the senior member but have no supervisory responsibility for the mission's work; the chief would be in charge of administrative and technical duties but have no authority. Economic, political, and military questions could not be separated from high policy. Success depended upon cooperation between the ambassador and the mission chief. The new guidelines, Griswold contended, would suggest division within the American command and undermine the Truman Doctrine.[12]

Griswold reminded the President that he had accepted his position as mission chief with the understanding that he would have "supreme authority" over the aid program. "Either [the] new instructions show that I no longer have your confidence and that of [the] Secretary of State, or else, as I hope, [the] new instructions were based on [a] misconception of [the] situation here and without realization of their practical effect." Regardless of the explanation, he insisted, they marked a dangerous change in policy. The mission was supposed to be an "entity separate from the Embassy although working in close collaboration," and the ambassador was to remain in charge of matters "not directly related to the activities of the mission." The new instructions conflicted with a stipulation contained in the report written by the Senate Foreign Relations Committee: the chief of mission would be "responsible for [the] entire program of assistance to Greece." The President had approved the report, and this statement became public during the congressional hearings on the supplemental appropriation bill for 1948. The new arrangement was unworkable because the chief of mission would be subject to the authority of the ambassador.[13]

Griswold threatened to resign: "Under [the] new instructions it would not be possible for me to remain here as I could not do effective or efficient work." The United States would find it "physically impossible" to change spokesmen with the Greek government every time a matter of high policy arose. A division of authority would invite the Greeks to play off the ambassador against the chief. Whatever the final decision of the White House, Griswold recommended against notifying the Greek and British governments of any change in responsibilities. Observers would interpret this move as a split between the two men and a repudiation of his work at the mission. The aid effort would sustain a severe blow.[14]

In light of Griswold's objections, the White House held up action on the new instructions until it could reappraise the relationship between the ambassador and the chief of mission. One possibility was to implement the new instructions without notifying either the Greek or British governments. Another was to devise a cooperative arrangement between Griswold and MacVeagh. A third was to name Griswold as ambassador and integrate the mission's duties with those of the embassy.[15]

Another complication was MacVeagh's personal probems. In addition to the exhaustion caused by the daily strain of events in Greece, he had become seriously ill following the death of his wife in early September. State Departmen colleagues had recommended moving him from Greece because of his noticeable decline in energy and drive. They agreed with him that Americans had to maintain the impression of Greek sovereignty even though that nation must follow America's directives. And they supported MacVeagh's insistence on having policy emanate from the embassy, not from agencies or missions. But they also knew that MacVeagh was not a sound administrator and that he could not supervise economic and military aid. MacVeagh had come into sharp conflict with Griswold over philosophy, personality, and diplomatic style. Now, in the midst of this controversy, MacVeagh had accompanied his wife's body home for burial and, while in Washington, met in the State Department for nearly a week of consultations. After returning to Athens in the latter part of the month, he came back to the United States in mid-October and soon went on sick leave.[16]

At this point, the embassy counselor in Athens, James Keeley, volunteered his views on the MacVeagh-Griswold problem. Keeley was "very fond" of MacVeagh but thought that both parties shared blame for the dissension. The aid program had originally been workable under the embassy with mission operations directed by a deputy acting for the ambassador, but the relationship had deteriorated to the extent that such an arrangement now would disrupt the program and hurt staff morale. "I see no satisfactory alternative at this stage than to keep Governor Griswold at [the] head of AMAG [American Mission for Aid to Greece] and to strengthen cooperation by increasing [the] liaison staffs of [the] Embassy and AMAG." The ingredients most needed were "good will and forbearance on both sides." The interrelatedness of America's efforts in Greece made it "impossible without detriment to [the] aid program to compartmentalize their respective responsibilities." If MacVeagh should not return to Greece (he was hospitalized in Washington after major surgery), Keeley recommended that the State Department refrain from sending another ambassador while Griswold was there. The embassy should remain under a chargé until the present aid program came to an end. A chargé, Keeley explained, was "less likely than an Ambassador to be sensitive to real or imagined affronts to his dignity and prerogatives."[17]

The White House desperately tried to avoid a public confrontation over the issue. Since Griswold guaranteed good relations between the mission and the embassy, the State Department expressed a willingness to follow his exhortations against changing the instructions. Truman directed the National Security Council to withdraw nearly all of the statement, leaving only the parts declaring that military and naval aid would go through the mission's military and naval units, and that the mission chief's military and naval subordinates would be responsible for operational advice not affecting mission policies. Greek and British officials were to learn only that additional military personnel would join the military section of the mission to provide operational advice. The President returned the matter to the National Security Council for further study.[18]

But the differences between Griswold and MacVeagh were now becoming public. The White House had received a number of messages from Griswold's supporters, urging MacVeagh's recall and the designation of Griswold as ambassador. Rumors were spreading that Griswold would run for Vice President on the Republican ticket and in the campaign attack the administration's Greek policy. In late November, the House of Representatives arranged an inquiry into the matter under the direction of Republican Karl Stefan of Nebraska, Griswold's home state. The chances for impartiality seemed even slimmer since Stefan had recently publicized demands for replacing Mac-Veagh with Griswold. When a member of the press asked Griswold the next day about the disagreement with MacVeagh and whether someone was en route from Washington to investigate, he brusquely replied, "All I know about it is what I read in the newspapers." The tension was difficult to hide. In Greek politics, Griswold favored the Liberals, MacVeagh the Populists. Neither approved the tactics of the other. Each insisted on primary control over relations with the Athens government.[19]

Faced with the choice, Truman relieved MacVeagh of his duties as ambassador and, in accordance with Keeley's suggestion, did not immediately appoint a successor. The embassy would be under the care of Keeley and the chargé, Karl Rankin, and Griswold would remain as mission chief. Perhaps to point in that direction, Lovett informed Griswold and the press that Mac-Veagh's surgery might prevent him from resuming his position in Greece. Henderson was unhappy with the President's decision. He did not approve of Griswold's abrupt and "highhanded" behavior, and he attributed the outcome to Griswold's being a "politician who had an inside track" to the President because he had been in Truman's regiment during World War I. When Acheson and Henderson informed MacVeagh of his recall, he broke down and wept.[20]

The arguments between MacVeagh and Griswold had revealed serious problems inherent in a foreign aid program. The administration faced an unavoidable dilemma: it realized the importance of cultivating an amicable relationship with the host government, and yet it recognized the political necessity of securing and holding congressional support by maintaining control over the program. MacVeagh was an experienced diplomat, learned and devoted to respecting the country in which he served. Griswold was a politician who had received his appointment to Athens primarily out of political expediency. Rather than working quietly through diplomatic channels, Griswold preferred bold and public movements designed to place pressure on the Greek government to bend to America's wishes. Tsaldaris and other officials, however, immediately recoiled at what they considered to be unwarranted and arrogant attempts to interfere with their internal affairs. They understood that, even though they were recipients of American aid, the Truman administration regarded Greece as vital to American security and would give in to many of their demands. In this instance, the tail wagged the dog, making a clash all but inevitable not only between the Greeks and the Americans but among the Americans themselves.

II

The driving force behind American policy in Greece remained the belief that the Soviets were instigating most of the region's problems and that the Kremlin had recently adopted more aggressive tactics. Some advisers in Washington thought that America's overall foreign aid program had hurt the Soviet position in Europe and caused this escalation in policy. The CIA believed that the recent establishment of the Cominform suggested particular concern about the impending Marshall Plan. Even though such a view now appears to have been myopic, the CIA argued that the communists had reacted to American pressures by setting aside the concepts of the "democratic front" and "socialist unity" and moving toward a "purer" concept of their mission as leaders of the masses. Hard-line militants were seeking revolution in Western Europe, while in Eastern Europe they were pushing toward "absolute Communistic totalitarianism." In the eastern Mediterranean, communist guerrillas were operating under "Soviet superior direction" and were receiving increasing support from allies that could lead to the creation of a communist regime in northern Greece. A State Department figure was convinced that the Cominform marked the beginning of Soviet support for Yugoslavia's efforts to enhance "the Communist/Slavic thrust at Greece."[21] As perceptions became reality, every event in Greece took on the character of a Soviet inspiration that, in turn, required a stronger response by the United States.

In Greece, the chief manifestation of this perceived change in Soviet tactics would be the guerrillas' establishment of Free Greece, followed by Soviet and allied recognition. John Jernegan in the State Department pointed to several options should this series of events occur. Greece might declare the act of recognition a "new aggression" that violated General Assembly recommendations and necessitated UN action under the right of collective self-defense guaranteed in Article 51 of the Charter. The General Assembly might condemn the move as a "violation of the spirit, if not the letter," of the UN Charter. If neither approach succeeded, the United States might increase aid to the Greek armed forces, urge other UN nations to send troops, and itself send troops and naval units to give moral support and protect strategic points. The State Department concluded that even though recognition was a political act that could not be construed as aggression, assistance to the guerrillas following recognition would constitute an armed attack within the meaning of the Charter.[22] The United States would have to make its opposition clear to such a regime—hopefully short of a military confrontation.

The Greek question had meanwhile resurfaced in the UN, this time in the General Assembly where the issue again would be assigned to a special border commission. After Greece was removed from the Security Council agenda in mid-September, the General Assembly took on the question and on October 21 established a Special Committee on the Balkans; but, like the Security Council's commission, the new committee offered little hope for resolving Greece's problems and undercutting the creation of a guerrilla regime in the north. The committee held its first meeting in Paris on November 21, before moving to Athens and then to its principal headquarters in Salonika. The committee had formally asked Poland and the USSR to become members but they did not respond. The committee sought to establish observation groups along both sides of the borders adjoining Greece with Yugoslavia, Albania, and Bulgaria. Yugoslavia declared that it could handle its own affairs; Albania and Bulgaria, not members of the UN, refused entry to observers and accused the British and Americans of interfering in Greek internal matters. Consequently, the observation groups worked only within Greece, except for a single instance when one group received permission to enter Bulgaria. The committee sat in virtually continuous session in Salonika from early December until the following June 1948. In addition to the observation groups, it organized subcommittees on political problems, refugees, and minorities. Albania and Bulgaria accused Greece of border violations and claimed that victory by the Democratic Army was crucial to peace. As in the Security Council, the General Assembly served only as a sounding board for opposing complaints.[23]

The achievement of America's strategic objectives in Greece and elsewhere largely depended on a continuation of the British role. If Bevin brought up the matter before the Council of Foreign Ministers that autumn in London, Marshall was to thwart any attempt to use America's expanded role as an excuse for British withdrawal. Lovett stressed that the continued presence of the British Military Mission was of the "utmost importance to the policies of the US not only in Greece but in the whole Middle East." Indeed, British diplomatic and military figures in Greece were anxious to remain in that country and work with the Americans. British and American officials on the scene thought that the solution was to integrate their missions into a single military mission having Livesay as head and Rawlins as deputy. According to the argument, the British government might be willing to cooperate with the United States if the Americans alone extended operational advice. If a combined mission was not feasible, Americans in Greece recommended an integrated advisory and planning staff with Americans providing operational advice and supplies and the British continuing to furnish the training. Lovett made clear, however, that the United States must have the dominant role.[24]

British leaders in London did not favor a full integration of the Americans and British into one military mission; but they had earlier expressed interest in developing "parallel and respective policies" in the entire region and were now receptive to a joint advisory and planning staff. Bevin thought it possible to integrate the staff with the Americans responsible for operational advice and supplies while the British took care of training. He also wanted the British officers to be consulted on all matters. Bevin recommended that the head of the British Military Mission in Washington work out the matter with Eisenhower.[25]

The question of integrating the two missions had to wait while the White House took on the unpleasant task of informing Americans that the establishment of the joint advisory and planning group entailed a commitment extending beyond the termination date stipulated in the original aid bill. At a press conference, Lovett focused on several developments that the administration had not anticipated when first presenting the bill to Congress. The refugee problem was growing. The forecast was gloomy for wheat crops and prices on the world market. Funds under the post-UNRRA relief program were ten million dollars less than expected. For temporary relief, the United States had diverted nine million dollars from economic funds to military supplies and equipment.[26] Resolution of the crisis could come only from a long-range policy of assistance.

In truth, the Greek army had shown some improvement, but its performance was still so disappointing that an expanded American military role appeared increasingly probable. Eisenhower insisted that the United States had to take decisive action. Livesay complained that the Greeks' "continued cry is for more and more of everything." The consul general in Salonika, Raleigh Gibson, reported in late November that Greek morale was still declining and that the guerrillas were preparing their defenses against the expected army offensive. The press and the public seemed to have developed a cynical attitude toward the UN's Balkan Committee. People in Salonika blamed the American mission for the country's problems. Gibson expressed the feeling of many observers when he recommended "effective US control" in northern Greece in the form of a "joint American-Greek" effort. Eisenhower concluded that operational advice was necessary.[27]

More than a few Americans warned that the Soviet threat in Greece was real, if only because events had forced the United States to demonstrate its willingness to halt communist aggression. Keeley asserted that the outcome in Greece was in precarious balance and would affect freedom worldwide. The United States must "see the job through" and "preserve Greek independence from Communist (Soviet) domination." Allies must have no doubt about America's steadfastness. The United States was engaged not only in a "propaganda war on a large scale but a shooting war, sponsored by those whose way of life [was] inimical to ours." An embassy study concluded that the United States must hold the line against the Soviets and their "satellites." If they won control, "the balance [would] not return short of war." America must safeguard its "vital interests" in Greece and develop a "spearhead aimed directly at a vulnerable spot on the Communist periphery." Greece must not fall "behind the Iron Curtain."[28]

On Christmas Eve of 1947 Markos took the step feared most by American and British observers: he announced the establishment of the Provisional Greek Government. The Soviet stamp appeared to be on the organization, for all members of the cabinet were communists. The American ambassador in Moscow, Walter Bedell Smith, did not believe that recognition by the Soviet Union and its allies was inevitable, but he felt confident that Albania and Bulgaria would extend recognition and that the Soviets and others would defer pending further developments. Even before the announcement, A. C. Sedgwick in the *New York Times* had predicted that the declaration of a new state would have Russia's "blessing." Greece's northern neighbors would certainly extend recognition to the only country on the Balkan peninsula not under Soviet control. The British press regarded Markos's declaration as an act of rebellion and urged the West to help Greece through the UN. The "Truman plan" was weak, according to the Manchester *Guardian*, because "it tends to increase the very danger it seeks to avert by adding fuel to Russia's fears." Recognition seemed imminent. Two days before Markos's announcement, the Bulgarian government pushed for the organization of the "National Committee for Assistance to the Greek Democratic People." Enthusiastic approval of the new regime in the Greek north came from numerous spokesmen in Yugoslavia, Albania, and Bulgaria.[29]

The announcement of Free Greece coincided with the collapse of the London Council of Foreign Ministers meeting and, to American observers, thereby seemed to be part of a Soviet effort to achieve the upper hand in the Cold War. Cyrus L. Sulzberger of the *New York Times* had earlier asserted that the "Red Satellites" would extend recognition to Free Greece and thus help the Soviets in their battle against the Marshall Plan. Many observers had predicted that the impasse over the German question during the London talks would harden East-West lines and lead to a decision for a Free Greece. *Time* magazine thought that Soviet intentions regarding Greece were now in the open. The announcement was "adroitly timed" with the breakup of the London meeting; the twin developments would suggest to lukewarm supporters of the Marshall Plan that no aid progam could clear the chaos from Europe. Yugoslavia, Albania, and Bulgaria would extend recognition, followed by "Mother Russia" if things went well. Sulzberger believed that the declaration was the first step in the Soviet effort to shift the focus of its attack on the United States from Western Europe to the Mediterranean. Recognition would come from neighboring countries, although it was "highly dubious" whether Russia would do so—unless the move afforded a good bargaining point for future international negotiations. Although the Soviets were not strong enough to risk war by making Greece a "new Spain," they would resort to every method short of war to undermine the Truman Doctrine. *Nation* argued that Markos's declaration was Moscow's first attempt after the London Conference to balance off recent political losses in France and Italy.[30]

Events during the last part of 1947 were happening so quickly and in such seemingly logical progression that they appeared to be part of a Soviet design to bring world conquest. Given the assumption in Washington that nothing took place in the communist world without the knowledge and consent of the Kremlin, the developments in Eastern and Western Europe seemed inseparable. The Marshall Plan was threatening to solidify another soft spot in Western Europe, thereby necessitating a series of dramatic moves in Eastern Europe—particularly the establishment of the communist regime of Free Greece, followed by recognition from the Soviet Union and its allies. A communist coalition working against the weak government in Athens was a frightening apparition to American policymakers who were convinced that the communists took no steps without a plan, and made no plan without possessing the means for its fulfillment.

On Christmas Day, in a move probably intended to secure a physical headquarters for the new communist regime in Greece, the guerrillas launched an attack on Konitsa, a town of 5,000 inhabitants located five miles from Albania and at the foothills of the mountains in northwest Greece. Konitsa offered the only accessible route from central Greece—and also from most of Albania—to the Grammos region. The guerrillas soon encircled the government garrison in Konitsa and bombarded the area with artillery fire. The full-scale assault indicated that the Democratic Army had undergone a change in tactics. Zahariadis was becoming a convert to frontal warfare after realizing the futility in hoping that revolutionary situations would develop on their own in the towns. The move from guerrilla warfare into conventional fighting was always risky, but it could succeed—*if* the enemy was demoralized and in a state of collapse. The great uncertainty was whether the growing U.S. presence would raise the morale of Greek leaders and help bring about improved performance by the army. To bolster the army's morale, Queen Frederika arrived in Konitsa during the siege.[31]

Greek and American leaders could not have known, but a feud had erupted between Markos and Zahariadis. As early as September 1947 Zahariadis had been undergoing a change in attitude toward the strategy of the war. Whereas in late 1946 and early 1947 he had opposed full mobilization—when the Greek army was at its lowest performance level—he was now turning toward positional warfare and the occupation of towns. Markos violently disagreed with this policy, causing him to fall out of favor with the Central Committee of the KKE. On December 2, 1947, before the Political Bureau of the Greek Communist party, the battle raged between the men. "If we concentrate all our troops on Grammos," Markos warned, "we release a large part of the enemy's troops from their present tasks and enable him to concentrate the bulk of them round our 25,000 men." Zahariadis dismissed Markos's misgivings as "an adventurist, petty-bourgeois conception of strategy." Markos declared that "the enemy's plan consists precisely of trying to force us to . . . concentrate our troops so that he can undertake a decisive action against us. We must do the opposite, *decentralize* our forces. We have to enter towns to deal with our recruitment problem, but we should take them by surprise; we should not attack them frontally or try to hold them." Zahariadis countered with another bitter attack on Markos.[32] The schism was perhaps personal as well as philosophical, but the outcome had the potential for causing a wider division among the leaders which, if not brought under control, could prove catastrophic to the KKE.

Less than a week after Markos announced the establishment of Free Greece, the government in Athens took further action against the communists in the country. It had already suppressed the two major communist newspapers—*Rizospastis* and *Eleftheri Ellada*—and it now outlawed both the KKE and the EAM (or National Liberation Front). In a move that infuriated Americans in Greece, the government also prohibited the right to strike. The Labor Division of the American mission in Athens had tried to advise on labor and trade unionism. But the workers' demands for higher wages failed to match skyrocketing prices and threatened to cause a nationwide strike. Then, on December 7, 1947, the Greek government passed an anti-strike law that, in certain instances, imposed the penalty of death. The move stunned the American mission, which two days later persuaded Tsaldaris to issue a statement that the government would use the law only in matters endangering national security, the public health, or industry and commerce. In the meantime the Americans worked toward repeal of the law.[33]

Markos's announcement again raised the question of sending American troops. In a meeting in Washington the day after Christmas, Lovett wanted to know whether the United States could rely on Greece: "Specifically, we could not take action which might result in the loss of American lives if the Greeks were not also ready and willing to sacrifice Greek lives." Livesay (who had returned to the United States for consultations) complained about Greek soldiers who would rather fight at long range than in close combat. Morale had deteriorated to the level that Greek loyalists were now wondering whether they were fighting on the right side. Livesay recommended a big increase in the National Defense Corps. He also thought that the presence of American observers would encourage the Greek soldiers to fight better. Henderson and Lovett agreed with the U.S. Army's assistant chief of staff that a definite decision must be made on whether to send troops if such a move became necessary. Livesay insisted that American soldiers could not go with the same instructions given to the British—to fight only if attacked. Kennan, however, warned that the administration should give "very careful consideration" to sending troops, even if they were part of a UN force. The

United States might find itself in a "difficult position from which it would be hard to withdraw and equally hard to keep other nations from withdrawing the contingents they contributed." The meeting adjourned with no final decisions.[34]

Kennan and Henderson became the focal points of the ongoing controversy. Kennan had "grave misgivings" about Henderson's interest in committing American troops. Deciding when to send them was a simple matter, Kennan admitted; complexities developed in determining when and how to get them out. The United States lacked the capacity to adopt an equally strong stance in the rest of the Middle East and the Mediterranean. What, for example, was the relationship of such a move in Greece to the Palestinian issue? The White House must reassess its Greek policy in relation to the Middle East and Mediterranean world. Henderson likewise took the broad view but approached the issue from a different perspective. America's entire foreign policy was dependent on taking "an extremely firm stand" against communist aggression in Greece.[35]

Even though Kennan and Henderson sharply disagreed over the use of American troops, their arguments again demonstrated a common assumption: Greece was only one part of a growing global approach to combatting communism. Kennan had pointed in that direction by advocating containment. But whereas he interpreted the problem in Greece as political and ideological, Henderson regarded it as military. Both saw the ultimate remedy as economic rehabilitation, but they differed over the type of assistance necessary to achieving that goal. Kennan was cautious in analyzing the steps involved in putting in troops as well as taking them out; Henderson wanted to send the men as a signal to the Soviets that the United States would hold the line. Kennan was too willing to concede what the Soviets already had, Henderson complained; the United States and its allies needed to push them back. Despite these differences in priorities, both men realized that America's strategy was global and that the White House could make no decisions pertaining to Greece without considering the relationship of those decisions to other trouble spots in the world.[36]

Short of sending troops, the United States was prepared to take several steps in the event that Free Greece won recognition. Yugoslavia was admonished that recognition would violate the UN Charter as well as the General Assembly's recent October resolution guaranteeing Greek integrity. As a UN member, Yugoslavia had special responsibilities before the world. The State Department approved a larger National Defense Corps, a permanent increase of 12,000 in the Greek army, and, in accordance with Livesay's recommendations, more military equipment for the army—especially machine guns. If any country extended recognition to Free Greece, Henderson declared, the National Security Council should hurry a decision on the "eventual despatch" of American troops under either Article 51 of the UN Charter or a special motion by the General Assembly. On December 29 the Special Committee on the Balkans unanimously adopted a resolution proclaiming that "recognition, even *de facto*," of the "'Provisional Democratic Greek Government,'" followed by "direct or indirect aid and assistance to an insurrectionary movement" against the Greek government "would constitute a grave threat to the 'maintenance of international peace and security.'" Henderson insisted that in seeking more congressional aid, the administration should be "completely frank" in warning of the "Soviet assault" on Greece. The United States "must carry through in Greece no matter how long it takes nor how much money it costs."[37]

The threat of recognition might have hurried a process already under way, for only a week following Markos's proclamation, the secretaries of the army, navy, and air force formally established the Joint United States Military Advisory and Planning Group and appointed Livesay as director. The heads of the three divisions—army, navy, and air force—made up the executive committee, which would advise the director on military matters. Headquartered in Athens, the group would aid the Greek General Staff through four advisers who specialized in armed forces personnel, intelligence, plans and operations, and logistics. Teams in the field would provide advice (in cooperation with the British Military Mission) to the Greek commanders and staff and send information and suggestions to the director. The British would continue training duties while the Americans advised infantry units. The director would work through the mission chief in bringing military matters affecting high policy before the embassy (which was still without an ambassador) for approval. The United States would assign military observers, comprised of both army and marine officers, to all Greek units in the field. The Joint Chiefs of Staff explained that "since the threat to Greek independence is now primarily military, military corrective measures must be applied to overcome it."[38]

By mid-January 1948, the outlook seemed grim as the first of the American officers and enlisted men had arrived in Athens and begun work, some as staff members and the rest among the field teams. The move did not come too soon. Government troops from Ioannina had arrived in Konitsa and, with air support, forced the guerrillas into retreat; but the success only temporarily lifted spirits. A *Time* correspondent in Athens gloomily wrote that the Truman Doctrine was failing. American aid was not evident to the Greek people, for the guerrillas' destructive tactics were undermining all efforts at reconstruction and rehabilitation. Houses, shops, schools, public utilities, railroads, bridges, trains, animals, food—nothing was safe from the growing number of raids on towns and villages. The worst problem was the refugees— over 400,000 living in tents, shanties, mud huts, or abandoned public buildings and warehouses (with family quarters often marked on the floor)—and many of these evacuated by the government from guerrilla territory because the Greek army could not protect them. Government relief per day amounted to less than a pound of bread (or flour) and the equivalent of fifteen cents in cash. Clothing came as gifts from voluntary organizations or from supplies left over from UNRRA. The American mission's Health Division cooperated with the Greek Red Cross and municipal and private agencies in supervising health measures. According to a police officer in Salonika, communist agents were among the refugees "like flies." And all the while, the guerrillas' forced recruitment policies were terrorizing the population. During the winter of 1947–48, they launched a mortar assault on Salonika that hit a building inhabited by British soldiers and left one dead and two wounded. Another shell exploded near the UN hotel and shattered its windows.[39] The war in Greece was intensifying as the new contingent of Americans arrived.

CHAPTER
7

Corollaries of a Global Strategy

The chief corollary of the new global strategy was that the United States could not overextend itself in one country. This was a difficult tendency to control. In early 1948, problems were erupting all over the world that affected American interests: the Soviet coup of February in Czechoslovakia along with continuing economic and political desperation in Europe, which would encourage congressional approval of the Marshall Plan in April; unrest in the Middle East over the impending division of Palestine; growing tension in Berlin; indications of a rift between Yugoslavia and the Soviet Union that could have widespread ramifications; the movement toward the establishment of a military pact in Europe; and the intensifying civil war in China. Greece was only one part of the picture: every decision in that country hinged upon holding the line against the communists in other places as well. More than a few observers, however, continued to insist that the Cold War would be won (or lost) in Greece. The government in Washington had to resist immense pressures from those who wanted to send combat troops. The insufficient number of men in the service provided a practical barrier to such action. Another consideration was that America's global strategy had subjected the aid program in Greece to limitations dictated by developments elsewhere in the world. To safeguard America's interests throughout the world, the Truman administration had to maintain rigid controls over its involvement in individual countries—including Greece.

I

The global emphasis of America's foreign policy reinforced the central objective in Greece of helping the government defeat the guerrillas without allowing the war to spread outside of the country. Marshall emphasized that the "destruction [of the] guerrilla forces and [the] establishment of internal security . . . have clearly assumed paramount importance" and should "take precedence over any portions [of the] present program which do not directly support them." Griswold agreed not to insist upon "economic programs and reform measures that do not directly or indirectly support [the] military effort." The prognosis was not good. Clifford noted that the guerrillas in Greece were so strong that the question became "whether or not we might ultimately have to send some troops." The army was preparing to move against Markos's headquarters in the Grammos-Vitsi area, just inside northern Greece along the Albanian border, and where his emplacements numbered about 8,000. Not only was Greece in jeopardy but so too was America's overall foreign policy: it had become dependent upon the early defeat of the guerrillas.[1]

The government in Athens could not have known, but the war had reached a crossroads and the decisions on both sides in the next few months were going to have profound impact on the outcome. The guerrillas had been driven from Konitsa and were in a state of disarray regarding tactics. Markos was convinced that the battle demonstrated the need for a returned emphasis on guerrilla warfare, and went to Belgrade to argue this stand before the Balkan Joint Staff. But Zahariadis insisted that this approach was wrong and countered with a demand for a unified command system that would permit the establishment of a formal army capable of seizing towns and fighting the Greek soldiers by conventional means. The KKE was divided and emerged with a shaky strategy that attempted to combine the two viewpoints. And, at precisely the time that the guerrillas were arguing over tactics, their reversal at Konitsa had awakened the Greek people to the necessity of a general mobilization of the war effort. In early 1948 the gradual change from British to American weapons began, and Greek leaders reorganized their army to facilitate better use of the greater firepower provided by the more than doubled supply of machine guns. The danger was that both sides appeared poised to launch a new and more aggressive approach to the war which would escalate the ferocity of the fighting and spread it beyond the northern frontier.[2]

In mid-January the KKE drew up operational plans that attempted to blend conventional organization with guerrilla tactics. The guerrillas improved their tactical and supply systems, and they organized into divisions, brigades, and battalions—a far cry from the independent bands who had earlier engaged in scattered raids. To counter discipline and loyalty problems, the leaders instituted political commissars as a special corps under the Supreme Council. Perhaps because the number of recruits (forced and voluntary) was lower than expected, the reliance upon women was increased to the point that they soon comprised between 10 and 25 percent of the fighting force. The guerrillas had been growing by about a thousand a month discounting casualties. Without outside help, they could field nearly 28,000 forces by March 1948—armed with rifles, machine guns, mortars, artillery, flamethrowers, time bombs, bazookas, and anti-tank weapons. Instead of full-fledged frontal engagements, however, the political leaders ultimately compromised by approving raids that would take place mostly at night. Despite poor weather conditions in the mountains—fog, snow, freezing rain—the guerrillas' terrorist actions spread the conflict into new areas, including the large islands.[3]

The difficulties in containing the war were compounded by the growing intensity of longstanding ethnic hostilities and border problems in the Balkans that had non-ideological origins and were not communist-inspired. The central irritant in Greek-Yugoslav relations concerned the Yugoslavs' desire for an outlet to the Aegean Sea. The bases of Greek-Albanian tensions lay in the Greek claim to Northern Epirus and in the Albanians' participation both in Italy's invasion of Greece in 1940 and in the succeeding occupation. The real problem in Greek-Bulgarian relations was the Bulgarian claim to the Greek province of Western Thrace, which had an opening to the Aegean. According to UN observers, Balkan "action committees" in each country were "openly and systematically" providing moral, political, and material assistance to the guerrillas. These committees operated under the sponsorship of "quasi-official organizations" but received official support from government-controlled radio stations. On numerous occasions, Markos sent representatives to meetings of these Balkan committees.[4] These Balkan problems were entangled with events in Greece, causing the war to take on additional international dimensions.

The Yugoslavs were engaged in numerous efforts to help the guerrillas. The United Trade Union led the way, assisted by the People's Youth Organization and the Anti-Fascist Women's Front. An aid committee was established in Belgrade in early January, and a system of committees soon collected money, medicines, clothing, and other goods. Less than two weeks later, a Croatian Committee of Assistance, sponsored by the Federation of Trade Unions in Zagreb, began raising funds. The following day a Macedonian Committee was organized and soon spread into numerous cities. Near the end of the month the Yugoslav War Invalids Central Committee presented a huge supply of clothing to those wounded in the "Greek liberation struggle." By March, the Yugoslavs had collected materials equivalent to about 150,000 American dollars.[5]

The Bulgarians also were openly supporting the guerrillas. In early 1948 they organized huge demonstrations for Markos in several cities. And, as sympathizers had done in other countries, they instituted "voluntary" wage deductions (as high as 10 percent) that went into the Greek Aid Fund. Every month Bulgarians bought coupons inscribed "for the aid of the Greek Democratic People." The Bulgarian Red Cross donated medical and other supplies, and the following month it issued a special stamp "for the aid of the Greek refugees." On the day after New Year's, the National Committee of the Fatherland Front sought contributions for "moral and political aid" as well as "material assistance to the refugees from Greece." A "victory of the Greek people" was "definitely in the interests of Bulgaria."[6]

A further complication was that Albania and Bulgaria accused the Greek government of violating their borders. From early January through mid-April 1948, the Albanian government lodged over a hundred complaints with the UN secretary-general that the Greeks, among other transgressions, had sent planes into Albanian air space more than seventy times and that their army was repeatedly firing shots and shells into Albanian territory. The Bulgarian government likewise informed the secretary-general of similar grievances.[7]

The Yugoslavs, however, filed no protests against Greece, which suggested that their government was undergoing a change in policy brought by increasing trouble with Moscow. Tito had repeatedly irritated Stalin by taking an independent stance on Balkan matters, albeit Marxist-Leninist in thrust. Now, in early January, Tito assured American Ambassador Cavendish Cannon that Yugoslavia was "not going to do anything dramatic or engage in any adventure" in Greece. "Yes, I know that you Americans are worried about Communism thrusting out into other areas but do not forget Yugoslavia's chief national task is internal development and we need peace." Tito, according to Cannon, appeared reluctant to extend recognition to Free Greece unless forced to do so by Moscow. Tito was also uneasy about America's plans. From his vantage point, he had reason for concern. The same day that Cannon's note arrived in Washington, the State Department sent a note to its embassies, including the one in Belgrade, warning that recognition of Free Greece would be a "flagrant violation" of the UN Charter and of the General Assembly resolution of October 1947 guaranteeing Greek integrity.[8]

Even with the onset of winter, the war in Greece threatened to escalate as the government made hurried efforts to use airpower. During the buildup of the Royal Hellenic Air Force in summer 1947, the British sent 250 planes, including Spitfire fighters, C-47s ("Dakotas"), Wellington bombers (later found to be ineffective), and other surplus aircraft. Plans called for the Greeks' single-engine AT-6s ("Harvards") to conduct reconnaissance, the Spitfires and Wellingtons to carry out strafing and bombing, and the twin-engine C-47 (or DC-3) transports to protect ground troops and drop supplies. The Greek air force developed three fighter-bomber squadrons, each composed of twenty Spitfires (equipped with rockets, cannons, and bombs) and three reconnaissance units, each made up of four Harvards (armed with a single machine gun and later fitted to haul fragmentation bombs). One squadron and one reconnaissance unit were located at each of three bases: at Salonika, for operations in the northeastern sector of the country; at Larisa, for those in central Greece; and at Elevsis, for the south.[9]

For months the air effort was only minimally successful. The air force had inadequate equipment and facilities, and an insufficient number of trained pilots and maintenance men. The planes struggled against rugged airstrips and high-velocity crosswinds that repeatedly caused the cancellations of flights and disrupted the ground war. Pilots found it difficult to locate guerrilla strongholds hidden in the mountains. When the enemy was spotted, the pilots were unable to establish effective communication and coordination with ground units. The Spitfires were vulnerable to ground fire and could not retaliate effectively because of their limited space for ammunition and their short-range flying capacity. The Greeks later tried to adapt the C-47 for bombing expeditions, but they could not correct the plane's problems in accuracy. These obstacles notwithstanding, the air combat units flew nearly 9,000 sorties during the campaigns of early 1948, while the transports made nearly 10,000 flights. They incurred fewer than fifty casualties, never encountered enemy aircraft, furnished valuable reconnaissance information, protected ground troops, provided supplies, and dropped propaganda leaflets. But in the air-ground part of the war—the bombings and strafings—the planes could have no measurable impact unless the Greek air force improved the methods of identifying targets. The implication should have been clear: the way to defeat guerrillas was in hand-to-hand combat.[10]

But the seemingly magical appeal of air warfare persisted, which ultimately led to pressure for the use of napalm (or liquid fire). In late 1947, Major Nelson H. Russell of the Air Section of the Joint U.S. Military Advisory and Planning Group met with Greek officers to discuss the manufacture of tanks for carrying the substance. The Greeks were certain that necessary raw materials were available in their country and that the State Aircraft Factory could have experimental models within ten days. But they would need to requisition the napalm and igniters from the United States. If the tanks proved satisfactory, the sheet metal necessary for manufacturing could come from either the United States or England. The Greek government wanted the napalm ready for the spring 1948 military operations.[11]

The truth was that if the air force worked in conjunction with the ground troops, it could help win the war. The Greek soldiers had shown signs of improvement, especially when working in cooperation with the air force. They had received assistance from the air in freeing Konitsa, even though Livesay complained that they had failed to engage in organized pursuit, thereby allowing the guerrillas to escape and to retain their stronghold in Western Epirus. During February, 4,000 guerrillas attacked Florina but were driven back by air assaults. In the ravines west of town, the planes inflicted most of the casualties sustained by the guerrillas—more than 900 killed or captured. With better air-ground coordination, Livesay believed, the Greeks could accomplish the job.[12]

But the development of such a program required time and careful training, which further highlighted the importance of America's operational advisers in promoting an end to the war before it expanded in scope and the nation's involvement reached a higher level. With or without air support the primary objective remained to amass an army offensive against the guerrillas that would kill them or drive them permanently out of the country.

The potential dangers in extending operational advice became clear during Livesay's briefing of the first twenty American officers who were preparing to go into the field. In a meeting attended by British officers (and kept secret from the Greeks), he told the Americans to "go out among the troops and see what is going on." Above all, "neither your actions *nor your talk*" should leave the impression that you are acting as a "combatant." This would not be easy. "You carry no arms. Your conduct, if you are caught in an operation, is more or less entirely up to you. The thing for you to do is to take cover. You are not armed and you take the best cover you can and see what you can but don't get involved in the combat." This was "rather a large order," Livesay admitted, and yet he proceeded to add another difficult command: "If you get ambushed without arms and take off down the road you will lose prestige among the Greeks[;] so don't give the Greeks the idea you are afraid when you take cover." In still another curious statement, he declared, "You are not armed and that is your protection." Livesay gave an example. "If I were lying in a hole and there was [a] Greek rifle close to me and I knew a bandit was coming to shoot me, there is not much doubt what I would do. You can be judged in the same way. In the final analysis observe combat but don't get involved in it."[13]

While the men were doubtless puzzling over the ramifications of such a policy, Livesay emphasized that America's goal was to advise, not to remake the Greek army into an American army. Advisers must give advice in a way that "the individual Greek officer will think it was his idea in the first place." Final decisions rested with the Greek commanders. The United States had furnished the army with equipment and now must establish one integrated unit of logistics, training, organization, and operation. World War II had virtually destroyed the Greek army, forcing a total reorganization of the armed forces and the insertion of untrained officers in key positions. Americans must encourage the Greeks "to do the job with what they have." The task would not be easy. Livesay tried to illustrate the magnitude of the problem. General Rawlins once asked a Greek battalion commander what he would do if guerrillas were nearby. The commander said he would launch a twenty-five-pounder on the spot. What if the area was beyond range? After a pause, he replied that he could set up an ambush along a trail through the mountains. Though the commander had a battalion with him, he never considered going after the guerrillas. Livesay insisted that security could come only through aggressive action by the Greek army, which must be encouraged by "our push, energy and, to use the old American expression, 'needling' all the time to get them going."[14]

Within a month, the predictable happened: charges appeared in the news media that Americans were participating in the fighting. The most widely publicized story came in February 1948, when United Press correspondent Dan Thrapp in Salonika declared that Colonel Augustus J. Regnier "personally led a Greek platoon up a mountain slope under heavy machine gun fire." Regnier, who was the commanding officer of a U.S. Army detachment assigned to the Greek army corps headquarters in Salonika, said he "took the lead when the Greek major commanding the battalion was hesitant about pushing his troops forward in the face of heavy fire." According to the story, Regnier asked the Greek major: "Will you go forward if I do?" He replied,

"Sure pal." To this Regnier declared: "I led one platoon to the topmost mountain peak south of the lake though I had to hit the dirt often." Confirmation seemingly came from CBS correspondent George Polk, who informed the American embassy in Athens that the U.S. colonel there told him that American military advisers were leading the Greek troops because their commanders from the brigade level up were "not worth a damn." The story drew what journalist and critic Constantine Poulos called "half a dozen feeble denials, a brief flurry of censorship on the part of the American Mission for Aid to Greece, and Colonel Regnier's transfer out of Salonika." Despite this and other examples, Poulos complained, the White House stood behind its bland statement that "United States military advisers will neither participate in combat nor command Greek troops." He concluded that "the report is obviously far behind actual events."[15]

The charges pertaining to Regnier's conduct drew the most public attention and led the White House to order an immediate investigation. A directive from the Joint Chiefs of Staff had admitted that for assistance and advice, American advisers might find it necessary to "participate in advisory or observant capacities," but such contact was to be limited to "higher levels." The only exception was that in implementing the above duties, American personnel could join "any channel in the Greek armed forces to advise and observe operations." But if Regnier *led* a Greek platoon, he violated the directive and became a "combatant"—even if he took over because the Greek major seemed hesitant under heavy fire. In a message to USAGG and the Joint U.S. Military Advisory and Planning Group in Athens, Colonel Richard W. Mayo of the U.S. Army's Plans and Operations division emphasized that no American military personnel were to "take command of or lead Greek troops." Nor was anyone to "participate as a combatant." America's "role [was] that of coach not player." This assignment was "especially delicate due to the domestic as well as international aspects."[16]

An inquiry led by Brigadier General Truman Thorson sent from Washington exonerated Regnier. After interviewing Regnier, Thrapp, and others in Salonika, Thorson concluded that the United Press story was wrong. Regnier did not lead or command Greek units; he had merely accompanied the men and offered operational advice. Regnier declared that he had advised the Greek major on "how to deploy his troops for the battle since he was taking no action and seemed to be helpless in this situation. I also suggested a rapid advance up the mountain slopes and accompanied a Greek Second Lieutenant in command of a platoon in the center of the line." Regnier and his fellow officers understood that they were only "observers" and were to act in an "advisory capacity only on operations and supply." Thrapp admitted that he had gotten his information from Greek and American civilians, and that the Regnier quote was a "misstatement" and had not come from American military personnel. He "regretted" the trouble caused.[17]

The Regnier incident illustrated again the dangers in the type of war being waged in Greece. *New York Times* correspondent Cyrus L. Sulzberger recorded in his notebook that the Americans "appear to be in charge of operations and there is not much disguising this fact, although everyone pretends it isn't so." And British observer Christopher M. Woodhouse wrote: "Both on the ground and in the air, American support was becoming increasingly active, and the theoretical line between advice, intelligence and combat was a narrow one." Combat participation was a matter of interpretation, and yet policymakers in Washington had attempted to draw a fine line between an American officer serving as "combatant" and as "adviser." Even in theory, the division of responsibility was minuscule; in reality the separation was virtually nonexistent. An American officer standing beside Greek soldiers firing at the guerrillas became part of the fighting force, whether or not he pulled the trigger. Moreover, advising and carrying out the advice rendered were both integral and related parts of combat. An American shot on the battlefield would be a casualty, whether or not he was an observer. Such an event would raise a cry for reprisals in kind. Regnier admitted that he had advised the Greek officer on how to use his men in battle, and that he had accompanied another Greek officer and his platoon at "the center of the line." The enemy would be hard-pressed to distinguish between observers and combatants when both were advancing on him in the heat of battle. In truth, however, such a distinction was a matter of debate only to the soldier behind the desk. A captured guerrilla claimed that his men were under orders to shoot *any* Americans "interfering with operations."[18]

II

Although Greece remained central to America's security interests in the Mediterranean and Near East, the Truman administration had come to regard the country as only one part of the global effort against the communists. The Joint Chiefs of Staff admitted that withdrawal from Greece would lead to a "substantial loss of prestige." However, they warned that if Americans became militarily involved in the ongoing crisis in Palestine, the White House would have to reassess the aid program in Greece. The National Security Council agreed. While still insisting that in Greece the administration must make "full use of its political, economic, and, if necessary, military power," the Council recognized that such a policy must be considered in relation to other matters and coupled with a British agreement to maintain their position in the region. A firm policy in Greece rested on "overall political and strategical considerations." The CIA also saw the broad picture but was more alarmist. A communist victory in Greece would cause "international panic" and a "greater risk of collision with the USSR" by exerting pressure on the United States to extend more aid to countries in trouble. The Office of Naval Intelligence concluded that the fall of Greece would be an "example of the futility of US policy" and would have major impact on the political direction of Europe and the Near East.[19]

The White House sought the National Security Council's advice regarding the steps to take if either the Soviets or their allies extended recognition to Free Greece. The Council recommended that if Markos won recognition, the United States should consult with the British, French, and other UN member nations to determine whether they would support military action under the Charter. If "non-Greek nationals in significant numbers" became involved in the hostilities, they would have engaged in an armed attack as comprehended in Article 51. If the Balkan nations refused to withdraw recognition of Markos's junta (the administration refused to use the word government), the United States should support a Greek resolution asking UN members for assistance. The resolution should not specifically refer to military aid, but "extreme care should be taken to insure that the General Assembly resolution does not in its language exclude direct military assistance."[20]

The President approved the National Security Council report in mid-February, but not without having to override considerable misgivings from other advisers. The joint chiefs reminded the White House that a decision to send armed forces would raise the politically unpopular question of mobilization. They also were concerned that another recommendation, the assignment of additional functions to the naval commander in the Mediterranean, would confuse the lines of authority. The joint chiefs wanted to leave all policy direction in Greece to America's senior representative in that country—the ambassador. Henderson likewise believed that final authority should reside in the ambassador, who had the best military advisers and should therefore supervise the American effort. But Henderson had seen similar difficulties develop between the mission chief and MacVeagh. Indeed, the White House had not yet replaced MacVeagh. Griswold had an overbearing personality and might threaten to resign over this matter as well. Such a development could have an unfavorable political impact in Greece as well as cause unfortunate repercussions for the Marshall Plan. Henderson recommended that the President and Department of State first deal with the problem of authority.[21]

Henderson was particularly unhappy that the National Security Council report did not contain a statement that in "certain circumstances" the United States would send troops to Greece. He had wanted to insert the following: "Such overt attack by troops of a foreign government would of course be an act of war against Greece." Perhaps influenced by Kennan's earlier warnings, Henderson had attached safeguards. First, the administration must establish the specific mission of armed forces—whether to garrison or protect certain areas, seal off valleys from invasion, or deter neighboring nations from attempting an armed coup. Second, it must determine the steps by which the troops would be withdrawn. The United States could announce that the troops would leave Greece once their mission was over. But they must not be "worn down by Soviet persistence."[22]

Henderson, however, was not immovable in his support for American troops: he realized that the nation's aid program was subject to global limitations and that the Greek government must put forth a greater effort.

Because of worldwide ramifications, the United States must prevent "the slow strangulation of Greece by the Soviet Union and its satellites." In a conversation with the Greek ambassador to the United States, however, Henderson warned that the Greeks "must not lay [sic] down on the job and simply wait for American military assistance." The White House must find a balance between too much aid and too little—with the amount determined by whatever was required to motivate the Greeks to help themselves. Their nation was "the test tube which the peoples of the whole world are watching in order to ascertain whether the determination of the Western powers to resist aggression equals that of international Communism to acquire new territory and new bases for further aggression."[23]

As the administration continued to explore the troop option, it discovered additional uncertainties. In an observation that at least implicitly questioned the performance of Livesay and other military advisers, the State Department's Policy Planning Staff (directed by Kennan) concluded that no one in Greece (or the entire Middle East) was qualified to make judgments on such an important matter. The issue of authority was part of the problem. Another was the quality of information received. The State Department declared that it could not rely on telegrams and reports arriving from various sources. The National Security Council was in agreement. It asserted that a buildup of the military establishment in Greece was advisable—including American soldiers—if "reliable evidence" from "qualified sources" showed that without them Greek independence was in jeopardy. Marshall summed up the problem by noting that no one seemed sure about the purpose of an expedition, the number of soldiers needed, the logistical support they would require, and whether the American public would be supportive. There was more. The deputy director of the Office of European Affairs, Llewellyn Thompson, warned the administration about making references to "indirect aggression" because the term had many meanings; troops were not advisable unless the aggression was "very thinly disguised." Confirmation came from a legal adviser in the State Department, Ernest Gross, who argued that outside military aid did not constitute an "armed attack" that fell within the meaning of Article 51 of the UN Charter. Nor would the use of non-Greek volunteers fit that category unless they were directed and controlled by an outside government. An armed attack must be an attack by one state with military force (whether with regulars or guerrillas) against another, with or without a declaration of war.[24]

The strongest objection to the use of American soldiers again came from military advisers in Washington, who continued to emphasize that the United States did not have enough men in uniform to send to every trouble spot in the world. A call for armed forces was unreasonable without determining the number of men in service, making an "educated guess" on the likelihood of mobilization, considering the time required to achieve mobilization and deployment, and making "some decision as to the most important places where U.S. forces . . . should be used if there aren't enough of them to use everywhere that we might wish." An adviser added, "We can't continue to proceed on the assumption that (a) we have enough U.S. military forces to go everywhere, and (b) we will face only one crisis at a time instead of a possible series of simultaneous crises in Italy, Greece, Iran and Palestine." The White House must consider the whole picture—Greece in relation to everything else.[25]

The Truman administration was nonetheless convinced that the Soviet threat made some form of decisive action necessary. The Soviets and their allies could soon extend recognition and overt aid to Free Greece and justify such moves as comparable to American assistance to the Athens government under the Truman Doctrine. The Soviets knew that recognition could lead to some action by the United States or the UN. And they realized that open assistance to the guerrillas could cause the West to adopt policies that might precipitate a larger war—which the USSR was not ready to fight. But from Moscow's point of view there was another and perhaps more critical consideration: Markos's collapse would hurt the prestige of international communism. Chances therefore seemed good that the Soviets would continue their growing commitment as long as Markos appeared capable of success, and as long as the Western reaction did not escalate into all-out war.

The irony is that, even though the Truman administration could not have known, its policies were having a major impact on the Soviet Union. Two communist contemporaries from Yugoslavia, Milovan Djilas (the country's vice president, and one of Tito's closest confidants) and Vladimir Dedijer (a leading journalist), years afterward declared that by early 1948 Stalin believed the Greek revolution could not succeed now that the United States was involved.[26]

By January 1948 the United States was aware of a few signs pointing to a diminished Soviet interest in the Greek guerrillas, but at the time these developments did not seem important enough to suggest a shift in the Kremlin's policy. Marshall saw no major reference in a recent Cominform paper of the Markos regime, which seemed indicative of "the present Soviet and satellite attitude in withholding a firm commitment on Markos in the face of their uncertainty regarding the reaction of the U.S." That same month Georgi Dimitrov, the Bulgarian Communist leader, told a press conference that when the question of a Balkan federation became an issue, "the nations of people's democracy, Romania, Bulgaria, Yugoslavia, Albania, Czechoslovakia, Poland, Hungary, and Greece—mind you, and Greece!—will settle it." According to Dedijer, "[T]he Kremlin reacted furiously to Dimitrov's statement." Stalin was so incensed with Dimitrov and with a series of treaties Yugoslavia had signed with various Balkan communist states that he summoned Bulgarian and Yugoslav leaders to Moscow. Dimitrov led his delegation, whereas Tito feigned illness and did not attend.[27]

In Moscow in February 1948, Stalin made an angry announcement to the Bulgarian and Yugoslav representatives that neither Markos nor Zahariadis could have known about: the conflict in Greece had to end. Stalin had changed his ambivalent stance on the Greek civil war to outright opposition—probably because the Truman Doctrine had injected the United States into the situation and thereby posed a potential danger to the Soviet alliance system in Eastern Europe. If he had ever offered any encouragement to the guerrillas—either directly or through Greece's neighbors—that was over. If he had given the struggle his tacit approval by turning the other way, that too had ended. The conflict had originally been between only the guerrillas and the Greek army, thereby permitting the Soviets to attack the British in the UN for refusing to bow out of a domestic controversy in Greece, and to launch a propaganda campaign against the Greek government in the press and on radio. Together, these actions worked to further unsettle an already unsettled situation. But in the summer and fall of 1947, the deepening involvement of the United States constituted a threat to Stalin's interests in the region. Dedijer recalled that Yugoslavia had extended help to the guerrillas despite Stalin's opposition to interfering with Greece as part of the Western sphere of influence. Tito's compatriot, Svetozar Vukmanović-Tempo (who had organized the resistance during World War II in Yugoslav Macedonia), likewise noted Stalin's lack of interest in Greece because of its remote location from Russia and because the country lay outside the Soviet sphere. And Djilas, who was of unquestioned integrity, declared that the Soviet Union "took no direct action" in behalf of the Greek guerrillas. But Yugoslavia and Bulgaria were now assuming independent stances in the Balkans that encouraged more Western involvement. In January 1948, Stalin had given his reply to a speech by Tito of the previous September advocating militant communist expansion. An article in *Pravda* vehemently rejected a Balkan federation encompassing Greece.[28]

Contemporary and firsthand support for Stalin's decision to abandon the Greek guerrillas came from Djilas and Dedijer. After Molotov brought up the matters of the press conference and Balkan federation, Stalin lashed out: "We see Comrade Dimitrov abandons himself fervently at press conferences; he does not mind his tongue. Whatever he says, whatever Tito says, is thought abroad to have been said with our knowledge." Dimitrov apologized and admitted, "It is true I was carried away at the press conference." But Stalin did not accept the apology. "You wanted to shine with new words; that's all wrong, because such a federation is an impossibility." When Dimitrov insisted that there was "no essential difference between the foreign policy of Bulgaria and that of the Soviet Union," Stalin shot back, "There are huge differences." Barely containing himself, he declared: "We do not agree with the Yugoslav comrades that they should help further the Greek partisans; in this matter, we think that we are right and not the Yugoslavs." Thus "the uprising in Greece has to fold up." When Yugoslav Vice-Premier Edvard Kardelj interjected that a Greek guerrilla victory was possible "if foreign intervention does not grow and if serious political and military errors are not made," Stalin angrily retorted: "If, if! No, they have no prospect of success at all. What do you think, that Great Britain and the United States—the United States, the most powerful state in the world—will permit you to break their line of communication in the Mediterranean Sea! Nonsense. And we have no navy. The uprising in Greece must be stopped, and as quickly as possible."[29]

Stalin's position was a product of several realities, the most important being the best interests of his country. He had accepted the percentages agreement of 1944 that safeguarded neighboring countries in Eastern Europe at the cost of recognizing British interests in Greece. During the December uprising of 1944, he had not interfered when British troops put down the communists. In succeeding months, he perhaps looked with favor on the growing unrest in Greece that broke out in guerrilla warfare in 1946. If the guerrillas could topple the Greek government on their own, the Soviets would be ready to exploit the situation by supporting the new communist state. But the situation abruptly changed after the United States proclaimed the Truman Doctrine and sent in aid and advisers; continued trouble in Greece would invite deeper American intervention and create a potential hazard to surrounding communist regimes that already were showing signs of discontent with Soviet control. Stalin reasoned that the continued attempt to establish a Greek communist state was not wise at a time when allies in the Balkan region were not reliable. Such a move, Djilas declared, would "endanger his already-won positions" and cause "possible international complications." Yugoslav policies regarding Greece could hurt Soviet efforts to consolidate power in Eastern Europe.[30] Out of Soviet interests, the guerrilla war had to be terminated.

In retrospect, by early 1948 the Truman Doctrine had virtually fulfilled the purpose intended by its creators: the undercutting of Soviet influence in Greece by convincing the Kremlin that the United States was determined to hold the line against communism. But two problems remained: the Truman administration was not aware of this success, and neither were the Greek guerrillas.

III

Ironically, at the same time that the Soviets were ordering an end to the guerrilla war in Greece, the White House thought that more stringent action was necessary because of word from various sources that the "Balkan Satellite States" were enhancing their efforts to incorporate Greece as a communist state into the "Balkan Bloc." Even if Markos and Zahariadis had known of Stalin's directives in Moscow, there was no guarantee that they would have obeyed. Indeed, events following the Moscow meeting demonstrate that the Yugoslavs (and, to some extent, the Bulgarians) did not buckle under to Soviet pressure: both countries continued to assist the guerrillas. And, not surprisingly, the White House continued to believe that the Soviets were directing events. Just as Greece had become the "bastion of the Western way of life in Eastern Europe," Truman's advisers explained, the country was a "major source of annoyance" to the Soviet Union. Domination of Greece would be a "triumph of Soviet policy and add considerably to her prestige amongst the satellite States and communist parties throughout the world, while fear of Soviet power would increase elsewhere, particularly in the Mediterranean and the Middle East." A "closely interlinked network of Soviet-controlled Communist States in South East Europe" would be a "bulwark for defense and a bridgehead for expansion whether military or political." Greece's neighbors would not organize armies to assist the guerrillas because this would be an act of war; but they could accomplish the same results in the "guise of international volunteers." The "satellite countries," along with France, Italy, Austria, and others, were providing money, clothing, and medical supplies through private societies.[31]

The Truman administration realized that the situation in Greece was so precarious that effective air support from the outside might have tipped the balance in favor of the guerrillas. The Soviet air force had pulled out of Bulgaria, but not without leaving stockpiles which could facilitate a re-entry into Bulgaria and a later attack on Greece. The Yugoslav air force had over a hundred fighters and light bombers near the Greek border and a regiment equipped with the same type of British aircraft possessed by the Greek air force. The Yugoslavs also had two squadrons of Russian fighters manned by Russian personnel in Albanian uniform and two squadrons of medium bombers piloted by Yugoslavs and Albanians and commanded by Russians. However, a U.S. Army Staff study concluded that before such "Satellite Air Forces" could come into use, the guerrillas would have to seize enough land inside Greece "for it to appear at least possible for the aircraft to be operating from Greek territory."[32]

Even if an air threat developed, the key to the Greek government's success remained an improved army. If Greek soldiers could prevent the enemy from securing suitable land for staging operations, the chances for help in the air seemed remote. The solution lay in organizing and implementing a huge offensive.

That objective in mind, Marshall pushed for a "more impressive personality" to head the American military group in Greece, and he found him in Major General James A. Van Fleet. Born in New Jersey in 1892, Van Fleet was a graduate of the U.S. Military Academy and a heavily decorated officer during World War II. He had commanded a regiment during the D-Day landing on Normandy Beach, and then went on to become a division and later a corps commander. Marshall thought Livesay sound on the supply end of the aid effort, but he believed that operational advice must come from a new officer with more personal drive and combat experience. American Army Staff records were blunt: the reason for the change in command was the "lack of progress of the anti-guerrilla campaign." Marshall considered Van Fleet to have been one of the most hard-nosed and aggressive corps commanders in Europe. Eisenhower concurred: Van Fleet was "definitely *not* the intellectual type, but [was] direct and forceful and [had] a fighting record that would make anyone respect him." After Congress approved Van Fleet's appointment, Livesay received notification in early February of his dismissal as director of the Joint U.S. Military Advisory and Planning Group and chief of USAGG, along with a request that he remain in Greece to handle the logistics of the aid program. Livesay, however, was disappointed and asked Eisenhower to relieve him of all duties. Eisenhower's decision to do so was correct, according to Griswold, "because of [the] Greek psychology which will embarrass Livesay and make him ineffective in Greece." Following Van Fleet's briefing in Washington, he prepared for a departure to Athens around the middle of the month.[33]

Van Fleet's appointment aroused both public and private discussions concerning the possibility of sending combat troops to Greece; for the first time, the United States had a high-ranking and combat-experienced officer on the scene who was qualified to offer recommendations regarding such matters. *Time* magazine called Van Fleet a "burly" and "battle-wise" combat soldier who had learned speed, daring, surprise, and audacity from General George S. Patton in World War II. Choosing to spend half of his work week in the field raising morale, Van Fleet quickly demonstrated a remarkable talent for instilling a fighting spirit into the Greek soldiers. The U.S. Army's Joint Strategic Plans Committee had recently formulated an elaborate set of contingency plans involving the marines, army, air force, and navy, which approximated the mobilization time required if dispatch orders arrived. The committee wanted the planning in place should Americans be needed on short notice, and it recommended that the President be in the position to implement them without needing special powers. Public opinion, however, was a deterrent to such action. Perhaps coincidentally with news of Van Fleet's appointment, the National Opinion Research Center conducted a survey that revealed strong opposition to a troop dispatch. Although nearly 60 percent of the respondents expressed support for continued military assistance, only 25 percent were in favor of sending American troops—even "if it appeared that Russia might get control" of Greece.[34]

In mid-February, at a meeting of the National Security Council, the question of sending troops surfaced again. Marshall asked how many men might be sent to Greece without causing serious political repercussions. Forrestal thought the least uproar might result from a regiment of marines. Marshall agreed that the arrival of marines "might be a less war-like gesture." The assistant secretary of the air force offered a compromise. He noted the interest in beginning flight training programs in strategic areas of the world, and he recommended that the United States send B-29s to Greek airfields and "accomplish at least a part of the purpose in mind in considering the dispatch of ground forces." Marshall approved and the National Security Council opted to move in that direction. He warned, however, that the only way to resolve the deficiency in fighting men was through a program of universal military training. But that approach remained politically unattractive—if not impossible. The Greek government had to resolve the issue before American troops were needed. At the same time, Marshall emphasized, the United

States must exercise extreme care not to suggest a lack of resolve. Any appearance of weakness would "lose the game and prejudice our whole national position"—in particular America's support for the Marshall Plan. "[W]e are playing with fire while we have nothing with which to put it out."[35]

The joint chiefs again put the quietus on the issue by emphasizing that the Free World's problems were more pressing elsewhere. Would the Greek government consider American troops "as the first step of a commitment by us to take over the job?" Would this step deter the communists or stir them to stiffer actions? Token American forces would do little good unless they were sent as "evidence of our intention to back them up to any extent that might reasonably become necessary and unless, further, it is *known* that we are ready and able to do so effectively." Two obstacles were evident: the United States was not "ready and able to do so effectively," and the use of combat forces in Greece would make them unavailable for "more critical emergency use" in other places. Furthermore, American and Greek ground forces *combined* were "numerically far inferior" to those of neighboring Soviet allied states. The joint chiefs highlighted the dilemma: American troops "will probably be unnecessary if Soviet satellites do not initiate open warfare and will be insufficient if the Soviet satellites do attack." The chief considerations were "our own strength, together with our prospective or actual commitments elsewhere, and the latest and best estimate as to whether or not such overt action by us will precipitate overt action by Soviet satellite or USSR forces." A decision to send ground forces would necessitate using America's reserve, which, because of "our extended military position, is already dangerously low."[36] Regardless of their number, the arrival of American troops would greatly expand the nation's involvement in a country that, because of the nature of global strategy, was no longer considered the focal point of the Cold War.

The joint chiefs nonetheless left the door open for sending a few troops—*if* such a move fitted global military strategy. They recommended the immediate beginning of mobilization measures to develop the minimum force necessary for emergency action, and they urged that it be done in such a way that "it will be practicable to extend their scope to [an] all-out war effort without avoidable delay." After declaring that these procedures would require statutory authorizations similar to those during World War II, the joint chiefs reminded policymakers that such laws "would naturally entail consideration additionally, at that time, as to whether or not to commit further forces if the initial commitment should prove insufficient." For the present, the joint chiefs had no intention of Americanizing the war by sending enough troops to Greece to meet operational needs. Whether or not the Soviets or their allies sent armed forces in response, the number of Americans needed would be too high in view of "the over-all world situation and our own state of readiness."[37] But the restraint advocated by the joint chiefs could come to an abrupt end if the Greek army did not soon win the war.

Largely because of global considerations, the issue of American troops was again dropped from discussion. The Truman administration had considered every conceivable aspect of the question and had reconfirmed its opposition to sending troops. As the time approached for the Greek government's spring offensive, the White House thought that the military aid program was having a favorable impact and that American soldiers would not be necessary. The first contingent of operations advisers was ready to begin work. The Greek army, with the present ceiling of 132,000 to be raised to 147,000 in May, was well-equipped and nearing a state of discipline and experience that might undergird a spirited drive northward. General Napoleon Zervas had called for "a quick, constant unstopping counter attacking action" that followed the tactics of "governmental guerrilla warfare." The National Defense Corps was in place, soon to be increased from its present 20,000 to 50,000 men. The Americans had a new and more forceful leader in General Van Fleet, who possessed the qualities needed to inspire a Greek following. The United States, McGhee declared, should "continue to utilize the Greeks as an instrument of our policy."[38] Since Greece was but one part of Washington's broad strategy of halting communism, the solution was to convince the Greeks that this was their war and that only they could win it.

But before the winter snows had passed, another complication arose. The guerrillas had apparently expanded their abductions of men and women to include children.

CHAPTER
8

The Greek Children

In early 1948 the war seemed to reach a new level of atrocity as the Truman administration began receiving reports that the guerrillas were evacuating thousands of children from Greece and relocating them in Yugoslavia and other neighboring communist states. The Greek government accused the guerrillas of kidnapping its youths and preparing to convert them to communism. The episode quickly took on the appearance of a calculated effort to destroy Greece as a nation as leaders in Athens charged the guerrillas with genocide and appealed to the UN and then directly to the United States for help. This seemingly new communist threat, which the Greeks called *paedomazoma* or "stealing of the children," aroused nationwide indignation by its violations of family sanctity and basic humanitarian principles. But broader considerations were also involved. Some American observers suspected that the evacuations were another device intended to deepen the chaos in Greece and undermine the Truman Doctrine.[1] The motives behind the displacement of Greek children are impossible to determine because the files in the Eastern European states and in Greece remain closed.[2] But regardless of the reasons, the impact of the evacuations threatened to widen the Greek war by adding a highly emotional issue to an already intense national and international atmosphere.

Accessibility to American documents permits a one-sided examination of the subject, but even this approach demonstrates again the Truman administration's flexibility in confronting the larger issues of the Cold War. Its advisers were dubious about the charges of mass kidnapping and genocide, although they believed that the communists had taken a few youths to prove the inability of the Greek government to guarantee the safety of even its young citizens. The most frustrating aspect was the lack of realistic options for remedial action. Military measures were too risky—for the children as well as for the impact such actions would have on escalating the war. The

Greek government did not know where the youths were, nor could it assure their protection during any sort of rescue attempt. An appeal for worldwide condemnation seemed possible, although a public campaign against the Balkan region's communists would not bring the children back. Indeed, such tactics might encourage the spread of the Greek struggle beyond national borders. The White House hoped to keep the issue under control while making a dispassionate decision about whether there was proof of the Greek government's charges.

Cold War considerations dictated other reasons for restraint. The Truman administration had to stay true to its purpose in Greece—to establish domestic security—without becoming involved in Greece's problems with other countries. The President's advisers knew, of course, that the furor over the children was an inseparable part of both internal and external matters, and that it could become intertwined with the Cold War. Not only would the argument invite outside exploitation by keeping Greece and the entire region in an uproar but the continual pressure on the White House to take a resolute stand in behalf of its Balkan ally could prove costly to another objective: the prospect of exploiting a crack in the Soviet alliance that was afforded by the growing troubles between Yugoslavia and the Cominform. The Truman administration was reluctant to criticize Tito's government (or any other potential dissident in Eastern Europe) over the issue of the children.[3] No strong policy, whether in action or word, was possible.

And yet, the pressure on the United States to do something was so intense that it threatened to override the most fundamental reality: the charge of kidnapping was impossible to prove. Many observers believed that the evacuations had taken place primarily to save the children from starvation and the war. Others allowed that humanitarian intentions had guided the first removals, but that the actions so unsettled the Greek government that the guerrillas had decided to take advantage of the situation by greatly exaggerating the numbers. The reason for the action, whatever it was, seemed irrelevant. Whether the guerrillas initiated the removals as either a humanitarian or propaganda effort, or even to destroy the nation, the decision ultimately aroused worldwide sympathy and deeply alienated large numbers of Greek people.[4] The issue also had political implications inside the United States, for numerous Greek-American organizations demanded that Washington take action. Unless the war ended soon, the United States would either have to forsake its commitment to an ally, or pursue some high-sounding and threatening policy that had no chance for success.

I

The White House suspected that both sides in the controversy over the children were guilty of exaggeration, but it nonetheless had to deal with the issues raised because they were basic to the ongoing civil war and could affect the outcome of the Truman Doctrine. The Athens government complained that the Yugoslavs were again attempting to undermine the Greek nation as part of their longstanding effort to construct a Balkan federation. Greek loyalists asserted that the child abductions were proof of the darkest kind of crime: the forced transportation of the youths to neighboring states, where in ideological camps they were converted to communism before being trained to return to Greece as guerrilla fighters. A spokesman in Athens insisted that the scheme "was intended to destroy Greece by destroying Greece's future—her youth." The Greek government amassed a considerable amount of documentation affirming the evacuations. The UN Special Committee on the Balkans interviewed witnesses of the removals. Red Cross agencies and independent observers verified the presence of thousands of Greek children outside the country. *Time* magazine's correspondent in Greece reported that the "Reds" had taken the youths into the "people's democracies" to receive a "Marxist education." The evidence for kidnapping, however, was circumstantial and motive remained undetermined. Most governments accepting the youths publicly defended their actions as humanitarian attempts to save the children from "monarcho-fascist" Greek armies allied with Anglo-American imperialists.[5] The belief was growing that neither the Athens government nor its American ally could guarantee the safety of Greek youths.

By pronouncing the evacuations as kidnappings, the Greek government made the matter regional in scope and elevated it into a potential Cold War issue. The United States did not want to broaden its Greek commitment to encompass a Balkan problem, especially when Yugoslavia was involved. Tito's relationship with the Soviet Union seemed tenuous, making it unwise to alienate his government. But the child controversy seemed impossible to contain within Greek borders. Given the panicky atmosphere of civil war, many Greek loyalists probably believed what they were saying: Slavic communists had abducted the youths with the intention of indoctrinating them for a later round in the civil war. Furthermore, according to contemporary belief, the Soviets were involved: Moscow wanted to incorporate Greek Macedonia into an independent Macedonian state, which would become part of the Federal State of Yugoslavia. Once the Russians were assured an outlet to the Aegean Sea, they would install a communist regime in Athens, cut off Turkey from the West, and secure access to the eastern Mediterranean. Regardless of whether all of the Greek charges were valid, many Americans were certain that the Eastern European communist regimes did nothing without Stalin's approval.[6]

The origins of the controversy, of course, lay in the civil war. The removals of children began perhaps as early as January 1948, but the first confirmed instances took place soon after a Balkan States Youth Conference in Belgrade the following month. There, a Cominform arrangement provided that children three to fourteen years of age should be relocated for safety in foster homes in Yugoslavia, Albania, Bulgaria, Czechoslovakia, Hungary, Poland, and Rumania. In early March, Markos called for the evacuation of eighty thousand youths from northern Slavophone villages in western Macedonia.[7] At the outset, it appears, the guerrilla command was reacting to the necessity of evacuating the north, which would soon become the target of a Greek army offensive.

The problem was that the countries providing refuge for the children did not hesitate to publicize their actions and to inflame the situation further by claiming that they were saving the youths from the reactionary Greek government. Radio Sofia announced in early March that Hungary had welcomed the youths and other Greek refugees "in response to the appeal of the People's Councils of Free Greece." Parents in fifty-nine villages "have given 4,684 children aged three to thirteen, who will be transferred to Hungary, Czechoslovakia, Poland, Rumania, and Yugoslavia." *Eleftheri Ellada*, the communist voice of Markos's guerrilla forces, listed over half a dozen Greek villages and the numbers of children taken from each. Radio Free Greece declared that over 4,000 children had been relocated, and in April Radio Belgrade reported the arrival of 7,000 more. Three days later it claimed that 12,000 would be divided among Yugoslavia, Albania, Czechoslovakia, and Hungary. One communist publication contained a story that was headlined "We save Greek children" and featured a photograph of two exhausted boys over the caption: "The first picture of persecuted children of democratic Greece shows two of these courageous young comrades who had to flee their homeland before monarchic terror. Entirely without means, they are dependent on international solidarity of people's democratic and progressive countries."[8]

The public declarations drew a strong reaction from Americans and Britishers abroad, who confirmed the mass removals of Greek children while noting that the program did not come without complications for Greece's neighboring states. The Joint U.S. Military Advisory and Planning Group reported that in mid-March the guerrillas had attacked a number of villages and taken both adults and children. The most widely circulated story concerned a sixteen-year-old orphan girl, who died from the mountain cold and snow while saving her two younger brothers from the guerrillas. American diplomatic sources noted the arrival of three hundred Greek youths in Rumania, five hundred in Yugoslavia, and eight hundred in Czechoslovakia. Numerous children denied being of Greek nationality—probably because most of them had come from Macedonia, where feelings of autonomy were strong. According to reports from Hungary, many Greek youths had to be "indiscriminately billeted" because of a "lack of popular enthusiasm."[9]

At this point, in February 1948, the uproar over the children became entangled with other wartime issues when the Greek delegation in the UN General Assembly made an official protest. The Greek foreign minister charged that "the abduction of Greek children was more than a mere violation of treaty pledges"; it was a "crime against humanity." Other Greek spokesmen maintained that witnesses reported strong and bitter opposition to the removals. Markos's guerrilla bands had instituted a census of children in northern Greece for the purpose of funneling them into nearby countries for "re-education" in communist ideology. The guerrillas were attempting to destroy the "Greek race" and were guilty of the "crime of genocide."[10]

The General Assembly authorized the Balkan border committee to investigate the charges. Half a dozen observation groups prepared to conduct inquiries along the Greek side of the northern frontier (Yugoslavia, Albania, and Bulgaria maintained their ban against the entry of committee members). Those questioned would be chosen at random, coercion was forbidden, and, to ensure safety, the witnesses would not be sworn or identified.[11]

The UN committee encountered numerous problems in gathering information. The teams had great difficulty reaching remote villages, and in several instances along the border they were fired on from outside the country. The guerrillas accused them of being under the control of the "Anglo-Saxons and their satellites" and warned that any member of the committee who entered areas under their jurisdiction would be arrested and treated as a prisoner of war.[12]

Though compiling what the committee termed a "considerable body of evidence," that evidence failed to prove kidnapping. The guerrillas had transported large numbers of Greek youths by trains, trucks, and ox-drawn carts into neighboring states. The committee could not prove the official complicity of Yugoslavia, Albania, and Bulgaria, although repeated communist radio broadcasts suggested that the program had the "approval and assistance of these Governments." The UN observers came across more than a few cases of voluntary relocation of children by parents, particularly in the Slavic-speaking region of western Macedonia. Of twenty-eight removals in a village in Kastoria, the investigatory teams discovered that in five instances (randomly chosen), the children had willingly joined their fathers who were members of the guerrilla force. A "fairly large number of parents" who supported the removals were also sympathetic with the guerrillas.[13]

According to a member of the UN teams, the chief consideration was personal. In villages supporting the guerrillas, the parents decided whether to send their children; in "hostile villages," the committee had "little doubt that the approach was different and a process of virtual conscription enforced." In one town in Bulgaria, the UN member continued, most of the children came from guerrilla-occupied areas in Greece and "their relatives who are still there—and for the most part are themselves combatants—do not wish their children to be sent back yet." A girl of twelve "neatly summed up the situation" when asked if the children had left on their own: "Yes," she replied, "the children whose fathers are in the mountains wanted to go. My father was not a guerrilla, therefore I didn't want to go."[14]

The UN committee was unable to resolve the two central issues: the number of children relocated against their will and whether the purpose was to indoctrinate the youths with communist ideology. The London *Times* in early December 1948 reported an estimate by the League of Red Cross Societies that nearly 24,000 abducted Greek children were now living in the "satellites of Russia." Six months later the figure had grown to 28,000. The paper had no evidence of kidnapping, but the tone of its coverage suggested that it believed the charge.[15] Despite widespread beliefs and various forms of suggestive evidence, most observers realized that there was no reliable way to determine how many children went involuntarily and whether the objective was to spread communism. Again, however, the motives behind evacuating the children were less important than the public impression left by the antagonists on both sides of the issue.

Although the UN team was unable to enter communist countries, several individuals, including Americans, were permitted to visit homes for the Greek children. A British news correspondent, Kenneth Matthews, joined an American newsman in securing visas from the Bulgarian government and inspecting a children's home in the town of Plovdiv. The building, formerly the town hall, sat in a wooded public park and housed two hundred Thracian children. Upon the arrival of the two visitors, the children marched from their rooms to present themselves. Older boys joined them from the garden nearby, carrying spades and singing in unison: "We're giving the death-blow to Fascism; we're marching to civilization." Many of the children were orphans and either did not know their own names or were too frightened to say. Matthews believed that the Greek government had converted "an act of politically motivated charity" into a diabolical plot. The American was skeptical about this assessment and hesitated to dismiss all of the Greek accusations.[16]

In another instance, the American embassy's cultural attaché in Sofia accompanied French, British, and Canadian newsmen in inspecting a Greek Children's Home outside the city. Once a hotel, bombed during the war but now rebuilt, the home housed over five hundred children in clean, comfortable surroundings. The American claimed that the schools in Bulgaria emphasized a "pattern of thought" that was communist in orientation. When someone entered the room, the youths stood, extended a clenched fist salute, and declared, "Welcome, Drugario [comrade]." They addressed adults as "synagonistes," or fellow fighters, the designation used by the guerrillas. Wherever the children went in groups, they moved in march step while singing partisan songs that substituted the word "foreigners" for "Germans" or "Nazis." Slogans chanted were "Forward with Markos," "Let us struggle for liberty," and "Down with imperialism and fascism." The school textbook opened with the Greek National Anthem and a picture of Markos, and it included poems and stories praising the guerrillas' wartime efforts against the Nazis and the British, while urging a campaign to drive all "foreigners and barbarians" from Greece.[17]

Reports also came from American visitors to children's homes in Yugoslavia and Poland. Homer Bigart, a correspondent for the New York *Herald Tribune*, described in positive terms the care received by the youths. According to Bigart, all of the children had left Greece voluntarily. Two members of the American embassy in Warsaw observed Greek children in their quarters in Poland. The Americans were not granted permission to talk with the youths, but their observations assured them that the children received satisfactory care. A Greek teacher noted that the children would remain in Poland until the war at home was over.[18]

These on-site inspections did not resolve the issue; if anything, they convinced the government in Athens of the accuracy of its charges. The lodgings were clean, the food ample, the supervision and education better than what most children experienced in Greek villages. Thus the stories that the newsmen and other observers carried home would serve as excellent propaganda. And yet the uniform behavior of the youths suggested an effort to convert them to communism. If the original purpose of the relocations was humanitarian, they nonetheless bolstered a perception held by many in Washington: the communists were engaged in a new kind of warfare aimed at undermining the enemy on all fronts—including attempts to change the loyalties of youths.

The UN committee concluded that if there were "humanitarian grounds" for relocating the children, the Greek government—not someone on the outside—should assume the leading role. Whatever the motive of the guerrillas, the removal of children "without their parents' free consent" raised "the issue of the inherent rights of parents" and broke "accepted moral standards of international conduct." Furthermore, the act violated Greek sovereignty and endangered relations between Greece and its northern neighbors. In a move supported by the United States and Britain, the committee recommended that the Greek government attempt to resolve the issue by bringing it up for discussion with the governments of the countries accepting the children. Should this approach fail and the need for assistance become clear, the committee would assure that needed evacuations took place "through the intermediary of an appropriate international organization." By June the Greek government had made contact with Yugoslavia, Albania, Bulgaria, Czechoslovakia, Hungary, and Poland. All governments had either ignored or rejected the appeals.[19]

II

Leaders in Athens had already taken measures to safeguard the remaining children in northern Greece by arranging for their transportation to "colonies" or "children's cities" established in the country's interior and on its islands. In addition, Queen Frederika helped to establish the Northern Provinces Relief Fund to relocate children in privately endowed homes. An American embassy official in Salonika learned that among the thousands of youths relocated by the government, none had gone without the parents' consent. Agencies responsible for the program were local welfare groups, Greek War Relief, philanthropy organizations working under the Ministry of Welfare and the Greek Red Cross, the Ministry of Social Welfare, and the Committee for the Welfare of the Northern Provinces of Greece (founded by the queen). Whether to protect the children from the guerrillas or from the approaching military operations in the north, the Ministry of Social Welfare

President Truman before a joint session of Congress, asking for aid to Greece and Turkey, March 12, 1947 (*Wide World Photos. Courtesy Harry S. Truman Library*)

Dean Acheson and President Truman (*U.S. Department of State. Courtesy Harry S. Truman Library*)

Loy Henderson (*Harry S. Truman Library*)

From left to right: Warren R. Austin, President Truman, George C. Marshall, and Arthur Vandenberg (*National Park Services, Abbie Rowe. Courtesy Harry S. Truman Library*)

General Markos Vafiades (front left), ca. 1946 (*Courtesy John O. Iatrides*)

Nikos Zahariadis (*Courtesy John O. Iatrides*)

Lincoln MacVeagh and King George II in Athens, October 1946 (*Courtesy John O. Iatrides*)

Mr. and Mrs. Dwight Griswold and General and Mrs. William L. Livesay (*Harry S. Truman Library*)

From left to right: Karl Rankin, Dwight Griswold, George McGhee, and Henry F. Grady in Athens (*Harry S. Truman Library*)

Signing the ECA agreement in Athens, 1948. From left to right: Karl Rankin, Constantine Tsaldaris, M. Ailenos (Minister of Press and Information), and Dwight Griswold (*Harry S. Truman Library*)

A SNAPSHOT OF STARVING GREEK CHILDERN
UNDER THE ENEMY OCCUPATION OF GREECE
(MAY 1941—SEPTEMBER 1944)

THE SAME SNAPSHOT REPRODUCED THREE YEARSL ATER
IN «LA VOIX OUVRIÉRE». EDITOR: LÉON NICOLE
(GENEVA, 27 MAY, 1948. No 119.)

Over the caption, "Victims of Athens Monarchofascists," the Greek guerrillas in May 1948 released a photograph of starving Greek children, allegedly under the present government's rule. In actuality, the guerrillas had changed the caption on a photograph of Greek children taken during the Nazi occupation of Greece. (*National Archives*)

Picture on the pamphlet sent to Secretary of State Marshall (*National Archives*)

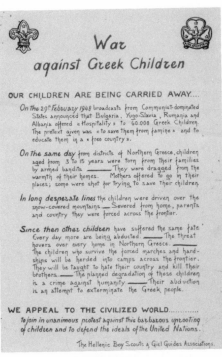

(left) Pamphlet sent to Secretary of State George C. Marshall in May 1948 (*National Archives*)

(right) Photograph of Greek elementary school student sent to President Truman in March 1948. Inscription on back reads: "To our highly respected and beloved Uncle Truman a Greek boy respectfully submits an appeal that he may protect our nation from the inhuman abduction of children by the bandits, now taking place in Greece." (*National Archives*)

Government investigation of alleged massacre of forty Greek children by the guerrillas in the Mount Ghiona area during the Greek army's Roumeli offensive in 1948 (*National Archives*)

Queen Frederika (middle, facing camera) visiting Children's Colony in Athens suburb in 1948 (*National Archives*)

Guerrilla strong point in Grammos area (*National Archives*)

American and Greek officers observing attack on Grammos during Operation Crown in 1948 (*National Archives*)

Guerrillas captured by Greek army in Grammos during Operation Crown (*National Archives*)

Generals James A. Van Fleet and (to his left) Alexander Papagos visiting Epirus headquarters in western Macedonia during Operation Rocket in 1949 (*National Archives*)

Undamaged guerrilla pillbox found in Tsouka area in Vitsi during Operation Torch (*National Archives*)

(left) Greek army preparations for assault on Vitsi during Operation Torch in 1949 (*National Archives*)

(right) American officer instructing Greek troops in the use of 75-mm recoilless rifle at Kozani Training Center in 1949 (*National Archives*)

Guerrilla equipment and stores captured in Vitsi during Operation Torch (*National Archives*)

Guerrilla radio equipment captured in Vitsi during Operation Torch (*National Archives*)

75-mm howitzer provided by United States for use against Grammos during Operation Torch (*National Archives*)

Battery support for Greek assault on Grammos during Operation Torch (*National Archives*)

U.S. Navy Hell-Divers being off-loaded from American aircraft carrier in Phaleron Bay for use in Grammos during Operation Torch (*National Archives*)

Greek army officer instructing refugees to return to their villages following Grammos campaign of Operation Torch (*National Archives*)

had taken more than 5,000 youths from Macedonia (including over 2,000 in Salonika), and nearly half of 5,000 from Thrace. In a housing program staffed by volunteers and having the enthusiastic support of the queen, the government eventually resettled nearly 15,000 youths, from both communist and loyalist backgrounds, in forty-eight children's homes.[20]

By late March of 1948 Griswold reported that Markos's announcement of child evacuations had had the additional impact of disrupting the Greek government's war preparations and thus working to the advantage of the guerrillas. The queen and others had overreacted to the communists' "unusually effective psychological warfare" by establishing a counter-program that necessitated expensive child-care arrangements and added to the enormous refugee burden. And, even more important, the program hampered the military's efforts by requiring the use of army transport units in moving the children. Americans on the scene thought the threat not as great as depicted by the Greek government, and recommended that it establish refugee centers in large towns where parents might choose to send their children. Griswold insisted that Markos's strategy was to "snatch" a few youths from time to time "to support propaganda of mass abductions and continue [to] produce [a] demoralizing result among Greeks." His assessment found support in Salonika, where Gibson believed that the guerrillas were waging an "effective war of nerves" designed to prove the army incapable of guaranteeing security.[21]

But the fear persisted. Suspicion had spread among the people in Greece that the abductions were part of an effort to dismember their country and establish a free Macedonian state dominated by either Slavs or Bulgars. The Greek chargé in Prague was convinced that the guerrillas sought to further the "Slav-ization" of the children in communist surroundings. Such a belief was encouraged by radio broadcasts, press releases, and statements of public officials in Yugoslavia and Bulgaria, all calling for the separation of Greek or Aegean Macedonia from Greece. In Greece the National Liberation Front called for an independent Macedonian state within the "confederation of democratic Balkan peoples." During a huge demonstration in Patras against the abductions, one speaker warned: "Do not forget that Greek children are kidnapped to be turned into Bulgarians." Another proclaimed that the Slavs intended to "annihilate the Greek race by their satanic plans." The Greek press denounced the abductions as atrocities aimed at destroying the country from within. One paper lashed out at the "hateful and barbaric action by Slav-led bands of gangsters," while another accused the UN of being indifferent to the "extermination of a race."[22]

In Athens, Rankin dismissed the Greek government's accusations but discerned a potential advantage to be derived from the guerrillas' recent behavior in the war: he urged the State Department to use the child removals and a recent newspaper report of a mass murder of other youths as propaganda against the communists. His sources revealed that "senior Communist officials in [the] Slav states" had not expected the evacuations to arouse such public resentment; they now sought to return to their original policy of taking "only the willing children of willing members of the rebel army and its followers." Another related event further promoted the image of atrocity. Press reports in Greece alleged that during the government's recent military actions in Roumeli its soldiers had come across the bodies of forty children along the slopes of Mount Ghiona. According to the account, the leader of the retreating guerrilla force had feared that the children would reveal its place of refuge and ordered them strangled. The day following the discovery, the Greek Ministries of War and Justice sent an investigatory team under American leadership. Rankin suggested that if the story proved accurate, the United States should expose the mass murder and take the initiative in the propaganda war against the communists.[23]

But the information gathered at Roumeli did not confirm a massacre. Despite the testimonies of three witnesses about multiple murders, the team found only two bodies. The officer in charge of the investigation, however, insisted that the lack of evidence did not exonerate the guerrillas. The army had failed to safeguard the area after discovering the bodies, causing him to believe that "the children originally were there and that they were since removed by radio instructions and dumped into snow crevices in Ghiona, where no one will ever find them."[24]

The State Department's advisers remained skeptical about the Greek government's most extreme charges pertaining to the children, even while they knew that only a few instances of forced abduction were enough to undermine the people's faith in their leaders. British and American sources in Greece and within the "iron-curtain area" believed that guerrilla propaganda had twisted the original purpose of the evacuation effort to draw praise for humanitarianism while terrorizing Greek loyalists. Marshall concluded that the guerrillas had taken a few thousand youths from Greece, some by force from loyalist families, but the majority from the "guerrilla infested area, where they constituted [a] welfare problem for Markos, and departed with more or less willing consent [of the] slavic minority or communist parents." The child removal program appeared to be more "convenience and psychological warfare than planned 'genocide,' but [was] of course no less reprehensible for that reason."[25]

Members of the intelligence community in Washington believed that the Kremlin was linked in some uncertain way with the abductions, and that its purpose was to promote unrest injurious to the American aid program. Although no reports had appeared of active involvement by the Soviets, the analysts suspected them of at least an indirect role. It seemed "reasonable to assume that all action in support of Markos takes place with the prior knowledge and approval of Moscow and with the participation of Soviet coordinators on the spot." The Soviets intended to keep Greece in a "constant state of turmoil" in an effort to obstruct economic stability and "undermine Greek morale." The objectives of the "war of attrition" in Greece were to erode faith in the Athens government, drain American sources, and facilitate a communist takeover.[26] By implication, the analysts seemed to say, the

Soviets tacitly approved the child evacuation program because it interfered with the Truman Doctrine.

In retrospect, the growing division between Tito and the Cominform raises questions about the assumption that the Soviets had some degree of control over the evacuation program. There were signs of discontent among communist leaders, but no one in Washington at that time could have been sure about the extent of the rift. Events were happening too quickly in the Balkans to allow a careful analysis of whether great changes were under way in the Soviets' alliance system. For the time being, the wisest approach was to observe what was happening while relying upon the standard presumptions about communist behavior. With understandable reason, more than a few observers preferred to believe that virtually no decision could take place without Stalin's approval.

Whether or not the Soviet Union was involved in Markos's efforts to remove the children, the Truman administration recognized the wisdom in averting a confrontation with the Kremlin and working through the UN. Proof of Soviet complicity was not available (even if it did exist), and there was no way to establish that the motive was to disrupt Greece and undermine the Truman Doctrine. Any bold American action (and there were no practical steps to consider) would have subjected the administration to charges of blatant intervention in Balkan affairs; worse, such action could have precipitated a greater crisis. If the Soviets bore any responsibility for the abductions, they had either devised or merely approved another ingenious weapon in the new kind of war being waged in Greece. If they had had nothing to do with the program, they were in the position of exploiting the results. The only feasible alternative left to the United States was the UN.

Disclosure of the Balkan committee's findings in May indicated that even within the UN only one action was possible—an appeal for the repatriation of only those youths taken against their will. The State Department was not happy with this approach. In a dispatch released to the press in late June, Marshall explained that even in the cases of children who went voluntarily, their "protracted retention" was "contrary to the accepted moral standards of international conduct." He found it "difficult to understand the 'humanitarianism' of harboring foreign children of uncertain family status without having the means to care for them, and of refusing their repatriation because of political considerations."[27] The White House realized, however, that the inability to prove kidnapping severely restricted its response.

But this appeal, no matter how soundly based in morality, was not enough for Americans following the controversy. The Truman administration came under public pressure to condemn the abductions and demand the restoration of all of the children. *Time* magazine featured an article that contained a picture of fifteen Greek children over the caption "Abductions for instruction" and which quoted Lenin: "Give us the child for eight years, and it will be a Bolshevist forever." The *New York Times* carried a front-page story by Cyrus L. Sulzberger, who asserted that Markos's purpose was to establish a

Slavophone minority in Greece grounded in "new ideologies" acquired in communist education camps. Expressions of indignation also came from boy and girl scout organizations, whose members protested the inhumane treatment of fellow youths.[28]

The Greek government likewise thought the American policy inadequate and prepared to tie in the Soviet Union with kidnapping charges brought before the General Assembly. In late March 1948 Ambassador Vassili Dendramis in Washington handed William Baxter, specialist in Greek, Turkish, and Iranian affairs, a draft note concerning the child removals which the Greek delegation intended to take before the UN. For added impact, Dendramis wanted the note sent to the UN secretary-general at the same time the Greek Foreign Office published the text and forwarded copies to the UN committee and all foreign missions in Athens. This approach would exert pressure on those countries holding the youths in "protective custody" to permit repatriation.[29]

The State Department advised against this effort and managed to quiet the issue—but only for a time. Before Baxter forwarded the Greek government's proposal to his superiors, he sought to avert a confrontation with the Soviets by making several alterations in the note. The Greek government, according to the draft, condemned "Soviet Communism" ["Soviet" struck] for a "diabolical international conspiracy" designed to kidnap their children. Radios in "Soviet dominated" [both deleted] Belgrade, Sofia, Bucharest, Budapest, and Tirana had announced the children's arrival. The purposes of the abductions, the note asserted, were to scare the Greek people into supporting the guerrillas and to increase the government's refugee burden by driving villagers into the cities. "In the long run the Communist objective is to warp the minds of the kidnapped children of Greece in order that they may become agents in the enslavement of their native land."[30] Without proof for the allegations, Baxter saw the necessity of eliminating references to the Soviet Union. Moreover, the Greek government was still unable to establish that the actions were kidnappings and not evacuations based on humanitarian considerations. The State Department feared that such charges brought before the UN would raise questions about the character of a government that would make such serious charges without having supporting evidence. But even more important, a revived controversy over the children would turn attention from the real issues of the war.

The guerrillas' removals of Greek children posed a major dilemma for the United States. On the one side, the Truman administration had a public commitment to Greece and believed that stability in that country was vital to the success of the Truman Doctrine. On the other side, the White House could not alienate Yugoslavia, which was, according to the Greek government, a major perpetrator of the abductions. The State Department was probably correct in believing that the program had originated solely to evacuate those Greek children in danger of war and starvation. But it also seems possible that the guerrillas had exploited the emotional reaction in an attempt to undermine the Greek people's faith in their government. From there the matter became enormously complicated. The Greek government charged that the removals were kidnappings designed to destroy Greece by genocide, leaving the Mediterranean and Balkan peninsula open to slavic-communist infiltration. Each side in the civil war had apparently exploited the act in an effort to put the other in the worst possible light. In the emotional atmosphere of civil war, both sides had developed well-conceived policies of psychological warfare, making any charge believable and therefore conducive to deeper American involvement.

During the early part of 1948, the speculations by Washington of deteriorating relations between Yugoslavia and the Soviet Union precluded any action stronger than an appeal to humanitarianism. The Truman administration had to maintain a low-key posture. Not only would a call for repatriation on humanitarian grounds allow the United States to take a stand which was morally unquestionable but it would keep the White House out of Balkan affairs while providing an opportunity to widen the suspected rift in the Soviet alliance system with the enticement of American economic aid to Yugoslavia.[31] Only a victory in the Greek war would resolve the controversy over the children.

CHAPTER

9

Toward the Spring Offensive of 1948

Shortly after General Van Fleet took command in late February 1948, the deputy chief of the Greek General Staff, Lieutenant General Stylianos Kitri-lakis, presented him a study describing the war as "unconventional, many-sided and simultaneously civil and international." The guerrillas received help from a significant part of the population—about 150,000 people, including women and young males—who comprised the "reserve and potential army" and followed the "KKE line consciously and actively." A large number of Greeks—the "fellow travellers"—were not communists but were "so confused in their ideological thinking" that they became supporters. The rural people were passive: they would not fight the guerrillas, nor would they provide the army with information. The government in Athens had to convince its people that this was not a struggle against dissidents, but a war aided by outsiders and threatening to the nation.[1]

The central paradox in this kind of war was that even though the Greek government's professed objective was to restore democracy as soon as practicable, the country's democratic tradition itself weakened the war effort. In a declared war, proof of guilt was not required to arrest and incarcerate suspects. But this type of conflict had the mistaken appearance of a mere domestic quarrel that necessitated evidence of subversion before legal proceedings could begin. The enemy exploited the protection offered by the "peace-time laws of a democracy," making the government's counter-measures appear to be persecution. "Ideas and principles should be respected in a democratic society but it would be suicidal on the part of a democratic state to allow its enemies to take advantage of the civic liberties it offers in order to destroy these very liberties." In war the only rule can be survival.[2]

Another feature of the war that was difficult to counteract was its fifth-column activity. Communists held state positions in the capital and provinces. They comprised that "mysterious force so often responsible for certain characteristic administrative lapses, and unexplainable cases of inertness, procrastination and irregularity." The guerrillas had access to secret documents and knew beforehand what actions the government planned, whereas the government's information was "somewhere drowned mysteriously without ever reaching its destination." To clear the "internal front" of communists, the army must destroy their "self-defense units"—those supply and intelligence agencies bearing respectable titles and whose members laid mines, engaged in sabotage, and secured recruits.[3]

This staff study indicated that not only had Greek military leaders grasped the multifaceted nature of the war, they had finally developed the aggressive attitude long advocated by British and American observers: the way to defeat guerrillas was through brutal, relentless pursuit. The army must launch a sustained assault along the northern border, followed by an occupation to prevent the "recontamination" of the area before public security forces took over. The army must also defeat those guerrillas in the interior who were operating as "highway brigands." As Kitrilakis later declared: "We have flushed the hares. Now we must hunt them down and kill them." Above all, the army must "inspire [the guerrilla] with terror and with the feeling that there is no place in the country where he may stay in safety by night or by day."[4]

But a gap remained between intention and action. The same drive had to permeate the ranks, a development which depended on finding field leaders capable of providing tactical and logistical advice and of inspiring their men to sacrifice everything for victory. The army had ample matériel and was slowly acquiring discipline and training. Morale was still in the rebuilding process, however, continually hampered by fifth-column and terrorist activities. The spring offensive would demonstrate whether America's operational advice would have its desired effect.

I

As the Greek army prepared for the northern offensive, the Truman administration continued to explore the ramifications of its global strategy of combatting communism. A U.S. Army planning committee warned that if Greece fell and the Soviets threatened to seize the Middle East's oil deposits, the Americans and British must be prepared for the "timely and proper plugging of oil producing wells in the Middle East and for destroying the transportation, refining and loading facilities by demolition." The National Security Council called for compulsory military service, an updated arms industry, and continued atomic superiority. The United States must help non-communist nations build their own military forces by providing them with machine tools, technical knowledge, and military goods. The government in Washington should encourage its citizens to establish non-communist trade unions in those nations that affected America's security. Finally, the United States should engage in a "vigorous and effective ideological campaign" and a "coordinated program to support underground resistance movements in countries behind the iron curtain, including the USSR." Marshall believed that a program of universal military training would prove that the United States refused to retreat from communism. The nation must also emphasize the Marshall Plan (which Congress enacted in early April 1948) and the Western Union (or Brussels Pact of 1948) as "anti-communist association[s] of states" designed to assure others of America's support, as well as to convince Americans that their security was at stake.[5]

This continuing analysis of the nation's foreign policy threatened to reopen the debate over the use of troops in Greece. The Department of State had inquired about the legality of such action, and Ernest Gross from the legal office concluded that sending troops to Greece would be lawful "from the standpoint of international law." After citing instances in Latin America and the Far East where the United States had sent troops, he declared that "forces of all branches of the armed services have been used in foreign non-enemy territory at different times to further United States interests. While the type of forces used has no doubt been dictated by the nature of the function to be performed, it seems to be a fact that marines have most frequently been used in peace time to perform quasi-police functions or to defend United States interests abroad as distinguished from the carrying on of combat operations." The use of marines would minimize "the psychological impact" on the American public.[6]

The troop question suddenly lost popularity, however, when the British informed the Americans of an important decision: they would retain their forces in Greece for an indefinite period. At a conference in London that Van Fleet attended, members of both the British Joint Chiefs of Staff and the Foreign Office inquired about the use of American soldiers in Greece. Van Fleet emphasized the importance of maintaining British troops along with their mission, and he artfully evaded the question by replying that "American troops for Greece was a matter for the American Congress to decide." The United States won a reprieve from a hard decision when Lord Arthur Tedder, who was marshall of the Royal Air Force, chief of the Air Staff, and presiding officer over the meeting, stated that despite criticism in England, his government had no plans to remove or reduce its troops in Greece. Tedder had earlier emphasized in a staff meeting that the presence of British soldiers lifted Greek morale. Bevin agreed and noted the necessity of cooperating with the Americans in establishing Greek stability. A high-ranking British diplomatic official emphasized the aim of "*not* joint but parallel policies in the Middle East."[7]

The British troop retention allowed the United States to continue its emphasis on military aid and operational advice. Every kind of practical reason argued against sending American troops—particularly the insufficient number of men in uniform—but had the British decided to pull out their soldiers, the Truman administration would have been forced to make the decision of either advocating a politically dangerous mobilization program or undermining the cornerstone of the nation's foreign policy by abandoning Greece. If only for symbolic reasons, a Western troop presence was essential to upholding Greek morale and preventing a further erosion of support for the government. Moreover, the lack of commitment under pressure would have endangered support for America among its allies as well as within those countries still undecided about which direction to take in the Cold War. The British decision bought time—time for American advisers to upgrade the morale and the performance of the Greek army by stressing discipline and training in the use of newly arrived weapons from the United States.

The British move had relieved the Truman administration of another major concern about having to send soldiers: even a small contingent might leave the impression that the United States was preparing for war and convince the Soviets to take advantage of their postwar military improvements to expand across Europe and into the Middle East. Although the CIA and other intelligence agencies believed that the Russians would not resort to direct military action during 1948, this prognosis could change if the United States made some move that the Kremlin could interpret as an attack on either the USSR or its allies. The outcome could be disastrous for the West. Postwar reorganization of the Soviet army had improved its mobility, firepower, and leadership. The air force was equipped with jets and long-range bombers. Improvements in radar and the acquisition of jet interceptors had allowed the Soviets to install an air defense system along their eastern and western borders. Evidence suggested that they were developing long-range, high-speed submarines. Though the Soviets would probably not begin a military action until they had atomic bombs or achieved economic stability, they would alter their thinking if they suspected the United States of preparing for a strike.[8]

With the British troops still in place, the White House remained convinced that victory in Greece and in Europe depended upon the careful and restrained use of military means toward achieving the ultimate goal of economic stability. As long as the United States did not take on the appearance of an aggressor, the administration believed that the Soviets would continue their indirect tactics of trying to obstruct the Marshall Plan by disrupting life in France, Italy, and other countries. The Soviets realized that an attempt to seize Western Europe and the Near East entailed great risks, but these dangers would pale in significance if the United States appeared ready to attack. The Joint Chiefs of Staff intended to reassess the matter in the autumn of 1948 to determine America's military strength at that time, the range of its commitments elsewhere, and the likelihood of evoking an overt response by either the Soviet Union or its allies. General Albert C. Wedemeyer, director of Plans and Operations in Washington, likewise warned that

the Truman administration had to avoid any unilateral actions and to consider the Greek matter in relation to other matters. Forrestal was concerned
about letting the Soviets "miscalculate the degree of our determination to
resist further Soviet encroachment."[9]

Though the chances of sending troops were remote, the Truman administration could not share this information with the Greek government because
of the certain deleterious effect on morale. In early March, during secret
testimony before the House Foreign Affairs Committee, Marshall declared
that even if the United States sent a token force, these men would either have
to be backed up or withdrawn "ignominiously" if the Soviets countered with
men of their own. Marshall remarked that he was under the same pressure he
had experienced as army chief of staff—to send soldiers to several trouble
spots in the world at the same time. He had to resist then and now because of
the nation's limited military strength. Major General Arthur M. Harper,
deputy commanding general of USAGG, was likewise opposed to sending
combat forces to Greece. From a strategic viewpoint, such a commitment
would be a "mousetrap" operation having no beneficial effect on the rest of
the Mediterranean. Henderson noted that even though the "general line of
thinking" was not favorable to troops, the United States could reveal nothing
to the Greek government because of the certain negative impact on morale.
When Republican Senator Henry Cabot Lodge, Jr., tried to put Marshall on
public record that the administration would not send combat troops, Marshall explained the ramifications and the senator dropped the matter.[10]

The Truman administration kept its options open, adhering to the policy
of flexibility advocated from the beginning of the Greek crisis. In every form
of assistance—whether economic or military—the White House refused to
lock itself into a position that prevented either the escalation or de-escalation
of involvement. If never an attractive alternative, the use of combat troops
remained a last resort as long as the British withdrawal seemed imminent. But
now that the British had elected to stay, the issue seemed virtually dead. Their
contribution enabled the White House to concentrate on other means that, in
conjunction with the British troops, might halt the communist threat in
Greece.

America's global strategy rested on the principle of flexibility, but the
White House concern about the broad range of Cold War problems had an
unexpected harmful effect on Greek army morale. From Washington's perspective, Greece was only one part of an overall strategy designed to undercut
the spread of communism. But in imposing so many restrictions on its
involvement and in placing so much emphasis on the relationship of Greek
affairs to events elsewhere, the Truman administration inadvertently convinced more than a few Greek leaders that the only thing that mattered was
how the war affected America's struggle with the Soviet Union. More than
once, Greek spokesmen expressed fear that their American (and British) allies
might abandon them and turn to some other problem area. When a *Time*

correspondent asked a Greek lieutenant about the lack of spirit among his men, he shrugged and replied: "This war in Greece is a battle between the United States and Russia. It happens that it's being fought here. That is our bad luck. But you can't expect us to fight your battle single-handed—at least not with the old spirit."[11]

The global thrust of America's foreign policy nonetheless seemed justified as reports grew of increased foreign involvement in the guerrilla war. French sources told of three international divisions quartered along the Greek border, one each in Yugoslavia, Albania, and Bulgaria, and totaling about 45,000 men. *Time* magazine cited State Department reports that an international brigade (again, never substantiated) of 30,000 Greeks, French, Italians, Czechs, Poles, Germans, and Spaniards were ready to invade Greece out of Albania and Yugoslavia. The French military attaché in Belgrade saw thirty-five Yugoslav officers in Tirana, along with an unspecified number of Russian officers and about a hundred Soviet doctors and surgeons. Despite Tito's disclaimers, the Yugoslav government continued to provide the guerrillas with sanctuary, along with economic, diplomatic, and military aid. The most pronounced military preparations were in Albania. Observers noted newly formed combat units of partisans, heavy truck traffic south, an increased number of training camps, and an enlargement of the airfield at Oortcha. The French mission in Tirana reported the departure of Albanian army officers and the southerly movement of cavalry equipment. One night the police halted Albanian reservists in Tirana en route south by truck convoy. The French thought military operations would soon begin along the Albanian-Greek border.[12]

The threat of expanded international involvement in the Greek war added to the urgency of Van Fleet's tasks. To lift morale, he had to establish personal contact between the Greek commanders and their men in the field. Van Fleet and the Greek chief of staff, General Dimitrios Yiadjis, spent considerable time in the north, encouraging the men to believe that they were capable of defeating the guerrillas. Because of the increased personnel in the National Defense Corps, they explained, the army could resume the offensive and leave the occupation duties to the corps. Van Fleet discovered that in the Peloponnese operations, no one had attempted to determine potential problems by inspecting the mountainous areas northwest of Tripolis. He made his way into the Peloponnese, where he recommended several changes in Greek command that would assure aggressive leadership. If these alterations had no results, he would call for more troops by the beginning of May.[13]

Another complication, Van Fleet noted, was that the war had "to be fought with a great deal of protocol." The outcome rested almost as much on bureaucratic procedures as on successful combat. Meetings were interminable, leaving him little time to be in the field. His agenda was filled with conferences called by the embassy, the aid mission, and the numerous ministers of the Greek government. Once a decision was reached, the British missions had to be notified so that only one advisory opinion would go to the Greek armed forces. But coordination was difficult to maintain, for the British had five different agencies—the British Military Mission, the Royal Air Force Mission, the Royal Naval Mission, the Military Training Mission, and the British Police Mission—and they operated independently of each other. After adhering to these intricate and time-consuming procedures, Van Fleet had to explain everything again to the Greek commanders and their staffs.[14]

The American command needed more men to take care of responsibilities not directly related to field operations. Van Fleet recommended raising the group's ceiling to 299, consisting of 274 for the army, 18 for the air force, and 7 for the navy. Griswold agreed that the move would release the officers to perform their advisory role. The "leading factor in improved GNA [Greek National Army] morale and demonstrated fighting ability has been [the] presence [of] US Army officers in [the] field as advisers." The army chief of staff in Washington approved the new personnel ceiling in late April.[15]

Van Fleet also had to rectify certain administrative aspects of the military advisory program. Although the American and British missions had reached an agreement in January 1948 assigning operational and logistical duties to the former and organization and training to the latter, the agreement had not been formalized. A blurring of responsibilities had resulted, leading to confusion in the allies' relationship. The British War Office had recently assigned seventy-five more officers to Greek army units in the field. But many of the new men held higher rank than did the Americans at the division level. General Rawlins and his successor at the British Military Mission, General Ernest E. Down, both had suggested a merger of the American and British groups. Van Fleet did not like the proposal because the British favored a detailed list of responsibilities for the men in the field, whereas he wanted America's officers to have broad lines of authority that would allow flexibility in meeting unexpected problems. The British feared that such an approach could lead to the Greek army's receiving conflicting advice. Van Fleet thought the solution might be a combined planning staff in Athens in which American, British, and Greek leaders would discuss proposals before reaching decisions.[16]

Van Fleet sought an arrangement that would assure Anglo-American coordination in dispensing advice to the Greek army. The heads of the British missions had received a directive in January ordering them to avoid participation in combat. Though free to cooperate with USAGG in advising Greek leaders, no mission members could "IN ANY CIRCUMSTANCES . . . take any executive part [in] operations" or "engage in political activities of any kind." When Van Fleet learned of this British directive, he sought an agreement (secured in mid-May) that guaranteed cooperation. The American and British missions would work separately, but they would attempt to offer single advisory opinions to the Greek army. USAGG would focus on supplies, logistics, and operations, whereas the British Military Mission would be responsible for organization and training. Members of both missions could enter the combat zones, but they could take "no executive part" in the campaigns. The objective was to maintain unity before the Greeks.[17]

Van Fleet was also concerned about having too many American and British advisers at the division level and none below. He attempted to have some assigned to lower units so that the number of British officers at lower levels would be equal to that of American officers. Van Fleet also suggested having both American and British advisers at the Greek General Staff and corps level, but he wanted to assign one team, American or British, to lower units. He knew that both Congress and the State Department believed that advisory groups had been limited to division level or above, and yet he saw justification for seeking additional officers to work with the regiments and brigades. Wedemeyer, however, notified Van Fleet that in view of the information furnished to Congress and the State Department, the White House could not comply with his request.[18]

Despite the administration's opposition, it is doubtful that American advisers stayed away from the lower units. Legal bases existed for working with the soldiers as well as with the officers. The Joint Chiefs of Staff directive creating the military advisory group in Greece emphasized that contact with the Greek army would be "restricted normally to the higher levels." An added provision allowed exceptions "when considered necessary to carry out the functions outlined herein, in order to place personnel in any channel in the Greek armed forces to advise and observe operations." Van Fleet surely understood the political dangers in seeking congressional support for allowing American advisers to accompany Greek soldiers. But more important than this consideration, he recognized the impracticality of extending advice at the division level without having firsthand awareness of the problems confronting the soldiers. In the President's report to Congress in May, he left the matter open to interpretation by declaring that U.S. officers accompanied Greek "operational units" in the field but did not take part in combat or command.[19]

The "almost final chapter" in preparation for the spring offensive, Van Fleet noted with satisfaction, came when Greek armed forces underwent a major reorganization that resulted in a unified command. The Supreme National Defense Council granted the army chief of staff full authority to carry out the war. Too many unqualified lieutenant generals remained on the active list, Van Fleet thought, but legislation took care of that problem. The American aid mission drafted the remedy, the Greek Parliament put it into final form, and the king affixed his signature. At a meeting of the Council, with Prime Minister Sophoulis and Deputy Prime Minister Tsaldaris present, all lieutenant generals, except for Yiadjis, were placed on the retirement roll. That same afternoon, the Higher Military Council recommended eight men as major generals. Four days later the Supreme National Defense Council approved the list.[20]

With these changes in place, Van Fleet was confident that "Operation Dawn," scheduled to begin in April, would succeed in clearing an estimated

3,000 guerrillas from the Roumeli area of central Greece and constitute the first step toward victory. To raise morale, the king would soon leave for the Peloponnese and then to Lamia to witness the beginning of operations. According to plans coordinated by the Americans, British, and Greeks, a force of 30,000 men, supported by planes and artillery, would close in on the guerrillas from three sides, attempting to encircle them. Van Fleet assured Washington: "Keep those Soviets or their satellites from crossing the border, and we will mop up everything in Greece right up to the border this year."[21]

Although Van Fleet was pleased with the first reports from Roumeli, he knew that despite the Greek military's reluctance expressed as early as March, more severe measures—perhaps napalm or incendiary bombs— would be needed in the offensive. The king visited the front in late April, where Van Fleet joined him and remained for about a week. Van Fleet was encouraged by the army's performance; the Greek soldier was "all right." Leadership from the top down to the divisions appeared sound, although improvement was still needed at the brigade, battalion, and company levels. As the war grew in ferocity, the American advisers debated for a considerable time before approving the use of napalm. Greek spokesmen, however, looked with "disfavor" on the idea because of the danger of forest fires and the fear of retaliation in kind from the guerrillas. The Americans nonetheless in May assigned a team of six men to train the air force in deploying the substance from the Spitfires.[22]

By late May the army broke the guerrillas' hold on Roumeli—only to see them regroup as the soldiers failed to complete the clearing operation. Casualty figures were not exact, but the guerrillas suffered many more losses than did the army. The National Defense Corps attempted to restore security. But the guerrillas continued their activities and by mid-July had used forced recruiting to raise their strength to about 1,400.[23]

The Greek forces proceeded to the second stage of the offensive—"Operation Crown," which was to begin during the first week in June with an assault by six divisions on the guerrillas' headquarters in the Grammos Mountains. That area was the backbone of the enemy; if Grammos fell, the Greek army could concentrate more commando units in the Peloponnese. If the commandos cleared that area, the army could prepare for winter fighting in the north.[24]

For the first time in the war, the government's forces appeared ready for a concentrated offensive. Van Fleet seemed to have succeeded in smoothing the organization of the Greek military establishment, in promoting the installation of officers capable of courageous leadership, and in raising morale by demonstrating to soldiers in the field that they were not isolated from the government in Athens. By that time, the American mission had furnished the Greek soldiers with more than 2,800 vehicles, 7,000 tons of ammunition, and 75,000 weapons, including machine guns, mortars, and rifles. Soon to arrive would be a large number of howitzers.[25] The army had always had superior numbers and equipment; it now possessed the will to win.

II

Had the Greek government and its Anglo-American allies been able to focus on the military aspects of the struggle, the way to victory would have been clear. But the effort was complicated by seemingly unrelated factors that kept emerging as obstacles to success. The war on the home front (both in the United States and in Greece) was as critical as that in the field. Anarchy seemed imminent in Athens, as the government appeared incapable of keeping order. The impact of the guerrillas' fifth-column activities was such that nearly all towns and villages had a network of communist agents, spies, saboteurs, and propagandists.[26] In the meantime, terrorist activities had reached a new level—and not coincidentally with the army's drive north. Nothing seemed safe from attack—including Van Fleet, Griswold, leading Greek public figures, the Greek government's policies against the enemy, and the newsmen who covered the war.

Frederick Ayer, who was in charge of security forces attached to the American mission in Greece, had learned that the KKE's leaders had sent out orders to assassinate at least one important Greek figure and perhaps one American leader. High on the KKE's list was Christos Ladas, the left-wing member of the Center party and minister of justice who had supported the government's execution of prisoners. Indeed, on May 1 Ladas was assassinated at the entrance of an Athens church, drawing international attention to the heightened level of terror in Greece. That same day the Democratic Army radio in Belgrade praised the act and appealed to members of the KKE in Athens to kill Sophoulis, Tsaldaris, and the minister of public order, Constantine Rendis. Ayer had earlier recommended bodyguards for both Van Fleet and Griswold. But despite the Greek government's claim to have uncovered two assassination plots with them as targets, they refused. However, when a hundred pounds of TNT were removed from a spot just in front of a northbound train with Van Fleet on it, they reconsidered. From then on, both men consented to protection.[27]

The drive for vengeance by the Greek government was clear during the Easter holidays; authorities made a number of preventive arrests and on May 4 began executing communist prisoners. The Soviet government joined a host of Western nations in protest. Three days later Sophoulis assured a reporter that the government was not engaged in acts of revenge and that it had "decided to clear out the files of all those sentenced to death long before the murder of Christos Ladas. It was also decided that all the files on which proceedings had ended, including rejections of appeals for pardon, be forwarded to the public prosecutor to order the execution of the sentenced, according to the law. No change has been made in these proceedings." That same day Rendis denied to another reporter that the mass executions were acts of vengeance. The government, he explained, had implemented a nationwide martial law and ordered the executions of those sentenced to death for crimes committed before 1944. Despite these official disclaimers, the message was unmistakable: in a three-day span, 238 resistance members were shot and their bodies scattered in every town in Greece. Court proceedings were hurried to facilitate the execution of almost 3,000 more by the middle of the month.[28]

The multifaceted nature of the struggle became more evident as the Truman administration had to counter growing criticism in the United States of the Greek government's recent actions. An editorial in *Nation* called the executions atrocities, and a New York City Council member complained to President Truman of the "Nazi like execution" of over a hundred Greeks and of the "threatened execution" of more than eight hundred more. How could the United States support such a government? New York Representative Kenneth B. Keating asked Marshall about charges of mass executions. Eleanor Roosevelt, wife of the former President and now chairman of the UN Human Rights Commission, forwarded to the secretary of state a telegram from the American Council for a Democratic Greece which indignantly inquired whether the executions were part of a mass reprisal for the Ladas assassination. Petitioners from Illinois expressed objections, the American Labor Party in New York City protested against executions of "Greek Democrats," and the National Maritime Union, comprised of 90,000 members, pleaded with Truman to intercede in behalf of "Greek Patriots" victimized by "fascist brutality."[29]

The White House had difficulty answering critics. To the British, Marshall admitted that the Greek government may have speeded the legal process as retaliation for Ladas's assassination, but he thought that those executed had been convicted murderers denied freedom only after a long series of appeals. Other State Department spokesmen assured Americans that the only ones put to death were those found guilty of the most heinous crimes. Even then, the offenders had the right to go through a lengthy process of judicial appeal. In Athens, Rankin reported that the executions resulted from fair trials and that they constituted warnings to the guerrillas that they could not escape punishment. Marshall recommended ignoring a Soviet note criticizing the Greek government. Markos probably ordered Ladas's assassination under higher communist orders "as [a] diabolically clever, double-edged propaganda weapon." To calm the uproar, Marshall urged the Greek government to approve the executions of only those guilty of the most atrocious crimes.[30]

In mid-May the Greek conflict expanded into a new kind of savagery when the body of the well-known CBS news correspondent for the Middle East, George Polk, was found floating face down in the shallow edges of the most heavily trafficked section of Salonika Bay. Polk, eyes bandaged shut and bound hand and foot with heavy rope, had been shot at close range in the back of the head. His body showed no other injuries and no signs of resistance, suggesting that he had willingly submitted to being tied but then was executed gangland style. His assailants had left his money and papers intact, and the only items missing were his small black address book and his war correspondent's accreditation card. Authorities surmised that the killing had taken place at sea but that the body had been thrown close to shore to ensure quick discovery. The police in Salonika soon received an envelope containing Polk's accreditation card. The murderers wanted to leave no doubt about the identity of their victim.[31]

More than one observer believed that Polk's murder was not a guerrilla action, but a political execution by right-wing supporters of the Greek government. British news correspondent Kenneth Matthews thought so, as did *Nation*, which termed the circumstances of the death "ominously political." The American Council for a Democratic Greece urged President Truman to send a special investigatory team. The Standing Committee of UN Correspondents called on UN Secretary-General Trygve Lie to bring the matter before the UN's Human Rights Commission. The evidence for political motivations seemed convincing. Polk had been outspoken in his opposition to the regime and monarchy as fascist. In *Harper's Magazine*, he claimed that "anyone daring to criticize government policies was likely to be labelled 'Communist' and given a oneway ticket to a barren Aegean island." Polk proclaimed his views in news broadcasts and in writings; in turn, he had been denounced as favoring the guerrillas. To the American columnist, Drew Pearson, Polk had told of threats from reactionaries within the Greek government: "The right wing is trying to get a number of us discredited or removed from Greece. . . . [T]here are a number of vague hints that 'somebody is likely to get hurt.'" Polk's widow declared that both the police and right-wing extremists had threatened him just before the killing. The editor of *Nation* urged the State Department and Griswold to investigate the matter. That sentiment was repeated by Senator Lodge, who cited a number of editorial opinions from newspapers all over the country that called the murder a threat to journalists worldwide. Lodge announced in the Senate chamber that he was asking the secretary of state to arrange an inquiry.[32]

Shortly before his death, Polk had claimed that he was about to make contact with Markos. All reporters in Athens dreamed of such an interview, but the increasing bitterness of the war made it difficult for anyone to cross the ever-changing battle lines. Polk was persistent, however, and eventually assured friends in America that he had made "contacts with contacts" and soon would meet the guerrilla chieftain. Mystery surrounded the last days of Polk's life. After arriving by plane in Salonika on May 7, he visited the American consulate and then checked into the Astoria Hotel. The following evening, Polk hastily left the hotel. No one could remember seeing him afterward, even though he was decidedly recognizable—a uniquely featured man, tall, light-haired, visiting a city that regarded strangers with suspicion. A little over a week later, a boatman came across his body in the bay.[33]

Americans were outraged. The Department of State assured the Senate Foreign Relations Committee that the Greek government was making every effort to find the guilty parties. Journalists in Greece shared the department's concern that if the leaders in Athens failed to find the murderers, freedom of the press would cease to exist. CBS newsman Howard K. Smith concluded

that the act was a "deliberate execution." "There is no doubt that the murder
. . . was a cold, deliberate political demonstration, planned to be spectacular,
planned to intimidate. If the murderers are not discovered, an invisible but
inevitable pressure of intimidation will rest on every American correspondent
abroad." Resentment swelled among reporters when Greek authorities speculated that the reasons for Polk's death lay in his "personal life." But the
authorities could find no evidence for this theory. The Greek government
then attributed the murder to the communists as part of their effort to bring
disfavor to leaders in Athens. This charge was so senseless, Matthews
claimed, that no one believed it.[34]

Many observers suspected the Greek government of a cover-up. When its
officers did not seem inclined to conduct an impartial inquiry, the Overseas
Writers' Association (headed by Walter Lippmann) offered a $10,000 reward
to anyone with information on Polk's assailant and asked William Donovan,
head of the Office of Strategic Services during World War II, to conduct an
investigation. Though at first receiving little cooperation in Athens, he eventually was able to assure American journalists that the Greek government had
consented to help. The authorities, he declared, were "handling the case
satisfactorily." But three top CBS staff figures—Howard K. Smith, Edward
R. Murrow, and Don Hollenbeck—were skeptical. Donovan's chief investigator, Lieutenant Colonel James Kellis of the U.S. Air Force, soon reported "an
attempted right-wing cover-up" stemming from both Greek officials and their
American supporters. Americans in Greece "were concerned that if the extreme Right committed this murder and were discovered," the news would
"upset our aid program to Greece." Kellis said he came under pressure from
Rankin, the Greek police, and others "to pin this murder on the Communists." When he resisted, Rankin angrily urged the investigator's recall, and a
short time afterward the Air Force complied.[35]

Only the threat of direct American involvement in the case led to its
apparent resolution. When a month passed with no arrests, Marshall announced that he was preparing to leave for Athens and inquire into the matter
himself. Timed on the night of Marshall's scheduled arrival, the Greek
minister of justice, George Melas, called a news conference to announce that
his people had broken the case. They had identified the handwriting on the
envelope containing Polk's accreditation card as that of a sixty-eight-year-old
widow, who had written the note at the bidding of her son, Gregorios
Stachtopoulos, a newsman and alleged communist employed by a local paper
in Salonika, the *Makedonia*. He confessed to serving as liaison between Polk
and the two men who killed him: Adam Mouzenides, former communist
member of Parliament who had done the shooting, and Evangelos Vasvanas,
also a communist and an accomplice.[36]

The judicial proceedings threatened to become a travesty. A surprise
witness, Nicolas Zaferiou, who was a former member of the Soviet police
force, appeared at the opening day of the trial to declare that the slaying had
been planned in Markos's headquarters in an effort to stop American aid to

Greece by making it appear that the rightists had killed Polk. At one point in the trial, anti-communist demonstrators marched in front of the court building and forced a cancellation of the afternoon session to avoid trouble. Greek authorities could not locate Mouzenides and Vasvanas, even though both of the men's wives were questioned. Only Stachtopoulos and his mother went to trial. Despite stories that the two accomplices were in the mountains, guerrilla leaders declared that Mouzenides had died in the war long before Polk's murder and that the Greek police had disposed of Vasvanas some time ago— "as the government well knew," Matthews asserted. The government, however, claimed that Mouzenides was alive and in Salonika on the night of Polk's murder. To counter the guerrillas' argument that Mouzenides had been killed some time before, the prosecution brought in the accused murderer's brother and sister-in-law, who both testified that he had been in the city the night of the killing. Donovan had followed up this claim by securing a private interview with the two relatives. He was confident that their statements had not come under duress.[37]

Stachtopoulos's testimony bore out the worst guesses of what had happened to Polk. He claimed that the Cominform had plotted Polk's murder, and that the KKE had carried out the execution in an effort to discredit the Greek government, arouse American public opinion, and force an end to the aid program. Stachtopoulos had served as the intermediary between Polk and the two communists who claimed they would take him to Markos. According to Stachtopoulos, he and Polk had taken a taxi to a restaurant on the wharf where a boat was to pick them up at 10 p.m. When the boat arrived, the two men climbed in; Mouzenides was manning the oars. A short distance upstream, they stopped alongshore, and Vasvanas and another man (Nikos) got in. As the boat moved farther from land, the men told Polk he would have to be blindfolded to safeguard the secrecy of Markos's headquarters. Polk consented. Even when the men said they would have to tie his feet and hands, he offered no resistance. Not long afterward, Mouzenides eased behind Polk, pressed a gun against the back of his head, and killed him instantly. "Polk's ghost pursues me night and day," Stachtopoulos emotionally declared in court; "I see him crumpling dead to the bottom of the boat." The men rowed back to the waterfront, where they directed Stachtopoulos to mail Polk's accreditation card to the police.[38]

The results of the trial were peculiar but almost predictable. On April 21, after only three hours of deliberation, the jury convicted Stachtopoulos and sentenced him to a life sentence as an accessory after the fact; his mother was acquitted despite her admission to being an accessory. Mouzenides and Vasvanas, in absentia, were sentenced to death. Donovan thought the trial was "honestly and efficiently conducted." The *New York Times* and the U.S. consul general in Salonika, Raleigh Gibson, agreed.[39]

Matthews, however, raised several questions about the Greek government's involvement. Though Stachtopoulos testified to having ridden with Polk in a taxi, no driver could recall either of the men. Stachtopoulos identified the restaurant in which they had eaten; that establishment did not have lobster and green peas on the menu that night, the foods that a post-mortem investigation revealed as having been Polk's last meal. No questions arose during the trial about the identity of the fifth man who boarded the rowboat with Vasvanas and was with them at the time of the murder. Four Greeks were to have appeared in court to give evidence of Stachtopoulos's character; all four said they were too ill to attend. If the leaders in Athens were not guilty of murder, they had done little to remove suspicion.[40]

Frederick Ayer, however, had participated in the investigation and did not believe the government to be responsible for Polk's death. He discounted the claims by Markos Radio that Vasvanas had not been in Greece at the time of the murder and that Mouzenides had died months before. Ayer explained that he had learned a year after the trial from "absolutely accurate sources" that Vasvanas had been transferred to Prague, and that Mouzenides was in Paris working for the Cominform. Stachtopoulos had insisted (Ayer did not explain how he had gotten this information from Stachtopoulos) that when he took Polk to the boat to meet Mouzenides and Vasvanas, all four men first ate dinner on board—lobster and green peas. Ayer believed that Stachtopoulos was telling the truth; only the coroner and four or five of the Greek government's investigating officers had known the contents of Polk's last meal.[41]

Journalists and other friends of Polk's were irate over what they considered to be a whitewash of the government. Winston Burdett, who had been ordered from his post in Rome to cover the trial for CBS, charged that the whole process was a masquerade to clear the Greek government by hanging the murder on the communists. No one questioned the claim that the communists' sole reason was to discredit Greece and stop American assistance. If the communists murdered Polk, according to the critics, the act would have underlined their terrorist reputation and *strengthened* the aid commitment. The prosecutors' questions were formulated in such a way as to leave no vagueness about the answers. "Who do you think killed George Polk?" "Who had most to gain by killing him and then advertising the murder?" Witnesses had little hesitation in replying that "Communists must have done it." Marquis Childs called the trial a "cover-up," and Irving Gilman termed it "a sham." Another CBS correspondent, Alexander Kendrick, hit upon the fear shared by American and other reporters in Greece: "It was sometimes hard to figure out whether this was a trial for the murder of Polk or a trial *of* Polk and of other foreign correspondents who have tried to report the Greek story objectively. . . . The most shocking thing about some of the testimony was the undercurrent of feeling that the United States had nothing to complain about, because only one American correspondent had been murdered, whereas several others might have been and perhaps should have been."[42]

Questions remain about who was responsible for Polk's death. The only certainty is that those who accused the government did not prove their case. The theory most difficult to refute is that KKE terrorists murdered him, hoping that the government's supporters would be blamed and thereby lead to a disruption of the American aid program. Ayer insisted that the only ones who could profit from the act were the communists. Even though it was not clear who had fired the shot, the bullet under the left ear was the KKE's "standard method of execution." Lippmann never doubted the State Department's belief that the communists had killed Polk, although he noted discrepancies in the evidence that suggested involvement by the Greek government and the CIA. Another theory, also difficult to dismiss, is that set out by Matthews. He attributed the murder to one of the secret nationalist societies then thriving in Greece. A year before, these right-wing extremists had denounced foreign interference in Greek affairs and had shot a member of the Communist party's Central Committee as he walked the streets during daylight. Matthews believed that Polk had been singled out as a communist sympathizer whose death would serve as a warning to others. In civil war, Matthews concluded, "men are killed for their religion, their politics, their wealth, their relations, friends and acquaintances, or simply because they happened to be in the way at the moment."[43]

Whatever the truth of Polk's murder, severe measures taken by the Greek government against the guerrillas and their sympathizers had made it and its supporters vulnerable to charges of repression and murder—even of journalists.

By the end of May the prospects for military success in Greece had improved. Van Fleet had instilled an aggressive spirit among the Greek forces and inspired them to carry the assault to the end. The government's forces had not totally secured Roumeli but were now preparing to hit the guerrillas' headquarters in the Grammos Mountains. The materials necessary for the use of napalm would soon arrive from the United States. The guerrillas were having trouble replacing casualties and had to draw upon reserves in border countries. The National Security Council received a report that outside aid to Markos was diminishing because of "deliberate Soviet policy." The CIA concluded that the Kremlin's failure to help, "after evident preparations to do so," must have been especially discouraging. Surely the guerrillas were experiencing "misgivings" about their communist friends. Perhaps the realization was growing that the Kremlin's goal was not to install Markos in Greece but to use the Greek communists to sap America's strength in the interest of Soviet expansion elsewhere.[44]

In early June Washington began receiving reports that the communists were switching tactics and, as after the setbacks during the December war of 1944, preparing to pursue a political offensive. Sophoulis rejected another peace offer made by Markos over Radio Free Greece in late May. The American ambassador in Belgrade, Cavendish Cannon, thought that Zahariadis's recent return to Greece signified the offer of "Moscow's olive branch." Cannon declared that he would not be surprised if Zahariadis "the politician take[s] [the] foreground and Markos the guerrilla recede[s]." The outcome of the war in Greece would determine the policies of Yugoslavia and other Eastern European countries. Rankin agreed that the military results would have a distinct effect on the Balkans. Cannon and Rankin were doubtless alluding to Tito's growing rift with the Cominform. The guerrillas realized that support for the Soviet Union in this controversy would mean the end of aid from Yugoslavia. In an effort to relieve themselves of having to make a choice between the adversaries, the guerrillas recommended a negotiated settlement of the war in Greece. But Rankin warned that for the Greeks to negotiate now would be appeasement and a sign of weakness; they must not give in to the enemy's peace offensives. The communists were seeking to save their forces for a later campaign and to blunt the impact of the final report by the UN Special Committee on the Balkans. Victory on the battlefield must come *before* negotiations.[45]

The State Department was meanwhile taking steps toward coordinating all aspects of America's involvement in Greece. Griswold resigned as chief of mission, smoothing the way for a new ambassador to become his replacement and hold both positions. For the first time, the ambassador would be responsible for America's political, economic, and military goals in Greece. President Truman asked Henry F. Grady to assume the responsibilities. Then ambassador in India, Grady had had business, economic, and diplomatic experience, and he had headed the Allies' March 1946 observation of Greek elections. He would arrive in Athens in July 1948. As ambassador and chief of mission, Grady would supervise all assistance to the Greeks.[46]

Every sign pointed to victory by the end of the year.

CHAPTER
10

Grammos and Vitsi

I

In June 1948 the Greek army was ready to launch the Grammos offensive ("Operation Crown") into the border area of northwest Greece, followed by the attack on Vitsi, which stretched along the Greek-Albanian-Yugoslav frontier. Many more guerrillas would soon join the 8,000 already in Grammos, a 225-square-mile area that the Joint U.S. Military Advisory and Planning Group called the "main bandit stronghold in Greece" and the "principal center of resistance and main entrance" into the country. The battle would not be easy. Markos's forces held the rugged, mountainous terrain with well-fortified positions surrounded by numerous minefields. If the army broke the resistance and forced the guerrillas to evacuate, it would still have to spend months in searching out stragglers and supplies before turning over the area to the gendarmerie. Furthermore, the army would have to occupy many spots along the border to prevent the guerrillas' re-entry and to put an end to outside involvement. Without these mopping-up operations, the result would be similar to the previous year's campaign in which the government failed to take adequate security measures, thus undoing the successes in the field and necessitating the present offensive.[1]

Plans called for a four-week campaign intended to encircle and eliminate the guerrillas in Grammos before they could escape into Albania. Though the operation was officially a secret, the guerrillas had somehow learned the details of the planned assault. They were stationed in a horseshoe shape, the bow fronting the advancing army and the tips pointing northwest and joined by the highest ridge of the Grammos Mountains—which also was the border of Albania. The army must break through the bow and seize the ridge before the guerrillas escaped. The key elements were surprise and quick execution.[2]

After several days of air and artillery bombardment, the soldiers opened the offensive on June 20. The initial assault on "D" day consisted of a

169

squadron of Spitfires, working in coordination with the artillery barrage and followed by the infantry's advance. While Harvards performed reconnaissance functions and C-47s dropped food and medical supplies, the Spitfires raked the area with rockets, bombs, cannon fire, machine guns, and, for the first time in the war, napalm. As one division prepared to scale the mountainsides, army engineers dynamited passageways through the granite walls to facilitate the use of pack animals in making the tortuous climb. The guerrillas had positioned almost forty pieces of artillery on the mountain, and they had blocked the passes with trees cut and tied into huge bunches. On the first day of the offensive, the army resorted to hand-to-hand combat in closing one of the enemy's principal supply routes.[3]

But on June 22, just two days into the attack, the army's advance ground to a halt along the edge of the mountains. Its intention had been to move rapidly between Grammos and Albania by using tanks to take Mount Ammouda in the northern cornerstone of Grammos. But the tanks—eighteen-ton British Centaurs, armed with small 50-millimeter cannon—were obsolete and underpowered, unable to make the climb by themselves. A tank recovery team had to enter the area first with a crane mounted on a U.S. Sherman chassis, which towed up the Centaurs with its power winch. Only two of the seven Centaurs made the grade. And getting them down proved almost as difficult. In the meantime, the fire bombs had only briefly boosted morale, for the air force had encountered many problems in their use and the incendiary impact was not as great as hoped. The army was unable to seize the Grammos ridge and close the guerrillas' main avenue of escape. A stalemate resulted, assuring a long and bloody siege.[4]

Yet the initial reports from Grammos were uniformly good—so good that the Truman administration found it necessary again to remind observers that victory in the field would only shift the struggle to the political front. Otherwise, Americans would assume the war had ended and demand a massive cutback in military aid, and UN members might take the communists' peace overtures at face value. Marshall warned both the American mission and the embassy to guard against feelings of false security. Griswold added another dimension to the danger: the appearance of a reduced threat from communism would renew the political fighting in Athens among noncommunist leaders and undermine the Populist-Liberal coalition. A purely rightist government could come to power. Such a regime could not keep peace because of a certain "blood-feud" with the great number of Greeks who did not share the right's political views. A broadly based government was necessary. Officials were needed whose social, political, and economic beliefs were "a little to the left rather than those who are ultra rightists."[5]

Another repercussion of the early jubilation was a brief push by some members of the State Department to send American troops—for political reasons. The director of the Office of European Affairs, John Hickerson, had been disturbed by the declaration of the National Security Council and the Joint Chiefs of Staff that a decision to send troops would be "militarily unsound." Both groups had missed the point. The crucial consideration was political: "The purpose of sending forces to Greece would be to indicate America's determination to clean up the situation in Greece and not effectively to conduct military operations if a shooting war started with Russia." Combat troops should go to Greece only to raise morale. "We have told the military boys time after time that we recognize that if we sent military forces to Greece and a shooting war with Russia started, the first thing we would do would be to get all of our forces out of Greece as rapidly as God would let us. All of us recognize that Greece is not the place to conduct military operations if World War III starts." Leonard Cromie of the Division of Greek, Turkish, and Iranian Affairs agreed with Hickerson. "The present struggle for Greece should be considered primarily as a last opportunity of avoiding World War III and only incidentally as the preliminary skirmish of an eventual new global conflict. Political rather than military considerations should therefore be paramount."[6]

Even though this suggestion went no farther than a few exchanges of notes, it further demonstrated the global thrust of America's aid program. To Hickerson and Cromie, the apparent success at Grammos afforded a safe opportunity to emphasize the nation's pledge to an ally by sending a token force as a signal of support. Such a show of strength would testify to America's tenacity and help to ward off threats elsewhere. They knew that the administration no longer regarded Greece as the showdown between East and West; attention had shifted to a crisis in Berlin caused by the passage of the Marshall Plan and the Russians' installation of a blockade, and to the outbreak of war in the Middle East following the declaration in May proclaiming the state of Israel. At minimal risk because the war seemed almost over, the assignment of a small number of American soldiers to Greece would send a message to the world that the administration intended to honor its pledges everywhere.

Partly because of these changing priorities in world affairs, however, the Truman administration had come to regard a troop dispatch as having less impact than would a dramatic demonstration of the results of American aid and advice. The White House recognized that a troop involvement would have appeared drastic no matter how large the force, and that the mere presence of these men would have automatically made Greece a vital interest of the United States. Such an act would have focused concern on Greece and undermined all efforts to fit that country within the perspective of global strategy. The United States had to prove its capacity to engage in sustained struggles against shadow-like forces. But it must do this, wherever possible, without participating in combat. In this instance, the arrival of American soldiers could induce a total commitment to a country now regarded as only one part of the strategic front against communism. The Greek war would become an American war—and against an elusive enemy who freely crossed international borders and received assistance from vaguely defined outside sources. American advisers had to supervise the reconstruction of a nation that was anti-communist and that rested on a sound political, economic, and military base. They had to develop a fighting force in Greece that was capable of achieving victory on its own. If the Greek army could win the guerrilla war while the rest of the world watched, the results would be more advantageous to American strategy than if Americans had done the fighting.

Despite the warnings of Marshall and others, the early successes of the Grammos campaign created the illusion of imminent victory in the war. The impact was far-reaching, shaping the outlook toward events inside the United States and Greece, as well as the larger issues of the Cold War.

Even before the Grammos offensive was under way, the State Department had had to counter the high expectations of victory that encouraged Congress to make cuts in the Greek-Turkish aid program. Now, with the initial good news from the field, congressional members were convinced that the Greek army would defeat the guerrillas by the end of 1948. But the truth was that the outcome hung in the balance. Any reduction in the appropriation would endanger the prospect for victory and force the State Department to find another way to maintain a steady influx of aid. Marshall was prepared for that problem. He decided not to make specifications on what proportion of future funds would go to either Greece or Turkey. Consequently, he declared, the "Turkish allocation may be called on for [a] portion of [the] cut in [the] event circumstances of [the] guerrilla war make it necessary." That tactic ready for implementation, he promised there would be no reduction in support for the Grammos assault throughout the remainder of the year.[7]

Another counterbalance to reductions in the Greek aid program was the congressional passage of the Marshall Plan in April. The new program encompassed economic assistance to Greece for four years, thereby permitting an even greater share of the funds allotted under the Truman Doctrine to go toward winning the war. The establishment of the Economic Cooperation Administration (to implement the Marshall Plan) included administrative adjustments intended to streamline the aid program and avoid problems similar to those between the embassy and the aid mission. The steady decline of inflation in Greece also encouraged many observers to believe that America's assistance program had almost fulfilled its purpose. In late June the Department of State and the ECA reached an agreement designed to minimize duplication in the aid program by coordinating economic, military, and political aims. Under the Foreign Assistance Act, the ECA would handle economic matters through a special mission in Greece responsible to the ECA administrator. The ECA Mission would make recommendations pertaining to aid requests and offer advice to the Greeks on economic matters. The new ambassador and chief of mission, Henry F. Grady, would arrive in July and coordinate all aid in accordance with the June agreement.[8]

Critics of the Truman Doctrine have correctly, although misleadingly, argued that despite the Marshall Plan and the administration's oft-repeated economic objectives in Greece, the great bulk of American aid was military. There can be little question that funds from the Marshall Plan in Greece allowed the emphasis of the Truman Doctrine to shift even more from economic to military aid. By the end of the first year of the assistance program, the State Department's planned use of the $300 million sum for Greece—50 percent for military expenses, 48.5 percent for economic, and 1.5 percent for administration—had been changed to an actual allotment of 57.7 percent for military, 41 percent for economic, and the balance for administration. But this alteration did not reflect a purposeful move toward a military solution. The administration recognized that the problem in Greece was multifaceted in nature, and that no part of the improvement program was separable from the rest. As noted repeatedly by administration spokesmen, the vital prerequisite to economic recovery was military success in the field. Consequently, depending upon one's definition of the goods sent, some of the matériel normally regarded as "economic" was integral to the war effort and thus subject to redefinition as "military" assistance. The distinction between "economic" and "military" goods was not always easy to make. Indeed, the attempt to compartmentalize the type of American aid was as pointless as trying to do the same with America's foreign policy: every step was dependent on all of the others. As General Schuyler wrote General Wedemeyer: "Our economic policy is primarily directed toward the support of the military operations of the Greek Government." An ECA official put it best when he later told Congress that economic reconstruction could not take place in Greece until there was security.[9]

The timing of the final report of the UN Special Committee on the Balkans was advantageous to the Truman administration, for on June 30 the findings confirmed its argument that the Greek conflict was not over. The report contained no surprises; nearly all of the information had been publicized piecemeal over the period of the investigation. Even though committee members had been unable to conduct any investigatory work outside Greece, they were convinced that Yugoslavia, Albania, and Bulgaria were virtually sponsoring terrorist and propaganda activities against the government in Athens by providing the guerrillas with military and economic aid, along with places of refuge and hospitalization. Many witnesses reported a steady stream of guerrillas moving back and forth across Greece's northern border at official checkpoints. When the army pushed the guerrillas into retreat, they escaped to safety beyond the Greek frontier. Radio stations and newspapers in the three neighboring countries praised the guerrillas, exhorting them to carry on the cause of democracy against the monarcho-fascist government in Athens. The problem was that this wealth of information did not prove official complicity by neighboring states. The committee was forced to make the following admission: "No definite conclusions can be drawn as to the origin of armament from the evidence. The quantity of mortar bombs and mines being used by the guerrillas in this remote mountain zone, however, leads to a strong presumption that the source of origin lies outside Greece."[10] Although the report could not fix responsibility for the continued border troubles, the point at this moment was that no sign had appeared of a relaxation of hostilities.

The impact that the UN report might have had on supporting the administration's view of the war was softened, however, by two developments during July that were undoubtedly related: the expanding peace offensive by the communist states—including an offer of mediation by the Soviet Union—and the rupture between Yugoslavia and the Soviet Union that finally became public. Was the rift indicative of a deeper division within the Soviet alliance system that would have, as one of its ancillary effects, an initiative taken by the Kremlin to wind down the Greek war and allow time for the communists to regroup?

In a move that could not have been coincidental with the Greek army's northern offensive and the growing rumblings of discontent within the Cominform, the Soviets made private overtures about mediating an end to the Greek conflict. The Soviet chargé in Athens, Nikolai Tchernychev, secretly approached Tsaldaris in late June (just before the Cominform issued a denunciation of Tito) with a proposal for secret talks between the Greek and Soviet governments that would aim at bringing the fighting to a close. The only condition was that Tsaldaris alone must hold the discussions to assure secrecy. Tchernychev implied that the topics could include the relations of Greece with northern neighbors as well as questions concerning Northern Epirus and Cyprus. Tsaldaris was non-committal until he could consult his Anglo-American allies. He was concerned that the Soviets designed the move either to divide the government by discrediting him if he entered secret negotiations, or to initiate a Soviet "mediation" between the Greek government and Markos that would establish the legitimacy of the guerrilla regime.[11]

The governments in Washington and London showed only cautious interest in the Soviet offer. Both were dubious of Soviet sincerity, but they also knew that an outright rejection of the proposal would lead to communist propaganda accusing the West of wanting to divide the world into opposing camps. The Soviet guidelines, however, were unacceptable. Tsaldaris should inform Tchernychev that the Greek government was willing to hear Soviet views pertaining to problems of mutual concern or to those affecting relations among UN member states. But the talks must not encompass regional matters, nor should they take place without Tsaldaris keeping the rest of his government informed. Bevin warned that the overture might be a "Soviet trap" designed to aggravate Tsaldaris's uneasy partnership with Sophoulis.[12]

Ambassador Grady warned Washington that the Soviet mediation offer did not mean that the communists had given up their goal of undermining the Greek government; failure on the battlefield had caused them to change tactics. News of the Greek army's early advances on Grammos had caused the Soviets to seek a political settlement designed to preserve the guerrillas' forces and as much prestige as possible. Latest reports suggested that communist leaders wanted to "jettison Markos" by making him the scapegoat for the military failure. Then, to throw the onus on the government in Athens, the Soviets would bring charges before the UN concerning the executions in

Greece; to the Russians this was the "very heart" of the Greeks' successes at home against the communists. The Grammos developments made the timing of the contact between Tsaldaris and Tchernychev "particularly significant." Tsaldaris recalled a conversation in Paris in 1946 during which he had asked Molotov what his government's policy toward Greece would be in case the Soviet Union failed in its efforts to expand into the Mediterranean. Molotov crisply replied that he would discuss the matter if that time ever came. Grady agreed with Tsaldaris that the time had arrived.[13]

The growing troubles between Stalin and Tito, along with other noteworthy changes in the Balkans, added credibility to the belief that the Kremlin wanted to end the Greek war. According to one of the closest students of the Soviet-Yugoslav split, the essential issue was political: Tito refused to be Moscow's instrument. On June 28, at a conference in Bucharest, the Cominform issued a communiqué denouncing Tito for "discrediting the Soviet Union," and invited Yugoslav communists to install new leaders attuned to Moscow's wishes. Tito's example could encourage other communist states to follow. If the Soviets were intending to focus on squelching him, such a strategy dictated that the communist effort in Greece was expendable. Other events affecting the Balkans confirmed this observation. The previous March, Bevin had told the U.S. ambassador in London of reports of a softer Soviet line regarding Greece, and in May, Albanian officials seemed conciliatory and Bulgaria publicly spoke of re-establishing diplomatic relations with Greece. In June the American ambassador in Belgrade, Cavendish Cannon, suggested that the communists' recent call for UN action in the war was part of a "new Stalinist strategy," and claimed that Zahariadis had arrived in Greece "bearing Moscow's olive branch."[14]

The Truman administration confronted another dilemma. It had to discern whether the communists now regarded problems other than Greece as more important, or whether the peace overtures were designed to buy time either for the guerrillas to prepare for the Greek army's assault or for the communists to switch to political weaponry. Indeed, the two considerations were not mutually exclusive.

Whatever the Kremlin's thinking, the Yugoslav-Soviet rift turned the focus of the communists' attention from Greece and had a potentially favorble impact on the Athens government's efforts to win the war. Neither the Soviets nor the Yugoslavs were interested in the war—which meant that the guerrillas would soon be on their own. At the time of the breach, little evidence had appeared to suggest a slowdown in Yugoslav aid to the guerrillas—probably because Tito had to prove loyalty to the international movement and maintain his position in the communist world. But the possibility of a cutoff in assistance now seemed real. Tito hinted that Greece was not his primary concern when he assured the United States that his government would do nothing dramatic pertaining to the struggle. A Yugoslav official expressed surprise that the United States had not softened its stance toward Tito in view of his problems with the Soviet Union. The Yugoslav government, he told the American chargé in Belgrade, R. Borden Reams, wanted the troubles in Greece liquidated because of the strain that refugees placed on the Yugoslav economy. When Reams remarked that Yugoslavia could settle the unrest by simply discontinuing aid to the guerrillas, the official dodged the implied accusation of past assistance and blandly responded that his country would give none. Additional corroboration came from Moscow, where the American ambassador, Walter Bedell Smith, reported a meeting he had with Stalin and Molotov that suggested that Tito's defection and other communist failures in Europe had modified the Soviet attitude. Stalin seemingly needed time to solidify his holdings and deal with Tito. Smith was certain that the Soviets wanted a political solution in Greece.[15]

Further support for the administration's assessment came from the well-known and respected contemporary writer, Edgar Snow, who argued that Tito's defection had caused the Soviets to reassess their strategy for expansion in Europe. According to Snow, Tito had rejected the infallibility of the Kremlin and repudiated the Soviets' dictatorial rule. The resulting collision was between "two sets of nationalisms"—not a deviation from the "Russian model so much as because of a too exact emulation of it." The rift had caused the Soviets to ease pressure temporarily while they sought to consolidate economic and political control over territories already under military domination. Above all, the Soviets had to disengage from a war crisis with the West—at least until they developed the atomic bomb, revamped their economy, and reconstructed the internal framework of their alliance system. Thus, in their game of chess, the Russians would rely upon patience and cunning in seeking a peace by stalemate. But, he warned, they would pursue this "cold armistice" only until they had stronger moves to make.[16]

Several other events suggested that the Greek communists as well as the Soviets wanted to bring the war to a close. Rankin was convinced that a division was growing between the KKE's military and political leaders. On the battlefield, of course, the guerrillas could not appear to be weakening in resolve. According to the communists' radio broadcasts, Markos had ordered his men to fight to the last drop of blood. At the same time, however, he called for peace negotiations, which suggested the existence of a strong opposing view within the KKE. Furthermore, in mid-July the party's Central Committee, along with the communist newspaper *Eleftheri Ellada*, announced the willingness of Free Greece "to accept any kind of honest democratic agreement which would bring to Greece and suffering Greek people peace and tranquility." Rankin believed this inconsistency to be a sign that the Democratic Army was breaking under the strain of the Grammos offensive. But at least one other observer was convinced that more was involved than the events of the war. Reams discerned a new Soviet strategy regarding Greece. Under Kremlin pressure, both the Democratic Army and the Provisional Democratic Government would make a "temporary exit" from the battlefield. The Soviets would then seek a resolution of the Greek problem *before* the General Assembly could publicly discuss the findings of the Balkan committee. The important observation was that the KKE was taking the lead in declaring a policy that would promote the Kremlin's goals.[17]

But the Greek government remained uninterested in negotiations. The fighting had lasted too long and was too embittered to end at a peace table. Besides, not enough had been won. Both government and opposition leaders called for unconditional surrender and agreed with the Greek press and public that Markos's peace proposal was insincere. According to American army officers in Athens, the Greek government suspected the KKE of attempting to slow the Grammos offensive, which was a sign of the guerrillas' weakness and confusion, "particularly in view [of the] almost simultaneous appearance [of] another Markos statement calling for greater resistance and increased sabotage."[18]

In anticipation of the Soviets' taking the peace offer before the UN General Assembly and using the occasion to denounce Greek domestic policies, the State Department urged the government in Athens to relax its stand on capital punishment. If the Soviets' strategy was to intensify the peace offensive, they would atempt to discourage UN action pertaining to the war by citing Markos's recent offer to compromise as well as the willingness of Albania and Bulgaria to resume diplomatic relations with Greece. A negotiated settlement would appeal to the UN, in part because the communists' propaganda had argued persuasively that Greek policies were repressive. Marshall recommended that the Greeks at least temporarily follow a lenient policy toward surrendered and captured guerrillas. This approach might undercut communist propaganda and bring the country together by easing the bitterness among relatives and friends. If for no other reason, "simple political expediency" required a cutback of executions until the General Assembly session was over. Marshall's exhortations were possibly having an effect. The Greek government had recently established clemency boards to review past sentences of executions.[19]

In the midst of this concern, the issue regarding the children arose again and threatened to become entangled with the communists' protests against the executions. The Truman administration found itself in the awkward position of having to resist the Greek government's attempt to bring kidnapping charges before the General Assembly. Marshall did not support the effort for at least two reasons. First, the charge of kidnapping was the weakest argument that the General Assembly could make against the communist states. No hard evidence tied these governments to the removals; they had admitted only to providing a haven for the children. Marshall explained to the Greek government that the "only group which could be definitely indicted as responsible for [the] removal [of] children from Greece [was] guerrillas, and no useful purpose would be served by endeavoring [to] obtain GA [General Assembly] condemnation of guerrillas." Second, the communist governments had posed an unassailable defense in calling their reception of the children a humanitarian act. Denunciation of these countries would invite countercharges that the repressive practices of the Athens government had driven these people from Greece.[20]

Marshall might have added a third reason: the United States's interest in establishing ties with Tito and widening the crack in the communist alliance. Although American officials in Belgrade called upon Washington to support Tito immediately, the State Department urged caution in an effort to determine whether the division with Stalin was real and whether other communist states might follow Yugoslavia out of the Cominform. Moreover, the Soviets would use any interventionist attempts by the West to persuade Tito to return to the communist camp or to convince other Cominform members to remain. The State Department nonetheless knew that the West could not turn its back on Tito and permit the Soviets to argue that his only alternative to isolation was repentance. The Truman administration decided only to consider any suggestions made by Yugoslavia for improving economic relations; for the time being it could do no more for fear of discrediting Tito among his Balkan communist neighbors.[21] Now, in light of the Tito-Stalin rift, the United States could not denounce Yugoslavia for taking in the Greek children. Not only would such an approach allow that government and people to feign innocence in motive, but it might cost the White House an excellent opportunity to drive the wedge deeper between Tito and Stalin.

For tactical reasons, the State Department preferred that the Greek government avoid a confrontation in the General Assembly and appeal for the repatriation of the children on a humanitarian basis. Marshall understood the justice of the Greek complaint, but he would not support any effort to "fix blame for [the] removal [of] children or sheltering them [by] neighboring countries." A less provocative approach seemed wise. The Economic and Social Council in Geneva was expected to pass a resolution urging the return of displaced children from all countries. Such a resolution would become a subject for discussion by the General Assembly's Economic and Social Committee. In that setting, the Greek government could seek the children's return for humanitarian reasons. If the Geneva Council failed to adopt the resolution, the Greeks could take the issue before the General Assembly's Political Committee. The State Department had received encouraging reports about repatriation efforts by the International Red Cross Societies. Should these groups succeed, Marshall thought, the Greeks might not have to take the matter before the General Assembly.[22]

Whether or not attributable to State Department pressure, the indirect approach was adopted. The Economic and Social Council in Geneva passed a resolution that called for reuniting "unaccompanied children" with their parents and for repatriating orphans and unaccompanied children whose nationality was not clear—with the stipulation that "the best interests of the individual child shall be the determining factor." This was somewhat different from the American position, which had called for "the best interests of the child" to be "a guiding principle in determining final plans for the unaccompanied displaced child." An irony became apparent. Depending on the definition of "best interests," the Greeks could advocate the repatriation of all children, whereas the countries housing the youths could refuse to repatriate any of them. Perhaps with that problem in mind, the General Assembly in late November resolved that the International Red Cross agencies should seek the return of those children whose "father or mother, or in his or her absence, their closest relative, express a wish to that effect."[23]

Once again in the controversy over the children, the Truman administration had succeeded in buying time for the Greek forces to win the war and thereby resolve this issue. The Greek government could not have been satisfied with this UN arrangement, but it was coming to realize that the United States had concerns elsewhere that transcended issues even as emotional as those involving the children. Such a stance by the White House had not done much to promote a harmonious relationship with Greece, but considerations outside the country as well as those relating to the Greek war itself required that there be no further intensification of that issue. The State Department had averted a public confrontation with the communists that would have failed to secure the return of the children while exposing the West to charges of interfering with their safety. The focus of concern could return to the war.

While the diplomats were waging their successful battle, the Greek army in August was breaking the deadlock at Grammos. When Operation Crown had first begun, the Greek commander in charge, Lieutenant General Panos Kalogeropoulos, had made an ill-advised decision: to promote morale, he allowed his staff to bring wives and children on the campaign. Furthermore, for six weeks, he forbade his men to advance beyond rigidly defined limits. With the Greek offensive at a standstill, Van Fleet visited the front with several dignitaries from Washington, including Undersecretary of the Army William H. Draper and the chief of Plans and Operations, General Albert C. Wedemeyer. They were shocked at the lull in fighting. In front of the group, Van Fleet demanded that the Greek commanders resume the attack and laced into them with such blunt language that his visitors from Washington moved out of earshot. Now, because of what Van Fleet could only regard as cowardice, he insisted that Kalogeropoulos be given an extended leave. In mid-August the Grammos command went to Lieutenant General Kitrilakis—the main architect of the Crown operation. Under the new leadership, the Greek forces mounted another move northward, hitting the Grammos Massif and closing the gap in the center. Though the terrain made the area nearly impenetrable, the men made it to the summit of Mount Grammos and occupied the enemy's stronghold. The guerrillas had one way out—an opening six miles wide that they used to retreat into Albania.[24]

Sensing victory, and yet at a cost too terrible to comprehend, the Greek government urged the United States to extend more military assistance and, in a surprising reversal of policy, to bring the matter before the Russians for discussion. In Washington, Dendramis complained to Lovett about mounting casualties and urged the United States to push for a rapid settlement by interjecting the Greek issue into a series of ongoing talks in Moscow. Lovett replied, however, that his reports about the army were encouraging and that most of its casualties were attributable to enemy mines rather than to the fighting. Additional military aid at this point would serve no purpose. As for the Moscow discussions, the Greek issue was not a proper subject for the agenda; the focus was on Berlin. Dendramis then expressed dissatisfaction with the Spitfires' inability to provide adequate support for the ground troops and inquired about the possibility of the United States sending bombers. But Lovett noted that, as in Okinawa during World War II, bombers were of little value in destroying guerrilla fortifications in mountainous areas. A former airman, Lovett was convinced that strafing by fighter planes was almost as debilitating as bombing to enemy morale. The way to defeat the guerrillas was with artillery fire and hard ground fighting. Their escape into Albania was inconsequential as long as they did not *want* to return to Greece.[25]

The recent developments at Grammos so encouraged McGhee that, after a visit to Athens, he thought the country no longer required special treatment by the United States. The guerrillas' supply lines were in jeopardy, and their command was having difficulty controlling its men because of the pressure exerted by the Greek military. Once the Grammos operation was over, the communists should never again be able to amass a large force. McGhee nonetheless urged caution. Even after mopping-up operations, a "residual guerrilla movement" would necessitate a lengthy holding action by the army and gendarmerie. Only then should the government reduce the size of its army. The great masses of Greek people now understood that the communists had used the guerrilla movement in an effort to seize control of the government and separate Greek Macedonia and western Thrace from Greece. These changes evident, McGhee believed that the United States could place Greek needs within the broader perspective of strategy.[26]

McGhee insisted, however, that the United States's obligations to Greece could not end with victory on the battlefield. Policymakers in Washington must continue to recognize their nation's long-range interests in Greece. "At no point," he emphasized (and Marshall reinforced in instructions to the embassy in Athens), "must the impression be given either to the Greeks or to the rest of the world that the US has lessened its determination to assist Greece in maintaining her independence and territorial integrity."[27]

McGhee's optimism was premature. The State Department saw no evidence of the guerrillas' collapse; they had not reduced their activities and were still forcibly recruiting new members. Uncertainty remained as to when the guerrillas would be "brought under control." Army Secretary Kenneth C. Royall warned McGhee that even though the offensive had forced the guerrillas from Grammos with casualties as high as 30 percent, the Greek army had still not inflicted a "decisive, conclusive defeat."[28]

The public impression in Greece nonetheless remained that the army had emerged triumphant by driving the guerrillas from their stronghold. Celebrations began on the spot, highlighted by the soldiers using flares as fireworks, joining in a doxology, and engaging in a ceremonial laying of the foundation of a chapel. Loyalists rang bells and raised flags in many cities. A communiqué from the KKE's Central Committee had the tone of defeat. The condition of the guerrillas' headquarters at Grammos added to the appearance of victory. Despite the anxieties caused by the establishment of Free Greece, the capital consisted of fifty crude wooden huts scattered over a number of acres and hidden by woods. In addition to Markos's quarters, the ramshackle buildings included a hospital, a central telephone center, a bakery, and several workshops and storehouses. Many border settlements lay in ruins, leveled by bombing sweeps and strewn with bodies of guerrillas. Standing out of the devastation was a heavily damaged church building which had these words on a wall: "Fight the mercenaries of American imperialism!"[29]

When the battle finally ended on August 22, Van Fleet and several American and British officers went to the front and returned with a favorable assessment of the outcome. The cost had been high. The Greek government's forces had sustained 7,000 casualties, and the air force had suffered serious groundfire damage to over twenty aircraft and slight damage to more than a hundred others. The guerrillas' light anti-aircraft fire hit twenty-three Spitfires, driving one from the air in a fiery crash that killed the pilot. Markos had eluded his pursuers and escaped with 6,000 of his followers, along with their heavy guns. Furthermore, his very existence remained the subject of mystery—to both enemies and allies. When a woman was asked if she had seen Markos, she replied: "He was here, but no one saw him. The sun did not shine on him by day, nor the moon at night." But the Greek army had cleared the area of guerrillas and destroyed their installations, seized huge supply stores and nearly seven hundred mulepacks of war goods (including a large cache of British ammunition), inflicted 10,000 casualties, and, according to the first field reports, achieved the "liquidation of 'Free Greece.'"[30]

As more field reports arrived in Athens, however, the realization grew that the initial enthusiasm had been unwarranted. Some of the guerrillas had passed through the army's advancing lines and were soon launching raids in southern and central Greece. The area hardest hit was the Peloponnese, forcing the army to divert some of its men back to deal with this problem. But most of the guerrillas escaped into Albania. As UN representatives examined the remains of Free Greece, they saw Hungarian canned vegetables and fruit, Yugoslav canned meat, Albanian cigarettes, and Bulgarian books, including *Thirty Years in the Soviet Army*, *This Is How We Fought at Stalingrad*, and *The American Plan for the Enslavement of Europe*. They also recognized the potential for new problems. Fresh trenches and mortars were located along the Albanian border, and the guerrillas were using Albanian territory for positioning guns and establishing rest areas and communication centers. Near two of the Greek frontier posts, the guerrillas had already launched a mortar and machine gun attack out of Albania. The Greek army was virtually powerless because it remained under orders not to fire back, and to avert international incidents by avoiding major operations closer than five miles from the border. The Greek government sent Albania a note through the UN secretary-general calling for a halt to such practices. Albania did not reply.

Van Fleet gloomily observed that "too much optimism" had resulted from the battle.[31]

The Grammos assault had mixed results—some not apparent at the time. The Greek government's forces had driven the guerrillas from their headquarters and widened the divisions within their leadership. Unrest had spread throughout the guerrillas' ranks, and Markos bore the brunt of the criticism. At the Fourth Plenary Session of the KKE, Zahariadis attributed the Grammos defeat to cowardice and poor military leadership and called for a purge. Though Markos held onto his position only after a bitter struggle, one of his officers was executed, another was exiled to Prague, and others were demoted or given unimportant assignments. But the guerrilla force remained potentially strong. In addition to those who had withdrawn to Albania, 17,000 others were still in Greece.[32]

Most of the guerrillas eventually relocated in the mountainous region of Vitsi and in the equally rugged area of Epirus, which lay about forty miles south of Grammos. By the end of the month, over 3,000 guerrillas had erected new headquarters near Lake Prespa. The outcome of Grammos confirmed the observation of a Greek spokesman that one of the most fundamental problems in the war against the guerrillas was "an open frontier in their rear." The army's campaign had called for an assault on Vitsi when the Grammos operation came to a close. The war was far from over.[33]

II

In late August three divisions of the Greek army were prepared to open the offensive on Vitsi. The plan was the same as that undertaken at Grammos, except on a smaller scale; two brigades would hit from the right and two from the left, while another would push the guerrillas to a "killing ground" on the shores of Lake Prespa. After reconnaissance planes located the enemy, Spitfires began divebombing and strafing operations. The initial results were successful. Advancing ground forces scattered 1,500 guerrillas in less than two weeks. But, as at Grammos, the army's weaknesses became apparent again as the drive broke down because of confusion in command complicated by bad weather. By mid-September the guerrillas, now 6,000 strong, had turned the army around and into a near rout before it finally held and inched back northward. Van Fleet at first had estimated that the offensive would take most of the month. Now the end could not be seen. Indeed, the government base at Florina was suddenly in danger. And even if Greek forces cleared the entire north, the guerrillas would escape into neighboring countries, where they would regroup and hit in a different spot.[34]

The fighting in Vitsi demonstrated again that without a smoothly functioning, aggressive offensive, the Greek army could not defeat mobile bands of guerrillas who had outside assistance and avenues of escape from the field. The soldiers remained weak in discipline and training, subject to mercurial rises and falls in morale brought by changing fortunes on the battlefield. Rather than dictating the intensity and direction of combat, the army followed the flow of events. Without a strong, charismatic leader, the men lacked the inspiration to move forward, encircle the enemy, and close the border. Assistance was still coming out of Yugoslavia, though on a smaller scale than before; the degree of aid from Albania and Bulgaria remained about the same. Since the army was unable to seal off outside aid, these three countries continued to underwrite the guerrillas' war efforts and remained the chief places of sanctuary.[35]

The illusion of imminent victory died hard in Washington. Even after the first negative reports from Vitsi, Van Fleet had to ward off a move by the Department of the Army to reduce Greek armed forces to a size supportable by their country's economy. When Colonel E. A. Walker arrived in Athens to discuss a reduction, Van Fleet argued that this was out of the question. No cut in the army was possible before the spring of 1949, at which time a reduction by 12,000 might be acceptable—*if* domestic security permitted. Assuming an improvement in the war by December of 1948, the National Defense Corps could be cut by 20,000, the gendarmerie reduced to 22,000, and category "C" personnel discontinued. But Van Fleet warned against optimism. The elimination of guerrillas from one border pocket did not prevent them from moving to others. As if to prove the accuracy of his assessment, the guerrillas launched a counterattack that, by late September, took them south almost to Kastoria before the army blunted their drive. Van Fleet insisted that the "overall picture has worsened rather than improved since the Grammos victory."[36]

As at Grammos, the fighting in Vitsi eventually mired into a stalemate, leading the Greek government to repeat its arguments for an expanded military force. In response to an American proposal to cut Greek military expenditures 20 percent, Tsaldaris argued for an increase in the army from 132,000 to 250,000 soldiers by the spring of 1949. Since American funds were not sufficient to cover these additions, he wanted aid outside the Marshall Plan that would meet all expenses necessary to end the war—including relief to guerrilla-stricken areas. The army, he insisted, must wage an offensive at the same time it conducted a defense to protect people and property in the wake of the advance. Both Tsaldaris and Sophoulis reminded Americans that Greece was the only country in Europe in which the communists were using armed force against American rehabilitation efforts.[37]

The Greek government's argument for military expansion seemed to gain credibility when another critical situation developed in the Peloponnese. The guerrillas had regained considerable control in that predominantly royalist area by taking advantage of the army's concentration in the north and the continual strife in the Peloponnese among right-wing groups. Movement between garrisoned towns could take place only under military protection, and guards had to be at bridges, power plants, and railway stations. The Chamber of Deputies pressed local commanders to spread out their troops to defend the area. Another problem was the British, Van Fleet complained. They were in "violent disagreement" with the Americans and the Greek command over what to do about this problem. Whereas Van Fleet supported Greek military and political leaders who wanted to concentrate on the Peloponnese, General Down wanted everything hurled at eastern Macedonia and Thrace. Grady thought that clearing the Peloponnese was a "must." Only then could the army focus on the northern frontier.[38]

The British notified Van Fleet that they did not support the Greek government's call for a bigger army, but they did recommend retaining its present size while improving its leadership and training and enlarging the air force. British observers feared that the situation would worsen if the scheduled reduction of 15,000 men went into effect by the end of October. The number of National Defense Corps battalions would fall from ninety-six to sixty, increasing the static defense requirements of the army and cutting the number of divisions available for operations. Fifteen divisions were needed: ten to seal the border, one each to garrison Thessaly, Roumeli, and the Peloponnese, and a strike force of two divisions to combine with the preceding three in destroying the guerrillas inside Greece. All niney-six battalions of the National Defense Corps were required to secure cleared areas. More army training centers were essential to building a qualified officer corps and a more effective fighting machine. The air force needed expansion, with the number of planes limited only by the availability of crew and maintenance personnel. According to an attached proposal, the necessary changes could not be completed until April 1950.[39]

The British recommendations offered little consolation to Van Fleet. He agreed that the greatest need was to improve the army, but a training program required time—which was in short supply because of growing demands for aid cuts in accordance with Washington's global strategy. The first essential was to close the border, which seemed possible either by a lightning-like offensive (which the army had been unable to conduct), or by a marked size increase in troops (which assured nothing positive and had no chance for approval in Washington). The only option left was to pursue the same policies: military aid and operational advice while hoping that some Greek military figure would emerge who was both inspiring to his men and capable of leading an offensive.

As the war remained in deadlock, however, America's military advisers in Athens moved toward the Greek position of enlarging the armed forces. The northern frontier stayed open, which necessitated an encirclement by government forces to prevent the guerrillas' escape. Van Fleet thought this action required "great superiority in numbers" and that the request for additional ground forces now seemed reasonable. Support came from the acting director of the Joint U.S. Military Advisory and Planning Group, Brigadier General Reuben E. Jenkins, who argued that the Greek government would lose the war unless the army was enlarged and the soldiers learned how to conduct a "modern small-arms fight." General William A. Matheny, chief of the Air

Section of the Joint U.S. Military Advisory and Planning Group, argued that an expanded air support system was needed to give the army the mobility it required. The soldiers could not by themselves pursue small guerrilla groups in such rough terrain.[40]

As the Americans pondered how to break the stalemate, events elsewhere reminded the White House of the necessity of keeping the Greek problem within the global perspective. The CIA warned that the chances of the Soviets risking war during 1948–49 had "slightly increased" because of setbacks in the Cold War that had put pressure on the Kremlin to engage in dangerous "diplomatic ventures." The Soviets had to counter the Marshall Plan, the movement toward the establishment of a West German government, the failure of communist strategy in Western Europe, and the growing solidity of the Western powers against Soviet expansion, along with the increased military unity among Western European nations. The Russians had not exhausted their non-military tactics in Western Europe. But recent events—particularly the Soviet blockade of Berlin—had heightened tension and caused talk of war. The Soviets wanted the United States "to over-extend its commitments and exhaust its resources." America's aid effort in Greece was only one part of the strategic picture.[41]

The Truman administration realized that even though the war was still going on in Greece, the sense of emergency had passed and a clarification of policies was needed to establish global priorities. All decisions affecting Greece must take place in relation to broad strategic concerns. As one State Department official noted, there were "no plans for making Greece into a military bastion against Soviet aggression." General Wedemeyer agreed that in comparison with the Western Union and Canada, Greece came second, along with Turkey and Italy. But in the interests of America's overall strategy, he warned, military aid and operational advice must continue during fiscal year 1950. To do otherwise would cause "undesirable political and strategic effects" and inflict a crippling blow to American prestige.[42] Global strategy did not permit the White House to approve a dramatic enlargement of either the Greek army or the American presence.

The ramifications for Greece of the administration's policy of restraint became evident during Marshall's visit to Athens in mid-October. Grady told him that the Greeks relied too heavily on outside aid and that a government information campaign was necessary to convince the people that the guerrilla war was their war. Furthermore, according to *Nation* magazine, the ambassador "strongly implied" to American journalists (by refusing to answer the question) that the State Department suspected the Greek government of failing to push the fight against the guerrillas in a deceitful effort to secure more U.S. aid. Grady insisted that the solution did not lie in more of anything material; what was needed was a more aggressive attitude among Greek soldiers. After he talked with Marshall, the secretary emerged with a compromise intended to placate all sides concerned. Marshall agreed to an increase in the army of 15,000 men which, even though considerably less than what the

Greek government wanted, might demonstrate that the United States had not turned its back on the problem. But the move only temporarily eased the growing fears among Greek leaders that the solution to their problems had become dependent upon international events and that their country was now merely a pawn between East and West. As the secretary left for Paris, a Greek newsman remarked: "There goes the wisest statesman who has come to Greece in a long time. He promised nothing—and didn't try to tell us that the situation was fine."[43]

Marshall reaffirmed the administration's priorities by placing the Greek problem within the global dimensions of strategy. The situation in Greece fitted the "local circumstances of the general Soviet or Communist plot" in that the communist guerrillas had turned from military measures in an attempt to exploit the country's widespread political and economic instability. General Schuyler agreed that Moscow had switched to political tactics out of fear that the continued escalation of events in Greece could lead to war. "The great deterrent to the Soviet bloc" was "not material U.S. aid but the fact that overt aggression against Greece might result in war with the U.S." Marshall warned, however, that even though the focal point of concern would shift to other places, Greece was still an integral part of America's defense strategy. Americans must realize that the dangers they encountered at any spot in the world were "but a piece or a portion of the front of the general Soviet effort, and that what we do regarding Berlin or any other Communist effort, subversive or otherwise, has a direct effect on the effort in Greece." Without expanding its involvement, the United States must maintain a strong front in Greece against the "machinations of the Soviet Union."[44]

As the administration continued its strategy assessment, the fighting resumed in Vitsi. Van Fleet had spent almost a week in the area with Greek division, brigade, and battalion commanders, and he was not confident when the assault was renewed on October 10. Greek forces had "everything available to win a quick and decisive victory, with the possible exception of the greatest requirement—morale." At one point, Greek commandos reduced the Mount Vitsi salient and prepared to strike deep into the rear of the guerrilla position. But this operation ended in failure. Within two weeks, Van Fleet called off the offensive and declared that the Greek army was "incapable, due to a thousand and one reasons but mainly one of command." Everything accomplished was by air and artillery, not by hard-nosed fighting. Exasperated, Van Fleet declared that "what is urgently needed is a *better* army." For the present the Greek command should concentrate on Thessaly and the Peloponnese and leave the border pockets alone save for "containing them with minimum forces" for the winter. The prognosis was not good. Although few thought a government collapse and communist takeover possible, the U.S. Army's policymakers in Washington were taking no chances. In the event of such an emergency, the ambassador was authorized to implement an "Internal Security Plan," which was designed to evacuate the 6,000 Americans in Greece, including the more than six hundred military personnel.[45]

The government's inability to close the border was the decisive factor at Vitsi as it had been at Grammos. When the army turned its attention to the interior during the following winter, many of the guerrillas in Vitsi made their way back into Grammos. The events at Vitsi had demonstrated what Van Fleet termed the Greek army's "total lack of aggressiveness and will to fight." The results were "embarrassing and discouraging," Lovett admitted to the embassy in Greece. The United States would continue to send sufficient military aid to re-establish internal security but, in a stance illustrative of strategy, not enough to seal the border. Such a move would risk involvement in Balkan concerns. The Greek army would have to close the border.[46]

To raise troop morale, the Truman administration gave in to proponents of an expanded air war and, in early November, approved the establishment of the United States Air Force Group, Greece, which provided advice on operations, air installations, and the procurement and delivery of matériel. Americans had reported that in good weather, the pilots strafed and bombed enemy positions with "great accuracy." To combat climatic difficulties, the Greeks had begun converting the airfield at Argos Orestikon into all-weather use by laying a pierced steel plank runway. In addition, the Americans attempted to improve the use of napalm. General Matheny pointed out that during World War II fighter pilots called napalm the "most effective type of munitions which they could drop." The fiery substance left a "trail of burned jungle, Japs and Japanese supplies from Guadalcanal to Tokyo." Since Spitfires could carry only two tanks of the liquid, Matheny recommended a modification of all aircraft for use in the northern operations. More support from the air would raise the Greek army's morale even if inflicting only minimal damage on the guerrillas.[47]

Meanwhile, the Greek government tried to resolve the army's leadership problem by offering the position as commander-in-chief to a well-known military figure, General Alexander Papagos; but the appointment was held up for months as Papagos made heated demands for an increase in the army to 250,000 men and for total control over military decisions. Both Van Fleet and Down had approved the government's decision to turn to Papagos. He had been victorious in the Albanian war against the Italians in 1940, and he had conducted himself admirably during the German occupation. Sophoulis was confident that Papagos's prestige, his support for the king, and his nonalignment with any political party would improve the situation. A few days later the State Department approved a new Greek army ceiling of 147,000 in response to Marshall's recommended increase of 15,000 men. The timing of this move undoubtedly left the impression that the White House was bending to Papagos's demands and that more expansion would come. But his appointment was held up by the United States's refusal to finance an even larger army and by the reluctance of Greek political leaders to grant absolute military authority to one person. Until the Greeks realized that a military commander must have the power to make his own decisions, their army would continue to lack a strong leader.[48]

In almost every way the fighting in Greece had become an American war, which presented the false notion that firepower would determine the outcome. The *New York Times*'s news correspondent, Cyrus L. Sulzberger, privately remarked in his notes that Americans "appear to be in charge of operations and there is not much disguising that fact, although everyone pretends it isn't so." Grady lamented that Van Fleet and other American military advisers had adopted the Greek argument that the way to victory was "always more: more men, more money and more equipment." The army was fighting with arms, rations, and uniforms bought in America, depending on an air force and navy financed by America, relying upon vehicles and pack animals supplied by America, and following the orders of officers trained and advised by Americans. Rather than instilling incentive, the abundance of military aid received by the Greeks nurtured a sense of carelessness that undermined the need for an aggressive spirit. During the Grammos offensive, Grady declared, "I watched Greek artillerymen using expensive ammunition irresponsibly, send repeated volleys against rocky slopes of mountain ridges, knowing only that [the] area was not occupied by [the] GNA [Greek National Army] much in [the] manner of American children setting off firecrackers on July 4." Another increase in size and matériel would do more harm than good. "Each numerical increase, with corresponding increase in supplies, has added proof to Greeks that this, in [the] first instance, is America's war rather than Greece's."[49]

The Truman administration recognized the necessity of making the leaders in Athens understand that their country was no longer the critical area in combatting communism. Grady warned that they would find this difficult to accept because the Greek politicians and press had long claimed that their country was the "focal point on [the] democratic front." The Soviet focus had shifted to other areas, causing America's strategists to regard Greece as secondary to other problem spots. The Greek government must learn the "realities of life"—that they could not "live indefinitely on American bounty." The United States must take steps toward "revitalizing the nation's strength through self-help rather than sustaining it artificially through foreign grants." Worldwide demands on American production and capital made it incumbent on the White House to maintain a continuing assessment of the place of Greece within America's general strategy. In response to constantly shifting priorities, the Defense Department recommended a sharp reduction in Van Fleet's budget request for fiscal year 1950 from $451 million to $200 million, primarily because of "the relatively low priority accorded Greece strategically vis a vis Western Union, from the standpoint of U.S. long range strategic interests."[50]

Thus the White House considered Greece less important than Turkey in strategic military terms, and yet, paradoxically, of high symbolic value to the global framework of the Cold War. Turkey was strategically located in relation to air, land, and sea routes from the Soviet Union to the Cairo-Suez area and to the oil fields of the Middle East. Even though Greece did not have that kind of geopolitical importance, a communist victory there might embolden the Soviets into taking reckless actions in strategic areas that would be conducive to all-out war. The danger of example still permeated the administration's thinking. The State Department warned that if the United States halted aid to Greece, "it would be impossible to explain why we had abandoned a small country which it was well within our capability to support against communist pressure applied by political means and by the use of guerrillas." At the same time, however, the Greek government must learn that the United States would not go beyond the limitations set by overall strategic considerations. Somewhere in the aid program a balance must be struck between too much and too little. The Soviet Union "undoubtedly counts on eventually exhausting Greek U.S. morale, bringing about the cessation of U.S. aid, and thereby winning Greece by default."[51]

A further complication had developed: disputes had erupted between Van Fleet and Grady over the nature of the aid effort which now forced Truman to send the secretary of the army to investigate. This was not the first time Van Fleet had had differences with colleagues. Before Griswold had left Greece, he had tried to convince the State Department to transfer Van Fleet after the Grammos operation. Although the general was good on instilling spirit, Griswold explained, he had no grasp of financial and political problems and was unable to withstand pressure from Greek political leaders for more aid. The new complaints from Grady convinced the President to inquire into the matter. He informed Royall that a "good deal of feeling" existed within the State Department "that we ought probably to send somebody there . . . who gets along better with the other American officials and who does not just run a one-man show." Truman added, "I may have to choose between the ambassador . . . and Van Fleet."[52]

Royall's assessment relieved the President of having to make a choice between Grady and Van Fleet. Since Grady was then in Washington, Royall talked only with the general. Upon arrival in Athens, the secretary accompanied Van Fleet to meet the king and queen, the latter of whom lavishly praised the general and declared that her country "couldn't get along without him." On the matter of troop enlargement, however, Royall confirmed Grady's view that the nation's armed forces had sufficient manpower and matériel but lacked discipline and leadership. The best approach to fighting communism was for both the Economic Cooperation Administration and the Greek government to shift the bulk of economic aid from the cities to the outlying provinces: "The growth of communism and the resulting support of the guerrilla cause appears to be making the greatest headway in the rural areas of Greece." For now there was no need for change. "Everything's all right in Greece. Just leave Van Fleet alone, and—ambassador or no ambassador—he'll win this war."[53]

A few changes had taken place in Greece that offered some bases for Royall's optimism. UN observers reported that Yugoslavia's assistance to the guerrillas had markedly decreased and that the only matériel still arriving was unofficial or merely the result of termination orders not having reached subordinates. The guerrillas were perhaps becoming more desperate; Markos had announced another plan for peace that the Greek government and Americans rejected as propaganda and regarded as a confession of weakness. In the Peloponnese, the guerrillas caused a brief sensation by kidnapping and soon releasing two men—including BBC news correspondent Kenneth Matthews. But these events could not overshadow the government's success in exterminating or capturing many "self-defense personnel" during the recent military operation in that region known as "Operation Pigeon." In a move suggesting a more stringent crackdown, the government in late October proclaimed martial law throughout the country.[54]

Other changes had occurred—major alterations in the guerrillas' leadership and direction of the war. At the November Politburo meeting, Zahariadis lashed out at Markos: "[Y]ou'll become a worm and crawl before me, . . . or you'll leave your head in Moscow because you insulted Stalin." Zahariadis and his supporters on the KKE's Central Committee proceeded to secure a no-confidence vote against Markos and to shift the Democratic Army almost totally into conventional warfare. Although Markos remained officially in command for a few more months, word went out that he was ill and had been sent on sick leave to Albania and then to Yugoslavia. Zahariadis was in control. In a move reflecting his pro-Moscow feelings, he secured a resolution (kept secret from his followers) to support the Cominform in its battle with Tito. Although his decision assured the eventual end of Yugoslav aid to the guerrillas, it guaranteed a continuation of Bulgarian and Albanian assistance and prevented his forces from being isolated in the communist world. But the decision (when revealed) also carried the potential of destroying the Democratic Army from within: support for the Cominform entailed a renewed commitment to Macedonian independence and a deeper threat to Greek territorial integrity that would further divide the guerrilla forces. Another decision was equally important. Despite the heavy losses sustained in holding off the government's attacks on Grammos and Vitsi, Zahariadis convinced the KKE that the fault did not lie in using the Democratic Army in a static defense role; Markos's emphasis on guerrilla tactics had obstructed victory. The Democratic Army should be more thoroughly reorganized along regular army lines to enable it to take the offensive. His strategy approved, Zahariadis ordered a series of assaults on the towns of Karditsa, Edessa, and Naoussa, and established a defense concentration in Grammos and Vitsi that was intended to beat the Greek army into submission. Although not discernible at the time, the Greek government finally had the opportunity to make full use of its firepower to seize the advantage on the field that it had long enjoyed on paper.[55]

But the ramifications of these changes remained obscured. As winter enveloped Greece, the dark clouds overshadowing the mountains seemed expressive of the national mood.

CHAPTER
11

The Communists' Peace Offensive

By early 1949 the chances for a collapse of the Greek government seemed remote, but the military situation remained threatening. Although Van Fleet predicted certain victory, he prepared a special operations plan in the event of a communist takeover. News correspondents on the scene were not optimistic. Homer Bigart claimed that the United States had become "inextricably involved" in a stalemated war, and *Time* correspondent Robert Low reported that "wherever the Greek army is not, the guerrillas are—if not physically, then in influence and authority." Anne O'Hare McCormick declared: "Everywhere the atmosphere was heavy with suspense. In such fearful quiet must the early settlers in the West have waited the descent of the Indians." According to a member of the American mission in Athens, many villagers sat out long nights, protected only by barbed wire. Despite the successes of Operation Pigeon, about 3,000 guerrillas remained active in the Peloponnese, both in urban centers and in outlying settlements. Less than a hundred miles west of Salonika, over 2,000 guerrillas attacked Naoussa and shot the mayor in the town's square (renamed Truman Square the year before at the mayor's request) as a "lackey of the Americans." Less than a week afterward, guerrilla "sabotage squads" opened an assault on Karpenisi in central Greece that quickly led to the town's collapse. In desperation a woman in Athens screamed at Low: "You Americans must put an end to this war—or leave us to the Russians. Between you we are being crucified!"[1]

The Karpenisi attack provided another complication: the guerrillas accused the United States of direct involvement in the war. Their ground fire had forced down a Greek plane with two military figures aboard—the Greek pilot accompanied by an American military officer. Four days later, the head of the guerrilla forces summoned the town's leaders to a space a short distance away and told them the plane had crashed, killing its two pilots, one Greek

191

and the other American. He wanted the citizens to sign a paper testifying that Americans were now participating in the strafing and bombing of defenseless civilians.[2]

The story aroused immediate suspicion. Though the Greek people saw the bodies, they were not permitted to examine them for injuries. The plane, according to one eyewitness account, showed no damages caused by an alleged crash. Afterward, a group of schoolchildren came across the American's body—later identified as Lieutenant Colonel Selden R. Edner—about two hundred yards from the landing site. No longer wearing a uniform, Edner had been scalped, a wire was wound tightly around his throat, his head was crushed, and his body had been stripped and mutilated. The Greek pilot's body had disappeared, and the guerrillas had burned the plane.[3]

American officials found themselves in the unlikely position of having to counter two charges of direct military involvement in the war—one from the guerrilla command that soon went as a formal complaint before the UN Security Council, the other in the form of a public explanation from the Greek government. The Greek Air Ministry issued an explanation implying that the American aboard had been involved in combat operations. According to the official statement, an armed AT-6 carrying an American had been on a reconnaissance mission from Larisa to Arazos when hit by enemy fire and forced to land near Karpenisi. In light of the Greek government's dissatisfaction with the American aid effort, its officials either wanted to exert more pressure on the United States to expand assistance, or they hoped that publicity claiming direct American involvement might break the will of the guerrillas. Whatever the reason, the Americans would have none of it. They admitted that an American had been on the plane, but staunchly denied that his duties went beyond observing events and offering advice. According to a USAGG investigation, Edner had been lynched within two hours of the crash. Witnesses claimed that they had been forced to certify that he had been found dead from injuries sustained in the crash. The Greek government had purposely given out misleading and "erroneous information." Edner's orders had been "to make occasional flights over bandit-held terrain" that allowed him only "to observe, advise, and report" on the fighting. He was "not authorized to participate in combat flights against the enemy," nor was he "to take an executive part in operations."[4] If the Greek government intended to convey the impression that the United States was now involved in combat, the Truman administration was seeing the truth of the maxim that in war an ally can become one's worst enemy.

The endless array of complexities that continued to emerge in Greece proved over and over that the United States was involved in what Anne O'Hare McCormick called "a new kind of war." In a series of articles in the *New York Times* in late 1948 and early 1949, she warned that victory over the guerrillas rested on the "inner stamina" of the West and its allies. The guerrilla takeover of Naoussa and the assassination of the mayor showed that the Greeks were fighting a "shadow army" whose purpose was to terrorize the people into submission. Greece was the "hot spot in the cold war" and an "index" of Stalin's intentions, comparable to the Berlin airlift in "symbolic significance." The situation in Greece proved that "cooperation must be carried into all fields to win a contest that is extended into all fields." With the communist overthrow of the Czech republic barely a year in the past, McCormick declared that Greece must not become "another Czechoslovakia."[5]

I

As the fighting continued in Greece, disagreements developed between the American and Greek military officers over the use again of napalm. To improve its effectiveness, the State Aircraft Factory had built the first two types of sway braces designed to carry wing tanks on Spitfires. The first successful test had an incendiary impact that was, according to witnesses, both accurate and "devastating." Yet Greek pilots repeated their earlier opposition to napalm because of the danger of forest fires and because of their fear of enemy retaliation. Greek commanders also were hesitant. They were reluctant to order their pilots to use the substance in low altitude attacks because of the possibility of setting fire to themselves. The objections became so strong that Americans suggested another type of incendiary bomb containing gelled gasoline mixtures. Spitfires could carry a combination of these and napalm bombs. By the end of March the State Aircraft Factory had produced over six hundred tanks considered "very satisfactory" for operational use. But the Greek Air Ministry gave in to the pilots' pressure and ordered a halt to the project.[6]

If the differences over the use of napalm suggested that all was not well within the alliance, relations became testy as the Greek government demanded more assistance in the war and the Americans urged its leaders to make better use of what they had. Greek officials repeatedly appealed for help under the self-defense guarantees contained in Article 51 of the UN Charter. But, White House advisers noted, even though the "presumed operational direction" came from the outside, no evidence suggested "direct participation in military operations against Greece by the armed forces of the USSR or Greece's three northern neighbors." The CIA cautioned that Greece was beginning to look like a "running sore" that needed "constant doctoring" but would be "unable to respond to treatment."[7] Others in the administration, however, were certain that the emergency had passed and that the completion of the job belonged to the Greek government. The Truman Doctrine had succeeded in preserving the country's independence and territorial integrity. Though the northern borders were not sealed, outside assistance now came mainly from Albania and was not large enough to do more than maintain small-scale guerrilla activity. The communists' peace proposals suggested their realization that the military standstill could shift against them. Either the guerrillas had changed to political tactics to permit the Kremlin to turn attention elsewhere, or they had decided that the way to victory did not lie through the battlefield. Whatever the truth, the United States had to convince the Greek government that it must win the war without additional assistance.

Another issue had erupted that threatened the aid program: according to Grady, some Americans and Greek loyalists were ready to take matters into their own hands by granting dictatorial powers to General Papagos. In early January (while Grady was in Washington, delayed by plane difficulties), W. Averell Harriman visited Athens, where, in his capacity as special representative for the Economic Cooperation Administration in Europe, he met with the organization's director in Greece, John Nuveen. Upon Grady's return to Athens less than a week later, he discovered that Nuveen had warned Harriman that the ECA program in Greece would fail unless the United States adopted a "tough policy." Harriman and Nuveen had then approached King Paul about the need for what Grady called a "semi-dictatorship under General Papagos." Chances for the approval of such a recommendation seemed good, Grady declared, because the king was already leaning toward that idea, and Papagos was "a member of the palace household and warmly devoted to the King." Toward that objective, Harriman and Nuveen privately approved Paul's proposal to remove the present government in Athens and himself appoint a cabinet. If one could not be formed, Papagos would be asked to assemble a government of his own. Should Parliament disapprove, the king would dissolve that body and leave Papagos as a virtual dictator. Harriman later denied giving approval to the king's proposal, and the ECA director in Europe, Paul Hoffman, sent a telegram to Harriman and Nuveen, insisting that the United States "cannot take [the] initiative in overthrowing [the] parliamentary government" and establishing a "dictatorship" or "authoritarian regime." Such a development might occur on its own, but the "ECA will not agitate for powerful pressure by [the] US Mission to reconstitute [the] present government by drastic steps."[8]

Grady was infuriated and tried to combat a move that would surely undermine the Truman Doctrine. He first talked with the British ambassador in Athens, Sir Clifford Norton, who agreed that such an attempt would be disastrous to the aid program. But the key person in defeating the proposal was British Vice-Admiral Lord Mountbatten, who was a guest of the king and talked all night with him in an effort to dissuade him from such a course. In the meantime Bevin in London sent a message through Norton, expressing opposition to a Papagos dictatorship. Grady warned the king that "little dictatorships tend to become big ones," and remarked that the plan "might ultimately result in the King's joining other ex-sovereigns on the Riviera." Fortunately, Grady asserted, Papagos was not enthusiastic about the proposal. The king finally gave up the idea and agreed to the installation of a new center-right government.[9]

Grady's anger over the attempt to grant dictatorial powers to Papagos was fueled by his earlier failures to have Nuveen removed from his ECA post in Greece. Grady had expressed misgivings about his own appointment to

Greece when for a time it appeared that he would not become head of both the embassy and the aid program. Hoffman had informed him that legal difficulties prevented the ambassador from heading the ECA in Greece. Grady was aware of MacVeagh's problems with Griswold and did not intend to go through the same kind of experience. He offered to withdraw from the post and remain in India. But Hoffman assured him that any ECA appointee to Greece would require Grady's approval and would act as his deputy in carrying out aid operations. Nuveen at first seemed acceptable. He was a banker and a "man of ideals," Grady noted with satisfaction. But he quickly became convinced that Nuveen "was not fitted for the responsibilities" assigned to him, and that he spent most of his time recruiting personnel because of an "obsession with regard to the need of a large organization." Grady complained to Washington. Hoffman talked with Acheson and others in the State Department and, offering no explanation, assured Grady that the matter was settled and Nuveen would present no further problems. But Nuveen did not change his attitude. America's aid, he believed, entitled it to impose policy on the Greek government—in Grady's words, to "dictate, in effect, the personnel and method of operation of the government of a sovereign country." Grady could not convince Nuveen that such a policy would vindicate the critics who accused the United States of using money to spread its political influence throughout the world.[10]

At this point Grady's feud with Nuveen meshed with his concern over a Papagos dictatorship as well as with his growing opposition to Van Fleet's approach to the war. Grady was already indignant with Harriman, a veteran diplomat, for violating the ambassador's prerogative by arranging a direct approach to the king. Then, when Grady asked Harriman and Nuveen about the subject of their talks with the king, they denied having discussed political issues. "This was not true," Grady later declared. He saw the memoranda of the conversations dictated by the king afterward. Grady was also infuriated with Van Fleet and General Down from the British mission, who were likewise favorable to a non-parliamentary remedy—a Papagos regime—with the general as prime minister. Had they succeeded, Grady declared, Papagos would not have become commander-in-chief and the military outcome "might have been very different."[11]

This controversy was still smoldering when the Greek government, on January 19, passed an emergency law calling Papagos out of retirement and making him commander-in-chief of the nation's armed forces. During Marshall's visit to Greece the previous October, he had urged Sophoulis and other leaders to grant full powers to Papagos; Marshall's own experiences during World War II had shown that commanders-in-chief must have full authority over their generals. Marshall's arguments probably had an effect, for Papagos won all of his demands and would be free of political interference. His first exhortation to his men came two days later: "[E]verything [was] at stake"— their country's territorial integrity, independence, tradition, and future—their "very survival as a race and a Nation." The basic need was "moral rearmament." The soldiers must talk only of victory, and they must take the offensive everywhere. "There are no obstacles which cannot be overcome for one who wants and is determined to win." Papagos intended to win the war by the end of 1949, and made a favorable impression on Van Fleet by asking his advice on how to do so.[12]

Van Fleet praised the government for granting its new field commander the broad powers needed to achieve victory. Papagos would demand discipline and was "very sound in his views and firm in his decisions." He recognized that the major weakness in the war effort were in command and training, and he wanted to cooperate with the Americans in seeking improvements. Three days after his appointment, Papagos replaced the large and unwieldy Supreme National Defense Council with the War Council, which was comprised of the premier and deputy premier; the leaders of the four parties participating in the government; Grady; Van Fleet; and Down. In response to Van Fleet's call for action, Papagos authorized his officers "to shoot on the spot anyone under his command who showed negligence or faintheartedness."[13]

Another striking change, Van Fleet asserted, was the recall to active duty of Lieutenant General Constantine Ventiris as inspector general—the former chief of the Greek General Staff and later field commander who had resigned for political reasons about a year before. Of "strong character," Ventiris was regarded by many as "the best military commander in Greece." He had been among the few Greek commanders to argue that the size of the army was sufficient and that the problem was to improve quality. The powers of inspector general had been expanded to make Ventiris a virtual "roving army commander." He insisted upon the reassignment of aggressive and obedient battalion and brigade commanders. "This will be a godsend," Van Fleet declared.[14]

Grady, however, did not share Van Fleet's enthusiasm regarding Papagos's leadership. Before the War Council in early February, Grady came under enormous pressure from Papagos to support an enlargement of the army. The general argued for two hours that the army was too small and that he had become commander-in-chief with the understanding that he would get whatever size army he felt necessary. Grady assured Washington that he had written a letter to the Greek prime minister disassociating the United States from any agreements in connection with Papagos's appointment. The ambassador repeated these thoughts to Tsaldaris and noted that Marshall was displeased as well. Papagos, however, attributed failure on the battlefield to an inadequate number of troops. He complained that requests for a 250,000-man army had gone to Grady, Marshall, and Royall, and that nothing had happened. Grady asserted that the previous November he had told Sophoulis that both Van Fleet and Down had recommended improvements in command, organization, training, and will to fight—*not* more men. Grady noted that Papagos's tone was disturbing. "In the vernacular, he was telling us off." Papagos quoted his letter of the preceding fall to the prime minister in which he asserted that if the army was not expanded to 250,000 within four months of his assumption of command, he would resign.[15]

Grady was irate over Papagos's behavior. Although no one had sought Grady's views at the meeting, he volunteered some bitter remarks to several ministers afterward. He had never heard nor read anything more upsetting. The general was violating the aid agreement by calling up conscripts without paying attention to the authorized ceiling. He was promising raises in officers' salaries and special funds for families of officers and soldiers—all of which entailed huge expenditures. If the allies did not provide funds, Papagos declared, the Greek government would institute confiscatory taxes. He appeared to have no understanding of the financial or economic side of the Greek problem.[16]

If Grady's feelings were justified, even he could not dispute the claim that the appointment of Papagos as commander-in-chief soon led to a vastly improved army. The general brought discipline to the army's senior officers, dismissed incompetents and insubordinates, ordered his soldiers into the training program provided by the American advisers, and demanded field operations that emphasized the offensive. One observer praised him for bringing coordination between the ground and air forces. Under Papagos's leadership, the army prepared a campaign designed to assault every guerrilla stronghold in Greece.[17]

Despite the continued elusiveness of victory, Americans at home remained confident that the White House could reduce its aid commitment without endangering the outcome. Whether they refused to believe the official caution expressed by observers in Greece, or because they considered issues more urgent elsewhere, the pressure mounted to cut assistance funds. Public Law 472 called for $200 million of military aid for Greece during FY 1949, which broke down into nearly $170 million for ground forces, $12 million for the navy, nearly $15 million for the air force, and over $3 million for administrative expenses. Congress, however, reduced the total figure for Greece and Turkey by $50 million, forcing the administration to implement Marshall's earlier contingency plan of shifting funds within the overall allotment to provide more for Greece.[18]

The aid cuts nonetheless meant that Greek leaders were going to have to do more to help themselves. In early January, the State Department argued that they must set aside political squabbles and recognize that recovery was not an American or Allied problem. The Greek government received a million dollars a day from the Truman Doctrine and the Marshall Plan. American assistance to Greece was greater, on a per capita basis, than to any other country. Now, as President Truman indicated in his inaugural address of January, he advocated a "Point Four" program of technical assistance to underdeveloped nations. The new aid effort, he later declared, had grown out of the Truman Doctrine, which had succeeded "magnificently" in Greece and Turkey. The Greek government must stop trying to embarrass the administration by accusing the United States of not being sufficiently generous. Even though America had global responsibilities, the political independence and territorial integrity of Greece were still vital to the Free World. The United States's support remained firm.[19]

The Truman administration's reluctance to expand its commitment to Greece seemed justified when the war suddenly took a turn toward peace: the guerrillas had made another call for negotiations and, in a move that was far-reaching in implications and probably related to the first, announced that Markos was no longer in command. On January 25 the Markos regime declared over guerrilla radio that it was willing to enter negotiations with the Greek government. Three days later the Athens Press Ministry expressed no surprise, dismissing the offer as a "new maneuver" designed to persuade the American Congress to cut aid further because the war was over. But in view of the events at Grammos and afterward the guerrillas this time seemed sincere. A British journalist was perhaps correct in declaring that the battle of Grammos had proved more costly to the enemy than surmised. The offer to negotiate suggested that the guerrillas' leadership had undergone major changes and that, combined with the Soviets' overture (to Tsaldaris from Tchernychev the preceding June), the move toward ending the war was real. But the greatest evidence of a shift in policy came within a week, when Markos lost command of the Democratic Army. The KKE's Central Committee announced that because of Markos's continued poor health, he had been removed from his positions as premier, as minister of war, and as commander, and as a member of the party's Politburo. The top spots now belonged to Zahariadis, who became secretary general and military commander. Yiannis Ioannides, vice premier and member of the Politburo, became acting premier. In a statement carrying deep implications, Free Greek radio announced that the party would allow no more "nationalist diversions."[20]

These alterations in guerrilla leadership caused immediate speculation that Markos had been ousted because he was pro-Tito and the KKE favored the Cominform. The Greek press adopted this line of reasoning, as did *Time* magazine in the United States. American and British officials in Greece also tied Markos's fall to his opposition to full-scale warfare and his Greek nationalism, which was manifested in his lack of enthusiasm for an independent Macedonia. Grady thought the change reflected a move to establish Cominform control over the guerrillas, whereas Acheson declared that Markos had achieved "undue personal prestige." Harriman believed that Moscow was behind the change—that it was trying to avoid new problems in the Balkans while attempting to secure positions already held. The State Department noted that a "primary motive" was Markos's lack of effectiveness in the field, but it believed that his "liquidation" was chiefly due to a strict "Cominform-Moscow line" taken by Zahariadis and his followers. The change in leadership would permit closer coordination with Albania and Bulgaria in encircling Yugoslavia. The KKE's leadership elected eight new permanent members of the Central Executive Committee, all of whom were staunch adherents to Cominform policy. The purge in the KKE was in line with those in Poland, Czechoslovakia, and Albania in 1948–49, along with the "more or less constant purges" in Bulgaria and Rumania.[21]

Even though the communists seemed confused and divided about command and tactics, the White House believed that they remained true to their goal of subjugating Greece and that they were turning their struggle into different channels. A pattern would doubtless become apparent. At first the communists would praise their allies for contributing to the military effort aimed at furthering their revolutionary cause. Then would follow their demands for positions within the Greek government. The initial phase was already under way. For the first time spokesmen for the guerrilla movement and the Greek Communist party publicly announced the importance of outside aid: "In the Popular Democracies," the KKE declared, "we found great and wholehearted support, without which we could not have made progress." To rally its followers and perhaps to exert more pressure on the Greek government to enter negotiations, the KKE insisted that victory would come in 1949, when a "solid popular revolutionary army" seized control of Greece on the basis of "indispensable fire power." The executive secretary of the National Security Council, Sidney W. Souers, assured his colleagues that even though the Soviet Union realized that American aid had undermined the guerrillas' military efforts, it still hoped to keep the country in turmoil. There was no basis for believing that the Kremlin would "permit any political settlement with Greece which would not result in or pave the way for communist domination of the country."[22]

The Truman administration was convinced that the call for a Macedonian state was the major disruptive force in the communist front. The issue was integral to the Yugoslav-Cominform rift, to Yugoslavia's relations with Bulgaria and Albania, to the division within the KKE, and to the establishment of a Balkan federation. Unrest had resulted from rumors claiming that in exchange for Tito's aid, Markos would cede much of Greek Macedonia to Yugoslavia, and would award the National Liberation Front some important positions in the Free Greek regime. The rumors were essentially correct, for the Bled agreements of August 1947 had authorized aid to the KKE from Yugoslavia, Albania, and Bulgaria in exchange for the establishment of a Slavo-Macedonian state that included parts of Greek Macedonia. Ambassador Cannon in Yugoslavia thought that since the end of World War II, the communists had developed a "closely coordinated political strategy" that involved the questions of Macedonian unification, the talks pertaining to a south Slav federation, and the guerrilla efforts in Greece. He was convinced that when the "secret history" of this period became available, the United States would find that Stalin in 1945, along with the Yugoslavs and Bulgarians, "laid down lines of guerrilla activity in Greece," and that the secret protocol of the Bled agreements would refer to these plans. The announcement of a forthcoming Free Greece at the same time as the Bled negotiations was not coincidental. Thus, as Cannon saw it, the central ingredient in the

Macedonian issue was the rise and fall of the Communist party of Yugoslavia as the Soviets' instrument for organizing the Balkans. Although the State Department suspected some sort of agreement but was likewise unaware of the terms, it believed that most guerrillas were patriots who opposed the partition of Greece and that Markos had now decided against sacrificing his country for any arrangement. His deal with Tito had become a critical "stumbling block" to KKE unity.[23]

The White House was correct in believing that the internal struggle over Macedonia had meshed with problems regarding leadership of the struggle to cause widespread dissension within the KKE. Although American and British observers in Greece estimated that 70 percent of the guerrillas at one time favored Markos, the defeat at Grammos convinced most of his supporters that he was expendable. But Ioannides had received training in Moscow and, like Zahariadis, supported a Macedonian republic at Greek expense. The secret arrangements Zahariadis had made with the KKE in November 1948 now became public as the party's official policy. In an attempt to placate the Slavo-Macedonians, the KKE announced in early February that Macedonia would soon be independent. Elaborating on that point, Zahariadis called for "the unification of the Macedonian people into a single Macedonian state, independent and with equality of rights, within the framework of a peoples' republican federation of the Balkan peoples." At a conference the following month, he criticized Tito and praised Georgi Dimitrov, leader of the Bulgarian Communist party. The Free Greek regime now looked to Bulgaria as the hub of a Balkan federation.[24]

The removal of Markos and the conflict over the Macedonian question exposed the deep divisions among the Greek communists over strategy and tactics. Zahariadis urged adherence to the Cominform program, and called for a further modernization of the army in preparation for conventional engagements (at the same time American military officers were advising the Greeks to convert infantry units to commando tactics). In February, his forces launched a raid on Florina, a snow-covered and garrisoned town of 11,000 residents that was located along the borders of Albania and Yugoslavia. Some 4,000 guerrillas engaged in a four-day battle with government soldiers, later joined by the air force, which ended in a rout of the guerrillas that cost nearly half of their forces. Indeed, the siege of Florina was the Democratic Army's last frontal operation of the war. The push for an independent Macedonian state also had important repercussions. Zahariadis welcomed all Macedonians—whether Greek, Yugoslav, Bulgarian, Albanian, or Turk—which caused a sudden infusion of recruits into the Democratic Army that drove the number of Slavo-Macedonians to 14,000, or nearly two-thirds of the army's strength. Whether this move had effectively internationalized the Greek war remains a matter of debate. Whatever the nationality of the Macedonians, the great masses of Greek guerrillas became distraught with their leaders' willingness to sacrifice the homeland to the Slavs. All but the most fervent adherents of Moscow left the party. Declarations of repentance among Greek Communists in royalist prisons became so widespread that the government had to draw up a shortened version of the standard form used for renouncing the party.[25]

Profound changes in the Balkans were under way, according to Cannon. The switch in communist leadership seemed indicative of a sincere drive for peace in the Greek war that would free the guerrilla movement to pursue the Cominform's anti-Tito program. The changeover to Zahariadis would save face by allowing the communists to blame Markos for the outcome of the war. Their peace offer should be taken "very seriously." The United States might encounter "highly aggressive conciliatoriness" from the Cominform states at the next UN General Assembly meeting. But a winding down of the war in Greece would give the Kremlin a chance to promote a communist takeover through subversion and infiltration while allowing the KKE to purge its "Titoists" and move toward closer cooperation with Albania and Bulgaria. Tito was in a tough position. He must publicly support conciliation even while his status in Macedonia was being undermined. Otherwise, the Cominform might accuse him of making secret arrangements with the government in Athens, and attempt to destroy his regime. The United States should do nothing regarding Yugoslavia's policy toward Greece. Events must convince the Yugoslavs of their "strategic vulnerability."[26]

Concurrence with Cannon's observations came from more than one source. Gerald A. Drew, the acting U.S. representative on the UN Special Committee on the Balkans, noted that Yugoslavia had to move cautiously because of certain Soviet reprisals. The Yugoslav War Ministry held back shipments for the guerrillas, including a huge supply of Swiss, Swedish, and Belgian arms (flamethrowers, hand grenades, machine guns, ammunition, infantry cannon) which had recently arrived in Yugoslavia on a Yugoslav vessel. The War Ministry also ordered home all Yugoslavs among the guerrillas. The United States should do no more than ask Yugoslavia to seal the border (*Time* magazine reported that the Yugoslavs had begun erecting barbed-wire barriers along the border in January), close refugee camps, return the children, and establish commercial and diplomatic relations with Greece. Marshall was encouraged by the prospects of improved Yugoslav-Greek relations, even if Tito's move in that direction stemmed only from self-preservation. Since pressure from the UN or from any of the major powers could embarrass Tito before the Cominform and his people, Marshall agreed that the progression of events should determine the outcome.[27]

Thus events on the battlefield had combined with troubles within the KKE to suggest that the American aid effort in Greece was moving toward success. The appointment of Papagos had brought an end to the army's defeatist attitude and had led to its improved performance. The new coalition government (led by Sophoulis and Alexander Diomedes) received an overwhelming vote of confidence from Parliament and was making progress in its economic recovery plan. The military campaign in the Peloponnese was coming to a triumphal close as government forces cleared the peninsula.

During the operations of early 1949, the army broke the guerrillas' intelligence and supply network, preventing them from further surprise attacks on the soldiers and permitting the army to launch surprise attacks of its own. The guerrillas' strength had dipped to 19,000, which was a marked decline from 26,000 just a year earlier, and of this smaller number nearly 25 percent were women. Amid this surge of hope, the United States made plans to establish economic relations with Yugoslavia. Although some British military leaders were now calling for a substantially enlarged army to finish the job, Grady saw no need for that. He wrote the secretary of state in early March: "Please tell the President for me that I feel we are getting hopefully near the full realization of the faith he showed in the evolution of the Truman Doctrine for Greece."[28]

II

The guerrillas' major objective during the spring of 1949 was to regain control of Grammos. Such a success would permit the re-establishment of a major base of operations connected with the Sarandaporos River valley and other supply routes. Toward this objective, the guerrillas established supply depots in Albania, just across from the main points of entry into the Grammos region. During the first night of April they joined newly arrived brigades from Vitsi in opening an offensive on a Greek army outpost on Height Alevitsa. Three times the guerrillas failed to take the point. By dawn the government's forces turned the attack and drove the enemy northward.[29]

The Greek command in Athens prepared to divert some forces from the central part of the country into Grammos. After assigning the National Defense Corps to safeguard Florina and Kastoria, it dispatched planes to assist a contingent of 20,000 soldiers in a day and night advance to the north. The ensuing battle at Grammos tipped back and forth until by the end of the first week in April each side had held the same height two times. Nearly 5,000 guerrillas armed with eight artillery pieces managed to hold off a much larger government force that included ten brigades, two commando groups, and air and artillery support.[30]

By mid-April the guerrillas held two hundred square miles of Grammos—which they quickly lost again. To regain the initiative, they launched an attack on Amindaion. But Greek intelligence had learned of the move, allowing the army to deal an effective counterblow. The guerrillas retreated to Vitsi, leaving behind more than three hundred dead and over ninety prisoners. The declining strength of the guerrillas became evident in that half of their attack force was female. Meanwhile the army pushed the enemy from the ridges along Boliana-Tambouri. For a brief time the guerrillas held a narrow piece of land south of the Sarandaporos River, but a nighttime commando attack soon drove them from that spot as well.[31]

By the end of the month government forces had dislodged the guerrillas from Grammos. The outcome was costly for both sides. The Greek army suffered over 1,400 casualties, whereas the guerrillas lost almost half that figure. But the guerrillas were hard-pressed for replacements and were now confined to a strip of territory along the Albanian frontier west of the Sarandaporos River. Albania remained their last refuge, their sole avenue for moving troops, and their only base for launching artillery and mortar fire into Greece.[32]

With Grammos clear, Greek forces were able to implement "Operation Rocket," which was designed to sweep southern and central Greece. Phase "A" began on May 2, intended to push the guerrillas out of Roumeli and northward into Agrafa. After two weeks of what American observers called "hide-and-seek," the army surrounded the enemy at Stayia and, at minimal loss, inflicted over a hundred casualties and forced the guerrillas to disperse into small groups. Slowly the army pursued the enemy northward, overrunning Angistron and seizing many weapons and materials. Later in the month, the army routed a large band of guerrillas northeast of Konitsa and confiscated more weapons and supplies. Phase "B," a full-scale offensive in Agrafa and Tsoumerka, began on May 5. Two divisions and several light infantry battalions prepared to surround over 2,000 guerrillas who had the Pindus Mountains at their backs. One division pushed toward the major Pindus ridge while the other advanced from the west. According to the plan, the guerrillas would be unable to retreat north, and, facing additional soldiers due to arrive from Roumeli, they could not escape south. But breakdowns in timing allowed the guerrillas to elude the trap.[33]

After the failure in Roumeli, Greek leaders made alterations in their military effort to prevent such a recurrence. They established a temporary command headquarters at Epirus and western Macedonia that would coordinate the pursuit operations in south-central and central Greece with the offensive in southern Grammos. The forces under Lieutenant General Ventiris would sweep the rear areas, hold the guerrillas where they were in the north, and prepare for a major offensive in the latter part of the year.[34]

In late May the army began an assault that within four days drove an entire guerrilla division out of Agrafa. West of Karditsa, the soldiers forced more of the enemy into retreat. Commandos and light infantrymen pursued the guerrillas across the Ossa-Pilion mountain range and scattered them in the Mount Olympus area. During the night a brigade and a commando group began a pursuit operation that within a month drove the last stragglers into Albania.[35]

The guerrillas attempted to concentrate in Thrace and in central and eastern Macedonia. Most of their actions consisted of attacks on villages, but each time the Greek army countered by pushing the guerrillas farther north. Near the end of the month, the guerrillas had established a series of defense posts in Vitsi and had moved in nearly thirty artillery pieces. The show of strength was misleading. The recent attack force on Florina had included 30 percent women, and the withdrawal had left two hundred casualties—about 40 percent of the original number.[36]

The Greek army was making progress, but Van Fleet warned that continued outside help to the guerrillas kept the outcome in question. The diversion of men to Grammos had dealt the guerrillas a severe setback, and the army expected to clear central Greece by July. The war was going well, Van Fleet assured General Bradley. But, in a curious and unsubstantiated statement, he warned that the communists, "with increased Russian assistance," remained capable of resistance in northwest Greece. The "continued open and flagrant help" from Albania was "most provoking." Corps commanders had a tendency to operate against guerrilla border bases, which drained troops from central Greece. The commandos had few reserves, many divisions remained engaged in static defense, and not one complete battalion was engaged in field training. Van Fleet warned Bradley against aid cuts and declared this the time to demonstrate strength.[37]

The momentum gained by government forces encouraged British military observers to increase their calls for an enlargement of the army that would permit the lethal blow; but American spokesmen opposed the idea. "Being British," Grady caustically remarked, the recommendations were "cast in terms of Empire defense and being a British soldier's report it makes its recommendations without giving consideration to [the] cost either to [the] US taxpayer or [to the] Greek recovery program." A sure way to slow the offensive was for stories to circulate that the army was too small and would soon be increased. The White House must not raise the troop ceiling. American and Greek military officials had enough problems with the present army in matters relating to training, equipment, and use of units. Van Fleet conceded that an increase was not practical. No money was available for additional troops and equipment, and the men could have no operational impact before the summer of 1950. He repeated these feelings to Sophoulis.[38]

The primary obstacle to victory now was the assistance from Albania, which led the Greek government to place pressure on the Truman administration to stem that nation's involvement in the war. Dendramis explained to the State Department that Balkan politics was enormously complicated. Developments in Macedonia were interrelated with Cominform pressure on Yugoslavia, which in turn bore heavily on Greece. If the Cominform overthrew Tito, Dendramis warned, the consequences would be "extremely dangerous" for Greece, Turkey, and Italy. The West must take "strong and decisive" measures against Albania—including a naval action. This would protect Tito's western flank and Greece's north, while giving the West a "valuable pawn" for securing "improved Soviet behavior in the Balkans." Aid to Greece "should be accordingly adjusted."[39]

The Albanian question became the subject of a series of UN talks on the Balkans at Lake Success, New York. Some participants recommended that the Greek government defuse the growing problem with Albania by renouncing claims to Northern Epirus. Grady immediately opposed the suggestion. He agreed that the move would provide good propaganda, but he did not consider it politically advisable for Greece to take an action so favorable toward a hostile government that was providing support to guerrillas out of Northern Epirus. The *quid pro quo* must be good relations with Greece's northern neighbors. Otherwise the renunciation would appear to be a capitulation.[40]

Although the Greek government continued to call for help from Washington, the White House refused out of fear that sanctions against the Albanians would elevate the Greek struggle into an international issue and thereby jeopardize America's overall strategy. Participation in a UN action might have been acceptable, but unilateral involvement in an issue relating to Northern Epirus and Albania (as in the case of Macedonia and other Balkan matters) was out of the question, no matter what the ramifications were for Greece. The Truman administration had to downgrade assistance to Greece in accordance with other problems.[41] The United States was successfully reducing the guerrilla threat to a level that the government in Athens could handle. White House efforts stopped below the northern border: although clearly exacerbated by outside interference and regional issues, the conflict was still officially termed a civil war.

Even though the United States felt the necessity of steering clear of Balkan matters, it must have been tempted to take the Macedonian controversy before the world because of its relationship to the Tito-Stalin rift. From Belgrade, Cannon noted that the chief issue in the Macedonian question might turn out to be the United States's ability to support Yugoslavia in the "first successful rebellion in [the] Soviet Empire." The White House must not leave the impression with the Soviets that it dismissed the matter as unimportant; neighboring communist states might use military force to put down Tito and feel unrestrained in halting any fledgling upheavals in their own countries. The embassy in Belgrade recommended that the United States block Soviet intentions in Macedonia and Yugoslavia by proposing a pact before the UN by which Yugoslavia, Albania, and Bulgaria would enter into mutual border guarantees with Greece. Such a pact would focus attention on Macedonia and convince the Soviets that they could not engage in any aggression against Tito without arousing public notice.[42] Nothing came of Cannon's suggestion—again because of the United States's resistance to any Balkan involvement that might internationalize the Greek war.

The guerrillas' failure at Grammos had apparently added a sense of urgency to other Cold War concerns, for in late April the Soviets expressed interest in working with the United States and Britain in negotiating an end to the war. The Soviets' willingness to go farther than their earlier proposal of private mediation now seemed clear. They did not want an intensification of the Cold War—as further evidenced by their efforts to defuse the ongoing crisis in Berlin.

The attempt to bring about a negotiated settlement actually got under way with Dean Rusk, who was an American representative to the UN. Following a dinner at UN Secretary-General Trygve Lie's house in New York on April 26, Andrei Gromyko, deputy foreign minister of the Soviet Union and a delegate to the General Assembly, became involved in a discussion of UN matters with Hector McNeil, Britain's minister of state and delegate to the assembly, and Rusk, America's assistant secretary of state for UN Affairs. Rusk steered the conversation to the war in Greece and inquired whether the three of them might find a way to normalize that situation. Gromyko turned to McNeil and remarked that if the British withdrew their troops, the Greeks themselves could resolve the matter. When McNeil rejoindered that the major problem was the influx of military aid from the north, Gromyko interrupted by noting that that charge had never been proved. Rusk supported McNeil by declaring that the United States had sent military aid because the guerrillas had received outside assistance. The result was a "desultory exchange," Rusk later recorded, primarily between Gromyko and McNeil. Before tempers flared, Rusk interjected an expression of hope that the three men could use their influence to pacify the Greek situation and suggested that they rejoin others at the party.[43]

That brief and animated conversation aroused interest in Moscow, for, in less than two weeks, on May 4, Gromyko invited Rusk and McNeil to meet with him that same day to discuss the Greek matter in "more concrete terms." Rusk called on McNeil to discuss a response to Gromyko's invitation. Rusk emphasized that he could not become involved in formal talks with Gromyko but would listen on an informal and personal basis. McNeil was pleased. He had already made an appointment for the two of them to see Gromyko that afternoon and had learned from the British embassy in Washington that Rusk had agreed to the meeting. Rusk said he had heard nothing but would go along to avoid complications.[44]

At 3:45 p.m., the three men met in Gromyko's office, where he reported his government's interest in ending the war. His superiors in Moscow were encouraged by Rusk's remark during the April 26 conversation that he hoped the three of them could use their influence to settle the Greek situation. McNeil understood that everything discussed was to be personal, informal, and not for the press, but he would listen to what Gromyko had to say— especially if he had specific proposals. Rusk insisted that his objective was to facilitate a settlement that would allow the Greeks to focus on reconstruction. Any talks must be "purely informal" and "imply no change in the forum for discussing the Greek question from existing United Nations channels." Gromyko agreed that everything said would be "informal and confidential."[45]

Gromyko turned the conversation toward bringing the war to a close. He referred to peace proposals of April 20 made by Miltiadis Porfirogenis, minister of justice of Free Greece, in which he called for a negotiated peace with UN mediation. But McNeil declared that this approach entailed formal negotiations and was unacceptable because the guerrillas did not constitute a legitimate government. When Rusk expressed unfamiliarity with the guerrillas' peace terms, Gromyko took from his desk a Russian text of the proposals and explained that he had not prepared an English translation for fear of altering the meaning. The first steps toward a final settlement were a cease-fire, general amnesty, and new elections, "in the administration of which," Gromyko emphasized, "the guerrilla forces would participate." After some discussion regarding how to end hostilities, Rusk noted that Gromyko did "not exclude a request by the great powers on both sides in Greece."[46]

Other difficulties became apparent. Rusk suggested that the vehicle toward resolving the conflict should be the UN Special Committee on the Balkans. But the Soviet seat on the committee remained vacant, and the Soviet attitude had not changed: Gromyko dismissed the committee as illegal and improper because it sought intervention in the Balkan countries' internal affairs. Rusk emphasized that the main issue was the illegal provision of goods to the guerrillas and that the UN was the appropriate forum. Gromyko responded that if the fighting stopped and parliamentary elections took place, the way would be open for "a normalization of other relations." What did Gromyko mean by "election"? Rusk inquired. A parliamentary election of a government under the existing constitution, or a plebiscite on other issues? Of a government, Gromyko curtly replied. Pleased with Gromyko's apparent willingness to shelve the Macedonian issue and other Balkan matters, Rusk asked how participation in election arrangements could take place. Since the guerrillas were scattered in the north, would there be a division of territorial responsibilities? Gromyko did not foresee this happening but thought it advisable to delegate ad hoc authority to a higher body established from the groups responsible for conducting the elections. When McNeil asked whether Gromyko was recommending a new UN body with Soviet participation, Gromyko left that possibility open by replying that the matter was subject to discussion. His only concerns were that the three governments agree on the methods to end the war and on the holding of parliamentary elections.[47]

Gromyko had concluded the discussion and wanted reactions to his proposals. McNeil could offer no comment on their merits; he could only convey suggestions to London. He did, however, warn of problems. The British could not treat the guerrilla regime as a government; they could not tell the Greek government how to handle internal affairs; and they would not infringe upon UN responsibilities. When Gromyko turned to Rusk, the response was predictable: this was an unofficial discussion and the White House could agree to no change in the forum for dealing with the Greek question. Rusk admitted that he had originally raised the possibility of using all three nations' influence in reaching a settlement—but the only acceptable procedure was through UN channels so that the Greek government could participate. Would there be a reply?, Gromyko wanted to know. Rusk promised to discuss the matter with his colleagues in Washington.[48]

The conversation left several questions. Gromyko had not raised the issue of withdrawing British troops or ending American military aid, both of which he had mentioned at Lie's home in late April. Nor had Gromyko criticized the present government in Greece, despite his disparaging remarks at the earlier meeting. By Gromyko's implied consent to restrict elections to a government, he seemed to deny Soviet interest in a free Macedonia. The State Department believed that the Soviets feared that the only way to keep the war going was to bring in non-Greeks—which Zahariadis was doing by inviting in all Macedonians. But this would risk a major war. Rusk thought it possible that the Soviets were attempting to reduce their foreign commitments at minimal political costs. Gromyko showed an "unusual degree of courtesy and affability" and appeared disappointed at receiving no specific replies to his proposals. In light of the recent relaxation of Soviet pressure on Berlin, Gromyko's attitude regarding Greece might have been another signal that Moscow had changed its strategy regarding expansion. Perhaps the Soviets needed a period of stability in Europe to allow them to exploit their seemingly favorable position in Asia. Or, they might have thought that a time of cooperation would weaken Western resolve and permit a renewed political offensive at a later date. In any case, Rusk insisted, the Soviet focus was shifting, and Washington needed to re-examine the Greek question with the intention of gradually terminating the military aid program. The administration must prepare counter-measures for the next Soviet move.[49]

Rusk's views regarding the Gromyko talks became the basis of White House policy. Although Rusk denied that the State Department had authorized him to discuss the Greek issue with Gromyko, it is probable that someone had told him to raise the matter on an informal basis. When Acheson reported to the President on Rusk's initial conversation with Gromyko, Truman expressed interest but emphasized that no formal talks could take place without Greek participation. The State Department observed that the communists had experienced sufficient bloodshed and would stop the war as soon as the Greek government guaranteed no more loss of life, assured general amnesty, and allowed the communists, in the words of the offer, "to contribute substantially toward such a peaceful democratic settlement of the home problem." The United States, according to directives received by Rusk, would "join in any approach" aimed at ending outside assistance, but would accept no settlement conditional upon any arrangement between the Greek government and its people. The Russians must have no role in Greek domestic affairs. To provide them a face-saving pretext for ending their support of the guerrilla movement, the Greek government should assure elections within the current year, agree to impose no death penalty on guerrillas who laid down their arms, and guarantee their fair treatment afterward.[50]

The timing of the diplomatic thaw in the Greek war—while the Soviets were lifting the blockade of Berlin—suggested that the opportunities for peace were real. Both peace offers—the one by the guerrillas, followed by Gromyko's overtures—came within the context of the Greek army's advances on the battlefield and America's diplomatic successes in Europe. Acceptance of these terms, however, would have infringed upon both the sovereignty of the Greek government and the responsibilities of the UN in regard to member states. Since the guerrillas were on the brink of annihilation, the Soviets were interested in saving what they could. The day following the May 4 meeting, the diplomatic correspondent of the Manchester *Guardian* tied together the two peace offers. In an article entitled, "Greek Rebels Want to End War—May Be Part of Moscow's General Peace Offensive," he explained that the Soviet Union had begun a general move for peace that was evident in its "more conciliatory approach" toward both Berlin and Greece. *Nation* expressed a similar view. For the first time the guerrillas were willing to negotiate without a prior withdrawal of the American mission and British troops, and without demanding an end to American aid. Czech Foreign Minister Vladimir Clementis had urged the president of the UN General Assembly, Herbert V. Evatt, to use the UN's good offices to help Porfirogenis secure an American visa to allow him to begin negotiations at Lake Success. "It need hardly be pointed out that a seasoned Communist in Dr. Clementis's position would no more dream of underwriting such a project without Russian sanction than of dropping a bomb on the Kremlin."[51]

The peace effort seemed legitimate for other reasons as well. The Soviets were only three months from detonating their own atomic device, and the spring of 1949 might have seemed a propitious time to arrange a cease-fire on the battlefield, negotiate or elect favorites to governmental positions, and then, hopefully, rely on atomic threats and continued subversion to recoup losses in Europe. Furthermore, once the war came to an end, the Soviets could deal with Tito. Had not the American chargé in Moscow alerted the State Department less than two months before that the liquidation of Tito was the "No. 1 objective in the Balkans," and that the Soviets' Greek policy would be "adapted as required"?[52] Even if that were not the case, Gromyko was undoubtedly aware of Yugoslavia's imminent termination of aid to the guerrillas and might have been looking for an honorable way out of the Greek affair. Whether the Soviet efforts were guiding the guerrillas' policy or paralleling them, the Kremlin wanted the war in Greece to stop.

On May 14, at Flushing Meadow, New York, the three men met a third time to discuss the war. Rusk initiated this meeting, largely to avoid misunderstandings that would allow Gromyko to claim that he had been unable to get a reply to his peace proposals. Rusk visited McNeil in his room at the Essex House and explained the wisdom of seeing Gromyko. But McNeil reported Bevin's interest in delaying any decisions pertaining to the conversations until he had discussed the Balkan situation with Acheson at the Council of Foreign Ministers meeting in Paris. To attract no attention, Rusk and McNeil secretly met with Gromyko that evening in a small room off the main hall of the General Assembly. When McNeil emphasized that no one could interfere in Greek internal affairs, Gromyko acknowledged with a "slight grunt" and turned to Rusk. The American repeated his earlier stand. Rusk and McNeil remained intractable because they believed that events in Greece and elsewhere had weakened the Soviets' position. The only negotiations possible, Rusk insisted, were through an "appropriate international forum which provided for full participation by the Greek Government." Gromyko was not interested in this approach and took from his pocket a short typed paper that contained three counter-proposals: the Soviet Union would partic- ipate in a commission of great powers to supervise a Greek parliamentary election, and in a commission of great powers to "control" the northern border of Greece; and all foreign military aid and personnel must withdraw from Greece. Even though McNeil thought Gromyko was "fishing very hard," Rusk believed that the situation remained unchanged. The three men adjourned.[53]

Rusk soon met with White House advisers to recommend that the time seemed right for peace and to urge them to inform Greek leaders of the Gromyko conversations before the news came from someone else and aroused suspicions that the United States was participating in unauthorized and private negotiations. He thought that an end to the war would allow the United States to take advantage of the situation in Yugoslavia and spread Western influence into the Balkans. The northern frontier of Greece must not take on the appearance of a line dividing two spheres of influence—especially with Yugoslavia on the other side of that line. Furthermore, a resolution of the border problems would ease the threat to Tito posed by the Macedonian issue and help him counter Soviet pressure. Rusk raised another considera- tion that affected the administration's general strategy: a continuation of the Greek struggle could require a diversion of American military resources from "more profitable areas." The Soviets were in a poor bargaining position. Rusk recommended that the United States offer to terminate military aid to Greece on condition that outside aid to the guerrillas also stopped. Although Rusk's observations required some thought, his warning about informing the Greek government did not. That same day, Acheson sent the necessary instructions to the embassy in Athens.[54]

But Gromyko had already informed the Greek embassy in Washington of the talks. He told Dendramis of the peace proposals presented to McNeil, who passed them to the British government. Dendramis was alarmed. Think- ing Gromyko had submitted the same offer to Rusk, Dendramis became wary of his allies. Had not they already shown reluctance to grant additional aid? Was Greece a mere instrument to be used by its allies in the Cold War? His home government feared the ramifications of any settlement without its participation and for that reason did not want the Greek question raised during the ongoing meeting of the Council of Foreign Ministers. The issue must remain in the UN where the Greek government had representation and could protect its interests. The Soviet Union, Dendramis knew, would make no concessions without gaining something in return. And now, with the British and Americans seemingly working behind his country's back, he could not be sure that they would resist Soviet demands. Dendramis agreed with his superiors in Athens that the Soviets' interest in peace was a sign of the guerrillas' weakness and that military power alone would end the war on the best possible terms.[55]

On May 20, the Soviets went a step farther and exerted public pressure on the West by announcing through the Tass news agency in Moscow that they were interested in settling the Greek war. Rusk and McNeil had made unofficial proposals for ending the conflict, Tass declared, and Gromyko had reacted in a way that proved his government's interest in a just peace. He would participate in peace talks only if they satisfied the conditions proclaimed by the Provisional Greek Democratic Government. After these agreements were in place, outside military aid to the Greek government should end and all foreign forces should pull out of the country. The Soviets were waiting for a reply from Washington and London.[56]

The same day that Tass released the story, Dendramis and other Greek embassy officials went to the State Department to complain that neither Rusk nor McNeil had informed them of the Gromyko conversations. Rusk assured them that the talks were informal and explained the specific proposals. Somewhat calmed, Dendramis expressed concern that the Russians wanted to publicize the talks to enable the communists' "fellow-travellers" to influence Congress to reduce aid. Soviet objectives remained the same even though tactics and strategy had changed. Rusk agreed with Dendramis's analysis and noted that when Gromyko was asked his understanding of "elections," he referred to parliamentary elections and not a plebiscite on Macedonia or some other matter. Rusk thought this was evidence of Soviet sincerity in wanting to end the fighting and return to political tactics. Dendramis was relieved that the United States had no plans for more talks regarding Greece.[57]

The Truman administration had to refute the implication in the Tass story that the Americans and British were responsible for prolonging the conflict. In a press release, the State Department claimed that, at the first gathering in New York, Rusk expressed hope that the three nations would use their influence to end the war in Greece. When Gromyko replied that the withdrawal of British troops would resolve the problem, Rusk countered that British and American military assistance had become necessary because of the armed rebellion aided by Greece's northern neighbors.[58] Tass did not mention these charges of outside interference. Nor did it cite the peace efforts by the UN Special Committee on the Balkans. The Soviets had refused to participate in these, perhaps because the battlefield forecast in late 1947 had looked promising. Now, when the guerrillas were faltering, the Soviets could not change their stand without losing face. Consequently, Gromyko had ignored these issues and concentrated on the peace terms proposed by the guerrillas. The Soviet Union could pose as a disinterested observer whose only concern was peace. Although the White House was certainly aware of these points, it could not prove them and did not want to become involved in a bitter public exchange with the Kremlin.

The American response to Gromyko's overtures nonetheless brought focus to the wide gulf between East and West over events in Greece. The Truman administration insisted that the conflict was internal, a civil war that had been fomented from the outside, and that should be handled by Greece and the UN. A cease-fire, amnesty, and elections were domestic concerns, subject only to the decisions of the Greek government. White House advisers had recognized that because of the guerrillas' misfortunes in the war, the Soviet Union was willing to participate in commissions for resolving the problems—which was a change from its earlier attitude toward the UN Special Committee on the Balkans. To join that committee would be a concession damaging to prestige, whereas membership in newly created commissions, no matter how narrowly distinguishable from the original, would be acceptable. In the interests of peace, the White House might have been willing to play this game in semantics. But a vital issue was at stake: Soviet participation in the commissions would open the door for direct involvement in Greek affairs, which neither Greece nor its Western allies could allow.

In accordance with the American assessment, the Greek government regarded Gromyko's overtures as a "Russian trap" and more vehemently demanded total victory. Sophoulis felt "gratitude and relief" with the American position. The king's political adviser, Panayiotis Pipinelis, feared that this "very clever Russian propaganda move" would hurt Greek morale. If the Greek government rejected the Soviet offer, its soldiers might come to believe that their leaders were not interested in peace. Cabinet members added other considerations. Peace talks could undermine the army's offensive by convincing its men to await the diplomats' verdict rather than risk life in a war that might soon end. Such discussions would interfere with the chances for better relations with Yugoslavia. A premature withdrawal of British troops would be a boost to the communists. The outcome of the war must depend on the battlefield, not the negotiating table.[59]

Grady agreed that peace discussions were unwise now that victory lay within reach. The Greeks were correct in opposing Soviet involvement in their domestic affairs and in resisting the legalization of the KKE, which would result in renewed subversive activities. There could be no discussions concerning elections, amnesty, and the KKE, for these matters were internal. But talks could take place regarding outside aid to the guerrillas, the return of Greek children, the establishment of diplomatic relations between Greece and its neighbors, and favorable frontier agreements—all international topics subject to UN consideration.[60]

Not all Americans supported this position. Despite British and American assurances that the Greek question should not come before the Council of Foreign Ministers, the American chargé in Moscow, Foy Kohler, saw no way to separate developments in Greece from other matters under discussion. Any agreement regarding Berlin would suggest that the Kremlin was shifting toward a relaxation of tensions in Europe, which, in turn, would raise hope that the Soviets wanted an end to the Greek war. A settlement in Greece would nonetheless be only a "temporary *détente*," as the fighting in the mountains would change into a "classic internal political struggle." Drew

agreed with his colleagues on the Balkan committee that insistence on unconditional surrender would discourage war-weary Greek people and jeopardize
public and congressional support in America. Aid from Yugoslavia was about
to end, and the situation in Thrace and eastern Macedonia was "relatively
rosy." Tito assured a high-ranking British official that the guerrillas would no
longer receive refuge or assistance, and Cannon learned from Edvard Kardelj,
Yugoslavia's minister for foreign affairs and member of the Politburo of the
Communist party, that the situation was "all different" and that orders had
gone out to stop material aid. Kardelj did not deny aiding the guerrillas in the
past but now seemed tired of the Greek involvement: "[W]e have no friends
[in Greece] any more. . . . [P]erhaps something will come of Gromyko's
proposal." Drew believed that with Greek participation, the Americans and
British might work out an arrangement with the Soviets to replace the Balkan
committee with a new body charged with conciliatory functions.[61]

The Rusk-McNeil-Gromyko talks did not lead to a settlement in Greece,
but the Soviet participation in the peace effort suggested a deeper concern
about defusing relations with the West that might have as one of its subsidiary
results a termination of the war. For the time being, however, the gap between
the opposing sets of proposals was too wide. The communists may have been
sincere in wanting to end the fighting, but the conditions they required for
holding discussions paradoxically assured that the outcome of the war would
rest on the battlefield, not at the negotiating table. Both sides had defensible
arguments. The communists could not approve any ground rules suggesting
that they lacked legitimacy as a viable political group. The Greek government
could not accept any arrangement that constituted recognition of the communists' legitimacy or that condoned Soviet participation in the country's domestic affairs. From either perspective, peace at such price was tantamount to
defeat.

As the chances for negotiations diminished, hopes soared for victory as
attention returned to the war in the mountains. In June the air force reversed
its stand and approved the use of napalm on a large scale. One official
assessment noted that the decision brought "excellent results." Spitfires
dropped the deadly containers of liquid fire, driving the guerrillas into the
open where they became easy targets for machine guns. Enemy recruitment
fell along with morale as the Greek army advanced northward. Guerrilla
sabotage units desperately worked behind the army, vainly trying to break its
thrust. Nothing could stop the onslaught. Operation Rocket was a success,
and plans were in place for the final phase of the northern assault—"Operation Torch"—to begin in August on 12,000 guerrillas entrenched in Vitsi and
Grammos and armed with Albanian artillery and mortars. Greek forces had
apparently turned the corner in the war. Van Fleet thought so. "Every effort is
being made to press home the victory this year. I believe it is within our
grasp."[62]

CHAPTER
12

Dénouement

I

By the summer of 1949, the war was clearly turning in the government's favor. Yugoslavia's reductions in aid to the guerrillas were having a serious impact on their war effort. The Greek army was severely restricting the guerrillas' contact with the rural population, leading to a sharp decline in abductions and to larger and more rapid withdrawals to the north.[1] Aid from Albania and Bulgaria continued, although not on the scale formerly provided by the Yugoslavs. The key to peace was a normalization of relations between Greece and Yugoslavia, which would result in a complete cessation of Yugoslav assistance to the guerrillas.

Evidence seemed conclusive that Yugoslavia was preparing to halt all help to the guerrillas when, in a speech at Pola on July 10, Tito announced the "progressive closure" of the Yugoslav-Greek border. Tito had attacked the guerrillas for making claims over Free Greek radio that Yugoslavia was helping the government in Athens. The guerrillas were "slandering us" to "blame us for [the] defeat [of the] Democratic Greek army." Tito's close associate, Svetozar Vukmanović-Tempo, later declared, "We gave them everything we could, but Stalin ordered them to slander us. . . . When they refused to stop, we closed our borders in 1949." Americans nonetheless remained cautious. Cannon warned that Tito's decision might mean "much or little." The border was already under strict control except for a few points left open for channeling communications. The United States, Cannon declared, had been pushing Yugoslavia to close it completely, "and I personally believe we have achieved it." Tito's appeal to the Americans and British to end "Greek provocations" was in "friendly terms"—perhaps an overture— whereas he used "bitter language" against Moscow. Acheson urged Tito to

214

regard the border closing as a step toward compliance with General Assembly resolutions calling for the repatriation of the Greek children and the re-establishment of good relations with the government in Athens.[2]

Van Fleet was uncertain about the impact of Tito's decision to close the border. On the one hand, Tito's apprehension regarding the Soviets was greater than his interest in winding down the Greek war and opening relations with the West. "It cannot be expected that Tito will effectively seal the Greek-Yugoslav border." His enemies were not in Greece, and "it cannot logically be expected that he will move the bulk of his forces along the Greek border." Yugoslavia's decision to stop aid to the Democratic Army would lead to increased assistance from Albania and Bulgaria. The guerrillas could still cross the Yugoslav border—unless Tito stationed troops there, which was not likely. On the other hand, Yugoslavia would no longer be a "haven" for the guerrillas, and the Greek army would not have to guard the border as carefully to stop the flow of men and supplies. The general situation would improve.[3]

Despite evidence that Tito soon completed the border closing and ordered the dismantling of guerrilla camps and hospitals, doubts lingered about whether the assistance had ceased. The Yugoslav ambassador in the United States, Sava N. Kosanovic, had assured Acheson on July 1 that his country was only receiving refugees and keeping them in camps. No one was sending material aid. Drew was cautious. Even if Belgrade had ordered a stop, a "twilight zone" would exist in which border police would be unwilling or unable to implement such a directive. Soon thereafter the Yugoslav foreign minister, Edvard Kardelj, accused Greek communist leaders of supporting the Cominform's "open policy of hostility against Yugoslavia" and an-nounced that his government had withdrawn "moral and political support" from the guerrillas. In early August, the UN Special Committee on the Balkans reported that Yugoslav aid had "diminished and may have ceased." Acheson expressed satisfaction and noted that Yugoslavia had to move cautiously in re-establishing relations with Greece. A rebuff of the Comin-form—demonstrated by an alliance with Greece, a partner of the West—could force Soviet intervention in Yugoslavia, either through its Balkan allies or by direct military action. Yet the time was appropriate to stabilize the frontier and bring order to the Balkans.[4]

As Yugoslav aid came to an end, the Greek government again sought outside assistance in halting Albania's growing involvement. Dendramis hoped that a UN recommendation might provide the basis for American action. But he encountered opposition from his ally. Van Fleet agreed with Brigadier General Reuben E. Jenkins and Admiral Forrest P. Sherman, commander of the Sixth Fleet in the Mediterranean, both of whom noted that a victory at Vitsi would take care of that problem by enabling the army to close the border. Grady warned that the Albanians did not heed public condemnations and that the United States could not risk a larger war by landing troops in Albania or blockading its coasts. McGhee and Cromie doubted the practicality of issuing a threat and could suggest no effective measures to adopt. The purpose of America's aid program was to restore internal order in Greece without, Grady emphasized, making that country part of a "*cordon sanitaire*" around the Soviet Union. America's chief consideration remained the danger of internationalizing the Greek war.[5]

But Greek officials would not drop the issue. During the first week of August, representatives of the British and French embassies in Athens became fearful of a Greek invasion of Albania. Tsaldaris offered no assurances to the British chargé, Ponsonby Crosthwaite, when he complained that Albanian aid to the guerrillas was intolerable and insisted that "if the Greek Army went into Albania it would be purely on military grounds rather than to achieve any political objective." Crosthwaite warned against expanding the war and repeated his feelings to Pipinelis and the minister of war. But Pipinelis had likewise told the French ambassador that the army would be caught in a dilemma if it won at Vitsi and approached the Albanian frontier. The Greek people and army wanted an invasion, regardless of whether the act created a "difficult international situation." Cromie assured the French embassy representative in Washington, Jean-Claude Winckler, that the United States had not changed its position—despite the impression left by Pipinelis that the White House "did not appear to oppose Greek military intervention in Albania." Grady felt confident that responsible Greek officials were not planning an invasion. Indeed, Cromie speculated that Tsaldaris and Pipinelis intended to use their allies' opposition to relieve them of public accountability. Winckler agreed.[6]

The British and the Americans, however, were not confident that all Greek leaders would act with restraint. In a private conversation, Diomedes (who was now prime minister after Sophoulis's death) warned Crosthwaite that the guerrillas' continued use of Albania as a base might lead to military measures. The American chargé in Athens, Harold B. Minor, reported that even though various Greek dignitaries had assured against an invasion, the army might engage in isolated crossings of the border for tactical reasons or in reaction to harassment. The Greeks were infuriated with the Albanians and, in the heat of battle, might not respect the border.[7]

In late August, as the war was again raging in the north, the Greek government placed more pressure on the United States, Britain, and France to take action against Albania. Dendramis wanted the Truman administration to support his government's call for UN assistance regarding the Albanian threat. Rusk offered no encouragement. The White House had no remedies to offer and would be "in the position of being forced to sit down at a table with other nations without having any course of action to propose." Acheson expressed hope to the British that one of the following circumstances might force the Albanians to change policy: their physical isolation from the Cominform; Greek success in the war; Cominform discouragement over the Greek situation. The Albanian matter was embarassing to the Western powers because they lacked the means of forcing a smaller and weaker country to end a practice that not only hurt their ally but prolonged unrest and created the potential for a wider war. Although the Western powers had "completely convincing evidence" of Albania's involvement, they could only appeal to that government for cooperation.[8]

Even while the Albanian problem intensified, the propensity in Washington remained to pronounce the war as all but over and reduce the size of the Greek armed forces. Van Fleet warned that figures on paper were misleading because not all soldiers were available for combat. More than 30,000 were engaged in gendarmerie and police duties, in training and supply operations, and in guarding areas against attacks. The enemy's considerably smaller size was likewise deceiving, for its number did not include either the troops training across the border, or those people outside Greece providing supplies. The Greek army needed superior manpower to root out the guerrillas. Before the summer was over, the army should clear central and northern Greece. But even then the trouble would not cease. American military aid was needed in FY 1950 to prevent future uprisings. "In this case the winning of the battle is not the winning of the war."[9]

Despite the skepticism, the war was nearing an end in the late summer of 1949 as the army prepared for "Operation Torch," the final assault on Vitsi and Grammos. About 8,000 guerrillas were in Vitsi, backed to the frontiers of Yugoslavia and Albania and fortified by mines, mortars, artillery, barbed wire, and machine guns emplaced in pillboxes protected by concrete or logs and dirt. But this defensive network was not capable of withstanding an air and artillery assault, followed by a massive invasion of ground troops. Under American supervision, the Greek officers ordered soldiers and supplies to the north, set up a road and radio communications network, planned tactics, and established a special training center at Drepanon-Kozani for the units about to engage in the battle. To prevent the guerrillas from escaping into Yugoslavia, the Greek army secured its rear by occupying the regions around Kaimaktchalan-Vermion. By late July the air force had delivered a week-long series of "softening blows" on Vitsi and Grammos, and Greek forces had eliminated the guerrillas' base in Kaimaktchalan, scattering them northward and closing a major route out of Greece. By August 1 Torch was ready to commence.[10]

The outcome of the offensive largely depended upon an initial deception. The army intended to trick the guerrillas into believing that its major operation was against Grammos, hoping that the enemy command would send reinforcements out of Vitsi. Then the Greek forces planned to encircle the guerrillas in Grammos and prevent their escape. On August 2, Torch "A" began with a series of minor attacks designed to close an escape route out of Grammos and into Vitsi. One division, supported by artillery, began a diversionary attack, while another division moved against southern Grammos to leave the impression that a full-scale assault was under way. During the first week of August, the air force dropped napalm bombs that were "terrifying," according to a prisoner taken during the battle. Three assault waves were extremely costly to Greek forces and led to mixed success, but military leaders redeployed their troops in preparation for Torch "B," the big push on Vitsi that Papagos called "D" Day, August 10. The first part of the plan had worked: the primary offensive on Vitsi was a surprise to the guerrillas.[11]

The army's advantages in manpower and resources became evident during Torch B. The air force opened the attack with a fourteen-hour bombardment by almost two hundred planes armed with bombs, rockets, and napalm. Half an hour after the initial air assault, artillery began shelling the area in preparation for an invasion by infantry-tank units. On the second day of the campaign, the air force encountered intense anti-aircraft fire but flew 150 sorties over the mountain approaches in front of the advancing ground troops. Greek soldiers destroyed many pillboxes and artillery pieces by using what Van Fleet claimed was the army's most effective weapon—the 75-millimeter recoilless rifle. Lightweight and mobile, it provided frontline forces with direct-fire capabilities at fixed defenses.[12]

The Greek army now moved toward the liberation of Vitsi. The decisive battle came at Tsouka, where the guerrillas numbered about 2,500. As one section stalemated against the guerrillas' positions at Lesits during the night of August 10-11, the other moved toward Tsouka and at midnight began a pounding of the area that lasted four hours. In the air-to-ground exchanges, one Spitfire was hit and burst into flames as it plunged to the ground, killing the pilot. The Greek soldiers gained a foothold and held onto Tsouka despite heavy losses. The next day the guerrillas conceded both areas. Greek units advanced northward during the following night, cutting off the guerrillas and exposing them to an artillery pummeling that, along with the air attack, drove them into retreat west toward Grammos and Albania. About a third of the guerrillas and senior leaders got away; the Greek army had not been able to close the escape routes. On August 16, the army, supported by an armor, air, and artillery barrage, forced more guerrillas out of Vitsi. Not all of them escaped. Almost two hundred guerrillas trying to enter Yugoslavia were turned back by Yugoslav soldiers. Eight hundred guerrillas made it into Albania at Lemos alone, but the Greek army soon blocked that outlet with tanks and a division of men. Van Fleet observed the fighting at Vitsi and, in a burst of emotion that belied his earlier exasperation with the Greek forces, congratulated Papagos on the "outstanding" courage of his "magnificent" army and air force.[13]

The army had overrun Vitsi—at staggering expense for the enemy. Only one guerrilla brigade escaped intact; two were wholly destroyed; three stood at half-strength. Greek forces had killed a thousand guerrillas, taken more than five hundred prisoners, and seized all of their heavy equipment and supplies, including harvested grain stacked in the fields. American observers had not been impressed by the infantry's reliance on air and artillery fire. But the air force had been instrumental in breaking the outer edge of the enemy's defense posts, penetrating the area, and driving the guerrillas into a hasty retreat and consequent loss of arms and equipment. "This is the beginning of the end," Van Fleet triumphantly announced.[14]

Torch "C"—the final offensive on Grammos—would be more difficult than Vitsi because of the area's rugged terrain. The Grammos stronghold contained about 5,000 guerrillas, although that number would grow because of the influx of those who escaped from Vitsi. With King Paul, Van Fleet, and a host of other officials in attendance, Papagos set the attack date but postponed it for three days to await the arrival of nearly fifty of the American navy's Helldivers. These deadly fighter-bombers added another dimension to the offensive, for they could engage in sweeping, low-level bombing while accurately dispensing cannon, rockets, and small arms fire.[15]

After King Paul gave the formal order, the army began a three-pronged assault on August 24. Various feints had revealed that the guerrillas were vulnerable along their northern sector touching the Albanian frontier. The army gained the element of surprise by attacking earlier than expected— before the guerrillas from Vitsi could relocate in Grammos. The assault opened at night with a single division and two brigades beginning the bombardment and Spitfires unleashing a stream of rockets. The army moved forward, shielded by the Helldivers, which in the first twenty-four hours dropped forty-eight tons of incendiary bombs on the center of the guerrillas' defense high on Tsarno Ridge. Though the guerrillas held their ground throughout the night, the Greek brigades seized the areas between the heights and prepared to move north toward Tsarno. That stronghold finally fell to a bayonet attack on August 26—but only after its occupants put up staunch resistance to the greatest concentration of artillery in the war and a larger number of bombers in a confined area than at any time since the organization of the air force. The guerrillas abandoned Grammos on August 31 and retreated into Albania. Less than a week earlier, however, the Albanian leader, Enver Hoxha, had announced that armed Greeks in his country would be disarmed and detained. The expulsion of Yugoslavia from the Cominform and the imminent defeat of the Greek guerrillas had left Albania physically isolated in the Balkans. Furthermore, Hoxha could not be certain that either the United States or Great Britain could restrain a Greek invasion. The war was over.[16]

Communist leaders, however, did not announce a cease-fire until October 16; even then they insisted that the struggle for Greece had merely changed form. At the Sixth Plenum of the KKE's Central Committee a week earlier, Zahariadis conceded his army's defeat but claimed that the economic and political revolution would continue. After a denunciation of Tito (whom Zahariadis blamed for the failure), the Sixth Plenum voted to "discontinue the armed struggle for the time being, leaving only small guerrilla detachments as a means of exerting pressure." But the cease-fire announcement was accompanied by the warning that "the monarcho-fascists would be mistaken if they think that the struggle has ended and that the Democratic Army has ceased to exist." Support for this view came from Moscow, where American Ambassador Alan G. Kirk insisted that the cease-fire was a "Soviet tactical lull." The United States should take advantage of this "short breathing spell" to push the rehabilitation of Greece.[17]

Tensions remained along the border. Even though guerrilla radio in early November confirmed the end of military resistance, the KKE urged the continuation of subversive actions. Its spokesmen asserted that the decision to end the military struggle was a temporary expedient brought by Tito's defection and by America's aid to the Greeks. The cease-fire was not an admission to defeat. Less than two weeks later, guerrilla radio declared that the KKE had established political commissar groups of ten to fifteen members whose duty was to distribute political materials in Greece. Skirmishes continued into December, although the last major battle took place the previous October, when the guerrillas attacked a Greek army brigade in the mountains and the air force had to use napalm bombs to drive them away. Until the end of the year, the army remained along the Yugoslav, Albanian, and Bulgarian borders and engaged in daily "search and ambush actions." The air force carried out over three hundred armed reconnaissance missions. Neither it nor the army uncovered anything more than minimal guerrilla movement.[18]

President Truman was satisfied that the war had come to a close. He proclaimed victory in his report to Congress on November 28.[19]

II

Three years of civil war had brought enormous destruction to the country and guaranteed a difficult transition to peace. The vendetta-like character of the conflict had resulted in atrocities by both sides that assured lasting bitterness. Casualty figures are in dispute because neither side kept careful records, and no one made an exact count of civilian casualties. Indeed, the attempt to arrive at an accurate comparison of figures almost loses meaning when one remembers that both sides in the war were Greek. A rough estimate is that the army suffered about 13,000 dead or missing and over 26,000 wounded, whereas about 38,000 guerrillas were dead and over twice that many wounded. In addition, 5,000 civilians had been killed—mostly by mines and executions—and about 28,000 children remained outside Greece. Another casualty was the large number of Greeks who had been displaced and were now homeless. By the end of September 1949 the army had returned less than a third of the more than 700,000 refugees to their village homes—which meant that the majority still sought security in urban relocation centers established during the war. Many Greek loyalists remained insecure because of threats from those fellow Greeks who had helped the guerrillas. To prevent reprisals, American military advisers approved the distribution of 15,000 rifles to returning villagers; the chief of the aid mission already had authorized over 56,000 rifles for the same purpose.[20]

The end of the war nonetheless seemed to have come as quickly as it had begun. By late August, the guerrillas in Greece numbered fewer than 4,000; by December 31 the total had dropped to scarcely more than eight hundred, with most of them scattered in the north. In March 1950 that number had fallen below five hundred, after eleven consecutive months of decline. The previous month, the government lifted martial law throughout the country. But few in Athens believed that the guerrillas' actions would cease. Though their forces were small and they no longer possessed a stronghold along the frontier, they could remain active in remote areas by re-establishing intelligence networks, promoting propaganda, maintaining supply lanes into Albania and Bulgaria, and engaging in raiding and looting expeditions. American military observers warned that future guerrilla actions depended on assistance from those two neighboring countries, which, in turn, acted according to directives from the Cominform.[21] Yet Albanians and Bulgarians had problems of their own, and the Cominform's focus had turned elsewhere. With minimal internal controls, the government in Athens should maintain order.

After the cease-fire, pressure intensified for a cutback in the military program in Greece. As of August 31, the Joint U.S. Military Advisory and Planning Group was authorized to have 274 men on duty, but it had only 191, among them 108 commissioned officers and 83 enlisted men (half of whom were in communications). Thirteen field detachments remained, but only six advised the army on operations, logistics, and training. By the end of the year the United States had cut its advisers to 128. Grady concurred with Van Fleet in wanting a smaller American military mission. Since the struggle was now political and economic, the Greek government must draw up a budget designed to relieve the economy of the military burden. The guerrilla threat had been reduced to police proportions, and American officials in that country recommended a cut in its armed forces. Such a move would allow the government to conserve American military matériel for the long-range maintenance of a smaller Greek army.[22]

The British also reduced their military presence in Greece. Although the training missions would remain, the Foreign Office wanted to withdraw the garrison at Salonika and assign it elsewhere. The war over, Van Fleet now favored total withdrawal of British troops in an effort to encourage Greek self-reliance. Grady added that the move might have a favorable impact on world opinion. Jernegan, however, was concerned about the Greek reaction. The purpose of the British presence had been "ninety-five per cent psychological"—to raise Greek morale. But by the end of 1949 the Greek government favored British troop withdrawal as a sign of national stability. The process of withdrawal began in late November.[23]

The explanation for the Greek government's victory has long been the subject of debate. Some writers, then and now, have attributed the outcome to international developments, whereas others have emphasized changes that were more national in nature. Although both arguments are valid in many ways, no one has presented a broadly based assessment that brings together the international and national considerations. Furthermore, no one has given sufficient attention to the role of America's global strategy in effectively confronting the threats posed by this new kind of war.

Several observers tied the victory to events in the Balkans, most notably to the rift between Yugoslavia and the Soviet Union. According to the argument, the crucial ingredient was the shift in Balkan alignments that ultimately forced Yugoslavia to withdraw support from the guerrillas. There can be no doubt that the defection of Yugoslavia created grave problems for the guerrillas. In January 1948, when the Tito-Stalin troubles were becoming evident, the Democratic Army included 11,000 Slavophones (Slavic-speaking Greeks)—almost half of its fighting component. They suddenly faced a critical choice: declare loyalty to the Cominform, which would cost them the assistance of Yugoslavia in the war; or follow Yugoslavia, which would incur the wrath of the Soviet Union. Not surprisingly, the KKE became bitterly divided over the question. By January 1949, Yugoslavia's aid to the guerrillas was barely a trickle. Furthermore, Tito's decision to close the border denied the guerrillas a protected spot for maneuverability in the north and effectively neutralized about a third of their strength. The closing isolated 4,000 guerrillas in Yugoslavia and another 2,500 in Bulgaria who were cut off from the forces in Vitsi and Grammos. In addition, the Greek army's control of the plains between the mountainous areas and Thrace inserted a wedge between the battle sites and another 3,000 guerrillas in Thrace and Macedonia. When asked about the impact of Yugoslavia's defection, Henderson admitted that it was a "great help," and McGhee gave "full credit" to Tito for the victory.[24]

Numerous writers have emphasized the guerrillas' change in tactics to conventional warfare. When Zahariadis in 1947-48 approved the organization of their light infantry into divisions and prepared for full military engagements, he was taking a high risk because of his inability to provide enough additional arms. Guerrilla warfare cannot emerge with a final victory unless it either receives outside conventional support (which was drying up in 1948), or is able to make a successful transition to conventional warfare. As Christopher M. Woodhouse has noted, "[T]he timing of that transition is crucial, because if it is chosen wrongly there can be no going back." In guerrilla warfare, few (if any) opportunities become available for switching to conventional tactics. The timing must be exactly right—when the morale, discipline, and fighting capabilities of the enemy are at their lowest. Zahariadis realized that his forces could not turn back if he chose the wrong moment. Over Markos's protests, Zahariadis made the decision to reorganize his forces into larger units and to engage in frontal assaults while preparing for positional warfare at Grammos and Vitsi. That decision was wrong. The conventional tactics used at Konitsa and Florina cost them popular support, demonstrated their officers' lack of training in that type of warfare, and led to deeper strife within the military and political command. But even more devastating to the Democratic Army, the Greek army had markedly improved its morale and discipline, and in the final offensive fully exploited its material and manpower advantages.[25]

Other views on the components of victory are also persuasive. Military spokesmen have given credit to Anglo-American military assistance, and to Papagos for consolidating his country's war effort. The presence of British troops and American advisers helped to restrain direct intervention and aid from the outside. American assistance sustained the Greek government while its leaders improved the military establishment. Papagos argued that the decisive factors were the "ruthless suppression" of the fanatic leaders, and the "continuous, relentless, unremitting pursuit, especially at night, so as to exhaust them and to force them either to fight or disintegrate." In early 1949, the army undercut the guerrillas' intelligence network by arresting and interring many known communists and their sympathizers. The army then turned the guerrillas' strategy against them by conducting surprise attacks of its own, followed by the systematic destruction of the guerrillas' underground and the expansion of government control over well-defined areas. The Greek air force provided reconnaissance and ground troop support—especially important in a war where the terrain limited the effectiveness of artillery and mortars and the guerrillas used strategic retreat to advantage. The guerrillas, however, had no air or naval support, which meant that they were forced to depend on their intelligence system and overland movement of goods, both of which proved severely limited. An official American history of the war considered the advisers' training program significant in raising the Greek army's morale and combat ability. On the other side, the morale of forced recruits was dependent on continuous political indoctrination, a program that was difficult to maintain once the Greek army kept the guerrillas on the move. Still other assessments have emphasized the importance of the communists' failure to win popular support.[26]

One observation seems certain: American military aid alone had not brought victory. The communists could have gone on indefinitely if they had stayed with guerrilla tactics and continued to receive refuge and outside assistance. But Zahariadis made an ill-advised decision to change to conventional warfare, and Tito's defection forced him to shore up his affairs at home and to cut off the major source of the guerrillas' aid and sanctuary. The conclusion is tempting—that Tito's defection broke the guerrillas' resistance and allowed Greek (and American) firepower to finish the task. It would follow that the United States was not controlling events so much as taking advantage of them. But the full explanation does not lie in either American military assistance and advice or events in the Balkans.

An important part of the explanation lies in the multifaceted nature of the American assistance program. Lieutenant General Ventiris was correct in later insisting that U.S. help had saved Greece from communism—but only in the broadest sense of the word. Military and economic aid enabled the Greek government to maintain the army and to raise morale among the soldiers and the civilians. Operational advice and improved training procedures (with British help) molded a respectable military establishment that ultimately proved itself on the battlefield. American diplomatic efforts meanwhile kept the war from escalating internationally. Inside Greece, American representatives had exerted direct influence on Greek political affairs in an effort to temper the extreme right while making known their preference for a broadly based government. American economic leverage was implicitly present—especially as Congress stepped up its calls for air reductions and lower troop ceilings. Greek officials knew that the United States considered the eastern Mediterranean and Middle East vital to national security; but they also realized that the United States considered Turkey more valuable militarily than Greece, that trouble spots in other areas of the world were attracting more of America's attention, and that Congress and the American people had come to believe by the summer of 1948 that their mission in Greece was almost fulfilled. The U.S. presence in Greece allowed an undeniable—if not always subtle—direction over internal and external affairs. Even then, Grady later declared, the success was attributable to the entire program—not to any specific part of it. "It is evident that neither military aid nor economic aid alone could have been successful. The combination of the two won the war in Greece."[27]

But even Grady's expanded conclusion is inadequate, for another vital part of the explanation lies in the impact that the Truman Doctrine had in placing pressure on Stalin to order the Yugoslavs and Bulgarians to wind down the war. The central contribution of the Truman Doctrine, according to Woodhouse, was the American *commitment* to Greece, not the amount of goods that went into the military and economic aid effort. The Greek communists were less vulnerable to American assistance than "to the vagaries of Stalinism, which had little regard for any consideration other than the security of the Soviet Union." Early in the Greek struggle, the Soviet premier would doubtless have welcomed a communist triumph—*if* it could have come primarily on its own and without prompting American intervention. Thus the various pieces of information held by the White House may have been correct—that the Soviets were engaged in a new kind of war aimed at undermining (or permitting their allies to do so) the Greek people's faith in their government and promoting its collapse. Stalin could not risk a confrontation with the United States, but he might achieve his expansionist objectives by resorting to indirect means—propaganda, subversion, infiltration, and, perhaps, some forms of assistance. As shown earlier, however, Stalin abruptly turned his back on the Greek communists when the White House announced the Truman Doctrine and steadily escalated its military involvement. He knew that a continuation of the war would deepen the American presence in Greece and endanger the already unsettled Soviet alliance system in Eastern Europe. The Greek communists, Woodhouse has concluded, finally learned in 1949 that the "rank and file of the KKE, and in particular its leaders, were expendable. Without a trace of compunction, Stalin let them go to their doom."[28]

And yet, even the Truman Doctrine was the mere instrument of strategy: in a broad sense, the administration achieved its objectives in Greece because of a flexible foreign policy that was global in theory and restrained by reality.[29] White House advisers had defined the nation's interests in Greece in relation to the rest of the world, developed a strategy that had manageable goals, and worked within the recognized limitations of America's capacity to control events and people. Most important, they cultivated a Greek people who had a democratic tradition and a base of nationalism, and who were opposed to communism and favorably inclined to the United States. All the while, America's policymakers insisted upon keeping the struggle within the technical confines of a civil war, repeatedly refusing to allow the conflict to encompass regional matters and grow into a larger war. Furthermore, knowing that victory in this struggle was of a different measure than that of past wars, the administration pursued a public information campaign designed to maintain popular support (in what some advisers called an ideological war) as the basis for sound foreign policy. After the White House had won congressional and popular support for the aid bill, the administration toned down its rhetoric to avoid confrontation with the communists, quietly urged its British ally to remain in Greece as part of an international effort, and thus provided time and opportunity for the strategy to work.

The Truman Doctrine in Greece was an integral part of a global strategy that rested upon equivalent responses to carefully defined levels of danger. In 1947 the military emergency in Greece necessitated military aid and operational advice; once that threat had subsided in late 1949, the United States concentrated on the ultimate goal of economic rehabilitation. During the Greek involvement, the administration considered every option—from outright withdrawal to full-scale intervention and the use of American troops. Decisions resulted from proposals thrashed out not only by specialists in Greek, Turkish, and Iranian affairs but also by those who brought both European and Asian perspectives to the problem. Information came from foreign and domestic sources that included British and Greek observers, the State and Defense Departments, National Security Council, Joint Chiefs of Staff, CIA, and other intelligence groups. Any decision rested on hard considerations: its impact on Greece and neighboring states, on America's allies and the nonaligned countries, and on Americans at home; how to persuade Britain to remain openly involved and thus avert a unilateral American intervention; whether the possibility remained for graceful de-escalation or even withdrawal; how the adopted measure related to the central objectives of preserving Greek independence and integrity while safeguarding America's security and prestige; and how the actions in Greece affected global strategy. In light of constantly changing situations both in Greece and in the rest of the world, the White House relied upon continuing assessments of the Greek situation as the means by which the administration kept its commitment reversible and under control.

The administration's strategy worked because the advisers maintained the distinction between the ideal and the reality. Means and goals remained constant, related, and in balance, as the Americans sought only to help Greece stand on its own. Truman's advisers recognized that strategy must not become negative by resting on anti-communism alone; they worked toward the establishment of reforms that the Greek people could support. The Greek experience constituted a victory for America's foreign policy.

CHAPTER
13

"On All Fronts"

The internal and external problems continuing to face Greece and its allies substantiated their belief that the communists had changed tactics without giving up the struggle. Both inside and outside the country, the government had to deal with demands for amnesty and leniency toward those who had been its enemies, while also having to resolve matters regarding Albania. In the course of attempting to settle these issues, the Greek government increasingly realized that the United States had become occupied with problems elsewhere. The focus of the Cold War was shifting to Asia, causing the White House to adjust its strategy. Attention had turned to the communists' victory in China and, soon, to the outbreak of war in Korea. As the public attacks on the West by the Soviets and their allies became more embittered, the Truman administration experienced the uneasy satisfaction of having dealt a blow to the Soviet Union's expansionist drives in Europe, the Mediterranean, and the Middle East. According to prevailing theory, the Soviets would shift probing operations to other soft spots, forcing the Truman administration to move its emphasis elsewhere and to re-evaluate again its commitments to Greece.

I

On the domestic front, the end of the war in Greece brought a sense of urgency to amnesty and other leniency considerations. The Greek government made tentative plans to divide the guerrillas into three categories: the top leaders, who would face imprisonment and probable execution; "hard-core leaders," who would be assigned to "reindoctrination centers" on the islands of Makronissos or Leros before being allowed to return to normal life; the "rank and file," who would be screened and sent home. In the interests of world opinion, the government planned to announce a declaration against executions. Furthermore, the Diomedes government released a number of prisoners-of-war in September and subjected all death sentences to reviews by the State Council of Pardons. The State Department urged the Greek government to go farther by proclaiming a policy of leniency toward the guerrillas—before the General Assembly convened—to prevent the impression that demands by member nations had led to generous terms. The Greek government should also seek UN advice on a program promoting the political and economic rehabilitation of the guerrillas. In compliance with the constitution, general elections must occur by March 1950. The United States did not recommend voter participation by the communists, but considered it wise to accompany the elections with a plebiscite on whether to remove the ban on the KKE.[1]

On the foreign front, Albania's involvement in the war and afterward remained an issue that threatened to divide the West. Despite the cease-fire and Hoxha's claim to have stopped assisting the guerrillas, the Greek government was convinced that the Albanians were still providing enough aid to encourage a resurgence of guerrilla activity in the north. The British now favored an interventionist action by the major powers. France would go along, although without enthusiasm. But Americans remained hesitant. They continued to believe that even if the Greek charges were warranted, such a step would have no impact on Albania. Drew insisted that the West must not make an "empty dramatic gesture" and then himself proceeded to recommend several of them: a warning to the Albanian government that "continuation of such actions . . . can only lead to stigmatizing the present regime as . . . an outlaw group with no claim to membership in the community of nations"; voluntary removal of the guerrillas in Albania, either to Greece under guarantees of good treatment or to non-Balkan countries; resubmitting the question to the Security Council; bringing Albania (and Bulgaria) before the International Court to demand reparations; withdrawing diplomatic representatives of UN members from Albania; authorizing the UN Balkan committee to arrange a blockade of Albania's frontier along the sea; encouraging the General Assembly to determine that Albania (and Bulgaria) were engaged in an undeclared war against Greece.[2]

But the Truman administration rigidly opposed any conspicuous role in matters pertaining to Albania. The only feasible approach was to accept the Balkan committee's recommendation that the General Assembly call on Albania and Bulgaria to permit UN verification of charges that they were helping the guerrillas.[3]

The matter caused sharp disagreement between Greece and the United States. The Greek government opposed public discussions within the General Assembly and preferred private consultations among only those UN members directly affected by the dispute. Greek leaders feared that the Soviets would shift the focus of general UN discussions to domestic matters—amnesty, restoration of "democratic elements" in Greece, protection of Slav minorities, recognition of the present Greek-Albanian border as permanent (which meant a renunciation of Greek claims to Northern Epirus). The West would either have to grant concessions damaging to Greece, or turn down Soviet proposals and appear to be obstructing a settlement. Public discussions would elicit hard-line stances; realistic adjustments could come only by quiet negotiations. The United States should discreetly pursue the possibility of private talks in Belgrade and Sofia as well as a diplomatic approach to Albania. The Truman administration rejected the Greek argument, however, and offered assurances that member states in the General Assembly would be supportive of the complaints against Albania. When the United States suggested taking the initiative in calling for open forum discussions, the Greek government balked.[4]

The State Department tried to find an approach consonant with the Greek position. It proposed consultations among the Big Four (the United States, United Kingdom, Soviet Union, and France), with the participation of Greece, Yugoslavia, Albania, and Bulgaria. Greek internal matters would not come under discussion. If this effort failed, the United States would publish a report exposing the Soviets' insincerity and then work with the British and French in securing a General Assembly resolution calling on Albania (and Bulgaria) to stop aiding the guerrillas and to allow on-site UN verification. The resolution should also express concern that other states, especially Rumania, had been supporting the guerrillas, and, in relation to an emotionally charged accusation, that these same states were now returning the children to northern Greece as guerrillas. The State Department urged the Greek government to accept the UN Conciliatory Commission's suggestions for bilateral agreements with Yugoslavia, Albania, and Bulgaria.[5]

Britain's response was mixed but cautious. The Foreign Office supported conciliation talks in the General Assembly, but did not favor the establishment of separate committees to deal with relations between Greece and its northern neighbors. The Foreign Office opposed UN supervision of the repatriation of guerrillas: the UN could not guarantee their safety, and Soviet participation would be a "nuisance." In a meeting in Washington, Acheson urged Bevin to exercise caution in dealing with the Russians: "If we are anxious, the price goes up." Bevin agreed that patience was the key—Stalin might want "to write off the Greek situation as a bad job." On the Albanian matter, Bevin was straightforward. His government felt an "unrelenting hostility" toward the communist regime, and wondered whether the British and Americans should "try to bring down the Hoxha government when the occasion arises." Acheson agreed that getting rid of Hoxha would be better than trying to entice him to follow Tito's example, but the secretary of state was opposed to any action "precipitating" his fall. Such a move might cause the Greek army to launch an invasion and provide Russia with a pretext for intervening.[6]

The Greek government would have to handle both the leniency and the Albanian issues on its own—and short of any measure endangering peace in the Balkans. Its spokesmen recognized the need to present themselves in the best possible way before the world. Thus they would support guerrilla rehabilitation, suspension of executions, and elections. But they would not approve any approach that carried the potential for Soviet involvement in Greek affairs. The Truman administration realized that the pursuance of some action regarding Albania might furnish the Soviets with an excuse to intervene there and in Yugoslavia. Perhaps to obviate such a move, Yugoslav Assistant Foreign Minister Aleš Bebler in early September emphasized his country's lack of interest in close relations with either Albania or Bulgaria. Nearly two weeks later, Tito expressed concern to Cannon about Soviet intervention. A Greek move against Albania would place Yugoslavia in a "most difficult situation." The Greeks must not "settle things their way." Cannon assured him that the United States had given "strong advice" to the Athens government not to take precipitous action. Tito remained uneasy: "It would be very hard for us if there should be intervention from outside. Let Greeks again be told."[7]

These issues then combined with broader developments in the Cold War to cause an acrimonious debate in the General Assembly during late September. The Soviet minister for foreign affairs, Andrei Vyshinsky, angrily denied that Albania and Bulgaria posed a threat to Greek sovereignty and attributed the troubles in the Balkans to the presence of "foreign troops and military missions." The "monarcho-fascist" government was in alliance with the British and Americans against "Greek patriots." But the problem included more than the events in Greece. The North Atlantic Treaty Organization was an effort "to frighten States which were not willing to obey the orders of the Anglo-American alliance." The Marshall Plan was "one of the cornerstones in the political and military system of Western States which was being set up against the USSR and the people's democracies." The representative from Czechoslovakia, Vladimir Clementis, joined the attacks by calling the Balkan committee one of the "undisguised instruments of Anglo-American power policy." The Polish representative, Julius Katz-Suchy, accused the Anglo-American governments of endangering Albanian independence. These charges drew immediate replies. Lebanon's Charles Malik announced support for any efforts to protect Greece, and Constantine Tsaldaris, now chairman of the Greek delegation, insisted that the threat to Balkan peace came from those countries "under the control of the Cominform."[8]

Emotions flared again when the issue arose of executions of war criminals. The Soviet delegation proposed the suspension and repeal of all death sentences in Greece. The Greek government was vulnerable on this matter; although it had announced a suspension of executions, the press reported that military authorities had forced a retreat on that policy. At the least, according to the State Department, the Greek government must end capital punishment for crimes other than murder. The "psychological moment" was right to extend leniency to the 2,500 prisoners awaiting the death sentence. The Greek government responded with a compromise. Only those charged with multiple murders would be executed, and specially established civilian pardon boards would review death sentences stemming from courts-martial.[9]

The United States could not support a UN appeal for leniency by the Greek government. Grady warned that such a move would revive the "discredited theory" that the "Greek Communist rebellion reflected political and economic dissatisfaction of [a] large number of Greeks and was not solely [a] Communist bid for power." Besides, a General Assembly resolution calling for leniency would serve no purpose because it would be directed at "fanatic leaders" who were "quartered and fed in satellite countries. They are only pawn[s] in Russia's Balkan strategy and not individuals free to direct their own destiny." Leniency plans for the disillusioned followers were in place. The Athens government was trying "to make good Greeks out of former bandits."[10]

The Albanian issue was also subject to attack, for the communist states could label any action taken by Greece as an aggression instigated by its Western allies. The United States recommended that Tsaldaris announce a warning that Greece would defend itself in the event of an Albanian armed attack. A punitive invasion of Albania, the State Department believed, would open Greece to the charge of aggression. If the Greeks attacked Albania, the White House would have to reconsider its entire policy toward Greece.[11]

President Truman understood Greece's feelings on these matters, but Cold War considerations forced him to authorize "Drastic Measures" to prevent trouble. He admitted that the Greek government's interest in punishing Albania "was like any other dog who has been down in a fight and then gets on top." An invasion, however, would cause additional trouble in the Balkans. The United States would cooperate with Britain and France in preventing the Greeks from launching an invasion except in retaliation for direct military aggression by the Albanians. To prevent such an assault, the State Department instructed its mission chiefs in Europe to block attempts by Albania to secure military goods. The United States began placing restrictions on arms shipments through Italy, Trieste, and Austria.[12]

More than Albanian assistance to the guerrillas was involved: nations north of Greece—in particular Bulgaria and Rumania—continued to provide material aid and refuge. The General Assembly urged these three states to stop these practices and then appealed to all UN members to cease encouraging "any armed group fighting against Greece." The Soviet delegation countered with resolutions encapsulating its demands. Observers must have experienced a sense of *deja vu* as the General Assembly resolved that aid to the Greek guerrillas from Albania, Bulgaria, Rumania, and other countries should cease because such action ignored the Assembly's resolutions, violated the UN Charter, and threatened peace in the Balkans.[13]

The issue involving the children similarly lingered after the war. Indignation had swelled both inside and outside the United States as news continued to arrive about their use as guerrillas. State legislatures and members of Congress protested, and a veritable deluge of letters and telegrams to the

President that had begun in August 1948 did not abate until the autumn of 1951. Correspondence came from fourteen countries and more than thirty American states, and included complaints from university students, private citizens, Greek-American organizations, Greek church groups, and the Greek Orthodox Archbishop of North and South America. Both houses of Congress passed resolutions urging the administration to halt the abductions and to secure repatriation of the children through the UN and other international agencies. In accordance with the General Assembly's resolution of November 1948, the President promised to cooperate with the UN and the International Red Cross in seeking the youths' return.[14]

Few of the 28,000 evacuated Greek youths returned to their homes immediately after the war. The International Red Cross reported that, as of April 1951, requests had arrived for the repatriation of only 10,344. Fewer than three hundred of over 9,000 Greek children in Yugoslavia had returned home by May, but over 7,000 of these children were living in Yugoslavia with their parents, who were mostly Greek Macedonians. In November 1952 a high-ranking British foreign affairs official told the House of Commons that the International Red Cross had received no help from the governments "within the Soviet orbit" and had halted efforts to secure the children's return.[15]

II

In the aftermath of the Greek war, General Van Fleet declared that the United States had experienced an "obvious measure of success" in halting Soviet advances into Western Europe and the Mediterranean. Future efforts must "roll back the iron curtain still farther in the Balkans." The Truman Doctrine had saved Greece and encouraged Yugoslavia's rift with the Cominform and its tilt toward the West. Albania was beset with domestic unrest, and if the present regime fell, that country likewise might lean toward the West. To spread the West's influence in the Balkans, the United States and the United Kingdom must maintain a "strong combined posture in Greece." To promote America's "long range strategic concepts," the United States had established a "solid belt" around Western Europe and through the Mediterranean that included Greece and, perhaps soon, Yugoslavia.[16]

Despite the shift in emphasis to other areas of strategic concern, the United States was not ready to return the leadership in Greece to the British. The Joint Chiefs of Staff urged the White House to maintain its "predominant position" and to be nothing less than the "senior partner" in a "senior-junior" arrangement with the United Kingdom. When the British Chiefs of Staff suggested the establishment of an Anglo-American Military Mission that would integrate all functions in Greece, the joint chiefs rejected the plan because they wanted the United States to maintain control over military assistance. America was "here to stay." Greece was a vital part of global strategy—"the keystone of the defense line from Western Europe to Middle

East." The United States, the joint chiefs insisted, "must hold the predominant position on all fronts."[17]

The Truman administration was aware of the diverse considerations that determined the success of communism. The large majority of communists in Greece were not ideologically attuned to Marxist teachings; they had aligned with the KKE out of desperation caused by the lack of alternatives. To more than a few Greek people, their chief concern was that the war come to an end. A peasant refugee put it best: "I want to go back to my farm. All I ask is peace and security." Van Fleet, however, had dismissed the communists as fanatics who would stop at nothing to achieve their objectives. His attitude was typical of those observers who made no effort to question the ideological base of the trouble and to discern whether a substantial number of the guerrillas were merely disillusioned patriots. If the problem had been purely economic, the economic aid provided under the Truman Doctrine should have been sufficient to remove the threat of communism. But the problem until 1949 was predominantly military—and made even more serious by the widespread belief that the government in Athens was calloused and non-caring about the people's well-being. Once the fighting phase of the communist struggle had ended in government victory, attention could turn to economic aid and the restoration of faith in the leaders in Athens. Reconstruction and rehabilitation had a chance to instill a sense of security only after the guerrillas were no longer able to pursue their terrorist actions.[18]

The re-establishment of domestic order appeared to be under way by March 1950. In the first national election after the war, fifteen political parties submitted candidates, and after a month of controversy General Nicholas Plastiras emerged as premier. A republican in philosophy, he headed a "Center" coalition regime that leaned toward liberalism. The Greek government consolidated the army, navy, and air force into a National Defense Ministry and appointed Papagos commander-in-chief of that and the Home Guard units, as well as chief of the National Defense General Staff. With the military situation under control, the government could concentrate on economic reconstruction. By early 1952 the economy had attained a shaky stability.[19]

America's experience in Greece provided a glimmer of a policy that would become known in the 1950s as "nation building." During the early part of that decade, a former member of an American aid mission to Greece wrote an essay entitled "The Reconstruction of Greece: An American Experiment in Administration," in which he declared that the Truman Doctrine was indicative of the "unprecedented challenge" facing the United States in the new "science" of public administration. America's "pioneering" effort had succeeded because the Greeks were a "sovereign, friendly, and civilized people." In a statement implicitly making reference to America's ongoing experiments in nation building, he asserted that the Greek experience might have "lessons for the administrators of a future 'Greece,' Korea, or any other war-plagued nation that might need, in a hurry, to be saved from Communism." To some policymakers at least, the program in Greece had provided a model for the future.[20]

The American involvement in Greece had an impact upon the administration's reaction to the outbreak of war in Korea in June 1950. During the dark hours following news of the North Korean attack, President Truman met with several of his advisers to prepare a statement to the nation. At one point, he crossed his White House office to spin the globe in front of the fireplace so that the colorful ridges of the Middle East became visible. To George M. Elsey, an aide who remained after the others had left, the President declared half to himself, "I'm more worried about other parts of the world. The Middle East, for instance." Pointing to Iran, he said, "Here is where they will start trouble if we aren't careful." He then asserted, "Korea is the Greece of the Far East. If we are tough enough now, if we stand up to them like we did in Greece three years ago, they won't take over the whole Middle East."[21]

Conversely, the Korean War affected Greece by causing the White House to extend the American commitment. Not only might the Soviets take advantage of the Korean conflict to instigate a similar assault on Greece from the north but Greece had become the symbol of the United States's ability to help nations threatened by communists. The attack on South Korea convinced the National Security Council that the country was just one objective in a series of expected communist assaults worldwide and that Greece remained a "target of Soviet ambition." In February 1951 the Council recommended enough military aid to Greece for "repelling an attack by satellite forces" and "causing maximum practicable delay . . . to an attack involving direct Soviet participation." Full Greek membership in NATO seemed advisable—which constituted a change of policy from that earlier supported by the Joint Chiefs of Staff. Western European nations had opposed the admission of Greece (and Turkey) as provocative to the Soviet Union, and the joint chiefs had recommended only "associate status." But in late 1951 Greece (and Turkey) received full membership status and by autumn concluded an agreement with Washington that authorized the establishment in those countries of NATO military bases.[22]

The Greek example—both in the formulation and in the implementation of policy—repeatedly came up as the United States later deepened its commitment in Vietnam. In 1957 President Dwight D. Eisenhower explained that he viewed events in Vietnam through the lessons learned in Greece. Seven years later Democrat Adlai Stevenson argued that Greece and Korea were models for American action in Vietnam. And, after the United States had dispatched combat troops to Vietnam in 1965, President Lyndon B. Johnson referred to the Truman Doctrine in assuring Americans that they would win the war against communist aggression in South Vietnam as they had won the war in Greece. When the Senate Foreign Relations Committee asked Secretary of State Dean Rusk in early 1966 why the United States was in Vietnam, he quoted from President Truman's address to Congress in March 1947: "I believe it must be the policy of the United States to support free peoples who are resisting attempted subjugation by armed minorities or by outside pressures."[23]

Greece also provided experience in guerrilla fighting. President John F. Kennedy once compared the Vietnam War to the struggle against the communist guerrillas in Greece. Both before and after his administration, advisers cited the guerrilla fighting in Greece as valuable preparation for similar struggles in Vietnam. Indeed, some Greek veterans of the guerrilla war took their expertise to Vietnam. Walt Rostow, chairman of the State Department's policy planning council, told Rusk that if the Johnson administration adopted new counterinsurgency measures, "there is no reason we cannot win as clear a victory in South Viet-Nam as in Greece, Malaya, and the Philippines." Finally, Henry Cabot Lodge, Jr., who had supported the Truman Doctrine in its formative years, declared in a 1964 speech that "We, of the Free World, won in Greece. . . . And we can win in Viet-Nam."[24]

It is not within the domain of this work to do anything more than raise questions about whether Greece was a legitimate prototype for American actions in Vietnam. As noted earlier, several advisers in the Truman administration were instrumental in formulating President Kennedy's policy during the early 1960s. In both instances, they sought to establish a flexible and restrained policy that relied upon short-of-war tactics in combatting the challenges presented by limited warfare. Despite the claims of critics, the reasons for the intensification of the Cold War lay less in the Truman Doctrine than in its misuse by policymakers in the period afterward. Used in the manner advocated by Acheson and his contemporaries, the Truman Doctrine was part of a global strategy capable of handling most foreign policy problems by carefully controlled responses. But if strategy did not match the means within the objectives, the remedial methods used could get out of hand. The American experience in Greece demonstrated that only a multifaceted assistance program could prevail over a multifaceted danger. The United States had used a sound strategy and emerged triumphant in Greece. Whether or not the United States ultimately failed in Vietnam because it followed the lead of the Johnson administration and too readily resorted to the military option, the Greek experience provided a justification, though grossly distorted, for these actions.[25]

If history affords "lessons," the chief lesson to be gained from the Greek experience is that the Greek government and its people *wanted* American help. They continued to receive aid under the Marshall Plan and, with NATO in place, were drawing support from the National Security Council for extended political, economic, and military assistance, as well as for a similar defense pact for areas east of the NATO countries that would include Greece. A sound basis existed for close ties between Greece and the United States. Policymakers in Washington had approved the use of firepower during the Greek war as one means for facilitating strategy—not as strategy itself. They recognized that economic efforts were hopeless without first providing security for the Greek people and restoring their faith in the government. Only such confidence could give them enough strength to withstand the communists' pressure. By a combination of American strategy, British willingness to keep their troops in place, the Greek military offensive, and Balkan factors largely beyond Washington's control, the communists had become convinced that they could not achieve victory by military means. As an American contemporary wrote, the triumph rested on an "interdependence of the elements" that promoted the "moral and economic revival of the countryside."[26]

Greece had been beset with many of the problems of the postwar era and therefore provided an important battlefield of the Cold War. McGhee was correct in proclaiming "*We won.*"[27] But his statement misleadingly implies that the result was attributable to American firepower. He and others in the administration realized that the use of military force was not the solution, but only one instrument in resolving the long-range economic problem. They understood that the Greek situation was enormously complicated—that the struggle had social, political, and economic dimensions as well as military. Finally, they grasped the importance of keeping the nation's Greek policy within the perspective of global events. In a broad sense, the Truman administration's advisers recognized the danger in establishing rigid guidelines in foreign policy and then seeking to apply them to all peoples and situations. America's strategy in Greece exemplified the wisdom in pursuing a flexible and restrained policy in meeting the challenges posed by the new kind of war.

Appendix I
Message of the President
of the United States
March 12, 1947

Mr. President, Mr. Speaker, Members of the Congress of the United States. The gravity of the situation which confronts the world today necessitates my appearance before a joint session of the Congress.

The foreign policy and the national security of this country are involved.

One aspect of the present situation, which I wish to present to you at this time for your consideration and decision concerns Greece and Turkey.

The United States has received from the Greek Government an urgent appeal for financial and economic assistance. Preliminary reports from the American Economic Mission now in Greece and reports from the American Ambassador in Greece corroborate the statement of the Greek Government that assistance is imperative if Greece is to survive as a free nation.

I do not believe that the American people and the Congress wish to turn a deaf ear to the appeal of the Greek Government.

Greece is not a rich country. Lack of sufficient natural resources has always forced the Greek people to work hard to make both ends meet. Since 1940, this industrious and peace-loving country has suffered invasion, four years of cruel enemy occupation, and bitter internal strife.

When forces of liberation entered Greece they found that the retreating Germans had destroyed virtually all the railways, roads, port facilities, communications, and merchant marine. More than a thousand villages had been burned. Eighty-five percent of the children were tubercular. Livestock, poultry, and draft animals had almost disappeared. Inflation had wiped out practically all savings.

As a result of these tragic conditions, a militant minority, exploiting human want and misery, was able to create political chaos which, until now, has made economic recovery impossible.

Greece is today without funds to finance the importation of those goods which are essential to bare subsistence. Under these circumstances, the people of Greece cannot make progress in solving their problems of reconstruction. Greece is in desperate need of financial and economic assistance to enable it to resume purchases of food, clothing, fuel, and seeds. These are indispensable for the subsistence of its people and are obtainable only from abroad. Greece must have help to import the goods necessary to restore internal order and security so essential for economic and political recovery.

The Greek Government has also asked for the assistance of experienced American administrators, economists, and technicians to insure that the financial and other aid given to Greece shall be used effectively in creating a stable and self-sustaining economy and in improving its public administration.

The very existence of the Greek state is today threatened by the terrorist activities of several thousand armed men, led by Communists, who defy the Government's authority at a number of points, particularly along the northern boundaries. A Commission appointed by the United Nations Security Council is at present investigating disturbed conditions in northern Greece, and alleged border violations along the frontier between Greece on the one hand, and Albania, Bulgaria, and Yugoslavia on the other.

Meanwhile, the Greek Government is unable to cope with the situation. The Greek Army is small and poorly equipped. It needs supplies and equipment if it is to restore the authority of the Government throughout Greek territory.

Greece must have assistance if it is to become a self-supporting and self-respecting democracy.

The United States must supply that assistance. We have already extended to Greece certain types of relief and economic aid, but these are inadequate.

There is no other country to which democratic Greece can turn.

No other nation is willing and able to provide the necessary support for a democratic Greek Government.

The British Government, which has been helping Greece, can give no further financial or economic aid after March 31. Great Britain finds itself under the necessity of reducing or liquidating its commitments in several parts of the world, including Greece.

We have considered how the United Nations might assist in this crisis. But the situation is an urgent one requiring immediate action, and the United Nations and its related organizations are not in a position to extend help of the kind that is required.

It is important to note that the Greek Government has asked for our aid in utilizing effectively the financial and other assistance we may give to Greece, and in improving its public administration. It is of the utmost importance that we supervise the use of any funds made available to Greece, in such a manner that each dollar spent will count toward making Greece self-supporting, and will help to build an economy in which a healthy democracy can flourish.

No government is perfect. One of the chief virtues of a democracy, however, is that its defects are always visible and under democratic processes can be pointed out and corrected. The government of Greece is not perfect. Nevertheless it represents 85 percent of the members of the Greek Parliament who were chosen in an election last year. Foreign observers, including 692 Americans, considered this election to be a fair expression of the views of the Greek people.

The Greek Government has been operating in an atmosphere of chaos and extremism. It has made mistakes. The extension of aid by this country does not mean that the United States condones everything that the Greek Government has done or will do. We have condemned in the past, and we condemn now, extremist measures of the right or left. We have in the past advised tolerance, and we advise tolerance now.

Greece's neighbor, Turkey, also deserves our attention.

The future of Turkey as an independent and economically sound state is clearly no less important to the freedom-loving peoples of the world than the future of Greece. The circumstances in which Turkey finds itself today are considerably different from those of Greece. Turkey has been spared the disasters that have beset Greece; and, during the war, the United States and Great Britain furnished Turkey with material aid. Nevertheless, Turkey now needs our support.

Since the war Turkey has sought financial assistance from Great Britain and the United States for the purpose of effecting that modernization necessary for the maintenance of its national integrity.

That integrity is essential to the preservation of order in the Middle East.

The British Government has informed us that, owing to its own difficulties, it can no longer extend financial or economic aid to Turkey.

As in the case of Greece, if Turkey is to have the assistance it needs, the United States must supply it. We are the only country able to provide that help.

I am fully aware of the broad implications involved if the United States extends assistance to Greece and Turkey, and I shall discuss these implications with you at this time.

One of the primary objectives of the foreign policy of the United States is the creation of conditions in which we and other nations will be able to work out a way of life free from coercion. This was a fundamental issue in the war with Germany and Japan. Our victory was won over countries which sought to impose their will, and their way of life, upon other nations.

To insure the peaceful development of nations, free from coercion, the United States has taken a leading part in establishing the United Nations. The United Nations is designed to make possible lasting freedom and independence for all its members. We shall not realize our objectives, however, unless we are willing to help free peoples to maintain their free institutions and their national integrity against aggressive movements that seek to impose upon them totalitarian regimes. This is no more than a frank recognition that totalitarian regimes imposed on free peoples, by direct or indirect aggression, undermine the foundations of international peace and hence the security of the United States.

The peoples of a number of countries of the world have recently had totalitarian regimes forced upon them against their will. The Government of the United States has made frequent protests against coercion and intimidation, in violation of the Yalta agreement, in Poland, Rumania, and Bulgaria. I must also state that in a number of other countries there have been similar developments.

At the present moment in world history nearly every nation must choose between alternative ways of life. The choice is too often not a free one.

One way of life is based upon the will of the majority and is distinguished by free institutions, representing government, free elections, guarantees of individual liberty, freedom of speech and religion, and freedom from political oppression.

The second way of life is based upon the will of a minority forcibly imposed upon the majority. It relies upon terror and oppression, a controlled press and radio, fixed elections, and the suppression of personal freedoms.

I believe that it must be the policy of the United States to support free peoples who are resisting attempted subjugation by armed minorities or by outside pressures.

I believe that we must assist free peoples to work out their own destinies in their own way.

I believe that our help should be primarily through economic and financial aid which is essential to economic stability and orderly political processes.

The world is not static, and the status quo is not sacred. But we cannot allow changes in the status quo in violation of the Charter of the United Nations by such methods as coercion, or by such subterfuges as political infiltration. In helping free and independent nations to maintain their freedom, the United States will be giving effect to the principles of the Charter of the United Nations.

It is necessary only to glance at a map to realize that the survival and integrity of the Greek nation are of grave importance in a much wider situation. If Greece should fall under the control of an armed minority, the effect upon its neighbor Turkey, would be immediate and serious. Confusion and disorder might well spread throughout the entire Middle East.

Moreover, the disappearance of Greece as an independent state would have a profound effect upon those countries in Europe whose peoples are struggling against great difficulties to maintain their freedoms and their independence while they repair the damages of war.

It would be an unspeakable tragedy if these countries, which have struggled so long against overwhelming odds, should lose that victory for which they sacrificed so much. Collapse of free institutions and loss of independence would be disastrous not only for them but for the world. Discouragement and possibly failure would quickly be the lot of neighboring peoples striving to maintain their freedom and independence.

Should we fail to aid Greece and Turkey in this fateful hour, the effect will be far reaching to the West as well as to the East.

We must take immediate and resolute action.

I, therefore, ask the Congress to provide authority for assistance to Greece and Turkey in the amount of $400,000,000 for the period ending June 30, 1948. In requesting these funds, I have taken into consideration the maximum amount of relief assistance which would be furnished to Greece out of the $350,000,000 which I recently requested that the Congress authorize for the prevention of starvation and suffering in countries devastated by the war.

In addition to funds, I ask the Congress to authorize the detail of American civilian and military personnel to Greece, and Turkey, at the request of those countries, to assist in the tasks of reconstruction, and for the purpose of supervising the use of such financial and material assistance as may be furnished. I recommend that authority also be provided for the instruction and training of selected Greek and Turkish personnel.

Finally, I ask that the Congress provide authority which will permit the speediest and most effective use, in terms of needed commodities, supplies, and equipment, of such funds as may be authorized.

If further funds, or further authority, should be needed for purposes indicated in this message, I shall not hesitate to bring the situation before the Congress. On this subject the executive and legislative branches of the Government must work together.

This is a serious course upon which we embark.

I would not recommend it except that the alternative is much more serious.

The United States contributed $341,000,000,000 toward winning World War II. This is an investment in world freedom and world peace.

The assistance that I am recommending for Greece and Turkey amounts to little more than one-tenth of 1 percent of this investment. It is only common sense that we should safeguard this investment and make sure that it was not in vain.

The seeds of totalitarian regimes are nurtured by misery and want. They spread and grow in the evil soil of poverty and strife. They reach their full growth when the hope of a people for a better life has died.

We must keep that hope alive.

The free peoples of the world look to us for support in maintaining their freedoms.

If we falter in our leadership, we may endanger the peace of the world—and we shall surely endanger the welfare of our own Nation.

Great responsibilities have been placed upon us by the swift movement of events.

I am confident that the Congress will face these responsibilities squarely.

Harry S. Truman

Appendix II
Public Law 75, To Provide Assistance to Greece and Turkey, 80th Congress, 1st Session, Approved May 22, 1947

AN ACT To provide for assistance to Greece and Turkey

Whereas the Governments of Greece and Turkey have sought from the Government of the United States immediate financial and other assistance which is necessary for the maintenance of their national integrity and their survival as free nations; and

Whereas the national integrity and survival of these nations are of importance to the security of the United States and of all freedom-loving peoples and depend upon the receipt at this time of assistance; and

Whereas the Security Council of the United Nations has recognized the seriousness of the unsettled conditions prevailing on the border between Greece on the one hand and Albania, Bulgaria, and Yugoslavia on the other, and, if the present emergency is met, may subsequently assume full responsibility for this phase of the problem as a result of the investigation which its commission is currently conducting; and

Whereas the Food and Agriculture Organization mission for Greece recognized the necessity that Greece receive financial and economic assistance and recommended that Greece request such assistance from the appropriate agencies of the United Nations and from the Governments of the United States and the United Kingdom; and

Whereas the United Nations is not now in a position to furnish to Greece and Turkey the financial and economic assistance which is immediately required; and

Whereas the furnishing of such assistance to Greece and Turkey by the United States will contribute to the freedom and independence of all members of the United Nations in conformity with the principles and purposes of the Charter:

Now, therefore,

Be it enacted by the Senate and House of Representatives of the United States of America in Congress assembled, That, notwithstanding the provisions of any other law, the President may from time to time when he deems it in the interest of the United States furnish assistance to Greece and Turkey, upon request of their governments, and upon terms and conditions determined by him—

(1) by rendering financial aid in the form of loans, credits, grants, or otherwise, to those countries;

(2) by detailing to assist those countries any persons in the employ of the Government of the United States; and the provisions of the Act of May 25, 1938 (52 Stat. 442), as amended, applicable to personnel detailed pursuant to such Act, as amended, shall be applicable to personnel detailed pursuant to this paragraph: Provided, however, That no civilian personnel shall be assigned to Greece or Turkey to administer the purposes of this Act until such personnel have been investigated by the Federal Bureau of Investigation;

(3) by detailing a limited number of members of the military services of the United States to assist those countries, in an advisory capacity only; and the provisions of the Act of May 19, 1926 (44 Stat. 565), as amended, applicable to personnel detailed pursuant to such Act, as amended, shall be applicable to personnel detailed pursuant to this paragraph;

(4) by providing for (A) the transfer to, and the procurement for by manufacture or otherwise and the transfer to, those countries of any articles, services, and information, and (B) the instruction and training of personnel of those countries; and

(5) by incurring and defraying necessary expenses, including administrative expenses and expenses for compensation of personnel, in connection with the carrying out of the provisions of this Act.

SEC. 2. (a) Sums from advances by the Reconstruction Finance Corporation under section 4 (a) and from the appropriations made under authority of section 4 (b) may be allocated for any of the purposes of this Act to any department, agency, or independent establishment of the Government. Any amount so allocated shall be available as advancement or reimbursement, and shall be credited, at the option of the department, agency, or independent establishment concerned, to appropriate appropriations, funds or accounts existing or established for the purpose.

(b) Whenever the President requires payment in advance by the Government of Greece or Turkey for assistance to be furnished to such countries in accordance with this Act, such payments when made shall be credited to such countries in accounts established for the purpose. Sums from such accounts shall be allocated to the departments, agencies, or independent establishments of the Government which furnish the assistance for which payment is received, in the same manner, and shall be available and credited in the same manner, as allocations made under subsection (a) of this section. Any portion of such allocation not used as reimbursement shall remain available until expended.

(c) Whenever any portion of an allocation under subsection (a) or subsection (b) is used as reimbursement, the amount of reimbursement shall be available for entering into contracts and other uses during the fiscal year in which the reimbursement is received and the ensuing fiscal year. Where the head of any department, agency, or independent establishment of the Government determines that replacement of any article transferred pursuant to paragraph (4) (A) of section 1 is not necessary, any funds received in payment therefor shall be covered into the Treasury as miscellaneous receipts.

(d) (1) Payment in advance by the Government of Greece or of Turkey shall be required by the President for any articles or services furnished to such country under paragraph (4) (A) of section 1 if they are not paid for from funds advanced by the Reconstruction Finance Corporation under section 4 (a) or from funds appropriated under authority of section (4) (b).

(2) No department, agency, or independent establishment of the Government shall furnish any articles or services under paragraph (4) (A) of section 1 to either Greece or Turkey, unless it receives advancements or reimbursements therefor out of allocations under subsection (a) or (b) of this section.

SEC. 3. As a condition precedent to the receipt of any assistance pursuant to this Act, the government requesting such assistance shall agree (a) to permit free access of United States Government officials for the purpose of observing whether such assistance is utilized effectively and in accordance with the undertakings of the recipient government; (b) to permit representatives of the press and radio of the United States to observe freely and to report fully regarding the utilization of such assistance; (c) not to transfer, without the consent of the President of the United States, title to or possession of any article or information transferred pursuant to this Act nor to permit, without such consent, the use of any such article or the use or disclosure of any such information by or to anyone not an officer, employee, or agent of the recipient government; (d) to make such provisions as may be required by the President of the United States for the security of any article, service, or information received pursuant to this Act; (e) not to use any part of the proceeds of any loan, credit, grant, or other form of aid rendered pursuant to this Act for the making of any payment on account of the principal or interest on any loan made to such government by any other foreign government; and

(f) to give full and continuous publicity within such country as to the purpose, source, character, scope, amounts, and progress of United States economic assistance carried on therein pursuant to this Act.

SEC. 4 (a) Notwithstanding the provisions of any other law, the Reconstruction Finance Corporation is authorized and directed, until such time as an appropriation shall be made pursuant to subsection (b) of this section, to make advances, not to exceed in the aggregate $100,000,000, to carry out the provisions of this Act, in such manner and in such amounts as the President shall determine.

(b) There is hereby authorized to be appropriated to the President not to exceed $400,000,000 to carry out the provisions of this Act. From appropriations made under this authority there shall be repaid to the Reconstruction Finance Corporation the advances made by it under subsection (a) of this section.

SEC. 5. The President may from time to time prescribe such rules and regulations as may be necessary and proper to carry out any of the provisions of this Act; and he may exercise any power or authority conferred upon him pursuant to this Act through such department, agency, independent establishment, or officer of the Government as he shall direct.

The President is directed to withdraw any or all aid authorized herein under any of the following circumstances:

(1) If requested by the Government of Greece or Turkey, respectively, representing a majority of the people of either such nation;

(2) If the Security Council finds (with respect to which finding the United States waives the exercise of any veto) or the General Assembly finds that action taken or assistance furnished by the United Nations makes the continuance of such assistance unnecessary or undesirable;

(3) If the President finds that any purposes of the Act have been substantially accomplished by the action of any other intergovernmental organizations or finds that the purposes of the Act are incapable of satisfactory accomplishment; and

(4) If the President finds that any of the assurance given pursuant to section 3 are not being carried out.

SEC. 6. Assistance to any country under this Act may, unless sooner terminated by the President, be terminated by concurrent resolution by the two Houses of the Congress.

SEC. 7. The President shall submit to the Congress quarterly reports of expenditures and activities, which shall include uses of funds by the recipient governments, under authority of this Act.

SEC. 8. The chief of any mission to any country receiving assistance under this Act shall be appointed by the President, by and with the advice and consent of the Senate, and shall perform such functions relating to the administration of this Act as the President shall prescribe.

Notes

ABBREVIATIONS

ABC	American-British Correspondence, War Department Records, Modern Military Division, National Archives, Wash., D.C.
AMAG	American Mission for Aid to Greece
BMMG	British Military Mission Greece
CCS	Combined Chiefs of Staff, Modern Military Division, National Archives, Wash., D.C.
CIG	Central Intelligence Group, Modern Military Division, National Archives, Wash., D.C.
DS	Department of State, United States
DSDF, NA	Department of State, United States, General Records, Decimal File, U.S.-Greek Internal Political Affairs, 1945-49, Diplomatic Branch, National Archives, Wash., D.C.
FO	Foreign Office, Great Britain
FRC	Federal Records Center, Suitland, Maryland
FRUS	*Foreign Relations of the United States*, Department of State
GPO	Government Printing Office, United States
"History of JUSMAGG"	History of Joint U.S. Military Assistance Group, Greece (25 March 1949 to 30 June 1950), Office of the Chief of Military History, U.S. Army, Historical Manuscript File (8-4.4 AC V C2), Records and Reports Section, Joint U.S. Military Advisory Planning Group, Greece, Modern Military Division, National Archives, Wash., D.C.
JCS	Joint Chiefs of Staff, Records, Modern Military Division, National Archives, Wash., D.C.
JIC	Joint Intelligence Committee
JUSMAPG	Joint U.S. Military Advisory and Planning Group Greece
Maxwell AFB	Maxwell Air Force Base, Montgomery, Alabama
MS Divis., LC	Manuscript Division, Library of Congress, Wash., D.C.
NA	National Archives, Wash., D.C.

NSC	National Security Council
P & O	Plans and Operations Division, U.S. Army Staff Records, Modern Military Division, National Archives, Wash., D.C.
PRO	Public Record Office, Kew Gardens, London, England
R & A	Research and Analysis Branch, National Archives, Wash., D.C.
SANACC	State-Army-Navy-Air Force Coordinating Committee
SWNCC	State-War-Navy Coordinating Committee
TS	Top Secret
UK	United Kingdom
UNGA	United Nations General Assembly
UNSC	United Nations Security Council
UNSCOB	United Nations Special Committee on the Balkans
USAFGG	United States Air Force Group Greece
"USAFGG History"	JUSMAGG Air Adjutant Section 314.7 Military Histories (USAF Section), JUSMAGG, Modern Military Division, National Archives, Wash., D.C.
USAGG	United States Army Group Greece

INTRODUCTION

[1] *New York Times*, Feb. 5, 1949. Clipping encl. in Francis F. Lincoln Papers, Truman Lib. Although McCormick was 5'2" tall and 67 years old, she made her way up and down the mountains with the soldiers, visiting outposts, refugees, and prisons. See *Time*, Jan. 10, 1949, p. 45.

[2] The term *andartes* was used during the Balkan Wars against Turkey and became widely known in relation to the resistance against Nazi occupation. According to a State Department specialist in Greece during the 1940s, an *andarte* was a Greek national hero who had operated out of the mountains in resisting the rule of the Ottoman Turks until Greece won independence during the 1820s. Afterward, the *andartes* opposed centralized government. During the 1940s the guerrillas took on the name to signify true patriots and folk-heroes. See Francis F. Lincoln, *United States' Aid to Greece, 1947–1962* (Germantown, Tenn.: Professional Seminars, 1975), 13–14.

[3] B. H. Liddell Hart, *The Revolution in Warfare* (New Haven, Conn.: Yale U. Press, 1947). See also Stephen G. Xydis, "The Truman Doctrine in Perspective," *Balkan Studies* 8 (1967): 239–62. Xydis argues that the United States developed a new foreign policy after the atomic bomb, and that Greece became the "focal point, a testing ground, a symbol between 1944–47." Ibid., 241.

[4] *New York Times*, Dec. 29, 1948, p. 20. Xydis argues that as early as 1944, Greece provided a "testing ground" for Great Power cooperation and that many elements of limited warfare became apparent during the civil war: subversion, revolution, token troops, guerrilla warfare, propaganda, "privileged sanctuary," and use of the UN for "symbolic warfare." See his article entitled "America, Britain, and the USSR in the Greek Arena, 1944–1947," *Political Science Quarterly* 78 (Dec. 1963): 581–96.

[5] At one stage in the Greek struggle of 1946–49, Stalin ordered the Bulgarian leader, Georgi Dimitrov, to call off the war because of the superior military strength of the United States and Great Britain. A British observer in Greece, Christopher M. Woodhouse, admitted that Stalin sought an outlet to the Mediterranean, that the Yugoslavs and Bulgarians wanted Greek Macedonia, that the Slavophones (Greek-speaking Slavs) desired autonomy, and that the KKE sought power. But, he adds, to argue that Stalin dictated events is to overlook the fierce rivalries between him and the Yugoslav communist leader, Josip Broz Tito, between Dimitrov and Tito,

between Greeks and Albanians, and between Slavo-Macedonians and Greeks. No one could have controlled Balkan events. Woodhouse, *The Struggle for Greece, 1941–1949* (Brooklyn Heights, N.Y.: Beekman-Esanu, 1976), 181–82, 194–95. See also Stefanos Sarafis, *Greek Resistance Army: The Story of ELAS* (London: Birch Books, 1951), 225; Edgar O'Ballance, *The Greek Civil War, 1944–1949* (N.Y.: Praeger, 1966), 78, 122, 131; Vojtech Mastny, *Russia's Road to the Cold War: Diplomacy, Warfare, and the Politics of Communism, 1941–1945* (N.Y.: Columbia U. Press, 1979), 205; Lawrence S. Wittner, *American Intervention in Greece, 1943–1949* (N.Y.: Columbia U. Press, 1982), 8; Milovan Djilas, *Conversations with Stalin* (N.Y.: Harcourt, Brace, 1962), 181–82. On the "percentages agreement," see Albert Resis, "The Churchill-Stalin Secret 'Percentages' Agreement on the Balkans, Moscow, October 1944," *American Historical Review* 83 (April 1978): 368–87; Stephen G. Xydis, "The Secret Anglo-Soviet Agreement on the Balkans of October 9, 1944," *Journal of Central European Affairs* 15 (Oct. 1955): 248–71; Winston Churchill, *Triumph and Tragedy* (Boston: Houghton Mifflin, 1953), 226–35; Thomas G. Paterson, *On Every Front: The Making of the Cold War* (N.Y.: Norton, 1982), 37–38. For the Soviets' refusal to intervene in behalf of the Greek communists in 1944–45, see John O. Iatrides, *Revolt in Athens: The Greek Communist "Second Round," 1944–45* (Princeton: Princeton U. Press, 1972), 221–24, 279. The "First Round" of the Greek struggle was an attempted communist overthrow that began in late 1943 and ended in failure in early 1944. The "Third Round" was the civil war of 1946–49. See also Heinz Richter, *British Intervention in Greece: From Varkiza to Civil War, February 1945 to August 1946* (London: Merlin, 1985), 536. Mastny believes that during the latter part of World War II, the Greek communists probably acted without authorization from the Soviets, but also with no directives against them. *Russia's Road to Cold War*, 236. This suggests a pattern of Soviet behavior toward Greece consistent with the early part of the civil war. Stalin preferred policies that guaranteed success. On this latter point, see John O. Iatrides, "Civil War, 1945–1949: National and International Aspects," in Iatrides, ed., *Greece in the 1940s: A Nation in Crisis* (Hanover, N.H.: U. Press of New England, 1981), 208.

[6]See Bruce R. Kuniholm, *The Origins of the Cold War in the Near East: Great Power Conflict and Diplomacy in Iran, Turkey, and Greece* (Princeton: Princeton U. Press, 1980), 402–05, 426–27; Van Coufoudakis, "The United States, the United Nations, and the Greek Question, 1946–1952," in Iatrides, ed., *Greece in 1940s*, 278; C. E. Black, "Greece and the United Nations," *Political Science Quarterly* 63 (Dec. 1948): 551–68; Charles E. Bohlen, *Witness to History, 1929–1969* (N.Y.: Norton, 1973), 261; George M. Alexander, *The Prelude to the Truman Doctrine: British Policy in Greece, 1944–1947* (Oxford, Eng.: Clarendon Press, 1982), 251; Dimitrios G. Kousoulas, *The Price of Freedom: Greece in World Affairs, 1939–1953* (Syracuse, N.Y.: Syracuse U. Press, 1953), 178; Soviet complaint lodged by UN delegate Andrei Gromyko, Jan. 21, 1946, in UNSC, *Official Records*, 1st Year, 1st series, supplement 1, pp. 73–74. Kousoulas believes that Stalin at first supported the guerrilla war but reversed his policy as Greek government forces appeared likely to win. See his work, *Revolution and Defeat: The Story of the Greek Communist Party* (London: Oxford U. Press, 1965), 236.

[7]Memo of conversation among Bidault, Byrnes, and H. Freeman Matthews, May 1, 1946, Byrnes Papers, folder 638, Clemson U.; "Draft of Information Policy on Relations with Russia," July 22, 1946, Acheson Papers, Truman Lib.; Oral History Interview with Clifford (March 1971–Feb. 1973), 87–88, ibid.; Oral History Interview with Elsey, II (April 9, 1970), 263, ibid.

[8][?] Smith to sec. of state, June 21, 1946, Byrnes Papers, folder 638, Clemson U.

[9]Kuniholm, *Origins of Cold War in Near East*, 59, 356, 379–80; Joseph M. Jones, *The Fifteen Weeks (February 21–June 5, 1947)* (N.Y.: Viking, 1955), 60; Dean Acheson, *Present at the Creation: My Years in the State Department* (N.Y.: Norton, 1969), 269; Theodore A. Couloumbis, *The United States, Greece, and Turkey: The Troubled Triangle* (N.Y.: Praeger, 1983), 11–12. By the Montreux Treaty of 1936, the signatory nations of Bulgaria, France, Great Britain, Greece, Japan, Rumania, Turkey, the Soviet Union, and Yugoslavia set out regulations for using the Dardanelles, Sea of Marmora, and Bosporus in such a way as to guarantee

the security of Turkey and other riparian states in the Black Sea area. Article I upheld "the principle of freedom of transit and navigation by sea in the Straits" for, as Article 28 states, an indefinite period, while the treaty was to be in force for twenty years. See Harry N. Howard, *The Problem of the Turkish Straits* (Wash., D.C.: GPO, 1947), 2, 36–37; Melvyn P. Leffler, "Strategy, Diplomacy, and the Cold War: The United States, Turkey, and NATO, 1945–1952," *Journal of American History* 71 (March 1985): 807–25.

[10]Jones, *Fifteen Weeks*, 59, 61; John L. Gaddis, *The United States and the Origins of the Cold War, 1941–1947* (N.Y.: Columbia U. Press, 1972), 336; Robert L. Messer, *The End of an Alliance: James F. Byrnes, Roosevelt, Truman, and the Origins of the Cold War* (Chapel Hill: U. of North Carolina Press, 1982), 192; "State Dept. Briefing Book," July 1, 1946, p. 8, Byrnes Papers, Clemson U.; Howard, *Problem of Turkish Straits*, 39; Elbridge Durbrow (chargé in Moscow) to sec. of state, Aug. 5, 1946, DSDF, NA. A recent intelligence report from the Netherlands confirmed the White House beliefs regarding Soviet objectives. According to the report, the Russians were engaged in a "strategic offensive" aimed at "World revolution in the Middle East" and eventual "world supremacy." See N.E.F.I.S. Netherlands Intelligence #141: "The Aims, Methods and Means of Soviet Russia in Asia and the Middle East," May 16, 1946, pp. 8, 11, 24, in William D. Leahy Files, Records of JCS, NA.

[11]After the President completed his explanation, he asked if the general was satisfied. Eisenhower joined in the laughter and declared that he was. Interview with Acheson (Feb. 17, 1955), 2–3, Truman Papers, Post-Presidential Files, "Memoirs File," box 1, Truman Lib. See also Robert J. Donovan, *Conflict and Crisis: The Presidency of Harry S Truman, 1945–1948* (N.Y.: Norton, 1977), 251; Acheson, *Present at Creation*, 263–64; Jones, *Fifteen Weeks*, 63–65. General Lauris Norstad, director of the Army's Plans and Operations Division, believed that the birth of the Truman Doctrine took place at this meeting when the President decided to support Turkey against Soviet demands. Xydis, "Truman Doctrine in Perspective," 248 n.4. The *Missouri* had returned the ashes of the Turkish ambassador in Washington, who had died during the war. Jones shows that in February, Forrestal had wanted to send a task force to the Mediterranean, but that Byrnes had finally turned down the proposal after considerable indecision. Sending the *Missouri* was a compromise. Jones, *Fifteen Weeks*, 62.

[12]Donovan, *Conflict and Crisis*, 251; Xydis, "Truman Doctrine in Perspective," 248–49; Acheson, *Present at Creation*, 265; Jones, *Fifteen Weeks*, 64–65; Couloumbis, *United States, Greece, and Turkey*, 11–12; Kuniholm, *Origins of Cold War in Near East*, 373; Gaddis, *United States and Origins of Cold War*, 336–37; Harry S. Truman, *Memoirs: Years of Trial and Hope* (Garden City, N.Y.: Doubleday, 1956), 97–98; Howard, *Problem of Turkish Straits*, 39–43. Feridun Erkin, the secretary general of the Turkish Foreign Ministry (later foreign minister) called the crisis "one of the most vigorous diplomatic initiatives in history launched by Russia to obtain control of the Straits." He attributed the outcome to Turkish resistance, suspicions aroused by Soviet intentions regarding the straits, and American support. Cited in Kuniholm, *Origins of Cold War in Near East*, 373 n.193.

[13]Clifford, "American Relations with the Soviet Union," Sept. 24, 1946, Conway File, Truman Lib.; Donovan, *Conflict and Crisis*, 221.

[14]Clifford, "American Relations with the Soviet Union," 1, 3–4, 12–14, 60–62, 68, 71, 73–74, 78–79; Oral History Interview with Elsey, II (April 9, 1970), 261–66; Gaddis, *United States and Origins of Cold War*, 321–22, 322 n.7; Donovan, *Conflict and Crisis*, 221–22; George F. Kennan, *Memoirs, 1925–1950* (Boston: Little, Brown, 1967), 247–51, 301–4.

[15]Oral History Interview with Clifford (March 1971–Feb. 1973), 89–90; Clifford, "American Relations with the Soviet Union," 75.

[16]Kennan, *Memoirs, 1925–1950*, 247–51, 301–4.

[17]"Soviet Military Intentions," Sept. 18, 1946, CIG Special Study No. 4, pp. i–ii, 2. Truman Papers, President's Secretary's Files, Truman Lib.

[18]Memo for Leahy from Hoyt S. Vandenberg, director of Central Intelligence, Sept. 25, 1946. Enclosure: Strategic Services Unit, War Dept., Subject of Soviet Activity in Shanghai, from Source "Z"—Field Evaluation C-3, July 7, 1946. In Leahy Files, Records of JCS, NA. The documents consulted did not include Araniev's first name.

[19]Ibid.; William Benton to Asst. Sec. of State William L. Clayton, Oct. 15, 1946, Clayton-Thorp Files, Truman Lib.

[20]"Revised Soviet Tactics in International Affairs," Jan. 6, 1947, CIG, ORE 1/1, pp. 1, 2, Truman Papers, President's Secretary's Files, Truman Lib.

[21]Ibid., 2, 3. The Americans' estimates about the size of the Red Army were greatly inflated. Although it is impossible to be sure, the Soviets' postwar demobilization had been rapid. From the maximum of 11,365,000 in May 1945, the figure had dropped to less than 3 million by early 1948 (including the air force). Comparatively speaking, of course, the U.S. military establishment was considerably weaker, having been reduced from about 12 million to over 1.5 million by July 1947. However, the British had over a million in the armed services, and the United States had the atomic bomb and a strategic bombing force. See Daniel H. Yergin, *Shattered Peace: The Origins of the Cold War and the National Security State* (Boston: Houghton Mifflin, 1977), 270–71; Paterson, *On Every Front*, 155–56. As in many matters during the period, however, the perception was more important than whatever the reality was.

[22]"Revised Soviet Tactics," 3.

[23]Ibid., 4–5.

[24]Ibid.

[25]"The Greek Situation," Feb. 7, 1947, CIG, ORE 6/1, pp. 1–2, 12, ibid. For an analysis of these suppositions by an adviser in the Truman administration, see Jones, *Fifteen Weeks*, 11.

[26]Appendix "A" of aide-mémoire to US: extract of report from Brit. representative in Greece, Feb. 5, 1947, DSDF, NA; "Soviet Military Intentions," 2. See John O. Iatrides, "Perceptions of Soviet involvement in the Greek Civil War, 1945–1949," in Lars Baerentzen, John O. Iatrides, and Ole L. Smith, eds., *Studies in the History of the Greek Civil War, 1945–1949* (Copenhagen, Denmark: Museum Tusculanum Press, 1987), 225–48. Iatrides argues that by 1947 both the American and the British governments believed that the Soviets were involved in some way in the civil war. In regard to Greek perceptions, the government in Athens adopted a "diplomatic posture" that was perhaps different from its real views. But until the Greek documents are open, Iatrides shows, the only message sent to Washington and London was that their perceptions were correct. Ibid., 242–45.

[27]"State Dept. Briefing Book," 7, 10, 11; Jones, *Fifteen Weeks*, 72. EAM stood for Ethnikon Apeleftherotikon Metopon.

[28]"State Dept. Briefing Book," 14; State-War-Navy Coordinating Subcommittee for Near and Middle East—"U.S. Security Interests in Greece," Sept. 7, 1946. Enclosure: memo for sec. of state, ABC-400.336 Greece, sect. I-A, pp. 1, 3, War Dept. Records, NA. MacVeagh to sec. of state, Feb. 7, 1947, *FRUS*, V: *The Near East and Africa* (Wash., D.C.: GPO, 1971), 16; "U.S. Security Interests in Greece," 1.

[29]"U.S. Security Interests in Greece," 1, 2; "Background Memorandum on Greece," March 3, 1947, by Joseph M. Jones, Jones Papers, Truman Lib.; notes on cabinet meeting, March 7, 1947, Patterson Papers, General Correspondence, box 19, MS Divis., LC. For a summation of the State Department's position, see Public Information Program on U.S. Aid to Greece: FPI 30, append. A: General Survey of Greek Situation, March 3, 1947, pp. 4–5, DSDF, NA.

[30]"Estimate of the Situation—Greece," attached to memo from Chamberlin to Norstad, director, P & O, War Dept., ca. early Dec. 1946, P & O 092 (TS), Dec. 17, 1946, p. 1, Army Staff Records, NA; Norstad to Chamberlin, Dec. 17, 1946, encl. in ABC-400.336 Greece, sect. I-A, p. 2, War Dept. Records, NA.

CHAPTER 1.   HOLDING THE LINE IN GREECE

[1]For the December events, see John O. Iatrides, *Revolt in Athens: The Greek Communist "Second Round," 1944–1945* (Princeton: Princeton U. Press, 1972). See also Christopher M. Woodhouse, *The Struggle for Greece, 1941–1949* (Brooklyn Heights, N.Y.: Beekman-Esanu, 1976), chap. 5; Dimitrios G. Kousoulas, *The Price of Freedom: Greece in World Affairs, 1939–1953* (Syracuse, N.Y.: Syracuse U. Press, 1953), 151; Dimitrios G. Kousoulas, *Revolution and Defeat: The Story of the Greek Communist Party* (London: Oxford U. Press, 1965), 232; Lawrence S. Wittner, *American Intervention in Greece, 1943–1949* (N.Y.: Columbia U. Press, 1982), 37ff. Although "civil war" is probably the correct label for these events in Greece, even that term causes problems. As John O. Iatrides notes about the civil war of 1946–49, the guerrillas did not have a revolutionary government recognized as a belligerent by either the lawful government in Athens or foreign governments. The United States and Greece regarded the insurgents as "bandits" or "rebels" engaged in an armed rebellion against the state. The insurgents nonetheless had a fairly substantial "army" that worked under a "government"—and it was in communication with foreign governments. Thus, Iatrides concludes that so fine was the distinction between a "civil war" and an "insurgency" in Greece that they were almost one and the same. See his "Civil War, 1945–1949: National and International Aspects," in Iatrides, ed., *Greece in the 1940s: A Nation in Crisis* (Hanover, N.H.: U. Press of New England, 1981), 196. Another writer (as well as an official in the Greek government during the 1950s and 1960s) agrees that even though the guerrillas received outside aid, the conflict was a civil war because it was among Greeks. See Evangelos Averoff-Tossizza, *By Fire and Axe: The Communist Party and the Civil War in Greece, 1944–1949* (New Rochelle, N.Y.: Caratzas Brothers, 1978), 356–57. Originally published as *Le Feu et la hache Grèce '46–'49, histoire des guerres de l'après-guerre* (Paris: Editions de Breteuil, 1973). Trans. by Sarah Arnold Rigos. For a Marxist view of the war as the guerrillas against monarcho-fascism and Anglo-American imperialism, see Zizis Zografos, "Some Lessons of the Civil War in Greece," *World Marxist Review* 7 (Nov. 1964): 43–50. On causes of the war, see Iatrides, "Civil War," 199, 203; Heinz Richter, *British Intervention in Greece: From Varkiza to Civil War, February 1945 to August 1946* (London: Merlin, 1985), 450, 506, 508, 536. KKE stood for Kommunistikon Komma Ellados.

[2]William H. McNeill, *The Greek Dilemma: War and Aftermath* (Philadelphia: Lippincott, 1947), 231, 233–35; Frank Smothers, William H. McNeill, and Elizabeth D. McNeill, *Report on the Greeks: Findings of a Twentieth Century Fund Team which Surveyed Conditions in Greece in 1947* (N.Y.: Twentieth Century Fund, 1948), 29; John O. Iatrides, "American Attitudes Toward the Political System of Postwar Greece," in Theodore A. Couloumbis and John O. Iatrides, eds., *Greek-American Relations: A Critical Review* (N.Y.: Pella, 1980), 60–61; Richter, *British Intervention in Greece*, 442–43; speech by Grady before Commonwealth Club of Calif., May 10, 1946, Grady Papers, Truman Lib.; Henry F. Grady, "Report of the Allied Mission to Observe the Greek Elections" (Wash., D.C.: GPO, 1946), 20, in ibid.; memo for Truman from Acheson, May 7, 1946, Truman Papers, Official File, ibid. Several small leftist-socialist parties also boycotted the elections. See Bickham Sweet-Escott, *Greece: A Political and Economic Survey, 1939–1953* (London: Royal Institute of International Affairs, 1954), 50–52.

[3]Iatrides, *Revolt in Athens*, 269–75; Stephen G. Xydis, *Greece and the Great Powers, 1944–1947: Prelude to the "Truman Doctrine"* (Thessaloniki: Institute for Balkan Studies, 1963), 210.

[4]KKE quote in Averoff-Tossizza, *By Fire and Axe*, 162; Partsalidis quote in Iatrides, "Civil War," 203. See also Xydis, *Greece and Great Powers*, 181. For the Moscow meeting, see Iatrides, "Civil War," 203; Dimitrios G. Kousoulas, "The Truman Doctrine and the Stalin-Tito Rift: A Reappraisal," *South Atlantic Quarterly* 72 (Summer 1973): 427–39; Kousoulas, *Revolution and Defeat*, 239; Bruce R. Kuniholm, *The Origins of the Cold War in the Near East: Great Power Conflict and Diplomacy in Iran, Turkey, and Greece* (Princeton: Princeton U. Press, 1980), 399, 404.

[5]Richter, *British Intervention in Greece*, 507–8; Kuniholm, *Origins of Cold War in Near East*, 399; Averoff-Tossizza, *By Fire and Axe*, 172–73. Ole L. Smith claims that Zahariadis ordered the

attack on Litokhoron as a warning to the Greek government to halt the "white terror." Smith admits, however, that many later regarded the assault as the beginning of the civil war. See his essay entitled "Self-Defence and Communist Policy, 1945–1947," in Lars Baerentzen, John O. Iatrides, and Ole L. Smith, eds., *Studies in the History of the Greek Civil War, 1945–1949* (Copenhagen, Denmark: Museum Tusculanum Press, 1987), 159, 168–70. ELAS stood for Ethnikos Laikos Apeleftherotikos Stratos.

6"History of JUSMAGG," 64; Woodhouse, *Struggle for Greece*, 184; Xydis, *Greece and Great Powers*, 195, 229, 617 n. 16; Moscow quoted in ibid., 229; Christopher M. Woodhouse, *Apple of Discord: A Survey of Recent Greek Politics in Their International Setting* (London: Hutchinson, 1948), 267; Geoffrey Chandler, *The Divided Land: An Anglo-Greek Tragedy* (London: Macmillan, 1959), 152–53; Chamberlin to Amer. embassy in Moscow, June 15, 1946, Leahy Files, Records of JCS, NA. According to the *New York Times* correspondent in Athens, Cyrus L. Sulzberger, King George II was convinced that the Russians were stirring the trouble and that they had two special brigades helping Yugoslavia and Albania funnel in arms to the Greek guerrillas. Sulzberger claimed that the king had a "phobia about communism," but he (Sulzberger) admitted to "incontrovertible evidence" by early December 1946 that Yugoslavia, Albania, and Bulgaria were causing a civil war in northern Greece. See Sulzberger, *A Long Row of Candles: Memoirs and Diaries [1934–1954]* (N.Y.: Macmillan, 1969), 324, 335.

7"The Greek Situation," Feb. 7, 1947, CIG, ORE 6/1, pp. 11, 12, Truman Papers, President's Secretary's Files, Truman Lib. It is impossible to be sure how much aid the Greek guerrillas ultimately received from Yugoslavia and other Eastern European communist states (not to mention the Soviet Union), but Vladimir Dedijer, a Yugoslav journalist of the period and an associate of Tito, offered some figures in 1984 that, according to Elisabeth Barker, perhaps approximate the truth. By late 1946 the guerrillas had established ties with Yugoslav security forces led by Aleksander Ranković who, according to Dedijer, was responsible for dispensing aid. Dedijer himself was secretary of a commission attached to the Yugoslav Communist party's Central Committee and was, in that capacity, involved in the aid program. Dedijer says that Yugoslavia furnished 35,000 rifles, 3,500 machine guns, 2,000 German heavy machine guns, 7,000 German anti-tank weapons, 10,000 land mines, clothing for 12,000, and 30 wagons of food. The Albanians furnished a few weapons from their small supply, and the Bulgarians sent weapons originally from Yugoslavia, along with food and first-aid items. Other countries extending aid included: Hungary, which sent first-aid goods and a colonel to serve as liaison officer; Rumania, blankets; either the Czechs or the Hungarians, gramophone records of Russian war songs. Poland sent nothing. Finally, according to Dedijer, the Soviet Union sent 30 anti-aircraft guns. Vladimir Dedijer, *Novi Prilozi za Josipa Broza Tita, Treći Tom* (Belgrade, 1984), 266–67. Cited in Elisabeth Barker, "The Yugoslavs and the Greek Civil War of 1946–1949," in Baerentzen, Iatrides, and Smith, eds., *Studies in the History of the Greek Civil War*, 303.

8George M. Alexander, *The Prelude to the Truman Doctrine: British Policy in Greece, 1944–1947* (Oxford, Eng.: Clarendon Press, 1982), 199; Kousoulas, *Revolution and Defeat*, 237; Woodhouse, *Struggle for Greece*, 183, 190–91, 193–94; Sweet-Escott, *Greece*, 44; Richter, *British Intervention in Greece*, 490–91, 539; Averoff-Tossizza, *By Fire and Axe*, 212; Iatrides, "Civil War," 202. See also Edgar O'Ballance, *The Greek Civil War, 1944–1949* (N.Y.: Praeger, 1966), 122, 124–26, 128; Dominique Eudes, *The Kapetanios: Partisans and Civil War in Greece, 1943–1949* (N.Y.: Monthly Review Press, 1972), 284. Originally published as *Les Kapetanios: La Guerre civile grecque de 1943 à 1949* (Paris: Librarie Arthème Fayard, 1970). Trans. by John Howe.

9"The Greek Situation," 12. See also Woodhouse, *Struggle for Greece*, 179–80; Intelligence Divis. of War Dept., ca. late Feb. 1947, P & O 092 (TS), sect. VI-A, case 95, Army Staff Records, NA.

10Averoff-Tossizza, *By Fire and Axe*, 177; Woodhouse, *Struggle for Greece*, 193–94; Eudes, *Kapetanios*, 284; *Time*, Jan. 5, 1948, p. 2.

11Averoff-Tossizza, *By Fire and Axe*, 171–73. Averoff was a high-ranking Greek government official during the 1950s and 1960s. Another writer believes that the decision to begin a rebellion took place at a meeting of the Central Committee of the KKE in Athens in June 1945. See

Evangelos Kofos, *Nationalism and Communism in Macedonia* (Thessaloniki: Institute for Balkan Studies, 1964), 165. On Bulkes, see Nicholas Pappas, "The Soviet-Yugoslav Conflict and the Greek Civil War," in Wayne S. Vucinich, ed., *At the Brink of War and Peace: The Tito-Stalin Split in a Historic Perspective* (N.Y.: Columbia U. Press, 1984), 222. Zahariadis later noted that Bulkes provided "a solid, healthy, nursery for the elevation and creation of cadres." Quoted in ibid.

[12]Richter, *British Intervention in Greece*, 488–89; Iatrides, "American Attitudes Toward the Political System of Postwar Greece," 72; Woodhouse opinion cited in Wittner, *American Intervention in Greece*, 311. Ole L. Smith admits to division within the KKE, but rejects the Markos view that he was deliberately restrained by Zahariadis from an offensive. See Smith, "A Turning Point in the Greek Civil War, 1945–1949," *Scandinavian Studies in Modern Greek* 3 (1979): 35–46.

[13]Richter, *British Intervention in Greece*, 484–88; McNeill, *Greek Dilemma*, 241.

[14]"State Dept. Briefing Book," July 15, 1946, 13, Byrnes Papers, Clemson U.

[15]J. M. MacKintosh, *Strategy and Tactics of Soviet Foreign Policy* (London: Oxford U. Press, 1962), 11 n.1; Xydis, *Greece and Great Powers*, 254; Sweet-Escott, *Greece*, 55; Woodhouse, *Struggle for Greece*, 184–85; Joseph M. Jones, *The Fifteen Weeks (February 21–June 5, 1947)* (N.Y.: Viking, 1955), 68.

[16]Smothers et al., *Report on Greeks*, 29–30; "The Justice for Greece Committee" to Sec. of Treasury John W. Snyder, Nov. 12, 23, 1946, Snyder Papers, Truman Lib.; George E. Phillies, chman. of Public Relations Committee of Justice for Greece Committee, to Byrnes, Nov. 13, 1946, Byrnes Papers, Clemson U.; append. "A" to aide-mémoire to U.S.: extract of report from Brit. representative in Greece, Feb. 5, 1947, DSDF, NA; MacVeagh to sec. of state, Dec. 5, 1946, cited in John O. Iatrides, ed., *Ambassador MacVeagh Reports: Greece, 1933–1947* (Princeton: Princeton U. Press, 1980), 700; Sweet-Escott, *Greece*, 55–56. One writer calls both the election and the September plebiscite "elaborate charades" that provided a justification for the KKE's decision to undertake arms. George Th. Mavrogordatos, "The 1946 Election and Plebiscite: Prelude to Civil War," in Iatrides, ed., *Greece in 1940s*, 181–94.

[17]Alexander, *Prelude to Truman Doctrine*, 173, 193, 214.

[18]"State Dept. Briefing Book," July 15, 1946, 10; Lord Inverchapel, Brit. ambassador to U.S., to F.O., Jan. 22, 1947, in FO 371, vol. 61074, AN 350/350/45, PRO. Inverchapel's remarks were a reaction to a paper written by Cornelius Van H. Engert (acting diplomatic adviser, UNRRA) and circulated throughout the Foreign Office: "Some Observations on the Strategic Importance of the Middle East to the United States," Sept. 26, 1946. In ibid. Xydis, *Greece and the Great Powers*, 363, 474; Wittner, *American Intervention in Greece*, 228.

[19]Alexander, *Prelude to Truman Doctrine*, 214, 225–27, 234.

[20]Ibid., 227, 234–35.

[21]Intelligence Divis. of War Dept., ca. late Feb. 1947, P & O 092 (TS), sect. VI-A, case 95, Army Staff Records, NA; "Estimate of the Situation—Greece," attached to memo from Norstad, director, P & O, Dec. 13, 1946, pp. 1–2, ibid.; Woodhouse, *Struggle for Greece*, 179–80, 187–88.

[22]Eudes, *Kapetanios*, 274, 278; Averoff-Tossizza, *By Fire and Axe*, 191; Woodhouse, *Struggle for Greece*, 186–87, 193, 199, 205–6; O'Ballance, *Greek Civil War*, 129; Rawlins, HQ, BMMG, to Gen. William Morgan, Brit. Joint Staff Mission, CCS, Sept. 18, 1947, P & O 091 Greece (TS), sect. II, cases 8–17, p. 1, Army Staff Records, NA; "The Greek Situation"—Report to Chief of Staff by Chamberlin, Oct. 20, 1947, files of sec. of defense, CD 2-1-6, sheet 2, ibid.; Intelligence Divis. of War Dept., ca. late Feb. 1947, P & O 092 (TS), sect. VI-A, case 95, ibid.; append. "A" to aide-mémoire to U.S., Feb. 5, 1947, DSDF, NA; J.P. (47) 5 (Final), Chiefs of Staff Committee, Joint Planning Staff, Report on Greek Armed Forces, Jan. 25, 1947, ABC-400.336 Greece, sect. I-A, p. 2, War Dept. Records, NA.

[23]Intelligence Divis. of War Dept., ca. late Feb. 1947, P & O 092 (TS), sect. VI-A, case 95, p. 1, Army Staff Records, NA; "An Analysis of the Greek Air Force," May 23, 1946, HQ, AAF Air

Intelligence Report, No. 100-41-10142.048-41, Air Intelligence Divis. Study No. 41—append. "A," p. 3, Simpson Lib., Maxwell AFB; M. A. Campbell et al., *The Employment of Airpower in the Greek Guerrilla War, 1947–1949* (Montgomery, Ala.: Air U., Maxwell AFB, 1964), 8. In Simpson Lib. See also Averoff-Tossizza, *By Fire and Axe*, 190–91.

24Author's interview with McGhee, May 24, 1979; O'Ballance, *Greek Civil War*, 131–33; guerrilla's quote from Oral History Interview with Harry N. Howard (June 5, 1973), 60, Truman Lib.; Ethridge to sec. of state, Feb. 21, 1947, *FRUS*, V: *The Near East and Africa* (Wash., D.C.: GPO, 1971), 38; MacVeagh to sec. of state, Feb. 21, 1947, ibid., 39 n.3; MacVeagh to sec. of state, Feb. 20, 1947, DSDF, NA.

25Rep. Hugh D. Scott, Jr., of Pa. to Byrnes, Nov. 16, 1946, folder 541 (2), CFM S NYC-Nov. & Dec. 1947, Byrnes Papers, Clemson U.; Mayor Bernard Samuel of Philadelphia to Byrnes, Nov. 19, 1946, ibid.; Public Information Program on U.S. aid to Greece: FPI 30, append. D, pp. 2–4, March 3, 1947, DSDF, NA; Acheson Papers, box 6, file on Marshall Plan—reports, Greece and Turkey, Truman Lib.; "Report of UNSCOB," Dec. 3, 1946, suppl. 8, UNGA, *Official Records*, 3 sess., 1948, 1; Acheson Papers, file on Marshall Plan, Truman Lib.; "The Greek Situation," CIG, ORE 6/1, p. 5. See also Sweet-Escott, *Greece*, 57; Stephen G. Xydis, "The Truman Doctrine in Perspective," *Balkan Studies* 8 (1967): 239–62; Evan Luard, *A History of the United Nations*. Vol. I: *The Years of Western Domination, 1945–1955* (London: Macmillan, 1982), chap. 8. Wittner believes that the Soviets also sought to embarrass Yugoslavia by exposing its assistance to the Greek guerrillas. Such argument, however, rests on the premise that Stalin opposed the civil war at this time. Although the Soviet premier made his opposition known by early 1948, there is no conclusive evidence that he worked to undermine it at this early point. As long as the guerrillas were effectively discrediting the government in Athens, and as long as they were not pulling in the United States, Stalin appears to have been content to look the other way. In this early stage of the Greek war, he was in a no-lose situation. See Wittner, *American Intervention in Greece*, 59–60.

26"Report of UNSCOB," Dec. 19, 1946, suppl. 8, UNGA, *Official Records*, 3 sess., 1948, p. 1; Acheson Papers, file on Marshall Plan, Truman Lib.; FPI 30, append. D., p. 1, March 3, 1947, DSDF, NA; Kousoulas, *Price of Freedom*, 156–57; Jones, *Fifteen Weeks*, 68; Sweet-Escott, *Greece*, 58; Kenneth Matthews, *Memories of a Mountain War Greece: 1944–1949* (London: Longman, 1972), 14, 136–51. The Central Committee of the KKE chose Markos to head the Democratic Army in August 1946. See O'Ballance, *Greek Civil War*, 123; Woodhouse, *Struggle for Greece*, 193–94. Several commission members from communist states met Markos in March 1947. During the interview he denounced the British and Americans as imperialists and praised his army's fight for independence and the people's rights. See Eudes, *Kapetanios*, 282–88.

27Ethridge to sec. of state, Feb. 17, 1947, *FRUS*, V: *Near East and Africa*, 24; Ethridge to sec. of state, Feb. 21, 1947, ibid., 38–39.

28Rankin, Amer. chargé, to sec. of state, April 15, 1946, Foreign Service Posts of DS, Athens embassy, General Records, FRC; UP correspondent Robert Vermillion, story in *Life*, Jan. 6, 1947, pp. 13–17; *New York Times*, ed. sect., Sept. 1, 1946, p. 1; Xydis, *Greece and Great Powers*, 180–81; David S. McLellan, *Dean Acheson: The State Department Years* (N.Y.: Dodd, Mead, 1976), 113. Byrnes, Forrestal, and Leahy had all emphasized the importance of Middle East oil in World War II. Kuniholm, *Origins of Cold War in Near East*, 301, 301 n.247, 382.

29Xydis, *Greece and Great Powers*, 364–65. The United States withdrew from UNRRA in 1946, partly because of claims that communist nations in Eastern Europe were distributing foods only to political allies. By mid-1947 UNRRA had come to an end after its establishment in Washington, D.C. in November 1943. See Jones, *Fifteen Weeks*, 74; Dean Acheson, *Present at the Creation: My Years in the State Department* (N.Y.: Norton, 1969), 271.

30Xydis, *Greece and Great Powers*, 232.

31"State Dept. Briefing Book," July 15, 1946, pp. 6, 14.

[32]Acheson to Truman, Aug. 7, 1946, Truman Papers, PSF-Subject File, Truman Lib.; Xydis, *Greece and Great Powers*, 261–62.

[33]Harry S. Truman, *Memoirs: Year of Decisions* (Garden City, N.Y.: Doubleday, 1955), 522; Truman, *Memoirs: Years of Trial and Hope, 1946–1952* (Garden City, N.Y.: Doubleday, 1956), 99; McLellan, *Acheson*, 108; Acheson, *Present at Creation*, 268; William H. Taylor & Edward H. Foley to Snyder, Oct. 1, 1946, Snyder Papers, Truman Lib.; Acheson to Truman, Aug. 7, 1946, Truman Papers, PSF-Subject File, ibid.

[34]Xydis, *Greece and Great Powers*, 317, 318, 637 n.3; Francis F. Lincoln, *United States' Aid to Greece, 1947–1962* (Germantown, Tenn.: Professional Seminars, 1975), 31, 48. The Greek undersecretary of foreign affairs was Philip S. Dragoumis.

[35]McLellan, *Acheson*, 108, 110–11; Wittner, *American Intervention in Greece*, 51–52; Walter Millis, ed., *The Forrestal Diaries* (N.Y.: Viking, 1951), 210; Hickerson to chiefs of division, Sept. 27, 1946, DSDF, NA.

[36]FPI 30, append. C., pp. 2–3, DSDF, NA; "The Greek Situation," CIG, ORE 6/1, p. 14; Porter testimony, April 1, 1947, U.S. Senate, *Legislative Origins of the Truman Doctrine: Hearings Held in Executive Session Before the Committee on Foreign Relations, 80th Cong., 1 sess., on S. 938: A Bill to Provide for Assistance to Greece and Turkey* (Wash., D.C.: GPO, 1973), 70; Xydis, *Greece and Great Powers*, 437, 462–63; Lincoln, *United States' Aid to Greece*, 7; Sweet-Escott, *Greece*, 58.

[37]Porter to Clayton, Feb. 17, 1947, pp. 2–5, Porter Papers, Truman Lib.; Porter to Truman, March 3, 1947, ibid.; Porter testimony, U.S. Senate, *Legislative Origins of Truman Doctrine*, 70ff.; 99.

[38]Edwin P. Curtin (lieut. col.), "American Advisory Group Aids Greece in War on Guerrillas," *Armed Cavalry Journal* 58 (Jan.–Feb. 1949): 9; Wittner, *American Intervention in Greece*, 66–67; MacVeagh to sec. of state, Feb. 11, 1947, *FRUS*, V: *Near East and Africa*, 17; Porter to Clayton, Feb. 17, 1947, ibid., 20; Porter to sec. of state, Feb. 19, 1947, ibid., 26; Porter to sec. of state, Feb. 22, 1947, ibid., 40; Porter to Clayton, Feb. 17, 1947, p. 5, Porter Papers, Truman Lib.; Porter to Acheson, April 25, 1947, enclosure: tentative report of "American Economic Mission to Greece. Summary and Recommendations of the Report," in DSDF, NA; MacVeagh to Loy Henderson, March 6, 1947, ibid.; MacVeagh to sec. of state, Oct. 17, 1946, cited in Iatrides, ed., *Ambassador MacVeagh Reports*, 708; MacVeagh to Truman, Dec. 20, 1946, cited in ibid., 709. See also ibid., 713–14. Porter believed that the Greek government recognized the need for strong reform measures. Porter testimony, U.S. Senate, *Legislative Origins of Truman Doctrine*, 72. See also ibid., 75–77; "Report of the American Economic Mission to Greece," April 30, 1947, pp. 2, 5, Porter Papers, Truman Lib.; Porter diary, Porter Papers, box 1, entries for Jan. 20, 22, Feb. 1, 6, 1947, ibid.; *Time*, Feb. 24, 1947, p. 35.

[39]Averoff-Tossizza, *By Fire and Axe*, 169–70; "The Greek Situation," CIG, ORE 6/1, pp. 1, 2; MacVeagh to sec. of state, Jan. 11, 1947, *FRUS*, V: *Near East and Africa*, 5.

[40]Marshall to embassy in Athens, Jan. 21, 1947, *FRUS*, V: *Near East and Africa*, 10; Marshall to embassy in Athens, Feb. 17, 1947, ibid., 23. Marshall had unsuccessfully tried to bring about a coalition of Nationalist and Communist forces in China.

[41]Xydis, *Greece and Great Powers*, 464; "The Greek Situation," CIG, ORE 6/1, p. 3; Lincoln, *United States' Aid to Greece*, 42; Woodhouse, *Struggle for Greece*, 74; FPI 30, append. N, pp. 1–2, Feb. 14, 1947, DSDF, NA.

[42]Alexander, *Prelude to Truman Doctrine*, 241–43; Robert J. Donovan, *Conflict and Crisis: The Presidency of Harry S Truman, 1945–1948* (N.Y.: Norton, 1977), 277; Alan Bullock, *Ernest Bevin: Foreign Secretary, 1945–1951* (London: Heinemann, 1983), 368–69.

[43]Terry H. Anderson, *The United States, Great Britain, and the Cold War, 1944–1947* (Columbia: U. of Missouri Press, 1981), 173–74; Jones, *Fifteen Weeks*, 78, 81–82; FPI 30, append. E, pp. 1–4, DSDF, NA.

[44]FPI 30, append. E, pp. 1–4, DSDF, NA; Robert M. Hathaway, *Ambiguous Partnership: Britain and America, 1944–1947* (N.Y.: Columbia U. Press, 1981), 298; Alexander, *Prelude to Truman Doctrine*, 173, 193, 214; *Time*, March 27, 1947, p. 25.

[45]"The Greek Situation," CIG, ORE 6/1, p. 2; Gallman to sec. of state, Jan. 31, 1947, *FRUS*, V: *Near East and Africa*, 13–14; C.H.B.[?] memo for Norstad, Feb. 19, 1947, P & O 091 Great Britain (TS), sect. I, case 1, Army Staff Records, NA.

[46]Jones, *Fifteen Weeks*; Acheson, *Present at Creation*, 290; author's interview with Henderson, May 24, 1979; interview with Acheson (Feb. 18, 1955), 32, 34–35, Truman Papers, Post-Presidential Files, "Memoirs File," box 1, Truman Lib.

[47]Anderson, *United States, Great Britain, and Cold War*, 173–75; Hathaway, *Ambiguous Partnership*, 300–301; author's interview with Henderson; MacVeagh to sec. of state, Feb. 24, 1947, DSDF, NA; aide-mémoire from Brit. embassy to DS, Feb. 21, 1947, *FRUS*, V: *Near East and Africa*, 32–37; Truman, *Memoirs: Years of Trial and Hope*, 99; Acheson, *Present at Creation*, 290; Donovan, *Conflict and Crisis*, 278. A good account of the drama is in Jones, *Fifteen Weeks*, 3–8.

[48]Acheson, *Present at Creation*, 291; author's interview with Henderson; Oral History Interview with Henderson (June 14 & July 5, 1973), 87–88, Truman Lib.; Acheson to Marshall, Feb. 21, 1947, *FRUS*, V: *Near East and Africa*, 29–31; Marshall to Senator William F. Knowland, March 25, 1948, DSDF, NA; Kuniholm, *Origins of Cold War in Near East*, 409 n.80.

[49]Millis, ed., *Forrestal Diaries*, 245; interview with Acheson (Feb. 18, 1955), 36.

[50]Henderson to Gallman & Matthews in London, Feb. 24, 1947, DSDF, NA; R. Borden Reams to sec. of state, Feb. 24, 1947, ibid.

[51]Gallman to sec. of state, Feb. 28, 1947, ibid.; aide-mémoire from Brit. embassy to DS, March 4, 1947, *FRUS*, V: *Near East and Africa*, 80; Gallman to sec. of state, March 4, 1947, DSDF, NA; summary of conversation between DS and Brit. embassy, March 7, 1947, ibid.; memo of conversation drawn by Acheson and with Inverchapel, March 8, 1947, ibid.

[52]Leahy diaries, entry of Feb. 27, 1947, p. 17, Leahy Papers, MS Divis., LC.

CHAPTER 2.   THE TRUMAN DOCTRINE AND THE BEGINNINGS OF GLOBAL STRATEGY

[1]Critics of the Truman Doctrine include: William A. Williams, *The Tragedy of American Diplomacy* (N.Y.: World Publishing, 1959); J. William Fulbright, *The Arrogance of Power* (N.Y.: Random House, 1966); Richard M. Freeland, *The Truman Doctrine and the Origins of McCarthyism* (N.Y.: Schocken Books, 1970); Andreas Papandreou, *Democracy at Gunpoint: The Greek Front* (Garden City, N.Y.: Doubleday, 1970); Joyce and Gabriel Kolko, *The Limits of Power: The World and United States Foreign Policy, 1945–1954* (N.Y.: Harper & Row, 1972); Thomas G. Paterson, *Soviet-American Confrontation: Postwar Reconstruction and the Origins of the Cold War* (Baltimore: Johns Hopkins U. Press, 1973); Thomas G. Paterson, *On Every Front: The Making of the Cold War* (N.Y.: Norton, 1979); Daniel H. Yergin, *Shattered Peace: The Origins of the Cold War and the National Security State* (Boston: Houghton Mifflin, 1977); Lawrence S. Wittner, *American Intervention in Greece, 1943–1949* (N.Y.: Columbia U. Press, 1982).

[2]Among defenders of the Truman Doctrine, see: Robert H. Ferrell, *George Marshall* (N.Y.: Cooper Square, 1966), vol. XV of *The American Secretaries of State and Their Diplomacy*, ed. by Robert H. Ferrell and Samuel F. Bemis; Robert H. Ferrell, *Harry S. Truman and the Modern American Presidency* (Boston: Little, Brown, 1983); Cabell Phillips, *The Truman Presidency: The History of a Triumphant Succession* (N.Y.: Macmillan, 1966); Herbert Feis,

From Trust to Terror: The Onset of the Cold War, 1945–1950 (N.Y.: Norton, 1970); Gaddis Smith, *Dean Acheson* (N.Y.: Cooper Square, 1972), vol. XVI of *American Secretaries of State and Their Diplomacy*; John L. Gaddis, *The United States and the Origins of the Cold War, 1941–1947* (N.Y.: Columbia U. Press, 1972); John L. Gaddis, *Strategies of Containment: A Critical Appraisal of Postwar American National Security Policy* (N.Y.: Oxford U. Press, 1982); John L. Gaddis, *The Long Peace: Inquiries into the History of the Cold War* (N.Y.: Oxford U. Press, 1987); Richard F. Haynes, *The Awesome Power: Harry S. Truman as Commander in Chief* (Baton Rouge: Louisiana State U. Press, 1973); David S. McLellan, *Dean Acheson: The State Department Years* (N.Y.: Dodd, Mead, 1976); Robert J. Donovan, *Conflict and Crisis: The Presidency of Harry S Truman, 1945–1948* (N.Y.: Norton, 1977); Bruce R. Kuniholm, *The Origins of the Cold War in the Near East: Great Power Conflict and Diplomacy in Iran, Turkey, and Greece* (Princeton: Princeton U. Press, 1980); Donald R. McCoy, *The Presidency of Harry S. Truman* (Lawrence: U. Press of Kansas, 1984); Walter Isaacson and Evan Thomas, *The Wise Men: Six Friends and the World They Made* (N.Y.: Simon and Schuster, 1986).

[3]MacVeagh insisted that the northern tier was the "front line" between the "two parts of the world" and that the Greeks were in the "frontline trenches." MacVeagh testimony before House Foreign Affairs Committee, March 25, 1947, in U.S. House of Reps., *Military Assistance Programs, Part 2. Assistance to Greece and Turkey* VI (Wash., D.C.: GPO, 1976): 321. The Truman Doctrine only appeared to mark a revolution in America's foreign policy. When the President announced the nation's willingness to engage in European political and military affairs in peacetime, he suggested a drastic change in policy; but within the perspective of events since the close of the nineteenth century, his "doctrine" was part of an evolutionary process toward the assumption of world responsibility for peace that had picked up in intensity with America's involvement in foreign affairs during the 1890s. For those writers who perceive a revolution, see: Harry S. Truman, *Memoirs: Years of Trial and Hope, 1946–1952* (Garden City, N.Y.: Doubleday, 1956), 106; Joseph M. Jones, *The Fifteen Weeks (February 21–June 5, 1947)* (N.Y.: Viking, 1955), viii, 3; Francis F. Lincoln, *United States' Aid to Greece, 1947–1962* (Germantown, Tenn.: Professional Seminars, 1975), 166; Ferrell, *Marshall*, 74; Haynes, *Awesome Power*, 133; William H. McNeill, *Greece: American Aid in Action, 1947–1956* (N.Y.: Twentieth Century Fund, 1957), 35; Robert E. Osgood, *Limited War: The Challenge to American Strategy* (Chicago: U. of Chicago Press, 1957), 148; Robert W. Tucker, "The American Outlook," in Robert E. Osgood et al., contributors, *America and the World: From the Truman Doctrine to Vietnam* (Baltimore: Johns Hopkins U. Press, 1970), 40. Those arguing against a revolution include: Gaddis, *United States and Origins of Cold War*, 318; Kuniholm, *Origins of Cold War in Near East*, 427; Donovan, *Conflict and Crisis*, 279; Smith, *Acheson*, 47. One writer sees ideological ties between the Truman Doctrine and America's past emphasis on manifest destiny. The Truman Doctrine, he says, pledged the United States to a "messianic promise" of protecting freedom. See Henry Butterfield Ryan, Jr., "The American Intellectual Tradition Reflected in the Truman Doctrine," *The American Scholar* 42 (Spring 1973): 294–307.

[4]Interview with Acheson (Feb. 16, 1955), 29, Truman Papers, Post-Presidential Files, "Memoirs File," box 1, Truman Lib.

[5]Oral History Interview with Henderson (June 14 & July 5, 1973), 21, Truman Lib.; minutes of Special Committee to Study Assistance to Greece and Turkey, Feb. 24, 1947, *FRUS*, V: *The Near East and Africa* (Wash., D.C.: GPO, 1971), 45–47.

[6]Memo by chman. of Special Committee (Henderson) to Acheson, ca. Feb. 24, 1947, *FRUS*, V: *Near East and Africa*, 47–48; "Analysis of the Proposals," in ibid., 51–53.

[7]Minutes of meetings of secs. of state, war, and navy, Feb. 26, 1947, DSDF, NA; sec. of state to Truman, Feb. 26, 1947, *FRUS*, V: *Near East and Africa*, 58. Text underlined in the original.

[8]Memo for sec. of war, Feb. 26, 1947, P & O 092, sect. VI-A, case 95, Army Staff Records, NA.

[9]Agenda for meeting on "Implementation of Aid to Greece," Feb. 28, 1947, DSDF, NA; memo by Francis H. Russell, March 17, 1947, *FRUS*, V: *Near East and Africa*, 123; report of meeting

of SWNCC Subcommittee on FPI, Feb. 28, 1947, ibid., 67; meeting of SWNCC Subcommittee on FPI, Feb. 28, 1947, Lot 54D202, box 11569, Dipl. Branch, NA. Jernegan was from the Office of Near Eastern and African Affairs.

¹⁰Meeting of SWNCC Subcommittee on FPI, Feb. 28, 1947, Dipl. Branch, NA; House Report on H.R. 2616: Assistance to Greece and Turkey, in U.S. House of Reps., *Military Assistance Programs, Part 2*, VI: append. II, 429.

¹¹"Analysis of the Proposals," 54–55; "Study on U.S. Assistance to Greece," March 20, 1947, p. 1, encl. in ABC-400.336 Greece, sect. I-A, War Dept. Records, NA.

¹²Meeting of SWNCC Subcommittee on FPI, Feb. 28, 1947, Dipl. Branch, NA.

¹³Leften S. Stavrianos, "The United States and Greece: The Truman Doctrine in Historical Perspective," in Dwight E. Lee and George E. McReynolds, eds., *Essays in History and International Relations: In Honor of George Hubbard Blakeslee* (Worcester, Mass.: Clark U. Publication, 1949), 58–59.

¹⁴MacVeagh to sec. of state, March 11, 1947, DSDF, NA.

¹⁵Ibid.; MacVeagh to Henderson, March 6, 1947, ibid.

¹⁶Lippman quoted in Washington *Post*, April 24, 1947, cited in "An Analysis of U.S. Public Comment, Prepared by Division of Public Studies Office of Public Affairs," May 1, 1947, DSDF, NA; New York *Herald Tribune*, clipping encl. in Francis F. Lincoln Papers, Truman Lib. Baldwin article also in ibid. See also Jones, *Fifteen Weeks*, 85; minutes of Working Party— Information Themes, March 1, 1947, Lot 54D202, box 17569, Dipl. Branch, NA; notes on cabinet meeting, March 7, 1947, Leahy diaries, 1947, p. 20, Leahy Papers, MS Divis., LC.

¹⁷John Gange of DS to Gen. John H. Hilldring and Francis H. Russell, March 20, 1947, DSDF, NA; note by secs., March 5, 1947, encl. in ibid.; memo from Brig. Gen. George A. Lincoln, chief of P & O, for Gen. [?] Cook on aid to Greece, March 8, 1947, P & O 091, Greece, sect. II, cases 8–17, p. 1, Army Staff Records, NA; sec. of state to embassy in Athens, March 4, 1947, *FRUS*, V: *Near East and Africa*, 87; report by Subcommittee on FPI of SWNCC, early March 1947, ibid., 76–77; Public Information Program on U.S. Aid to Greece (FPI 30), March 3, 1947, pp. 3–5, DSDF, NA.

¹⁸FPI 30, pp. 14, 15, 16–17, 19–20.

¹⁹Notes on cabinet meeting, March 7, 1947, Leahy diaries, 1947, p. 20, Leahy Papers, MS Divis., LC; notes on cabinet meeting, March 7, 1947, Connelly Papers, Box 1, White House File (set I), Truman Lib.; Jones, *Fifteen Weeks*, 118–20; notes on cabinet meeting of March 7, 1947, Patterson Papers, Gen. Corresp., box 19, MS Divis., LC; cabinet meeting notes of March 7, 1947, Truman Papers, Connelly Files, Truman Lib.; Walter Millis, ed., *The Forrestal Diaries* (N.Y.: Viking, 1951), 251; Forrestal diaries, VI: 1513, 1515, Operational Archives, Naval History Divis., Wash., D.C. (photocopies of originals at Princeton U.).

²⁰Dean Acheson, *Present at the Creation: My Years in the State Department* (N.Y.: Norton, 1969), 293; Jones, *Fifteen Weeks*, 138, 138 n.3. The congressmen in attendance were Senator Vandenberg; House Speaker Joseph Martin; Representative Sam Rayburn, Democrat and Minority Leader; Representative Charles A. Eaton, Republican chairman of the Foreign Affairs Committee; Senator Styles Bridges, Republican and chairman of the Appropriations Committee; Senator Tom Connally, ranking Democrat on the Foreign Relations Committee; and Representative Sol Bloom, ranking Democrat on the Foreign Affairs Committee. Representative John Taber, Republican chairman of the Appropriations Committee, had to decline the invitation but was briefed later that afternoon. Ibid., 138.

²¹Jones (the adviser), *Fifteen Weeks*, 139; Acheson, *Present at Creation*, 293; Gaddis, *United States and Origins of Cold War*, 348–49; McLellan, *Acheson*, 115; Kuniholm, *Origins of Cold War in Near East*, 411–12. See also Truman, *Memoirs: Years of Trial and Hope*, 103–4.

²²Jones, *Fifteen Weeks*, 140–41; Terry H. Anderson, *The United States, Great Britain, and the*

Cold War, 1944–1947 (Columbia: U. of Missouri Press, 1981), 169–70; Acheson, *Present at Creation*, 293.

[23]Notes on meeting in cabinet room between Truman and cong. leaders of both parties, March 10, 1947, Leahy diaries, 1947, p. 21, Leahy Papers, MS Divis., LC; Acheson, *Present at Creation*, 293, 295; Anderson, *United States, Great Britain, and Cold War*, 170; Arthur H. Vandenberg, Jr., ed., *The Private Papers of Senator Vandenberg* (Boston: Houghton Mifflin, 1952), 340; Jones, *Fifteen Weeks*, 143. Eric F. Goldman claims that Vandenberg remarked on the way out of the meeting: "Mr. President, if that's what you want, there's only one way to get it. That is to make a personal appearance before Congress and scare hell out of the country." Goldman, *The Crucial Decade–and After: America, 1945–1960* (N.Y.: Random House, 1960), 59. Whether or not these were Vandenberg's words, others shared his feelings. Undersecretary of State for Economic Affairs William L. Clayton warned that the American people would not accept global responsibilities without being "shocked" into doing so. The State Department would have to present a program to Congress that would "electrify the American people." Clayton memo, March 5, 1947, Clayton Papers, folder entitled "Confidential Marshall Plan Memos," box 42, Truman Lib.

[24]Personal notes, March 7, 1947, Eban Ayers Papers, Truman Lib.

[25]Cabinet meeting notes of March 7, 1947, Truman Papers, Connelly Files, Truman Lib.; notes on cabinet meeting of March 7, 1947, Patterson Papers, Gen. Corresp., box 19, MS Divis., LC; Truman, *Memoirs: Years of Trial and Hope*, 101; Oral History Interview with Henderson (June 14 & July 5, 1973), 86–87, Truman Lib.; Jones, *Fifteen Weeks*, 117–25; personal notes, March 8, 1947, Patterson Papers, MS Divis., LC; author's interview with Henderson; "The Drafting of the President's Message of March 12, 1947," Chronology, ca. March 13, 1947, Jones Papers, Truman Lib. For a good account of the President's speech, see Jones, *Fifteen Weeks*, 17–23.

[26]*Public Papers of the Presidents: Harry S. Truman, 1947* (Wash., D.C.: GPO, 1963), 176–79. The President's speech came two days after the opening of the Council of Foreign Ministers meeting in Moscow. Though the agenda of that meeting focused on Germany and Austria, the four principal powers there, the United States, Great Britain, France, and the Soviet Union, could not ignore the ramifications of America's new policy for areas other than Greece and Turkey. Lincoln, *United States' Aid to Greece*, 6, 30. Indeed, American press and radio interpreted the President's speech as part of the administration's battle with the Soviet Union over the future status of Germany. Jones, *Fifteen Weeks*, 227.

[27]Jones, *Fifteen Weeks*, 23; *Life*, March 24, 1947, p. 40.

[28]*New York Times*, March 12, 1947, p. 24. McCormick in ibid., March 15, 1947, and Reston in ibid., April 1, 1947, both in Democrat Clipping File, Truman Lib.; survey in *New York Times*, March 23, 1947, p. E5; *Time*, March 24, 1947, pp. 17, 20, 25; *Newsweek*, March 10, 1947, pp. 23–24, and March 31, 1947, p. 25; Wilson W. Wyatt (national chman. of ADA), "The Application of Truman Doctrine," *The New Leader*, April 28, 1947, pp. 1, 3; Russell quoted in *Time*, March 10, 1947, p. 17. For the range of congressional feeling, see *Congressional Record*, 80 Cong.,1 sess., vol. 93, part 1, p. 1984, and *Appendix*, part 10, pp. A997, A1073, A1123–24, A1155–56.

[29]Jones, *Fifteen Weeks*, 177; *Time*, April 7, 1947, p. 24; *Nation*, March 8, 1947, p. 261, March 15, 1947, p. 289, March 29, 1947, pp. 356–58, 364–65; La Guardia quoted in Wittner, *American Intervention in Greece*, 82; Gaddis, *United States and Origins of Cold War*, 338–41; Edward L. & Frederick H. Schapsmeier, *Prophet in Politics: Henry A. Wallace and the War Years, 1940–1965* (Ames: Iowa State U. Press, 1970), 170; J. Samuel Walker, *Henry A. Wallace and American Foreign Policy* (Westport, Conn.: Greenwood, 1976), 168–69; Lincoln (the adviser), *United States' Aid to Greece*, 5.

[30]Ronald Steel, *Walter Lippmann and the American Century* (N.Y.: Random House, 1980), 438–40; sampling of Lippmann's articles in New York *Herald Tribune*, March 15, 22, 1947, Chicago *Sun*, March [?], 1947, Washington *Post*, April 8, 1947, all in Democrat Clipping File, Truman Lib.

[31]Wittner, *American Intervention in Greece*, 83; *Izvestia* editorial reprinted in *New York Times*, March 15, 1947, Democrat Clipping File, Truman Lib.; British figure quoted in *Time*, March 24, 1947, p. 25. For global reaction to Truman's speech, see numerous newspaper quotations contained in various dispatches from State Department representatives abroad dated March 13, 1947 ff., DSDF, NA.

[32]George F. Kennan, *Memoirs, 1925–1950* (Boston: Little, Brown, 1967), 315; author's interview with Dean Rusk, Nov. 3, 1978; Charles E. Bohlen, *Witness to History, 1929–1969* (N.Y.: Norton, 1973), 261; T. Michael Ruddy, *The Cautious Diplomat: Charles E. Bohlen and the Soviet Union, 1929–1969* (Kent, Ohio: Kent State U. Press, 1986), 72; Forrest C. Pogue, *George C. Marshall: Statesman* (N.Y.: Viking, 1987), 172–73.

[33]On the Turkish matter, see Kuniholm, *Origins of Cold War in Near East*, 413, and Jones, *Fifteen Weeks*, 162. Controversy has arisen over Kennan's involvement in the making of the Truman Doctrine. In preparing his memoirs, Kennan at first recalled his involvement in all meetings that led to the bill. Indeed, Jones wrote that Kennan chaired the staff meetings that began in Washington during the weekend following receipt of the British notes on Friday, February 21. But years afterward, Henderson wrote Acheson that the decisions were already made by the time Kennan joined the deliberations—which was no sooner than Monday, February 24. Jones's account, Henderson declared, was incorrect. Acheson agreed and, in accordance with Henderson's comments, revised his manuscript that later became *Present at the Creation*. In reply to a letter from Kennan of March 29, 1967, Henderson wrote that the passage of time had "blurred" Kennan's memory. Despite Kennan's complaint that his ideas had been changed *after* his participation, Henderson asserted: "So far as the Department was concerned . . . the decision to render aid to Greece and Turkey was made before you were brought into the consultations." Clifford, McGhee, and Elsey agreed that Kennan's influence was minimal. See Kennan, *Memoirs, 1925–1950*, 314; Jones, *Fifteen Weeks*, 132–34, 154–55; Henderson to Acheson, April 4, 1967, Henderson Papers, box 8: Greece folder, MS Divis., LC; Acheson to Henderson, April 6, 1967, ibid.; Henderson to Kennan, April 28, 1967, ibid.; Oral History Interview with Clifford (March 1971–Feb. 1973), 86–87, 89–90, Truman Lib.; author's interview with McGhee, May 24, 1979; Margaret Truman, *Harry S. Truman* (N.Y.: William Morrow, 1973), 309; Robert M. Hathaway, *Ambiguous Partnership: Britain and America, 1944–1947* (N.Y.: Columbia U. Press, 1981), 303. On domestic issues, see Gaddis, *United States and Origins of Cold War*, 261–63, 282–84, 312–18, 337 ff. The domestic problem was clearly seen in the opposition to the $3.75 billion loan to Britain during the first half of 1946. Ibid., 342. Gaddis claims that the administration got caught up in a "new cycle of rhetoric and response which in years to come would significantly restrict the Administration's flexibility in dealing with Moscow." Ibid., 317–18. See also Kuniholm, *Origins of Cold War in Near East*, 415. On the 80th Congress, see Susan M. Hartmann, *Truman and the 80th Congress* (Columbia: U. of Missouri Press, 1971). It convened with 51 Republicans and 45 Democrats in the Senate, and with 245 Republicans and 118 Democrats in the House. Jones, *Fifteen Weeks*, 90–91.

[34]Kennan to Henderson, March 27, 1947, DSDF, NA; Kennan, "Comments on the National Security Problem" in Europe and Asia, 1–4, 9–12, 15–17, encl. in ibid.

[35]For Kennan's views, see his Long Telegram to sec. of state of Feb. 24, 1946, in *FRUS*, VI: *Near East and Africa* (Wash., D.C.: GPO, 1970), 696–709, and his article signed "X," "The Sources of Soviet Conduct," in *Foreign Affairs* 25 (July 1947): 566–82. See also Kennan's *Memoirs, 1925–1950*, 354–57; Kennan, "Containment Then and Now," *Foreign Affairs* 65 (Spring 1987): 885–90. In this last article of 1987, Kennan declared that Russia was no military threat in 1947 and that the real danger was "ideological-political"—again, a disagreement with the White House over the nature of the Soviet peril, not the peril itself. Ibid., 886.

[36]Author's interview with McGhee; Lincoln, *United States' Aid to Greece*, 5, 40.

[37]George M. McGhee, "The Impact of Foreign Commitments upon the Coordinative Responsibilities of the Department of State," *International Commitments and National Administration* (Charlottesville: Bureau of Public Administration, U. of Virginia, 1949), 39–55.

[38]Acheson's testimony, April 2, 1947, U.S. Senate, *Legislative Origins of the Truman Doctrine: Hearings Held in Executive Session Before the Committee on Foreign Relations, 80th Cong., 1 sess., on S. 938: A Bill to Provide for Assistance to Greece and Turkey (Wash., D.C.: GPO, 1973)*, 2, 26, 79-80, 83, 153; DS Analysis of S. 938—Greece, encl. in Acheson to Henry Cabot Lodge, March 28, 1947, pp. 1-3, DSDF, NA; Acheson's written replies to Senate questions, 18, 35, 56, 86, encl. in Acheson to Vandenberg, March 24, 1947, ibid.; MacVeagh's testimony, March 25, 1947, U.S. House of Reps., *Military Assistance Programs, Part 2*, VI: 354.

[39]Acheson's written replies to Senate questions, 6, 23; Acheson's testimony, March 13, 1947, U.S. Senate, *Legislative Origins of Truman Doctrine*, 7, 9, 19; statement by Clayton before Senate For. Relats. Committee, March 25, 1947, cited in ibid.; Interim Greece-Turkey Assistance Committee summarizing testimony before House and Senate Committees on Aid Program, April 24, 1947, ibid.

[40]For the State Department's establishment of the aid program's "Administrative Facilities," see "Organization and Administrative Implementation of the Greek Public Assistance Program," March 28, 1947, append. 7, p. A-19, DSDF, NA. Ibid., pp. A-28, 1-3, 6-12, 14-22; memo for record by Gen. George A. Lincoln, April 11, 1947, P & O 091 Greece, case 10/2, Army Staff Records, NA.

[41]Acheson's written replies to Senate questions, 10, 22, 49, 58; Acheson before House For. Affairs Committee on Greek-Turkish Aid Bill, March 20, 1947, in Frank McNaughton Papers, Truman Lib. Acheson assured Senator Theodore Green of Rhode Island that the administration would judge each aid applicant on its "individual merits." Acheson to Green, April 18, 1947, DSDF, NA. Circumstances alone would determine whether to extend aid, he insisted. Acheson, *Present at Creation*, 300-301. See also Lincoln, *United States' Aid to Greece*, 4. Gaddis and McLellan agree that the Truman Doctrine was not a blanket, global commitment. Gaddis, *United States and Origins of Cold War*, 351; McLellan, *Acheson*, 403-4. Despite Acheson's efforts, his answers were, according to a knowledgeable British observer, Christopher M. Woodhouse, "unilluminating, and the doubts remained." See his *The Struggle for Greece, 1941-1949* (Brooklyn Heights, N.Y.: Beekman-Esanu, 1976), 201. Evidence indicates that the President wanted the aid proposal to be global in application. Years afterward, Henderson recalled a discussion with Acheson concerning a meeting that the acting secretary of state had had with the President sometime before the March 12 address to Congress. Acheson claimed that when he showed the President a draft of the proposed speech, Truman asked: "Why limit it to the Middle East? Why not leave the thrust of the message 'general' in application?" Author's interview with Henderson. See also Oral History Interview with Henderson (June 14 & July 5, 1973), 86-87, Truman Lib. The British encouraged the White House to realize that the problem was not confined to Greece and Turkey, but arose everywhere there was a threat of Soviet communist expansion. Orme Sargent to sec. of state, March 18, 1947, FO 371/61086/1947—Aid to Greece and Turkey, PRO. Acheson's testimony, March 13, 1947, U.S. Senate, *Legislative Origins of Truman Doctrine*, 17; Jones, *Fifteen Weeks*, 193, 196, 262. *Time* magazine grasped the meaning of Acheson's statement. Hungary, for example, was outside American reach because of Red Army occupation, whereas France and Italy were subject to American economic and political pressure. *Time*, June 9, 1947, p. 27.

[42]Acheson's written replies to Senate questions, 4, 58, 65, 94, 111; "Statement by Acting Secretary of State Dean Acheson Before the House Foreign Affairs Committee," March 20, 1947, Clifford Papers, #6 (Greece & Turkey), Truman Lib.; notes on Acheson's testimony before House For. Affairs Committee, March 21, 1947, McNaughton Papers, ibid.; *Time*, March 31, 1947, p. 21.

[43]Author's interview with McGhee; Hurley to Roosevelt, Dec. 21, 1943, Acheson Papers, Truman Lib.; Acheson to Edward Stettinius, Jan. 28, 1943, ibid.; Acheson's written replies to Senate questions, 29-30.

[44]MacVeagh's testimony, March 28, 1947, U.S. Senate, *Legislative Origins of Truman Doctrine*, 66, 67.

45"Personal Memorandum for Clark Clifford" from Don Kingsley, ca. March 1947, Clifford Papers, #6 (Greece & Turkey), Truman Lib.

46Jones, *Fifteen Weeks*, 160; Oral History Interview with Elsey, II (July 7, 1970), 354, 356–57, ibid.; Acheson's written replies to Senate questions, 1–4, 67–68, 95; author's interview with Henderson; Connally quoted in his *My Name Is Tom Connally* (N.Y.: Crowell, 1954), 318; Vandenberg, Jr., ed., *Private Papers of Senator Vandenberg*, 340–41, 343; Vandenberg's testimony, March 13, 1947, U.S. Senate, *Legislative Origins of Truman Doctrine*, 13, 14; Acheson to Sen. Charles Tobey, March 31, 1947, DSDF, NA. Vandenberg told members of the Senate committee that the United States was engaged in an ideological war and had to use "ideological resources" to win.

47George T. Mazuzan, *Warren R. Austin at the U.N., 1946–1953* (Kent, Ohio: Kent State U. Press, 1977), 70–73; Acheson, *Present at Creation*, 298; Lincoln, *United States' Aid to Greece*, 4.

48European Recovery Program interview with Constantine Tsaldaris (May 4, 1964), 15–16, Truman Lib.; Oral History Interview with Anthony Bernaris (April 30, 1964), 11, ibid.; British Minister of State Hector McNeil's letter to members of Parliament, March 27, 1947, *Parliamentary Debates*, House of Commons. vol. 435, p. 234; McNeil before House of Commons, April 23, 1947, ibid.; vol. 436, p. 1010; Reston's article entitled, "U.N. Held a Poor Scapegoat in Debating New U.S. Policy," *New York Times*, March 18, 1947, p. 8; author's interview with Rusk.

49Acheson's testimony, March 13, 1947, U.S. Senate, *Legislative Origins of Truman Doctrine*, 9; Wilson's testimony, March 28, 1947, ibid., 47–48, 56; Wilson's testimony, March 26, 1947, U.S. House of Reps., *Military Assistance Programs, Part 2*, VI: 357; JCS to secs. of war and navy, March 13, 1947, DSDF, NA.

50Durward V. Sandifer, DS legal adviser, to Acheson, March 26, 1947, DSDF, NA; Alsop quoted in "An Analysis of U.S. Public Comment, Prepared by the Division of Public Studies, Office of Public Affairs," May 1, 1947, ibid.; Shepard Jones to Joseph Jones, March 27, 1947, Jones Papers, box 2 (Greece—newspaper clippings), Truman Lib.; "Latest Public Opinion Survey on Greece and Turkey," memo by Divis. of Public Studies to Interim Greek and Turkish Assistance Committee, April 29, 1947, DSDF, NA.

51Acheson's written replies to Senate questions, 26, 51, 77, 92; Acheson's testimony before House Hearings on Aid Bill, March 20, 1947, summary in McNaughton Papers, Truman Lib.; "Source of Supply of Equipment for the Greek Armed Forces," ca. mid-March 1947, unlabeled, DSDF, NA; MacVeagh's testimony, March 25, 1947, U.S. House of Reps., *Military Assistance Programs, Part 2*, VI: 334.

52*PM*, March 21, 1947, Democrat Clipping File, Truman Lib.

53*New York Times*, March 15, 1947, p. 4 (congressional concern over troops); Lincoln's testimony, April 2, 1947, U.S. Senate, *Legislative Origins of Truman Doctrine*, 160, 162–64; U.S. House of Reps., *Military Assistance Programs, Part 2*, VI: append. IV, 454; Interim Greece-Turkey Assistance Committee summarizing testimony, April 24, 1947, DSDF, NA.

54John O. Iatrides, ed., *Ambassador MacVeagh Reports: Greece, 1933–1947* (Princeton: Princeton U. Press, 1980), 709; MacVeagh to sec. of state, March 4, 1947, *FRUS* V: *Near East and Africa* (Wash., D.C.: GPO, 1971), 89–90; memo for record: conferences concerning Greek situation, March 5, 6, 1947, ABC-400.336 Greece, sect. I-A, pp. 2–3, War Dept. Records, NA; Acheson's written replies to Senate questions, 73; memo for record: conferences concerning Greek situation, March 6, 1947, ABC-400.336 Greece, sect. I-A, p. 4, War Dept. Records, NA.

55Patterson to sec. of state, ca. March 11, 1947, *FRUS*, V: *Near East and Africa*. 105–6; sec. of war to sec. of state, March 11, 1947, P & O 092, sect. VI-A, case 95, p. 2, Army Staff Records, NA; all testimonies, March 13, 1947, U.S. Senate, *Legislative Origins of Truman Doctrine*, 5–6, 10–11.

56Acheson's testimony in U.S. Senate, *Legislative Origins of Truman Doctrine*, 11; author's interview with Henderson; author's interview with McGhee; Bohlen, *Witness to History*, 310; author's interview with Rusk.

[57]Author's interview with McGhee; Oral History Interview with Clifford (March 1971–Feb. 1973), 83–84, 151–55, Truman Lib.; author's interview with Rusk; M. Truman, *Harry S. Truman*, 343, 359–60; author's interview with Henderson.

[58]Sargent to sec. of state, March 18, 1947, FO 371/61086/1947—Aid to Greece and Turkey, PRO; Chancery to Southern Dept. of FO, April 9, 1947, FO 371/67119/1947—Greek-U.S. Relations, PRO; conversation between Lavrischev and Ethridge quoted in Stephen G. Xydis, *Greece and the Great Powers, 1944–1947: Prelude to the "Truman Doctrine"* (Thessaloniki: Institute for Balkan Studies, 1963), 489. See also Oral History Interview with Ethridge (June 4, 1974), 36–37, Truman Lib.

[59]Acheson's testimony, March 13, 1947, U.S. Senate, *Legislative Origins of Truman Doctrine*, 20; "Foreign Policy Series": "Why are we helping Greece?", March 15, 1947, Jones Papers, Truman Lib.; draft of Henderson's speech of April 4, 1947, in ibid.

[60]Address entitled "The Government's Policy on Aid to Greece and Turkey: Some Questions Answered," March 20, 1947, in DSDF, NA.

[61]For congressional objections, see U.S. Senate, *Legislative Origins of Truman Doctrine*; U.S. House of Reps., *Military Assistance Programs, Part 2*, VI; Acheson's testimony, April 11, 1947, ibid., 411; Donovan, *Conflict and Crisis*, 286; *Time*, March 31, 1947, p. 21; Vandenberg, Jr., ed., *Private Papers of Senator Vandenberg*, 341–42, 344–49; notes on cabinet meeting of April 4, 1947, Millis, ed., *Forrestal Diaries*, 260–61; "Analysis of Comment Upon the Proposals by Senator Vandenberg Concerning Aid to Greece and Turkey," ca. April 5, 1947, in Jones Papers, Truman Lib.; Jones, *Fifteen Weeks*, 184; Acheson, *Present at Creation*, 299; Smith, *Acheson*, 48; hearings of April 3, 1947, U.S. Senate, *Legislative Origins of Truman Doctrine*, 182; "Comparison of Treasury and State Drafts of Agreement on Assistance to Greece," May 22, 1947, in Elsey Papers, Truman Lib.; DS Draft of "Agreement on Aid to Greece," May 22, 1947, encl. in memo for President from Acheson, May 23, 1947, in Truman Papers, Confidential File, ibid.

[62]Acheson's testimony, April 1, 1947, U.S. Senate, *Legislative Origins of Truman Doctrine*, 90; Connally's testimony, April 2, 1947, ibid., 135; Barkley's testimony, April 2, 1947, ibid., 137; Hatch's testimony, April 2, 1947, ibid., 138.

[63]Lodge's testimony, April 2, 1947, ibid., 141. See also *Cong. Record*, 80 Cong., 1 sess., vol. 93, part 3, April 11, 1947, pp. 3335–36; William J. Miller, *Henry Cabot Lodge: A Biography* (N.Y.: Heineman, 1967), 190.

[64]Acheson to Green, April 18, 1947, DSDF, NA; Wittner, *American Intervention in Greece*, 17–22, 232; Paterson, *Soviet-American Confrontation*, chap. 9; Forrestal diaries, VII, entry for May 2, 1947, pp. 1610–11; Arnold A. Rogow, *James Forrestal: A Study of Personality, Politics, and Policy* (N.Y.: Macmillan, 1963), 180; Michael B. Stoff, *Oil, War, and American Security: The Search for a National Policy on Foreign Oil, 1941–1947* (New Haven: Yale U. Press, 1980), 178, 207–8; McLellan, *Acheson*, 115; Kuniholm, *Origins of Cold War in Near East*, 301 n.247. Writers and others often use "Near East" and "Middle East" interchangeably, although Near East usually is used to encompass Greece and Turkey. See ibid., xv n.2. Uranium in Africa was also at stake, according to one White House adviser. Jones, *Fifteen Weeks*, 47.

[65]*Time*, March 24, 1947, pp. 83–84; J. H. Carmichael, "Oil Is Big Factor in Aid to Greece," *New York Times*, March 16, 1947, III, p. 3; Phillips's article in ibid., April 6, 1947, IV, p. 5, McLellan, *Acheson*, 112; Kuniholm, *Origins of Cold War in Near East*, 427–28, 431.

[66]Oral History Interview with Henderson (June 14 & July 5, 1973), 57, Truman Lib.; Stephen J. Randall, *United States Foreign Oil Policy, 1919–1948: For Profits and Security* (Montreal: McGill-Queen's U. Press. 1985), 237, 241.

[67]See Oral History Interview with Henderson (June 14 & July 5, 1973), 53–54; Clifford, "American Relations with the Soviet Union," Sept. 24, 1946, p. 63, Conway File, Truman Lib.; Truman, *Memoirs: Years of Trial and Hope*, 95; Wittner, *American Intervention in Greece*, 18–19, 60; Stoff, *Oil, War, and American Security*, 178, 206–8, 212–14; John A. Loftus, "Middle East Oil:

The Pattern of Control," *Middle East Journal* 2 (Jan. 1948): 17–32; Michael J. Hogan, "The Search for a 'Creative Peace': The United States, European Unity, and the Origins of the Marshall Plan," *Diplomatic History* 6 (Summer 1982): 267–85.

68Editorial, "The Truman Doctrine," *The Economist*, March 29, 1947, encl. in Lewis Douglas, U.S. ambassador in London, to sec. of state, April 1, 1947, DSDF, NA; Wittner, *American Intervention in Greece*, 20–22, 60–63. Actually, the British and Americans had earlier tried (and failed) to reach an amicable arrangement by the Anglo-American Petroleum Agreement of August 1944. U.S. oil companies opposed the agreement out of suspicion of the government in Washington trying to gain control over corporations. In September 1945 a similar agreement failed to secure Senate approval because the oil companies feared domestic competition from Arab oil, were worried about government controls, and were concerned that the deal helped only the larger American firms. Ibid., 21.

69Wiley's questioning of Acheson, April 1, 1947, U.S. Senate, *Legislative Origins of Truman Doctrine*, 94.

70Baxter to Acheson, April 2, 1947, *FRUS*, V: *Near East and Africa*, 135; Lincoln's testimony, April 2, 1947, U.S. Senate, *Legislative Origins of Truman Doctrine*, 161; Patterson's testimony, April 3, 1947, U.S. House of Reps., *Military Assistance Programs, Part 2*, VI: append. IV, 454; meeting of Interdepartmental Interim Greek Assistance Committee, April 9, 1947, DSDF, NA.

71Mundt's testimony, April 11, 1947, U.S. House of Reps., *Military Assistance Programs, Part 2*, VI: 410; Javits's testimony, April 11, 1947, ibid., 404.

72Patterson's testimony, April 11, 1947, ibid., 403–5, 409; Acheson's testimony, April 11, 1947, U.S. House of Reps., *Military Assistance Programs, Part 2*, VI: 408; Interim Greece-Turkey Assistance Committee summarizing testimony, April 24, 1947, DSDF, NA.

73Sandifer to sec. of state, May 9, 1947, *FRUS*, V: *Near East and Africa*, 164; Jones, *Fifteen Weeks*, 197–98.

74"Assistance to Greece and Turkey," April 22, 1947, section entitled "Background of the Greek Assistance Program," pp. 4, M-5, DSDF, NA; A. N. Overby to Willard Thorp, chman., Interde-partmental Interim Greek Assistance Committee, encl. in Snyder to Clifford, May 21, 1947, Truman Papers, Confidential File, Truman Lib.; PL 75, 61 Stat. 103; PL 271, 61 Stat. 610, 613; Interim Greece-Turkey Assistance Committee summarizing testimony, April 24, 1947, DSDF, NA; DS Draft of "Agreement on Aid to Greece," ibid.; "Comparison of Treasury and State Drafts," Elsey Papers, Truman Lib.

75House Report on H.R. 2616: Assistance to Greece and Turkey, April 25, 1947, U.S. House of Reps., *Military Assistance Programs, Part 2*, VI: append. II, 424; append., IV, 454; "USAFGG History," 5, 8; "Assistance to Greece and Turkey," April 22, 1947, p. M-5, DSDF, NA; meeting of Interdepartmental Interim Greek Assistance Committee, May 1, 1947, ibid.; Maj. Gen. Lauris Norstad, director, P & O, to Col. Charles Lehner, May 19, 1947, Records of Interservice Agen-cies, box 49, 322 JUSMAPG 1947–48, P & O 091 Greece, Army Staff Records, NA; Interim Greece-Turkey Assistance Committee summarizing testimony, April 24, 1947, DSDF, NA; memo from Capt. M. M. Dupre, Jr., U.S. Navy, for chman., Interdepartmental Committee on Greece and Turkey, May 4, 1947, ibid.; "Assistance to Greece and Turkey," April 22, 1947, p. M-5, ibid.; M. A. Campbell et al., *The Employment of Airpower in the Greek Guerrilla War, 1947–1949* (Montgomery, Ala.: Air U., Maxwell AFB, 1964), append. 2, pp. 63–64; "USAFGG His-tory," 15, 17; Interim Historical Report—USA Group, Amer. Mission to Greece. Encl. in General William L. Livesay (became head of U.S. Army Group Greece in June 1947) to director, P & O, Aug. 8, 1947, P & O 091 Greece (TS), Sect. V, cases 74–86, p. 1, Army Staff Records, NA; note for record, May 16, 1947, P & O 091 Greece, case 10/6, ibid.; instructions to Lehner, May 19, 1947, P & O 091 Greece, (TS), sect. II-A, case 13, ibid.; Interim Greece-Turkey Assis-tance Committee summarizing testimony, April 24, 1947, DSDF, NA.

76McGhee, "Impact of Foreign Commitments," 46–48.

77Wittner, *American Intervention in Greece*, 101–2; notes on cabinet meeting of April 4, 1947, Millis, ed., *Forrestal Diaries*, 261; handwritten notations on conversations in cabinet, early June (?) 1947, Truman Papers, Confidential File, Truman Lib.; "The White House Washington," ibid.; Truman to Griswold, June 3, 1947, ibid.; Griswold to Truman, June 5, 1947, ibid.; Lincoln, *United States' Aid to Greece*, 40. Over radio in April 1945, Griswold had explained his relationship with Truman: "We soldiered together—we loafed together; between real friends . . . party lines are forgotten." Quoted in Wittner, *American Intervention in Greece*, 102.

78Case to Truman, May 10, 1947, Truman Papers, Official File, Truman Lib.

CHAPTER 3. THE NEED FOR AMERICAN MILITARY ASSISTANCE

1M. A. Campbell et al., *The Employment of Airpower in the Greek Guerrilla War, 1947–1949* (Montgomery, Ala.: Air U., Maxwell AFB, 1964), 27–28; Rawlins to Morgan, Brit. Joint Staff Mission, CCS Sept. 18, 1947, P & O 091 Greece (TS), sect. II, cases 8–17, pp. 1–2, Army Staff Records, NA: James Keeley to sec. of state, April 19, 1947, DSDF, NA.

2Rawlins to Morgan, Sept. 18, 1947, P & O 091 Greece (TS), sect. II, cases 8–17, pp. 1–2, Army Staff Records, NA; "History of JUSMAGG," 64–65; George McGhee, "U.S. and Soviet Actions and Reactions in Middle East," Oct. 6, 1955 (Air War College lecture), K239.716255 26, Maxwell AFB. In Simpson Lib. Edgar O'Ballance, *The Greek Civil War, 1944–1949* (N.Y.: Praeger, 1966), 140, 142, 147–48. William H. McNeill, at that time military attaché in Athens, later alluded to the principle of flexibility underlying the Truman Doctrine when he declared that the "first phase" of American assistance was military, and that the other objectives had to wait. See his *Greece: American Aid in Action, 1947–1956* (N.Y.: Twentieth Century Fund, 1957), 38.

3Porter's testimony, April 1, 1947, U.S. Senate, *Legislative Origins of the Truman Doctrine: Hearings Held in Executive Session Before the Committee on Foreign Relations. 80th Cong., 1 sess., on S. 938: A Bill to Provide for Assistance to Greece and Turkey* (Wash., D.C.: GPO, 1973), 26; Campbell et al., *Employment of Airpower in Greek Guerrilla War*; Edwin P. Curtin (lieut. col.), "American Advisory Group Aids Greece in War on Guerrillas," *Armed Cavalry Journal* 58 (Jan.-Feb. 1949): 10–11. In April the United States had approved a Greek request to increase its army by 15,000 men. Christopher M. Woodhouse, *The Struggle for Greece, 1941–1949* (Brooklyn Heights, N.Y.: Beekman-Esanu, 1976), 205; "History of JUSMAGG," 65; D. M. Condit, *Case Study in Guerrilla War: Greece During World War II* (Wash., D.C.: Special Operations Research Office, Dept. of Army, 1961), 188–89. For a description of Greece's land features, see C. A. Munkman, *American Aid to Greece: A Report on the First Ten Years* (N.Y.: Praeger, 1958), 35–39. For outside aid to the Greek guerrillas, see Chapter 1, above, n. 7.

4Kenneth Matthews, *Memories of a Mountain War Greece: 1944–1949* (London: Longman, 1972), 28.

5Condit, *Case Study*, 141–42; William H. McNeill, *The Greek Dilemma: War and Aftermath* (Philadelphia: Lippincott, 1947), 99–100.

6O'Ballance, *Greek Civil War*, 137; Woodhouse, *Struggle for Greece*, 203; Lawrence S. Wittner, *American Intervention in Greece, 1943–1949* (N.Y. Columbia U. Press, 1982), 119–20; Dominique Eudes, *The Kapetanios: Partisans and Civil War in Greece, 1943–1949* (N.Y.: Monthly Review Press, 1972), 291. Originally published as *Les Kapetanios: La guerre civile grecque de 1943 à 1949* (Paris: Librarie Arthème Fayard, 1970). Trans. by John Howe. Keeley (the counselor), to sec. of state, April 3, 1947, DSDF, NA: Rankin to sec. of state, May 22, 1948, ibid.; Cyrus L. Sulzberger, *A Long Row of Candles: Memoirs and Diaries [1934–1954]* (N.Y.: Macmillan, 1969), 391. In Greece's tense atmosphere, rumors spread that King George had been assassinated. Woodhouse is noncommittal on the possibility, but one of the guerrilla leaders, Kapitan Orestis Moundrikhas, told him in 1969 that he, Orestis, had had three agents inside the palace at the time. See Woodhouse, *Struggle for Greece*, 203 n. The rumors were not taken seriously then or later.

[7]Evangelos Averoff-Tossizza, *By Fire and Axe: The Communist Party and the Civil War in Greece, 1944–1949* (New Rochelle, N.Y.: Caratzas Brothers, 1978), 203–4. Originally published as *Le Feu et la hache Grèce '46-'49, histoire des guerres de l'après-guerre* (Paris: Editions de Breteuil, 1973). Trans. by Sarah Arnold Rigos.

[8]Matthews, *Memories of a Mountain War Greece*, 158–59.

[9]Condit, *Case Study*, 143; British Minister of State Hector McNeil's account of terrorist activities in Greece, in *Parliamentary Debates*, House of Commons, vol. 435, p. 14; Constantine Poulos, "Fruits of the Truman Doctrine," *Nation*, Dec. 6, 1947, p. 614; *Time*, Aug. 25, 1947, p. 27; Wittner, *American Intervention in Greece*, 137; Eudes, *Kapetanios*, 306. The London paper was the *Daily Mirror*, Nov. 11, 1947. Cited in ibid. The Greek government's spokesman was the minister of justice under the Liberals in late 1947, Constantine Rendis. Ibid.

[10]By the end of 1947, the refugees numbered more than 400,000. Woodhouse, *Struggle for Greece*, 208.

[11]Ibid., 7–9; George M. Alexander, *The Prelude to the Truman Doctrine: British Policy in Greece, 1944–1947* (Oxford: Clarendon Press, 1982), 197; Bickham Sweet-Escott, *Greece: A Political and Economic Survey, 1939–1953* (London: Royal Institute of International Affairs, 1954), 173–74. For a history of the Macedonian question from the 1870s to 1949, see Elisabeth Barker, *Macedeonia: Its Place in Balkan Power Politics* (London: Royal Institute of International Affairs, 1950). See also Evangelos Kofos, *Nationalism and Communism in Macedonia* (Thessaloniki: Institute for Balkan Studies, 1964).

[12]Christopher M. Woodhouse, *Apple of Discord: A Survey of Recent Greek Politics in Their International Setting* (London: Hutchinson, 1948), 93; Richard V. Burks, *The Dynamics of Communism in Eastern Europe* (Princeton: Princeton U. Press, 1961), 97, 98. Slavophones were the Slavo-Macedonian minority living in the northwestern section of Aegean or Greek Macedonia. Ibid, 236.

[13]Acting director of Office of European Affairs ([?]Reber) to Henderson, July 28, 1947, *FRUS*, V: *The Near East and Africa* (Wash., D.C.: GPO, 1971), 263–64.

[14]Ethridge to sec. of state, May 8, 1947, *FRUS*, V: *Near East and Africa*, 846; MacVeagh to Greek Prime Minister Dimitrios Maximos, April 11, 1947, ibid., 142-43; Marshall to embassy in Athens, May 10, 1947, DSDF, NA: "Knife Edge in Greece," *The Economist*, July 5, 1947, encl. in Robert Coe of Amer. embassy in London to sec. of state, July 8, 1947, ibid. According to McNeil, these policies included blocking food from guerrilla areas and nearly forcing evacuation of villagers; preventing those remaining in the villages (mostly leftist sympathizers) from tending their flocks or working their fields; suppressing civil liberties; allowing poor treatment of guerrillas who had surrendered under amnesty terms; engaging in arbitrary persecution, imprisonment, and beating of innocent civilians by gendarmes and rightists. Keeley to sec. of state, April 11, 1947, ibid. McNeill became a historian and wrote, among many publications, several accounts dealing with Greece during this period and after.

[15]Constantine Poulos (the observer), "The Greek Frontier," *Nation*, May 24, 1947, pp. 620-22; Wittner, *American Intervention in Greece*, 3; Francis F. Lincoln, *United States' Aid to Greece, 1947–1962* (Germantown, Tenn.: Professional Seminars, 1975), 41; Frank Smothers, William H. McNeill, Elizabeth D. McNeill, *Report on the Greeks: Findings of a Twentieth Century Fund Team Which Surveyed Conditions in Greece in 1947* (N.Y.: Twentieth Century Fund, 1948), 32; Lincoln to Peg and Rune [?], March 16, 1947, Lincoln Papers, "Personal Corresp.," Subject File: Greece-Personal, box 3, Truman Lib.; Marshall to embassy in Athens, May 5, 1947, *FRUS*, V: *Near East and Africa*, 160; MacVeagh to sec. of state, May 7, 1947, ibid., 163; Col. A. Frondistis, Greek intelligence officer for C Corps, to Gibson, Sept. 18, 1947, encl. in Gibson to sec. of state, Sept. 27, 1947, DSDF, NA. EDES stood for Ethnikos Demokratikos Ellinikos Syndesmos.

[16]Copy of May 23 report in Acheson Papers, box 6, file on Marshall Plan—reports, Greece and Turkey, Truman Lib.; "US Draft Conclusions," May 12, 1947, encl. in Ethridge to sec. of state, May 12, 1947, *FRUS*, V: *Near East and Africa*, 850-60. It is not clear whether the military equipment in the guerrillas' hands at this time had come from neighboring countries (as the UN commission believed), or was that left after the December Revolution of 1944. Possibly some supplies were already coming from the outside.

[17]"US Draft Conclusions," 850–60.

[18]Sec. of state to Ethridge, May 16, 1947, *FRUS*, V: *Near East and Africa*, 863.

[19]Proposals by Commission of Investigation, May 23, 1947, in Acheson Papers, box 6, file on Marshall Plan—reports, Greece & Turkey, Truman Lib.; Russian vetoes of proposals of Commission of Investigation, ibid. From June through August, the Security Council debated the possibility of bringing the border under international surveillance by the establishment of international border commissions, but it was unable to implement any program because of five Soviet vetoes. A White House adviser, Francis F. Lincoln, argued that the vetoes showed Soviet support for Yugoslavia and the Greek guerrillas. Lincoln, *United States' Aid to Greece*, 34. See also Dimitrios G. Kousoulas, *The Price of Freedom: Greece in World Affairs, 1939-1953* (Syracuse, N.Y.: Syracuse U. Press, 1953), 171. *Nation* supported the UN attempts. See editorial in July 19, 1947, pp. 57–58.

[20]"USAFGG History"; Livesay diary, entries of May 29, June 13, 1947, Livesay Papers, U.S. Army Military History Institute, Carlisle Military Barracks, Pa.; "Interim Historical Report," USAGG, AMAG, encl. in Livesay to director, P & O, Aug. 8, 1947, P & O 091 Greece (TS), sect. V, cases 74–86, pp. 1, 8, Army Staff Records, NA; memo from Col. Benjamin F. Taylor for DS (McGhee), June 12, 1947, P & O 091 Greece (TS), sect. II-A, case 13, ibid.; Norstad to Livesay, June 12, 1947, P & O 091 Greece (TS), ibid. General Dwight D. Eisenhower, who was army chief of staff, claimed that Livesay replaced Lehner for political reasons. He did not elaborate on the claim. See Eisenhower to Lehner, June 17, 1947, P & O 091 Greece (TS), sect. II-E, case 13, ibid.

[21]War Dept. Summary Sheet on U.S. Military Assistance to Greece & Iran, by Norstad, June 9, 1947, P & O 400, case 39, p. 1, Army Staff Records, NA. For the treaty, see Lincoln, *United States' Aid to Greece*, Append. I.

[22]Marshall to embassy in Athens, May 7, 1947, *FRUS*, V: *Near East and Africa*, 162; MacVeagh to sec. of state, May 26, 1947, ibid., 179; Henderson memo, June 13, 1947, ibid., 195.

[23]Livesay diary, entries of June 19, 20, 21, July 1, 18, 1947, Livesay Papers, U.S. Army Military History Institute; "Interim Historical Report," Aug. 8, 1947, p. 8, Army Staff Records, NA; chief of staff, minister for public order, to commanding officer, Amer. mission, July 7, 1947, P & O 091 Greece (TS), sect. I-A, case 3, p.1, Army Staff Records, NA.

[24]Livesay to Griswold, June 24, 1947, P & O 092, sect. VI-A, case 95, pp. 2–4, Army Staff Records, NA.

[25]Ibid., 4–5. The Greek General Staff had asked the Currency Control Committee for funds to buy ammunition from Italy, but the committee rejected the request because of certain international complications. The staff then requested 10,000 rifles and 500,000 rounds of ammunition. The committee likewise turned this down because of international problems. Ibid.

[26]Ibid., 5.

[27]"History of JUSMAGG," 2; Marshall to Griswold, July 11, 1947, *FRUS*, V: *Near East and Africa*, 220–23.

[28]Marshall to Griswold, July 11, 1947, *FRUS*, V: *Near East and Africa*, 224, 227.

[29]John O. Iatrides, ed., *Ambassador MacVeagh Reports: Greece, 1933-1947* (Princeton: Princeton U. Press, 1980), 4–5, 706–7, 717–18. MacVeagh's wife studied classical languages and knew modern Greek.

[30]For a hint of Griswold's concern over this potential problem, see notes on conference of July 9, 1947, in DS, in Forrestal diaries, VIII: 1718, Operational Archives, Naval History Divis., Wash., D.C. (photocopies of originals at Princeton U.).

[31]Constantine Poulos, "Meet Our Greek Allies," *Nation*, June 28, 1947, pp. 761–63.

[32]See Kennan's article in *Foreign Affairs* 25 (July 1947): 566–82. See also Oral History Interview with Elsey, II (April 9, 1970), 263, 354, Trum Lib.; Kennan, *Memoirs, 1925–1950* (Boston: Little, Brown, 1967), 315.

[33]Memo for President from Rear Admiral R. H. Hillenkoetter, director, CIG, June 6, 1947, Truman Papers, President's Secretary's Files, Truman Lib.; Greek embassy to DS, June 7, 1947, *FRUS*, V: *Near East and Africa*, 196–98. The term "international brigade" is derived from the Spanish Civil War of 1936, during which several foreign units (but not government forces) participated in the fighting. The day following Truman's address to Congress, March 13, the Greek communist newspaper, *Rizospastis*, predicted that the President's "undisguised declaration of American imperialism" would lead to the establishment of an "International Brigade" as in Spain during the 1930s. Quoted in Woodhouse, *Struggle for Greece*, 202. According to one contemporary, Soviet aid to the Greek guerrillas consisted of only 30 anti-aircraft guns. See Chapter 1, above, n. 7.

[34]Sec. of state to U.S. ambassador to UN (Warren R. Austin), June 26, 1947, *FRUS*, V: *Near East and Africa*, 867; Brit. embassy to DS, July 21, 1947, ibid., 248; Marshall to Griswold, July 11, 1947, DSDF, NA; "Global Estimate of the Situation," Joint Planning Staff report of June 30, 1947, pp. 1–2, in ABC-381 Global Estimate, War Dept. Records, NA.

[35]*New York Times*, July 15, 1947; p. 1; *Time*, July 28, 1947, p. 11; *Newsweek*, July 28, 1947, pp. 32–33; Johnson quoted in *Nation*, July 26, 1947, pp. 86–87; "Greek Town Fights 'Bandit' Attackers Based in Albania," *New York Times*, July 14, 1947, p. 1. See also "Greek Skirmishes Cause War Scare," *Life*, July 28, 1947, p. 34.

[36]Averoff-Tossizza, *By Fire and Axe*, 224; Cyrus L. Sulzberger, "World Reds Study Division of Greece," *New York Times*, June 29, 1947, p. 1; Lovett memo for sec. of state, July 15, 1947, DSDF, NA; Porfirogenis quote in MacVeagh to sec. of state, July 11, 1947, ibid.; memo prepared in DS, July 17, 1947, *FRUS*, V: *Near East and Africa*, 239–40; MacVeagh to sec. of state, July 19, 1947, ibid., 245–46.

[37]Memo for JCS from sec. of state, July 17, 1947, ABC-400.336 Greece, sect. I-A, pp. 1, 3, 4, War Dept. Records, NA; memo prepared in DS, July 17, 1947, *FRUS*, V: *Near East and Africa*, 240; MacVeagh to sec. of state, July 24, 1947, ibid., 260–61.

[38]McNeill, *Greece*, 35–37; William H. McNeill, *The Metamorphosis of Greece since World War II* (Chicago: U. of Chicago Press, 1978), 85; Lincoln, *United States' Aid to Greece*, 42; Wittner, *American Intervention in Greece*, 108–9; Averoff-Tossizza, *By Fire and Axe*, 162–63; MacVeagh to sec. of state, July 13, 1947, *FRUS*, V: *Near East and Africa*, 231–32; Marshall to embassy in Athens, July 18, 1947, ibid., 243–44; MacVeagh to sec. of state, July 15, 1947, DSDF, NA. Sophoulis was prime minister from November 1945 until after the elections of March 1946.

[39]"Memorandum for the President," from sec. of state, July 16, 1947, Truman Papers, PSF-Subject File, Truman Lib.; "Memorandum Re Greek Conditions," July 17, 1947, Truman Papers, Official File, ibid.; Leahy diaries, 1947, pp. 60–61, Leahy Papers, MS Divis., LC; Marshall to AMA, July 29, 1947, *FRUS*, V: *Near East and Africa*, 267; memo for JCS from sec. of state, July 17, 1947, ABC-400.336 Greece, sect. I-A, pp. 1, 3, 4, War Dept. Records, NA.

[40]Livesay to DS, July 28, 1947, P & O 091 Greece (TS), sect. I-A, case 3, pp. 2 (enclosure no. 4), 4, Army Staff Records, NA; Wittner, *American Intervention in Greece*, 227.

[41]"Monthly Historical Report," USAGG, AMAG, Aug. 1947, in Livesay to director, P & O, P & O 091 Greece (TS), sect. V, cases 74–86, pp. 9, 10, Army Staff Records, NA; Brit. Chargé John Balfour to sec. of state, July 30, 1947, *FRUS*, V: *Near East and Africa*, 268. The matter of

Britain's troop withdrawal had repeatedly come before the British Parliament for discussion. In late April, Under-Secretary of State for Foreign Affairs Christopher P. Mayhew had told the Commons that the government would withdraw the final contingent of soldiers "as soon as it is practicable." *Parl. Debates*, House of Commons, vol. 436, p. 1524. See also previous discussions of question in ibid., vol. 434, pp. 454–56. In early June, Foreign Secretary Ernest Bevin told the Commons that a little more than 5,000 British soldiers remained in Greece other than those in British Service Missions. Ibid., vol. 438, p. 181. In late July, Mayhew declared that since the end of March 1947, about 9,000 British troops had been withdrawn but that more than 5,000 remained. Ibid., vol. 440, p. 9. See also Mayhew before Commons, ibid., p. 108.

[42]Lincoln, *United States' Aid to Greece*, 60–61.

[43]Matthews, *Memories of a Mountain War Greece*, 160–61; "Interim Historical Report," Aug. 8, 1947, p. 10. Aid soon arrived in Salonika, an area close to military operations. Thus the psychological impact was not yet felt in Athens. Woodhouse, *Struggle for Greece*, 203. On American aid in Greece, see McNeill, *Greece*.

CHAPTER 4. THE CALL FOR AMERICAN COMBAT TROOPS

[1]*Time*, Sept. 8, 1947, p. 20; Terry H. Anderson, *The United States, Great Britain, and the Cold War, 1944–1947* (Columbia: U. of Missouri Press, 1981), 152. By early 1948 the Soviets' Red Army (including the air force) had been reduced from its high of over 11 million in May 1945 to less than 3 million. See Daniel H. Yergin, *Shattered Peace: The Origins of the Cold War and the National Security State* (Boston: Houghton Mifflin, 1977), 270–71; Thomas G. Paterson, *On Every Front: The Making of the Cold War* (N.Y.: Norton, 1982), 155–56.

[2]Special briefing for chief of staff from Brig. Gen. Walter E. Todd, deputy director of intelligence, after July 30, 1947, P & O 091, Great Britain (TS), sect. I, case 1, Army Staff Records, NA. British withdrawal from Greece would violate their earlier assurance that they would maintain troops until ratification of the Bulgarian treaty. The move was part of a massive retrenchment effort led by left-wing members of the British government who wanted an immediate cut of 500,000 in the armed forces to meet a severe manpower shortage at home. The British government had agreed to pull out all troops from Greece and Italy (except 5,000 in Trieste) and to reduce the numbers in Germany, Austria, and India before schedule. Ibid. JIC 400/1—"Estimates of the Situations in Greece and Italy," Aug. 28, 1947, ABC 370.5 Greece-Italy, sect. I-A, p. 1, War Dept. Records, NA.

[3]Memo by representatives of Brit. Chiefs of Staff (C.C.S. 972), Aug. 29, 1947, ABC 370.5 Greece-Italy, sect. I-A, War Dept. Records, NA.

[4]Bohlen to Lovett, Aug. 1, 1947, *FRUS*, V: *The Near East and Africa* (Wash., D.C.: GPO, 1971), 271–72; Lewis Douglas, Amer. ambassador in London, to sec. of state, Aug. 3, 1947, ibid., 277–78; Bevin to sec. of state, ca. Aug. 20, 1947, ibid., 301–2; Douglas to sec. of state, Sept. 1, 1947, ibid., 321–23.

[5]Marshall to Brit. sec. of state for for. affairs, Aug. 1, 1947, ibid., 273–74; Marshall to embassy in London, Aug. 1, 1947, ibid., 274–75; Marshall to embassy in London, Aug. 7, 1947, ibid., 287; Marshall to embassy in London, Sept. 8, 1947, ibid., 331; notes on cabinet meetings, Aug. 8, 1947, Connelly Papers, box 1, White House File, set I, Truman Lib. For the argument that British troop withdrawal was attributable less to economic concerns than to forcing the United States into international matters, see Robert Frazier, "The Bevin-Marshall Dispute of August–November 1947 Concerning the Withdrawal of British Troops from Greece," in Lars Baerentzen, John O. Iatrides, and Ole L. Smith, eds., *Studies in the History of the Greek Civil War, 1945–1949* (Copenhagen, Denmark: Museum Tusculanum Press, 1987), 249–61.

[6]Marshall to embassy in London, Aug. 1, 1947, P & O 091.7 (TS), sect. II-E, case 47, Army Staff Records, NA; Marshall to Lovett, Aug. 25, 1947, *FRUS*, V: *Near East and Africa*, 313.

[7]Walter Millis, ed., *The Forrestal Diaries* (N.Y.: Viking, 1951), 302–3; Marshall to embassy in London, Aug. 7, 1947, *FRUS*, V: *Near East and Africa*, 287; notes on cabinet meetings, Aug. 8, 1947, Connelly Papers, box 1, White House File, set I, Truman Lib.

[8]See Inverchapel to Foreign Office, Jan. 22, 1947, FO 371, vol. 61074, AN 350/350/45, PRO. The American adviser was Cornelius Van H. Engert, and his paper was entitled, "Some Observations on the Strategic Importance of the Middle East to the United States." See also Frazier, "The Bevin-Marshall Dispute," 252, 257.

[9]MacVeagh to sec. of state, Aug. 2, 1947, *FRUS*, V: *Near East and Africa*, 276–77.

[10]JCS to Brit. Chiefs of Staff, after Aug. 29, 1947, pp. 1–2, encl. in Forrestal to sec. of state, Sept. 1, 1947, P & O 091 Greece (TS), Army Staff Records, NA; JCS 1801/1: Report by Joint Strategic Survey Committee to JCS—"Military Implications of Withdrawal of British Troops from Greece and Italy," Aug. 30, 1947, pp. 7–10, 16, ABC 370.5 Greece-Italy, sect. I-A, War Dept. Records, NA; memo for Joint Staff Planners for JCS from F. H. Schneider, sec. of ad hoc committee to consider plan of action regarding British withdrawal of troops from Greece, Sept. 2, 1947, pp. 1–3, ibid.; Royall and Forrestal to sec. of state, Sept. 5, 1947, *FRUS*, V: *Near East and Africa*, 327–29.

[11]MacVeagh to sec. of state, Aug. 4, 1947, *FRUS*, V: *Near East and Africa*, 278–79; JCS 1801/1, pp. 14–15.

[12]Memo for record by H. A. B. (Col. Byroade), Aug. 5, 1947, P & O 091.7 (TS), sect. II-E, case 47, p. 1, Army Staff Records, NA; special briefing for chief of staff by Todd, after July 30, 1947, P & O 091 Great Britain (TS), sect. I, case 1, ibid.

[13]Symington to sec. of state, Aug. 1, 1947, P & O 091.7 (TS), sect. II-E, case 47, pp. 1–2, ibid.

[14]Memo by Rear Admiral R. H. Hillenkoetter, director, CIG, "Soviet Intentions," Aug. 8, 1947, in JCS—Leahy Files, CIG, #129 (1942–48), NA.

[15]Ibid.

[16]Ibid.

[17]Ibid.

[18]Schuyler to Glover et al., Aug. 12, 1947, enclosure of staff study: "Deployment of Forces to Greece," ABC 370.5 Greece-Italy, sect. I-A, pp. 1–3, War Dept. Records, NA.

[19]Kerwin to HQ, EUCOM, Frankfurt, Germany: to Royall, Aug. 1, 1947, P & O 091.7 (TS), case 47, Army Staff Records, NA; JIC 400/1, pp. 3, 5; Royall to sec. of state, Sept. 11, 1947, P & O 091.7 (TS), sect. II-E, case 47, ibid.

[20]Schuyler to commanding general, USFMTO, Leghorn, Italy, Aug. 11, 1947, P & O 092 (TS), sect. VI-A, case 95, ibid., NA; Schuyler to Glover et al., Aug. 12, 1947, "The Greek Situation," ABC 370.5 Greece-Italy, sect. I-A, War Dept. Records, NA; Lieut. Col. [?] Osmanski, Strategic Plans, "Planning Bases for Dispatch of Task Force to Greece," Aug. 20, 1947, P & O 320.2 (TS), sect. V, cases 74–86, p. 1, Army Staff Records, NA. See also Brig. Gen. A. W. Kissner to commanding general, Army Air Forces, "Availability of Forces for Movement to Greece," Sept. 5, 1947, P & O 320.2 (TS), sect. V, cases 74–86, ibid.

[21]Kissner to commanding general, Army Air Forces, "Availability of Forces for Movement to Greece," Aug. 21, 1947, P & O 320.2 (TS), sect. V, cases 74–86, pp. 1–2, Army Staff Records, NA. The force designated "Parrakeet" was thought sufficient to carry out the mission in Greece. About 8,500 officers and men in number, it consisted of the following tactical and support service units: 1 Fighter Group (P-51), 1 Light Bomb Group (A-26), 1 Tactical Reconnaissance Squadron (FA-264), 1 Troop Carrier Squadron (C-82), and 1 Liaison Squadron (L-4). Ibid., p. 2. Memo for Major Gen. S. E. Anderson from Schuyler, Sept. 8, 1947, ABC 370.5 Greece-Italy, sect. I-A, War Dept. Records, NA.

[22]Quotes in Lawrence S. Wittner, *American Intervention in Greece, 1943–1949* (N.Y.: Columbia U. Press, 1982), 236.

[23]MacVeagh quoted in ibid., 109. See also ibid., 259. Transcript, David E. Bell, Oral History Interview (Sept. 12, 1968), p. 114, Truman Lib. The Marshall Plan, or European Recovery Program, became law in April 1948 and established an economic aid program for Europe.

[24]*Time*, Aug. 11, 1947, p. 23; ibid., Aug. 18, 1947, p. 24.

[25]Bickham Sweet-Escott, *Greece: A Political and Economic Survey, 1939–1953* (London: Royal Institute of International Affairs, 1954), 76; Griswold memo encl. in MacVeagh to sec. of state, Sept. 2, 1947, DSDF, NA; MacVeagh to sec. of state, Aug. 9, 1947, ibid.; *New York Times*, Aug. 28, 1947, pp. 1, 14; Villard to sec. of state, Aug. 7, 1947, *FRUS*, V: *Near East and Africa*, 282; quotes in John O. Iatrides, ed., *Ambassador MacVeagh Reports: Greece, 1933–1947* (Princeton: Princeton U. Press, 1980), 722. A friend of the State Department's specialist on Greece, Harry N. Howard, wrote him a personal letter in late August that recorded his firsthand observations of Griswold's behavior in Greece. "The more I see of them the more I have my doubts of Mr. Griswald [*sic*] (strictly between you and me). He came with his whole family (son in laws [*sic*], daughters in law, brother, wife's relations, etc.) plus golf clubs and tennis rackets. All the inner circle are old political cronies. MacVeigh [*sic*] is meeting him 90-10 by going completely out of his way to be cooperative and helpful, but I am afraid Griswald [*sic*] is in to [*sic*] much of a dilema [*sic*] to listen to anyone." Personal letter from [illegible] to Howard, Aug. 24, 1947, Howard Papers, Gr-Sp, box 3, Truman Lib.

[26]Griswold to sec. of state, Aug. 5, 1947, *FRUS*, V: *Near East and Africa*, 279–80.

[27]Ibid., 280; Griswold to McGhee, ca. Aug. 12, 1947, ibid., 295–96.

[28]MacVeagh to sec. of state, Aug. 5, 1947, ibid., 280–81; MacVeagh to sec. of state, Aug. 19, 1947, ibid., 300–301; MacVeagh to sec. of state, Aug. 20, 1947, ibid., 303; MacVeagh to sec. of state, Aug. 15, 1947, DSDF, NA.

[29]McGhee to Griswold, Aug. 21, 1947, DSDF, NA; Griswold to Major Gen. Harry H. Vaughan, military aide to Truman, Sept. 20, 1947, enclosure: monthly report on Greek Mission regarding "The Political Crisis," Truman Papers, PSF-Subject File, Truman Lib.

[30]Griswold to Vaughan, Sept. 20, 1947, enclosure: monthly report on Greek Mission regarding "The Political Crisis," Truman Papers, PSF-Subject File, Truman Lib.

[31]Griswold to sec. of state, Aug. 27, 1947, *FRUS*, V: *Near East and Africa*, 319.

[32]HQ, USAGG, AMAG, to director, P & O, Aug. 29, 1947, P & O 091.7 Greece (TS), sect. I-A, case 3, Army Staff Records, NA.

[33]MacVeagh to sec. of state, Aug. 1, 1947, *FRUS*, V: *Near East and Africa*, 270–71; Livesay to director, P & O, Aug. 2, 1947, encl. in Monthly Historical Report (Aug.), USAGG, AMAG, Sept. 10, 1947, P & O 091 Greece (TS), sect. V, cases 74–86, p. 11, Army Staff Records, NA; [?] Haven in Turin to sec. of state, Aug. 5, 1947, DSDF, NA; W. Clyde Dunn in Rome to sec. of state, Aug. 6, 1947, ibid.; memo by Robert G. Miner of Divis. of Near Eastern Affairs, Aug. 11, 1947, *FRUS*, V: *Near East and Africa*, 292–93. Miner found much "circumstantial evidence" presented by American missions pertaining to campaigns to raise volunteers from Italy, Germany, Rumania, Poland, France, and Czechoslovakia. He had "no definite information," but the volunteers were allegedly taken to Yugoslavia to pose as "Yugoslav nationals" and to receive military training. Ibid. See also [?] Greene in Leghorn, Italy, to sec. of state, Aug. 21, 1947, DSDF, NA.

[34]Dimitrios G. Kousoulas, *The Price of Freedom: Greece in World Affairs, 1939–1953* (Syracuse, N.Y.: Syracuse U. Press, 1953), 176–77; Evangelos Averoff-Tossizza, *By Fire and Axe: The Communist Party and the Civil War in Greece, 1944–1949* (New Rochelle, N.Y.: Caratzas Brothers, 1978), 234. Originally published as *Le Feu et la hache Grèce '46–'49, histoire des guerres de l'après-guerre* (Paris: Editions de Breteuil, 1973). Trans. by Sarah Arnold Rigos.

Averoff was the writer. According to Richard V. Burks, the Yugoslavs led these discussions regarding Macedonia and were lax about keeping Moscow informed. See his *Dynamics of Communism in Eastern Europe* (Princeton: Princeton U. Press, 1961), 99–101. See also Edgar O'Ballance, *The Greek Civil War, 1944–1949* (N.Y.: Praeger, 1966), 150; Christopher M. Woodhouse, *The Struggle for Greece, 1941–1949* (Brooklyn Heights, N.Y.: Beekman-Esanu, 1976), 210; Adam B. Ulam, *Titoism and the Cominform* (Cambridge: Harvard U. Press, 1952), 93–94; Evangelos Kofos, *Nationalism and Communism in Macedonia* (Thessaloniki: Institute for Balkan Studies, 1964), 161; Nicholas Pappas, "The Soviet-Yugoslav Conflict and the Greek Civil War," in Wayne S. Vucinich, ed., *At the Brink of War and Peace: The Tito-Stalin Split in a Historic Perspective* (N.Y.: Columbia U. Press, 1982), 223; William H. McNeill, *The Metamorphosis of Greece since World War II* (Chicago: U. of Chicago Press, 1978), 84–85. For aid figures from Yugoslavia, Albania, and Bulgaria, see Chapter 1, above, n. 7. One of Tito's associates, Vladimir Dedijer, declares that the Yugoslav leader made the decision in September 1946 to help the Greek guerrillas. According to Dedijer, Tito feared British imperialist designs on Yugoslavia, and he considered it his duty to help other revolutions. It seems possible that the Bled agreements formalized assistance to the guerrillas that had already been under way on a smaller scale. See Vladimir Dedijer, *Novi Prilozi za Biografiju Josipa Broza Tita, Tréci Tom* (Belgrade, 1984), 265, 268. Cited in Elisabeth Barker, "The Yugoslavs and the Greek Civil War of 1946–1949," in Baerentzen, Iatrides, and Smith, eds. *Studies in the History of the Greek Civil War*, 301. Barker adds another reason for Tito's interest in the Greek conflict: a united Macedonia inside a Balkan federation. Ibid., 302.

35John O. Iatrides, *Balkan Triangle: Birth and Decline of an Alliance Across Ideological Boundaries* (The Hague: Mouton, 1968), 22; Dominique Eudes, *The Kapetanios: Partisans and Civil War in Greece, 1943–1949* (N.Y.: Monthly Review Press, 1972), 297. Originally published as *Les Kapetanios: La guerre civile grecque de 1943 à 1949* (Paris: Librarie Arthème Fayard, 1970). Trans. by John Howe. One writer, who was the Greek foreign minister during the late 1950s and early 1960s, declared that at Bled, Markos renegotiated agreements of 1946 with Albanian and Bulgarian officers, and that a few Soviet officers were present. Averoff-Tossizza, *By Fire and Axe*, 234. Woodhouse asserts that Stalin had received word of the Tito-Dimitrov agreement beforehand and had expressed no objection. Kardelj insisted that the agreement was only a "preliminary statement of intent." If so, this fits Averoff's claim that Soviet officers were there. Woodhouse, *Struggle for Greece*, 229. Kardelj quoted in ibid.

36Livesay to Griswold, Aug. 21, 1947, P & O 091 Greece (TS) sect. I-A, case 3, p. 1, Army Staff Records, NA.

37Livesay diary, entry of Aug. 31, 1947, Livesay Papers, U.S. Army Military History Institute, Carlisle Military Barracks, Pa.

38Memo from director, P & O, for Lieut. Col. Theodore J. Conway, Aug. 25, 1947, P & O 091 Greece (TS), sect. IV, case 39, pp. 1–3, Army Staff Records, NA.

39Griswold to sec. of state, ca. Aug. 23, 1947, Truman Papers, Official File, Truman Lib.; Livesay to director, P & O, Sept. 10, 1947, encl. in Monthly Historical Report (Aug.), USAGG, P & O 091 Greece (TS), sect. V, cases 74–86, pp. 1, 7, Army Staff Records, NA; Wittner, *American Intervention in Greece*, 231. One problem obstructing the distribution of military vehicles in the field was the absence of spare parts. Though ordered, they were not shipped until September. Ibid., 1. For the directive to stay out of combat, see SWNCC 358/3, "Policies for Execution of Assistance Program to Greece," Aug. 18, 1947, annex to append. B, p. 43, in DSDF, NA.

40Livesay to director, P & O, Sept. 10, 1947, enclosure: Monthly Historical Report (Aug.), USAGG, AMAG, P & O 091 Greece (TS), sect. V, cases 74–86, pp. 12–13, Army Staff Records, NA; Livesay to director, P & O, Oct. 10, 1947, P & O 091 Greece (TS), sect. V, cases 74–86, pp. 20–22, ibid.; memo of conversation in Amer. embassy in Athens among Brit. and Amer. representatives regarding report by Lieut. Col. Miller of UN Sub-committee on situation in Thrace, Sept. 10, 1947, P & O 091 Greece (TS), sect. I, cases 1–7, pp. 1–6, ibid.; Keeley to sec. of state, Sept. 12, 1947, *FRUS*, V: *Near East and Africa*, 336–37; Miller quoted in MacVeagh to sec. of state, Aug. 22, 1947, ibid., 307; JIC 401/1: "United States Assistance to Greece," Sept. 16, 1947, pp. 1–4, ABC 370.5 Greece-Italy, War Dept. Records, NA; Fritz A. Voight, *The Greek Sedition* (London: Hollis and Carter, 1949), 168, 179–80.

[41]Paper prepared by Rawlins and sent to his embassy: "A Military Review of the Situation in Greece," Sept. 1, 1947, P & O 091 Greece (TS), sect. I-A, case 3, pp. 1–3, Army Staff Records, NA. Rawlins also recommended the appointment of a "Greek Supreme Commander," but Livesay did not mention this in his letter to Bradley. Ibid., 3. Livesay diary, entry of Sept. 10, 1947.

[42]Griswold to sec. of state, Sept. 15, 1947, *FRUS*, V: *Near East and Africa*, 337–39; Rawlins, "A Military Review of the Situation in Greece," pp. 2–3; Livesay diary, entry of Sept. 11, 1947.

[43]Livesay to director, P & O, Oct. 10, 1947, encl. in Monthly Historical Report (Sept.), USAGG, AMAG, P & O 091 Greece (TS), sect. V, cases 74–86, pp. 18–20, Army Staff Records, NA.

[44]Keeley to sec. of state, Sept. 12, 1947, *FRUS*, V: *Near East and Africa*, 336–37.

[45]JIC 401/1, pp. 8–9, 56–57, 59–60; Intelligence Report #3899, "United States Assistance to Greece," Sept. 12, 1947, P & O 091 Greece (TS), sect. II-A, case 13, pp. 9, 13–14, Army Staff Records, NA.

[46]Intelligence Report #3899, pp. 3–8, 14–15. The report declared that the Soviets had 476,000 ground forces in Bulgaria, Rumania, and nearby areas that could be sent immediately in the event of an attack on Greece. The number would be 693,000 if one included air and naval personnel. Ibid., 7. See also JIC 401/1, pp.1–3, 52, 54–56, 65–67. As shown earlier, contemporary estimates of Soviet ground strength were much higher than what it now seems to have been. See n. 1, above.

[47]JIC 401/1, pp. 1–4, 10. In late November 1947 the UN General Assembly voted to partition Palestine into Arab and Jewish states. The Arab delegates stalked out of the General Assembly in protest.

[48]Ibid., pp. 1, 3–4, 14–15.

[49]Ibid., pp. 12–13, 16, 25, 32.

[50]Millis, ed., *Forrestal Diaries*, entry of Sept. 16, 1947, p. 316.

[51]Memo by Schuyler on meeting with DS representatives on the Greek situation, Sept. 17, 1947, P & O 319.1 Greece (TS), sect. IV-A, case 46, Army Staff Records, NA.

CHAPTER 5.   THE DECISION TO EXTEND OPERATIONAL ADVICE

[1]Memo by Schuyler on meeting with DS representatives, Sept. 17, 1947, P & O 319.1 Greece (TS), sect. IV-A, case 46, Army Staff Records, NA; memo for Chamberlin: instructions from Gen. J. Lawton Collins, Sept. 19, 1947, CSUSA 091 Greece, encl. in P & O 091 Greece (TS), sect. I, cases 1–7, p. 1, ibid.; memo for record by Lieut. Col. E. S. Hartshorn, Sept. 18, 1947, P & O 320.2 (TS), encl. in P & O 091 Greece (TS), sect. I, cases 1–7, p. 2, ibid.; instructions from Collins to Chamberlin, Sept. 19, 1947, CD 2-1-6, files of sec. of defense, NA; Lovett to Keeley and Griswold, Sept. 19, 1947, DSDF, NA.

[2]Memo of meeting of DS representatives, Sept. 17, 1947, P & O 091 Greece (TS), sect. I, cases 1–7, p. 1, Army Staff Records, NA; memo for record by Hartshorn, Sept. 18, 1947, P & O 320.2 (TS), encl. in P & O 091 Greece (TS), sect. I, cases 1–7, p. 1, ibid.; note for record: "Increase in Strength of the Greek Army," by Lt. Col. [?] Goss, Sept. 22, 1947, P & O 320.2 Greece (TS), sect. I-A, case 3, pp. 1–2, ibid. William Rountree from the State Department pointed out that the

diversion of funds from civilian to military goals would have a profound effect on the economic program. Nine million dollars had been shifted already; the pattern suggested that the total losses to the economic program could be about $114 million. Rountree to Walter Wilds, deputy coordinator for aid to Greece and Turkey, Oct. 13, 1947, DSDF, NA.

[3]Francis F. Lincoln, *United States' Aid to Greece, 1947–1962* (Germantown, Tenn.: Professional Seminars, 1975), 42; British Foreign Office quoted in Lawrence S. Wittner, *American Intervention in Greece, 1943–1949* (N.Y.: Columbia U. Press, 1982), 111; ibid., 111–13; Bickham Sweet-Escott, *Greece: A Political and Economic Survey, 1939–1953* (London: Royal Institute of International Affairs, 1954), 77. Henderson was not happy with the outcome. Tsaldaris was strong and what the country needed, but he would not alter his policies; Sophoulis would waver before difficult decisions. Another State Department adviser thought that Sophoulis's chances for ending the war were slim because his government was "so heavily tinged with foreign participation." Oral History Interview with Henderson (June 14 & July 5, 1973), 95–96, Truman Lib.; Lincoln (the DS adviser) to Peg & Mead, Sept. 18, 1947, Lincoln Papers, Subject File: Greece Personal, box 3, ibid.; MacVeagh to sec. of state, Sept. 2, 6, 1947, DSDF, NA; Keeley to sec. of state, Sept. 16, 1947, ibid. The British ambassador in Athens reported to his home office that, although Henderson did not want to dictate the outcome, he was "up to the neck in this wasps' nest." Quoted in Wittner, *American Intervention in Greece*, 353 n.21. Griswold had not been involved in the Henderson-MacVeagh talks with Tsaldaris; both Henderson and MacVeagh had no regard for Griswold's political tactics and considered him overly favorable to the Liberals. Ibid., 111.

[4]Oral History Interview with Henderson (June 14 & July 5, 1973), 92–93, 96, Truman Lib.

[5]Sweet-Escott, *Greece*, 74; Lincoln, *United States' Aid to Greece*, 43; minutes of meeting of Supreme National Defense Council, Sept. 17, 1947, P & O 337 (TS), encl. in P & O 091 Greece (TS), sect. I, cases 1–7, pp. 1–2, Army Staff Records, NA; Wittner, *American Intervention in Greece*, 112–13. Sophoulis had headed a center government after his election as prime minister in November 1945. Ibid., 37. Although State Department officials had approved an enlargement of the Greek army, they had done so the very day that Livesay was meeting with Sophoulis. The general was doubtless unaware of the action in Washington. In any case, the implementation of the move would have required some time.

[6]Rawlins to Morgan, Sept. 18, 1947, P & O 091 Greece (TS), sect. II, cases 8–17, pp. 1–3, Army Staff Records, NA; note for record by Lieut. Col. [?] Crawford: "Estimate of the Greek National Army," Sept. 18, 1947, P & O 091.7 Greece (TS), sect. I-A, case 3, ibid. To encourage the offensive, Rawlins insisted that the Greek army withdraw from the villages and join the advancing forces. He recommended deployment of the Greek's paramilitary organizations (MAD and MAY) as a military force much like Britain's Home Guard. The United States would have to arm and clothe these additional 50,000 men. If the guerrillas received help from an international brigade, he recommended the elimination of troop ceilings so that the country could double its military strength by using its full potential of nearly 400,000 men. Ibid., p. 3.

[7]Walter Millis, ed., *The Forrestal Diaries* (N.Y.: Viking, 1951), entry of Sept. 26, 1947, p. 321; CIA Report 1, "Review of the World Situation as It Relates to the Security of the United States," Sept. 26, 1947, summary, p. 5, Truman Papers, President's Secretary's Files, Truman Lib. The National Security Act of 1947 established both the National Security Council and the CIA. In the Pentagon Talks of October 1947, the United States and Great Britain discussed the importance of halting Soviet expansion into the Middle East. To stop the Soviets from securing the region's oil, the two allies agreed to follow parallel policies and to use political, economic, and military means. Bruce R. Kuniholm, *The Origins of the Cold War in the Near East: Great Power Conflict and Diplomacy in Iran, Turkey, and Greece* (Princeton: Princeton U. Press, 1980), 423; Wittner, *American Intervention in Greece*, 230, 284–85.

[8]Griswold to Henderson, Sept. 2, 1947, *FRUS*, V: *The Near East and Africa* (Wash., D.C.: GPO, 1971), Griswold to sec. of state, Oct. 9, 1947, ibid., 361, 363; memo by Wilds of conversa-

tion, Oct. 15, 1947, ibid., 367–68; Cromie to Henderson, Sept. 2, 1947, Foreign Service Posts of DS, Athens Embassy, Confidential File 1947: 711.3-800, box 15, FRC; Wittner, *American Intervention in Greece*, 233–34. In mid-October, Lovett expressed disagreement with Griswold's recommendations. If the British left, Lovett did not think an American military mission should replace them. Existing law did not authorize American combat forces. The United States could take no action until consideration by both Truman and the National Security Council and until after a final vote in the UN General Assembly on the Greek border difficulties. And, finally, Lovett believed that twenty-five American officers were enough to be "quietly fed" to Livesay as "observers." *FRUS*, V: *Near East and Africa*, 368.

[9]Christopher M. Woodhouse, *The Struggle for Greece, 1941–1949* (Brooklyn Heights, N.Y.: Beekman-Esanu, 1976), 211; Lincoln, *United States' Aid to Greece*, 41; Vladimir Dedijer, *Tito* (N.Y.: Simon & Schuster, 1953), 292–93; Svetozar Vukmanović-Tempo, *How and Why the People's Liberation Struggle of Greece Met with Defeat* (London: Merritt & Hatcher, 1950), 6, 82. The Cominform replaced the Comintern (Communist International), which had been disbanded during World War II.

[10]Dimitrios G. Kousoulas, *The Price of Freedom: Greece in World Affairs, 1939–1953* (Syracuse, N.Y.: Syracuse U. Press), 176.

[11]Caffery to sec. of state, Oct. 1, 9, 1947, DSDF, NA.

[12]Note for record by Goss, Oct. 2, 1947, P & O 091 Greece (TS), sect. I, cases 1–7, Army Staff Records, NA; address by Henderson, "Some Current Problems of Modern Greece," Oct. 4, 1947, pp. 2–3, 7–9, in Jones Papers, Truman Lib.; establishment of "Special Balkan Committee," Oct. 11, 1947, encl. in Acheson Papers, box 6, file on Marshall Plan—reports, Greece and Turkey, Truman Lib. The resolution recommended negotiations among the parties concerned for the resumption of normal diplomatic and good neighborly relations, new frontier conventions, settlement of the refugee problem, and a study of the practicability of voluntary exchange of minorities. Ibid. Address by McGhee over CBS radio, Oct. 15, 1947, p. 4, Jones Papers, Truman Lib.

[13]Ed. note, *FRUS*, V: *Near East and Africa*, 366–67; JCS 1798/1—"United States Assistance to Greece," Oct. 15, 1947, pp. 57–58, ABC 370.5 Greece-Italy, War Dept. Records, NA; JCS 1798/1, pp. 49–54, 61–65; HQS U.S. Air Force, Air Intelligence Report No. 100-41/1-10 (142.048-41 A), "An Air Study of Greece (Including Dodecanese Islands)," Oct. 7, 1947, pp. 1–4, 7, 18, Maxwell AFB. In Simpson Lib. The Royal Hellenic Air Force (RHAF) had 238 "obsolescent aircraft," 77 of which were in tactical units. The total included 9 medium bombers (Wellingtons), 113 fighters (Spitfires), 108 Liaison (Ansons, Harvards, Austers, Oxfords, Tiger Moths, L-5s), and 8 transports (C-47s). They were capable of maintaining internal order but incapable of combat effectiveness against modern combat planes. The main offensive air potential consisted of 40 Spitfires in two squadrons, but even these planes would be ineffective because of poor maintenance and inadequate pilot reserves. According to the intelligence study, the RHAF defensive air potential was "negligible" except in operations against the guerrillas. The planes lacked radar, and probably had insufficient anti-aircraft artillery guns. Ibid., 1, 4, 7, 18; JCS 1798/1, pp. 50, 54–56, 58–61, 64–67; J.P.S. 858—Joint Staff Planners, The Greek Situation Subcommittee Report, Oct. 16, 1947, pp. 1–2, 6–7, 9, P & O 091 Greece (TS), sect. II-A, case 13, Army Staff Records, NA.

[14]Joseph Alsop, "Decide We Must," New York *Herald Tribune*, Oct. 20, 1947, p. 13; Lovett to embassy in Athens, Oct. 21, 1947, P & O 091 Greece (TS), sect. IV, case 48, Army Staff Records, NA; Chamberlin report to chief of staff, "The Greek Situation," Oct. 20, 1947, CD 2-1-6, p. 1, files of sec. of defense, NA; Wittner, *American Intervention in Greece*, 234.

[15]Chamberlin report, 1–2, 50. See also *Time*, Oct. 27, 1947, p. 25.

[16]Chamberlin report, 2–3; *Time*, Oct. 27, 1947, p. 25.

[17]Chamberlin report, 51.

[18]Ibid., 52–53.

[19]Ibid., 55.

[20]Ibid., 1, 53–57, 59, Enclosure 16, tab B, p. 1.

[21]Ibid., 56.

[22]Ibid., 55.

[23]Eisenhower memo to sec. of army, Oct. 22, 1947, CD 2-1-6, pp. 1–3, files of sec. of defense, NA. A copy of this memo is also in P & O 091 Greece (TS), sect. II, cases 8–17, pp. 1–3, Army Staff Records, NA.

[24]Draft memo by MacVeagh to Henderson, ca. Oct. 27, 1947, *FRUS*, V: *Near East and Africa*, 385–86.

[25]Admiral Sidney W. Souers, executive sec. of NSC, to NSC, Oct. 23, 1947 (encl. in Oct. 30, 1947), in ibid., 393–94; "Statement of Department's Position on Organization of America's Activities in Greece," Oct. 23, 1947 (attached to memo for President from Marshall, Nov. 3, 1947), Truman Papers, Confidential File, Truman Lib. This statement is also in P & O 091 Greece (TS), sect. II, cases 8–17, pp. 1–2, Army Staff Records, NA. Henderson and Lovett supported MacVeagh and were upset about Griswold's attempts to use economic leverage to interfere with the ambassador's authority in political matters. Lovett was particularly irritated by a *New York Times* article entitled, "Griswold, Most Powerful Man in Greece." See John O. Iatrides, ed., *Ambassador MacVeagh Reports: Greece, 1933–1947* (Princeton: Princeton U. Press, 1980), 725–28.

[26]Griswold to sec. of state, Oct. 24, 1947, *FRUS*, V: *Near East and Africa*, 378–79.

[27]Memo for chief of staff from Norstad, director, P & O, Oct. 22, 1947, P & O 091 Greece (TS), sect. II, cases 8–17, Army Staff Records, NA; draft letter from Forrestal, Oct. 24, 1947, brought before NSC on Oct. 27, 1947, *FRUS*, V: *Near East and Africa*, 377–78; Jernegan to Henderson, Oct. 27, 1947, ibid., 384; memo for NSC from Souers, Oct. 30, 1947, enclosure A, pp. 1–3, ABC 400.336, War Dept. Records (General and Special Staffs), NA; memo for President from Marshall, Nov. 3, 1947, Truman Papers, Confidential File, Truman Lib.

[28]Memo of briefing of House Armed Services and Appropriations Committee (on Oct. 27, 1947) by Col. Smith, Nov. 19, 1947, pp. 7–11, Livesay Papers, U.S. Army Military History Institute, Carlisle Military Barracks, Pa.

[29]Ibid., 12–13.

[30]Souers to NSC, Nov. 4, 1947, *FRUS*, V: *Near East and Africa*, 393 n. 4; Griswold to sec. of state, Nov. 4, 1947, ibid., 395–96; Marshall to embassy in Athens, Nov. 4, 1947, DSDF, NA.

[31]Lovett to Griswold, Oct. 29, 1947, *FRUS*, V: *Near East and Africa*, 390; note for record: "Increase in Greek National Army," by Goss, Nov. 5, 1947, P & O 091 Greece (TS), sect. I-A, case 3, pp. 1–15, Army Staff Records, NA; Livesay to director, P & O, Nov. 6, 1947, encl. in Monthly Historical Report (Oct.), USAGG, AMAG, P & O 091 Greece (TS), sect. V, cases 74–86, pp. 8–10, ibid. McGhee noted that the American military group in Athens had just made an agreement with the Greek government to give to the national guard $6 million earlier designated for the army. Memo by Jernegan of conversation, Oct. 28, 1947, *FRUS*, V: *Near East and Africa*, 387; recommendation for action by Wedemeyer, director, P & O, Nov. 5, 1947, P & O 091 Greece (TS), sect. I-A, case 3, Army Staff Records, NA. See Woodhouse, *Struggle for Greece*, 213.

[32]Livesay to director, P & O, Nov. 6, 1947, encl. in Monthly Historical Report (Oct.), USAGG, AMAG, P & O 091 Greece (TS), sect. V, cases 74–86, pp. 12–13, Army Staff Records, NA.

[33]Ibid., 13–15. See Woodhouse, *Struggle for Greece*, 210.

[34]Livesay to director, P & O, Nov. 6, 1947, encl. in Monthly Historical Report (Oct.), USAGG, AMAG, P & O 091 Greece (TS), sect. V, cases 74–86, pp. 4, 15–16, Army Staff Records, NA; Lincoln, *United States' Aid to Greece*, 44.

CHAPTER 6. THE JOINT U.S. MILITARY ADVISORY AND PLANNING GROUP

[1]Memo for Wedemeyer from Major Gen. W. H. Arnold, chief, Operations Group, P & O, Nov. 5, 1947, P & O 091 Greece (TS), sect. I-A, case 3, pp. 1–2, Army Staff Records, NA; note for record on JUSMAPG, Nov. 14, 1947, P & O 091 Greece (TS), sect. II-A, case 13, ibid.; Marshall to Griswold, Nov. 6, 1947, *FRUS*, V: *The Near East and Africa* (Wash., D.C.: GPO, 1971), 399; Joint Strategic Plans Committee (JSPC) 859—"Establishment of a Joint Advisory and Planning Group in Greece," Nov. 6, 1947, p. 5, ABC 400.336 Greece, sect. I-B, War Dept. Records, NA; memo for chief of staff, U.S. Army, from Schuyler, Nov. 4, 1947, ABC 400.336 Greece, sect. I-B, p. 1, ibid.; Marshall to Forrestal, Nov. 7, 1947, CD 6-1-23 (TS), files of sec. of defense, NA; Forrestal to Marshall, Nov. 10, 1947, ibid.; Marshall to embassy in Athens and AMAG, Nov. 7, 1947, Truman Papers, Confidential File, Truman Lib.; "USAFGG History," 11. Forrestal became secretary of defense after the National Security Act of 1947 created the National Military Establishment. Two years later, an amendment to the Act created the Department of Defense. See Allan R. Millett and Peter Maslowski, *For the Common Defense: A Military History of the United States of America* (N.Y.: Macmillan, 1984), 480–82.

[2]Walter Millis, ed., *The Forrestal Diaries* (N.Y.: Viking, 1951), entry for Nov. 7, 1947, p. 340; Royall to Vandenberg, Nov. 10, 1947, P & O 091 Greece (TS), sect. I-A, case 3, p. 1, Army Staff Records, NA; memo for record by Arnold, Nov. 13, 1947, P & O 091 Greece (TS), sect. I-A, case 3, p. 1, ibid., Captain J. B. Carter of U.S. Navy to Glover, Schuyler, and Brig. Gen. R. C. Lindsay, Nov. 10, 1947, ABC 400.336 Greece, sect. I-B, pp. 3, 6–7, 10, War Dept. Records, NA.

[3]Memo for record by Arnold, Nov. 13, 1947, P & O 091 Greece (TS), sect. I-A, case 3, pp. 1–2, Army Staff Records, NA.

[4]Griswold press conference with American press, Nov. 18, 1947, encl. in Griswold to sec. of state, Feb. 12, 1948, DSDF, NA. See also *New York Times*, Nov. 19, 1947, p. 10.

[5]Griswold press conference with American press, Nov. 18, 1947.

[6]Ibid.

[7]Ibid.

[8]Ibid.; press conf. of Nov. 21 encl. in Griswold to sec. of state, Jan. 21, 1948, DSDF, NA.

[9]Memo for Wedemeyer, Nov. 12, 1947, P & O 319.1 (TS), sect. IV-A, case 46, Army Staff Records, NA; Lieut. Col. T. J. Conway, acting chief, Strategic Plans Branch, to Wedemeyer, Dec. 1947, ibid. To counter the guerrillas, American advisers urged Wedemeyer to support the establishment of a "guerrilla warfare corps" and a "guerrilla warfare school" run by the American army. See [?] Biddle to Wedemeyer, March 3, 1948, P & O 319.1 Greece (TS), sect. IV-A, case 46, ibid. Memo for Glover, Lindsay, Carter, and sec., JSPC, from Schuyler, regarding "Greek Situation," Nov. 21, 1947, pp. 1–4, ABC 370.5 Greece-Italy, War Dept. Records, NA.

[10]Conference with Eisenhower, Nov. 14, 1947, P & O 091 Greece (TS), sect. I-A, case 3, Army Staff Records, NA; memo for record by Lieut. Col. Hartshorn regarding JCS 1798/1, Nov. 25, 1947, P & O 091 Greece (TS), sect. II, cases 8–17, ibid.

[11]Griswold to sec. of state, Nov. 13, 1947, *FRUS*, V: *Near East and Africa*, 402.

[12]Griswold to sec. of state, Nov. 14, 1947, Truman Papers, Confidential File, Truman Lib.

[13]Ibid.

[14]Ibid.

[15]Sec. of state to embassy in Athens, Nov. 15, 1947, *FRUS*, V: *Near East and Africa*, 408; Henderson and McGhee to Lovett, Nov. 18, 1947, ibid., 411–12.

[16]John O. Iatrides, ed., *Ambassador MacVeagh Reports: Greece, 1933–1947* (Princeton: Princeton U. Press, 1980), 717, 725; *New York Times*, Nov. 21, 1947, p. 19.

[17]Keeley to sec. of state, Nov. 18, 1947, DSDF, NA.

[18]Lovett to Griswold, Nov. 20, 1947, *FRUS*, V: *Near East and Africa*, 416–17; memo for secs. of defense, army, navy, air force, and chman. of National Security Resources Board, Dec. 5, 1947, CD 6-1-29, files of sec. of defense, NA; memo for President from Lovett, Nov. 24, 1947, Truman Papers, Confidential File, Truman Lib.

[19]Iatrides, ed., *Ambassador MacVeagh Reports*, 731; Griswold press conference of Nov. 21, 1947, encl. in Griswold to sec. of state, Jan. 21, 1948, DSDF, NA; Lawrence S. Wittner, *American Intervention in Greece, 1943–1949* (N.Y.: Columbia U. Press, 1982), 118. Stefan left for Athens on November 21. See *New York Times*, Nov. 21, 1947, p. 19.

[20]Lovett to Griswold, Nov. 20, 1947, *FRUS*, V: *Near East and Africa*, 417; Wittner, *American Intervention in Greece*, 118; author's interview with Henderson, May 24, 1979; Henderson to John O. Iatrides, Sept. 23, 1972, Henderson Papers, box 8: Greece folder, MS Divis., LC; Iatrides, ed., *Ambassador MacVeagh Reports*, 732; *New York Times*, Nov. 22, 1947, cited in ibid. MacVeagh was reassigned to Portugal. A few months after his recall from Greece, MacVeagh wrote his brother that "if we subordinate our experts all around Europe to the interruption and interference and dictation of politically ambitious amateurs, we certainly are heading for disaster." March 1948 letter quoted in ibid., 734 n. 27.

[21]CIA Report 2, "Review of the World Situation as It Relates to the Security of the United States," Nov. 14, 1947, pp. 1, 5; Wittner, *American Intervention in Greece*, 259. The CIA also warned that even though Iran had recently turned down the Soviet proposal for an oil concession, the United States must give as much aid consideration to that country as it was doing with Greece and Turkey. The Soviets had reacted mildly to the rejection, but this was deceptive. The CIA believed that the Soviets would probably increase their subversive activities in Iran in an effort to force that country into the Soviet alliance system. CIA Report 2, p. 5.

[22]Memo by Jernegan, Nov. 17, 1947, *FRUS*, V: *Near East and Africa*, 408–9; DS office memo (from [?] Mangano) to Jernegan, Dec. 16, 1947, DSDF, NA. Michael R. Wright of the British Foreign Office agreed with Henderson that Anglo-American safety was dependent on keeping Greece, Turkey, Iran, and Italy from Russian control. The Joint Chiefs of Staff affirmed that the Near East and eastern Mediterranean were of "critical importance to the future security of the U.S." See Forrestal diaries, entry of Nov. 7, 1947, p. 1916, Operations Archives, Naval History Divis., Wash., D.C. (photocopies of originals at Princeton U.); Leahy diaries, entry of Nov. 19, 1947, Leahy Papers, MS Divis., LC.

[23]"Report of the UNSCOB," Nov. 21, 25, 26, 28, 29, Dec. 1, 8, 23, 1947, UNGA, *Official Records*, 3 sess., 1948, suppl. 8, pp. 2, 3, 5; "Special Balkan Committee," Nov. 21, 25–29, Dec. 2, 1947, Acheson Papers, box 6, file on Marshall Plan—reports, Greece & Turkey, Truman Lib.; Harry N. Howard, "Greece and Its Balkan Neighbors (1948–1949): The United Nations Attempts at Conciliation," *Balkan Studies* 7 (1966): 3.

[24]Lovett to sec. of state, Nov. 25, 1947, *FRUS*, V: *Near East and Africa*, 419–20; Keeley to sec. of state, Dec. 3, 1947, ibid., 433–34; Lovett to embassy in London, Dec. 11, 1947, ibid., 452; Lovett to embassy in Athens, Nov. 25, 1947, DSDF, NA; Weekly Report of AMAG to DS, Dec. 9, 1947, ibid.

[25]Douglas to sec. of state, Dec. 13, 1947, *FRUS*, V: *Near East and Africa*, 453; Douglas to sec. of state, Dec. 17, 1947, ibid., 456–57. As noted earlier, the British had expressed interest in parallel policies during the Pentagon Talks in Washington from mid-October to early November 1947. Inverchapel and Lovett led the discussions. A British memo referred to the Middle East and eastern Mediterranean forming a "strategic whole." See F.O. minute by Michael R. Wright, assistant undersec. of state, record of talks from Oct. 16–Nov. 7, 1947, FO 371, vol. 61114, AN 3997/3997/45, and British memo (n.d.), AN 3999, PRO.

[26]Lovett to AMAG, Nov. 26, 1947, ibid., 422–23.

[27]Eisenhower to Morgan, Dec. 4, 1947, P & O 091 Greece (TS), sect. I-A, case 3, pp. 1–2, Army

Staff Records, NA; Livesay to Wedemeyer, Dec. 5, 1947, P & O 400 Greece, sect. I, case 1, ibid.; Gibson to sec. of state, Nov. 22, 25, Dec. 6, 1947, DSDF, NA.

[28]Keeley to sec. of state, Dec. 8, 1947, *FRUS*, V: *Near East and Africa*, 438-39; memo by Political Section of embassy in Athens, Dec. 6, 1947, encl. in ibid., 440-49.

[29]A. C. Sedgwick, "Communists Form 'Free' Government in North of Greece," *New York Times*, Dec. 25, 1947, p. 1; "Report of the UNSCOB," Dec. 22, 24-25, 27-28, 1947, Jan. 2, 1948, UNGA, *Official Records*, 3 sess., 1948, suppl. 8, pp. 14-16, 15 n. 126; Rankin to sec. of state, Dec. 24, 1947, *FRUS*, V: *Near East and Africa*, 462-64; memo by Jernegan of conversation (meeting between DS officers and Livesay), Dec. 26, 1947, ibid., 466-69; Smith to sec. of state, Dec. 27, 1947, ibid., 470; Sedgwick, "Broadcast from Belgrade," *New York Times*, Dec. 17, 1947, p. 14; Greek embassy in Wash., D.C., to DS, Dec. 26, 1947, DSDF, NA; "The Greek Challenge," London *Times* editorial, Dec. 31, 1947; "Greece," Manchester *Guardian* editorial, Dec. 31, 1947; "Greek Guerrillas Hold the Tactical Advantage," in ibid. All three articles enclosed in James C. Sappington, first sec. of embassy in London, to sec. of state, Dec. 31, 1947, ibid. "History of JUSMAGG," 64; Sedgwick, "Rebels' Offensive in Epirus Is Held By Greece's Army," *New York Times*, Dec. 27, 1947, p. 6. The stated objectives of Free Greece were: liberation of the country from imperialists; "popular justice," equality of minorities, and the establishment of a democratic state; free elections for a "People's National Assembly"; agrarian reform; organization of a "democratic army, fleet and air force"; "specially friendly relations with [the] Soviet Union, Balkan democracies[,] and other democratic states." See Edgar O'Ballance, *The Greek Civil War, 1944-1949* (N.Y.: Praeger, 1966), 158-60, 159 n.2; Christopher M. Woodhouse, *The Struggle for Greece, 1941-1949* (Brooklyn Heights, N.Y.: Beekman-Esanu, 1976), 218-21.

[30]Cyrus L. Sulzberger, "Rebel Manifesto in Greece Likely," *New York Times*, Dec. 17, 1947, p. 14; *Time*, Jan. 5, 1948, pp. 31-32; Sulzberger, "'Free Greece' Declaration Held Chiefly Propaganda," *New York Times*, Dec. 25, 1947, p. 24; "Truman or Stalin in Greece," *Nation*, Jan. 3, 1948, pp. 4-5.

[31]Woodhouse, *The Struggle for Greece*, 218-21; O'Ballance, *The Greek Civil War*, 161; Evangelos Averoff-Tossizza, *By Fire and Axe: The Communist Party and the Civil War in Greece, 1944-1949* (New Rochelle, N.Y.: Caratzas Brothers, 1978), 246. Originally published as *Le Feu et la hache Grèce '46-'49, histoire des guerres de l'après-guerre* (Paris: Editions de Breteuil, 1973). Trans. by Sarah Arnold Rigos. Dominique Eudes, *The Kapetanios: Partisans and Civil War in Greece, 1943-1949* (N.Y.: Monthly Review Press, 1972), 308-9. Originally published as *Les Kapetanios: La guerre civile grecque de 1943 à 1949* (Paris: Librarie Arthème Fayard, 1970). Trans. by John Howe. Sedgwick, "Rebels' Offensive in Epirus Is Held by Greece's Army," *New York Times*, Dec. 17, 1947, p. 1; *Time*, Jan. 5, 1948, p. 31; Heinz Richter, *British Intervention in Greece: From Varkiza to Civil War, February 1945 to August 1946* (London: Merlin, 1985), 491; Dimitrios G. Kousoulas, *Revolution and Defeat: The Story of the Greek Communist Party* (London: Oxford U. Press, 1965), 249-50.

[32]Eudes claims this division within the KKE was "the beginning of the end for the Democratic Army." *Kapetanios*, 303. Markos and Zahariadis quoted in ibid., 304-5. Because of his KKE sympathies, Eudes is not regarded as a reputable source by all writers. See Ole L. Smith, "Self-Defence and Communist Policy, 1945-1947," in Lars Baerentzen, John O. Iatrides, and Ole L. Smith, eds., *Studies in the History of the Greek Civil War, 1945-1949* (Copenhagen, Denmark: Museum Tusculanum Press, 1987), 161 n.8, 168 n.35. Eudes's account of the Markos-Zahariadis battle, however, fits succeeding events and therefore seems credible.

[33]Woodhouse, *The Struggle for Greece*, 177; Wittner, *American Intervention in Greece*, 155; Bickham Sweet-Escott, *Greece: A Political and Economic Survey, 1939-1953* (London: Royal Institute of International Affairs, 1954), 72; William H. McNeill, *Greece: American Aid in Action, 1947-1956* (N.Y.: Twentieth Century Fund, 1957), 198; Eudes, *Kapetanios*, 245, 359; *Time*, Jan. 5, 1948, p. 32; Francis F. Lincoln, *United States' Aid to Greece, 1947-1962* (Germantown, Tenn.: Professional Seminars, 1975), 55. The Greek government repealed the anti-strike law in May 1948. Wittner, *American Intervention in Greece*, 210.

34Memo by Jernegan of conversation (meeting between DS officers and Livesay), Dec. 26, 1947, *FRUS*, V: *Near East and Africa*, 466–69.

35Memo for Wedemeyer from T.W.P.[?]: "State Department Views Reference Greek Problem," Dec. 29, 1947, P & O 091 Greece (TS), sect. II, cases 8–17, pp. 1–2, Army Staff Records, NA.

36See Kennan, "The Sources of Soviet Conduct," *Foreign Affairs* 25 (July 1947): 566–82; author's interview with Henderson.

37Lovett to embassy in Belgrade, Dec. 27, 1947, *FRUS*, V: *Near East and Africa*, 471–72; Henderson to acting sec. of state, Dec. 29, 1947, ibid., 472–74; Lovett to AMAG, Dec. 30, 1947, ibid., 478; Henderson to Rankin, Dec. 31, 1947, ibid., 480–84; "Report of UNSCOB," Dec. 29, 1947, UNGA, *Official Records*, 3 sess., 1948, suppl. 8, p. 15. By the end of 1947, the Greek government's forces totaled about 232,500 men: 150,000 in the army; 50,000 in the National Defense Corps; 25,000 in the gendarmerie; and 7,500 in the civil police. M. A. Campbell et al., *The Employment of Airpower in the Greek Guerrilla War, 1947–1949* (Montgomery, Ala.: Air U., Maxwell AFB, 1964), 24.

38Royall to Forrestal, Dec. 31, 1947, CD 6-1-29, files of sec. of defense, NA; JCS 1798/3: "Proposed Joint U.S. Military Advisory and Planning Group in Greece," Dec. 2, 1947, pp. 1, 151–52, 154–55, encl. in memo for sec. of defense from Leahy, CD 6-1-29 (TS), ibid.; JCS 1798/3: JCS decision on JCS 1798/3—"Establishment of a Joint U.S. Military Advisory and Planning Group in Greece," Dec. 2, 1947, ABC 400.336 Greece, sect. I-B, pp. 1, 146–48, War Dept. Records, NA; "USAFGG History," 5–25; "History of JUSMAPG" (1 Jan. 48–31 Aug. 49), pp. 1–3, 65, P & O Geog L, Greece 314.7 JUSMAPG, Reports and Records Section (15 Sept. 49), Army Staff Records, NA; memo for chief of staff, U.S. Army, from Wedemeyer, Feb. 6, 1948, P & O 091 Greece (TS), sect. I-A, case 3, ibid.; Lovett to embassy in Athens, Dec. 6, 1947, *FRUS*, V: *Near East and Africa*, 436; Forrestal to Marshall, Jan. 5, 1948, ibid., 480; Campbell et al., *Employment of Airpower in Greek Guerrilla War*, 64; Lincoln, *United States' Aid to Greece*, 45.

39Kenneth Matthews, *Memories of a Mountain War Greece: 1944–1949* (London: Longman, 1972), 177; Woodhouse, *The Struggle for Greece*, 221–22; Kousoulas, *Revolution and Defeat*, 249; *Time*, Jan. 5, 1948, p. 31; Robert Low (the correspondent), "The Battle for Greece," *Time*, Nov. 17, 1947, p. 37; Lincoln, *United States' Aid to Greece*, 54.

CHAPTER 7.   COROLLARIES OF A GLOBAL STRATEGY

1Marshall to Griswold, Jan. 12, 1948, *FRUS*, IV: *Eastern Europe: The Soviet Union* (Wash., D.C.: GPO, 1974), 26; Griswold to sec. of state, Jan. 13, 1948, ibid., 27–28; Livesay to director, P & O , Jan. 31, 1948, encl. in Monthly Historical Report (Jan.), USAGG, Feb. 10, 1948, P & O 091 Greece (TS), sect. V, cases 74–86, pp. 5–6, Army Staff Records, NA; memo for DS from sec. of army, Jan. 23, 1948, p. 1, P & O 091 Greece (TS), sect. II, cases 8–17, ibid.; Oral History Interview with Clifford (March 1971–Feb. 1973), Truman Lib.; "History of JUSMAPG" (1 Jan. 48–31 Aug. 49), map insert following p. 3, P & O Geog L, Greece 314.7 JUSMAPG, Reports & Records Section (15 Sept. 49), Army Staff Records, NA; Christopher M. Woodhouse, *The Struggle for Greece, 1941–1949* (Brooklyn Heights, N.Y.: Beekman-Esanu, 1976), 226.

2Dominique Eudes, *The Kapetanios: Partisans and Civil War in Greece, 1943–1949* (N.Y.: Monthly Review Press, 1972), 309. Originally published as *Les Kapetanios: La Guerre civile grecque de 1943 à 1949* (Paris: Librarie Arthème Fayard, 1970). Trans. by John Howe. Evangelos Averoff-Tossizza, *By Fire and Axe: The Communist Party and the Civil War in Greece, 1944–1949* (New Rochelle, N.Y.: Caratzas Brothers, 1978), 254. Originally published as *Le Feu et la hache grèce '46–'49, histoire des guerres de l'après-guerre* (Paris: Editions de Breteuil, 1973). Trans. by Sarah Arnold Rigos. Edgar O'Ballance, *The Greek Civil War, 1944–1949* (N.Y.: Praeger, 1966), 162–63; Francis F. Lincoln, *United States' Aid to Greece, 1947–1962* (Germantown, Tenn.: Professional Seminars, 1975), 64; Woodhouse, *Struggle for Greece*, 221–22, 226, 233; *Time*, Jan. 12, 1948, p. 22. Averoff calls the Greek army's victories at Konitsa and Metsovon the "turning point" of the war because their outcomes led to internal conflict between the communists' political and military leaders. *By Fire and Axe*, 253.

[3]Averoff-Tossizza, *By Fire and Axe*, 253–55; Woodhouse, *Struggle for Greece*, 226.

[4]"Report of the UNSCOB," early Jan. 1948, UNGA, *Official Records*, 3 sess., 1948, suppl. 8, pp. 10, 15, 17–18.

[5]Ibid., Jan. 10–March 1948, p. 17.

[6]Ibid., early Jan. 1948, p. 16.

[7]Ibid., Jan.-mid–April 1948, p. 20.

[8]Ibid.; Cannon to sec. of state, Jan. 3, 1948, *FRUS*, IV: *Eastern Europe; Soviet Union*, 1055–56; Lovett to legations in Rumania et al., Jan. 3, 1948, ibid., 223. Lovett sent a copy of the note to Ankara, Athens, Belgrade, Bucharest, Budapest, London, Moscow, Paris, Praha, Rome, Salonika, Sofia, and Warsaw. He also sent one to the UN Special Committee on the Balkans. See also Lawrence S. Wittner, *American Intervention in Greece, 1943–1949* (N.Y.: Columbia U. Press, 1982), 7–8.

[9]Livesay to director, P & O, Jan. 31, 1948, encl. in Monthly Historical Report (Jan.), USAGG, Feb. 10, 1948, P & O 091 Greece (TS), sect. V, cases 74–86, p. 2, Army Staff Records, NA; memo to commanding general from Col. M. R. Kammerer, Infantry, P & O, JUSMAPG, Athens, Feb. 20, 1948, Livesay Papers, U.S. Army Military History Institute, Carlisle Military Barracks, Pa.; M. A. Campbell et al., *The Employment of Airpower in the Greek Guerrilla War, 1947–1949* (Montgomery, Ala.: Air U., Maxwell AFB, 1964), 34–41, 55–56, 66–69. Though the Wellington was the principal bomber used by Britain's Royal Air Force in the initial stages of World War II, this twin-engine plane was effective only against specific targets and not for bombing large areas. The RHAF found the Wellington useless in the guerrilla war and ordered it grounded. Ibid., 67. See also *New York Times*, June 20, 1948, p. 48, and Aug. 1, 1948, p. 4.

[10]Campbell et al., *Employment of Airpower in Greek Guerrilla War*, pp. 36–39, 48 n.70, 55–56.

[11]Memo to chief, Air Section, JUSMAPG, from Russell, Jan. 5, 1948, p. 1, JUSMAPG, Air Adjutant Section 471—Ammunition (Napalm), NA. John O. Iatrides noted that the question of napalm use was an emotional issue for the Greeks and is not mentioned in the official history of the civil war prepared by the Greek army staff. Letter from Iatrides to author, Aug. 23, 1987. See also Iatrides, "Civil War, 1945–1949: National and International Aspects," in Iatrides, ed., *Greece in the 1940s: A Nation in Crisis* (Hanover, N.H.: U. Press of New England, 1981), 391 n.87.

[12]Livesay to Wedemeyer, Jan. 15, 1948, P & O 091 Greece, sect. VI, case 73, Army Staff Records, NA; Livesay to director, P & O, Jan. 31, 1948, encl. in Monthly Historical Report (Jan.), USAGG, Feb. 10, 1948, p. 1, P & O 091 Greece (TS), sect. III, cases 18–25, ibid.; Livesay to director, P & O, Jan. 1948, encl. in Monthly Historical Report (Jan.), USAGG, Feb. 10, 1948, pp. 2–3, 6, P & O 091 Greece (TS), sect. V, cases 74–86, ibid.; memo for DS from sec. of army, Jan. 23, 1948, p. 2, P & O 091 Greece (TS), sect. II, cases 8–17, ibid.; Campbell et al., *Employment of Airpower in Greek Guerrilla War*, 47–48 n.68; Griswold to sec. of state, Jan. 29, 1948, *FRUS*, IV: *Eastern Europe; Soviet Union*, 37–38.

[13]Livesay's address to Amer. advisers to Greek army, Jan. 16, 1948, pp. 1–2, 6–7, Livesay Papers, U.S. Army Military History Institute, Carlisle Military Barracks, Pa. Livesay and others had become concerned over sharing information with the Greeks, and devised a system whereby the word "Henley" would be stamped on papers the Greeks were not to see. Ibid., 7.

[14]Ibid., 2–8. See also Griswold press conference on Jan. 16, 1948, encl. in Griswold to sec. of state, Jan. 21, 1948, DSDF, NA.

[15]Quoted excerpts from UP story in "Note for Record," Feb. 11, 1948, in P & O 000.7 (TS), sect. I, case 1, Army Staff Records, NA. See also *New York Times*, Feb. 13, 1948, p. 11. Polk

quote in Rankin to sec. of state, Feb. 13, 1948, DSDF, NA; Constantine Poulos, "The Lesson of Greece," *Nation*, March 27, 1948, pp. 343–45. Later that month of February, Major Morell Saxton, assigned to a Greek division in the mountains, was "hugging cold mother earth as guerrilla machine-gun bullets fanned the air above." In another incident reported by the Chicago *Daily News* correspondent on the spot, an unnamed American officer was told that a village taken by the advancing Greek army was friendly to the guerrillas. "'Well,' said the practical Yank, 'burn the village.'" Both incidents cited in ibid., 343.

16"Note for Record," Feb. 11, 1948, in P & O 000.7 (TS), sect. I, case 1, Army Staff Records, NA; Col. Richard W. Mayo, chief, Overseas Branch, P & O, to USAGG and JUSMAPG, Feb. 11, 1948, ibid.

17Mayo to USAGG and JUSMAPG, Feb. 11, 1948, ibid.; Regnier to commanding general, USAMPG, Athens, Feb. 12, 1948, encl. in ibid.

18Cyrus L. Sulzberger, *A Long Row of Candles: Memoirs and Diaries [1934–1954]* (N.Y.: Macmillan, 1969), 394; Woodhouse, *Struggle for Greece*, 260–61; *New York Times*, Feb. 13, 1948, p. 11.

19Report to NSC by Souers regarding NSC 5: "The Position of the United States with Respect to Greece," Jan. 6, 1948, *FRUS*, IV: *Eastern Europe; Soviet Union*, 2–7; NSC 5, ibid., 3–4; JCS 1826/3—"The Position of the United States with Respect to Greece," Feb. 3, 1948, pp. 46–52, P & O 091 Greece (TS), folder ABC 370.5 Greece, Army Staff Records, NA; memo for sec. of defense from Robert Blum, Feb. 3, 1948, CD 6-1-21 (TS), files of sec. of defense, NA; CIA Reports, ORE 69, "Possible Consequences of Communist Control of Greece in the Absence of U.S. Counteraction," Feb. 9, 1948, p. 1, Truman Papers, President's Secretary's Files, Truman Lib.; CIA Reports, ORE 69, pp. 1–3, 6–7, 9.

20NSC 5, *FRUS*, IV: *Eastern Europe; Soviet Union*, 7.

21JCS to Forrestal, Jan. 8, 1948, ibid., 8–9; Henderson to sec. of state, Jan. 9, 1948, ibid., 14; NSC 5/2: Report by NSC to Truman—"The Position of the United States with Respect to Greece," Feb. 12, 1948, ibid., 47–48; Souers to NSC, Feb. 16, 1948, OSA 091 Greece, P & O Greece (TS), Army Staff Records, NA; memo for sec. of defense from Blum, Jan. 8, 1948, p. 3, CD 6-1-21, files of sec. of defense, NA; memo for sec. of army from Wedemeyer, Jan. 9, 1948, ABC 370.5 Greece-Italy, sect. I-B, War Dept. Records, NA.

22Memo by Henderson to sec. of state, Jan. 9, 1948, *FRUS*, IV: *Eastern Europe; Soviet Union*, 10, 12–13; memo from Henderson to William J. McWilliams, asst. director of Executive Secretariat, Feb. 10, 1948, ibid., 39–40.

23Memo by Henderson to sec. of state, Jan. 9, 1948, ibid., 11–12; memo by Henderson of conversation with Vassili Dendramis (the ambassador), Feb. 20, 1948, ibid., 54. See also address by Henderson before Kentucky Women's Action Committee Forum, Feb. 18, 1948, pp. 2, 4, 6, 8–12, in Jones Papers, Truman Lib.

24Report prepared by Policy Planning Staff, PPS/18—"United States Policy with Respect to Greece," Jan. 10, 1948, *FRUS*, IV: *Eastern Europe; Soviet Union*, 22–26; memo by Kennan, Jan. 13, 1948, ibid., 27; memo by Thompson to Henderson, Jan. 9, 1948, ibid., 15; memo by Gross to McWilliams and Rusk, Jan. 9, 1948, ibid, 15–17.

25Marshall to AMAG, Jan. 12, 1948, ibid., 26; memo for sec. of defense from John H. Ohly, Jan. 12, 1948, pp. 1–3, CD 6-1-21, files of sec. of defense, NA.

26CINCNANEAST LANTMED, Admiral [?] Conolly, to COMNAVMED, Admiral [?] Bieri, Jan. 1, 1948, JCS—Leahy files, JCS Info Line/Messages on U.S. Policy on Greece—Messages between CNO & Greece, NA; memo for Truman by Rear Admiral R. H. Hillenkoetter, former director of CIG, Jan. 2, 1948, Truman Papers, President's Secretary's File, Truman Lib.; Stephen G. Xydis, *Greece and the Great Powers, 1944–1947: Prelude to the "Truman Doctrine"* (Thessaloniki: Institute for Balkan Studies, 1963), 540–41; Vladimir Dedijer, *Tito* (N.Y.: Simon & Schuster, 1953), 321–22; Wittner, *American Intervention in Greece*, 58–59. Lovett instructed the

American representative on the UN Special Committee on the Balkans, Alan G. Kirk (ambassador to Belgium), that if any government announced recognition of the Markos junta, he was to arrange a resolution condemning the action as contrary to the General Assembly resolution of October 21, 1947. Lovett to Kirk, Jan. 3, 1948, *FRUS*, IV: *Eastern Europe; Soviet Union*, 222.

[27]Marshall to certain Amer. missions, Jan. 12, 1948, box 2485, Athens Post Records, FRC; Dedijer, *Tito*, 316–17; Dimitrios G. Kousoulas, "The Truman Doctrine and the Stalin-Tito Rift: A Reappraisal," *South Atlantic Quarterly* 72 (Summer 1973): 430–32; Evangelos Kofos, *Nationalism and Communism in Macedonia* (Thessaloniki: Institute for Balkan Studies, 1964), 164.

[28]Dimitrios G. Kousoulas, *Revolution and Defeat: The Story of the Greek Communist Party* (London: Oxford U. Press, 1965), 250; Eudes, *Kapetanios*, 310; Vladimir Dedijer, *The Battle Stalin Lost: Memoirs of Yugoslavia, 1948–1953* (N.Y.: Viking, 1971), 269–70; Svetozar Vukmanović-Tempo, *How and Why the People's Liberation Struggle of Greece Met with Defeat* (London: Merritt & Hatcher, 1950), 3; Milovan Djilas, *Conversations with Stalin* (N.Y.: Harcourt, Brace, 1962), 131–32, 181–82; Kousoulas, "Truman Doctrine and Stalin-Tito Rift," 429–30; Dimitrios G. Kousoulas, *The Price of Freedom: Greece in World Affairs, 1939–1953* (Syracuse, N.Y.: Syracuse U. Press, 1953), 176. Djilas was among the Yugoslav representatives. Dedijer claims that Stalin sent a telegram to the Yugoslavs in March 1947, praising them for helping the Greek guerrillas. If so, Elisabeth Barker warns, this did *not* mean that Stalin was willing to send aid. And, she adds, the telegram was probably sent either before the Truman Doctrine was announced, or certainly before American assistance had begun to take effect. Barker, "The Yugoslavs and the Greek Civil War, 1946–1949," in Lars Baerentzen, John O. Iatrides, and Ole L. Smith, eds., *Studies in the History of the Greek Civil War, 1945–1949* (Copenhagen, Denmark: Museum Tusculanum Press, 1987), 304–5.

[29]Dedijer, *Tito*, 316–22; Dedijer, *Battle Stalin Lost*, 68–69; Kousoulas, "Truman Doctrine and Stalin-Tito Rift," 430–32; Djilas, *Conversations with Stalin*, 181–82. Elisabeth Barker believes Djilas's account reliable. See her essay entitled "Yugoslav Policy towards Greece, 1947–1949," in Baerentzen, Iatrides, and Smith, eds., *Studies in the History of the Greek Civil War*, 273.

[30]Djilas, *Conversations with Stalin*, 131–32, 181–82; Kousoulas, "Truman Doctrine and Stalin-Tito Rift," 430–31. J. M. MacKintosh sees no evidence of Soviet responsibility for the beginning of guerrilla operations in 1946. "But there can be no doubt about the Soviet attempt to exploit the situation." See his *Strategy and Tactics of Soviet Foreign Policy* (London: Oxford U. Press, 1962), 11.

[31]"Russian Short Term Intentions in Greece," Feb. 4, 1948, encl. in memo for Leahy, Gen. Carl A. Spaatz, Admiral Louis Denfeld, and Gen. Omar Bradley, Feb. 26, 1948, pp. 1–3, 5, P & O 091 Greece (TS), sect. V. cases 74–86, Army Staff Records, NA.

[32]Ibid.

[33]Marshall to AMAG, Jan. 26, 1948, *FRUS*, IV: *Eastern Europe; Soviet Union*, 36–37; Marshall to embassy in Athens and AMAG, Feb. 5, 1948, ibid., 37 n.3; Griswold to sec. of state, Feb. 6, 1948, ibid., 37 n.3; Edwin P. Curtin (lieut. col.), "American Advisory Group Aids Greece in War on Guerrillas," *Armed Cavalry Journal* 58 (Jan.-Feb., 1949): 9; memo for DS from Lt. Col. Benjamin F. Taylor, Feb. 10, 1948, P & O 091 Greece, Army Staff Records, NA; memo for record (no author given), Feb. 11, 1948, P & O 091 Greece (TS), sect. I-A, case 3, ibid.; tab "E", sub-no. 13, Feb. 10, 1948, P & O 391.1 Greece (TS), sect. IV-A, case 46, ibid.; "History of JUSMAPG," 3, ibid.; Eisenhower to Marshall, Jan. 7, 1948, DSDF, NA; memo for chief of staff, U.S. Army, from Wedemeyer, Feb. 6, 1948, ABC 400.336 Greece, sect. I-B, War Dept. Records, NA; JCS 1798/6—memo by chief of staff, U.S. Army, to JCS, Feb. 10, 1948, p. 160, ABC 400.336 Greece, sect. I-B, ibid.

[34]*Time*, April 5, 1948, p. 26, and May 23, 1949, p. 28; memo for chief of staff, U.S. Army, from Wedemeyer, Feb. 5, 1948: JCS 1826/2—"Outline Plans for the Dispatch on Short Notice of United States Forces to Greece and for Their Deployment in That Country," ABC 370.5 Greece-

Italy, sect. I-B, War Dept. Records, NA; memo from S. Shepard Jones of Public Studies Division, DS, to McGhee, Feb. 16, 1948, with enclosure: Telegraphic Public Opinion Survey Conducted by the National Opinion Research Center (survey done Feb. 11–13, 1948), DSDF, NA. Van Fleet's work was cut out for him. One of America's advisers, Major Winston W. Ehrgott, had wanted to observe a Greek cavalry patrol at night. The Greek colonel offered him cognac and remarked that he was surely joking: "We never move cavalry at night. Horses fall down; you might run into ambushes." Ehrgott, however, finally convinced the colonel to send fifty cavalrymen into eastern Thrace. Ehrgott accompanied them and was unarmed, but the Greeks had rifles, Bren guns, and Tommy guns. Their arrival amazed the inhabitants of villages, who hung out windows, gaping as the troops went by. On a starlit night, Ehrgott was shocked to see the soldier at point riding a readily visible white horse; no security guards on the flanks; officers smoking cigarettes; and men talking loudly. The Greek patrol was inviting an ambush. In one almost deserted village, the soldiers' arrival caused dogs to bark, and from one house a light went on. When the Greek captain knocked, a woman called out, "Is that you, comrade? and opened the door enough to shove out two loaves of bread. She thought the Greek soldiers were guerrillas. Ehrgott, frustrated, asked where they could find the guerrillas. The Greek captain shrugged and said: "Everywhere—and nowhere." *Time*, Feb. 23, 1948, p. 35.

35Meeting of NSC, Feb. 12, 1948, summarized in Forrestal diaries, pp. 2069–71, Operational Archives, Naval History Divis., Wash., D.C. (photocopies of originals at Princeton U.); memo for Wedemeyer from Schuyler, Feb. 20, 1948, P & O 091 Greece (TS), sect. VII, case 93, Army Staff Records, NA; memo for JCS from Souers, Feb. 24, 1948, pp. 1–2, plus enclosure: "Comments on Certain Courses of Action Proposed with Respect to Greece and Answers to Specific Questions Contained in the Memorandum by the Secretary of the National Security Council dated 24 February 1948," pp. 1, 3, CD 6-1-21, files of sec. of defense, NA.

36JCS 1826/2, Jan. 29, 1948—Report by the JSPC to JCS on "Outline Plans for the Dispatch on Short Notice of United States Forces to Greece and for Their Deployment in That Country," 33–35, approved by JCS on Feb. 24, 1948, ABC 370.5 Greece-Italy, sect. I-B, War Dept. Records, NA; "Comments on Certain Courses of Action Proposed with Respect to Greece," 2–4.

37"Comments on Certain Courses of Action Proposed with Respect to Greece," 7–8.

38Woodhouse, *Struggle for Greece*, 237–38; McGhee to Marshall, Feb. 24, 1948, DSDF, NA; Zervas to Sophoulis, Dec. 22, 1947, encl. in Rankin to sec. of state, Jan. 28, 1948, ibid. American military goods sent to Greece included forage, rations, clothing, ammunition, petroleum, animals and heavy transportation equipment, mountain artillery, machine guns, mortars, howitzers, rifles, pistols, signal items, and aircraft. The United States also assumed responsibility for the maintenance of British goods previously furnished to the Greek fighting units. The use of British maintenance materials already in Greece alleviated the need for major replacements throughout the remainder of the year. Griswold again emphasized that "the economic front must be held while the military battle is being won." "History of JUSMAGG," 2; memo to commanding general from Kammerer, Feb. 20, 1948, Livesay Papers, U.S. Army Military History Institute, Carlisle Military Barracks, Pa.; memo of oral statement to Sophoulis and Tsaldaris by Griswold, on Jan. 5, 1948, encl. in Griswold to sec. of state, Jan. 7, 1948, DSDF, NA; Griswold to sec. of state, Jan. 14, 1948, *FRUS*, IV: *Eastern Europe; Soviet Union*, 28–29.

CHAPTER 8. THE GREEK CHILDREN

1See Howard Jones, "The Diplomacy of Restraint: The United States' Efforts to Repatriate Greek Children Evacuated During the Civil War of 1946–49," *Journal of Modern Greek Studies* 3 (May 1985): 65–85. For the Greeks' references to the removals of the 1940s as *paedomazoma*, see Amer. embassy in Athens to sec. of state, April 17, 1948, Athens Post Records, Confidential File, 1948: 624.4-800, box 20, Military Intelligence, FRC. See also Lars Baerentzen, "The

'Paidomazoma' and the Queen's Camps," in Lars Baerentzen, John O. Iatrides, and Ole L. Smith, eds., *Studies in the History of the Greek Civil War, 1945–1949* (Copenhagen, Denmark: Museum Tusculanum Press, 1987); 127–57.

[2]Brief accounts of the practice are in: Bickham Sweet-Escott, *Greece: A Political and Economic Survey, 1939–1953* (London: Royal Institute of International Affairs, 1954), 71–72; Edgar O'Ballance, *The Greek Civil War, 1944–1949* (N.Y.: Praeger, 1966), 169; John Campbell, "The Greek Civil War," in Evan Luard, ed., *The International Regulation of Civil Wars* (N.Y.: N.Y.U. Press, 1972), 52; Kenneth Matthews, *Memories of a Mountain War Greece: 1944–1949* (London: Longman, 1972), 177–83; Christopher M. Woodhouse, *The Struggle for Greece, 1941–1949* (Brooklyn Heights, N.Y.: Beekman-Esanu, 1976), 249-50; Evangelos Averoff-Tossizza, *By Fire and Axe: The Communist Party and the Civil War in Greece, 1944–1949* (New Rochelle, N.Y.: Caratzas Brothers, 1978), 260–62, 269. Originally published as *Le Feu et la hache grèce '46–'49, histoire des guerres de l'après-guerre* (Paris: Editions de Breteuil, 1973). Trans. by Sarah Arnold Rigos. Lawrence S. Wittner, "The Truman Doctrine and the Defense of Freedom," *Diplomatic History* 4 (Spring 1980): 183–84; Wittner, *American Intervention in Greece, 1943–1949* (N.Y.: Columbia U. Press, 1982), 161–62, 366 ns.70, 72; Van Coufoudakis, "The United States, the United Nations, and the Greek Question, 1946–1952," in John O. Iatrides, ed., *Greece in the 1940s: A Nation in Crisis* (Hanover, N.H.: U. Press of New England, 1981), 285–88. The most extended and emotional discussion is by a contemporary British journalist in Greece, who openly advocated the royalist cause. See Fritz A. Voight, *The Greek Sedition* (London: Hollis and Carter, 1949), 14–19, 74, 135–36, 144–46, 182–93, 196–98. For a dramatic personal account of the child removals, see Nicholas Gage, *Eleni* (N.Y.: Random House, 1983), 245ff.

[3]In 1949 the Truman administration was sending economic assistance to Yugoslavia. See Lorraine M. Lees, "The American Decision to Assist Tito, 1948–1949," *Diplomatic History* 2 (Fall 1978): 407–22; Coufoudakis, "Greek Question," 417 n.47.

[4]Gage, *Eleni*, 245ff.

[5]Athens spokesman quoted in *Time*, March 15, 1948, p. 35; correspondent quoted in ibid., May 28, 1949, p. 26.

[6]For the Greek argument that the Soviets sought to establish a free Macedonia that would lead to the Mediterranean, see Soterios Nicholson, "The U.S.S.R. Scheme on Macedonia," *Atlantis*, July 30, 1950, reprinted in *Cong. Record, House, Appendix*, 81 Cong., 2 sess., vol. 96, part 17, Aug. 7, 1950, p. A5676. Richard V. Burks argues that the Greek civil war was partly aimed at Macedonian unification, which was integral to Balkan federation and involved a sacrifice of much of Greece. See his *The Dynamics of Communism in Eastern Europe* (Princeton: Princeton U. Press, 1961), 99–101. For Americans who believed that the communist states of Eastern Europe did not act without Stalin's consent, see OIR (Office of Intelligence Research) Report 4664: "Prospects for the Preservation of the Independence of Greece," April 17, 1948, p. 22, Research and Analysis Lists, DS, NA. For American concern regarding the Truman Doctrine, see Griswold to sec. of state, June 16, 1948, *FRUS*, IV: *Eastern Europe; The Soviet Union* (Wash., D.C.: GPO, 1974), 107.

[7]Sweet-Escott, *Greece*, 71; Bohlen to Repres. Ralph Gwinn of N.Y., March 30, 1948, DSDF, NA. See *New York Times*, March 4, 1948, p. L3, and March 15, 1948, p. L8; London *Times*, March 4, 1948, p. 4e, and March 6, 1948, p. 3e. Greek propagandists decried *paedomazoma* as the "rape of the children." Matthews, *Memories of a Mountain War Greece*, 177. A writer for the London *Times* labeled the removals a "general plan" to abduct 80,000 children of loyalist Greek families. See issue of March 16, 1948, p. 4e.

[8]Voight, *Greek Sedition*, 188, 189, 198, 198 n.3. See London *Times*, March 12, 1948, p. 3e; UNGA, *Official Records*, 3 sess., suppl. 8, 1948, p.19; UNSCOB report A/574, annex 2, in ibid., 29, 31. See also *New York Times*, April 11, 1948, p. L28, and June 23, 1948, p. L23. Communist publication (*Mlada Fronta*) encl. in Laurence Steinhardt, Amer. legation in Prague, to sec. of state, April 28, 1948, DSDF, NA.

[9]JUSMAPG Report No. 6 to JCS, March 25, 1948, P & O 091 Greece (TS), sect. III-A, Army Staff Records, NA; JUSMAPG Report No. 7 to JCS, April 1, 1948, ibid.; JUSMAPG Report No. 9 to JCS, April 15, 1948, ibid. The girl's name was Eutychia Kalyva. Memorialists inscribed a tribute on a column of white marble erected near the spot of her death outside Karpenisi. Matthews, *Memories of a Mountain War Greece*, 179. See also "Children—or Slaves?," *Union Jack*, April 17, 1948, clipping encl. in Amer. embassy in Athens to sec. of state, May 12, 1948, Athens Post Records, Confidential File, 1948: 624.4-800, box 20, Military Intelligence, FRC. Rudolf Schoenfeld, Amer. legation in Bucharest, to sec. of state, April 17, 1948, DSDF, NA: Cannon to sec. of state, April 19, 1948, ibid.; Selden Chapin, Amer. legation in Budapest, to sec. of state, May 10, 1948, ibid.; Chapin to sec. of state, May 13, 1948, ibid.

[10]UNSCOB Report A/574, UNGA, *Official Records*, 3 sess., suppl. 8, 1948, p. 18; UNSCOB Report A/574, annex 2, ibid., 29, 31.

[11]UNSCOB Report A/574, UNGA, *Official Records*, 3 sess., suppl. 1948, p. 18; UNSCOB Report A/935, annex 3, UNGA, *Official Records*, 4 sess., suppl. 8, 1949, p. 23.

[12]Guerrillas quoted in Voight, *Greek Sedition*, 190–91; Woodhouse, *Struggle for Greece*, 248; Matthews, *Memories of a Mountain War Greece*, 177–78; UNSCOB Report A/574, annex 2, UNGA, *Official Records*, 3 sess., suppl. 8, 1948, p. 29.

[13]UNSCOB Report A/644, UNGA, *Official Records*, 3 sess., suppl. 8A, 1948, pp. 9, 16–17; UNSCOB Report A/574, annex 2, ibid., 3 sess., suppl. 8, 1948, pp. 19, 30–31; UNSCOB Report A/574, ibid., p. 29; UNSCOB Report A/644, annex 3, ibid.

[14]Kenneth Spencer, "Greek Children," *The New Statesman and Nation* 39 (Jan. 14, 1950): 31–32.

[15]London *Times*, Dec. 3, 1948, p. 3d, and May 30, 1949, p. 3e; quote in UNSCOB Report A/574, annex 2, UNGA, *Official Records*, 3 sess., suppl. 8, 1948, p. 31.

[16]Matthews, *Memories of a Mountain War Greece*, 177, 180–82.

[17]Donald Heath, Amer. legation in Sofia, Bulgaria, to sec. of state, July 21, 1948, DSDF, NA.

[18]Dispatch by Bigart, New York *Herald Tribune*, June 14, 1948; C. H. Hall, Jr., second sec. of Amer. embassy in Warsaw, to DS, Dec. 23, 1949, DSDF, NA.

[19]UNSCOB Report A/574, UNGA, *Official Records*, 3 sess., suppl. 8, 1948, pp. 19, 20; UNSCOB Report A/644, ibid., 3 sess., suppl. 8A, 1948, pp. 4, 5; London *Times*, June 3, 1948, p. 3f, and June 25, 1948, p. 3g.

[20]*New York Times*, June 21, 1948, p. L1; Gibson (consul general in Salonika) to sec. of state, April 16, 28, 1948, DSDF, NA; Rankin to sec. of state, April 23, May 2, 1948, ibid.; UNSCOB Report A/935, UNGA, *Official Records*, 4 sess., suppl. 8, 1949, p. 5; UNSCOB Report A/574, UNGA, *Official Records*, 3 sess., suppl. 8, 1948, pp. 19, 20; UNSCOB Report A/574, annex 3, ibid., p. 31. The Greek government's relocation program cost 10,000 drachmas (about $6) per day per child. Ibid.

[21]Griswold to sec. of state, March 23, 1948, DSDF, NA; Gibson to sec. of state, April 28, 1948, ibid.

[22]Speakers quoted in L. Pittman Springs, Amer. consul in Patras, Greece, to sec. of state, March 27, 1948, DSDF, NA; Greek press quotes in Rankin to sec. of state, April 19, 1948, ibid.

[23]Rankin to sec. of state, April 3, May 10, 1948, ibid. For a newspaper account of the alleged massacre near Mount Ghiona, see London *Times*, May 10, 1948, p. 4b.

[24]Report encl. in Amer. embassy in Athens to DS, June 14, 1948, DSDF, NA. The officer was Captain James Hurley, Jr.

[25]Marshall to Amer. legations in Athens, Budapest, Bern, Salonika, and Moscow, April 29, 1948, ibid.

[26]OIR Report 4340.4 (Soviet For. Affairs), July 3, 1947, p. 41, Research and Analysis Lists, DS, NA; OIR Report 4664: "Prospects for the Preservation of the Independence of Greece," April 27, 1948, pp. 20, 22, 26–27, ibid.

[27]Gibson (in Salonika, headquarters of UNSCOB) had already forwarded the substance of the UNSCOB report a few weeks before, making it conceivable that the State Department had been waiting for its release before acting. Marshall to Amer. embassies in Athens, Paris, London, Belgrade, Sofia, Budapest, Prague, Warsaw, and Moscow, June 23, 1948 (released the following day), *FRUS, IV: Eastern Europe; Soviet Union,* 249–50; *New York Times,* June 25, 1948, p. L14.

[28]*Time,* March 15, 1948, p. 35; Sulzberger story in *New York Times,* June 21, 1948, p. L1; Gertrude Engstrom (commissioner of Girl Scouts in Pittsburgh) to Marshall, May 25, 1948, DSDF, NA; Bohlen to Gwinn, March 30, 1948, ibid. (Gwinn had submitted a letter of protest from the director of the Boy Scouts International Bureau in Greece); Baxter to Engstrom, June 18, 1948, ibid.

[29]Memo by Baxter of conversation with Dendramis, March 24, 1948, DSDF, NA.

[30]Ibid. See also Coufoudakis, "United States, United Nations, and Greek Question," 286, 417 n.39.

[31]Adam B. Ulam, *Titoism and the Cominform* (Cambridge, Mass.: Harvard U. Press, 1952), 106–8, 131, 135; Ulam, *Expansion and Coexistence: Soviet Foreign Policy, 1917–73* (N.Y.: Praeger, 1968; 2d ed., 1974), 464; Lees, "American Decision to Assist Tito," 409.

CHAPTER 9. TOWARD THE SPRING OFFENSIVE OF 1948

[1]Kitrilakis, Greek General Staff, "A Survey of the War Against the Bandits in Greece," March 8, 1948, pp. 1–2, P & O 091 Greece, sect. IX, case 129, Army Staff Records, NA.

[2]Ibid., 2–3.

[3]Ibid., 8–9.

[4]Ibid., 5–8; Kitrilakis quoted in *Time,* May 3, 1948, p. 29.

[5]CIA Situation Report 10—Greece, summary, 1. See also memo from Biddle for Wedemeyer, March 3, 1948: "Demolition of Middle East Oil," 1–2, P & O 319.1 Greece (TS), sect. IV-A, case 46, Army Staff Records, NA; NSC Report #7, "The Position of the United States with Respect to Soviet-Directed World Communism," March 30, 1948, pp. 1–8, NSC Lists, NA; Forrestal diaries, entry for March 4, 1948, p. 2115, Operations Archives, Naval History Divis., Wash., D.C. (photocopies of originals at Princeton U.). Western Union was an alliance of Britain, France, and the Benelux countries, the first step toward a joint defense pact among the noncommunist countries of Europe. Western Union later became the Western European Union when West Germany and Italy joined the alliance. The Marshall Plan—or Economic Cooperation Act—was part of the Foreign Assistance Act of April 2, 1948. It supplemented the Greek-Turkish aid bill of 1947, and encouraged Greeks to realize that the United States intended to promote economic reconstruction after the guerrilla war had been won. In mid-April an international convention in Paris established the Organization of European Economic Cooperation to draw up plans for economic recovery and make recommendations for ECA fund distribution. See Francis F. Lincoln, *United States' Aid to Greece, 1947–1962* (Germantown, Tenn.: Professional Seminars, 1975), 62, 75 n.5, 85; John Gimbel, *The Origins of the Marshall Plan* (Stanford: Stanford U. Press, 1976); Imanuel Wexler, *The Marshall Plan Revisited: The European Recovery Program in Economic Perspective* (Westport, Conn.: Greenwood, 1983); Michael J. Hogan, *The Marshall Plan: America, Britain, and the Reconstruction of Western Europe, 1947–1952* (Cambridge: Cambridge U. Press, 1987).

[6]Gross to Henderson, March 4, 1948, DSDF, NA.

[7]JCS 1841/4, note by secs. to JCS on reports by commanding general, HQs, USAGG, AMAG, March 24, 1948, P & O 091 Greece (TS), sect. III-A, case 21, Army Staff Records, NA; minutes of Chiefs of Staff Committee Meeting, Nov. 21, 1947, FO 371, vol. 61114, AN 400, PRO; minute by Orme Sargent, Dec. 3, 1947, vol. 68041, AN 45/45, ibid.

[8]CIA Report, ORE 22-48, "Possibility of Direct Soviet Military Action during 1948," April 2, 1948, pp. 1–3, files of sec. of defense, NA.

[9]Ibid., 3; JCS 1826/8—append., April 1, 1948, pp. 69, 72–79, P & O 091 Greece (TS), sect. II-A, case 13, Army Staff Records, NA; "Brief of Appendix"—"Comments on Certain Courses of Action Proposed with Respect to Greece and Answers to Specific Questions Contained in the Memorandum by the Secretary of the National Security Council dated 24 Feb. 48," encl. in memo for chief of staff, U.S. Army, from Wedemeyer, April 6, 1948, pp. 1–2, P & O 091 Greece (TS), sect. II-A, case 13, ibid.; memo for chief of staff, U.S. Army, from Wedemeyer, April 6, 1948, pp. 1–2, P & O 091 Greece (TS), sect. II-A, case 13, ibid; memo for the NSC from Forrestal, April 13, 1948, CD 6-1-21, files of sec. of defense, NA; author's interview with Wedemeyer, July 3, 1987. Lieut. Gen. Russel L. Vittrup agreed with Wedemeyer that the aid program in Greece had to remain a "limited type of operation." Author's interview with Vittrup, July 3, 1987. Vittrup was chief of the Policy Branch in the Pentagon in 1946–47, and was chief of the Army Division of the Military Assistance Group in Greece from 1952–53. General Wedemeyer later declared that he "was opposed to the Truman Doctrine pertaining to Greece" and that the United States "should not assume or accept the responsibility of world policeman." Rather, it "should scrupulously adhere" to the charter of the UN and other international organizations. Wedemeyer to author, Feb. 1, 1988. Letter in author's possession. In regard to a criticism often made about the Truman Doctrine, America's intervention was not unilateral as long as the British mission and troops remained.

[10]Henderson to Rankin, March 25, 1948, *FRUS*, IV: *Eastern Europe; The Soviet Union* (Wash., D.C.: GPO, 1974), 64–65.

[11]*Time*, April 5, 1948, p. 26.

[12]Caffery to sec. of state, March 16, 1948, DSDF, NA; Cannon to sec. of state, March 22, 1948, *FRUS*, IV: *Eastern Europe; Soviet Union*, 62–63; *Time*, March 29, 1948, p. 37.

[13]Van Fleet report to Wedemeyer, encl. in JCS 1841/8, April 22, 1948, pp. 58–60, P & O 091 Greece (TS), sect. III-A, case 21, Army Staff Records, NA.

[14]Van Fleet report to Wedemeyer, encl. in JCS 1841/9, April 27, 1948, pp. 63–64, P & O 091 Greece (TS), sect. III-A, case 21, ibid.

[15]Ibid., 64–65; Van Fleet recommendation encl. in memo by chief of staff, U.S. Army, to JCS, March 31, 1948, CD 6-1-29 (TS), files of sec. of defense, NA; memo by chief of staff, U.S. Army, to JCS, April 21, 1948, CD 6-1-29 (TS), ibid.; Griswold to sec. of state, April 9, 1948, *FRUS*, IV: *Eastern Europe; Soviet Union*, 96 n.2.

[16]Lawrence S. Wittner, *American Intervention in Greece, 1943–1949* (N.Y.: Columbia U. Press, 1982), 239–40; Van Fleet to Wedemeyer, April 20, 1948, p. 1, P & O 091 Greece (TS), sect. I-A, case 3, Army Staff Records, NA; Wedemeyer to [?] Templar, July 27, 1948, P & O 091 Greece (TS), sect. IV, case 32, ibid.; James A. Van Fleet, "How We Won in Greece," *Balkan Studies* 8 (1967): 390.

[17]JCS 1798/10—note by secs. to JCS, May 7, 1948, pp. 175–77, 182–83, P & O 091 Greece (TS), sect. I-A, case 3, ibid.; Van Fleet to Wedemeyer, encl. in JCS 1841/8, April 22, 1948, pp. 78–84, P & O 091 Greece (TS), sect. III-A, case 21, ibid.

[18]Van Fleet to Wedemeyer, April 20, 1948, p. 2, P & O 091 Greece (TS), sect. I-A, case 3, ibid.; memo for Wedemeyer from Col. Richard W. Mayo, chief, Europe-Middle East Branch, P & O, May 5, 1948, P & O 091 Greece (TS), sect. IV, cases 26–35, ibid.; Wedemeyer to Van Fleet, May 6, 1948, ibid.; memo for record by Lieut. Col.[?] Poinier, May 6, 1948, p. 1, ibid.

[19]See JCS 1798/5 quoted in memo from Mayo for Wedemeyer, May 5, 1948, P & O 091 Greece (TS), sect. IV, cases 26–35, ibid.; "President's Third Quarterly Report on Greek-Turkish Aid," May 12, 1948, p. 12, in Truman Papers, Official File 426, Truman Lib.

[20]Van Fleet report to Wedemeyer, encl. in JCS 1841/9, April 27, 1948, pp. 65–66, P & O 091 Greece (TS), sect. III-A, case 21, Army Staff Records, NA; Campbell et al., *Employment of Airpower in Greek Guerrilla War*, 28. See also Leften S. Stavrianos, *Greece: American Dilemma and Opportunity* (Chicago: Regnery, 1952), 190–91.

[21]Van Fleet report to Wedemeyer, encl. in JCS 1841/9, pp. 66–68; "USAFGG History," 38; JUSMAPG Report No. 7 to JCS (covers March 20–31, 1948), April 1, 1948, P & O 091 Greece (TS), sect. III-A, case 21, Army Staff Records, NA; JUSMAPG Report No. 8 to JCS (covers April 1–6, 1948), April 8, 1948, in ibid.; JUSMAPG Report No. 12 (covers April 28–May 4, 1948), May 6, 1948, in ibid.; "History of JUSMAGG," 136; Edgar O'Ballance, *The Greek Civil War, 1944–1949* (N.Y.: Praeger, 1966), 167–68.

[22]Van Fleet to Wedemeyer, April 20, 1948, pp. 2–3, P & O 091 Greece (TS), sect. I-A, case 3, Army Staff Records, NA; JUSMAPG Report No. 13 to JCS, May 13, 1948, P & O 091 Greece (TS), sect. III-A, case 21, ibid.; Campbell et al., *Employment of Airpower in Greek Guerrilla War*, 49. Controversy exists over the alleged use of napalm this early in the war. John O. Iatrides has pointed out that the Greek official history of the war prepared by the Army Staff does not mention napalm, and Christopher M. Woodhouse has asserted that even though "Communist apologists report napalm in use in 1948, Greek historians say that requests for napalm were refused; its use is only certain in the closing stages." Letter from Iatrides to author, Aug. 23, 1987; Woodhouse, *The Struggle for Greece, 1941–1949* (Brooklyn Heights, N.Y.: Beekman-Esanu, 1976), 237; Walter Wilds, deputy coordinator for aid to Greece and Turkey, to Major Gen. Arthur M. Harper, deputy commanding general, USAGG, March 4, 1948, JUSMAPG Air Adjutant Sect. 471 Ammunition (Napalm), NA.

[23]"History of JUSMAGG," 136; Campbell et al., *Employment of Airpower in Greek Guerrilla War*, 40–41; Jenkins on "Greek Army Operations, 1948," Oct. 1, 1948, p. 1, P & O 091 Greece (TS), sect. V, case 40, Army Staff Records, NA: O'Ballance, *Greek Civil War*, 168. The guerrillas downed one plane and inflicted damages on ten others.

[24]Van Fleet to Wedemeyer, April 20, 1948, p. 2, P & O 091 Greece (TS), sect. I-A, case 3, Army Staff Records, NA.

[25]"President's Third Quarterly Report."

[26]Cyrus L. Sulzberger, "Greek Rebel Fifth Column Seen Big Athens Handicap," *New York Times*, Dec. 19, 1948, p. 10.

[27]Evangelos Averoff-Tossizza, *By Fire and Axe: The Communist Party and the Civil War in Greece, 1944–1949* (New Rochelle, N.Y.: Caratzas Brothers, 1978), 263–64. Originally published as *Le Feu et la hache Grèce '46–'49, histoire des guerres de l'après-guerre* (Paris: Editions de Breteuil, 1973). Trans. by Sarah Arnold Rigos. Wittner, *American Intervention in Greece*, 145–46; Frederick Ayer, Jr., *Yankee G-Man* (Chicago: Regnery, 1957), 239, 241, 261–62. Critics referred to Van Fleet as "The Butcher" and Griswold as "Gauleiter." Ibid., 241. Ladas's assassin was Stratis Moutsoyiannis, who said he had acted under the KKE's orders. Averoff-Tossizza, *By Fire and Axe*, 263. In mid-March and again in April, the Greek government claimed that it had uncovered plots in Athens by communists to assassinate Van Fleet and senior Greek officials, including Papagos. The government made only a few arrests in the first instance, but arrested over eighty communists in the second. London *Times*, March 12, 1949, p. 4c, April 12, 1949, p. 30; *New York Times*, March 12, 1949, p. 4. Assassination plots were not Ayer's only concern; he also had to deal with indiscretions and outright gaffes that also threatened to undermine the American aid effort. In one case, American wives had urged AMAG to provide them and their children with a beach of their own in Athens. The Corps of Engineers obliged and cleaned up a beach and brought in new sand. But the spot was a favorite of Athenians and led to ill feelings. Engineers erected a barbed wire fence stretching down to the water, while at the access point, a guard was posted by the narrow gate in daylight next to a sign on a billboard declaring in two languages: "This beach is reserved exclusively for the use of American Personnel of the Mission." Greeks complained that not even the Nazis had done this during the occupation. Within forty-eight hours, the Greek press had the story, and it caused a furor. Ayer worked with Burton Berry, the former U.S. ambassador to Sofia in Bulgaria and now political adviser to AMAG, to get the wire, guard, and sign removed. Ayer, *Yankee G-Man*, 266–67.

[28] Averoff-Tossizza, *By Fire and Axe*, 264; Dominique Eudes, *The Kapetanios: Partisans and Civil War in Greece, 1943–1949* (N.Y.: Monthly Review Press, 1972), 321. Originally published as *Les Kapetanios: La guerre civile grecque de 1943 à 1949* (Paris: Librarie Arthème Fayard, 1970). Trans. by John Howe. For a critical account of the Greek government's policies, see Wittner, *American Intervention in Greece*, chap. 5.

[29] *Nation*, May 15, 1948, p. 518; Eugene P. Connolly, New York City Council, to Truman, May 5, 1948, DSDF, NA; Keating to sec. of state, May 6, 1948, ibid.; Eleanor Roosevelt to sec. of state, May 6, 1948, ibid.; Aurora, Illinois petition to sec. of state, May 6, 1948, ibid.; American Labor Party to Truman, May 7, 1948, ibid.; National Maritime Union to Truman, May 7, 1948, ibid.

[30] Marshall to embassy in London, May 7, 1948, *FRUS, IV: Eastern Europe: Soviet Union*, 82; Marshall to embassy in Athens, May 15, 1948, ibid. 85–86; Leonard R. Cowles, chief, Public Views & Inquiries Section, Divis. of Public Liaison, DS, to Connolly, June 7, 1948, DSDF, NA; Rankin to sec. of state, May 10, 1948, ibid. Assistant Secretary of State Willard L. Thorp assured one writer that those recently executed in Greece had been convicted of murdering fellow Greeks during the Nazi occupation of World War II and the communist uprisings of the winter of 1944–45. Official Greek records showed that Greek authorities had unconditionally freed the vast majority of captured guerrillas, but that the "active and dangerous Communists" remained imprisoned after courts-martial. Only the "most vicious ringleaders" received the death penalty. Thorp to A. F. Whitney, president, Brotherhood of Railroad Trainmen, May 17, 1948, ibid. Reports from Athens assured Washington that the KKE had been responsible for Ladas's murder. See embassy in Athens to sec. of state, May 24, 1948, ibid.; John B. Howard, acting chief, AMAG, to sec. of state, May 28, 1948, ibid. One writer argues that the increased number of executions directly resulted from Ladas's assassination. O'Ballance, *Greek Civil War*, 168.

[31] Kenneth Matthews, *Memories of a Mountain War Greece: 1944–1949* (London: Longman, 1972), 185, 187; *New York Times*, May 17, 1948, pp. 1, 8; London *Times*, May 17, 1948, p. 4c. A good account of the Polk episode is in Ayer, *Yankee G-Man*, 275–99. Polk was thirty-four years old and a navy fighter and dive-bomber pilot in World War II. *Time*, May 24, 1948, p. 68.

[32] Matthews, *Memories of a Mountain War Greece*, 184–85; *Nation*, May 29, 1948, p. 589; *New York Times*, May 18, 1948, p. 12, and May 28, 1948, p. 7; London *Times*, May 18, 1948, p. 4d; Wittner, *American Intervention in Greece*, 159; *Cong. Record*, 80 Cong., 2 sess., vol. 94, part 5, p. 6550 (May 27, 1948); *Cong. Record, Appendix*, 80 Cong., 2 sess., vol. 94, part 11, p. A3960 (June 15, 1948). Editorial opinions found in ibid., pp. A3960–61. See also *New York Times*, May 24, 1948, p. 8. For letters containing Polk's views of the Greek situation, see his correspondence with his brother William, which the latter allowed to be printed in *Nation*, "Letters to the Editors," as "George Polk—His Own Memorial," June 16, 1948, pp. 726–27.

[33] Matthews, *Memories of a Mountain War Greece*, 185, 187. Matthews was not surprised that Polk's body was found in Salonika; that city had always been comprised of an uneasy mixture of nationalities and the scene of violence for years. Even though Salonika's location suggested the status of a buffer zone, it instead became a choice battle site of hostilities that burst into violence again with the civil war. Ibid., 186.

[34] Ibid., 187–88; Bohlen to Senator Tom Connolly of For. Relations Committee, May 24, 1948, DSDF, NA; *Time*, July 5, 1948, p. 57.

[35] Matthews, *Memories of a Mountain War Greece*, 188; Wittner, *American Intervention in Greece*, 159; *New York Times*, May 22, 1948, p. 5; ibid., May 25, 1948, p. 8; ibid., Oct. 5, 1948, p. 9; London *Times*, Oct. 19, 1948, p. 3b; *Time*, July 5, 1948, p. 56. For the argument that a cover-up took place that involved the Greek government, American officials, and the American press, see Yiannis P. Roubatis and Elias Vlanton, "Who Killed George Polk?," *More* 7 (May 1977): 12–32. According to the writers, the "conspirators" were determined to block any investigation of the extreme right's role in the murder.

[36] Matthews, *Memories of a Mountain War Greece*, 188; Wittner, *American Intervention in Greece*, 159; *New York Times*, March 12, 1949, p. 6.

[37]Matthews, *Memories of a Mountain War Greece*, 188–89, 191; *New York Times*, Jan. 9, 1949, p. 5; ibid., March 1, 1949, p. 21; ibid., April 13, 1949, p. 16; ibid., April 15, 1949, p. 3.

[38]*Time*, Oct. 25, 1948, p. 56; ibid., May 2, 1949, pp. 56–57; *New York Times*, Oct. 18, 1948, pp. 1, 6, and April 14, 1949, p. 15; Matthews, *Memories of a Mountain War Greece*, 189.

[39]Matthews, *Memories of a Mountain War Greece*, 189; *Time*, May 2, 1949, p. 57, and April 22, 1949, pp. 1, 22; London *Times*, April 22, 1949, p. 3c. Stachtopoulos spent twelve years in prison. He later claimed that his "confession" had resulted from two months of torture by government officials. He was innocent, according to his statements made years afterward. Roubatis and Vlanton, "Who Killed George Polk?," 13, 18. Greek law permits a verdict in absentia. If persons convicted in this manner were later arrested, however, they could ask for and receive a new trial. Ibid., 32.

[40]Matthews, *Memories of a Mountain War Greece*, 189.

[41]Ayer, *Yankee G-Man*, 282–83, 295–96.

[42]Matthews, *Memories of a Mountain War Greece*, 189–90; Wittner, *American Intervention in Greece*, 160.

[43]O'Ballance, *Greek Civil War*, 176; Ayer, *Yankee G-Man*, 278, 296; Matthews, *Memories of a Mountain War Greece*, 191–92; Ronald Steel, *Walter Lippmann and the American Century* (N.Y.: Random House, 1980), 487. British correspondent Fritz A. Voight was convinced that the KKE was responsible for Polk's murder. See his study, *The Greek Sedition* (London: Hollis & Carter, 1949), 218. A reporter in Greece for the *Christian Science Monitor*, Constantine Hadjiargyris, believed that British intelligence was involved in the murder as part of an effort to regain the British position in the area by complicating the Greek situation and causing the United States to seek help. In 1975 he published a book in Athens entitled *The Polk Affair: The Role of Foreign Agencies in Greece*. Roubatis and Vlanton, "Who Killed George Polk?," 22.

[44]Wedemeyer to Van Fleet, April 29, 1948, Records of Interservice Agencies, box 55: 312–Correspondence of Gen. Van Fleet, 1948–50, Army Staff Records, NA; Campbell et al., *Employment of Airpower in Greek Guerrilla War*, 49–50; JUSMAPG Report No. 14 to JCS (covers period May 12–18, 1948), May 20, 1948, P & O 091 Greece (TS), sect. III-A, case 21, Army Staff Records, NA; NSC 5/3—"The Position of the United States with Respect to the Use of US Military Power in Greece," May 25, 1948, *FRUS*, IV: *Eastern Europe: Soviet Union*, 93–94; CIA 5–48: "Review of the World Situation as It Relates to the Security of the United States," May 12, 1948, and CIA 6–48 (same title), June 17, 1948, both in Truman Papers, President's Secretary's Files, box 203—NSC Meetings #11 and 13, Truman Lib.

[45]Cannon to sec. of state, June 6, 1948, *FRUS*, IV: *Eastern Europe: Soviet Union*, 105 n.1; Cannon to sec. of state, June 8, 1948, ibid., 1070, 1072; Rankin to sec. of state, June 12, 1948, ibid., 106. See also Rankin to sec. of state, May 15, 1948, DSDF, NA; O'Ballance, *Greek Civil War*, 170; Woodhouse, *Struggle for Greece*, 254.

[46]McGhee to Lovett, May 19, 1948, *FRUS*, IV: *Eastern Europe: Soviet Union*, 88–91; Lovett to Harriman, March 1, 1948, CD 9-2-8 (TS), files of sec. of defense, NA; message (authorized by the President) to Grady, May 11, 1948, Grady Papers, Truman Lib.; Marshall to Grady, ca. mid-May 1948, ibid.; John O. Iatrides, ed., *Ambassador MacVeagh Reports: Greece, 1933–1947* (Princeton: Princeton U. Press, 1980), 732.

CHAPTER 10.   GRAMMOS AND VITSI

[1]"USAFGG History," 39; plan for "Operation Crown"—Greece, ca. June 15, 1948, P & O 091 Greece (TS), sect. III-A, case 21, Army Staff Records, NA; Griswold to sec. of state, June 8, 1948, *FRUS*, IV: *Eastern Europe; The Soviet Union* (Wash., D.C.: GPO, 1974), 103–5; Fran-

cis F. Lincoln, *United States' Aid to Greece, 1947–1962* (Germantown, Tenn.: Professional Seminars, 1975), 66. *Time* called it "Operation Coronet." Edition of July 5, 1948, p. 24.

[2]Plan for "Operation Crown"—Greece, ca. June 15, 1948, Army Staff Records, NA; memo for record by Poinier, June 29, 1948, P & O 091 Greece (TS), sect. IV, cases 26–35, ibid.; Van Fleet to Wedemeyer, June 11, 1948, pp. 3–4, P & O 091 Greece (TS), sect. I-A, case 3, ibid.; "USAFGG History," 40; Edgar O'Ballance, *The Greek Civil War, 1944–1949* (N.Y.: Praeger, 1966), 170–71; Christopher M. Woodhouse, *The Struggle for Greece, 1941–1949* (Brooklyn Heights, N.Y.: Beekman-Esanu, 1976), 241–42. Woodhouse does not explain how the guerrillas learned the details of the Greek government's planned assault.

[3]M. A. Campbell et al., *The Employment of Airpower in the Greek Guerrilla War, 1947–1949* (Montgomery, Ala.: Air U., Maxwell AFB, 1964), 42–44. On several occasions, the Harvards used fragmentation bombs. Ibid. The approaching campaign led to the decision to use napalm. In early June two American Air Force officers and four enlisted men from the Military Advisory and Planning Group prepared to train the Greeks in its use. By the middle of the month the Americans made arrangements for moving the napalm equipment and crews from Elevsis Airfield to Kozani. Van Fleet agreed with Matheny that it was time to seek the American aid mission's approval for napalm attacks. Orders went out for over 5,000 pounds of napalm from the United States and 200 drop tanks from Germany which could hold 75 gallons of liquid each. On June 20, ten Spitfires launched their first napalm raid on targets chosen by the army. Although there were many problems in using the napalm and the incendiary impact was not as great as hoped, the fire bombs lifted Greek morale. Work then began to expand their use. The Greeks' State Aircraft Factory, with American technical assistance, developed bomb racks and release mechanisms under each wing that allowed the Spitfires to drop the napalm tanks. But the Spitfires could carry only 250 pounds on each wing, and only 35 gallons of napalm mix in each wing tank. In comparison with the number of other bombs and rockets, the amount of napalm used was small: the Greeks dropped only 14 napalm tanks from June until December 1948, whereas they fired almost 11,000 rockets and dropped over 7,000 bombs. See Major James B. Weeks, USAF, USAGG, to chief, "D" Branch, Greek Air Ministry, June 3, 1948, Air Adjutant Section 471 Ammunition (Napalm), JUSMAPG, NA; Matheny to chief of Air Staff, Air Ministry, Athens, June 8, 14, 1948, ibid.; Col. S. B. Knowles, Jr., USAF Air Operations, to Matheny, June 14, 1948, ibid.; "USAFGG History," 39, 49, 161, 212; *New York Times*, June 19, 1948, p. 2, and June 20, 1948, pp. 1, 49; Kenneth Matthews, *Memories of a Mountain War Greece: 1944–1949* (London: Longman, 1972), 207; O'Ballance, *Greek Civil War*, 171; JUS-MAPG Report No. 23 to JCS (covers July 14–20, 1948), July 23, 1948, p. 9, P & O 091 Greece (TS), sect. III-A, case 21, Army Staff Records, NA; U.S. Army message from Athens to sec. of state, June 25, 1948, DSDF, NA; Griswold to sec. of state, June 16, 1948, *FRUS*, IV: *Eastern Europe; Soviet Union*, 107–8.

[4]*Time*, Aug. 16, 1948, p. 28; Lawrence S. Wittner, *American Intervention in Greece, 1943–1949* (N.Y.: Columbia U. Press, 1982), 243; Woodhouse, *Struggle for Greece*, 240–42; O'Ballance, *Greek Civil War*, 170–73. For an account of the Grammos battle, see *Time*, July 5, 1948, p. 24. During the Olympic Games of mid-July, the guerrillas cut the relay route (the entire length of Greece) of the Olympic torch. To counteract this interference, the plan was for the team to take the torch to a spot twenty miles from the nearest port, where a British destroyer would take it to Italy, en route to London. Ibid., July 19, 1948, p. 28.

[5]Griswold to Henderson, June 24, 1948, *FRUS*, IV: *Eastern Europe; Soviet Union*, 112; sec. of state to embassy and AMAG in Athens, June 26, 1948, ibid., 113.

[6]Hickerson to Lovett, June 1, 1948, ibid., 98–99; Cromie to Jernegan, June 1, 1948, ibid., 99 n.1.

[7]Sec. of state to AMAG, June 23, 1948, *FRUS*, IV: *Eastern Europe: Soviet Union*, 108–09. See also Jernegan to Joe Satterthwaite (DS adviser), June 23, 1948, DSDF, NA.

[8]Agreement between DS and ECA on aid to Greece, June 24, 1948, 109–11, DSDF, NA; George C. McGhee, "The Impact of Foreign Commitments upon the Coordinative Responsibili-

ties of the Department of State," in *International Commitments and National Administration* (Charlottesville: Press of U. of Virginia, 1949), 52; "History of JUSMAGG," 1; Lincoln, *United States' Aid to Greece*, 84–85. In July the economic branch of the American mission became the ECA Mission to Greece as part of the Marshall Plan program. Ibid., 74. For the relief and reconstruction story under the Marshall Plan and the American mission under the Truman Doctrine, see ibid., 86–97. Inflation was coming under control during the first half of 1948. The commodity price index rose 6 percent in the first six months of the year, as compared with a rise of 28 percent during the previous half-year. Inflation was largely under control from July 1948 through the end of the war in October 1949. Ibid., 69, 97. See also William H. McNeill, *Greece: American Aid in Action, 1947–1956* (N.Y.: Twentieth Century Fund, 1957), 47. Another writer, at the University of Thessaloniki, credits the Marshall Plan with saving Greece as a nation. See D. J. Delivanis, "Marshall Plan in Greece," *Balkan Studies* 8 (1967): 333–38. One writer points out that the Greeks did not benefit as much as other recipients of the Marshall Plan because of the enormous destruction of World War II and the civil war. Evangelos Averoff-Tossizza, *By Fire and Axe: The Communist Party and the Civil War in Greece, 1944–1949* (New Rochelle, N.Y.: Caratzas Brothers, 1978), 356. Originally published as *Le Feu et la hache Grèce '46–'49, histoire des guerres de l'après-guerre* (Paris: Editions de Breteuil, 1973). Trans. by Sarah Arnold Rigos.

[9]Wittner's account is critical. See *American Intervention in Greece*, 187–88. Lincoln, *United States' Aid to Greece*, 66; Michael M. Amen, *American Foreign Policy in Greece, 1944–1949: Economic, Military, and Institutional Aspects* (Frankfurt: Peter Lang, 1978), 135; Schuyler to Wedemeyer, Oct. 22, 1948, P & O 091 Greece, sect. X, Army Staff Records, NA; ECA official (Edward T. Dickinson, director of Program Relations) quoted in U.S. House of Reps., *Military Assistance Programs, Part 2. Assistance to Greece and Turkey* VI (Wash., D.C.: GPO, 1976): 81. U.S. strategy in the war was to have economic assistance play a greater role as the military situation improved. Edwin P. Curtin (lieut. col.), "American Advisory Group Aids Greece in War on Guerrillas," *Armed Cavalry Journal* 58 (Jan.-Feb. 1949): 34.

[10]"Report of the UNSCOB," June 30, 1948, UNGA, *Official Records*, 3 sess., 1948, suppl. 8, pp. 21–27.

[11]Sec. of state to embassy in London, July 21, 1948, *FRUS*, IV: *Eastern Europe; Soviet Union*, 115.

[12]Ibid., 115–16; sec. of state to embassy in Athens, Aug. 11, 1948, ibid., 129; sec. of state to embassy in Athens, Aug. 2, 1948, ibid., 117.

[13]Grady to sec. of state, Aug. 6, 21, 1948, DSDF, NA. One writer has speculated that the Soviets were trying to defuse the troubles in Greece in light of the growing crisis in Berlin. See Elisabeth Barker, "Yugoslav Policy towards Greece, 1947–1949," in Lars Baerentzen, John O. Iatrides, and Ole L. Smith, eds., *Studies in the History of the Greek Civil War, 1945–1949* (Copenhagen, Denmark: Museum Tusculanum Press, 1987), 277–78.

[14]Adam B. Ulam, *Titoism and the Cominform* (Cambridge: Harvard U. Press, 1952), 106–8, 131, 135; Ulam, *Expansion and Coexistence: Soviet Foreign Policy, 1917–73* (N.Y.: Praeger, 1968; 2d ed., 1974), 464; Wittner, *American Intervention in Greece*, 263–64.

[15]Woodhouse, *Struggle for Greece*, 253; Averoff-Tossizza, *By Fire and Axe*, 276–77; sec. of state to certain diplomatic offices, July 6, 1948, *FRUS*, IV: *Eastern Europe; Soviet Union*, 1084–85; Walter Millis, ed., *The Forrestal Diaries* (N.Y.: Viking, 1951), entry for Aug. 3, 1948 (dealing with Smith's meeting with Stalin and Molotov), 469; Smith to sec. of state, Aug. 19, 1948, DSDF, NA.

[16]See Edgar Snow, "Will Tito's Heretics Halt Russia?," in *Saturday Evening Post*, Dec. 18, 1948, pp. 23, 108–10. Snow was a noted correspondent who had written *Red Star Over China* after visiting Mao Tse-tung in the 1930s.

[17]Rankin to sec. of state, July 14, 1948, DSDF, NA; Reams to sec. of state, July 15, 1948, ibid. For State Department opposition to the peace feelers as a "Communist trap," see Satterthwaite to sec. of state, June 25, 1948, ibid.

[18]U.S. Army message from Athens to sec. of state, July 18, 1948, ibid.

[19]Sec. of state to embassy in Athens, Aug. 6, 1948, *FRUS*, IV: *Eastern Europe; Soviet Union*, 118–19. See Rankin to sec. of state, July 14, 1948, DSDF, NA.

[20]Marshall to embassy in Athens, Aug. 14, 1948, *FRUS*, IV: *Eastern Europe; Soviet Union*, 254. For a discussion of the Athens government's repressive practices, see Lawrence S. Wittner, "The Truman Doctrine and the Defense of Freedom," *Diplomatic History* 4 (Spring 1980): 161–87.

[21]Dimitrios G. Kousoulas, "The Truman Doctrine and the Stalin-Tito Rift: A Reappraisal," *South Atlantic Quarterly* 72 (Summer 1973): 436; Lorraine M. Lees, "The American Decision to Assist Tito, 1948–1949," *Diplomatic History* 2 (Fall 1978): 407–22. The United States did not succeed in establishing economic or political ties with Yugoslavia until 1949. Ibid., 407.

[22]Marshall to embassy in Athens, Aug. 14, 1948, *FRUS*, IV: *Eastern Europe; Soviet Union*, 254–55.

[23]"Comment Paper"—REFUGEES AND DISPLACED PERSONS, SD/A/C.3/112, Harry Rosenfeld Papers (commissioner, Displaced Persons Commission, 1948–52), box 1, folder on UN file, 1949, Truman Lib.; UNSCOB Report A/935, annex 1, UNGA, *Official Records*, 4 sess., suppl. 8, 1949, p. 21.

[24]Woodhouse, *Struggle for Greece*, 243; *Time*, Aug. 16, 1948, p. 28. The *Time* correspondent claimed that Kalogeropoulos preferred tending his flowers to fighting the war. Ibid. Van Fleet account in Homer Bigart, "Are We Losing Out in Greece?," in *Saturday Evening Post*, Jan. 1, 1949, p. 49. "USAFGG History," 39; Report by Lieut. Col. [?] Nagle, Europe and Middle East Branch, P & O 091 Greece (TS), sect. III-A, case 21, Army Staff Records, NA; Campbell et al., *Employment of Airpower in Greek Guerrilla War*, 44–45; Matthews, *Memories of a Mountain War Greece*, 207.

[25]Memo by Cromie of conversation among Lovett, Dendramis, and Cromie, Aug. 10, 1948, *FRUS*, IV: *Eastern Europe; Soviet Union*, 122–24. Royall likewise opposed adding fighter-bombers to the Greek air force. The U.S. Air Force, after a conference with State, Navy, and Army representatives, had recently turned down a request by Van Fleet and Grady for the transfer of 30 P-47s from Turkey to Greece. The Air Force recommended instead that all planning should focus on crushing the guerrillas with weapons and manpower already available. See Royall to McGhee, Aug. 13, 1948, ibid., 133; memo by Lieut. Col. [?] Sievers: "Transfer of Thirty Planes now in Turkey to Greece," Aug. 13, 1948, P & O 452.1, sect. II, case 38, Army Staff Records, NA.

[26]McGhee to Lovett, Aug. 11, 1948, *FRUS*, IV: *Eastern Europe; Soviet Union*, 124–27.

[27]Ibid., 128–29; sec. of state to embassy in Athens, Aug. 16, 1948, ibid., 135, 136.

[28]Jernegan to McGhee, Aug. 13, 1948, ibid., 131–32; Royall to McGhee, Aug. 13, 1948, ibid., 132–33.

[29]Amer. embassy in Athens to DS, Aug. 6, 1948, DSDF, NA; Matthews, *Memories of a Mountain War Greece*, 208.

[30]Matthews, *Memories of a Mountain War Greece*, 207–8; Woodhouse, *Struggle for Greece*, 242; O'Ballance, *Greek Civil War*, 173; Wittner, *American Intervention in Greece*, 243–44; "Greek Army Operations, 1948," encl. in Jenkins to asst. director, JUSMAPG, Oct. 1, 1948, p. 2, P & O 091 Greece (TS), sect. V, case 40, Army Staff Records, NA; "USAFGG History," 40; Campbell et al., *Employment of Airpower in Greek Guerrilla War*, 45; woman quoted in *Time*, Oct. 11, 1948, p. 33. Actually, Homer Bigart of the New York *Herald Tribune* had earlier interviewed Markos in the Grammos Mountains and published his story in a four-part series. *Time* called attention to this story in its edition of Aug. 1, 1948, p. 35. Controversy has arisen over the claim that Zahariadis tried to have Markos assassinated because of the defeat at Grammos. According to a left-wing author, Dominique Eudes, Markos had departed the Grammos area with ten companions on August 20 (less than a week before the final Greek army assault), quickly pursued by a small group under orders from Zahariadis to kill the guerrilla leader. The would-be assassins

caught up with Markos inside Albania, where shots alerted Albanian soldiers on patrol. They safeguarded Markos's entry into the Soviet military mission. Another writer, Evangelos Averoff-Tossizza (who was a high official in the Athens government during the 1950s and 1960s), agrees that Zahariadis was a fanatical follower of Moscow and that soon after Grammos he became the real commander of the Democratic Army. But Averoff considers Eudes's claim of an attempted assassination "seemingly improbable." Dominique Eudes, *The Kapetanios: Partisans and Civil War in Greece, 1943-1949* (N.Y.: Monthly Review Press, 1972), 330-31. Originally published as *Les Kapetanios: La guerre civile grecque de 1943 à 1949* (Paris: Librarie Arthème Fayard, 1970). Averoff-Tossizza, *By Fire and Axe*, 319-20, 322-23.

[31] *Time*, Aug. 30, 1948, p. 26; "USAFGG History," 40; Matthews, *Memories of a Mountain War Greece*, 208; "Supplementary Report of the UNSCOB" (17 June-10 Sept. 48), UNGA, *Official Records*, 3 sess., 1948, suppl. 8A, pp. 6-7; Amer. embassy in Athens to sec. of state, Aug. 25, 1948, P & O 091 Greece (TS), sect. V, case 36, Army Staff Records, NA; Woodhouse, *Struggle for Greece*, 242-43; O'Ballance, *Greek Civil War*, 173; Cyrus L. Sulzberger, *A Long Row of Candles: Memoirs and Diaries [1934-1954]* (N.Y.: Macmillan, 1969), 394. Actually, the Greek army crossed the Albanian border at least one time during the war. On August 14, 1948, General Thrasyvoulos Tsakalotos ordered his men to fire on Albanian artillery releasing a barrage from the Greek village of Sotira in Northern Epirus on the Albanian side. In the process the Greek shelling destroyed some houses. Then an infantry company invaded Albania and drove out the Albanian soldiers who had undoubtedly taken part in the artillery fire. Averoff-Tossizza, *By Fire and Axe*, 294.

[32] "USAFGG History," 40; Matthews, *Memories of a Mountain War Greece*, 208; Woodhouse, *Struggle for Greece*, 242-43. The officer executed was Yannoulis; Kikitsas was exiled to Prague. See Eudes, *Kapetanios*, 329-32. See also John O. Iatrides, "Civil War, 1945-1949: National and International Aspects," in Iatrides, ed., *Greece in the 1940s: A Nation In Crisis* (Hanover, N.H.: U. Press of New England, 1981), 213.

[33] Woodhouse, *Struggle for Greece*, 243; "History of JUSMAGG," 150; plan for "Operation Crown"; Campbell et al., *Employment of Airpower in Greek Guerrilla War*, 28-29, 43; "Greek Army Operations, 1948," 2; Matthews, *Memories of a Mountain War Greece*, 208-9; "USAFGG History," 40-41; "Supplementary Report of the UNSCOB" (17 June-10 Sept. 48), UNGA, *Official Records*, 3 sess., 1948, suppl. 8A, p. 14.

[34] "History of JUSMAGG," 65; "Estimate of the Situation Greece," 2, by British GHQ, Middle East Command, encl. in Van Fleet to Wedemeyer, Oct. 21, 1948, P & O 091 Greece (secret) sect. V, case 40, Army Staff Records, NA; "Greek Army Operations, 1948," p. 2, encl. in Jenkins to asst. director, JUSMAPG, P & O 091 Greece (TS), sect. V, case 40, ibid.; "Special Report, Vitsi Operation, 30 Aug. to 15 Oct. 1948," pp. 1-2, from JUSMAPG, encl. in Van Fleet to Wedemeyer, Oct. 21, 1948, P & O 091 Greece (secret), sect. V, case 40, ibid.; Van Fleet to Wedemeyer, Sept. 10, 1948, p. 1, P & O 091 Greece, sect. X, case 143/2, ibid.; Campbell et al., *Employment of Airpower in Greek Guerrilla War*, 45-46; report by Policy Planning Staff on U.S. aid to Greece, Nov. 24, 1948, *FRUS*, IV: *Eastern Europe; Soviet Union*, 197-98; *Time*, Oct. 11, 1948, p. 33.

[35] "Supplementary Report of UNSCOB" (17 June-10 Sept. 48), UNGA, *Official Records*, 3 sess., 1948, suppl. 8A, pp. 9-10.

[36] Grady to sec. of state, Sept. 29, 1948, *FRUS*, IV: *Eastern Europe; Soviet Union*, 152-53; "Special Report, Vitsi Operation," pp. 1-2.

[37] Acting military attaché in Greece, Major Harold A. Tidmarsh, to sec. of state, Oct. 1, 1948, *FRUS*, IV: *Eastern Europe; Soviet Union*, 156-57; memo of conversation, probably drafted by Henry S. Villard, adviser to U.S. delegation at UNGA, Sept. 30, 1948, ibid., 154-55; Greek government memo from prime minister to Grady, encl. in embassy in Athens to DS, Oct. 1, 1948, p. 4, P & O 091 Greece (TS), sect. V, case 40, Army Staff Records, NA.

[38] "Estimate of the Situation Greece," 2; Van Fleet to Wedemeyer, Sept. 10, 1948, pp. 1-2, P & O 091 Greece, sect. X, case 143/2, Army Staff Records, NA; "Greek Army Operations, 1948," p. 2.

[39]"Estimate of the Situation Greece," 3; Brit. assessment, Oct. 1, 1948, pp. 1–4, 7–8, P & O 091 Greece (TS), sect. V, case 40, Army Staff Records, NA.

[40]"Estimate of the Situation Greece," 6–8; Van Fleet to Grady, Oct. 7, 1948, pp. 1, 3, P & O 091 Greece (TS), sect. V, case 40, Army Staff Records, NA; Grady to sec. of state, Oct. 16, 1948, *FRUS*, IV: *Eastern Europe; Soviet Union*, 160; Wittner, *American Intervention in Greece*, 245. American observers believed the Greek navy strong enough to combat guerrilla activities and to supply movements at sea. Although an increase in the army by four divisions would raise demands for naval transport of supplies, the navy had never been fully used and its present size seemed sufficient. The navy could transport one army brigade for a beach assault, and it could transport additional units as well. The navy had 14,300 personnel, 115 vessels, and a shore establishment. See "Greek Army Operations, 1948," pp. 1, 3; report by J. A. Snackenberg, append.: "Naval Section," 1, Oct. 1, 1948, P & O 091 Greece (TS), sect. IV, case 40, Army Staff Records, NA; transcript of conference held by Jenkins in office of Lieut. Gen. [?] Vimblis, at HQ, Greek General Staff, Dec. 4, 1948, pp. 1–5, P & O 091 Greece (TS), sect. III, case 21, ibid.; Matheny, "Air Estimate of Situation," Oct. 1, 1948, pp. 1–7, P & O 091 Greece (TS), sect. V, case 40, ibid. The air force needed two fighter-bomber groups, two transport squadrons, two reconnaissance squadrons, and one medium bombardment squadron. These changes necessitated 7,620 additional officers and men, 180 fighter planes, 60 transports, 60 reconnaissance and trainer craft, and 30 bombardment planes. Ibid., 6–7.

[41]CIA Report ORE 22-48—"Possibility of Direct Soviet Military Action During 1948–49," Sept. 16, 1948, pp. 1–4, CD 2-1-26, files of sec. of defense, NA. The Office of Naval Intelligence was not convinced that the Russians would resort to direct military action during 1948–49, but it did agree that the possibility of military action stemming from "miscalculation" had "increased slightly" during the preceding six months. Ibid., 1 n.2. CIA Report ORE 58-48—"The Strategic Value to the USSR of the Conquest of Western Europe and the Near East (to Cairo) prior to 1950" (Appendices), 44–45, Truman Papers, President's Secretary's Files, Truman Lib.; CIA Report ORE 60-48—"Threats to the Security of the United States," Sept. 28, 1948, pp. 3–5, 10–11, in ibid.

[42]JCS 1826/12—report by Joint Strategic Survey Committee to JCS: "Future United States Support to the Armed Forces of Greece," Oct. 7, 1948, pp. 107–9, P & O 091 Greece (TS), sect. II-A, case 13, Army Staff Records, NA; memo by DS member, SANACC, enclosure: "Decision on Long-Range U.S. Military Interests in Greece and Turkey," Oct. 12, 1948, pp. 1–3, P & O 400, case 39, ibid.; memo for chief of staff, U.S. Army, by Lieut. Col. [?] Lawler, Oct. 29, 1948, ibid.; Major Gen. Ray T. Maddocks to TUSAG, Ankara, Dec. 9, 1948, P & O 091 Turkey (TS), sect. II, case 11, ibid.; memo for record by Sievers, Nov. 16, 1948, ibid.; memo for chief of staff, U.S. Army, from Wedemeyer, Oct. 19, 1948, pp. 1–2, P & O 091 Greece (TS), sect. II-A, case 13, ibid.; memo for Wedemeyer from Schuyler, Oct. 14, 1948, pp. 1–3, P & O 091 Greece, sect. X, case 155, ibid.; memo by John Jernegan, chief of Divis. of Greek, Turkish, and Iranian Affairs, to Ray L. Thurston, asst. chief of Divis. of South Asian Affairs, Oct. 11, 1948, *FRUS*, VI: *The Near East, South Asia, and Africa* (Wash., D.C.: GPO, 1977), 2–3.

[43]Memo of conversation between Marshall and King Paul of Greece, Oct. 17, 1948, DSDF, NA; Carter in Paris to Lovett, Oct. 21, 1948, pp. 1–2, CD 6-3-43 (TS), files of sec. of defense, NA; memo by sec. of state of conversation between Marshall and Grady, Oct. 18, 1948, *FRUS*, IV: *Eastern Europe; Soviet Union*, 162; sec. of state to Lovett, Oct. 20, 1948, ibid., 162–64; Grady to sec. of state, Oct. 22, 1948, ibid., 168–70; "History of JUSMAGG," 2; "The Shape of Things" (editorial), *Nation*, Oct. 30, 1948, p. 478; Greek newsman quoted in *Time*, Oct. 25, 1948, p. 33.

[44]Sec. of state to Lovett, Oct. 20, 1948, *FRUS*, IV: *Eastern Europe; Soviet Union*, 164; memo of conversation between Marshall and King Paul of Greece, Oct. 17, 1948, DSDF, NA; memo for Wedemeyer from Schuyler, Oct. 22, 1948, P & O 091 Greece, sect. X, case 150, Army Staff Records, NA.

[45]Van Fleet to Wedemeyer, Oct. 9, 1948, pp. 1–2, P & O 091 Greece (secret), sect. V, case 40, Army Staff Records, NA; Van Fleet to Wedemeyer, Oct. 21, 1948, p. 2, ibid.; memo for record: "Internal Security Plan" (for security and evacuation), Oct. 13, 1948, pp. 1–2, P & O 370.05, ibid. Color codes signified the degrees of emergency: "Yellow" meant a state of emergency; "Red" indicated internal disorder but the army and gendarmerie were still in control; "Black" denoted that a major disturbance or uprising was out of the Greek authorities' control. Ibid. See also Campbell et al., *Employment of Airpower in Greek Guerrilla War*, 46 n.65; Van Fleet to Wedemeyer, Oct. 25, 1948, Records of Interservice Agencies, entry 146, box 55: 312-Correspondence of Gen. Van Fleet, 1948–50, Army Staff Records, NA; Grady to sec. of state, Oct. 26, 1948, *FRUS*, IV: *Eastern Europe; Soviet Union*, 177 n.1.

[46]"History of JUSMAGG," 65; "Special Report, Vitsi Operation," 2; Lovett to embassy in Athens, Oct. 30, 1948, *FRUS*, IV: *Eastern Europe; Soviet Union*, 177–78; Lovett to embassy in Athens, Dec. 6, 1948, ibid., 209; memo for record: briefing of Royall by Gen. Thomas S. Timberman, Oct. 27, 1948, pp. 1–6, P & O 091 Greece, sect. X, case 152, Army Staff Records, NA.

[47]"USAFGG History," 44; Campbell et al., *Employment of Airpower in Greek Guerrilla War*, 46–47, 64; "History of JUSMAGG," 2; JUSMAPG Report No. 38 (27 Oct.–2 Nov. 48), Nov. 5, 1948, annex 5, p. 1 (Nov. 4, 1948), P & O 091 Greece (TS), sect. III-A, case 21, Army Staff Records, NA; Matheny to chief of Air Staff, RHAF, Oct. 22, Nov. 6, 9, 1948, Air Adjutant Section 471 Ammunition (Napalm), JUSMAPG, NA; Ch. [?] Potamianos, group captain, chief of Air Staff, Air Ministry, Athens, to chief, Air Section, JUSMAPG, Oct. 30, 1948, ibid.

[48]Grady to sec. of state, Oct. 26, 1948, *FRUS*, IV: *Eastern Europe; Soviet Union*, 176–77; Grady to sec. of state, Nov. 13, 1948, ibid., 183; Lovett to embassy in Athens, Oct. 31, 1948, ibid., 178–79; "USAFGG History," 44–45; Wedemeyer to JUSMAPG, Nov. 9, 1948, P & O 091 Greece (TS), sect. V, case 36, Army Staff Records, NA; Satterthwaite to Lovett, Nov. 9, 1948, DSDF, NA; Wittner, *American Intervention in Greece*, 247–48; Woodhouse, *Struggle for Greece*, 247. According to Wedemeyer, Papagos, now 59 years of age, had had a long and illustrious career. His first military experience came as a second lieutenant of the cavalry in the Balkan Wars of 1912–13. He later entered the Greek War Academy, and when World War I began, he took part in the campaigns in Asia Minor as a major and a lieutenant colonel. By 1935 Papagos was a lieutenant general, then commander of an army corps, and even served briefly in the Greek cabinet as minister of war. In 1936, he became inspector general of the army, then chief of the Greek General Staff before year's end. During the war against Italy and Germany, Papagos was commander-in-chief until he was captured. He spent two years in a German concentration camp. In 1945 he returned to Greece as general and became grand marshall of the court. Papagos was considered honest, intelligent, courageous, and an outstanding leader. He possessed a strong personality and had the quality of commanding respect. Though Papagos was a royalist and a confidant of the king, he had tried to stay out of politics. The Greek people liked him because of his achievements and his integrity. Sophoulis shared this confidence. The Department of the Army agreed with the State Department that Papagos's appointment was a wise move, as long as he remained free from political interference. See memo for acting sec. of army from Wedemeyer, Dec. 22, 1948, P & O 400 (TS), sect. II-A, case 13, ibid.; William H. Draper, Jr., acting sec. of army, to Lovett, Dec. 24, 1948, ibid.

[49]See Sulzberger, *Long Row of Candles*, 394; Grady to sec. of state, Nov. 22, 1948, *FRUS*, IV: *Eastern Europe; Soviet Union*, 187–89; JCS to Forrestal (SANACC 358/8), Nov. 24, 1948, ibid., 191–92; Grady to sec. of state, Dec. 7, 1948, ibid., 210–11. The Department of the Army believed that the present force was adequate to deal with 25,000 guerrillas. More than 240,000 Greeks were in arms, including 147,000 in the army, 50,000 in the National Defense Corps, 14,200 in the navy, 7,200 in the air force, and 22,000 in the gendarmerie. See memo for chief of staff, U.S. Army, from Maddocks, Dec. 14, 1948, p. 2, P & O 091 Greece (TS), sect. II-A, case 13, Army Staff Records, NA.

[50]Grady to sec. of state, Nov. 22, 1948, *FRUS*, IV: *Eastern Europe; Soviet Union*, 189–90; JCS to Forrestal, Nov. 24, 1948, ibid., 191; Grady to sec. of state, Dec. 7, 1948, ibid., 211–12; Maddocks

to Van Fleet, Dec. 9, 1948, P & O 091 Greece (TS), sect. V, case 40, Army Staff Records, NA; memo for chief of staff, U.S. Army, from Maddocks, Dec. 14, 1948, p. 2, P & O 091 Greece (TS), sect. II-A, case 13, ibid.; memo by Maddocks for deputy chief of staff for Plans and Combat Operations, Dec. 14, 1948, P & O 091 Greece (TS), sect. V, case 36, ibid.; memo for record by Robert J. Wood for sec. of defense (notes on Army P & O meeting of Dec. 17, 1948), Dec. 17, 1948, CD 6-3-43, files of sec. of defense, NA; Forrestal to sec. of state, Dec. 23, 1948, CD 6-3-43 (TS), ibid.

51Grady to sec. of state, Nov. 22, 1948, *FRUS*, IV: *Eastern Europe; Soviet Union*, 189; McGhee to Lovett, Nov. 24, 1948, ibid., 193–94; report by Policy Planning Staff on U.S. aid to Greece, Nov. 24, 1948, ibid., 196, 203; draft report by DS to NSC: "The Position of the United States with Respect to the Use of U.S. Military Power in Greece," Nov. 30, 1948, ibid., 207; memo for sec. of defense from Leahy, Nov. 24, 1948, pp. 1–2, CD 5-1-13, files of sec. of defense, NA.

52Griswold to sec. of state, July 26, 1948, DSDF, NA; McGhee to sec. of state, Aug. 13, 1948, ibid.

53Quotes in Wittner, *American Intervention in Greece*, 247.

54Lovett to embassy in Ankara, Oct. 21, 1948, *FRUS*, IV: *Eastern Europe; Soviet Union*, 166–67; memo for Wedemeyer regarding Royall's recommendations after trip to Greece and Turkey, Dec. 22, 1948, p. 2, P & O 400, case 39, Army Staff Records, NA; memo for Wedemeyer from Maddocks, Dec. 22, 1948, p. 2, P & O 091 Greece (TS), sect. II-A, case 13, ibid.; Draper to Lovett, Dec. 24, 1948, p. 2, ibid.; JUSMAPG Report No. 46 to JCS, Dec. 31, 1948, P & O 091 Greece, sect. III-A, case 21, ibid.; "History of JUSMAGG," 66, 151; "USAFGG History," 45–47; Campbell et al., *Employment of Airpower in Greek Guerrilla War*, 47; Matthews, *Memories of a Mountain War Greece*, 213–22, 231ff., 244–51, 258; *New York Times*, Oct. 28, 1948, p. 11; Woodhouse, *Struggle for Greece*, 245, 255. Markos's terms included a coalition government in Athens comprised of representatives of all political parties; free elections within six months of the formation of this coalition government; the withdrawal from Greece of all foreign missions, except representatives of the UN; legalization of trade unions; and a pardon of political prisoners. See [?] Penfield in Praha to sec. of state, Oct. 26, 1948, DSDF, NA.

55Woodhouse, *Struggle for Greece*, 253–57; Iatrides, "Civil War," 210–11; Averoff-Tossizza, *By Fire and Axe*, 276–77; Matthews, *Memories of a Mountain War Greece*, 263–67; Wittner, *American Intervention in Greece*, 252, 267; O'Ballance, *Greek Civil War*, 181–83; Dimitrios G. Kousoulas, *Revolution and Defeat: The Story of the Greek Communist Party* (London: Oxford U. Press, 1965), 252–53; Eudes, *Kapetanios*, 335–38. One writer believes that Tito decided to reduce aid to the guerrillas because of Western diplomatic pressure and the possibility of receiving Western economic aid. See Nicholas Pappas, "The Soviet-Yugoslav Conflict and the Greek Civil War," in Wayne S. Vucinich, ed., *At the Brink of War and Peace: The Tito-Stalin Split in a Historic Perspective* (N.Y.: Columbia U. Press, 1982), 224–25. Elisabeth Barker, however, admits to Tito's interest in receiving economic assistance but emphasizes that Zaharia-dis's triumph over Markos within the KKE was the crucial factor. It had moved the party into a pro-Stalinist stance in relation to the rift in the Cominform, and it had led to the removal of Markos, the man most responsible for attracting Yugoslav aid to the guerrillas. Indeed, in late 1948, Yugoslavia's vice foreign minister, Aleš Bebler, was in Paris, where he made informal contacts with Greek representatives that might have re-established relations had not some threats (presumably from the Soviet Union) intervened. Barker bases her conclusions largely on a recently published work by one of Tito's associates, Vladimir Dedijer: *Novi Prilozi za Biografiju Josipa Broza Tita, Treći Tom* (Belgrade, 1984), 265, 268. Cited in Barker, "The Yugoslavs and the Greek Civil War of 1946-1949," in Baerentzen, Iatrides, and Smith, eds., *Studies in the History of the Greek Civil War*, 300, 304–5. Another writer shows that Tito was unable to stop his country's aid to the Greek guerrillas as quickly as he wanted to because of protests from his Macedonian Communist friends. See Jože Pirjevec, "The Tito-Stalin Split and the End of the Civil War in Greece," in ibid., 316. NOF, the Slavo-Macedonian communist group working with the guerrillas, began purging those for Yugoslavia, and by December was making its "national claims" by calling for an independent Macedonia. KKE leaders thus had to make a decision on Macedonia—which meant making a choice between Yugoslavia and Bulgaria on that question. This also meant choosing between Tito and Stalin. Woodhouse, *Struggle for Greece*, 253–54. Zahariadis quoted in Pappas, "The Soviet-Yugoslav Conflict and the Greek Civil War," 227.

CHAPTER 11. THE COMMUNISTS' PEACE OFFENSIVE

[1]Memo prepared by Amer. embassy in Athens, Jan. 27, 1949, *FRUS*, VI: *The Near East, South Asia, and Africa* (Wash., D.C.: GPO, 1977), 242–44; "USAFGG History," 47–48; Van Fleet to Maddocks, Jan. 29, 1949, Records of Interservice Agencies, 312-Correspondence of Gen. Van Fleet, 1948–50, box 55, entry 146, Army Staff Records, NA; Homer Bigart, "Are We Losing Out in Greece?," *Saturday Evening Post*, Jan. 1, 1949, p. 19; *Time*, Jan. 3, 1949, p. 20, and Jan. 31, 1949, p. 26; McCormick quoted in ibid., Jan. 10, 1949, p. 45; Francis F. Lincoln (the American observer), *United States' Aid to Greece, 1947–1962* (Germantown, Tenn.: Professional Seminars, 1975), 80; Evangelos Averoff-Tossizza, *By Fire and Axe: The Communist Party and the Civil War in Greece, 1944–1949* (New Rochelle, N.Y.: Caratzas Brothers, 1978), 312–13. Originally published as *Le Feu et la hache Grèce '46–'49, histoire des guerres de l'après-guerre* (Paris: Editions de Breteuil, 1973). Trans. by Sarah Arnold Rigos. Woman quoted in *Time*, Jan. 31, 1949, p. 27; Fritz A. Voight, *The Greek Sedition* (London: Hollis & Carter, 1949), 3, 5–7; Edgar O'Ballance, *The Greek Civil War, 1944–1949* (N.Y.: Praeger, 1966), 184–85; Christopher M. Woodhouse, *The Struggle for Greece, 1941–1949* (Brooklyn Heights, N.Y.: Beekman-Esanu, 1976), 260–62. Van Fleet's plan, code-named "Lugworm," was generally approved and incorporated into CINCNELM's overall war plan by Christmas 1949. See "LUGWORM," JUSMAPG Special Operations Plan, Jan. 13, 1949, P & O 381 Europe (TS), sect. I-B, case 4, book 1, ibid. Documents consulted did not contain details regarding LUGWORM. The mayor of Naoussa had recently extended an official welcome to Van Fleet in a public celebration. After the killing, the mayor's body remained propped up against the bloodstained monument where he was shot until government forces drove out the guerrillas three days later. Many of Karpenisi's 3,000 residents escaped into the woods or hid in the sewers. Over a hundred died in the cold or during the brief resistance, and more than 700 were abducted. The Greek army pushed out the guerrillas in late March, but only after they had pillaged and destroyed all public buildings, including the hospital, school, and refugee home.

[2]*New York Times*, Feb. 19, 1949, p. 7; London *Times*, Feb. 19, 1949, p. 4e; Voight, *Greek Sedition*, 7–8; Woodhouse, *Struggle for Greece*, 260; memo for record, Jan. 27, 1949, P & O 091 Greece (TS), sect. I, case 2, Army Staff Records, NA.

[3]Ibid., all references.

[4]*New York Times*, Jan. 23, 1949, p. 26, and Feb. 19, 1949, p. 7; memo for record, Jan. 24, 1949, P & O 091 Greece (TS), sect. I, case 2, ibid.; USAGG in Athens to CSGPO, Dept. of Army, Jan. 26, 1949, P & O 091 Greece (TS), sect. I, case 2/2, ibid; memo for record, Jan. 27, 1949, P & O 091 Greece (TS), sect. I, case 2, ibid.

[5]*New York Times*, Dec. 29, 1948, p. 20; editions of Jan. 5, 31, Feb. 2, 5, 1949, encl. in Lincoln Papers, Truman Lib.

[6]Memo to Major Nelson H. Russell, Ordnance, Air Section, JUSMAPG, to chief, Air Section, JUSMAPG, Jan. 18, 1949, pp. 1–4, 6, Air Adjutant Section 471 Ammunition (Napalm), JUSMAPG, NA; Russell to chief, Air Section, JUSMAPG, March 3, 1949, ibid.; "USAFGG History," 212.

[7]NSC Action 173, approval of Policy Planning Staff paper, PPS 46 of Nov. 30, 1948—"The Position of the United States with Respect to the Use of United States Military Power in Greece," Jan. 10, 1949, *FRUS*, VI: *Near East, South Asia, and Africa*, 235–36; memo for sec. of defense from Blum, Jan. 5, 1949, pp. 1–6, CD 6-4-17, files of sec. of defense, NA; PPS 46, pp. 5–6;

SANACC 358/9—"Decision on Long-Range U.S. Military Interests in Greece and Turkey," Jan. 12, 1949, pp. 75–76, P & O 092 Europe (TS), sect. I, case 4, Army Staff Records, NA; CIA Report 1–49—"Review of the World Situation," Jan. 19, 1949, p. 6, in Truman Papers, President's Secretary's Files, Truman Lib. The CIA claimed that Moscow controlled the KKE through the party's leadership and through the Cominform, but that that control was weakened by the "conflicting nationalistic aspirations" for Macedonia. See CIA Report ORE 68-48—"Opposition to ECA in Participating Countries," Feb. 10, 1949, p. 29, ibid.

[8]Grady, "Adventures in Diplomacy" (unpublished memoirs), 202, Grady Papers, box 5, Truman Lib.; Hoffman to Harriman and Nuveen, Dec. 25, 1948, folder: "Greece-Correspondence, 1946–1951," box 3, ibid.; Cyrus L. Sulzberger, *A Long Row of Candles: Memoirs and Diaries [1934–1954]* (N.Y.: Macmillan, 1969), 428–31; Lawrence S. Wittner, *American Intervention in Greece, 1943–1949* (N.Y.: Columbia U. Press, 1982), 122–28.

[9]Grady, "Adventures in Diplomacy," 201–2; William Rountree to McGhee, Jan. 14, 1949, DSDF, NA; Grady to Harriman, Jan. 12, 1949, ibid.; Grady to sec. of state, Jan. 14, 18, 1949, ibid.; Rankin to sec. of state, March 8, 1949, ibid.; Grady to McGhee, Jan. 22, 1949, folder: "Greece-Correspondence, 1946–1951," box 3, Grady Papers, Truman Lib.

[10]Grady, "Adventures in Diplomacy," 198–200. Grady eventually won President Truman's support in having Nuveen removed. His replacement was Paul R. Porter (not to be confused with Paul A. Porter, who had headed the economic mission to Greece), at the time working for the ECA in Geneva. According to Grady, Harriman later expressed regrets for his efforts to keep Nuveen in Greece. Grady used the Nuveen experience to warn of the inherent danger in America's aid programs: the giver has a choice of seeking no control over expenditures (which was "absurd"); of taking absolute control of the recipient country (which was "equally unthinkable"); or of finding a "middle course" by offering advice through a "corps of experts" and exerting "influence . . . through a sympathetic approach to the country's problems" (which was the "only appropriate" approach). Only in this manner could there be the necessary coordination of economic, military, and political affairs. Ibid., 203–6; Acheson meeting with President Truman, May 16, 1949, Acheson Papers, memoranda of conversations, box 64, Truman Lib. Acheson later excused much of Nuveen's conduct as attributable to natural frustration with Greek business practices. Acheson to Harriman, March 15, 1949, ibid.

[11]Grady, "Adventures in Diplomacy," 200–201. Grady later wrote: "From the time [Papagos] took over the tide turned. Our Military Mission aided him beyond question and our vast quantities of supplies were of untold benefit, but, in the final analysis, it was the inspired leadership and military genius of General Papagos, supported by his valiant soldiers, that really saved the day for Greece." Ibid., 202. For supporting an authoritarian government, Grady vainly sought Van Fleet's removal from Greece after the civil war. Grady to sec. of state, Aug. 23, 1949, DSDF, NA.

[12]Grady, "Adventures in Diplomacy," 202–3; *Time*, Jan. 31, 1949, pp. 26–27; Wittner, *American Intervention in Greece*, 248; Woodhouse, *Struggle for Greece*, 247, 259; Emergency Law No. 882, cited in "Decision of the Council of Ministers," *Official Gazette* of Greece, Jan. 20, 1949, vol. I, no. 2, in Records of Interservice Agencies, 312-Correspondence of Gen. Van Fleet, 1948–50, box 55, entry 146, Army Staff Records, NA. By law, Papagos directed all military operations, assumed responsibility for the composition and establishment of army units, made changes in personnel, and recalled officers from retirement or reserve. Ibid. Order of the Day to the National Forces, encl. in Van Fleet to Maddocks, Jan. 29, 1949, ibid.; Papagos to Van Fleet, Jan. 27, 1949, ibid. Van Fleet noted that Papagos's request "moved me deeply." Van Fleet to Papagos, Jan. 29, 1949, ibid.

[13]Van Fleet to Maddocks, Jan. 29, 1949, vol. I, no. 2, in Records of Interservice Agencies, 312-Correspondence of Gen. Van Fleet, 1948–50, box 55, entry 146, Army Staff Records, NA; *New York Times*, Jan. 23, 1949, p. 26; Woodhouse, *Struggle for Greece*, 259; "History JUSMAPG—Greece, Jan. 1, 1948–March 25, 1949," 126; "Brief History, JUSMAPG, Jan. 1, 1948 to Dec. 31, 1949," 19; Wittner, *American Intervention in Greece*, 250.

[14]Van Fleet to Maddocks, Jan. 29, 1949, vol. I, no. 2, in Records of Interservice Agencies, 312-Correspondence of Gen. Van Fleet, 1948-50, box 55, entry 146, Army Staff Records, NA. Van Fleet claims that Ventiris was a Liberal who was *"persona non grata"* to Tsaldaris, the leader of the Populists. In October 1947 Ventiris resigned under pressure from the Greek General Staff to become army commander. Then, after the army's poor initial showing at Konitsa in early 1948, he came under heavy criticism and resigned in protest. Woodhouse, *Struggle for Greece*, 209, 221.

[15]Grady to sec. of state, Feb. 7, 1949, *FRUS*, VI: *Near East, South Asia, and Africa*, 245-46; Grady to Tsaldaris, Feb. 15, 1949, ibid., 248-49.

[16]Grady to sec. of state, Feb. 7, 1949, ibid., 246-47.

[17]"History of JUSMAGG," 159; M. A. Campbell et al., *The Employment of Airpower in the Greek Guerrilla War, 1947-1949* (Montgomery, Ala: Air U., Maxwell AFB, 1964), 12-13, 57; "History of JUSMAPG" (1 Jan. 48-31 Aug. 49), 16; *New York Times*, June 20, 1948, p. 48. Grady remarked years afterward that Papagos's appointment was the "turning point" in the war and that the outcome might have been considerably different had he not held that position. Grady, "Adventures in Diplomacy," 202. A British observer, Christopher M. Woodhouse, was not enthusiastic about Papagos's contributions. According to Woodhouse, the Greeks "had virtually won the war" before Papagos took command. If the general affected the outcome, "it has been rightly said that 'the Army was simply made to do what it was capable of doing.'" Woodhouse, *Struggle for Greece*, 270.

[18]"History of JUSMAGG," 3.

[19]Satterthwaite (director of Office of Near Eastern and African Affairs) to Lovett, Jan. 3, 1949, *FRUS*, VI: *Near East, South Asia, and Africa*, 228-30; memo by acting sec. of state of conversation, Jan. 4, 1949, ibid., 231-32; Harry S. Truman, *Memoirs: Years of Trial and Hope, 1946-1952* (Garden City, N.Y.: Doubleday, 1956), 230.

[20]Grady to sec. of state, Jan. 27, 28, 1949, DSDF, NA; Kenneth Matthews (Brit. journalist), *Memories of a Mountain War Greece: 1944-1949* (London: Longman, 1972), 15; O'Ballance, *Greek Civil War*, 185; Woodhouse, *Struggle for Greece*, 263; Fifth Session of Central Committee of Greek Communist party, Jan. 29-30, 1949, in *FRUS*, VI: *Near East, South Asia, and Africa*, ed. comment, 250 n.1. According to the "most reliable Greek intelligence reports from Bucharest via Ankara, Markos recently traveled from Bucharest to Sinaia, Rumania, where he was being held in custody. He reportedly had a bandage over one eye. See memo of conversation between Alexander Beinoglou, first sec., Royal Greek Assembly, and Cromie, March 15, 1949, DSDF, NA. *Time*, Feb. 21, 1949, p. 31. Ioannides had been a member of the Communist party since 1918. Ibid.

[21]Report by Harry N. Howard, DS specialist in Greek affairs, on "The Fifth Plenum of the Greek Communist Party (KKE), January 30-31, 1949," pp. 1-2, Howard Papers, Truman Lib.; *Time*, Feb. 14, 1949, p. 26; "History of JUSMAGG," 152; Amer. embassy in Athens, to sec. of state, Feb. 8, 1949, DSDF, NA: Douglas to sec. of state, Feb. 11, 1949, ibid.; Acheson to Amer. missions in Athens, Belgrade, Bucharest, Moscow, Praha, Sofia, and Warsaw, Feb. 18, 1949, ibid.; Grady to sec. of state, Feb. 24, 1949, ibid.; directors for European Affairs and Near Eastern and African Affairs, to sec. of state, March 2, 1949, ibid. The American ambassador in Paris, Jefferson Caffery, reported that a "source maintaining close relations with Comintern circles" declared that Central European Communists claimed that Markos had been "liquidated" because of his refusal to work exclusively along the Albanian-Greek border and to accept the Kremlin's use of growing numbers of Bulgarian guerrillas in the Salonika area to detach Macedonian Greece as a "Macedonian popular republic." Though the Parisian Communists remained silent in public, they privately referred to Markos as "Titoist." Caffery to sec. of state, Feb. 14, 1949, ibid.

[22]Report by Howard on "The Fifth Plenum of the Greek Communist Party," 1-4; Souers memo for NSC: "The Position of the United States with Respect to the Use of Military Power in

Greece," Dec. 20, 1948, p. 4, Truman Papers, President's Secretary's Files, box 203, NSC Meeting #12, Truman Lib.

23 Report by Howard on "The Fifth Plenum of the Greek Communist Party," 9, 11, 17, 23; Quarterly Report, DS Publication 3594, Economic Cooperation Series 21, *Seventh Report to Congress on Assistance to Greece and Turkey for the Period Ended March 31, 1949* (Wash., D.C.: GPO, 1949), 1–4, 6–9, Truman Papers, Official File, OF 426, Truman Lib.; Cannon to sec. of state, March 9, April 12, 1949, DSDF, NA; *FRUS*, VI: *Near East, South Asia, and Africa*, 378, ed. note.

24 "History of JUSMAGG," 152; Douglas to sec. of state, Feb. 11, 1949, DSDF, NA: Richard V. Burks, *The Dynamics of Communism in Eastern Europe* (Princeton: Princeton U. Press, 1961), 103–4.

25 "History of JUSMAGG," 153, 154; "USAFGG History," 56, 59; Averoff-Tossizza, *By Fire and Axe*, 327–29, 335; Bickham Sweet-Escott, *Greece: A Political and Economic Survey, 1939–1953* (London: Royal Institute of International Affairs, 1954), 62–63; Burks, *Dynamics of Communism in Eastern Europe*, 103 n.19, 103–4; Woodhouse, *Struggle for Greece*, 262; O'Ballance, *Greek Civil War*, 188–90; Matthews, *Memories of a Mountain War Greece*, 16, 267–68; Voight, *Greek Sedition*, 12; *Time*, Feb. 21, 1949, p. 31; London *Times*, Feb. 19, 1949, p. 4e. It is debatable whether the mass entry of Slavo-Macedonians into the Democratic Army had brought an internationalization of the war. As historians have noted, the question of the nationality of Slavo-Macedonians remains unanswered. Burks shows that their homeland was divided among the Yugoslav republic of Macedonia (or Vardar Macedonia), the Bulgarian section (or Pirin Macedonia), and the Greek part (or Aegean Macedonia). The Greeks called their small Slavo-Macedonian people "Slavophones," or Slavic-speaking Greeks. Thus the Slavo-Macedonians who entered the Democratic Army in February 1949 were probably a mixture of the three, but united behind the call for a free and independent Macedonian state. Burks, *Dynamics of Communism in Eastern Europe*, 91–92. Zahariadis had invited all Macedonians into his forces. See Hamilton Fish Armstrong, *Tito and Goliath* (N.Y.: Macmillan, 1951), 192.

26 Cannon to sec. of state, Feb. 16, 1949, *FRUS*, VI: *Near East, South Asia, and Africa*, 250–52.

27 Drew to sec. of state, Feb. 19, 1949, ibid., 253–54; sec. of state to embassy in Athens, Feb. 25, 1949, ibid., 257–58; [?] Baldwin in Trieste to sec. of state, Feb. 21, 1949, DSDF, NA; directors for European Affairs and Near Eastern and African Affairs to sec. of state, March 2, 1949, ibid.; *Time*, Feb. 14, 1949, p. 26.

28 Rankin to sec. of state, Feb. 4, 1949, DSDF, NA; Grady to sec. of state, March 8, 1949, ibid.; Grady to sec. of state, Feb. 21, 1949, *FRUS*, VI: *Near East, South Asia, and Africa*, 256–57; Grady to sec. of state, March 30, 1949, ibid., 281–84; Bevin to sec. of state, March 31, 1949, ibid., 286. Bevin wanted to expand the Greek army by one infantry division (9,000 men) and two infantry pursuit groups (total of 4,000 men), and the air force by two fighter-bomber squadrons and one reconnaissance squadron. Ibid., 287. JCS 1704/19, "Report on Greece by Chief of Imperial General Staff," March 31, 1949, pp. 98, 101–2, P & O 091 Greece (TS), sect. I, case 7/2, Army Staff Records, NA. To raise the morale of the Greek people, the government sponsored a week of national celebration called "For Work and Victory." The climax was the 128th anniversary of the independence of Greece on March 25. President Truman appointed Grady as his personal representative with the rank of "Special Ambassador." The culmination was a rally in Athens Stadium that drew 60,000 people inside and an equivalent number outside in the streets and nearby hills. Grady to sec. of state, March 30, 1949, *FRUS*, VI: *Near East, South Asia, and Africa*, 284, 284 n.2; Baxter to [?] Allen, March 4, 1949, DSDF, NA; Acheson to Grady, March 17, 1949, ibid.; Baxter to Satterthwaite, March 3, 1949, ibid.; Acheson to embassy in Athens, March 4, 1949, ibid. See also "History of JUSMAPG" (1 Jan. 48–31 Aug. 49), p. 17; report by NSC to President—"U.S. Objectives with Respect to Greece and Turkey to Counter Soviet Threats to U.S. Security," March 22, 1949, ibid., 269, 276, 278; President's Seventh Report to Congress on Assistance to Greece and Turkey, 7–9. According to the UN Special Committee on the Balkans, Albania was sending motor vehicle convoys to the Greek border for logistical

support. Ibid., 7. The chief of staff of one of the guerrilla brigades captured at Ioannina claimed that forced recruiting was necessary because over a third of the guerrillas in central Greece were women. "History of JUSMAGG," 15. Harriman considered Sophoulis and Diomedes "too old and weary" to run the Greek government, and recommended "strong discreet pressure." Acheson agreed. Harriman to Acheson, Feb. 28, 1949, Acheson Papers, memoranda of conversations, 1949, box 64, Truman Lib.; Acheson to Harriman, March 15, 1949, ibid. Sophoulis was in his eighties and had had two heart attacks, and Diomedes was in his seventies—an economist and Byzantine scholar with no political experience. *Time*, Jan. 31, 1949, pp. 26–27.

29"History of JUSMAGG," 11–12.

30Ibid., 12.; "USAFGG History," 64–65; Campbell et al., *Employment of Airpower in Greek Guerrilla War*, 30–31, 48.

31"History of JUSMAGG," 10–12.

32Ibid., 13–14.

33Ibid., 15–18, 40–41, 66.

34Ibid., 19–20.

35Ibid., 20–21.

36Ibid., 38–40.

37Van Fleet to Maddocks, May 12, 1949, Records of Interservice Agencies, 312-Correspondence of Gen. Van Fleet, 1948–50, box 55, entry 146, Army Staff Records, NA; Van Fleet to Bradley, May 12, 1949, ibid.; Van Fleet to Papagos, May 9, 1949, ibid.

38Van Fleet to Sophoulis, May 2, 1949, ibid.; Grady to sec. of state, April 7, 1949, *FRUS*, VI: *Near East, South Asia, and Africa*, 291–92; memo for chief of staff from Maddocks, April 18, 1949, P & O 091 Greece (TS), sect. I, case 7/1, Army Staff Records, NA.

39Memo by Cromie of conversation among Satterthwaite, Jernegan, Cromie, and Dendramis, April 1, 1949, *FRUS*, VI: *Near East, South Asia, and Africa*, 287–88.

40Grady to sec. of state, April 1, 1949, ibid., 289–90.

41Memo by Gordon P. Merriam of DS Policy Planning Staff, June 13, 1949, ibid., 32, 34–35, 40–42. At a press conference on March 23, 1949, the secretary of state declared, "In the compact world of today, the security of the United States cannot be defined in terms of boundaries and frontiers. A serious threat to international peace and security anywhere in the world is of direct concern to this country. Therefore, it is our policy to help free peoples to maintain their integrity and independence, not only in Western Europe or the Americas, but wherever the aid we are able to provide can be effective. Our actions in supporting the integrity and independence of Greece, Turkey and Iran are expressions of that determination." Ibid., 44.

Actually, that same month of March, a British delegation of Foreign Office and Secret Intelligence Service members had met with representatives of the State Department and the CIA's Office for Policy Coordination (OPC) in a three-day conference regarding broad Anglo-American intelligence cooperation against the Soviet Union. Nicholas Bethell argues that the central purpose of the visit was to discuss subversive techniques aimed at deposing the Hoxha regime in Albania. The previous November of 1948, the "Russia Committee" in London (which was primarily a Foreign Office body) had decided to move toward undercutting the USSR in the Cold War, and had agreed (due mainly to financial difficulties) to concentrate on Albania. At this meeting were several future British ambassadors and the air force chief, Lord Tedder. With Bevin's approval (at least "presumed by those close to the project"), planning for such a liberation movement began, and the following month the committee decided that there must be "coordination with the United States government." According to Bethell, the Americans at the March 1949 meeting in Washington approved. If so, it seems safe to assume that Acheson was aware of the project, for as Bethell notes, the secretary of state, with the NSC, was responsible for the OPC, whose mission, since its establishment in June 1948, was to engage in covert operations against the Soviets. The United States clandestinely supported the enterprise until its final failure in 1953. Bethell maintains that the initial attempts by Albanian exiles to overthrow Hoxha were betrayed by one of Britain's SIS participants in the operation, Kim Philby, who worked as a double agent for Stalin's secret service. Philby was later uncovered and defected to the Soviet Union in 1963. For this story, see Nicholas Bethell, *The Great Betrayal: The Untold Story of Kim Philby's Biggest Coup* (London: Hodder & Stoughton, 1984), esp. 1–6, 36–39, 94. See also Bruce Page, David Leitch, and Phillip Knightley, *The Philby Conspiracy* (Garden City, N.Y.: Doubleday, 1968), 197–202 (the three staff members of the *Sunday Times* in London who first revealed the plot against Hoxha); Kim Philby, *My Silent War* (London: Macgibbon & Kee, 1968); John Halliday, ed., *The Artful Albanian: Memoirs of Enver Hoxha* (London: Chatto & Windus, 1986), 80–83; John L. Gaddis, *The Long Peace: Inquiries into the History of the Cold War* (N.Y.: Oxford U. Press, 1987), 160. Cyrus L. Sulzberger, the *New York Times* correspondent in the Mediterranean area, wrote a story in March 1950 revealing the attempt. Bethell, *Great Betrayal*, 100–101; Sulzberger, *Long Row of Candles*, 476, 498. For the NSC's establishment of the OPC, see Robert J. Donovan, *Conflict and Crisis: The Presidency of Harry S Truman, 1945–1948* (N.Y.: Norton, 1977), 367.

42Cannon to sec. of state, April 8, 1949, *FRUS*, VI: *Near East, South Asia, and Africa*, 292–93.

43Memo by Rusk of conversation, April 27, 1949, ibid., 301–3. The initiative toward negotiations perhaps can be traced to a suggestion for cooperation among the major powers made by the U.S. representative to the UN, Philip Jessup, to the Soviets' UN representative, Yakov Malik, on March 21, 1949. Malik laughed about the assertion that the Kremlin had influence on the communist nations surrounding Greece but added that his government had influence with "*some* of them." See Wittner. *American Intervention in Greece*, 275.

44Memo by Rusk of conversation, May 5, 1949, ibid., 303–4; report on "Greece: The Evatt Conciliation Discussions," May 4, 1949, p. 44, Howard Papers, Truman Lib. Herbert V. Evatt was an Australian and at that time president of the UN General Assembly.

45Memo by Rusk of conversation, May 5, 1949, *FRUS*, VI: *Near East, South Asia, and Africa*, 304; "Greece: The Evatt Conciliation Discussions," 44.

46Memo by Rusk of conversation, May 5, 1949, *FRUS*, VI: *Near East, South Asia, and Africa*, 304–6, 305 n.3; "Greek Air Force Small But Able," *Air Intelligence Digest*, II, no. 9, p. 44, Maxwell AFB, 140.0371, in Simpson Lib.; "Greece: The Evatt Conciliation Discussions," 44. Less than a week after the guerrillas' peace offer, they denied over radio having made specific proposals. This probably resulted from the Russians telling Porfirogenis that they were in control and that he should not go on record with concrete terms from which they could not retreat with grace. See Cromie to Satterthwaite, Jernegan, and Baxter, May 17, 1949, DSDF, NA.

47Memo by Rusk of conversation, May 5, 1949, *FRUS*, VI: *Near East, South Asia, and Africa*, 306–7; "Greece: The Evatt Conciliation Discussions," 44.

48Memo by Rusk of conversation, May 5, 1949, *FRUS*, VI: *Near East, South Asia, and Africa*, 307–8.

49Ibid., 308–9; Satterthwaite to Rusk, May 9, 1949, DSDF, NA.

50Howard to Cromie, May 4, 1949, DSDF, NA: Satterthwaite to Rusk, May 9, 1949, ibid.; Rusk to Acting Sec. of State James E. Webb, May 19, 1949, ibid.; memo by Acheson of conversation with Truman, May 5, 1949, Acheson Papers, memoranda of conversations, 1949, box 64, Truman Lib.; author's interview with Rusk, Nov. 3, 1978.

51Howard to Cromie, May 4, 1949, DSDF, NA; Manchester *Guardian*, May 5, 1949, encl. in Douglas to sec. of state, May 11, 1949, ibid. The State Department specialist on Greece, Harry N. Howard, considered the Gromyko talks a serious move toward conciliation. Howard, "Greece and Its Balkan Neighbors (1948–1949): The United Nations Attempts at Conciliation," *Balkan Studies* 7 (1966): 11–12. See also "The Shape of Things" (editorial), *Nation*, May 14, 1949, pp. 541–42. Van Fleet scoffed at the peace terms and declared that if the communists wanted peace, they must first lay down their arms. *Time,* May 16, 1949, p. 33.

[52]Foy Kohler (the chargé) to sec. of state, March 28, 1949, DSDF, NA.

[53]Memo by Rusk of conversation, May 16, 1949, ibid.; Satterthwaite to sec. of state, May 17, 1949, ibid.; "Greece: The Evatt Conciliation Discussions," 44–45; ed. note based on various papers in DS, May 14, 1949, *FRUS,* VI: *Near East, South Asia, and Africa,* 320–21; memo by Cromie of conversation among Dendramis, Rusk, Economou-Gouras (Greek minister), and Cromie, May 20, 1949, ibid., 330–33; Acheson to Evatt, May 26, 1949, ibid., 33 n.1. On November 10, 1948, the UN General Assembly established a "Conciliation Committee," which was chaired by Evatt to examine ways to resolve Greek border problems. By the end of the Paris meetings in December, the committee had made some progress and was to meet again at Lake Success in New York in April 1949. See Howard, "Greece and Its Balkan Neighbors (1948–1949)," 1–26; Howard, "The Problem of Greece in the Third Session of the General Assembly," in *Documents and State Papers* 1 (Wash., D.C.: DS Publications 3438, no. 10, Jan. 1949): 545–614. Both explanations in *FRUS,* VI: *Near East, South Asia, and Africa,* 254 n.4. See also Wittner, *American Intervention in Greece,* 275–77.

[54]Memo by Rusk of conversation: "Preliminary U.S. Reactions to the Gromyko Balkan Proposals," May 19, 1949, *FRUS,* VI: *Near East, South Asia, and Africa,* 326–29; Acheson to embassy in Athens, May 19, 1949, DSDF, NA.

[55]Minor to sec. of state, May 19, 1949, *FRUS,* VI: *Near East, South Asia, and Africa,* 323–24.

[56]"Greece: The Evatt Conciliation Discussions," 42–43.

[57]Memo by Cromie of conversation, May 20, 1949, *FRUS,* VI: *Near East, South Asia, and Africa,* 330–33.

[58]"Greece: The Evatt Conciliation Discussions," 43.

[59]Jernegan to Rusk, May 24, 1949, DSDF, NA; Grady to sec. of state, May 26, 1949, *FRUS,* VI: *Near East, South Asia, and Africa,* 345–47.

[60]Grady to acting sec. of state, May 28, 1949, *FRUS,* VI: *Near East, South Asia, and Africa,* 348–49; Webb to sec. of state, June 3, 1949, ibid., 351–52; Grady to acting sec. of state, June 8, 1949, ibid., 353, 355.

[61]Memo by Rusk of conversation, May 19, 1949, ibid., 324; sec. of state to Amer. embassy in Athens, May 19, 1949, ibid., 322–23; Kohler to acting sec. of state, May 25, 1949, ibid., 338–39; Drew to acting sec. of state, May 25, 1949, ibid., 339–41; Brit. embassy to DS, June 30, 1949, ibid., 363–64; Cannon to sec. of state, June 9, 1949, ibid., 355; "History of JUSMAGG," 157.

[62]"Greek Air Force Small But Able," 36; "USAFGG History," 113; "History of JUSMAGG," 9, 41–42, 46–47, 66–67; Van Fleet memo for Wedemeyer, June 22, 1949, P & O 091 Greece (TS), case 15, Army Staff Records, NA. The guerrillas raided and burned Naoussa and abducted more than 300 inhabitants. Greek planes opened fire on them in the Vermion Mountains northwest of Salonika, breaking their retreat and allowing the hostages to escape. Resistance was declining as the guerrillas split into small pockets of men and women interested only in dodging the steady government barrage. Campbell et al., *Employment of Airpower in Greek Guerrilla War,* 50–51; "History of JUSMAGG," 17a; *New York Times,* Jan. 18, 1949, p. 10.

CHAPTER 12. DÉNOUEMENT

[1]Richard V. Burks, *The Dynamics of Communism in Eastern Europe* (Princeton: Princeton U. Press, 1961), 104, 104 n.20. From a high of 3,650 abductions in January 1948, the figure had dipped to 143 in July 1949. "History of JUSMAPG," 26.

[2]Cannon to sec. of state, July 13, 1949, *FRUS*, VI: *The Near East, South Asia, and Africa* (Wash., D.C.: GPO, 1977), 368; sec. of state to embassy in Belgrade, ibid., 369. Tempo quoted in Vladimir Dedijer, *The Battle Stalin Lost: Memoirs of Yugoslavia, 1948–1953* (N.Y.: Viking, 1970), 270. Dedijer claims that Yugoslav aid began in 1946 at the beginning of the liberation movement. Ibid., 269–70.

[3]Chief of AMAG to chief of JUSMAPG, "Questions and Answers on Military Program," July 12, 1949, p. 2, P & O 091 Greece (TS), sect. I, case 17, Army Staff Records, NA; Van Fleet to Major Gen. Stafford Irwin, director of Intelligence, Army General Staff, Records of Interservice Agencies, 312-Correspondence of Gen. Van Fleet, 1948–50, box 55, entry 146, Army Staff Records, NA.

[4]Memo of conversation with Kosanovic by John C. Campbell, acting chief of Divis. of Southeast European Affairs, July 1, 1949, *FRUS*, VI: *Near East, South Asia, and Africa*, 364, ed. note; Drew to sec. of state, July 12, 1949, ibid., 366–67; sec. of state to embassy in Belgrade, Aug. 11, 1949, ibid., 387; Kardelj quoted in *Time*, Aug. 1, 1949, p. 25; Christopher M. Woodhouse, *The Struggle for Greece, 1941–1949* (Brooklyn Heights, N.Y.: Beekman-Esanu, 1976), 273; Lawrence S. Wittner, *American Intervention in Greece, 1943–1949* (N.Y.: Columbia U. Press, 1982), 278.

[5]Memo by Cromie of conversation with Dendramis, McGhee, Grady, and Cromie, July 27, 1949, *FRUS*, VI: *Near East, South Asia, and Africa*, 373–76. Papagos likewise recognized the danger in spreading the war into Albania. Despite pressure from a retired Greek general and numerous army officers, he asserted that to invade Albania as part of the Vitsi campaign could put his men into a "trap" and lead to an extensive and debilitating engagement with the Albanian army. Ibid.

[6]Memo by Cromie of conversation among Brit., French, and DS representatives, Aug. 5, 1949, ibid., 381–84. That same day, according to one writer, Diomedes (then deputy prime minister) told Crosthwaite that he was aware of the plan to depose Hoxha. Papagos and Pipinelis had been informed of the plan the previous May by British spokesmen. They approved it. Nicholas Bethell, *The Great Betrayal: The Untold Story of Kim Philby's Biggest Coup* (London: Hodder & Stoughton, 1984), 51–52, 114. For an explanation of the plan, see Chapter 11, above, n. 41.

[7]Minor to sec. of state, Aug. 6, 1949, *FRUS*, VI: *Near East, South Asia, and Africa*, 385–86; Minor to sec. of state, Aug. 8, 1949, ibid., 386 n.4. Sophoulis had died on June 24. Diomedes was sworn in as prime minister six days later and retained most of Sophoulis's cabinet members. Tsaldaris remained as foreign minister and also became deputy prime minister. Ed. note, ibid., 363 n.3. One writer claims that the Greek forces on at least one occasion crossed the border into Albania. See Evangelos Averoff-Tossizza, *By Fire and Axe: The Communist Party and the Civil War in Greece, 1944–1949* (New Rochelle, N.Y.: Caratzas Brothers, 1978), 294. Originally published as *Le Feu et la hache Grèce '46–'49, histoire des guerres de l'après-guerre* (Paris: Editions de Breteuil, 1973). Trans. by Sarah Arnold Rigos. For explanation, see Chapter 10, above, n. 31.

[8]Memo by Rusk of conversation among Dendramis, Jernegan, and Rusk, Aug. 29, 1949, *FRUS*, VI: *Near East, South Asia, and Africa*, 389–90; sec. of state to embassy in London, Aug. 29, 1949, ibid., 392–93. The Greek government claimed to have taken Albanians as prisoners, but Woodhouse believes they might have been Chams who spoke Albanian and were Greek nationals. Woodhouse, *Struggle for Greece*, 273. As pointed out, the American and British governments went farther than an appeal and tried to arrange an overthrow of the Hoxha regime. See n.6 above.

[9]"Questions and Answers on Military Program," encl. in Van Fleet to Major Gen. Charles L. Bolte, director, P & O, July 19, 1949, pp. 1–2, P & O 091 Greece (TS), sect. I, case 17, Army Staff Records, NA.

[10]"History of JUSMAGG," 48–49, 67–71, 74–75; "USAFGG History," 68–71; M. A. Campbell et al., *The Employment of Airpower in the Greek Guerrilla War, 1947–1949* (Montgomery, Ala.: Air U., Maxwell AFB, 1964), 31, 53; London *Times*, Aug. 11, 1949, p. 3; Kenneth Matthews, *Memories of a Mountain War Greece: 1944–1949* (London: Longman, 1972), 268–69; Averoff-

Tossizza, *By Fire and Axe*, 345–46. The first two of a large installment of U.S. Navy Helldivers had arrived that month at Larisa, the newly established Headquarters Central Greece. The remainder of the aircraft—39 Helldivers and 10 additional surplus—were scheduled to arrive by carrier on August 15. In late July, U.S. Air Force advisers recommended the use of napalm to clear the guerrillas from the mountainsides. For several hours before the infantry attack, the Greek army was to use an artillery barrage to destroy land mines around the fortifications. Spitfires would sweep the area with guns, rockets, and bombs to keep the enemy inside the fortifications. Then 12 to 16 Helldivers would saturate the area with napalm, which would allow the infantry to advance. But these large-scale napalm attacks did not materialize because of the rapid deterioration of guerrilla resistance in Grammos during August. This was fortunate for the Greeks, for the U.S. Navy was not able to furnish the sheet metal needed for the liquid containers. "USAFGG History," 171–72, 174–75; Bolte to Van Fleet, July 18, 1949, P & O 091 Greece (TS), case 15, Army Staff Records, NA; Russell to commanding general, USAFGG, July 26, 1949, Air Adjutant Section 471 Ammunition (Napalm), JUSMAPG, NA. The Torch campaign was under the command of Lieut. Gen. Constantine Ventiris, brought in from the Epirus Western Macedonia Command, and Lieut. Gen. Thrasyvoulos Tsakalotos, placed in charge of "A" Corps. "History of JUSMAGG," 67. Woodhouse notes that for the first time in the war, a comparison of military strengths could be made. The Democratic Army was also organized into divisions, brigades, and other units. Both in manpower and matériel, the Greek government's forces held the decisive advantage. *Struggle for Greece*, 277.

[11]"History of JUSMAGG," 67–69; Campbell et al., *Employment of Airpower in Greek Guerrilla War*, 31, 51–52; London *Times*, Aug. 8, 1949, p. 3, and Aug. 12, 1949, p. 4; "USAFGG History," 69; Van Fleet to Wedemeyer, Aug. 5, 1949, Records of Interservice Agencies, 312-Correspondence of Gen. Van Fleet, 1948–50, box 55, entry 146, Army Staff Records, NA; Edgar O'Ballance, *The Greek Civil War, 1944–1949* (N.Y.: Praeger, 1966), 196–99; Woodhouse, *Struggle for Greece*, 278–83.

[12]"History of JUSMAGG," 73. The air force flew an average of 126 sorties a day during the first five days of the offensive. "USAFGG History," 70. Where the emplacements were stone (sometimes two feet thick), the recoilless rifle blew them apart. Where protected by heavy timber, the Greeks managed to fire a few strikes into the openings, killing the occupants either by the hit or by the resulting concussion. The flash of the gun was a problem; the enemy could spot locations and within minutes return heavy counterfire. The Greeks made adjustments by moving rapidly to alternate positions; placing the guns on reverse slopes or behind small trees or bushes; and wetting the ground to eliminate the dust raised in addition to the flash. Jenkins disagreed with Van Fleet's positive assessment. The primary purpose of the weapon had been for anti-tank defense in the infantry and only secondarily to help the support fire protecting a battalion. The rifle was effective to 1,800 yards, but it could not carry sufficient explosives to penetrate twelve inches of armor and was therefore of no value against pillboxes encased in rock, sealed by two-foot layers of mortar, and covered with logs and dirt. The enemy's ability to return fire so quickly was demoralizing to the army, for it meant that after firing the rifles the gun crew had to evacuate the area, leaving the advancing infantry exposed to the guerrillas' counter battery. Report by Jenkins to President, Army Field Forces Board No. 3, Fort Benning, Oct. 13, 1949, in "History of JUSMAGG," 128–32; Van Fleet to Lieut. Gen. Raymond S. McLain, army comptroller, office of chief of staff, U.S. Army, Sept. 8, 1949, Records of Interservice Agencies, 312-Correspondence of Gen. Van Fleet, 1948–50, box 55, entry 146, Army Staff Records, NA.

[13]"History of JUSMAGG," 75–79, 81–85; "USAFGG History," 70–71; Van Fleet to Papagos, Aug. 13, 1949, Records of Interservice Agencies, 312-Correspondence of Gen. Van Fleet, 1948–50, box 55, entry 146, Army Staff Records, NA. During the battle, the potential increased for a widened war as Greek soldiers exchanged fire with a company of Albanian troops along the common border. In addition, the Greek army underwent a barrage coming out of Albania that again raised the cry from within the Athens government to launch an invasion. Averoff-Tossizza, *By Fire and Axe*, 343–44.

[14]Campbell et al., *Employment of Airpower in Greek Guerrilla War*, 32, 64–65; "History of JUSMAGG," 81–85; notes by director of P & O, Aug. 18, 1949, P & O 091, Greece (TS), sect. I, case 14/13, Army Staff Records, NA; notes by director of P & O, Aug. 25, 1949, case 14/14, ibid.; "USAFGG History," 70–71; Van Fleet quoted in *Time*, Aug. 22, 1949, p. 20. At Vitsi the Greek army found the Albanian company commander's papers on the field, along with 20 dead Albanian soldiers; 7 others were taken prisoner. One writer called this a "curious episode." Averoff-Tossizza, *By Fire and Axe*, 344.

[15]"History of JUSMAGG," 68, 86, 88; "USAFGG History," 71; "Greek Air Force Small But Able," *Air Intelligence Digest*, II, no. 9, p. 38, Maxwell AFB, 140.0371, in Simpson Lib.; Campbell et al., *Employment of Airpower in Greek Guerrilla War*, 53–54; J. C. Murray, "The Anti-Bandit War," Part V, *Marine Corps Gazette* 38 (May 1954): 52; London *Times*, Aug. 26, 1949, p. 3; *Time*, Sept. 5, 1949, p. 25; Averoff-Tossizza, *By Fire and Axe*, 345–46.

[16]Notes of director of P & O, Aug. 25, 1949, P & O 091 Greece (TS), sect. I., case 14/14, Army Staff Records, NA; "History of JUSMAGG," 88–89, 91–96; "USAFGG History," 71–73; "History of JUSMAPG, " 22; Campbell et al., *Employment of Airpower in Greek Guerrilla War*, 32, 53–54, 65; London *Times*, Aug. 26, 1949, p. 3; Woodhouse, *Struggle for Greece*, 282; Averoff-Tossizza, *By Fire and Axe*, 346–47; O'Ballance, *Greek Civil War*, 200. The air force also dropped 2,440 pounds of leaflets, urging the guerrillas to surrender. "USAFGG History," 71. Woodhouse considered the air support in Torch "decisive." *Struggle for Greece*, 278. Zahariadis and his closest advisers had escaped into Albania before going on to Bulgaria. Ibid., 284.

[17]"History of JUSMAGG," 144; ed. note, Oct. 16, 1949, *FRUS*, VI: *Near East, South Asia, and Africa*, 434; Grady to acting sec. of state, Oct. 3, 1949, ibid., 431–33; Kirk to sec. of state, Dec. 18, 1949, ibid., 467; Woodhouse, *Struggle for Greece*, 285; O'Ballance, *Greek Civil War*, 201.

[18]"USAFGG History," 73–74; "History of JUSMAGG," 32–33, 141, 144–45. The Greek government's mopping-up operations continued through the end of June 1950. Ibid., 181, 188.

[19]Woodhouse, *Struggle for Greece*, 285.

[20]Matthews, *Memories of a Mountain War Greece*, 269; Wittner, *American Intervention in Greece*, 253; "History of JUSMAGG," 51, 104–5, 193–96. By March 1950, when it was clear that there would be no more guerrilla offensives, the remainder of the refugees returned home. Ibid., 186. The guerrillas' abductions had dropped dramatically to about 5,000 in 1949. The army's casualty figures are disputed. Woodhouse believes the number on the government side approached 70,000. O'Ballance arrives at a similar figure by claiming that a total of more than 158,000 had died in the war, about half of them from the Democratic Army and the rest from government troops, security forces, police, and civilians. See Woodhouse, *Struggle for Greece*, 286; O'Ballance, *Greek Civil War*, 202. Dimitrios G. Kousoulas says that the figures for the Greek armed forces and gendarmerie were 16,753 dead, 40,398 wounded, and 4,788 missing. Kousoulas, *Revolution and Defeat: The Story of the Greek Communist Party* (London: Oxford U. Press, 1965), 270 n.21. Averoff-Tossizza declares that 36,839 guerrillas were found dead on the battlefield, but that the total dead was probably close to 50,000 since the guerrillas tried to carry their dead away. The number of wounded was impossible to tell. The Greek government held 20,128 prisoners, and the guerrillas suffered 21,258 desertions. Depending on which figure is used on the dead, the guerrillas' casualties were either around 57,000 or around 70,000. The Greek government suffered 59,636 civilian and military casualties, including civilians and priests executed, civilians killed by mines, and dead and wounded army and gendarmerie. *By Fire and Axe*, 355. For the difficulties in determining casualty figures, see William H. McNeill, *Greece: American Aid in Action, 1947–1956* (N.Y.: Twentieth Century Fund, 1957), 45.

[21]"History of JUSMAGG," 52, 106–8, 137–38, 143, 156, 182, 184, 196–97, "History of JUSMAPG," p. 20; Van Fleet, "JUSMAPG-USAGG Monthly Report, Month of January 1950," Jan. 31, 1950, p. 1, JUSMAPG-USAGG Monthly Report, Records of Interservice Agencies, box 148, entry 156, Army Staff Records, NA; Van Fleet, "JUSMAPG-USAGG Monthly Report— Month of March 1950," March 31, 1950, pp. 1–2, ibid. According to Van Fleet and other

American military observers, about 10,000 guerrillas were in Albania and another 5,000 in Bulgaria. Greek intelligence estimated the total of guerrillas "fit" for fighting at 9,000 in Albania and 2,500 in Bulgaria. Van Fleet to Brig. Gen. Thomas S. Timberman, P & O, Dept. of Army General Staff, Sept. 16, 1949, Records of Interservice Agencies, 312-Correspondence of Gen. Van Fleet, 1948–50, box 55, entry 146, ibid. The KKE continued to disintegrate in the years after the war. Zahariadis was removed from the Central Committee in 1956, whereas Markos had his reputation restored, only to see it denigrated again the following year. By the end of the 1950s, all KKE leaders in the civil war had been expelled or they had died. Woodhouse, *Struggle for Greece*, 287–88.

22"History of JUSMAPG," 23; "USAFGG History," 22; "History of JUSMAGG," 58–59, 136, 148, 170. The actual size of the Greek armed forces by December 31, 1949 was 128,000 men. Ibid., 148. Grady to acting sec. of state, Oct. 3, 1949, *FRUS*, VI: *Near East, South Asia, and Africa*, 431–32; Grady to sec. of state, Oct. 15, 1949, ibid., 432 n.5. Recommendations were to cut 50 percent in the army and navy groups and 25 percent in the air group, the process to begin in January and to be completed on April 30, 1950. Then all three groups would be phased down to token strengths, the navy by June 30, the other two by December 31, 1950. The JCS approved Van Fleet's plan for reducing the American military groups to half their size by June 30, 1950. Grady to acting sec. of state, Oct. 3, 1949, ibid., 432–33; Van Fleet to Timberman, Sept. 16, 1949, Records of Interservice Agencies, 312-Correspondence of Gen. Van Fleet, 1948–50, box 55, entry 146, Army Staff Records, NA; memo for sec. of defense from Bradley, Jan. 23, 1950, p. 1, CD 6-1-29 (TS), files of sec. of defense, NA.

23Grady to sec. of state, Oct. 19, 1949, ibid., 443 n.3; Van Fleet to Dept. of Army, Oct. 27, 1949, ibid., 437 n.1; memo by Ben Franklin Dixon of conversation among W. D. Allen (counselor of Brit. embassy), Jernegan, and Dixon, Oct. 20, 1949, ibid., 435–36; Grady to sec. of state, Oct. 21, 1949, ibid., 437; memo by Jernegan of telephone conversation among Major Gen. Alfred M. Gruenther, director of Joint Staff, JCS; Raymond A. Hare, deputy asst. sec. of state for Near Eastern, South Asian, and African Affairs; and Jernegan, Oct. 27, 1949, ibid., 445–46; Grady to sec. of state, Oct. 28, 1949, ibid., 446 n.3; Sec. of Defense Louis A. Johnson to Acheson, Nov. 22, 1949, ibid., 447 n.4; "History of JUSMAGG," 140; Woodhouse, *Struggle for Greece*, 287.

24Matthews, *Memories of a Mountain War Greece*, 16, 261–63; Campbell et al., *Employment of Airpower in Greek Guerrilla War*, 18–20, 58; unsigned paper entitled, "The Counter-Insurgency Campaign (1947–1949)," ca. Oct. 1949, in Francis F. Lincoln Papers, Truman Lib.; Burks, *Dynamics of Communism in Eastern Europe*, 101–2. The British observer was Christopher M. Woodhouse. See his *Struggle for Greece*, 274. To encourage the rift, the United States sent aid to Yugoslavia. See Lorraine M. Lees, "The American Decision to Assist Tito, 1948–1949," *Diplomatic History* 2 (Fall 1978): 407–22; Robert W. Selton, "Communist Errors in the Anti-Bandit War," *Military Review* 45 (Sept. 1965): 66–77; Murray, "Anti-Bandit War," Part I, *Marine Corps Gazette* 38 (Jan. 1954): 14–23; ibid., Part IV (April 1954): 52–60; ibid., Part V (May 1954): 52–58; Dimitrios G. Kousoulas, "The Success of the Truman Doctrine Was Not Accidental," *Military Affairs* 29 (Summer 1965): 88–92; author's interview with Henderson; author's interview with McGhee. McNeill believes that the "real turning point" in the war came on June 28, 1948, when the Cominform denounced Tito for deviating from socialism. McNeill, *Greece*, 42. Another writer calls Tito's decision to close the border a "deadly blow" to the Democratic Army. O'Ballance, *Greek Civil War*, 195. Wittner considers Tito's defection *one* of the reasons for the outcome. *American Intervention in Greece*, 253. Averoff argues that the major reason for the Democratic Army's defeat was "the firm determination of the majority of Greeks to fight against it until the bitter end." *By Fire and Axe*, 357. See also ibid., 362. Others argue that Tito's decision was not the central military factor because the guerrillas were already backed into Grammos and Vitsi, and the rest of Greece had been cleared. These realities in mind, Kousoulas calls the border closing a "death sentence." "The Truman Doctrine and the Stalin-Tito Rift: A Reappraisal," *South Atlantic Quarterly* 72 (Summer 1973): 437. See also his *The Price of Freedom: Greece in World Affairs, 1939–1953* (Syracuse, N.Y.: Syracuse U. Press, 1953),

179. For a discussion of the changing literature on the impact of the rift on the Greek struggle, see Nicholas Pappas. "The Soviet-Yugoslav Conflict and the Greek Civil War," in Wayne S. Vucinich, ed., *At the Brink of War and Peace: The Tito-Stalin Split in a Historic Perspective* (N.Y.: Columbia U. Press, 1982), 236–37. According to Pappas, the issue no longer has as much impact in the writings. Ibid., 236.

[25]Matthews, *Memories of a Mountain War Greece*, 261–63; O'Ballance, *Greek Civil War*, 206–7, 219; Woodhouse, *Struggle for Greece*, 276; Selton, "Communist Errors in the Anti-Bandit War," 74–75, 77; Edward R. Wainhouse, "Guerrilla War in Greece, 1946–49: A Case Study," *Military Review* 37 (June 1957): 17–25; Dimitrios G. Kousoulas, "The Guerrilla War the Communists Lost," *U.S. Naval Institute Proceedings* 89 (May 1963): 66–73. See also his article, "The Success of the Truman Doctrine Was Not Accidental," 90. Murray, "Anti-Bandit War," Part II (Feb. 1954): 50–59; ibid., Part V (May 1954): 52–58; John O. Iatrides, "Civil War, 1945–1949: National and International Aspects," in Iatrides, ed., *Greece in the 1940s: A Nation in Crisis* (Hanover, N.H.: U. Press of New England, 1981), 217. One writer calls Zahariadis's decision for conventional warfare the "most basic error" made in the war. Kousoulas, *Revolution and Defeat*, 271. See also Wittner, *American Intervention in Greece*, 253.

[26]"History of JUSMAGG," 156; Wainhouse, "Guerrilla War in Greece," 24; Kousoulas, "The Guerrilla War the Communists Lost," 69, 71–72, 73; Alexander Papagos, "Guerrilla Warfare," in Franklin M. Osanka, ed., *Modern Guerrilla Warfare: Fighting Communist Guerrilla Movements, 1941–1961* (Glencoe, N.Y.: Free Press, 1963), 228–42. Robert E. Osgood argues that U.S. intervention was crucial: "It was, above all, America's dispatch of military advisers, its reorganization of the Greek army, its donation of enormous military supplies, its granting of economic aid, and even its intervention in internal political affairs, that kept this key position on the southern flank of Europe out of Russian control." See his *Limited War: The Challenge to American Strategy* (Chicago: U. of Chicago Press, 1957), 143–44. Burks believes that the communists probably would have taken over Greece had the United States and Britain refused to extend military aid. See his *Dynamics of Communism in Eastern Europe*, 48. "History of JUSMAGG," 34, 135; "History of JUSMAPG," 20–21. The air force used fewer than 7,500 men in the air phase of the war, and the entire operation cost less than 10 percent of what it took to keep the ground effort going. Campbell et al., *Employment of Airpower in Greek Guerrilla War*, 58. Some assessments criticized the Greeks for relying too heavily on the air force. See ibid.; "Greek Air Force Small But Able," 35–36. See also O'Ballance, *Greek Civil War*, 210; Woodhouse, *Struggle for Greece*, 233; Wainhouse, "Guerrilla War in Greece," 24–25; Kousoulas, "The Success of the Truman Doctrine Was Not Accidental," 89, 91; Murray, "Anti-Bandit War," Part III (March 1954): 48–57; ibid., Part V (May 1954): 52–58. Averoff acknowledges the importance of American military aid, but believes that the impact was not felt until the outcome of the war had already been decided. *By Fire and Axe*, 357, 360–62. Woodhouse agrees. See his "The 'Revolution' in its Historical Context," in Richard Clogg and George Yannopoulos, eds., *Greece Under Military Rule* (N.Y.: Basic Books, 1972), 9–10.

[27]Ventiris to Mrs. William G. Livesay, Oct. 15, 1956, Livesay Papers, U.S. Army Military History Institute, Carlisle Military Barracks, Pa.; outline for manuscript entitled "Summary Outline and Comments—U.S. Aid to Greece 1947–1962," n.d., p. 11, Lincoln Papers, Truman Lib.; Henry F. Grady, "Adventures in Diplomacy" (unpublished memoirs), 213, Grady Papers, box 5, ibid. Van Fleet later praised the Greeks for working with the Americans to win the war. See James A. Van Fleet, "How We Won in Greece," *Balkan Studies* 8 (1967): 387–93. John O. Iatrides considers U.S. military assistance "less significant" than political and economic aid, which he thought "decisive." The key to victory, he declares, was a combination of political, military, domestic, and foreign factors. Iatrides, "Civil War," 216. See also Richard F. Haynes, *The Awesome Power: Harry S. Truman as Commander in Chief* (Baton Rouge: Louisiana State U. Press, 1973), 133, 267, and C. A. Munkman, *American Aid to Greece: A Report on the First Ten Years* (N.Y.: Praeger, 1958), 275. Munkman was the chief of Audits and Surveys of the U.S. Economic Mission to Greece. It is virtually impossible to divide the American aid program into military

and economic compartments and then assign appropriate credit to each. As one AMAG report explained: "American military assistance has provided rations, forage, clothing, weapons, ammunition, vehicles, mules, petroleum, communications and other technical equipment, aircraft, boats, and many other items necessary to equip and maintain the Greek armed forces . . . ." Quoted in Francis F. Lincoln, *United States' Aid to Greece, 1947-1962* (Germantown, Tenn.: Professional Seminars, 1975), 84. Depending on how one defines "military" and "economic" aid, he can cite figures that will either refute or support the charge that the Truman Doctrine was overly military in orientation. As an example, an administration adviser, Francis Lincoln, claims that from 1947 to 1949, the United States provided almost twice as much economic aid as military. Ibid., Appendix II. McNeill has adopted the safest approach. He simply says that America's "financial contribution" to Greece was four times what President Truman had originally intended.*Greece*, 45. But McNeill cites figures suggesting that the economic aid allotment was only about a third more than that for military goods. See ibid., Append. 1, 229.

[28]Woodhouse, *Struggle for Greece*, 288-89. O'Ballance believes that Stalin had exerted pressure for a cease-fire. *Greek Civil War*, 201. Constantine Poulos called Stalin's decision a "betrayal" of the Greek communists. See Poulos, "Greece: Betrayal as Usual," *Nation*, Oct. 29, 1949, pp. 411-13.

[29]Many of Truman's policymakers fitted the category of the "wise men" discussed in Walter Isaacson and Evan Thomas, *The Wise Men: Six Friends and the World They Made* (N.Y.: Simon and Schuster, 1986). The six men were Acheson, Bohlen, Harriman, Kennan, Lovett, and John McCloy. More than a few of Truman's advisers played a major role in developing the "flexible response" policy of the presidential administration of John F. Kennedy: Acheson, Bohlen, Clifford, Harriman, Kohler, Lovett, McGhee, and Rusk. See Thomas G. Paterson, "Bearing the Burden: A Critical Look at J.F.K.'s Foreign Policy," *Virginia Quarterly Review* 54 (Spring 1978): 193-212; Herbert S. Parmet, *JFK: The Presidency of John F. Kennedy* (N.Y.: Dial, 1983). Years afterward, President Truman insisted that the Truman Doctrine was only one aspect of the administration's foreign policy. To Clark Clifford, he wrote: "Like the Marshall Plan, it [the Truman Doctrine] too was only a part of the foreign policy of the United States, and that is how history should refer to it." Truman to Clifford, March 18, 1957, in Robert H. Ferrell, ed., *Off the Record: The Private Papers of Harry S. Truman* (N.Y.: Harper & Row, 1980), 349.

CHAPTER 13. "ON ALL FRONTS"

[1]Minor to sec. of state, Aug. 16, 1949, *FRUS*, VI: *The Near East, South Asia, and Africa* (Wash., D.C.: GPO, 1977), 388; Minor to sec. of state, Aug. 23, 1949, ibid., 388 n.1; sec. of state to embassy in Athens, Aug. 26, 1949, ibid.; sec. of state to embassy in Athens, Sept. 10, 1949, ibid., 410-11; Bickham Sweet-Escott, *Greece: A Political and Economic Survey, 1939-1953* (London: Royal Institute of International Affairs, 1954), 74-75. A law of 1951 extended the outlawry of the KKE. Dominique Eudes, *The Kapetanios: Partisans and Civil War in Greece, 1943-1949* (N.Y.: Monthly Review Press, 1972), 359. Originally published as *Les Kapetanios: La guerre civile grecque de 1943 à 1949* (Paris: Librarie Arthème Fayard, 1970). Trans. by John Howe. The American ambassador in the Soviet Union, Alan G. Kirk, was skeptical about adopting a new conciliatory approach when the recent favorable turn of events in Greece made the Soviet overture a natural outcome. Although temporarily obstructed by guerrilla defeats and Tito's defection, the Soviets had not abandoned their goals and would now use every political or diplomatic opportunity to insert their friends in power. The United States must exercise the utmost care to keep the Soviets and the Greek Communists from turning military defeat into political victory. Dangers could arise from pushing too far on amnesty and elections. Kirk to sec. of state, Sept. 15, 1949, *FRUS*, VI: *Near East, South Asia, and Africa*, 417.

[2]Julius C. Holmes, Amer. chargé in London, to sec. of state, Sept. 3, 1949, *FRUS*, VI: *Near East, South Asia, and Africa*, 398; Ambassador David K. Bruce in Paris to sec. of state, Sept. 17, 1949,

ibid., 422; Donald R. Heath, Amer. minister in Bulgaria, to sec. of state, Sept. 3, 1949, ibid., 393 n.4; Drew to sec. of state, Sept. 2, 1949, ibid., 394-95; Drew to sec. of state, Sept. 2, 1949, ibid., 394-96.

³Sec. of state to embassy in Athens, Sept. 7, 1949, ibid., 400-401; Webb to embassy in Athens, Sept. 20, 1949, ibid., 422.

⁴Dendramis statement to DS, Sept. 8, 1949, ibid., 402 n.1; memo by Jernegan of conversation among Dendramis, Rusk, and Jernegan, Sept. 8, 1949, ibid., 401-4.

⁵Position Paper, Sept. 9, 1949, in Jernegan memo, ibid., 405-9. The reports concerning the children had arrived in the spring of 1949 and caused an angry outcry in the General Assembly. The British delegate, Hector McNeil, denounced the "satanic use" of children in war. International organizations protected youths from "harmful drugs, from indecent traffic, from pornography, from hunger and from disease." Surely, he proclaimed, the General Assembly could not be "uncritical of men who twisted a child's mind to throw his body into a struggle of which he knew little, perhaps against kith and kin." Despite the Polish representative's denials, the Greek General Staff insisted that children were among the 14,000 guerrillas in Yugoslavia, Albania, and Bulgaria. The Foreign Office believed the charges, as did McGhee, who reported that most of the children were receiving "intensive communist indoctrination." See UNSCOB Report A/935, UNGA, *Official Records*, 4 sess., suppl. 8, 1949, pp. 13-15; UNGA First Committee, ibid., 4 sess., 1949, 304th meeting, Oct. 31, 1949, p. 153; UNGA First Committee, ibid., 4 sess., 1949, 301st meeting, Oct. 28, 1949, p. 131; Greek General Staff cited in "History of JUSMAGG," 52; Southern Dept. of F.O. to U.K. Delegation in UNGA, June 17, 1949, FO 371/78362, File 10111: 1949—Abduction of Greek children, PRO; McGhee to sec. of state, Dec. 29, 1949, DSDF, NA; sec. of state to embassy in Athens, Sept. 10, 1949, *FRUS*, VI: *Near East, South Asia, and Africa*, 411. The UN Conciliatory Commission was headed by Herbert V. Evatt of Australia, who was that country's minister for External Affairs.

⁶Memo by Cromie of conversation among Lord Jellicoe (second sec. of Brit. embassy), Ben Franklin Dixon (DS Division of Greek, Turkish, and Iranian Affairs), Jernegan, and Cromie, Sept. 13, 1949, *FRUS*, VI: *Near East, South Asia, and Africa*, 412-13; Holmes to sec. of state, Sept. 15, 1949, ibid., 416; memo by sec. of state of conversation among Bevin, Ambassador Sir Oliver Franks, U.S. Ambassador-at-Large Philip Jessup, McGhee, Acheson, and others, Sept. 14, 1949, ibid., 414-15. On the Albanian issue, Acheson was also concerned about keeping the State Department clear of the ongoing and secret effort to depose Hoxha. Within a week of the September 14 meeting, an "Albanian committee" was denied a request to meet with the White House but did meet with members of the Committee for Free Europe (CFE), a group formed the previous June and chaired by the well-known former diplomat, Joseph Grew. Among the CFE's members were Dwight D. Eisenhower and Allen Dulles (future director of the CIA and brother of John Foster Dulles). Though the CFE was termed a "private organization," the Department of State had informed its major missions abroad that it had given "unofficial approval" to the CFE's goals and would cooperate where possible. Those goals were to gather émigrés from Eastern Europe into a political group that would promote the collapse of the Soviet alliance system. Nicholas Bethell, *The Great Betrayal: The Untold Story of Kim Philby's Biggest Coup* (London: Hodder & Stoughton, 1984), 105-06, 113-14. As mentioned earlier, the mission failed, and Hoxha remained in power from 1944 until his death in 1985.

⁷Grady to sec. of state, Sept. 16, 1949, *FRUS*, VI: *Near East, South Asia, and Africa*, 419-21; Cannon to sec. of state, Sept. 8, 1949, ibid., 427 n.2; Cannon to sec. of state, Sept. 21, 1949, ibid., 423.

⁸Vyshinsky speech on Sept. 22, 1949, UNGA, *Official Records*, 4 sess., 1949, 224th plenary meeting, p. 20; Vyshinsky speech on Sept. 23, 1949, ibid., 226th plenary meeting, pp. 36-37; Clementis speech on Sept. 26, 1949, ibid., 228th plenary meeting, pp. 63-64; Katz-Suchy speech on Sept. 22, 1949, ibid., 224th plenary meeting, p. 21; Malik speech on Sept. 26, 1949, ibid., 228th plenary meeting, p. 69; Tsaldaris speech on Sept. 26, 1949, ibid., p. 73. NATO was a military alliance of North Atlantic nations that included the United States as a member.

[9]Bebler speech on Nov. 18, 1949, ibid., 246th plenary meeting, p. 253; Soviet resolution, A/1080, Nov. 12, 1949, annex to plenary meetings, p. 68; ed. note on discussion of Oct. 24, 1949, *FRUS*, VI: *Near East, South Asia, and Africa*, 451–52; DS to embassy in Athens, Sept. 19, 1949, ibid., 424 n.4; Webb to U.S. mission to UN, Sept. 23, 1949, ibid., 424–25; memo by U.S. delegation to UNGA of conversation among Tsaldaris, Venizelos, and Howard (adviser to UN delegation in General Assembly), Sept. 24, 1949, ibid., 425 n.5; Grady to sec. of state, Sept. 28, 1949, ibid., 428.

[10]Grady to sec. of state, Nov. 1, 1949, *FRUS*, VI: *Near East, South Asia, and Africa*, 450–51.

[11]Webb to embassy in Athens, Sept. 23, 1949, ibid., 425–26.

[12]Memo by Webb of meeting with Truman, Oct. 1, 1949, ibid., 427–28; sec. of state to certain diplomatic offices (Athens, London, Paris, Rome), Oct. 21, 1949, ibid., 438; DS to Amer. missions in Europe, late Oct. 1949, ibid., 447 (ed. note).

[13]Report of First Committee, A/1062, Nov. 5, 1949, UNGA, *Official Records*, 4 sess., 1949, annex to plenary meetings, pp. 65–66. After the Soviets appealed to everyone to "cease military operations" and to declare a general amnesty, they set out the following terms: free parliamentary elections, which would include "representatives of Greek democratic circles at the head of the national freedom movement in Greece" and which would be supervised by representatives of all the powers; the creation of a "Joint Commission of the Powers" to patrol the northern borders; the end of foreign military aid to Athens and the setting of a deadline for the removal of foreign troops; the disbanding of the UN Special Committee on the Balkans. Ibid., 67–68. See also UNGA resolution, Nov. 18, 1949: "Threats to the political independence and territorial integrity of Greece," ibid., 246th plenary meeting, p. 9.

[14]Gross to Sen. Scott Lucas of Ill., Oct. 11, 1949, DSDF, NA; Jack McFall, asst. sec. of state, to Sen. Sheridan Downey of Calif., Dec. 22, 1949, ibid. For the memorials, remarks by congressional members, and House and Senate resolutions, see: *Cong. Record, Senate*, 81 Cong., 2 sess., vol. 96, part 1, Jan. 18, 1950, p. 507; part 2, Feb. 27, 1950, ibid., pp. 2366–67; *House, Append.*, 81 Cong., 2 sess., vol. 96, part 14, March 1, 1950, p. A1514; March 20, 1950, ibid., p. A2070; *House*, 81 Cong., 2 sess., vol. 96, part 3, March 22, 1950, p. 3812; *Senate, Append.*, 81 Cong., 2 sess., vol. 96, part 14, March 27, 1950, ibid., pp. A2215–16; *Senate*, 81 Cong., 2 sess., vol. 96, part 8, July 17, 1950, p. 10356; part 11, Sept. 13, 1950, ibid., p. 14667; *House*, 82 Cong., 1 sess., vol. 97, part 3, April 23, 1951, p. 4222. For correspondence to the President, see folder labeled "Greek Children" in Truman Papers, Truman Lib. See also Nicholas Skordilis to Truman, March 23, 1948, DSDF, NA. For the President's pledges, see: Truman to Greek Orthodox Archbishop Michael of North and South America, Jan. 6, 1950, doc. 7, in *Public Papers of the Presidents of the United States. Harry S. Truman. Containing the Public Messages, Speeches, and Statements of the President. 1950* (Wash., D.C.: GPO, 1965), 32; Truman to Sam Rayburn, speaker of House, April 19, 1950, doc. 90, ibid., 259; Truman to Vice-President Alben Barkley, Sept. 29, 1950, doc. 261, ibid., 663.

[15]UNSCOB Report A/935, UNGA, *Official Records*, 4 sess., suppl. 8, 1949, p. 13; UNSCOB Report A/1857, ibid., 6 sess., suppl. 11, 1951, p. 24; London *Times*, Aug. 16, 1948, p. 3d; Nov. 27, 1948, p. 5e; Nov. 29, 1948, p. 3b; Jan. 29, 1951, p. 3d; Sweet-Escott, *Greece*, 71, 72 n.1. For the November 1948 General Assembly resolution, see UNSCOB Report A/935, annex 1, UNGA, *Official Records*, 4 sess., suppl. 8, 1949, p. 21. Bevin had deplored the abductions as a violation of "fundamental human rights." Bevin to William Ross (Darvel Industrial Co-operative Society), Jan. 4, 1949, FO 371/78361, File 10111: 1949—Abduction of Greek Children, PRO. For a discussion of the difficulties involved in the repatriation process, see Lars Baerentzen, "The 'Paidomazoma' and the Queen's Camps," in Lars Baerentzen, John O. Iatrides, and Ole L. Smith, eds., *Studies in the History of the Greek Civil War, 1945–1949* (Copenhagen, Denmark: Museum Tusculanum Press, 1987), 146–52.

[16]Van Fleet to Dept. of Army, Nov. 7, 1949, *FRUS*, VI: *Near East, South Asia, and Africa*, 453–54. See Dimitrios G. Kousoulas, "The Truman Doctrine and the Stalin-Tito Rift: A Reappraisal," *South Atlantic Quarterly* 72 (Summer 1973): 427–39.

[17]Van Fleet to Dept. of Army, Nov. 7, 1949, *FRUS*, VI: *Near East, South Asia, and Africa*, 453, 455; Van Fleet to Dept. of Army, Nov. 10, 1949, ibid., 456 n.2; JCS 1798/24—"Report by the Joint Strategic Survey Committee to the J.C.S. on the United States' Position in Greece," Nov. 19, 1949, pp. 249, 252, 255–58, 263, 269, P & O 091 Greece (TS), sect. II, case 22/4, Army Staff Records, NA; memo for sec. of defense from Bradley, Jan. 23, 1950, pp. 1–2, CD 6-1-29 (TS), files of sec. of defense, NA; memo for sec. of defense from Rear Admiral A. C. Davis, Feb. 3, 1950, pp. 1–2, CD 6-3-43, ibid. The last British troops withdrew in February 1950. The British Military and Air Force Missions withdrew for economic reasons in April 1952, and negotiations for the withdrawal of the British Naval Mission began in autumn 1953. Sweet-Escott, *Greece*, 79 n.1.

[18]See Van Fleet, JUSMAPG Report: "Estimate of the Current Military Situation in Greece," ca. early 1950, p. 3, P & O 091 Greece (TS), sect. V, case 40, Army Staff Records, NA; Richard V. Burks, *The Dynamics of Communism in Eastern Europe* (Princeton: Princeton U. Press, 1961), 188, 190–92, 200. Burks argues that cultural variations and ethnic differences make it unrealistic to regard communism as a monolithic force in Eastern Europe.

[19]See "History of JUSMAGG," 173, 175–80, 187, 190–91. The Mutual Defense Assistance Program (enacted in 1949) had replaced the Truman Doctrine, signifying the fulfillment of the original aid effort. A short time afterward, the United States further coordinated its military missions in Greece by establishing the Joint U.S. Military Aid Group to Greece (JUSMAGG). The Marshall Plan was also extending economic assistance to Greece as part of the European effort. In the March election, the center and left won 63 percent of the votes. The Populists were reduced from 191 of the 250 seats in Parliament to 61, while the center parties got 133. The leftist Democratic Front held 22 seats. Lawrence S. Wittner, *American Intervention in Greece, 1943–1949* (N.Y.: Columbia U. Press, 1982), 286. The Economic Cooperation Administration planned the economic development program for FY 1950–51. The United States felt the necessity of compressing four years of Marshall Plan assistance into the two years left under the program. On December 31, 1951, the Mutual Security Act replaced the ECA with the Mutual Security Agency. Francis F. Lincoln, *United States' Aid to Greece, 1947–1962* (Germantown, Tenn.: Professional Seminars, 1975), 105–06, 108, 126. The Diomedes government had resigned in early January, leaving the governing functions to a transition regime. Sweet-Escott, *Greece*, 79.

[20]"History of JUSMAGG," 60, 62; NSC 103—"The Position of the United States with Respect to Greece," Feb. 6, 1951, p. 5, NSC Lists, NA. During FY 1950, Marshall Plan money financed almost 64 percent of the civilian goods imported into Greece. Ibid. Statement by the president of UNGA, Gen. Carlos P. Romulo from the Philippines, Dec. 10, 1949, UNGA, *Official Records*, 4 sess., 1949, 276th plenary meeting, p. 615; draft essay by J. P. Maynard, Nov. 1952, introd. page, in Lincoln Papers, Truman Lib. Maynard was a member of the Mutual Security Agency. Sweet-Escott, *Greece*, 84.

[21]Truman to Elsey cited in Margaret Truman, *Harry S. Truman* (N.Y.: William Morrow, 1973), 461.

[22]NSC 103, pp. 6–10; William H. McNeill, *Greece: American Aid in Action, 1947–1956* (N.Y.: Twentieth Century Fund, 1957), 64, 69, 195; Wittner, *American Intervention in Greece*, 289–90, 293–94.

[23]Bruce R. Kuniholm, *The Origins of the Cold War in the Near East: Great Power Conflict and Diplomacy in Iran, Turkey, and Greece* (Princeton: Princeton U. Press, 1980), 420; Ernest R. May, *"Lessons" of the Past: The Use and Misuse of History in American Foreign Policy* (N.Y.: Oxford U. Press, 1973), 108; Lyndon B. Johnson, *The Vantage Point: Perspectives of the Presidency, 1963–1969* (N.Y.: Holt, Rinehart & Winston, 1971), 31, 422; Richard J. Barnet, *Intervention and Revolution: The United States in the Third World* (N.Y.: World Publishing, 1968), 97ff.; Stephen G. Xydis, "The Truman Doctrine in Perspective," *Balkan Studies* 8 (1967): 256 n.74; Rusk quoted in Adam B. Ulam, *The Rivals: America and Russia Since World War II* (N.Y.: Viking, 1971), 346–47.

[24]Theodore C. Sorensen, *Kennedy* (N.Y.: Harper, 1965), 660–61; Wittner, *American Intervention in Greece*, 307–8, 407 n.58; Rostow quoted in ibid., 309; William J. Miller, *Henry Cabot Lodge: A Biography* (N.Y.: Heineman, 1967), 373. Todd Gitlin declares that "Greece was the Vietnam of the 1940s." Gitlin, "Counter-Insurgency: Myth and Reality in Greece," in David Horowitz, ed., *Containment and Revolution* (Boston: Beacon, 1967), 141.

[25]One writer asserts that by "dramatically drawing a distinction between ideologies . . . the Truman Doctrine lent a rigidity to foreign policy that for a generation inhibited a turn from the Cold War." See Robert J. Donovan, *Conflict and Crisis: The Presidency of Harry S Truman, 1945–1948* (N.Y.: Norton, 1977), 285. On the argument that "flexible response" failed in Vietnam, see John L. Gaddis, *Strategies of Containment: A Critical Appraisal of Postwar American National Security Policy* (N.Y.: Oxford U. Press, 1982), chap. 8. In an earlier work, Gaddis criticized the Truman Doctrine for encouraging a Cold War mentality conducive to involvement in Vietnam. "By presenting aid to Greece and Turkey in terms of an ideological conflict between two ways of life, Washington officials encouraged a simplistic view of the Cold War which was, in time, to imprison American diplomacy in an ideological straightjacket almost as confining as that which restricted Soviet foreign policy. Trapped in their own rhetoric, leaders of the United States found it difficult to respond to the conciliatory gestures which emanated from the Kremlin following Stalin's death and, through their inflexibility, may well have contributed to the perpetuation of the Cold War." *The United States and the Origins of the Cold War, 1941–1947* (N.Y.: Columbia U. Press, 1972), 352. See also ibid., 351. Richard J. Powers argues for a flexible foreign policy that would place the military means in "proper balance with the other essential elements of foreign policy, namely diplomacy, economics, trade, foreign aid and international law." See his article entitled "Containment: From Greece to Vietnam—and Back?," *Western Political Quarterly* 22 (Dec. 1969): 846–61.

[26]NSC 103/1—"The Position of the United States with Respect to Greece," Feb. 14, 1951, pp. 1–2; memo by sec. of state of conversation among Tsaldaris, Dendramis, Jernegan, and Acheson, Oct. 28, 1949, *FRUS*, VI: *Near East, South Asia, and Africa*, 448; quote from G. L. Reed, in essay entitled "Who Won the War," June 28, 1949, p. 2, in Lincoln Papers, Truman Lib.

[27]Author's interview with McGhee, May 24, 1979.

Index